Communications
in Computer and Information Scie

T0238805

Wenjun Zhang   Xiaokang Yang   Zhixiang Xu
Ping An   Qizhen Liu   Yue Lu (Eds.)

Advances on Digital Television and Wireless Multimedia Communications

9th International Forum on Digital TV
and Wireless Multimedia Communication, IFTC 2012
Shanghai, China, November 9-10, 2012
Proceedings

 Springer

Volume Editors

Wenjun Zhang
Shanghai Jiao Tong University, China
E-mail: zhangwenjun@sjtu.edu.cn

Xiaokang Yang
Shanghai Jiao Tong University, China
E-mail: xkyang@sjtu.edu.cn

Zhixiang Xu
Shanghai University, China
E-mail: xuzxiang@163.com

Ping An
Shanghai University, China
E-mail: anping@shu.edu.cn

Qizhen Liu
Fudan University, Shanghai, China
E-mail: qzliu@fudan.edu.cn

Yue Lu
East China Normal University, Shanghai, China
E-mail: ylu@cs.ecnu.edu.cn

ISSN 1865-0929   e-ISSN 1865-0937
ISBN 978-3-642-34594-4   e-ISBN 978-3-642-34595-1
DOI 10.1007/978-3-642-34595-1
Springer Heidelberg Dordrecht London New York

Library of Congress Control Number: 2012950367

CR Subject Classification (1998): I.4, I.5, I.2.10, H.5.2, H.3.1, H.3.3, K.8.1

Typesetting: Camera-ready by author, data conversion by Scientific Publishing Services, Chennai, India

Printed on acid-free paper

Springer is part of Springer Science+Business Media (www.springer.com)

Preface

Over the past few years, smart TV and multimedia communication have enjoyed tremendous growth, driven by communication, broadcasting, microelectronics industries and technologies, the wide deployment of digital television networks, and the proliferation of smart wireless devices. As digital broadcasting and broadband communications networks are both becoming more common, many people can now enjoy high-quality broadcasting content as well as a large variety of content provided via the Internet. Therefore, new-generation digital television is evolving toward many new features, such as controllable, rich/new media, ubiquitous, immersive, social, and new experiences. The evolution digital TV (DTV) and multimedia communications requires advanced image-processing techniques for content production, adaption, analysis and interactions, as well as new paradigms of next-generation DTV and wireless multimedia communication systems that enable more advanced services in terms of quality, diversity, and flexibility.

The annual International Forum on Digital Television and Wireless Multimedia Communication (IFTC) provides an international forum for extensively exchanging the latest research advances in DTV and wireless communication around the world as well as the relevant policies of industry authorities. The forum also aims to promote the technology, equipments and applications in the field of DTV and multimedia by comparing the characteristics, frameworks, significant techniques and their maturity, analyzing the performance of various applications in terms of scalability, manageability, and portability, and discussing the interfaces among various of networks and platforms.

IFTC 2012, the 9th international annual forum, took place in Shanghai during November 9–10, 2012. It brought together international and local researchers to share the visions on DTV and wireless multimedia communication. The forum was co-hosted by Shanghai Image and Graphics Association (SIGA), Springer CCIS, and The China International Industry Fair 2012 (CIIF 2012), and co-sponsored by Shanghai Jiao Tong University (SJTU), IEEE BTS Chapter of Shanghai Section, Shanghai Institute of Communication, and the Shanghai Society of Motion Picture and Television Engineers (SSMPTE). IFTC 2012 received 117 full submissions for ten sessions (Image Processing and Pattern Recognition, 3D Video, Multimedia Communication etc.). Among the submissions, 69 were accepted as regular papers, with an acceptance ratio of 58.97%. Each submission was rigorously reviewed by at least two Program Committee members.

We want to thank many people who contributed to the high quality of the technical program. Special thanks go to the Technical Program Committee members who accomplished their tasks with competence and timeliness, and the external reviewers who maintained a focus on high quality while providing their punctual reports, among their busy schedules. Our sincere thanks go to the authors for their excellent contributions that have resulted in a high-quality and exciting technical program that was enjoyed by all conference attendees. We are also grateful to the local organizers, coordinated by Shanghai Jiao Tong University, and volunteers for their valuable help; the sponsors, in particular BESTV for making the event financially viable; Celine Chang for coordination with the publication of the proceedings; and Springer for agreeing to print this volume. Finally, many other people contributed to the success of IFTC 2012, whose names cannot be listed here due to space limitation. However, we owe them our gratitude.

August 2012

Wenjun Zhang
Xiaokang Yang
Zhixiang Xu
Ping An
Qizhen Liu
Yue Lu

Organization

Honorary Chairs

Hequan Wu	CAE, China
Jiangxing Wu	NDSC, China
Wen Gao	AVS Workgroup of China, China

General Chairs

Wenjun Zhang	Vice President, SJTU, China
Zhixiang Xu	Executive Vice Chairman, SIGA, China

Program Chairs

Xiaokang Yang	EE, SJTU, China
Ping An	EE, SHU, China
Qizhen Liu	SIGA, China

International Steering Committee

Chang Wen Chen	SUY Buffalo, USA
Baichuan Du	SARFT, China
Jialun Hu	SAST, China
Thomas Huang	UIUC, USA
Xin Qiu	SMG, China
Huifang Sun	MERL, USA
Yiyan Wu	CRC, Canada
Yaqin Zhang	Microsoft China Company
Weihua Zhang	Shanghai Telecom, China
Jie Zheng	Shanghai Mobile, China

Finance Chairs

Jun Zhou	SJTU, China
Rong Xie	SJTU, China

Publication Chairs

Yue Lu	CS, ECNU, China
Qiudong Sun	CIE, SSPU, China

Publicity Chairs

Xiangyang Xue   CST, Fudan, China
Fuqiang Liu   IEIE, Tongji U, China

Industrial Program Chairs

Sijun Huang   BesTV, China
Yijun Zhang   SSV, China
Dingxiang Lin   OPG, China

Exhibits Chairs

Gang Hou   WeiPeng Co. Ltd.
Changsong Wang   SIAA, China
Shengjun Jin   Digi-graphic Co. Ltd.
Guang Tian   BoCom Co. Ltd.

Local Arrangements Chairs

Cheng Zhi   SIGA, China
Shouzhong Huang   SIAA, China

International Liaisons

Mark Richer   Advanced Television Systems Committee
Phil Laven   Digital Video Broadcasting

Table of Contents

Image Processing and Pattern Recognition

Image and Video Analysis

Image Quality Assessment

Text Image and Speech Processing

Content Retrieval and Security

Source Coding

Multimedia Communication

New Advances in Broadband Multimedia

Human Computer Interface

3D Video

Research on Networked Integration Technology of Remote Sensing Image Processing

Chao Jiang, Ze-xun Geng, Xiao-feng Wei, and Chen Shen

Institute of Surveying and Mapping, Information Engineering University
Zhengzhou 450052, China

Abstract. Traditional image process method cannot share data efficiently and realize process interoperately, this paper presents a server-side image process method based on JNI package the local process function, combined with the Web Processing Service standard which is formulated by OGC to design and realize a three-tier network architecture. This architecture is a network integration framework for image process function. The experimental demonstrates that the image process algorithms of local library can package as a WPS service and clients can call the service through the network.

Keywords: OGC WPS, Web Service, JNI, Image Process.

1   Introduction

With the development of earth observation technologies, we can easily obtain a large number of remote sensing images, remote sensing image as a large-capacity information carrier, which contains a lot of information available. It is a data sources which have such property of large area, dynamic, near real-time, and it plays an irreplaceable role in many areas of the military, resources, environment and disaster prevention. How efficient organization, management and use of these distributions, heterogeneous image data is a problem. The traditional image processing methods can not share data efficiently and realize process interoperability.

With the development of Web Service technology, it provided an opportunity to the people for solving the sharing and interoperability for the distributed and heterogeneous data. Web service can be characterized by cross-platform, cross-language, cross-hardware interoperability. Based on the above-mentioned advantages of Web service, the researchers consider whether in practice by providing geographic information data into a geographic information services. Thus, the organization OGC (Open Geospatial Consortium Open GIS Union) which committed to sharing and interoperability of spatial data proposed a series of Web Service standards such as: WMS (Web Map Service), WFS (Web Feature Service) and WCS (web coverage the Service). The release of these standards is better to solve the problem of spatial data sharing.

The all standards of Web Service's are generic and therefore can not be a good solution to specific professional disciplines. Such as geo-spatial information field in the transfer agreement does not contain spatial information metadata information, as well as the standardization of spatial information data, making the Web Service to resolve functional interoperability deficiencies[1]. Aim at the weakness of functional interoperability and increasing need for web-based spatial data process, OGC has

W. Zhang et al. (Eds.): IFTC 2012, CCIS 331, pp. 1–8, 2012.

developed a Web service standard WPS (Web Processing Service), the standard can packaging of any type of spatial data processing functions. WPS aims to describe the service, to provide processing services that can be performed through the Web, and allows the user to input data and call the service when the underlying mechanism is transparent to the user.

2   The Profile of OGC WPS

WPS[2][3] is a Web Service standard which is proposed by OGC and play a important role in process interoperability. WPS defines a standard interface, making the release of spatial processing steps, discovery and binding the process more easier. "Process" refers to the algorithm of the operation of spatial reference data, calculation or model. "Publish" means that can be obtain machine-readable binding information and human-readable metadata to run the service for finding and using.

The WPS interface specifies three operations that can be requested by a client and performed by a WPS server, all mandatory implementation by all servers. Those operations are:

GetCapabilities: This operation allows a client to request and receive back service metadata (or Capabilities) documents that describe the abilities of the specific server implementation. This operation also supports negotiation of the specification version being used for client-server interactions.

DescribeProcess: This operation allows a client to request and receive back detailed information about one or more process(es) that can be executed by an Execute operation, including the input parameters and formats, and the outputs.

Execute: This operation allows a client to run a specified process implemented by the WPS, using provided input parameter values and returning the outputs produced.

These operations have many similarities to other OGC Web Services, including the WMS, WFS, and WCS.

Figure 1 is a simple UML diagram summarizing the WPS interface. This class diagram shows that the WPS interface class inherits the GetCapabilities operation from the OGC Web Service interface class, and adds the DescribeProcess and Execute operations.

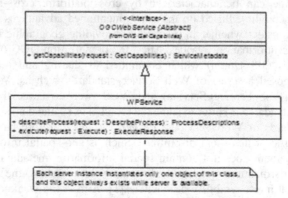

Fig. 1. The UML diagram of WPS interface

3   Design and Implementation od Integrated Framework Based on WPS

The OGC WPS as a solution to the spatial information sharing and processing interoperability, which can be realized in many way. Because three or multi-tier architecture can separation the display layer (ie, client), business logic layer(ie, the WPS service implementation layer) and the data layer to the logical and physical, ease of system maintenance and upgrades, reducing system coupling between the layers, therefore this architecture become the first choice for building Web-based application systems. Based on the above considerations and accord with the WPS standard specification, this paper reference the OpenGIS's three-tier network architecture[4] and propose the three-tier architecture of WPS service, shown in Figure 2.

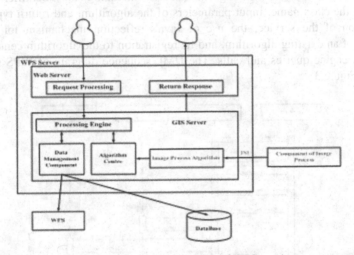

Fig. 2. The three-tier architecture of WPS service

The top level of the three-tier architecture for the client is responsible for receiving and sends the user's request, the user can use the browser to directly access, can also be via a standard Web service client calls the service provide by the business logic layer. The middle layer is the service layer, the core part of the whole architecture. Under the service layer is the data layer, data layer is responsible for the upper layer and provide the necessary data, data layer either realized by WFS service or spatial database directly.

The server side is based on existing Web container, the underlying algorithm module as a plug-in and can be dynamic load to the server. Each algorithm is transparent for the service code[1].

Service's realization were included in the the contents of two parts: WPS server and data management components. WPS server includes a processing engine and algorithms Center. The processing engine is the core part of the WPS service, each module is driven by it, structural response message and complete the service. Specifically, the processing engine's work is mainly reflected in the response of the three operations defined for the WPS specification: first, GetCapabilities request, the processing engine will query the algorithm center, access to the registered metadata information of all algorithms, including algorithms identifier, the name of the algorithm, and a description of the algorithm. Second, the DescribeProcess request, processing engine query algorithm centers according to the identifier of the request processing and returns the processing details, including input and output of the algorithm name, and each input and output's illuminate. Finally, for the Execute request, processing engine based on the user's request, decide whether to call the data service middleware to obtain the data, then the algorithm identifier in the request query algorithm Centre, algorithm implementation class is called after the class to complete processing and in accordance with the requirements of the request will return the result to the client. The algorithms center's main work is to maintain the metadata information of the algorithm class, including the identifier of each algorithm, the class name, input parameters of the algorithm, and return type. In the initialization of the service, the use of Java's reflection mechanism for dynamic discovery of an existing algorithm, and its registration to the algorithm center for the processing engine queries and calls. The UML sequence diagram of WPS service is shown in Figure 3.

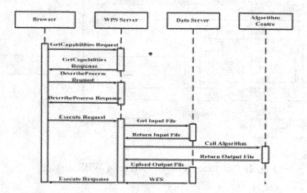

Fig. 3. The UML sequence diagram of WPS service

Data management components in the system plays the role of connecting the data and services, the bear's main job is to read the data from different data sources and standardization the data to provide to the WPS server to use. Vector files which need to process can be uploaded to the server by the client, there are two ways: the first is a direct HTTP send vector-based binary file, such as SHP files. Another approach is the input file on the client side transform to GML format and sent to the service side; after server-side processing is still in GML format back to the client [5]. Other than by the client upload, the WPS specification also supports access to a data file by calling the WFS service, we usually only need the data service middleware contains WFS client program can achieve this feature.

4   Server-Side Image Process Method Based on JNI Technology

The previous section, we have designed a functional integrated system framework, in this section, we introduce the server-side image processing algorithms to achieve and WPS packages.

The server-side algorithm is implemented by Java, Java to implement image processing algorithms can be implemented in two ways: 1、 an image processing package using Java itself, or to rewrite the image processing algorithms using the Java language; 2、 using JNI technology to call stable and mature third-party image processing library[6]. Image processing package provided by Java only provides some simple image processing class enables developers to write image-processing program has become very convenient, but Java provides the image processing package that contains only a small number of processing functions and image formats supported by default too less, can not meet the needs of users, to rewrite the image processing algorithms using the Java language also involves many time-consuming computing tasks, less time-consuming algorithms operating efficiency of Java than in C / C + +. At present, image processing library (such as OpenCV and CxImage)has been widely used In the open source community, these libraries are not only high operating efficiency, but also include the mainstream of the field of image processing algorithms. Using this method can directly call the library of image processing algorithms to greatly shorten the development cycle, so it is an excellent choice for server-side image processing algorithms.

This paper presents a server-side image processing module shown in Figure 4, the image processing functions is realized by a third-party image processing library, we use JNI technology as a interface between Java and third-party library so we can make a direct call to a third party processing functions in the library. The input of this module is the processed image file path name, the output is the results of image processing after the processing module of the algorithm.

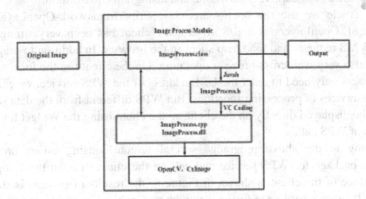

Fig. 4. The architecture of image process module

About the processing function packaged, we introduction of a server-side implementation of GeoServer[7]. GeoServer as an open source project, users can be downloaded directly to the source code for the entire project, the project provided the WPS service package interface, so the server-side can easily achieve the package through call the API provided by GeoServer.

In the specific of the packaging process, we define two classes, for example, we define ImageProcessFactory, and ImageProcess class, while the two classes inherit from the SingleProcessFactory and the SimpleProcess class which come from GeoTools. Process method in ImageProcess provide specific processing algorithms, the Create method in the class of ImageProcessFactory is used to register the process algorithm which realized in the class of ImageProcess in order to facilitate the client to make calls. Packaging process, as well as concrete implementation of the WPS services are shown in Figure 5:

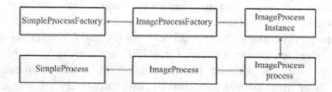

Fig. 5. The packing process of WPS service

5   Experiment Results and Analysis

The server-side's framework design and image processing's packaging and implementation are described in Section 3 and 4. Server-side processing algorithms implemented using JNI technology called the fusion of the OpenCV, Canny edge detection; CxImage's adaptive binarization and histogram equalization.

In this article we use the open-source JavaScript framework-OpenLayers as a client-side[8], OpenLayers as a B/S system, the client has been very strong, it can package WMS requests and load map slices in the browser. In addition to drag, zoom feature is also very well cross-browser operation. On the client use the form of a web browser, users only need to enter the URL address of the WPS service, we can easily obtain the services of processing functions. But WPS different from the data services, it can not be displayed directly on the client, so the client using the Widget for display the results of WPS call.

According to the above programs, several remote sensing image processing algorithms package for WPS service and call on the client through the Widget, the main interface of the client is shown in Figure 6, the results of process is shown in Figure 7a-7f (except for image fusion using the two original images(a and b), the rest results all use the original images one).

Fig. 6. The interface of client

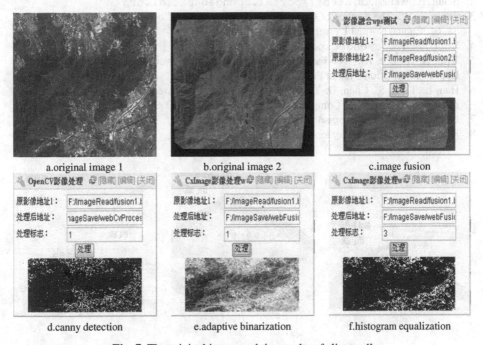

a.original image 1	b.original image 2	c.image fusion
d.canny detection	e.adaptive binarization	f.histogram equalization

Fig. 7. The original image and the results of client call

6   Conclusion and Outlook

With the continuous development of network technology, the demand of spatial data processing based on network are increasing. Remote sensing data because of its convenient access and contains a lot of available information, it would become an important part of spatial data. How efficient organization, and use of these distributions, heterogeneous image data is a problem which worthy of study. The traditional image processing methods can not share data efficiently and realize process interoperability. this paper presents a server-side image process method based on JNI package the local process function, combined with the Web Processing Service standard which is formulated by OGC to design and realize a three-tier network architecture. This architecture is a network integration framework for image process function. The experimental demonstrates that the image process algorithms of local library can package as a WPS service and clients can call the service through the network.

References

1. Sun, Y., Li, G.-Q., Huang, Z.-C.: Research on Implementation of OGC Web Processing Service. Computer Science, 86 (2009)
2. Schut, P.: Whitesidea, http://portal.opengeospatial.org/
3. Tang, G.-W.: The Service of Geographic Information Based on Digital Earth Platform, pp. 38–61. Capital Normal University, Beijing (2008)
4. http://www.opengeospatial.org/
5. Kim, H.-H., Lee, K.: Web-based GIS transportation framework data services using GML. Dept of Information System Engineering, 136–792 (2006)
6. Han, L., Li, Z.-S., Chen, D.-Y.: Object detection module based on implementation of Java and OpenCV. Journal of Computer Application, 773–776 (2008)
7. http://www.open-open.com/open130269.htm
8. http://www.openlayers.org/

Steganalysis in High-Dimensional Feature Space Using Selective Ensemble Classifiers

Bin Chen, Guorui Feng, and Fengyong Li

School of Communication and Information Engineering, Shanghai University,
Shanghai 200072, China
{chenbin99,grfeng,fyli}@shu.edu.cn

Abstract. Today, modern steganalysis needs to start using high-dimensional feature spaces, which makes the complexity of traditional classifiers such as support vector machine (SVM) increase rapidly. This paper proposes a frame of selective ensemble classifiers as an alternative to SVM for steganalysis by applying the selective theory that ensemble some instead of all the available base learners. A family of weak classifiers is built on random subspaces of the high-dimensional feature spaces. Then, assign a random weight to each classifier and employ genetic algorithm to evolve those weights based on a validation set. The Final classifier is constructed by fusing the decisions of individual classifiers whose weight is bigger than a pre-set threshold λ. Experiments with the steganographic algorithms nsF5 and MBS demonstrate the usefulness of the approach over current popular methods.

Keywords: steganalysis, high-dimensional feature space, random subspace, ensemble classifiers, selective strategy, fisher linear discriminants, SVM.

1 Introduction

Steganalysis is the art of detecting hidden information in cover objects with little knowledge about the steganography algorithm. Blind steganalysis tries to analysis any steganographic tools with little knowledge in advance, which makes blind steganalysis more practical than specific steganalysis. We also constrain our discussion to the blind steganalysis in this paper.

Today, most of modern blind steganalysis algorithms in digital images are usually implemented as supervised classifiers. The process of blind steganalysis comprises two important steps: feature extraction and classification. With the increased sophistication of steganographic algorithms, steganalysis has already begun extracting feature spaces of increased dimensionality, e.g., Shi proposed an efficient method using 324 features [1] based on JPEG blocks differences modeled by Markov processes and later extended to twice its size by Cartesian [2] calibration, Liu [3] proposed 216 neighboring joint density features extracted from the DCT coefficient array and the absolute array on both intra-block and inter-block. Once the features are extracted, a classifier such as SVM (Support Vector Machine) [7] is trained to distinguish the stego image from the cover. SVM always gives impressive results and

W. Zhang et al. (Eds.): IFTC 2012, CCIS 331, pp. 9–14, 2012.

seems to be by far the most popular choice. However, the complexity of SVM will be increased rapidly with the dimensionality of feature space growing. To address the complexity issues arising in staganalysis, Kodovsky [8,10] proposed ensemble classifiers built as random forests by fusing decisions of an ensemble of simple base learners that are inexpensive to train, their results demonstrated ensemble classifiers can achieve performance as good as or even better than the SVM with low cost. Zhou [4] proposed an ensemble theory that many could be better than all, which means that ensembling some instead of all the available base learners, a better result can be generated.

In this paper, we improve the ensemble classifiers by applying the theory of selective strategy [4] and propose a frame of selective ensemble classifiers for steganalyisis in high-dimensional feature space in section 3. Experiments with the steganographic nsF5 and MBS demonstrate the usefulness of the selective ensemble classifiers over current popular approaches.

2   Ensemble Classifier for Steganalysis

Hansen and Salam [5] firstly proposed an ensemble neural networks which shows that the generalization ability of a neural networks system can be significantly improved through ensembling a number of neural networks, i.e., training many neural networks and then combing their predictions. Since it behaves remarkably well, recently it has become a very hot topic in machine learning communities. Kodovsky [8] successfully proposed an ensemble classifier with the ensemble theory to solve the complexity issues of steganalysis in high-dimensional feature space. The ensemble classifier consists of a number of individual base learners. The base learners are Fisher Linear Discriminants (FLDs) rather than neural networks or SVMs because of its low complexity, weak, and unstable classifiers desirably increase diversity. All base learners are trained on feature spaces of a fixed dimension d_{sub} that can be chosen to be significantly smaller than the full dimensionality d. After collecting L base learners, the final class predictor is formed by combining their individual decisions. The performance of the ensemble classifiers is far better than that of each individual base learner and successfully solves the complexity issues of steganalysis in high-dimensional feature space.

3   Frame of Selective Ensemble Classifier

In general, a typical ensemble algorithm is constructed in two steps [9], i.e., training a number of base learners and then combining all the component predictions. As for the ensembling neural networks, Zhou [4] analyzed the relationship between the ensemble and its component neural networks and then proposed a selective ensemble theory that many could be better than all.

3.1   Selective Strategy

Zhou [4] proposed an effective selective strategy for the ensemble neural networks, we briefly introduce it and apply it to form the selective ensemble classifier. Assume each neural network(base learner) can be assigned a weight that could characterize the fitness of selecting network in the ensemble. Suppose the weight of the ith component neural network is w_i, $0 \le w_i \le 1$, Then we get a weight vector $w = (w_1, w_2, ..., w_N)$, N is the number of the component neural networks. The process of finding the optimum weights w_{opt} can be viewed as defining an optimization problem. Firstly, assign a random weight to each neural network and then employ genetic algorithm to evolve those weights based on a validation set. Finally it selects the networks whose weights are bigger than a pre-set threshold λ to make up the ensemble. In the experiments of this paper, we set the threshold $\lambda = 1/N$ as the default value as paper [4].

3.2   Selective Ensemble Classifiers for Steganalysis

We design a selective ensemble classifier by applying the selective strategy to the ensemble classifiers. Firstly, we randomly select about 30% of the Training set including cover and stego images as validation set for the genetic algorithm of selective strategy and the rest part as the final training set for the selective ensemble classifiers, denote N^{trn} and N^{val} the number of the final training and validation examples from each class.

Denote d as the dimensionality of the high-dimensional feature space, N^{tst} the number of testing examples from each class, and L the number of base learners. Furthermore, let $x^{(m)}$, $y^{(m)} \in \mathbb{R}^d$, $m = 1, ..., N^{trn}$, and $b^{(k)} \in \mathbb{R}^d$, $k = 1, ..., N^{tst}$, be the cover and stego feature vectors for the final training set, validation set and the testing set. The selective ensemble classifier is described using Algorithm 1. For $D \subset \{1, ..., d\}$, $x^{(D)}$ is the subset of features $\{x^{(k)}\}$ $k \in D$.

Algorithm 1. Selective Ensemble classifiers

1: Randomly select about 30% samples from the training set as validation set and the rest part as the final training set
2: **for** l=1 to L **do**
3: Randomly select $D_l \subset \{1, ..., d\}$, $|D_l| = d_{sub} < d$
4: Train a classifier F_l on cover features $x_m^{(D_l)}$ and stego features $y_m^{(D_l)}$, m =1, ..., N^{trn}. Each classifier is a mapping F_l: $\mathbb{R}^d \rightarrow \{0, 1\}$.
5: Make decisions on validation set using F_l:

$$F_l(b) \triangleq [F_l(b^{(1)}), ..., F_l(b^{(N^{val})})] \in \{0, 1\}^{N^{val}} \qquad (1)$$

6: **end for**
7: Assign a random weight to each base learner $w = (w_1, w_2, ..., w_L)$, then employ genetic algorithm to evolve those weights based on the decisions set F of validation and get the optimum weights $w_{opt} = (w_{o1}, w_{o2}, ..., w_{oL})$.

8: Get the indexes of the selected base leaner by the threshold λ.

if $w_{oi} > \lambda$, $S(i) = 1$; if $w_{oi} \leq \lambda$, $S(i)=0$, $i=1, ..., L$, S is the index vector of the selected base learners. L_{opt} is the number of the selected base learner.

$$L_{opt} = sum(S) \tag{2}$$

9: **for** $l=1$ to L **do**

   if $S(l)==1$, Make decisions on testing set using F_l:

$$F_l(b) \triangleq [\, F_l(b^{(1)}), ..., F_l(b^{(N^{tst})})\,] \in \{0, 1\}^{N^{tst}} \tag{3}$$

10: **end for**

11: Fuse all decisions of selected base learners by voting for each test example $k \in \{1, ..., N^{trn}\}$:

$$F(k) = \begin{cases} 1 & when \sum_{i=1}^{L_{opt}} F_{s(i)}(b^{(s(i))}) > L_{opt}/2 \\ 0 & otherwise \end{cases} \tag{4}$$

12: **return** F(k), k=1, ..., N^{tst}

Fig 1 gives the frame of the proposed selective ensemble classifier, $\bar{B} = [\bar{B_1}, ..., \bar{B_N}]$, $N = L_{opt}$, $\bar{B}$ is the set of the selected individual base learners, which produced by the individual base learners B_l, $l = 1, ..., L$. Because the seteganalysis methods always have a large simple sets with high dimensional feature spaces, it is critical important to select a weak and low complexity classifier as the base learners for the selective ensemble classifiers. The fisher linear discriminants would be the best choice as the base learner. The optimal L and d_{sub}, in fact the optimum is quite flat, we simply select d_{sub} by hand after a initial trails as the paper [8].

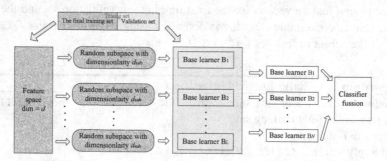

Fig. 1. The frame of proposed selective ensemble classifier

4   Experimental Results

We analyze the selective ensemble classifier on the steganographic algorithms MBS (Model-Based steganography) [11] and nsF5 (no-shrinkage F5) [12]. All experiments carried out on a database of 2000 images coming from the BOSSbase [6], JPEG compressed with quality 75 and resized to 512×512, use the MBS and nsF5 algorithms to create stego images carrying a range of different payloads. Each experiment consists of training samples and testing samples, both of the sample sets include 500 cover images and 500 stego images with a specified payload.

We extract 216 Liu [3] features and 648 SHI [1] features for the experiments. Compare the Selective ensemble classifiers with Ensemble classifiers [8] and SVM [7] as Table 1. Set d_{sub} = 200, L = 101 for the SHI features of the ensemble classifiers and the selective ensemble classifiers, Set d_{sub} = 80, L = 101 for the LIU features of the ensemble classifiers and the selective ensemble classifiers. After employing the selective strategy, selective ensemble classifiers select L_{opt} base learners to join ensemble finally. The value of L_{opt} is far less than L and always selects about 40% base learners to join ensemble. The results in Table 1 show that the selective ensemble classifiers have a better performance over the ensemble classifiers and SVM.

Table 1. Detection error rates of Ensemble classifiers, Selective ensemble classifiers and SVM

Embedding algorithm	Payload (bpac)	LIU-216			SHI-648		
		Ensemble[8]	**Selective**	SVM[7]	Ensemble[8]	**Selective**	SVM[7]
nsF5	0.05	36.85%	**36.23%**	38.71%	42.35%	**42.00%**	43.50%
	0.1	23.16%	**22.72%**	25.43%	34.14%	**33.22%**	37.32%
	0.15	11.43%	**11.05%**	15.27%	24.51%	**23.90%**	29.61%
	0.2	5.51%	**5.17%**	7.40%	14.61%	**13.93%**	21.30%
MBS	0.01	37.62%	**37.11%**	40.41%	42.65%	**41.52%**	42.90%
	0.02	30.57%	**29.73%**	33.12%	33.42%	**33.01%**	35.92%
	0.03	18.22%	**17.90%**	22.43%	26.31%	**25.27%**	29.84%
	0.04	12.78%	**12.35%**	16.46%	19.42%	**19.04%**	22.78%
	0.05	7.71%	**6.92%**	9.65%	15.33%	**14.40%**	17.80%

Fig.2 gives the steganalysis of nsF5 for SHI features using Ensemble classifiers, Selective ensemble classifiers and SVM. The performance of ensemble classifiers is far better than that of SVM for different payload and the selective ensemble classifiers can improve the performance of the ensemble classifier by about 1% with much less base learners.

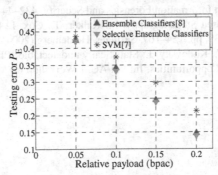

Fig. 2. Steganalysis of nsF5 for SHI features using Ensemble classifiers, Selective ensemble classifiers and SVM

5   Conclusion

In this paper, we apply the selective ensemble theory that ensemble some instead of all the available base learners and propose a frame of selective ensemble classifiers for steganalysis. The experiments show that the selective ensemble classifiers can improve the performance of the ensemble classifiers with much less base learners targeted at current popular embedding algorithms nsF5 and MBS. Our feature work will be directed towards designing a better selective strategy for the frame of selective ensemble classifiers.

References

1. Shi, Y.Q., Chen, C.-H., Chen, W.: A Markov Process Based Approach to Effective Attacking JPEG Steganography. In: Camenisch, J.L., Collberg, C.S., Johnson, N.F., Sallee, P. (eds.) IH 2006. LNCS, vol. 4437, pp. 249–264. Springer, Heidelberg (2007)
2. Kodovsk, J., Fridrich, J.: Calibration revisited. In: 11th ACM Workshop on Multimedia and Security, Princeton, NJ, pp. 63–74 (2009)
3. Liu, Q.: Steganalysis of DCT-embedding based adaptive steganography and YASS. In: 13th ACM Multimedia and Security Workshop, Niagara Falls, NY, pp. 77–86 (2011)
4. Zhou, Z.H., Wu, J., Tang, W.: Ensembling Neural Networks: Many Could Be Better than All. Artificial Intelligence 137, 239–263 (2002)
5. Hansen, H.K., Salamon, P.: Neural network ensembles. IEEE Trans. Pattern Anal. Machine Intelligence 12, 993–1001 (1990)
6. http://www.agents.cz/boss/BOSSFinal/index.php?mode=VIEW&tmpl=materials
7. Chang, C.C., Lin, C.J.: LIBSVM: A library for support vector machines (2001), Software, http://www.csie.ntu.edu.tw/cjlin/libsvm
8. Kodovsk, J., Fridrich, J.: Steganalysis in high dimensions: fusing classifiers built on random subspaces. In: 8th SPIE Electronic Imaging, Media, Watermarking, Security and Forensics, vol. 7880, pp. 1–13 (2011)
9. Li, N., Zhou, Z.H.: Selective ensemble under regularization framework. In: 8th International Workshop on Multiple Classifier Systems, Reykjavik, Iceland, pp. 293–303 (2009)
10. Kodovsk, J., Fridrich, J., Holub, V.: Ensemble classifiers for steganalysis of digital media. IEEE Transactions on Information Forensics and Security, 432–444 (2012)
11. Sallee, P.: Model-Based Steganography. In: Kalker, T., Cox, I., Ro, Y.M. (eds.) IWDW 2003. LNCS, vol. 2939, pp. 154–167. Springer, Heidelberg (2004)
12. Fridrich, J., Pevny, T., Kodovsky, J.: Statistically undetectable JPEG steganography: Dead ends, challenges, and opportunities. In: 9th ACM Workshop on Multimedia and Security, pp. 3–14 (2007)

Parallel-Friendly Patch Match
Based on Jump Flooding

Pei Yu, Xiaokang Yang, and Li Chen

Shanghai Key Labs of Digital Media Processing and Communication,
Shanghai Jiao Tong University, Shanghai, China
{fisher,xkyang,hilichen}@sjtu.edu.cn

Abstract. In this paper, we propose a parallel-friendly algorithm for k-nearest neighbor based patch match. Based on jump flooding algorithm, an efficient pattern of communication, our algorithm is fully parallelized at patch-level. To improve the performance, we propose and analyze its variants, and implement them with GPU. Compared with state-of-the-art approximate patch match algorithm, the GPU implementation of our algorithm achieves up to 100 times speedup over its CPU implementation, and 5 times faster than the GPU implementation of Barnes's algorithm, a most recently benchmark algorithm.

Keywords: Patch-matching, kNN, GPU, CUDA.

1 Introduction

As a fundamental problem of classification and clustering, the k-nearest neighbor (kNN) search is widely employed in many research domains [1]. Patch match is a specific occasion of kNN search problem. In this scenario, each patch in the image is one point in the d-dimension space, which can be defined by arbitrary descriptor. Many algorithms and subdomains of image processing and computer vision have to solve this basic issue at different levels, from video coding such as motion estimation, to image denoising such as non-local means [2] and block-matching and 3D filtering (BM3D) denoising [3], to image analysis such as image segmentation and completion. In some subdomains of image processing, approximate patch is eligible and can obtain significant speedup. In [4] of Connelly Barnes et al., a novel randomized algorithm for approximate nearest neighbor was proposed. In terms of memory usage, speed and even the error of match, this algorithm has outperformed tree structure based methods (e.g., kd-tree [5]). In [6], this algorithm has been generalized to address kNN problem. Nevertheless, for an image of 0.15 mega pixels and k equals to 3, it still takes more than 10 seconds.

Recently, numerous publications proposed parallel-friendly algorithms suitable to be implemented on GPU to gain significant speedup. Compute Unified Device Architecture (CUDA^{TM}) enables researchers to use GPU for general purpose computation easily. In [1], the general problem of kNN was solved by brute-force method using CUDA^{TM}. To the contrary, some constraints of the scale of

W. Zhang et al. (Eds.): IFTC 2012, CCIS 331, pp. 15–21, 2012.

kNN problem, e.g. the maximum number of points of the set is limited to 65536 because of the highly memory-consuming nature, prevent it to be widely used in other domains, such as image processing, in which the scale of problem is in the magnitude of million patches.

In this paper, we propose a parallel-friendly algorithm for kNN patch match and implement it on GPU. Compared with state-of-the-art approximate patch match algorithm. The GPU implementation of our algorithm achieves up to 100 times speedup over its CPU implementation, and 5 times faster than the GPU implementation of Barnes's algorithm with comparable matching accuracy. The rest of this paper is organized as follows. Section 2 presents our algorithm and its variants. Section 3 describes how we implement this algorithm through CUDA^{TM}, and how we optimize it for performance. Section 4 describes and analyzes the experiment results. Section 5 concludes this paper.

2 Algorithm

For nearest neighbor, nearest-neighbor field (NNF) is defined as a function $f : A \mapsto \mathbb{R}^2$ over all possible coordinates of patches (here coordinate of patch is defined as the coordinate of top-left corner) in image A [4]. The value of function f is the offset of matched patch to query patch, which means for a patch coordinate a in image A and its nearest neighbor b in image B, $f(a) = b - a$. $D(\mathbf{v})$ denotes the patch distance between the patch at (x, y) in image A and patch at $(x, y) + \mathbf{v}$ in image B. Under the context of k nearest neighbors, the k-nearest neighbor field (kNNF) f is a multi-valued map with k values, each of which indicating the offset of one of the k nearest neighbors, i.e. each $f_i(a)(i = 1 \cdots k)$ denotes the offset of one of the k nearest neighbors to query patch [6].

2.1 Approximate K-Nearest Neighbor Algorithm

The proposed algorithm is based on Jump Flooding algorithm, an efficient communication pattern proposed to compute an approximation to the Voronoi diagram [7]. For a grid containing $n \times n$ points, the flood process is completed in $\log n$ rounds with step lengths of $n/2, n/4, \cdots, 1$. In each flood round with step length l, each grid point at (x, y) passes its content, which contains information about its closest seed, to other grid points at $(x+w, y+h)(w \in \{-l, 0, l\}, h \in \{-l, 0, l\})$ as their new candidate.

Based on the above scheme, we propose our algorithm for k-nearest neighbor based patch match. It contains two fundamental components, initialization and propagation. The initialization process fills the originally vacant kNNF with randomized information needed in further improvement. And the propagation process improves the kNNF by passing kNN of each patch to its neighbors as candidates.

Initialization: Initialization builds the initial kNNF needed in further improvement. The k-nearest neighbor field is initialized with random offsets, which are independent uniform samples of all effective patch coordinates in image B. For

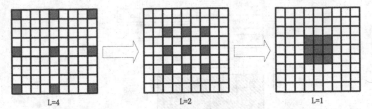

Fig. 1. Illustration of propagation. The step length is halved. In each round, each patch, e.g., the red patch, inquiries eight blue 8-neighbors, and takes $f_i(x + w, y + h)(i = 1 \cdots k, w \in \{-l, 0, l\}, h \in \{-l, 0, l\})$ as candidate offsets of kNN.

efficiency, we build a max-heap to store the patch distances D of the k-nearest neighbors of each effective patch in A. To avoid testing a patch already in the k-nearest list, a hash table is constructed for each patch in A.

Propagation: Propagation is to improve initial kNNF, which is far from the exact kNNF. This process contains many rounds. For $n \times n$ image A, there are $\log n + 1$ rounds with halved step lengths of $n, n/2, n/4, \cdots, 1$. Figure 1 illustrates how the information of kNN is propagated. In each round with step length l, for each patch at (x, y) in image A, we exhaustively inquiry each $\mathbf{v} = f_i(x + w, y + h)(i = 1 \cdots k, w \in \{-l, 0, l\}, h \in \{-l, 0, l\})$ as its new candidate offset. For each i, w and h, let

$$f_1(x, y) = \arg\min\{D(f_1(x, y)), D(f_i(x + w, y + h))\} \tag{1}$$
$$(i = 1 \cdots k, w \in \{-l, 0, l\}, h \in \{-l, 0, l\})$$

where $f_1(x, y)$ is the worst matched patch in max-heap. This new unit $f_1(x, y)$ is sifted down to an appropriate position in the max-heap. Then we test the next candidate.

2.2   Variants

As mentioned, the proposed algorithm only generates an approximation to the exact kNNF. To further improve kNNF, this subsection proposes some variants of our proposed algorithm. These variants modify the propagation module to propagate the information further. To reduce the occurrences of errors, Guodong Rong et al. proposed some variants of Jump Flooding algorithm [7], most of which added some additional rounds in propagation process. Similarly, we propose two variants of our original algorithm (JF). One $(JF + 2)$ adds two additional rounds with step lengths of 2 and 1, respectively. The other one $(JF + \log n + 1)$ adds $\log n + 1$ rounds with step lengths of $n, n/2, \cdots 2, 1$. In section 4, we will fully compare these two variants with the original one in terms of speed and the average distance between matched patches.

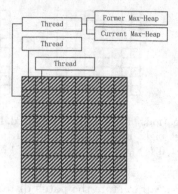

Fig. 2. Illustration of parallelism. In each round of propagation, the processes of all patches are run simultaneously. Each patch needs two max-heaps.

3   CUDA™ Implementation

In our implementations, the hardware is Core™ i7-2600k 3.4GHz(3.7GHz) and NVIDIA™ GeForce GTX 560Ti with 1GB dedicated graphic memory. Considering the inherently parallel-friendly nature, our algorithm can be implemented efficiently on GPU with CUDA™. In detail, it is parallelized at patch-level, i.e. each thread in the kernel computes k-nearest neighbors to one patch in image A as depicted in image 2. The patches of different threads are mutually exclusive. Only one kernel function for propagation is needed. Each launch of kernel completes one complete propagation round with step length of l. Since the threads of different blocks cannot be synchronized, we have to store two k-nearest neighbor heaps, one for the former round, and one for the current round. In initialization, two heaps share the same value. In the propagation process, each thread inquiries the offset stored in the former heap, compares it to the one in current heap, and completes the sift down operation in current heap if needed. After each round of propagation, value of current heap is copied back to the former one.

4   Experimental Results

In terms of the accuracy of kNNF and speed, this section analyzes our original algorithm (JF) and its two proposed variants $(JF + 2, JF + \log n + 1)$. We have applied algorithms, including CUDA™ implementations of Barnes's algorithm, our original algorithm and the ones of $JF + 2, JF + \log n + 1$, to real-world images chosen from Caltech-256 dataset [8]. We randomly choose 40 images from 20 categories of images in the dataset. The size of images spans from 0.06 MP to 0.35 MP. We also vary the patch size from 3×3 to 16×16 and the k of kNN from 3 to 16.

Table 1. Comparison of average error and speedup

	average error of same images	average error of less similar images	speedup
Ours	0.3045-22520	10.327-57369	3-115
Barnes's	0.3050-21564	9.213-56253	1-24

To assess the performance and the error of the approximate kNNF, we define two criteria, one of which is speedup,

$$speedup = T_0/T \tag{2}$$

where T_0 denotes the running time of Barnes's algorithm on CPU, T denotes the running time of new algorithm. The other one criterion is error rate. Before this, we qualify the average error of kNNF as

$$E = \sum_{x=1}^{n^2} \sum_{i=1}^{k} MSE(A(x), B(x + f_i(x)))/kn^2 \tag{3}$$

where MSE is the standard function for computing mean squared error between two patches located at x in image A and $x + f_i(x)$ in image B, n^2 is the amount of effective patches in image A. To intuitively compare the matching error of our algorithm with the one of Barnes's algorithm, a most recently benchmark algorithm, the second criterion error rate (ER) is defined as

$$ER = E/E_0 \tag{4}$$

where E and E_0 are the average errors of new algorithm and the original Barnes's, respectively. Considering different degrees of similarity between query patch and reference one, these algorithms are tested on same images, i.e. image A is the same as image B, and on less similar images, i.e. image A and image B are from the same category. The Barnes's algorithm runs for 5 iterations. Table 1 depicts the average error and speedup of CUDA[TM] implementations of our proposed $JF + 2$ algorithm and the Barnes's. All of the CUDA[TM] implementations are optimized under the same way as depicted in section 3. While attaining a comparable matching error, our algorithm achieves a substantial speedup.

To discuss efficiency and accuracy of our original algorithm and its variants, we implement these algorithms and test them on same images. Figure 3 shows the evolution of error rate and speedup as a function of k (of kNN), for patch size of 6 by 6 and 16 by 16, respectively. The error rate is roughly a convex function. And the speedup is roughly a linear increasing function of k. As more additional propagation rounds are added, the error rate ameliorates while the speedup deteriorates. Error rate of $JF + 2$ is much smaller than the original one, and very close to $JF + \log n + 1$. In practical, $JF + 2$ will be the best choice considering both error rate and speed.

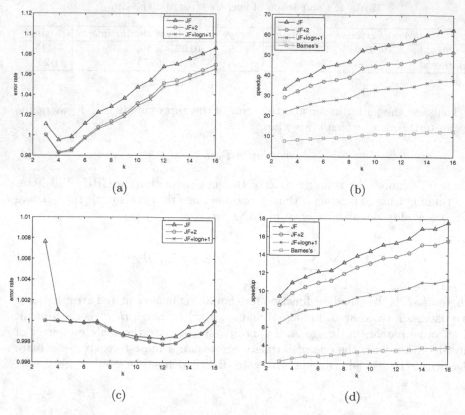

Fig. 3. The comparison of error rate and speedup of our original algorithm and its variants. Patch size of (a) and (b) is 6 by 6, and the one of (c) and (d) is 16 by 16; (a) and (c) denote the error rate of our algorithm and its variants; (b) and (d) depict the speedup of GPU implementation.

5   Conclusion

In this paper, we propose a parallel-friendly algorithm for approximate k-nearest patch match. This algorithm and its variants are implemented on GPU with CUDA^{TM}. The speedup and error rate are analyzed. Compared with Barnes's algorithm, the GPU implementation of our algorithm achieves up to 100 times speedup over its CPU implementation, and 5 times faster than the GPU implementation of Barnes's algorithm with comparable matching accuracy.

Acknowledgment. This paper was supported by NSFC (61025005, 60932006, 61001145), SRFDP (20090073110022), CPSF (20100480603), SPSF (11R21414200), 111 Project (B07022).

References

1. Garcia, V., Debreuve, E., Nielsen, F., Barlaud, M.: K-nearest neighbor search: Fast gpu-based implementations and application to highdimensional feature matching. In: International Conference on Image Processing, pp. 3757–3760. IEEE Press, Hong Kong (2010)
2. Buades, A., Coll, B., Morel, J.: A non-local algorithm for image denoising. In: IEEE Computer Society Conference on Computer Vision and Pattern Recognition, vol. 2, pp. 60–65. IEEE Press, San Diego (2005)
3. Dabov, K., Foi, A., Katkovnik, V., Egiazarian, K.: Image denoising by sparse 3-D transform-domain collaborative filtering. IEEE Trans. Image Process. 16, 2080–2095 (2007)
4. Barnes, C., Shechtman, E., Finkelstein, A., Goldman, D.: PatchMatch: a randomized correspondence algorithm for structural image editing. ACM Trans. Graphics 28, 24:1–24:11 (2009)
5. Hertzmann, A., Jacobs, C., Oliver, N., Curless, B., Salesin, D.: Image analogies. In: Proceedings of ACM SIGGRAPH, pp. 327–340. ACM Press (2001)
6. Barnes, C., Shechtman, E., Goldman, D.B., Finkelstein, A.: The generalized patch-match correspondence algorithm. In: 11th European Conference on Computer Vision, pp. 2049–2056. IEEE Press, Crete (2010)
7. Rong, G., Tan, T.-S.: Jump flooding in gpu with applications to vornoi diagram and distance transform. In: Proceedings of the Symposium on Interactive 3D Graphics and Games, pp. 109–116. ACM Press, New York (2006)
8. Caltech-256 Object Category Dataset, http://www.vision.caltech.edu/Image_Datasets/Caltech256/

Skew Estimation Based on Haar-Like Features

Bing Liu and Li Song

Shanghai Digital Media Processing and Transmission Key Lab,
Shanghai Jiao Tong University, Shanghai, China, 200240
{bingle,song_li}@sjtu.edu.cn

Abstract. This paper presents a novel approach for skew estimation of scanned documents. Haar-like features are firstly proposed to construct objective function and then a modified coarse-to-fine search strategy is implemented to reduce computation. Experimental results show that our skew estimation algorithm performs well on general printed documents with different contents, languages and layouts. The accuracy of skew angle estimation is comparable with or better than state-of-the-art methods.

Keywords: skew estimation, Haar-like feature, coarse-to-fine search.

1   Introduction

Document skew estimation and correction refer to estimate the skew angle of digital document and correct it to zero-skewed image. It is important for document analysis system (DAS) where page layout analysis, optical character recognition (OCR), or document retrieval usually need zero-skewed input image. Many skew estimation and correction algorithms have been developed for general document processing.

Projection profile analysis (PP) method [1,2] is a popular method, in which the horizontal or vertical projection profile of the document image at a number of angles close to the expected orientation is computed. The estimated angle responses to the angle where projection profile get its max value. Because of exhaustion computation, projection profile based approaches are computationally expensive. Sadri [2] modified the Projection Profile method using spline curves and defined a new objective function based on the difference between the global maximum value and the minimum value, at the same time, particle swarm optimization (PSO) is introduced to search for the best skew angle avoiding exhaustive search. Another widely important approach is HT based method [3-5], which applies the Hough transform to every black pixel in the binary image and the peak in the Hough space indicates the skew angle. HT method is typically slower than the non-iterative projection profile technique, however the accuracy is typically high. Recently, some new methods have been proposed for skew estimation. Chou [6] used piece-wise coverings of objects by parallelograms (PCP) to estimate skew angle of a scanned document. In this method, A document image is divided into a number of non-overlapping slabs in which each object is covered by parallelograms. Then skew angle is estimated when maximum white space occurs. One of limitation of this technique is that noises in the

W. Zhang et al. (Eds.): IFTC 2012, CCIS 331, pp. 22–28, 2012.

background area easily affect skew angle estimation. Alireza[8] proposed an efficient skew estimation technique based on Piece-wise Painting Algorithm (PPA) for scanned documents, in which two separate painted images are initially obtained after employing PPA on document image horizontally and vertically, subsequently candidate bands are selected from these painted images in which few lines are drawn based on the lists of points utilizing linear regression. The slope of the best-fit line indicates the final skew angle.

In this paper, we propose a novel method to estimate skew of document images. Firstly, we introduce Haar-like features when constructing objective function. Secondly, a coarse-to-fine search scheme is proposed to reduce computing complexity. The experimental results show our skew estimation approach can achieve high estimation precision for general printed documents.

The rest of our paper is organized as follows. In Section 2, we will explain our method in details. Experimental results are showed in Section 3. Second 4 draws our conclusion.

2   Methodology

In this section, we describe the details of our skew estimation algorithm. In the first subsection, Haar-like feature is introduced. At the same time, we will explain how to use Haar-like feature for skew estimate and give the corresponding objective function. Then in the next subsection, we give a brief description for the modified search strategy in order to reduce the computing complexity.

2.1   Haar-Like Features and Objective Function

Haar-like features are digital image features widely used in object recognition. Viola and Jones [7] adapted the idea of using Haar wavelets and developed the so called Haar-like features used for rapid objection detection. A Haar-like feature considers adjacent rectangular regions at a specific location in a detection window, sums up the pixel intensities in these regions and calculates the difference between them [9].

For general documents, usually they are composed of text lines and blank spaces between them. Given a document image without skewing, Haar-like features have a very high response where text lines transmit to blank space. However, for a skewed document image, no matter scanned horizontally or vertically, there are no such transitions that Haar-like features have relatively small response.

The simplest two-rectangle feature is used in this paper for skew estimation. The value of this feature is the difference between the sums of the pixels within two rectangular regions. The regions have the same size and shape and are horizontally or vertically adjacent (see Fig. 1).

In order to calculate the final objective function, first, we need to define the size of the sliding window, where two types of feature are calculated. For H-type and V-type feature, we define the size of the sliding widow as $C * H$(pixels) and $W * C$(pixels) respectively, where H, W are the height and width of the input image. And C can be odd numbers such as 2,4,6 ···.The sensitivity of our method to different value of C is given in Section 3.Then, we slide the window with the step of $C/2$ on the image and calculate the corresponding feature value within the sliding window. These two values are denoted by H(i) and V(j) respectively, where i, j is the column and row index of the sub image. In the end, these values are summed up as the final value of the Haar-like feature for the whole image using formulation (1)-(2),

$$\text{Feature}_H = \sum |H(i)|, i = 0, C/2, C \cdots. \tag{1}$$

$$\text{Feature}_V = \sum |V(j)|, j = 0, C/2, C \cdots. \tag{2}$$

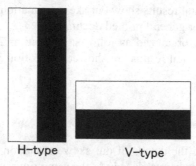

H-type   V-type

Fig. 1. Calculation of two-rectangle feature's value. The sum of the pixels within the white rectangle is subtracted from that in the black rectangle.

For the input image I, we rotate it from $-A°$ to $+A°$ ("-"means the image is rotated anticlockwise), with the step of some degree. For each rotated angle, we calculate two Haar–like features mentioned above on the image, denoted as Feature_H and Feature_V. It is worth mentioning that ether binary or normal 8 bit gray image can be used for this computation. By selecting the bigger one as the final response to the rotated angle, the objective function $F(\theta)$ can be defined as:

$$F(\theta) = \max\{\text{Feature}(\theta)_H, \text{Feature}(\theta)_V\}. \tag{3}$$

where, θ is the rotation angle. When $F(\theta)$ gets its maximum value, then the corresponding rotated angle θ is the skew angle estimated. That is,

$$\hat{\theta} = \arg\max[F(\theta)]. \tag{4}$$

2.2   Coarse-to-Fine Search Strategy

In order to estimate the skew angle, function (3) is calculated for each rotation angle. When adopting exhaustive search, such operation is time consuming. For example, suppose the range of the search angle is [-15°, 15°] and the search step length is 0.1 degree, it needs 300 times rotation operation on input image and 301 times evaluation of function (3).In order to reduce the number of the search, we do some modifications on the basic exhaustive search employing the so called coarse-to-fine search.

We assume that the skew angle of each document image is within the range $[-A°, A°]$. There are two main stages in our search strategy: coarse search and fine search. In the coarse search, we search the skew angle using $1°$ as the search step length. When this stage is finished, we obtain a coarse estimation of the skew angle denoted as $θ'$. Then in the next stage of fine search, first we search the finer skew angle from $θ' - 0.9°$ to $θ' + 0.9°$ with a smaller search step length of 0.2 degrees. After obtaining the skew angle $θ''$, we select the best skew angle from the following three angles: $θ'' - 0.1$, $θ''$ and $θ'' + 0.1°$ as the final estimation of the skew angle, which is denoted as $θ$. Adopting the improved search scheme, for the search range $[-15°, 15°]$, only 42 times of rotation operation and 43 times of evaluation of function (3) are needed.

In addition, the Haar-like feature can be computed in parallel way which will further accelerate the process speed when parallel computing can be used such as today's multicore CPU.

3   Experimental Results

3.1   Performance Evaluation and Dataset

In order to evaluate the proposed technique, we use the same dataset used in [6]. Two evaluation factors (average error and variance of errors) are explored for each group of data in our experiment. These factors are described as follows:

$$\text{Average Error: } \mu = \frac{1}{N}\sum_{i=1}^{N}(θ' - θ_i).$$

$$\text{Variance: } σ^2 = \frac{1}{N}\sum_{i=1}^{N}(θ_i - \mu)^2.$$

Where, $θ'$ is the ground truth of skew angle; $θ_i$ is the skew angle estimated in the proposed method and N is the number of the document image in the dataset.

The dataset [6] includes several types of objects such as horizontal textlines, vertical textlines, tables and figures. They are divided into five categories, that is, 1) English documents containing no figures or tables. 2) Documents in traditional/simplified Chinese or Japanese. 3) Documents with horizontal textlines and large scale figures. 4) Documents composed of horizontal textlines and tabular regions. 5) Document in several languages, including Greek, Arabic, Hindi, Nepalese, Bulgarian, Thai, Vietnamese and Hebrew. Each category has 100 document images and there are 500 test images in all.

3.2   Results and Analysis

We compare the results of our present work with that of recently published papers [6, 8]. Both PCP [6] and PPA [8] are representations of the state-of-the-art methods, and they have outperformed the other techniques in the literatures. A detailed comparison result of three techniques is shown in Table 1 where we set C=4. Fig.2 is the estimation results of the skew angle for sample document from 5 categories. The experiment was conducted on opencv/c++ platform. We directly select the original image as the input image to be processed.

As shown in Table 1, the proposed method has smaller average error and variance on pure text document images (English, Chinese&Japanese and Multilingual documents). However, its average error is a bit worse on documents containing large scale Figures. The main reason is that Haar-like feature of figures in this type document image disturbs the skew angle estimation. As is mentioned at the beginning of section2, the motivation of adopting Haar-like feature is that the transition from text line to space is helpful to estimation of the skew angle; however for document containing large scale figures, such figures have weakened this kind of effect. Therefore, the value of the Haar-like features of zero skewed figures does not necessarily get its maximum value any more in this case.

Table 1. Comparative of results of the different techniques on different categories of the dataset used in [6], C=4

Dataset	Algorithms	All images	
		Average Error	Variance
1st Category (English)	PCP[6]	0.1490	0.1290
	PPA[8]	0.1427	0.0830
	Ours	-0.0170	0.0788
2st Category (Chinese & Japanese)	PCP[6]	0.1390	0.1430
	PPA[8]	0.1237	0.0690
	Ours	-0.0790	0.0291
3st Category (Figure)	PCP[6]	0.2310	0.1350
	PPA[8]	0.2680	0.0980
	Ours	0.4950	0.0575
4st Category (Table)	PCP[6]	0.0770	0.0750
	PPA[8]	0.0600	0.0155
	Ours	0.1320	0.0278
5st Category (Multilingual)	PCP[6]	0.1110	0.1250
	PPA[8]	0.1075	0.0657
	Ours	0.0160	0.0045
All500images	PCP[6]	0.1414	0.1200
	PPA[8]	0.1404	0.0700
	Ours	0.1094	0.0814

To test the sensitivity of proposed method to different size of the sliding window, we set C=2, 4 and 8, results are listed in Table 2. We can see the proposed method is not very sensitive to the value of C used to vary the size of sliding window, although the bigger of the C usually results in the smaller average error and variance.

Table 2. Average and Variance of estimation errors (°) with different value of C for sliding window

C(pixels)		2	4	8
1st Category	μ	-0.0180	-0.0170	-0.0340
	σ^2	0.0877	0.0788	0.0910
2st Category	μ	-0.0780	-0.0790	-0.0660
	σ^2	0.0311	0.0291	0.0324
3st Category	μ	0.5250	0.4950	0.4590
	σ^2	0.1169	0.0575	0.0680
4st Category	μ	0.1350	0.1320	0.1210
	σ^2	0.0275	0.0278	0.0265
5st Category	μ	0.0160	0.0160	0.0150
	σ^2	0.0045	0.0045	0.0031
All Images	μ	0.1166	0.1094	0.0990
	σ^2	0.0045	0.0045	0.0031

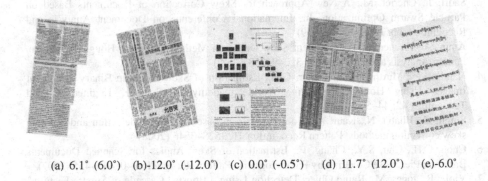

(a) 6.1° (6.0°)   (b)-12.0° (-12.0°)   (c) 0.0° (-0.5°)   (d) 11.7° (12.0°)   (e)-6.0°

Fig. 2. Estimated skew angle values (and ground truths) of sample images in (a) 1st Category. (b) 2st Category. (c) 3st Category. (d) 4st Category. (e) 5st Category.

It is easy to see that the speed of the proposed method depends on both the size of input image and search range. For a typical case in previous experiments, where input is an 8-bit grey image of A4 size with 300dpi (2480 × 3508) and search range is constrained as [-15°, +15°] with accuracy of 0.1°, current implementation still takes about 20s to finish on a PC platform with 2.33 GHz CPU and 2GB RAM. It is expected that speed can be improved a lot after parallel computation and code optimization are employed.

4   Conclusion

Skew estimation is an important step in document image processing system. In this paper, we proposed a new method of skew estimation for general printed documents. We introduced Haar-like features to construct objective function and speed up exhaustive search in a coarse-to-fine way to reduce computing complexity. Our experimental results show that our algorithm performs well on general documents with different contents, languages, and layouts. The present work is comparable with or better than several state-of-the-art methods. In the future, we are going to improve our technique in dealing with document with large scale figure, improve its speed and accuracy.

Acknowledgments. This work was supported by the 973 Program (2010CB731401, 2010CB731406), the NSF grants (60902073, 60902020, and 61102098), STCSM (12DZ2272600) and the 111 project.

References

1. Papandreou, A., Gatos, B.: A Novel Skew Detection Technique Based on Vertical Projections. In: International Conference on Document Analysis and Recognition, pp. 384–388 (2011)
2. Sadri, J., Cheriet, M.: A New Approach for Skew Correction of Documents Based on Particle Swarm Optimization. In: International Conference on Document Analysis and Recognition, pp. 1066–1070 (2009)
3. Amin, A., Fischer, S.: A Document Skew Detection Method Using the Hough Transform. Pattern Analysis and Applications 3, 249–253 (2000)
4. Nandini, N., Murthy, K.S., Kumar, G.H.: Estimation of Skew Angle in Binary Document Images Using Hough Transform. World Academy of Science, Engineering and Technology 42, 44–50 (2008)
5. Singh, C., Bhatia, N., Kaur, A.: Hough transform based fast skew detection and accurate skew correction methods. Pattern Recognition 41, 3528–3546 (2008)
6. Chou, C.H., Chu, S.Y., Chang, F.: Estimation of Skew Angles for Scanned Documents Based on Piecewise Covering by Parallelograms. Pattern Recognition 40, 443–455 (2007)
7. Viola, P., Jones, M.: Rapid Object Detection Using a Boosted Cascade of Simple Features. In: IEEE Computer Society Conference on Computer Vision and Pattern Recognition, pp. 511–518 (December 2001)
8. Alaei, A., Pal, U., Nagabhushan, P., Kimura, F.: A Painting Based Technique for Skew Estimation of Scanned Documents. In: International Conference on Document Analysis and Recognition, pp. 299–303 (2011)
9. http://en.wikipedia.org/wiki/Haar-like_features

An Efficient Synthesizing and Tone-Mapping System for High Dynamic Range Images

Tianle Zhao[1] and Yi Xu[2]

[1] Department of Electronic Engineering, Shanghai Jiao Tong University,
200240 Shanghai, China
[2] Shanghai Key Lab. of Digital Media Processing and Communication,
Shanghai Jiao Tong University,
200240 Shanghai, China
{colineeap,xuyi}@sjtu.edu.cn

Abstract. Current research works on high dynamic range (HDR) images put emphasis on the perception quality of the reconstructed image, where an enhanced low dynamic range (LDR) image is directly output as an HDR image from a sequence of LDR images. These works are useful to improve the limited ability of display devices. However, the dynamic range is not actually expanded and the physical properties of real scenes are unavailable in these works. For example, the radiance map of the surrounding scene cannot be recovered in such a direct way, which is an important issue in many industrial and aerospace applications. This paper proposes an efficient synthesizing and displaying system for HDR images. It focus on providing solutions of the following open problems: 1) LDR image registration under camera shaking and object motion; 2) HDR image reconstruction for physical property analysis of real scenes; 3) Structure preservation when compressing dynamic range of HDR image for LDR display devices.

Keywords: Motion compensation, Camera response function, High dynamic range image synthesis, Tone-Mapping.

1 Introduction

The dynamic range of a real scene can be extremely high, about $10^{9\sim14}$ levels in general, whereas that of a typical digital image keeps poorly 256 levels (or still just 65536 levels in even special cases). Although the existing display devices are still limited on dynamic range, there are indeed many situations where we need to analyze physical properties of the real scene. For instance, irradiance maps are widely used in the detection of mineral substance on a planet and the analysis of deep space.

However, current research works are mainly focused on the perception quality of the display devices. They use the information recorded in the sequence of differently exposed LDR images or even a single LDR image to reconstruct a so-called HDR image like the Apple iPhones, which indeed has the same dynamic range as LDR images but only enhanced in visual quality [1]. These works are very useful in the

W. Zhang et al. (Eds.): IFTC 2012, CCIS 331, pp. 29–36, 2012.

situations where visual effects are most concerned about. However, these works would be unavailable when we need the radiance maps of the captured scenes for analysis or display on some advanced HDR display devices.

In this paper, we aim to design a system which has the ability to reconstruct a genuine HDR image for recovering the radiance map of real scenes, and still to provide enhanced visual effects on LDR display devices. The proposed system contains 4 fundamental modules: (1) We obtain the registrated LDR image sequence after motion computation among the input LDR images. It should be noted that there exists motion among the sequential LDR images which is usually ignored in current HDR research works [2]. Thus, we propose an efficient motion compensation module to avoid motion blurring effects in reconstructed HDR image. (2) The module for camera response function (CRF) recovery. (3) Synthesizing module of reconstructing the radiance map of real scenes. (4) The terminal displaying module of the system is developed to obtain enhanced visual quality using tone-mapping technique when compressing dynamic range of HDR image for LDR display devices. The experimental results demonstrate that the proposed system can recover high dynamic range of real scenes and well preserve structure information when outputting HDR image on LDR display devices.

2   LDR Image Registration under Camera Shaking and Object Motion

In practical uses, it should be noted that the sequential LDR images are taken asynchronously. This phenomenon is usually incurred by camera shaking and moving objects. Also, varied lighting would introduce challenges to accurate motion estimation among LDR images. In fact, camera shaking would result in global motion between images while moving objects produce varied local motion distribution. In this section, we establish a two-layer motion computation scheme to registrate the sequential LDR images, so that ghosts or motion blurring effects would be avoided in following reconstructed HDR image.

To withstand noises, geometric distortions and sharp luminance changes during capture of LDR sequence, we adopt SURF features [3] to estimate global motion under camera shaking. We assume that the camera is far away from the scene or the camera shaking is not violent, so that we can ignore depth difference in motion estimation. Then two input images can be related by a three-dimensional transformation matrix, namely homography matrix.

Suppose there are two images, the reference image A and the source image B. If SURF point P located at (x, y) in image A has its corresponding point P' located at (x', y') in image B, we can establish homography transformation C between them using homogeneous coordinates $X = (x, y, 1)'$ and $X' = (x', y', 1)'$, that is

$$X' = CX \tag{1}$$

C is a 3×3 transformation matrix. There are quite a few ways to estimate matrix C, for instance the least square method (LSM). But considering that there are always some mismatched pairs encountered in LSM, we adopt the Random Sample Consensus (RANSAC) method to achieve robust estimation [4].

Moving objects in the scene will cause blurs and ghosts in the following HDR result even after camera shaking is compensated. It is necessary to conduct motion compensation for local moving objects. Actually, residual motion vectors after camera shaking compensation in layer 1 can represent the local object motion distribution.

In our system, we set a magnitude threshold for the residual vectors. Those SURF pairs whose residual vector magnitudes are greater than the threshold are assumed to belong to the region of moving objects. As for multiple moving objects, we categorize these dominant residual vectors and obtain local motion distribution using *k-means* method.

Motion compensation for camera shaking and moving objects can be conducted by six steps:

1) Extract SURF points and descriptors for two successive LDR images, and find the best matched pairs between them;
2) Randomly select three pairs of matched points whose location vectors are independent with each other, and calculate the transformation matrix C_j;
3) Iterate the second step for m times, and use RANSAC method to find the most accurate transformation matrix C;
4) Compensate global motion using matrix C.
5) Set magnitude threshold for residual motion vectors to find the region of moving objects.
6) Categorize these dominant residual motion vectors to locate each moving object and determine their central motion vector.

As shown in Fig. 1, ghosts are eliminated in the HDR reconstruction results if motion compensation module is added in our system.

Fig. 1. Effects of motion compensation: the left one is synthesized directly without motion compensation while the right one is synthesized after relatively accurate motion compensation

3   Camera Response Function Recovery and LDR Image Fusing

The recovery of CRF is a key module in our system. CRF is actually the composition of several non-linear mappings that occurred in the photographic process and easy to change when using different imaging systems or in varied situations. So, we need to recover it each time for reconstructing the radiance map.

Given the shutter time, we used D. & M.'s algorithm [2] to conduct camera response function recovery. This process can be formulated as:

$$O = \sum_{i=1}^{N}\sum_{j=1}^{P}\left[g\left(Z_{ij}\right)-\ln E_i - \ln \Delta t_j\right]^2 + \lambda \sum_{z=Z_{min}+1}^{Z_{max}-1} g''(z)^2 \tag{2}$$

where i is a spatial index and j indexes over exposure time $\triangle t$. Z and E represent pixel values of LDR images and the radiance map respectively. g'' is the second derivation of g, which is introduced to ensure the smoothness of CRF, and λ is a weighting coefficient. Finally, the recovered function g represents the CRF.

To reduce the errors caused by intensity truncation and noises, a weighting term is introduced to improve CRF estimation,

$$E_i = \exp\left\{\sum_{j=1}^{P} w\left(Z_{ij}\right)\left[g(Z_{ij})-\ln \Delta t_j\right]\bigg/\sum_{j=1}^{P} w\left(Z_{ij}\right)\right\} \tag{3}$$

where the weighting function shows a "hat shape",

$$w(Z) = 1 - \left(2\times\frac{Z}{255}-1\right)^{12} \tag{4}$$

It should be emphasized that the sample set should be selected to cover all of the gray levels and the whole image spatially, so that the estimation errors can be further reduced. See the left figure in Fig. 4.

4   Color Space Selection for Radiance Map Recovery and Fusing

Current research works are concerned about radiance map recovery (RMR) from gray LDR images, but color images contain much more useful information for RMR solution. In this section, we provide the guidance of rational selection of color space.

Fig. 2. Color HDR image synthesized in different color space. The left one is synthesized in RGB color space, while the heavily distorted one on the right is synthesized in HSI color space.

An intuitive approach to deal with a color image is in a monochrome way, that is, to treat each channel (R, G and B) as a gray image and process them separately. In image processing tasks, researchers used to select two kinds of color spaces, i.e. digital imaging color spaces and mathematical color spaces. RGB color space is a typical digital imaging color space with much inter-color redundancy. HSI color is a typical mathematical color space that decouples the brightness information from the color information.

Fig. 2 shows sample images synthesized in these two color spaces. The undistorted one on the left is synthesized in RGB color space while the heavily distorted one on the right is reconstructed in HSI color space. Thus, we can get two conclusion remarks: (1) RGB images are generated by a digital imaging system, so the CRFs recovered from each color channel are very close to each other, as shown by the right figure in Fig. 4. Therefore, no color distortion can be observed while radiance map E recovered from these CRFs in a fusion way. (2) Brightness cannot be completely separated as the I channel in HSI color space, so inter-color redundancy results in color distortion in the synthesized radiance map.

5   Display of HDR Image on LDR Device

Recently, tone-mapping techniques are utilized to compress images' dynamic range to fit LDR display devices. Then it should preserve structure information as much as possible according to Human Vision System properties like traditional contrast enhancement algorithms, i.e. gamma correction. Thus, the main challenge is how to enhance sharpness and details while compressing HDR images.

To fully utilize the limited dynamic range of display devices, just noticeable difference (JND) is taken into account to emphasize the noticeable structures. According to *Weber's law*, JND is proportional to brightness of background, which indicates that brighter regions can be more compressed. Hence, after comparing with recent tone-mapping works [5], [6] and [7], we adopt Global Optimized Linear Windowed (GOLW) algorithm to achieve LDR image with promising visual quality [1]. As for the regions exhibiting significantly high dynamic range but with smooth radiance shifting, we need to reduce their average intensity value to get compressed dynamic range. As for the regions exhibiting sharp and significant local radiance change, we compress local contrasts to further reduce the dynamic range of the whole image.

The algorithm performs adjustments on small overlapped windows over the entire input image. In the i-th window w_i, a simplest linear compression function is used

$$Z_j = p_i E_j + q_i, j \in w_i \tag{5}$$

where Z and E represent LDR image and HDR radiance map respectively. Parameter p_i controls the compression ratio of local contrast and q_i controls the average intensity value in the window. The compressed LDR image can be constructed by minimizing

$$f = \sum_i f_i = \sum_i \left\{ \sum_{j \in w_i} [Z_j - p_i E_j - q_i]^2 + \varepsilon c_i^2 (p_i - c_i)^2 \right\} \qquad (6)$$

c_i controls the compression ratios of local contrasts and is introduced to avoid trivial solutions. The inner minimization problem is easy to solve by setting the partial derivations of function f_i to zeros with respect to p_i and q_i. After that, Z can be obtained by solving a linear system.

6   Experimental Results

Fig. 3 shows two synthesized HDR images and their original LDR image sequences. It can be observed that the delicate textures of the sea surface, the ground and the clouds make these HDR images have pleasing visual effects. Fig. 4 shows the uniform distribution of the selected points for CRF recovery in gray level space, and CRFs recovered for each channel in a color image.

Fig. 3. HDR images displayed on an LDR device. Left: An HDR image that records the details from the darkest shadows to the brightest sun with its original sequence; Right: An HDR image that clearly records the brightest sun as well as the darkest ground and the original sequence.

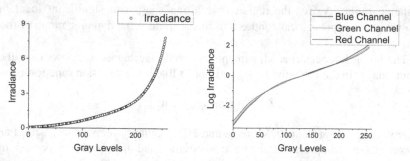

Fig. 4. Left: CRF recovered from the left photo in Fig. 3, using the selected points distributed uniformly in both spatial and gray level spaces; Right: CRFs for RGB channels of the right photo in Fig. 3

Fig. 5. HDR images synthesized using the algorithm proposed in [2] (the first row) and our system (the second row)

Fig. 5 shows another two examples which are compared with HDR images synthesized using the algorithm proposed in [2]. HDR images synthesized by our system lay on the second row, which show pleasing visual effects especially in the regions of the sky, the surface of sea and the ground.

Acknowledgement. This work was supported in part by Research Fund for National Natural Science Foundation of China (60902073), the National Basic Research Program of China (2010CB731401) and 111 project.

References

1. Shan, Q., Jia, J., Brown, M.S.: Globally Optimized Linear Windowed Tone Mapping. IEEE Transactions on Visualization and Computer Graphics 16(4), 663–675 (2010)
2. Debevec, P.E., Malik, J.: Recovering High Dynamic Range Radiance Maps from Photographs. In: Proceeding of ACM SIGGRAPH 2008, Article No. 31. ACM, New York (2008), doi:10.1145/1401132.1401174
3. Bay, H., Ess, A., Tuytelaars, T., Gool, L.V.: Speeded-Up Robust Features (SURF). Computer Vision and Image Understanding 110(3), 346–359 (2008)

4. Fischler, M.A., Bolles, R.C.: Random Sample Consensus: A Paradigm for Model Fitting with Apphcatlons to Image Analysis and Automated Cartography. Communications of the ACM 24(6), 381–395 (1981)
5. Liu, H., Guo, B., Feng, Z.: Pseudo-Log-Polar Fourier Transform for Image Registration. IEEE Signal Processing Letters 13(1), 17–20 (2006)
6. Duan, J., Bressan, M., Dance, C., Qiu, G.: Tone-Mapping High Dynamic Range Images by Novel Histogram Adjustment. Patten Recognition 43(5), 1847–1862 (2010)
7. Wu, X.: A Linear Programming Approach for Optimal Contrast-Tone Mapping. IEEE Transactions on Image Processing 20(5), 1262–1272 (2011)

Pathological Signal Quantitative Analysis Using Quaternion-Based Image Processing

Mingjia Han[1], Lin Zhou[2], and Yi Xu[1,3]

[1] Department of Electronic Engineering, Shanghai Jiao Tong University,
Shanghai 200240, China
[2] Department of Computer Science, Shanghai Jiao Tong University, Shanghai 200240, China
[3] Shanghai Key Lab. of Digital Media Processing and Communication,
Shanghai Jiao Tong University, Shanghai 200240, China

Abstract. Nowadays, IVF-ET (In Vitro Fertilization-Embryo Transfer) has become one of the best choices to treat infertility. For IVF-ET, the successful rate largely depends on the receptivity of the endometrium, while there is potential application of digital image processing to help the automatic assessment of the receptivity of the endometrium. This paper studies proper methods to get quantitative analysis of HE (Hematoxylin-Eosin) staining medical images in the womb, including the number, density, area and perimeter of the glands. Instead of using monochrome analysis for color images, we represent the color medical images in the form of quaternion matrix to well preserve interrelationship between color channels. Quaternion Singular Value Decomposition (QSVD) is imposed on quaternion matrix to conduct dimension reduction of color vector data and to obtain color texture segmentation using k-means technique. Quaternion-based edge detection and pattern matching are then implemented on segmentation results to locate glands. Consequently, the quantitative analysis is available based on the extracted glands. Rather than reading a large number of medical images all by themselves, doctors can provide diagnosis more efficiently and more accurately using the proposed automatic quantitative analysis of pathological signal.

Keywords: IVF-ET, quantitative analysis, Quaternion, QSVD, k-means, color texture segmentation, color edge detection.

1   Introduction

In recent years, infertility has become one of the most severe diseases involving both human multiply and population quality. Medical survey shows that all over the world, one of ten couples suffer from this disease. With the development of medical technology, the In Vitro Fertilization-Embryo Transfer (IVF-ET) has made great progress and becomes the first choice to treat infertility. However, the successful rate of IVF-ET is limited (only about 40%), which is considered the biggest obstacle to its application. The following medical investigation shows that the endometrial receptivity of womb plays an important role in IVF-ET.

As digital image processing has been widely applied in many aspects of medicine despite of IVF-ET, this paper focuses on how to automatically get quantitative data of

W. Zhang et al. (Eds.): IFTC 2012, CCIS 331, pp. 37–45, 2012.

the HE staining medical images such as the number, density, area and perimeter of the glands, which are regarded as key indicators for doctor's diagnosis, through digital image processing technics.

Since the traditional color image processing technics usually treat the three color channels (r,g,b) separately, the interrelationship between the color channels might be destroyed and erroneous analyses would be introduced in the processing results. In this paper, quaternion algebra is used to represent color vectors, which builds an efficient way to treat the color pixels as units. Then an automatic quantitative analysis scheme for glands is established on the basis of quaternion-based color texture segmentation and color edge detection. The experimental results demonstrate that the proposed quantitative analysis scheme can help doctors provide diagnosis more efficiently and more accurately.

2   Quaternion Representation of Color Image

Quaternion [1] is a kind of numbers which exist in four dimensions,

$$a = t + x \cdot i + y \cdot j + z \cdot k \tag{1}$$

RGB color vectors can then be represented using pure quaternions, i.e. the real part $t = 0$. For example, we can use the pure quaternion $Q_p = r \cdot i + g \cdot j + b \cdot k$ to represent color pixel $p = \{r, g, b\}$. The multiplication between two pure quaternions $a = \{x, y, z\}$ and $b = \{x', y', z'\}$ is computed as follow,

$$a \times b = (-xx' - yy' - zz') + (yz' - zy')i + (zx' - xz')j + (xy' - yx')k = (a \otimes b) - (a \cdot b) \tag{2}$$

where symbol ' $\cdot$ ' denotes dot product operator and ' $\otimes$ ' denotes the cross product operator. Thus, HE staining medical images can be represented as a quaternion matrix, that is, each element of the matrix is formulated as a pure quaternion. Accordingly, all the color vector operations can be realized with the rules of quaternion algebra operations.

3   Automatic Quantitative Analysis of Pathological Signal

As the HE staining medical images have such a high resolution as 2088×1550 pixels, we first down-sample the images to the size of 522×388 pixels for efficiency.

3.1   Color Texture Segmentation Using QPCA and K-means Clustering

After down-sampling, QSVD (singular value decomposition) is used to decompose an $m \times n$ quaternion matrix into its singular value form. Supposing an $m \times n$ quaternion matrix X_q, it can be written in the following form,

$$X_q = X_r + X_i \cdot i + X_j \cdot j + X_k \cdot k \tag{3}$$

where X_r, X_i, X_j and X_k are all $m \times n$ real matrixes. Then we can define the equivalent real matrix $X_{equ,r}$ of the quaternion matrix X_q [2],

$$X_{equ.r} = \begin{bmatrix} X_r & X_i & X_j & X_k \\ -X_i & X_r & -X_k & X_j \\ -X_j & X_k & X_r & -X_i \\ -X_k & -X_j & X_i & X_r \end{bmatrix} \tag{4}$$

To implement QSVD, we first transform quaternion matrix into its equivalent real form, then use SVD to get its singular values, finally transform these acquired singular values into quaternion form as,

$$x_q = [x_1] - [x_2] \cdot i - [x_3] \cdot j - [x_4] \cdot k \tag{5}$$

where x_q is the singular value vector of X_q, a $n \times 1$ quaternion vector; x_1, x_2, x_3, x_4 are $n \times 1$ real vectors, consisting of the singular value vectors of $X_{equ.r}$[3]. Thus, we can summarize QSVD as:

1. Use Equation 3 to get the equivalent real matrix $X_{equ.r}$ of the quaternion matrix X_q;
2. Use the traditional SVD to get the eigenvectors and singular values of matrix $X_{equ.r}$;
3. Use Equation 4 to get the quaternion eigenvectors and quaternion singular values of matrix X_q;

Given QSVD result, we present QPCA method to reduce the dimension of color images. After a quaternion matrix is decomposed by QSVD:

$$Q = U \cdot \Lambda \cdot V^H = \Sigma_{i=1}^{R} \lambda_i \cdot (u_i \times v_i^H) \tag{6}$$

where u_i and v_i are the i-th column and row of quaternion matrices U and V. λ_i is the ith element of diagonal matrix Λ. R is the rank of Q. Every $u_i \times v_i^H$ yields an eigen-image. Hence the color image can be considered as the linear combination of R color eigen-images. As i increases, λ_i would decrease and less low-frequency components of an image would be contained in ith color eigen-image. Therefore, we can just take use of the first several eigen-images to represent the main feature of a medical image.

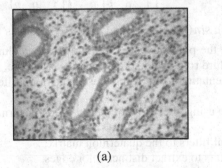 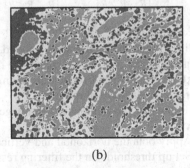

(a)   (b)

Fig. 1. Texture segmentation results using QPCA method and k-means clustering. (a) Original HE staining medical image. (b) Texture segmentation results, where red region and yellow region represent cell nucleus and cell wall respectively, and green region denotes both extracellular matrices and cytoplasm.

As for an $M \times N$ HE staining medical image, we divide it into overlapped $W \times W$ neighboring windows (total number is $M \times N$). The contents of each image window are approximated by projecting them onto the dimension-reduced basis space using QPCA method. Therefore, the projection results can then be used as the color texture feature for image segmentation. This procedure includes two steps:

1. Feature Extraction. We train the classifier on a small amount of samples from the image. By applying the QSVD algorithm to the matrix of training data T_q, whose size is $W^2 \times MN$. Each column of eigenvectors U represents a basis function of the transformation. Supposing that the first K columns of U can represent the dominant structures of the whole image, we can reduce the training data T_q to T_q^K, where $T_q^K = U_q^K \cdot T_q$. In the experiment, we found that K=1 would be the best choice for efficiency.

2. Texture Classification. We use K-means algorithm to realize classification step and thus achieve texture segmentation results. The number of kinds is set as 3 in the experiments. As shown in Fig.1, we can obtain 3 kinds of segmented textures: Red region and yellow region represent cell nucleus and cell wall respectively, and green region extracts both extracellular matrices and cytoplasm.

3.2   Location of Glands Using Quaternion Color Edge Detection

To realize automatic quantitative analysis of HE staining medical image, we should first locate the glands since the indicators of their number, density, area and perimeter are very useful to provide receptivity of the endometrium. With the texture segmentation result as the input image, we propose to use quaternion color edge detection to outline glands.

The following pair of masks is defined by Sangwine as a new filter to detect horizontal and vertical color edges [4][5]. The vertical color edge masks can be obtained from the horizontal ones with rows and columns transposed. These filters can be considered as the expansion of the famous Prewitt filter in quaternion domain.

$$\text{Horizontal: } \begin{bmatrix} 1 & 1 & 1 \\ 0 & 0 & 0 \\ \bar{R} & \bar{R} & \bar{R} \end{bmatrix} \times [\,] \times \begin{bmatrix} 1 & 1 & 1 \\ 0 & 0 & 0 \\ R & R & R \end{bmatrix} \text{ and vertical: } \begin{bmatrix} 1 & 0 & \bar{R} \\ 1 & 0 & \bar{R} \\ 1 & 0 & \bar{R} \end{bmatrix} \times [\,] \times \begin{bmatrix} 1 & 0 & R \\ 1 & 0 & R \\ 1 & 0 & R \end{bmatrix} \quad (7)$$

where R is defined as $R = [cos(\pi/2) + \mu \sin(\pi/2)]/\sqrt{6}$ and $\mu = \frac{i+j+k}{\sqrt{3}}$ defines the gray line. When these filters are applied, the pixels covered by the first row/column remain unchanged, while the ones in the third row/column are flipped by π. Hence, we can extract color edges from texture segmentation result using these quaternion filters. The procedure includes three steps:

1. Represent the segmentation image using the form of normalized quaternion matrix;

2. Apply both the horizontal and vertical filters to the quaternion matrix;

3. Set up thresholds on the filtering results to extract distinct color edges,

$$Threshold = \frac{average(\Delta)}{100}, \Delta = max(coef(i), coef(j), coef(k)) - min(coef(i), coef(j), coef(k)) \quad (8)$$

where $average(\Delta)$ computes the average value of Δ over the whole picture. Δ provides a measure to compute the distance between the coefficients of three imaginary parts. It is noted that the threshold is adaptively computed in varied image contents.

It is important to identify contours of glands from all the detected edges. Here we firstly apply the breadth-first search algorithm (BFS) to filter out all the closed curves. Then we define a shape factor for describing the shape complexity of the region of interest,

$$S = \frac{A}{P}$$

(9)

For a closed edge region, if the shape factor S is above 2.8, we consider it as the contour of glands, as shown in Fig.2. Once all the contours are located, we can easily calculate the number, area and perimeter of glands.

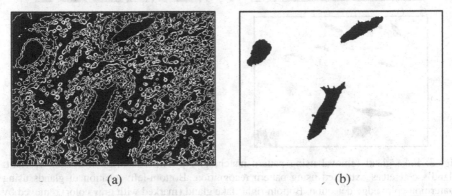

(a)   (b)

Fig. 2. Detection of glands using color edge map and shape facor. (a) Color edge map of texture segmentation image. (b) The glands filtered out by thresholding shape factor.

3.3   Outlier Detection Using Pattern Matching Method

However, there are still some areas falsely labeled as a gland. We called them "the fake gland" and choose simple pattern matching method to remove these outliers.

We manually cut out a part of the cells in the HE staining medical image as a sample and then compute its statistical chrominance distribution. For each pixel of the processed image, we extract its spatial neighborhood of size 6×6 pixels and compare its chrominance distribution with the sample,

$$dis = \Sigma_{6 \times 6pixel} \Sigma_{0 \sim \pi} [H(pic) - H(samp)]^2$$

(10)

where 'dis' is a similarity measure and H(.) computes the histogram of chrominance distribution. If it gets a smaller value than a given threshold, then the pattern around current pixel is considered to match the sample. All the matching areas are outlined as the cells. It should be noted that the area of the gland's cells is also a useful indicator for doctor's diagnosis.

To remove "the fake gland", we define a ratio factor as follows.

$$ratio = \frac{Area\ of\ CellWall}{Total\ Area}$$

(11)

As for a closed edge region, which is filtered out as a candidate gland in section 3.2, it would be labeled as a fake gland if its edge does not mainly consist of cells. That is, the gland is judged as "the fake gland" when the computed ratio is smaller than the empirical threshold 0.7. As shown in Fig.3, one fake gland is removed after pattern matching.

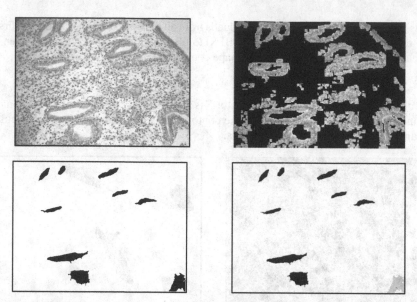

Fig. 3. Fake gland removal using pattern matching. Up-left: The original image. Up-right: Gland's cell areas extracted using pattern recognition. Bottom-left: location of glands using quaternion color edge detection. Bottom-right: fake gland (marked with gray color) removed by pattern matching.

4   Experimental Results

In this paper, the images are segmented before color edge detection. In fact, there are several traditional edge detection technic, such as Sobel operator and Canny operator. To demonstrate the efficiency of quaternion-based color image processing, for comparison, Fig. 4 shows the results -- using Sobel edge detector and Canny edge detector.

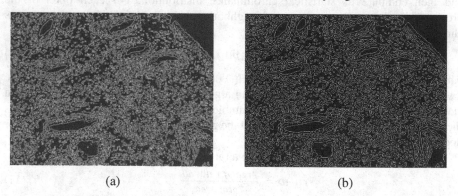

(a)   (b)

Fig. 4. Edge detection results of traditional methods. (a) Edge detection result of Sobel operator. (b) Edge detection result of Canny operator.

Compared with the proposed method using quaternion algebra, the traditional detection methods, Sobel operator and Canny operator, mainly have the shortcomings as follows: (1) The detected edges in region of interest is not clear and entire enough to form closed curves, which is necessary for glands to be detected (Fig. 5); (2) Monochrome processing technique cannot reliably segment color texture regions into cell nucleus, cell wall and matrices. Thus the related quantitative analysis is unavailable.

Through color texture segmentation, our quaternion-based processing scheme can remove trivial structures around glands, which enhances the contour strength of glands in the following color edge maps. Accordingly, we could extract these glands entirely as closed contours. In contrast, the traditional edge detection techniques only focus on the change of gray scale. As a result, the trivial structures around glands would be extracted together with the glands due to similar gradient variations. Thus, it is very difficult to segment glands as closed contours in the edge maps since gland's contour connected with trivial structures' edges formed an extremely complicated open area.

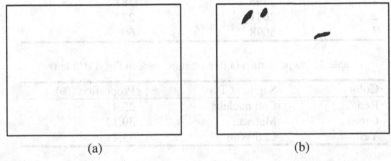

(a)   (b)

Fig. 5. Closed curve detection results of Fig. 3 (Up-left) using traditional methods. There are nine glands in Fig. 3 (Up-left). (a) Closed curve detection result of Sobel operator. None of the nine glands are detected. (b) Closed curve detection result of Canny operator. Six glands are missing.

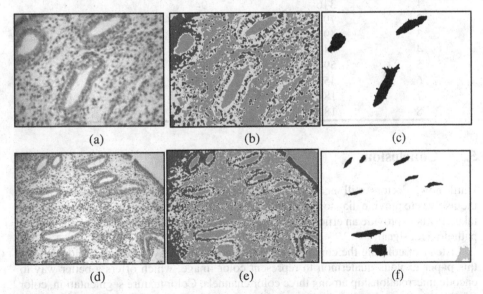

(a)   (b)   (c)

(d)   (e)   (f)

Fig. 6. Image processing results. (a) and (d): The original image; (b) and (e): Corresponding texture segmentation results of (a) and (d); (c) and (f): Corresponding detected glands of (a) and (d).

The quantitative analysis of HE staining medical images are shown in the four tables below:

Table 1. The proportion of three texture areas in Fig. 1

Color	Segment Type	Proportion (%)
Red	Cell nucleus	21.07
Green	Matrices	42.35
Yellow	Cell Wall	36.59

Table 2. The quantitative analysis for glands in Fig. 1

No.	Area(pixel)	Perimeter(pixel)
1	2896	381
2	2641	277
3	5098	608

Table 3. The proportion of three texture areas in Fig. 3 (Up-left)

Color	Segment Type	Proportion (%)
Red	Cell nucleus	25.47
Green	Matrices	39.13
Yellow	Cell Wall	35.41

Table 4. The quantitative analysis for glands in Fig. 3 (Up-left)

No.	Area(pixel)	Perimeter(pixel)
1	346	94
2	792	188
3	495	136
4	447	131
5	594	173
6	453	158
7	1849	329
8	1823	252

5   Conclusion

Until now, doctors still need to read a large number of medical images all by themselves to provide diagnosis. It is much exhausting and inefficient. In this paper, we take efforts to provide an efficient scheme to provide automatic quantitative analysis of pathological signal.

Instead of utilizing the commonly-used monochrome way to process color images, this paper exploits quaternion to represent color image, which offers a better way to encode interrelationship among three color channels. Color texture segmentation, color edge detection and color pattern matching methods are all employed to establish a highly-efficient analysis scheme to automatically obtain indicators of the receptivity of the endometrium. This scheme is applicable to a real system of pathological signal analysis.

Acknowledgements. This work was supported in part by Research Fund for National Natural Science Foundation of China (60902073), Shanghai Jiao Tong University Medical-Engineering Cross Projects (YG2011MS42) and 111 project.

References

1. Malonek, H.: Quaternions in Applied Sciences a Historical Perspective of Mathematical Concept. In: Proc. International Kolloquium Applications of Computer Science and Mathematics in Architecture and Building Industry, IKM, vol. 16 (2003)
2. Zhang, F.: Quaternions and matrices of quaternions. Linear Algebra and its Application 251, 21–57 (1997)
3. Xing, Y., Tan, J.: Color Image Decomposition Based on the SVD of Quaternion Matrix. Journal of Engineering Graphics (2) (2011)
4. Sangwine, S.J.: Colour image edge detector based on quaternion convolution. Electronics Letters 34(10), 969–971 (1998)
5. Sangwine, S.J., Evans, C.J., Ell, T.A.: Colour-sensitive edge detection using hypercomplex filters. In: Proceedings of the Tenth European Signal Processing Conference (EUSIPCO), Tampere, Finland, vol. I, pp. 107–110 (2000)

The De-nosing Algorithm of ECG Signal Based on Wavelet Packet

Gang Wang, Hairun Wang, Yue Zhao, and Longlong Zhao

School of Mechatronics Engineering and Automation, 200072 Shanghai, China
xingkong1210@shu.edu.cn

Abstract. There is always noise mixed with cardio-electric signal via hardware acquisition, which impede patients' diagnosis. Wavelet transform can well analyze regional signals, and achieve good result in separating signal and noise by taking advantage of their differences shown in both time and frequency domain. Yet wavelet decomposition focuses on approximate coefficient vector, which leads to loss of original features in time domain during the de-noising preprocess as it continues decomposing in lower frequency direction. Wavelet packet transform is proposed in order to overcome wavelet decomposition's low frequency resolution ratio in high-frequency section and weak time resolution ratio in low-frequency section. It's a more elaborate method for signal analysis, and well enhances resolution ratio in both time and frequency domain. This paper mainly presents application of wavelet packet transform in cardio-electric signal de-noising.

Keywords: ECG signal, wavelet, wavelet packet.

1   Introduction

Cardio-electric signal is a type of weak and low-frequency physical electric signal, usually in the range of 0.05Hz~100Hz, and its amplitude is less than 4mV [1]. Due to poor contact of electrode with patient's skin, frequent body movement, muscular tension, tachypnea, over gastrointestinal peristalsis and so forth, the distributed capacitance and wire loop of the electrode may be disturbed by 50 Hz power-line interference from electromagnetic field, which often adds noise to cardio-electric signal's collection. Basically, there are three kinds of interferences according to wave form classification, i.e. baseline drift, myoelectric high-frequency interference and strong noise interference.

Filter is the most traditional and simple tool to deal with the above problems, in which wavelet filtering is a common approach that can effectively reduce interference mixed in the signal. But it cannot partition signal during the high-frequency, which becomes a tough drawback. Based on wavelet filtering, wavelet packet transform is a good tool for time-frequency analysis, it has unique feature by dividing signal into different frequency sections without missing required information.

W. Zhang et al. (Eds.): IFTC 2012, CCIS 331, pp. 46–51, 2012.

2   Wavelet and Wavelet Packet

2.1   Wavelet Transform

For signal $f(t)$, its continuous wavelet transform [2] denotes as:

$$WT_f(a,\tau) = < f(t), \psi_{a,\tau}(t) >= \frac{1}{\sqrt{a}} \int_R f(t) \psi^*(\frac{t-\tau}{a}) dt \cdot \tag{1}$$

in which $\psi_{a,\tau}(t)$ is wavelet's primary function, a is the scale factor, τ is shift factor, $WT_f(a,\tau)$ is wavelet transform coefficient, and meets

$$\psi_{a,\tau}(t) = |a|^{-\frac{1}{2}} \psi(\frac{t-\tau}{a}), b \in R, a \in R - \{0\}. \tag{2}$$

As to continuous wavelet, the scale value a, time t and time-related offset τ are all continuous values. If calculating via computer, we must first discretize them to obtain the transform. For scale discrete currently the available approach is to adopt discrete of power series, i.e. set $a = a_0^j, a_0 > 0, j \in Z$, and its respective wavelet function :

$$a_0^{-\frac{j}{2}} \psi[a_0^{-j}(t-\tau)], j = 0,1,2.... \tag{3}$$

in which $\tau = ka_0^j\tau_0$. Usually we uniformly discrete τ so as to cover the whole time axis, and τ meets Nyquist sampling theorem. When $a = 2^j$, the responsive sampling interval is $2^j\tau_0$ along τ axis. And when $a_0 = 2$, if j increases by 1, a doubles but its respective frequency reduces to half. In this case, the sampling rate halves without losing the information we need. Usually, we set $a_0 = 2$, then $a = 2^j$, $\tau = 2^j k\tau_0$, so the sampling interval is $\tau = 2^j\tau_0$, and $\psi_{a,\tau}(t)$ becomes $\psi_{j,k} = 2^{-\frac{j}{2}} \psi(2^{-j}t - k\tau_0)$, and $WT_f(j,k) = \int f(t)\psi_{j,k}^*(t)dt$, $j=0,1,2..;k \in Z$. Furthermore, after normalizing τ_0, we get $\psi_{j,k}(t) = 2^{-\frac{j}{2}} \psi(2^{-j}t - k)$, and the respective WT_f is $WT_f(j,k) = \int f(t)\psi_{j,k}^*(t)dt$.

2.2   Wavelet Packet

In wavelet packet we denote a sequence function $\{W_n(x)\}$ and it meets the requirement below:

$$\begin{cases} W_{2n}(x) = 2^{j/2} \sum_k h_k W_n(2^{j/2}x-k) \\ W_{2n+1}(x) = 2^{j/2} \sum_k g_k W_n(2^{j/2}x-k) \end{cases} \quad (4)$$

in which $W_0(x)$ is scale function or primary function, $W_1(x)$ is the respective wavelet function, and $2^{j/2} \sum_k h_k W_n(2^{j/2}x-k)$ is denoted as wavelet packet function. As to h_k and g_k, they meet

$$\sum_{n\in Z} h_{n-2k} h_{n-2l} = \delta_{kl}$$

$$\sum_{n\in Z} h_n = \sqrt{2}, g_k = (-1)^k h_{1-k} \quad (5)$$

After deducing from format (4), we get wavelet packet's double-scale equation set:

$$\begin{cases} W_{2n}(x) = \sqrt{2} \sum_k h_k W_n(2x-k) \\ W_{2n+1}(x) = \sqrt{2} \sum_k g_k W_n(2x-k) \end{cases} \quad (6)$$

3　De-noising Model and Principle in Wavelet Packet

The filtering process of wavelet packet is generally completed in three steps. First we need to have wavelet transform and then deal with wavelet packet coefficient so as to filter the noises. In the end, reverse transformation is adopted. We assume the observed data is $f_i = g_i + \varepsilon_i; i = 1, 2, ..., N, (N = 2^2)$ It consists of signal g_i and noise ε_i, if we denote it by vectors, we get $f = g + \varepsilon$. Then our goal is to estimate g after observing the f. Assumme the observed data is being wavelet transformed, then we gain $w = \theta + \eta$. Denoting $D(\bullet,\bullet)$ and $W^{-1}(\bullet)$ to be wavelet packet transform and reverse transform operator respectively, then the above three steps of filtering can be described as $w = W(f), w_t = D(w,t), \hat{g} = W^{-1}(w_t)$, in which $D(\bullet,\bullet)$ is nonlinear filtering operator, and it is the core of filtering problem. Obviously, such fundamental summary does not address how has $W(\bullet)$ or $D(\bullet,\bullet)$ been functioned in certain signal, neither does it consider selection methods of different operators and their related filtering results. Through selecting of different $W(\bullet)$ or $D(\bullet,\bullet)$ can obtain different filtering approaches, as for wavelet filtering, in order to reduce or remove noise without losing two much useful signal, its core principle is to modify wavelet coefficients according to the regulation offered in step two. There are roughly two kinds of threshold filtering ways, i.e. soft and hard threshold filtering [3].

3.1   Threshold Function

We can get soft threshold filtering function expression $\eta(w) = wI(|w| > T)$ from Fig.1 on the right and get hard threshold filtering function $\eta(w) = (w - \text{sgn}(w)T)I(|w| > T)$ from Fig.1 on the left, the horizontal axis represents the original coefficient of the signal, vertical axis represents wavelet coefficient after thresholding. There is no denying the fact that hard threshold filtering function can comparatively better to preserve signal's saltation, while soft threshold filtering function can make signal much more smooth.

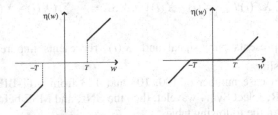

Fig. 1. Hardware and software threshold function

3.2   Common Threshold Estimation Methods

Uniform threshold de-noising method [4] aims at dealing with distribution of multi-dimensional independent normal variables, and getting optimal threshold between the limit of minimal and maximal estimation when dimensions approach to infinite. Its selection of threshold meets $T = \sigma_n \sqrt{2 \ln N}$.

Stein unbiased risk estimation threshold method is an adaptive threshold selection method based on Stain unbiased risk estimation [5]. For a certain threshold t, we first calculate its likelihood estimation and then get minimal t of non-likelihood estimation in order to obtain the threshold we need. Assume $P = \begin{bmatrix} p_1, p_2 \cdots p_n \end{bmatrix}$, the element of P is the square of wavelet packet coefficient arranged from smallest to largest. Defining risk vector R, of which the elements are as follows:

$$r_i = \left[N - 2i - (N - i)\, p_i + \sum_{k=1}^{n} p_k \right] / N \, , \ i = 1, 2, 3, \dots N \, . \tag{8}$$

Choosing minimal r_b as value-at-risk from elements set of R, and calculating respective threshold according to subscript of r_b, which is $T_2 = \sigma \sqrt{p_k}$.

Heuristic threshold method integrates the previous two methods. Assuming P is the quadratic sum of N wavelet packet coefficients, set $u = (P - N)/N$ and $v = (\log_2 N)^{3/2} \sqrt{N}$, then $T_3 = \begin{cases} T_1 & u < v \\ \min(T_1 T_2) & u > v \, , \end{cases}$

4   Simulation Analysis

This paper adopts cardio-electric signal with the sampling frequency of 333Hz, and the data source is from arrhythmia database of MIT. We set signal's length to N=500, the power interference is simulated via sine wave of 50Hz and myoelectric high-frequency interference is simulated via AWGN (Addictive-White Gaussian Noise).

We choose SNR and MSE as evaluation criterions for de-noising result, which are respectively defined as follows[6]:

$$SNR = 10\log(\sum_{i=1}^{n} X^2(i) / \sum_{i=1}^{n} \left[X(i) - \hat{X}(i) \right]^2), MSE = \frac{1}{N}\sum_{i=1}^{n}(X(i) - \hat{X}(i))^2. \qquad (20)$$

in which $X(i)$ represents pure signal and $\hat{X}(i)$ represents impure cardio-electric signal after de-noising.

Randomly select case number of 100, 103 and 123 from MIT-BIH database, and input different SNR, select Sym4 wavelet, then the SNR and MSE before and after de-noising are shown in the following tables.

Table 1. Software and hardware threshold method's SNR before and after de-noising

Case	Impure signal (dB)	Wavelet threshold method(dB)		Wavelet packet Threshold method(dB)	
		Software	Hardware	Software	Hardware
100	8.0884	12.9657	15.3407	13.4690	15.4380
103	8.7157	12.7411	15.5530	12.8931	15.8633
123	16.0792	20.8596	24.2335	20.9450	24.2854

Table 2. Software and hardware threshold method's MSE before and after de-noising

Case	Impure signal	Wavelet threshold method		Wavelet packet Threshold method	
		Software	Hardware	Software	Hardware
100	2.04%	67%	39%	69%	38%
103	2.04%	71%	43%	65%	43%
123	2.04%	65%	35%	65%	34%

From Table 1, we can conclude that wavelet packet via soft and hard threshold methods are all better than wavelet via soft and hard threshold methods. Besides, hard method is superior to software method generally. From Table 2 we can also conclude that MSE are relatively lower when wavelet packet threshold methods are adopted. Again, hard methods generally surpass soft methods.Taking case *No.* 100 as an example, seen from the wave form after de-noising via hardware method on the rightmost of Fig. 2, we know that it well reflects the characteristics of original signal without introducing redundant oscillation or resulting in cutting peak problem.

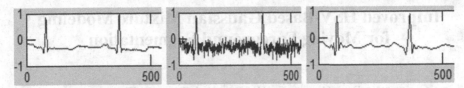

Fig. 2. From the leftmost to the rightmost are respectively original, impure signal with noise and de-nosied signal via wavelet packet hard threshold method

5   Conclusion

This paper adopts wavelet packet algorithm combined with threshold analysis, which takes the place of traditional wavelet transform as a way to deal with electromyography disturbance and power interference. Simulation shows wavelet packet's soft and hardware threshold algorithms can well preserve the signal while suppressing noises. And they have high SNR and low mean square error compared with wavelet threshold de-noising approaches, especially that the hardware threshold method can preserve singular points more perfectly, which is suitable for post-recognizing of feature points.

References

1. Gotchev, A., Nikolaev, N., Egiazarian, K.: Improving the Transform Domain ECG Denoising Performance by Applying Interbeat and Interbeat Decorrelating Transforms. In: IEEE International Symposium on Circuits and Systems, pp. 2–17 (2001)
2. Li, C.W., Zheng, C.X., Tai, C.F.: Detection of ECG characteristic points using wavelet transform. IEEE Trans. BME 42(1), 21–29 (2006)
3. Berkner, K., Wells, R.O.: Wavelet transforms and denosing algorithms. In: Signals, Systems & computers,1998 Conference Record of the Thirty-Second Asilomar Conference, pp. 1639–1643 (1998)
4. He, Q., Yao, C.: Feature Extraction Method of Hydraulic Pump Vibration Signal Based on Singular Value Decomposition and Wavelet Packets Analysis. Journal of Data Acquisition & Processing, 241–247 (2012)
5. Guo, D.F., Zhu, W.H., Gao, Z.M.: A study of wavelet thresolding denoising. In: Signal Processing Proceedings, pp. 329–332 (2000)
6. Brij, N., Singh, A.K.T.: Optimal selection of wavelet basis function applied to ECG signal denosing. Digital Signal Processing, 275–287 (2006)

Improved HSV-Based Gaussian Mixture Modeling for Moving Foreground Segmentation

Ye-Peng Guan[1,2], Jin-Hui Du[1], and Chang-Qi Zhang[1]

[1] School of Communication and Information Engineering, Shanghai University
[2] Key Laboratory of Advanced Displays and System Application, Ministry of Education

Abstract. It is crucial to get the moving foreground for variety video processing system in complex scenes. An improved GMM-based method is developed that can real-time segment moving foreground efficiently. The Gaussian mixture model is improved to effectively detect motion foreground objects even if the object moves slowly. Some relationships between *H* and *S* components in HSV space are adopted to suppress shadow caused by moving objects. The shortcoming in literature that more parameters are needed to remove shadow. Experimental results highlight that the proposed method is computationally cost-effective and robust to segment foreground by comparison.

Keywords: Foreground segmentation, shadow suppression, GMM.

1 Introduction

In recent years serious public safety situation made intelligent visual surveillance popular, as an active research topic in computer vision, intelligent visual surveillance attempt to detect, and track certain objects, further more understand the sense and the objects behaviors. To complete the task, it takes an important rule that segment the moving object (foreground) from the background quickly and accurately and affects the following works. It's the foundation of the system works well or not.

Moving detection is one important part of visual surveillance system. The representative schemes of moving object segmentation are frame difference [1], [2], Background subtraction [3], [4] and optical flow [5], [6]. Many literatures are proposed over the years which are based on the schemes of background subtraction [7], [8], [9]. The Gaussian mixture model (GMM) [10], [11] is one of the most commonly used methods for background subtraction. As time goes on, new pixel values update the mixture of Gaussians using an online approach [12]. Another background subtraction method is the codebook model [13], [14]. Sample background values at each pixel are quantized into codebooks which represent a compressed form of background model for a long image sequence. The background learning is required and robust threshold parameters cannot always be measured accurately, especially for highly compressed videos.

Shadow is one of challenging problem in segmenting foreground. The difficulties associated with shadow arise since shadows and moving objects share some important

W. Zhang et al. (Eds.): IFTC 2012, CCIS 331, pp. 52–58, 2012.
© Springer-Verlag Berlin Heidelberg 2012

visual features [15]. Color constancy is one of the fundamental abilities of human vision. Humans tend to assign a constant color to an abject even under changing illumination over time or space.

In this paper, improved GMM-based moving foreground segmentation is proposed with HSV color space video sequences. The proposed algorithm generates a mask of moving objects using GMM based background subtraction. To get more accuracy of background, different learning rates are adapted. Cast shadow areas are detected inside each moving object segmented. The integral moving foreground is obtained by using morphological methods.

2   Foreground Segmentation

The background modeling plays an important role in segmenting foreground. Since the background is changing, we need to constantly update the background by using the weighted average of the background and the current frames. Due to light mutation and other environmental impact, it is hard to get a very clean and clear background.

In GMM for one frame, K Gaussian distribution models are defined to describe the state of one pixel. K is usually takes between 3 to 5 [16]. The pixel is classified as background if it matches one of K Gaussian models. Assuming one pixel value is $\{X_1, X_2... X_t\}$, the probability of the pixel values X_t can be defined with K Gauss equation. If X_{t+1} meet one of K Gaussian distributions, it is classified as background pixels. Since the moving target, light conditions and noise will affect the background model, we need to update the Gaussian model in real time.

Three video sequences (laboratory, campus and running) are selected from public library to observe the change of the model parameters. In Fig. 1, d, e, f show the mean curves of four points selected from the above video sequences separately, and g, h, i show the curves of standard deviation. The background pixel (290, 19) (wall) and (33, 223) (table) without moving object have the curves in standard deviation and mean without any changes. The pixel (170, 188), (184, 220) and (170, 143) with moving objects have the ones with significant changes. So learning rate of variance should be more than that of mean to get an accurate model. Based on the fact, different update rates are set for variance and mean. The update equations are as follows:

$$\omega_{i,t+1} = \omega_{i,t} + \alpha \left(o_{i,t} - \omega_{i,t} \right) \tag{1}$$

$$\mu_{i,t+1} = \mu_{i,t} + o_{i,t} \left(\frac{\alpha}{\omega_{i,t}} \right) \delta_{i,t} \tag{2}$$

$$\sigma^2_{i,t+1} = \sigma^2_{i,t} + o_{i,t} \left(\frac{\beta}{\omega_{i,t}} \right) \left(\delta^T_{i,t} \delta_{i,t} - \sigma^2_{i,t} \right) \tag{3}$$

where $\delta_{i,t} = X_t - \mu_{i,t}$, $o_{i,t}$ is set to 1 for the component with largest $\omega_{i,t}$ and the others are set to zero.

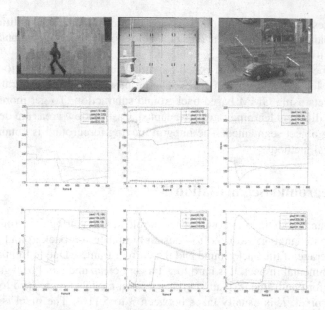

Fig. 1. Changes in the mean and variance. The first row is original images, the second and the third rows are results of mean and variance values corresponding to different pixels marked with green color in the original image, respectively.

For GMM based method, the background modeling needs learning over time. There is a problem that when the moving object keeps being stationary for a long time, the background updates slowly. To classify pixels robustly, combine Gaussian model with the frame difference method to improve the integrity of the foreground. By finding out the connected domain and filling the blank region, a more complete profile and better results can be gotten.

3   Shadow Suppression

The choice of color model is one of the problems associated with this view. The common two color models are RGB, and HSV. The RGB color model is an additive color model in which red (R), green (G), and blue (B) light is added together in various ways to reproduce a broad array of colors. In RGB color space, it is sensitive to illumination and view direction for shadow suppression. HSV color model is the most common cylindrical-coordinate representations of points in an RGB color model. HSV stands for hue (H), saturation (S), and value (V). In HSV color space, the luminance is separated from chrominance and the three components are orthogonal and independent. It has been proven that it is easier than the RGB space to set a mathematical formulation for shadow detection. By comparison, the HSV color space is fit for visible shadow.

By this reason, we analyze the moving shadow in the HSV color space. Cucchiara et al. [17] presented a non-model-based shadow detection approach. They defined a shadow mask for each point from motion segmentation, but there are multiple parameters that need to be adjusted, the choice of the parameters are less straightforward, and for now is done empirically.

In this paper, we proposed a quickly and efficiently method for shadow detection and exploit the relationship between H and S components in HSV space. By shadow suppression, two important features associated with visual experience come into play as figure 2 shows: First, the hue of the shadow is closer to the hue of background under the same lighting conditions; second, the shadow part has the lower saturation. Based on this fact, we check each pixel belonging to the objects resulting from the segmentation, if it is a shadow. First, we compare the saturation between the object and the background. In addition, we also consider the hue component which is proven experimentally to change within a certain limit. We now take care of this matter by applying the following conditions defined as:

$$p(x,y) = \begin{cases} 1 & \dfrac{S_I - S_B}{H_I - H_B} \geq \tau_s \\ 0 & otherwise \end{cases} \tag{4}$$

where $p(x, y)$ is the image mask used to label out the shadow pixels. S_I, S_B and H_I, H_B denote S, and H components of the current image and the background at point (x, y), respectively. In binary case, the mark $p(x, y) = 1$, if the pixel(x, y) is determined to shadow. Otherwise $p(x, y) = 0$. Fig. 2 shows some results of suppressing shadow. One can note that the shadow is suppressed efficiently. Some pixels may be misclassified because of the noise. In getting a better result, some morphological processing can be used to overcome this problem.

Fig. 2. Some results of shadow suppression. Original image, H component, S component and detected shadow results (marked as red color), from left to right, respectively.

4 Experimental Results

To demonstrate the validity and accuracy of the method, we have conducted experiments where five indoor and outdoor video sequences are employed: A: hall (indoor, 352×288 pixels); B: Intelligent Room (indoor, 320×240 pixels); C Lab (indoor, 320×240 pixels); D campus (outdoor, 352×288 pixels); E run (outdoor, 180×144 pixels). A is obtained from the standard test sequences. B, C and D are obtained from the CVRR database [18]. E is from the database in [19]. The results of experiments are given at an Intel Pentium E5300 2.6GHz, 2G RAM computer in MS Visual C++ development circumstance.

The experiments compared the time-consuming and the integrity of the foreground among the Gaussian mixture background modeling [11], the code book [14], and the proposed algorithm. We use the two metrics for characterizing the *TPR* and the *FPR* as following:

$$TPR = TP/(TP + FN), FPR = FP/(TR + FN) \tag{5}$$

where *TPR* is also called detection rate. TP (true positive) is the detected regions that correspond to moving objects. FP (false positive) is the detected regions that do not correspond to a moving object. FN (false negative) is the moving objects not detected. The experiments result is given in table 1. From table 1, one can notice that the proposed method can effectively deal with the interference of the shadow and noise, and get better performance.

Table 1. Comparison of different methods on five tested datasets

Data set	Detection rate(TPR/FPR)		
	GMM[11]	Codebook [14]	**Proposal**
Run	0.9821/0.1654	0.9832/0.023	**0.9812/0.0432**
Hall	0.6780/0.2143	0.5563/0.0122	**0.7631/0.0232**
Intelligent room	0.9120/0.5632	0.8194/0.0782	**0.9681/0.0937**
Lab	0.9644/0.5431	0.9527/0.3542	**0.9611/0.0983**
Campus	0.9424/0.5231	0.9251/0.3416	**0.9562/0.1325**

Some examples of foreground segmentation result are shown in Fig. 3.

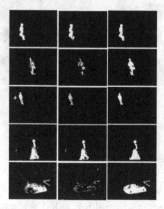

Fig. 3. Some examples of foreground segmentation result based on GMM, Codebook and proposal. The first column is results of GMM, the second column is results of Codebook, and the third is results of proposal.

Time consumed by three algorithms investigated over each video sequence is shown in Fig. 4.

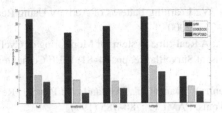

Fig. 4. Comparison of running time

5 Conclusions

This paper has presented an approach to segment the foreground and suppressing shadow from video sequences. We use Gauss mixture model to extract foreground, and the combination of HSV color space to effectively suppress the shadow. Based on the related video database testing, for the complex and simple scene, our algorithm has a good foreground extraction and shadow suppression effect. The proposed approach is more efficient and has better performance at accuracy, integrity, time-consuming. After it, we get effective and reliable movement region of the acquisition. In the future, with some stable detection information, we would like to get useful features to manifest movement.

Acknowledgments. This work is partly supported by the National Natural Science Foundation of China (Grant no. 11176016, 60872117).

References

1. Candamo, J., Shreve, M., Goldgof, D., Sapper, D., Kasturi, R.: Understanding Transit Scenes: A Survey on Human Behavior-recognition Algorithms. Trans. Intel. Transp. Syst. 11, 206–224 (2010)
2. Xiao, B., Lu, C., Chen, H., Yu, Y., Chen, R.: Moving Object Detection and Recognition Based on the Frame Difference Algorithm and Moment Invariant Features. In: 27th Chinese Control Conference, pp. 578–581. IEEE Press, New York (2008)
3. Sheikh, Y., Javed, O., Kanade, T.: Background Subtraction for Freely Moving Cameras. In: IEEE Int. Conf. Computer Vision, pp. 1219–1225. IEEE Computer Society, Los Alamitos (2009)
4. Kwak, S., Lim, T., Nam, W.: Generalized Background Subtraction Based on Hybrid Inference by Belief Propagation and Bayesian Filtering. In: IEEE Int. Conf. Computer Vision, pp. 2174–2181. IEEE Computer Society, Los Alamitos (2011)
5. Yilmaz, A., Javed, O., Shah, M.: Object Tracking: A survey. ACM Comput. Surv. 38, 1–45 (2006)
6. Denman, S., Fookes, C., Sridharan, S.: Improved Simultaneous Computation of Motion Detection and Optical Flow for Object Tracking. In: Digital Image Computing: Techniques and Applications, pp. 175–182. IEEE Computer Society, Los Alamitos (2009)

7. Stauffer, C., Grimson, W.: Learning Patterns of Activity Using Real-time Tracking. IEEE Trans. PAMI 22, 747–757 (2000)
8. Heikkila, J., Silven, O.: A Real-time System for Monitoring of Cyclists and Pedestrians. In: IEEE Workshop on Visual Surveillance, pp. 74–81. IEEE Computer Society, Los Alamitos (1999)
9. Wren, C., Azarbayejani, A., Darrell, T., Pentland, A.: Pfinder: Real-time Tracking of the Human Body. IEEE Trans. PAMI 19, 780–785 (1997)
10. Fazli, S., Pour, H., Bouzari, H.: A Novel GMM-based Motion Segmentation Method for Complex Background. In: 5th IEEE GCC Conference and Exhibition, pp. 1–5. IEEE Press, New York (2009)
11. Zivkovic, Z.: Improved Adaptive Gaussian Mixture Model for Background Subtraction. In: IEEE Int. Conf. Pattern Recognition, vol. 2, pp. 28–31. IEEE Computer Society, Los Alamitos (2004)
12. Jain, V., Kimia, B., Mundy, J.: Background Modeling Based on Subpixel Edges. In: IEEE Int. Conf. Image Process., pp. 321–324. IEEE Computer Society, Los Alamitos (2007)
13. Ilyas, A., Scuturici, M., Miguet, S.: Real Time Foreground-background Segmentation Using A Modified Codebook Model. In: 6th IEEE Int. Conf. Advanced Video and Signal Based Surveillance, pp. 454–459. IEEE Computer Society, Los Alamitos (2009)
14. Pal, A., Schaefer, G., Celebi, M.: Robust Codebook-based Video Background Subtraction. In: Int. Conf. Acoustics Speech and Signal Processing, pp. 1146–1149. IEEE Press, New York (2010)
15. Guan, Y.-P.: Spatio-temporal Motion-based Foreground Segmentation and Shadow Suppression. IET Computer Vision 4, 50–60 (2010)
16. Ding, B., Shi, R., Liu, Z., Zhang, Z.: Human Object Segmentation Using Gaussian Mixture Model and Graph Cuts. In: Int. Conf. Audio Language and Image Process., pp. 787–790. IEEE Computer Society, Los Alamitos (2010)
17. Cucchiara, R., Grana, C., Piccardi, M., Prati, A., Sirotti, S.: Improving Shadow Suppression in Moving Object Detection with HSV Color Information. In: IEEE Intelligent Transportation Systems, pp. 334–339. IEEE Press, New York (2001)
18. CVRR database, http://cvrr.ucsd.edu/aton/shadow/
19. http://www.wisdom.weizmann.ac.il/~vision/SpaceTimeActions.html

An Improved Algorithm Based on IHS Transform for the Fusion of Object and Scene

Youdong Ding[1], Xiaocheng Wei[2], and Jianliang Lan[1]

[1] School of Film & TV Arts and Technology
[2] School of Computer Engineering and Science,
Shanghai University, Shanghai, China
cookiecooki@hotmail.com

Abstract. Since the existing object-scene fusion method based on IHS transform has two defects: emergence of the scene image's illusion in target area and the illumination inconformity of the fusion object, this paper proposes an improved algorithm through rearranging the hue component and saturation component of the new scene image which are used to carry out IHS inverse transform. Subjective quality evaluation and objective quality assessment data of comparative fusion experiment results show that the new algorithm not only can get rid of the two drawbacks of the existing object-scene fusion method based on IHS transform effectively and achieve better fusion result in the application of object-scene fusion, but also performs fast.

Keywords: Fusion of object and scene, IHS transform, Image rearrangement, Quality evaluation.

1 Introduction

As a visual simulation technology and application branch of image fusion, fusion of object and scene (object-scene fusion) refers to segment the target object of interest from the original scene image then blend it into another scene graph through overlying, combination and processing. The fusion image must look real and natural. Object-scene fusion has been widely used in image editing field [1], [2], especially in the film production process. Many shots can not be obtained through on-the-spot shooting, such as embedding the actor's behavior which is conducted in the real world into a fantasy environment. These lenses can use object-scene fusion technology to realize [3]. The simplest method for the fusion of object and scene is to copy directly. What we need to do is no more than to adjust the size or orientation of object in order to suit its position in the new scenarios. When the illumination contrast between the object and the new scene is large, the fusion result will lack sense of reality. Fusion effect of Poisson image editing technique is inferior when a great texture difference exists between the object and the new scene graph, causing color distortion of the object. Alpha blending algorithm performs poorly when the object is inconsistent with the new scene in illumination. At present, three-dimensional (3D) illumination method is the most accurate. But it needs a certain number of images to rebuild 3D

W. Zhang et al. (Eds.): IFTC 2012, CCIS 331, pp. 59–66, 2012.

structures, and it requires more conditions and is complex to implement, this is unnecessary and not practical for general fusion applications [4]. Currently, image fusion method based on IHS transform is basically only used in remote sensing field and multi-focus image fusion applications.

2   Object-Scene Fusion Based on IHS Transform

The greatest advantage of the image fusion scheme based on IHS transform lies in simpleness and rapidness. It has become one of the basic methods in remote sensing image fusion since proposed by Haydan et al in 1982. One important application of this method is to fuse the multispectral (MS) image with the panchromatic (PAN) image in order to inject the spatial information from the PAN image into the MS image without overly modifying the spectral information of the latter. The main steps of using the standard IHS transform to carry out this fusion are: 1) Transform MS from RGB into IHS; 2) Replace intensity component I with PAN; 3) Convert MS back to RGB.

Since the correlation between intensity (I) component and the other two components, hue (H) component and saturation (S) component, is not obvious, we can process I independently.

Based on IHS transform and the concept of intensity modulation, a new framework for the fusion of object and scene has been proposed in [4] recently. The framework first uses IHS transform and intensity modulation as intensity fusion tools to generate an illumination mask image, then restores the object's details on the mask image to achieve the purpose of fusion. The main steps of it are:

1. Segment and overlie. First create a copy graph of the new scene image Image1 named Image1', then segment the target object from the original scene picture and overlie it onto a suitable position of Image1'. The overlap area of the target object and new scene is defined as target area and the rest areas are called background area. The overlying result is labeled Image2.

2. IHS transform. Transform Image1 and Image2 from RGB into IHS, the transformation results are Image1_ihs and Image2_ihs. Fetch I components of them which are labeled I1 and I2 respectively.

3. Intensity fusion. Fuse I1 with I2 to form fusion intensity I1' by means of a certain fusion algorithm.

4. IHS inverse transform. Replace I component of Image1_ihs with I1', and perform IHS inverse transform on the Image1_ihs to get the illumination mask image Maskimage.

5. Detail restoration. The final fusion image could not be gained until a proper detail restoration algorithm is employed to restore the details of the object on the Maskimage.

Intensity fusion is the core link of the framework. Standard IHS transform technique and weighted wavelet technique have already been introduced as intensity fusion tools to verify the framework's practicality and the experimental data suggest that standard IHS transform fusion scheme performs better than weighted wavelet fusion scheme [4]. Standard IHS transform fusion scheme do the intensity fusion like this: 1) I2 histogram matched to I1 , the result is I2'; 2) I1'= I2'. Histogram matching is adopted to minimize the modification of the spectral information of the original image during the fusion [5]. It accomplish the detail restoration by adding weighted Image2 to weighted Maskimage as below:

$$F = \alpha \cdot M + \beta \cdot S \qquad (1)$$

where $\alpha + \beta = 1$, M and S stand for Maskimage and Image2, F is the final fusion image. The metric α determines the illumination degree of the fused object, and metric β determines its details' richness degree. When α is too large (β is too small), the object's details should not be rich enough, and the target area will emerge an illusion of the scene image. On the contrary, if β is too large (α is too small), fused illumination of the object cannot be well demonstrated, and the object will look unnatural in new scene. So the choice of weights is very important. For fuse the same object into different scenes may require different weights, we must choose appropriate weights according to the actual situation.

Although this scheme is simple, it may cause two problems. First, through a large number of experiments, we have come to a conclusion that when the texture of the object is simple or the illumination contrast between object and new scene image Image1 is large, we must appropriately increase the value of α in (1). But if the texture of the object is simple and that of Image1 is complex, at the same time, the illumination contrast between object and Image1 is great, we have to amplify α to make the object commensurate with the illumination condition of Image1. Unfortunately, before we can achieve this goal, α may already be too large causing the target area emerge an illusion of the scene image. On the other hand, illumination of the fusion object is strongly dependent on the information of Image1 in target area because hue component and saturation component used to carry out IHS inverse transform are both from Image1. When the target area of Image1 owns different levels, that is to say, different subareas of the target region have different brightness and color, the fusion object may not be harmonious because different parts of the object will present different illumination.

In order to reveal these two defects, we conduct a fusion experiment with the same experimental pictures employed in [4]. Experiment results are shown in Fig. 1, where the spatial resolution of the new scene image is 900×675. Fig. 1(c) and Fig. 1(d) are both the fusion results of standard IHS transform fusion scheme. Detail restoration coefficients used in (c) are $\alpha = 0.2$, $\beta = 0.8$, and that used in (d) are $\alpha = 0.3$, $\beta = 0.7$. Meanwhile, we magnified the new scene image and (d) to fetch detail pictures of the identical regions of them. These detail graphs are shown in (e) and (f) respectively. (c) and (d) illustrate that increase of α makes brightness and color of the object more close to the new scene and natural. But (e) and (f) demonstrate the side-effect of this augment of detail restoration coefficient. We can catch sight of the illusion of scene image on the boy's body obviously which prevents us to amplify the value of α further. Moreover, neither (c) nor (d) have achieved a successful modulation since the illumination of the boy's body is reasonable in the new scene, but the head of the boy should not present such a high brightness under the dim light of background.

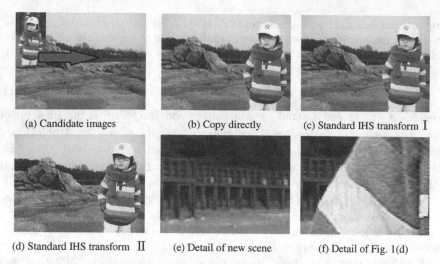

(a) Candidate images   (b) Copy directly   (c) Standard IHS transform I

(d) Standard IHS transform II   (e) Detail of new scene   (f) Detail of Fig. 1(d)

Fig. 1. Fusion experiment revealing the defects

Therefore, in order to overcome these shortcomings and also attain fast object-scene fusion without degrading fusion result, we improve the existing object-scene fusion method based on IHS transform and propose a modified algorithm.

3   Improved Algorithm

The main cause of the two drawbacks explained in Section 2 is that fusion process is heavily dependent on the information of the new scene image Image1 in target area. Since Image1 has its own texture and the illumination of its target area may vary from subarea to subarea, fusion object may contain the texture of the scene and display an inharmonious illumination. So what we need to do is to remove the texture in target area of Image1 and get rid of the illumination inconformity between subareas of target area in Image1. One useful tool to remove texture is smoothing filters, such as averaging filter and Gaussian filter. However, they could do little to eliminate illumination inconformity fundamentally.

We don't care about the content in the target area of Image1. What we need is only its color information. So we can rearrange the target area: replace the pixel value of one subarea with that of another subarea, then they will have the same illumination information. Further, we can select a pixel which is able to reflect the illumination that object will present after fusion process from the entire Image1 and pad the whole target area of Image1 with it. Thus, the target area not only contains no texture, but also has uniform illumination. In fact, since only the hue component and saturation component of Image1 are utilized in fusion process, we just need to rearrange the hue image and saturation image of Image1 respectively like this:

$$pixel(i,j) = \begin{cases} selected(M,N) & (i,j) \in target\ area \\ pixel(i,j) & (i,j) \in background\ area \end{cases} \tag{2}$$

where (i,j) is a pixel of the image that will be rearranged and $pixel(i, j)$ is the value of it, $1 \le i \le HR$, $1 \le j \le VR$, HR is the horizontal resolution of the image and VR is the vertical resolution. The $selected(M,N)$ is the value of the pixel which is selected to pad the target area, M and N are constants. In addition, since segmentation algorithm is not within the research scope of this paper, we will not discuss "segment and overlie" in detail but only focus on the fusion operation and assume Image2 is ready-made as the input of fusion algorithm. Then we can give the implementation steps of the improved algorithm as following:

1. Transform Image1 and Image2 from RGB into IHS, fetch the I components of Image1_ihs and Image2_ihs which are labeled I1 and I2 respectively.

2. I2 histogram matched to I1, the matched result is I2'.

3. Select an appropriate pixel (M,N) from the hue image H of Image1_ihs, then rearrange H using (2), the rearranged result is H'. Select the same pixel on the saturation image S of Image1_ihs and rearrange it using (2) too, the rearranged result is S'.

4. Replace I component of Image1_ihs with I2', and perform IHS inverse transform on Image1_ihs with I2', H' and S' to get the illumination mask image Maskimage.

5. Conduct detail restoration on Maskimage using (1).

(a) Improved algorithm   (b) Detail of Fig. 2(a)

Fig. 2. Fusion effect of improved algorithm

Fig. 2 shows the fusion effect of the improved algorithm. The central pixel of the blue rectangle marked on Fig. 2(a) serves as $selected(M,N)$. With the same detail restoration coefficients as that adopted by standard IHS transform fusion scheme in Fig. 1(d), new method can both accomplish the fusion of object and scene well and surmount the two defects of the existing algorithm effectively. Fig. 2(a) shows the intensity modulation is very successful because the illumination of the boy's head is consistent with that of the body. This makes the object more lifelike. Fig. 2(b) illustrates that illusion of the scene image no longer appears on the fusion object for the content in target area of the new scene image has been remove after rearrangement, only leaving color information. Hence, we could enlarge the value of α enough in detail restoration procedure to get a more vivid illumination on the object that is close to the background enough.

Fig. 3 demonstrates more fusion effects of the improved algorithm, where four images in the same row serve as a group. Four images in a group, from left to right, are original scene image, new scene image, effect of the existing object-scene fusion method based on IHS transform and the fusion effect of the improved algorithm respectively.

Fig. 3. More fusion effects of the improved algorithm

4   Quality Evaluation

Fig. 1 and Fig. 2 have shown a comparative fusion experiment and subjective quality evaluation has verified the superiority of the improved algorithm. In this section, we will carry out objective quality assessment on Fig. 1(b), Fig. 1(d) and Fig. 2(a) with four objective evaluation indexes:

1. Correlation Coefficient (CC). By calculating the CC between the background area of Image2 and that of fusion image, we can measure how the fusion process impact on the background area. The more CC is close to 1, the less this impact is.

2. Sum of mutual information (MI_F^{AB}). We can evaluate fusion quality of target area through computing the MI_F^{AB} of fusion image F, Image1 and Image2 in this area [6]. The greater MI_F^{AB} is, the better object information and scene information are fused within the area.

3. Average gradient ($\overline{G}$). For the sake of definition of fusion image and the ability of it expressing the tiny detail contrast and texture variation feature, we calculate the $\overline{G}$ of fusion picture. Generally speaking, the larger $\overline{G}$ is, the more levels fusion image has and the clearer it is [7].

4. Ratio of fusion time. We use fusion processing time as an index out of consideration of computation efficiency. Likewise, we only count the time consumed during image fusion procedure, without regarding to the time spent on "segment and overlie". Same operation will be implemented on the same algorithm 100 times, and the average execution time will serve as the final processing time. In order to eliminate the influence imposed by experiment environment on evaluation, we set the time taken by the standard IHS transform fusion scheme 1, then give the time ratios with it of other schemes.

Table 1 and Table 2 give the objective evaluation data on hue component and intensity component separately. Table 3 shows the ratios of fusion time. M1, M2 and M3 stand for copy directly, standard IHS transform and the improved algorithm respectively.

Table 1. Objective Evaluation Data on H

Fusion scheme	CC	MI_F^{AB}	$\overline{G}$
M1	1	None	1.3908e-004
M2	99.58%	2.7032	1.7256e-004
M3	99.58%	4.0763	1.5533e-004

Table 2. Objective Evaluation Data on I

Fusion scheme	CC	MI_F^{AB}	$\overline{G}$
M1	1	None	7.3182e-005
M2	99.86%	12.0661	7.0503e-005
M3	99.86%	13.4521	6.9564e-005

Table 3. Ratios of Fusion Time

	M2	M3
Time ratio	1	1.1025

Direct copy scheme hasn't fuse the information of object and new scene in target area, so MI_F^{AB} which reflects the amount of information extracted by fusion image from object and scene graphs is meaningless to it and corresponding table cell is filled with "None". Judging from CC, direct copy method makes no difference to information of background area, thus the CC is 1. The remaining two schemes both have certain influence on the hue and intensity of background area. These two methods which are both based on IHS transform modulate the intensity of object and that of the whole background area at the same time in order to make the target object look consistent in illumination in the new scene. However, CC of them are all above 99.58%, this impact is not evident. MI_F^{AB} and $\overline{G}$ both indicate that the improved algorithm performed better than the standard IHS transform method here. For fusion processing time, new algorithm is almost equivalent to standard IHS transform, it can also achieve fast object-scene fusion.

5 Conclusion

Object-scene fusion technique is increasingly being applied to the film production, which endows great practical significance to its research [8, 9]. This paper improves the existing object-scene fusion method based on IHS transform and proposes a modified algorithm. Quality evaluation of comparative fusion experiment results shows that the new method can not only accomplish the fusion of object and scene well and overcome the two defects of the existing algorithm effectively, but also performs fast. Thus, it has significant application value.

References

1. Pérez, P., Gangnet, M., Blake, A.: Poisson image editing. In: Proceedings of the SIGGRAPH Conference, pp. 313–318. IEEE Press, San Diego (2003)
2. Wang, D., Zhou, S.S., Sang, X.S.: Simulation for Pyrography Style Painting Based on Texture Transfer. Journal of System Simulation 22(12), 2929–2933 (2010)
3. Jia, J.Y., Sun, J., Tang, C.K., Shum, H.Y.: Drag-and-Drop Pasting. In: Proceedings of the SIGGRAPH Conference, pp. 631–636. IEEE Press, Boston (2006)
4. Ding, Y.D., Wei, X.C., et al.: A new framework for the fusion of object and scene based on IHS transform. In: Proceedings of the ICDIP, v8009: 80091W. IEEE Press, Chengdu (2011)
5. Song, Q., Wang, J.W., Zhang, H.B.: An Overview on Fusion of Panchromatic Image and Multispectral Image. In: International Conference on Information Engineering and Computer Science, pp. 1–4. IEEE Press, Wuhan (2009)
6. Qu, G.H., Zhang, D.L., Yan, P.F.: Information Measure for Performance of image fusion. Electronics Letters 38(7), 313–315 (2002)
7. Gu, H., Liu, Z., et al.: Research and recent development of image fusion at pixel level. Application Research of Computers 25(3), 650–655 (2008)
8. Hays, J., Efros, A.A.: Scene Completion Using Millions of Photographs. In: Proceedings of the SIGGRAPH Conference, pp. 1–7. IEEE Press, San Diego (2007)
9. Chen, T., Cheng, M.M., Tan, P., Ariel, S., Hu, S.M.: Sketch2Photo: Internet Image Montage. ACM Transactions on Graphics 28(5), 1–10 (2009)

A New Method Used in Moving Vehicle Information Acquisition from Aerial Surveillance with a UAV*

Fuqiang Liu, Xiaofeng Liu, Pingting Luo, Yingqian Yang, and Danqing Shi

BW&M Lab, School of Electronics and Information Engineering,
Tongji University, Shanghai, 201804, P.R. China
liufuqiang@tongji.edu.cn

Abstract. In this paper, a multiple moving vehicle detecting and tracking framework on aerial range data provided by the unmanned aerial vehicle (UAV) which is installed with a video camera is proposed. The system consists of two modules: moving vehicle detection, multi vehicle tracking. First of all, detect moving vehicles by clustering the singular points obtained after the motion estimation. Then, build a specific data structure to store multi-vehicle's data and track several vehicles in the shaking video sequence from the UAV. After tracking the vehicle in the video sequence, the speed of the vehicle and record them as traffic flow information would be estimated. Finally, the method on real aerial data and the experiments are estimated and demonstrate the effectiveness of approach.

Keywords: aerial video, dynamic background, multiple target tracking, cluster singular points.

1   Introduction

Compared with sensors located on the ground, UAV visual surveillance platform has many advantages. Low cost, easy to deploy, high mobility, UAV can save time and money to acquire information from a sparse highway system by just let the aircraft to patrol itself. The key point of UAV traffic information acquisition is to detect and sense the traffic element precisely.

The UAV visual surveillance system also brings exceptional problems to vehicle identification. Unlike the still background in traditional surveillance system, the background in the UAV surveillance platform changes frequently because of the high speed of the aircraft. To identify traffic status and incidents, the complex background should be filtered, traffic features should be detected, both of which should be accomplished en-route, so it has a very high demand of the performance of the algorithm [1].

To deal with these problems, a lot of relative works have been done widely. HulyaYalcin [2] and Hsu-Yung Cheng [3] proposed a detection approach of moving

---

* This research is supported by a grant from National High Technology Research and Development Program of China (863 Program) (2009AA11Z220).

W. Zhang et al. (Eds.): IFTC 2012, CCIS 331, pp. 67–72, 2012.

vehicles based on dense optical flow estimated by a Bayesian framework. But this method didn't achieve good performance under the condition of camera vibration and noise interference. So as to counteract the influence of vibration,

Wang Wen-long [4] developed a detection method with some restriction conditions and fuzzy classification in the context of varying background to identify moving and static vehicles. Although this method could differentiate the moving and static vehicles, it only worked well when the background is not complex.

2   Moving Vehicle Detection

In this stage, detect the moving vehicle based on singular points clustering for three times. But before that singular points first by selecting reliable singular points for motion estimation should be detected. Use restrictions to select the best image points to compute image motion. The first restriction selects the points whose gradient magnitude value is above a noise-adaptive threshold. The points are characterized by their large principal curvature along the edge. By adopt the approach of Harris and Stephen [5]. A non-maximal suppression is applied to obtain the final selection of singular points. K-means [6] clustering algorithm has been used in this system. First clustering classifies the singular points for three parts: the vehicle whose direction is opposite with the plane, the background, and the vehicle whose direction is same with the plane. The motion vector $Dis(P_i)$ of each singular points P_i is:

$$Dis(P_i) = Coordinate(P_m) - Coordinate(P_n) \qquad (1)$$

P_m, P_n are the matched points in consecutive images. The motion vector $Dis(P_i)$ of singular points in vehicle whose direction is opposite with the plane is larger than the background, which is larger than the vehicle whose direction is the same with the plane. So the result of clustering is well just with a little false clustering.

In the second clustering, the number of clusters is calculated first, and which is also the number of moving vehicles.

Third clustering: the singular points are clustering for two clusters: vehicle and the noise. And in two clusters, the distance between singular points is different. The vehicle is the cluster that has less distance. The noise is the cluster that has larger distance. The results of moving vehicle detection are shown in Fig. 5(a).

3   Vehicle Tracking and Velocity Estimation

There are several tracking algorithm being used in tracking targets including Kalman filter, Meanshift [7] tracker. But none of them can have a good performance in an aerial video capture in the UAV. The sudden shake can cause the tracker lost the target because the region of interest is too small for the tracker to find the target in the next frame during one shaking frame.

The region of interest value is set before the track begin to work. So it can not predict the vector lenth of shake in the video sequence there would be. if the shake is big enough to let the object goes out of the tracking field. The track will be lost.

In order to solve the tracking problem in a shaking video sequence, template match algorithm [8] is used to find the vehicle in the one frame first. Suppose we want to find a position which has the maximum correlation with the template image data in search position, the correlation degree by template matching can be computed.

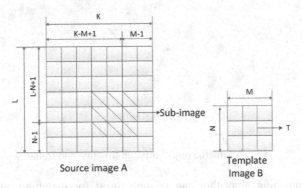

Fig. 1. A schematic diagram of template matching algorithm

Assumed that the template b is put to cover on the source image A and moving. The area that covered by template B is called sub-image $S_{i,j}$, in which "i" and "j" is the coordinate of the left up point in the source image that the sub-image is covering. From the Fig.1 the value range of i, j can be got as: $1 \leq i \leq K - M + 1$, $1 \leq j \leq L - N + 1$

Then measure the correlation between the template T and the sub-image $S_{i,j}$. the following measure can be used

$$D(i, j) = \sum_{m=1}^{M} \sum_{n=1}^{N} [S^{i,j}(m,n) - T(m.n)]^2 \tag{2}$$

Matching location algorithm can finish the entire small matching error point search in matching area, which is expressed as a formula (3):

$$D_{\min}(i, j) = Min \sum_{i=1}^{K-M+1} \sum_{j=1}^{L-N+1} \sum_{m=1}^{M} \sum_{n=1}^{N} [S^{i,j}(m,n) - T(m,n)]^2 \tag{3}$$

The impact of the size of template on the performance of the system and the calculation cannot be underestimated. In actual operation, when the template size is 32x16, the effect is perfect. So it had been done in the UAV tracking platform.

Realized that if the source image is big, the program needs to do a large number of looping according to the formula (3). Matching results shows that the matching error decreased rapidly near the matching point which is significantly different from other position. According to this feature, coarse-fine searching method can be used to lock up the target area quickly; this can reduce the times of global matching in the whole image. Use the image of the vehicle that is detected in the current frame as the template of matching in the next frame as Fig. 2 shows.

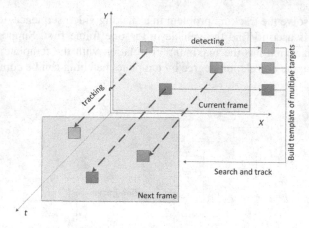

Fig. 2. Link the object through timeline and frame

Template matching algorithm can be only used for matching and tracking one target. It will link the coordination of the target through the time line. But now there are several targets appear in each frame and there are several frames containing targets. So it is very important to build a proper data structure to store and manage all matching and tracking data.

So a structure like this could be built:

Table 1. Data structure of tracking algorithm

variant	Type	comment
X,Y	float	The coordinate given by the detect module
Vehicleid	integer	The unique id of the target
Direction	bool	Direction of the vehicle
Velocity	integer	Velocity of the vehicle
Lastshifting	integer	The coordinate given by the last tracking loop
Shifting	integer	The coordinate given by the current tracking loop
Tpl	image	Template of the target vehicle
Similarity	float	Similarity in matching
Stats	integer	State of the target including enabled and disabled
Startframe	integer	The frame number that tracking starts
Stopframe	integer	The frame number that tracking ends

The table above refers to a certain data structure. Each target vehicle can be stored separately in the data structure and containing the property defined in the structure which ensures the possibility of tracking several targets in one frame. When the detect module give a signal that it detected a target. There will be a new object created in the database which inherits and initialize all of the property.

Now it is necessary to introduce a concept that is tracking period (Fig. 3) which is the time length of each object lives. In a tracking period, whether an object is valid or not depends on whether the object is in the field of frame. After one period, system will terminate tracking even if the target vehicle is in the field of frame and begin to calculate the velocity of the target vehicle.

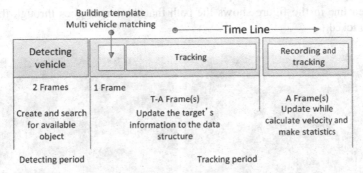

Fig. 3. Introduction of tracking period

From a target vehicle being detected, the tracking period is valid until the vehicle disappear or timeout. Some information such as vehicle speed can be acquired from the data structure.

Velocity: In one tracking period, we can calculate the distance (Fig. 4) that the target goes along the road to make out how many pixels there is between the startframe's coordination and endframe's coordination. Project the vector to the direction of the road. The real distance can be calculated if given the scale of the video.

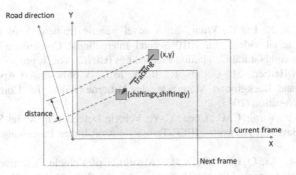

Fig. 4. Calculation of velocity

4   Conclusion

In this paper, by using an UAV platform in a sparse highway system, both detecting and tracking module are working correctly. Even in shaking video sequences, the velocity of vehicle estimation accuracy can be up to 88% and vehicle detecting accuracy can be up to 90%.

If using Kalman filter in tracking the objects in the same video sequence. The detecting accuracy can be up to 84%, but in some shaking scenes, the accuracy drops to 42%, which means only 21 in 50 vehicles can be detected in the whole sequence including the shaky scenes.

The red line in the figure shows the path that the target goes through the frames that are tracked.

(a)Vehicle detecting result   (b)vehicle tracking period result

Fig. 5. Vehicle detecting and tracking result

Not only the velocity information can be calculated, but traffic flow, vehicle coordination and direction information can also be collected.

References

[1] Tian, Y., Lu, J., Li, Y., Wang, J.: A novel generic framework of event detection in unmanned aerial videos. In: 2010 Second International Conference on Computational Intelligence and Natural Computing Proceedings (CINC), vol. 1, pp. 357–360 (2010)

[2] Yalcin, H., Herbert, M., Collins, R., Black, M.J.: A Flow-Based Approach to Vehicle Detection and Background Mosaicking in Airborne Video. In: Computer Vision and Pattern Recognition (2005)

[3] Cheng, H.-Y., Weng, C.-C., Chen, Y.-Y.: Vehicle Detection in Aerial Surveillance Using Dynamic Bayesian Networks. IEEE Transactions on Image Processing 21(4), 2152–2159 (2012)

[4] Wang, W.-L., Li, Q.-Q., Tang, L.-L.: Algorithm of Vehicle Detection in Low Altitude Aerial Video. Journal of Wuhan University of Technology 32(10), 155–158 (2010)

[5] Harris, C., Stephens, M.: A combined corner and edge detector (PDF). In: Proceedings of the 4th Alvey Vision Conference, pp. 147–151 (1988)

[6] Ding, C., He, X.: K-means Clustering via Principal Component Analysis. In: Proc.of Intel Conf. Machine Learning (ICML 2004), pp. 225–232 (July 2004)

[7] Zhou, K., Fan, R.-X., Li, W.-X.: A MeanShift-Particle Fusion tracking algorithm based on SIFT. In: 2010 29th Chinese Control Conference (CCC), pp. 2717–2720 (2010)

[8] Gonzalez, R.C., Woods, R.E.: Digital Image Processing, 3rd edn., pp. 132–135. Pearson, Prentice Hall (2008)

A Robust Bus Detection and Recognition Method Based on 3D Model and LSD Method for Public Security Road Crossing Application

Wenqi Ma[1,*], Hua Yang[1], and Yingkun Wang[2]

[1] Institution of Image Communication and Information Processing,
Department of EE, Shanghai Jiaotong University, Shanghai, 200240, China
Shanghai Key Laboratory of Digital Media Processing and Transmission
[2] Department of Optical-Electronic and Computer Engineering,
University of Shanghai for Science and Technology
{mawenqi2011,hyang}@sjtu.edu.cn, wmeggie@sina.com.cn

Abstract. Bus detection and recognition in real transportation scenes is a fundamental task for public security road crossing application. In this paper, a novel system is proposed to overcome the high computation complexity and the hard task of training large set of 3D models of the current algorithms. In the proposed system, the 3D model is built according to the contour information of the vehicle itself so that the system is more robust and practical. Meanwhile, the line features of the vehicle are extracted using the LSD (line segment detector) method. Finally, the line features are matched with the 3D model using a combined matching algorithm which reduces the computational complexity of the matching process. Experiments on real videos show the proposed method has a good performance in terms of the high recall ratio and low fall-out ratio.

Keywords: vehicle detection, vehicle recognition, 3D model, LSD, template matching method, combined matching method, computing efficiency.

1   Introduction

Model based vehicle detection and recognition in real transportation scenes is a fundamental issue for the public security road crossing application [1]. Since the bus is such an important vehicle in the urban road traffic that providing the information about the bus, such as the type and the location of it, would be very significant.

To recognize the vehicles, traditional algorithms, the tree search [2], the attributed graph search [3], the generalized Hough Transform [4] and so on, try to achieve the 2D-3D correspondence. 2D features like edge points, edge lines and vertices are first extracted as vehicle descriptions. Then recognition is realized by establishing the

---

* This research is supported by Shanghai Key Labs of Digital Media Processing and Transmission, NSFC (No.61102099) and STCSM (No.12DZ2272600, No.10231204002, No.11231203102).

W. Zhang et al. (Eds.): IFTC 2012, CCIS 331, pp. 73–81, 2012.
© Springer-Verlag Berlin Heidelberg 2012

match between the fixed model and the extracted features. However, the extraction and the matching of 2D geometric primitives such as lines and curves might be time-consuming and error-prone.

In recent years, most work in this field was based on fixed vehicle models (e.g., in [5]-[7]). In this case, vehicle recognition is based on comparing evaluation scores of different vehicle models. Success of the strategy depends strongly on how accurately the 3D model captures the geometry of the real vehicles. Since there are so many different states of vehicles in reality, a large set of models are needed to capture accurately their geometries, respectively, which is quite a difficult task. Even worse, the processing time of the fixed-model-based methods is linearly proportional to the number of vehicle models. Moreover, the focus of these algorithms [5][8][9] was on vehicle tracking instead of recognition.

To summarize, the mentioned algorithms could not directly be applied to bus recognition of the public security road crossing surveillance because of the high computational complexity and the low recall ratio. In this paper, a recognition system is proposed based on 3D model, which is constructed according to the contour information itself, thus there is no need to collect a large sample of 3D models in advance [5]-[7], which may be a formidable work. And in the matching stage, a novel algorithm is proposed which combines the template matching method and the minimized distance method. Since the minimized distance method just matches the points left by the template matching method, the compute time would be much lower than the traditional method [2][3][4].

The main object of our system is to assist the public security road crossing surveillance, providing the information about the bus, such as the type and the location of it. The remainder of this paper is organized as follows: the structure of the system is presented in section 2. Then the details of the bus recognition algorithm are discussed in section 3. In section 4, experiment results of the proposed system will be shown. Finally, the conclusion is made in section 5.

2   System Architecture

The system mainly includes two modules, which is shown in Fig. 1: module I denotes the vehicle detection process and module II denotes the vehicle recognition process.

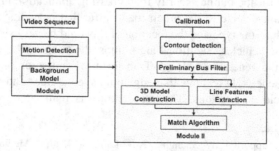

Fig. 1. System structure of vehicle detection and vehicle recognition

Referring to Fig. 1, in module I, motion detection segments foreground from the back-ground based on the mixture-of-Gaussian background modeling [8].

In module II, the calibration is firstly applied, which establishes a connection between world coordinate and image coordinate. Then, the contour information is extracted. Since it is time-consuming to construct the 3D model and apply the matching algorithm for all vehicles, a bus filter is applied to roughly get rid of the vehicles (except bus) according to the vehicle size in world coordinate. Next, the 3D model is constructed based on the contour information, the real size and the shape of the bus which are prior knowledge in our paper. Meanwhile, the line features of the vehicle will be extracted via the LSD method [11]. Finally, a combined matching algorithm is applied to the 3D model and the line features, the matching results will tell us whether the vehicle is a bus or not.

In the next section, we will focus on module II.

3   Vehicle Detection and Recognition

3.1   Calibration and Contour Detection

To construct the 3D model of the bus, contour detection is applied to the foreground image to extract the contour information of the vehicle. Since the real size of the bus is different from other vehicle, e.g. car, vehicles could be preliminarily filtered to avoid constructing the 3D model and implementing the match process for all vehicles.

First, the perspective transformation H between image coordinate and world coordinate should be computed. Then, the contour information of the vehicle is extracted. For each bus, a minimum rectangle R is gotten which contains all contours of the bus. The two bottom points of R are the base to construct the 3D model. After that, to reduce the workload of the follow-up procedure, a bus filter is applied to preliminarily judge whether the vehicle is a bus or not according to the position of the bottom points and the real length of a bus. Suppose all the buses have the same length l, using the bottom points p_1 and p_2, a new point p_m is created via Eq.1 in world coordinate. Since the length of bus is much longer than other vehicle, e.g. car, p_m would belong to R after converting to image coordinate if the vehicle is a bus. Fig. 2(a) shows an example of this relationship.

$$\begin{cases} p_m.x = (p_1.x + p_2.x)/2 \\ p_m.y = (p_1.y + p_2.y)/2 - l \\ p_m.z = p1.z \end{cases} \tag{1}$$

3.2   3D Model Construction

In this section, the 3D model [5][7][8][9] of each filtered vehicle is constructed based on the bus model. The two bottom points p_1 and p_2, the real length l, width w and height h of the bus have been known, then the 3D model could be constructed.

Step 1, the shape of the bus front is like a square so that we can get the top points p_3 and p_4 in world coordinate as described in Eq.2.

$$\begin{cases} p_3.x = p_1.x, \; p_3.y = p_1.y, \; p_3.z = p_1.z + h \\ p_4.x = p_2.x, \; p_4.y = p_2.y, \; p_4.z = p_2.z + h \end{cases} \qquad (2)$$

$$\begin{cases} \theta = \arctan\left(\frac{p_1.y - p_2.y}{p_2.x - p_1.x}\right) \\ p_j.x = p_i.x - l\sin\theta \quad (i,j) \in \{(1,5),(2,6)\} \\ p_j.y = p_i.y - l\cos\theta \end{cases} \qquad (3)$$

Step 2, the bottom points p_5 and p_6 of the bus rear could be computed by the geometric relationship through Eq.3, as shown in Fig. 2(b) and (c).

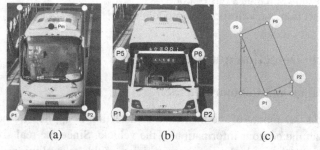

(a)   (b)   (c)

Fig. 2. An example of 3D model: (a) preliminary bus filter; (b) the top view of the bus; (c) geometric relationship

Step 3, the top points p_7 and p_8 of the bus rear are extracted as step 1 described. The generation process of the eight points is shown in Fig. 3.

Fig. 3. The generation process of the eight points

Step 4, now the bus lines could be decided as follows: (1) Fig. 4(a) shows six lines which could be caught by the front camera. (2) (p_5, p_6) is a line which could not be caught by our camera, as Fig. 4(b) shows. (3) (p_2, p_6), (p_6, p_8) are two lines which the camera might be caught according to the position p_6, if $p6 \in Rect(p_1, p_2, p_3, p_4)$, (p_2, p_6), (p_6, p_8) are invisible, as Fig. 4(b) shows. So do (p_1, p_5), (p_5, p_7). (4) The lines which are visible to the camera are selected as the lines of the 3D model.

(a)   (b)

Fig. 4. Lines of 3D model: (a) visible lines; (b) invisible lines

3.3　Line Feature Extraction

Now the line features of the vehicle need to be extracted to match with the 3D model. Here, a fast line segment detector (LSD) [11][12] will be adopted on the foreground image. LSD which is a linear time detector could give accurate results, a controlled number of false detections, and require no parameter tuning. Fig. 5 shows an example of LSD.

(a)   (b)

Fig. 5. An example of LSD: (a) original image; (b) line feature

3.4　Matching Algorithm

To match the line features and the 3D model, the template matching method and the minimized distance method are combined. As Fig. 6(b)-(d) show, φ is the line feature image extracted by LSD, ψ is the 3D model image whose pixel value belongs to $\{0,1\}$, $Dilate(I)$ means dilating image I and $Threshold_t^v()$ is defined as follows:

$$Threshold_t^v(I_{x,y}) = \begin{cases} v, & I_{x,y} \geq t \\ 0, & otherwise \end{cases} \qquad (4)$$

Then, the matching ratio η_1 could be calculated by the template matching method via Eq.5:

$$\eta_1 = \frac{\sum Threshold_2^1\{Threshold_{TH}^1[Dilate(\varphi)] + \psi\}}{\sum \psi} \qquad (5)$$

where $\varphi_0 = Threshold_2^1 \{Threshold_{TH}^1 [Dilate(\varphi)] + \psi\}$, representing the overlap region between the line features and the 3D model, as Fig. 6(e) shows. To compensate the missing detection of LSD, the line feature image is dilated. The ratio η_1 means the similarity between the line features and the 3D model and if η_1 is larger than a threshold (here 0.7 is selected), the vehicle could be preliminary judged as a bus and if η_1 is larger than a higher threshold (here 0.8 is selected), the vehicle could be confirmed as a bus, then the follow-up procedure would be ignored.

Suppose $\psi_h = \psi - \varphi_0$, representing the rest part of the 3D model except the overlap region, as Fig. 6(f) shows. $\varphi_h = Threshold_{TH}^1 [Dilate(\varphi)] - \varphi_0$, representing the rest part of line feature image except the overlap part. $I(\alpha)$ represents the gray scale value of the pixel α. $p(\alpha)$ represents the image coordinate of the pixel α. Then, the following algorithm is applied.

(a) Get the location $(p(\alpha))$ of the pixel α, where $\alpha \in \psi_h$ and $I(\alpha) \neq 0$. Then, a searching window w of $step \times step$ centered in $p(\alpha)$ is built.

(b) Search the point β_0 in the window w of the image ψ_h, where

$$d(\alpha) = \|p(\alpha) - p(\beta_0)\| = \min_{\beta \in w \in \psi_h} \|p(\alpha) - p(\beta)\|, I(\beta) \neq 0 \qquad (6)$$

(c) If $d(\alpha) < d_{TH}$, set $sum = sum + 1$ and $I(\beta) = 0$.
(d) Repeat step (a) until all the pixels in ψ_h have been iterated.

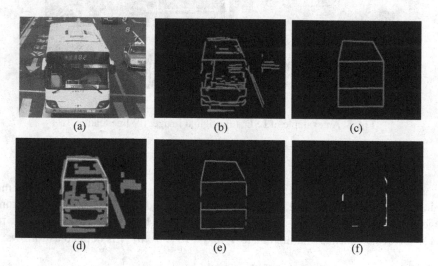

Fig. 6. an example of matching: (a) original image; (b) line feature image; (c) 3D model image; (d) dilated image; (e) overlap region; (f) rest of 3D model

Afterwards, the ratio η_2 is computed.

$$\eta_2 = \frac{sum}{\sum \psi_h} \qquad (7)$$

The image ψ_h is the 3D model point set except those that has been matched via the template matching method, the ratio η_2 represents the similarity between the line features and the rest 3D model points. When η_2 is also larger than a threshold (here 0.9 is selected), the vehicle can be confirmed as a bus.

In conclusion, a vehicle could be confirmed as a bus via Eq.8.

$$\begin{cases} \eta_1 > TH_h \\ \eta_1 > TH_l \ and \ \eta_2 > TH_d \end{cases} \tag{8}$$

4   Experiments and Results

In this work, the video sequences are captured from the public security road crossing application. The size of each frame in the test video is 1600x1200. The test video including 100 buses and 150 other vehicles (cars, trunks etc.) will be used as the experiment samples.

First, the bus filter proposed in subsection 3.1 is applied on the test video and the filter output is shown in table 1. This step aims to detect the buses as many as possible while get rid of some cars. Higher fall-out ratio occurs in the following cases: (1) two or more cars drive successively on the same road so that they are detected as a unity; (2) there are trucks or other vehicles whose shapes are similar to buses on the road.

Table 1. Output of the bus filter

Filter Output	Buses	Others(cars etc.)
Number	96	50

To decrease the fall-out ratio as much as possible while ensure the recall ratio remains in a proper level, the detected vehicles are recognized by the matching methods. The recognition results of the template matching method and the combined matching method are respectively shown in table 2.

From table 2, it can be seen the fall-out ratio declines rapidly after the vehicle recognition process because the line features of buses and other vehicles like trunks are different, which would be recognized through the matching methods. However, the recall ratio also decreases since the built 3D model is not so ideal and the omission of LSD exists.

The proposed combined matching method would decrease the fall-out ratio further as it will go on matching the rest points left by the template matching method. Meanwhile, it is not good for the recall ratio even in some cases the recall ratio will decline. From table 2, it can be seen the recall ratio of the combined method stays in the same level with the template matching method while the fall-out ratio falls.

We have achieved a recognition (process of module II) rate of approximately 0.7 fps using a standard PC machine (Intel i7-2600 3.4GHz). In the public security road crossing application, the algorithm is applied to the bus lane part of the image other than the whole scene so that it fits for the real-time application.

Table 2. Result of matching algorithms

Rate Method	Recall ratio	Fallout ratio	Omission ratio
template matching	90%(90/100)	6.8%(17/250)	10%(10/100)
combined matching	90%(90/100)	2.4%(6/250)	10%(10/100)

5   Conclusion

In this paper, a novel system is proposed to detect and recognize the bus for the public security road crossing application. In the proposed system, the foreground is firstly detected using the mixture-of-Gaussian background modeling and the contour information of the vehicle is then extracted. To reduce the workload of the follow-up procedure, a bus filter is applied. Afterwards, the 3D model is built according to the contour information and the real bus shape. Meanwhile, the line features of the vehicle are extracted through the LSD method. Finally, the line features are matched with the 3D model using a combined algorithm.

Since our 3D model is built on the contour information of the vehicle itself, the system does not need extra model database and the training process is also avoided. Thus the video surveillance system is more robust and practical. The bus filter avoids constructing the 3D model and implementing the match process for all vehicles and the combined matching algorithm combines the template matching method and the minimized distance method, both would reduce the computational complexity. Experiments on real videos show that the proposed method has a good performance in terms of the high correct detection rate.

References

1. Jones, W.: Keeping cars from crashing. IEEE Spectrum 38(9), 40–45 (2001)
2. Grimson, W.: The combinatorics of heuristic search termination for object recognition in cluttered environment. IEEE Trans. PAMI 13(9), 920–935 (1991)
3. Fan, T., Jain, A.: Recognizing 3D objects using surface descriptions. IEEE Trans. PAMI 11(11), 1140–1157 (1989)
4. Grimson, W., Huttenlocher, D.: On the sensitivity of Hough transform for object recognition. IEEE Trans. PAMI 12(3), 255–274 (1990)
5. Lou, J., Tan, T., Hu, W., Yang, H., Maybank, S.J.: 3-D model-based vehicle tracking. IEEE Trans. Image Process. 14(10), 1561–1569 (2005)
6. Tan, T.N., Sullivan, G.D., Baker, K.D.: Model-based localization and recognition of road vehicles. Int. J. Comput. Vis. 27(1), 5–25 (1998)
7. Tan, T.N., Baker, K.D.: Efficient image gradient based vehicle localization. IEEE Trans. Image Process. 9(8), 1343–1356 (2000)
8. Ottlik, A., Nagel, H.-H.: Initialization of Model-Based Vehicle Tracking in Video Sequences of Inner-City Intersections. IJCV 80(2), 211–225 (2008)
9. Hu, W., Xiao, X., Xie, D., Tan, T., Maybank, S.: Traffic accident prediction using 3D model based vehicle tracking. IEEE Trans. Vehicular Technology 53(3), 677–694 (2004)

10. Stauffer, C., Grimson, W.E.L.: Adaptive background mixture models for real-time tracking. In: IEEE Computer Society Conference on Computer Vision and Pattern Recognition, vol. 2 (1999)
11. von Gioi, R.G., Jakubowicz, J., Morel, J.-M., Randall, G.: LSD: A Fast Line Segment Detector with a False Detection Control. IEEE Trans. PAMI 32(4), 722–732 (2010)
12. LSD information,
    http://www.ipol.im/pub/algo/gjmr_line_segment_detector/
13. Ma, W.: Received the BS degree in EE department from Shanghai Jiao Tong University (SJTU), Shanghai, China. He is currently working toward the MS degree at SJTU
14. Yang, H.: Received her BS and MS degrees from Haerbin Engineering University, China, in, and, respectively. She has received the doctor degree in EE department from Shanghai Jiao Tong University, Shanghai, China. She is now an associate professor at SJTU. Her research interests are intelligent video surveillance and video analysis and understanding (1998)
15. Wang, Y.: Received the doctor degree in EE department from Shanghai Jiao Tong University, Shanghai, China. in She is now an associate professor at University of Shanghai For Science and Technology. Her research interest is video compression (2006)

Real-Time Human Intrusion Detection Using Audio-Visual Fusion*

Defu Wang[1], Shibao Zheng[1,2], and Chongyang Zhang[1,2]

[1] Institute of Image Communication and Network Engineering,
Shanghai Jiao Tong University, Shanghai 200240, China
[2] Shanghai Key Labs of Digital Media Processing and Transmission,
Shanghai 200240, China
{wonderwander,sbzh,sunny_zhang}@sjtu.edu.cn

Abstract. Human intrusion detection is widely used in intelligent video surveillance systems. It requires not only high accuracy but also real-time performance. In this paper, a real-time human intrusion detection algorithm is proposed to achieve good trade-off between detection accuracy and real-time performance: Firstly, fast HOG-based human recognition is designed, where HOG feature based human recognition is used to increase the detection accuracy, and one spatial-temporal joint detection region shrinking method is developed to reduce the computational load. Considering that the recognition accuracy of HOG-based human detection will drop markedly under occlusion, footstep recognition and a Bayesian Network based video-audio fusion model are proposed to achieve joint decision, which can improve the detection robustness further. Experimental results show that: compared with the existing methods, the proposed scheme can achieve better balance between the time consumption and detection accuracy.

Keywords: human intrusion detection, audio-visual fusion, HOG, footstep recognition, Bayesian network.

1 Introduction

Human intrusion detection is widely used in intelligent video surveillance. It requires not only high accuracy but also real-time performance. For most of existing methods, it is hardly to have good trade-off between accuracy and complexity. Some simple motion detection methods can achieve real-time performance, but with high false positive rate, such as frame difference method, background difference method. Since these methods are simply based on motion detection, they can't distinguish human intrusion from other intrusions accurately.

Dalal and Triggs [1] presented a Histograms of Oriented Gradients(HOG) based human detection algorithm : for each detection block with size of 16×16

---

* This work was supported by the NSF of China under grant No.61001147,61171172, the China National Key Technology R&D Program under grants No. 2012BAH07B01, and by the STCSM of Shanghai under grant No.12DZ2272600.

W. Zhang et al. (Eds.): IFTC 2012, CCIS 331, pp. 82–89, 2012.

pixels, a dense grid of HOG is computed to represent a detection window. Using a linear SVM, this representation is proved to be powerful enough to classify humans from other objects. Unfortunately, their method can only process 320×240 images at 1 FPS [2]. Additionally, when a portion of the pedestrian is occluded, the densely extracted blocks of HOG feature in that area may uniformly respond to the linear SVM classifier with negative inner products [3].

Audio-visual(AV) fusion algorithms in surveillance have attracted more attention in recent years. In [4], AV association is subsequently developed by constructing audio-video concurrence matrix. It can successfully detect and discriminate unusual AV event. However, under an unpredictable circumstance, it's difficult to distinguish human intrusion event from the other intrusion events caused by small animal or illumination variations. In [5], an incrementally structured HMM for detecting unusual events is trained, based on audio and visual patterns. Since it requires the length of raw audio signal segments is at least 2 seconds, the scheme can hardly be adopted in real-time applications. Events detection using AV fusion is much fewer than tracking, and it remains to be further studied.

In this work, an audio-visual fusion based real-time detection human intrusion detection method was proposed to solve these problems mentioned. 1) Real-time performance: when the detection area used for HOG feature extraction is limited to motion region instead of the whole image, the computational load can be reduced significantly. Thus, a spatial-temporal joint detection region shrinking method can be developed to achieve fast HOG-based human detection. 2) Robustness under occlusion: considering the fact that human intrusion must be accompanied with footsteps, footstep recognition is used to improve the detection robustness. One Bayesian Network (BN) is developed to fuse audio and video signals at decision level to detect human intrusion event. The proposed scheme can achieve better balance between the time consumption and detection accuracy.

The rest of the paper is organized as follows. In Section 2, fast HOG-based human recognition is elaborated, and footstep recognition is discussed in Section 3. Section 4 introduces Bayesian Network based video-audio fusion model. Experimental results are given In Section 5, followed by the conclusion of this work.

2   Fast HOG-Based Human Recognition with Detection Region Shrinking

HOG-based human recognition needs to extract and compare the HOG features in fixed-size blocks. Qiang Zhu [2] designed a much larger set of blocks that vary in size, location, and aspect ratio. Then they used AdaBoost to select the best blocks suited for human detection and construct the rejector-based cascade. However, the computational complexity can be decreased further if the search space can be limited into the motion region.

Since motion objects can be included in a small region, it can reduce much computation time when the area of HOG feature extraction is limited to the

Fig. 1. An overview of proposed fast HOG-based human detection

Fig. 2. The result of extracting detection region. Motion object spans two bins. The red rectangle is selected as the detection region, and the blue is discarded.

moving region instead of the whole image. An overview of the proposed fast HOG-based human detection is summarized in Figure 1.

Foreground is extracted using adaptive Gaussian mixture model(GMM) [6]. Since there are no events (motion objects) happened in most of the video clips, we can detect human intrusion only when motion objects appeared. We assume motion objects appeared when $R_{fg} > T_{fg}$, where $R_{fg} = Pix_{fg}/Pix_{total}$, Pix_{fg} and Pix_{total} represent the quantity of foreground pixels and the whole image pixels, respectively, and T_{fg} is the ratio threshold of the Pix_{fg}/Pix_{total}. Due to the walking speed of human is usually slow, the variance of inter frame can be very small. Thus, interval detection strategy (IDS) is adopted. For locating motion objects(LMO), the image is divided into K bins in width. Each bin is denoted by B_k, k varies from 1 to K. $V_k = Pix_k/Pix_{fg}$, Pix_k represents foreground pixels number of k-th bin. When $V_k > T_b$, the B_k is selected as the detection region, where T_b is the ratio threshold of the Pix_k/Pix_{fg}. Considering that one motion object may span two bins or more, it is necessary to extend the detection region from one bin to two bins or more. Since one of adjacent bins may include most of the other part of objects, unbalanced extension (UBD) is more suitable. If $V_{k-1} > V_{k+1}$, the detection region can be left-extended by a rate of η, and right-extended by a ratio of $(1-\eta)$, where η is a coefficient greater than 0.5. The extended bin is taken as the detection window. But when obtained two detection regions from LMO are adjacent, the two detection windows will have a lot of overlap after UBD. Thus, the detection region whose V_k is less than the other is discarded to avoid the unnecessary overlap detection. This step is named overlap elimination (OVE). The result of extracting detection region is shown in Figure 2. Finally, human detection bases on HOG feature in the extracting detection region.

3 MFCC-Based Real-Time Footstep Recognition Using GMM Classifier

As the recognition accuracy of HOG-based human detection based HOG may drop markedly under the condition of occlusion, footstep recognition can be applied with the HOG detection to improve robustness. We extract mel frequency cepstrum coefficient(MFCC) from raw audio signal and then use GMM classifier to recognize.

3.1 GMM Classifier

Given the training data, Maximum likelihood estimation (EM) can be used to finds the GMM model's optimal parameters with maximized the likelihood of the GMM. For a sequence of T training vectors $X = \{\vec{x_1}, \vec{x_2}, \ldots, \vec{x_T}\}$, the GMM likelihood can be written as $p(X|\lambda) = \prod_{t=1}^{T} p(\vec{x_t}|\lambda)$. Using EM algorithm [7] to get a new model $\vec{\lambda}$, making $p(X|\vec{\lambda}) \geq p(X|\lambda)$. The new model then is taken as the initial model for the next iteration and the process is repeated until a given convergence threshold is reached.

A group of N sound models N={1,2,...,N} is represented by GMM's $\vec{\lambda_1}$, $\vec{\lambda_2}$, ..., $\vec{\lambda_N}$. The target is to find the sound model which has the maximum a posteriori probability for a given observation sequence.

3.2 Real-Time Footstep Recognition

The MFCC+GMM scheme(MFCC+GMM) developed in [8] is used in this work to identify footstep event. However, the speaker recognition method in [8] is offline, which makes it impossible to realize the real-time footstep recognition without any improvement. In this work, we subdivide the audio signal into over-lapped temporal windows of fixed length W_a. For synchronizing with the video processing, W_a must be less than 0.2s(video detection interval). Overlapped temporal window is designed to avoid the case that segments may not be recognized as footstep, especially when the footstep spans two segments.

Human walks about 2 to 3 steps in 1 second. That's to say, there are more than two segments can be classified as non-footstep in a one-second audio clip. The precision of BN-based decision-level fusion must decline. Thus, we amend recognition result as footstep when at least two segments are recognized as footstep in the last 1s.

4 BN-Based Audio-Visual-Fusion Decision

Compared with pixels-level fusion and feature-level fusion, decision-level fusion are strong tolerance, little communication and strong anti-disturbance.

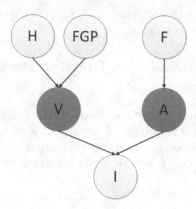

Fig. 3. Bayesian network structure of decision-level fusion

Moreover, It is more suitable for fusion in heterogeneous sensors [9]. We adopt Bayesian network to fuse audio and video at decision level for detecting human intrusion. Figure 3 shows the Bayesian inference model for performing fusion on the audio and video decision results. The observed evidence(E) is decision outputs from footstep recognition(F), fast HOG-based human recognition(H), and foreground proportion(FGP). Video decision(V) and audio decision(A) are the intermediate variables. The human intrusion event(I) is the final output of the total BN model. Each arrow represents a dependency side (with a conditional probability). The values of the observed evidence(E) are represented by F, H, FGP, respectively. With the observed evidence, the human intrusion event(I) node can be found using

$$p(I|E) = \frac{p(I,E)}{p(E)} = \frac{p(E|I)p(I)}{p(E)} \tag{1}$$

Applying the Bayesian Chain Rule, we can have

$$p(I|E) = \frac{\sum[p(I)\prod p(E_i|A=a_i,V=v_k)p(A=a_i|I)p(V=v_k|I)]}{\sum[p(I=i_m)\prod p(E_i|A=a_i,V=v_k)p(A=a_i|I=i_m)p(V=v_k|I=i_m)]} \tag{2}$$

Before the inference model can be used, each node is populated with its a priori knowledge, which can be obtained during an initialization run before the start of experiments and from other standalone experiments.

5   Experimental Evaluation

This section presents the experimental evaluation of real-time human intrusion detection using audio-visual fusion. There are two aims of this experiments: 1) to prove if the proposed algorithm can achieve real-time performance. 2) to find if the proposed algorithm can improve the robustness under occlusion condition.

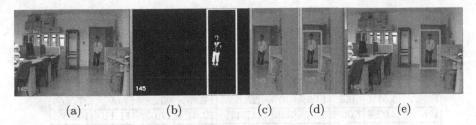

(a)   (b)   (c)   (d)   (e)

Fig. 4. (a) a test sequence (b) foreground (c) extracting detection region (d) HOG-based detection result of shrinking detection region (e) original HOG-based detection result

Table 1. Mean time consumption and accuracy of proposed and original schemes

	Mean time consumption		Accuracy	
	Proposed	Original	Proposed	Original
P2	162.21ms	1030.50ms	73.23%	81.89%
P3	151.12ms	1036.71ms	71.20%	71.20%
P4	170.14ms	1043.39ms	75.33%	80.67%

5.1 Dataset Description and Parameter Setting

Two scenarios are employed in our experiment: 1) human enter the room 2) a rolling basketball in the ground which simulates small animal intrusion. P1, P2, P3, P4 belong to the first scenario. Q1, Q2 are the second scenario. P1 and Q1 are used to train, and the test sequences are P2, P3, P4 and Q2. The video and audio data was recorded by a camera with build-in microphone. The sequences are 320×240, 25 frames per second. We set T_{fg}=0.05%, K=9, T_b=0.3, η=0.7. The audio signal was captured at 8kHz, and the samples were subdivided using temporal windows of length W_a=0.1s, and all the windows were overlapped by 50%. Footstep was modeled by 50-components GMM with a grand, diagonal covariance matrix, which is trained using 20 dimensional mel-cepstral vectors.

5.2 Real-Time Performance Evaluation

The proposed fast HOG-based detection was compared with original algorithm on a Pentium Dual 1.79 GHz desktop with 2 GB memory. We compared them from time consumption and detection accuracy.

Figure 4 shows the processing procedure of proposed method. It can successfully detect human when shrinking detection region includes the whole people. Table 1 lists the mean time consumption and the accuracy of proposed and original schemes. According to Table 1, the proposed scheme significantly reduces the time consumption and slightly impacted the accuracy. We process 1 frame every 5 frames. Thus, by shrinking spatial-temporal joint detection region, the proposed method can satisfy real-time requirement.

Table 2. Result comparison between multiple sensors and single sensor

	Fusion			Video(HOG+FGP)			Audio		
	FPR	FNR	FAR	FPR	FNR	FAR	FPR	FNR	FAR
P2	0%	0%	0%	0%	11.76%	10.45%	52%	0%	10.24%
P3	3.51%	0%	1.05%	0%	25.63%	17.28%	99.28%	0%	27.35%
P4	3.92%	7.06%	5.33%	3.92%	17.17%	12.67%	17.65%	11.11%	13.33%
Q2	0%	–	0%	0%	–	0%	6.45%	–	6.45%

5.3   Detection Result Comparison between Multiple Sensors and Single Sensor

The final performance evaluation is false positive rate(FPR), false negative rate(FNR), and false alarm rate(FAR).

$$FPR = \frac{N_{false\_positive}}{N_{positive}}$$
$$FNR = \frac{N_{false\_negative}}{N_{negative}} \qquad (3)$$
$$FAR = \frac{N_{false\_positive} + N_{false\_negative}}{N_{total}}$$

The performance of three different methods is shown in Table 2. Since Q2 is a sequence about rolling basketball without human intrusion, the FNR is null.

FPR of Audio detection is higher than others. It can be explained as follows: 1) Human is out of room but footstep can be identified, especially P2, P3 sequences. 2) Since sound models are not enough, some similar sound is recognized as footstep.

Higher FNR of video detection can be explained as follows: 1) when human entry and leave the room, the camera only captured a part of people but not the whole. 2) Human poses are obviously different from the normal upright pose, such as bow. 3) The main reason is occlusion.

Obviously, the experimental results turn out that human intrusion detection using audio-visual fusion significantly improve robustness. FAR of the proposed scheme is much lower than single sensor detection.

6   Conclusion

The proposed real-time human intrusion detection using audio-visual fusion takes full advantage of video and audio information. Compared with single sensor detection, it distinctively enhances robustness. Spatial-temporal joint detection region shrinking method makes it easy to meet real-time requirement. The proposed scheme can achieve better balance between the time consumption and detection accuracy.

References

1. Dalal, N., Triggs, B.: Histograms of oriented gradients for human detection. In: CVPR, pp. 886–893 (2005)
2. Zhu, Q., Yeh, M.-C., Cheng, K.-T., Avidan, S.: Fast Human Detection Using a Cascade of Histograms of Oriented Gradients. In: CVPR, pp. 1491–1498 (2006)
3. Wang, X., Han, T.X., Yan, S.: An HOG-LBP human detector with partial occlusion handling. In: ICCV, pp. 32–39 (2009)
4. Cristani, M., Bicego, M., Murino, V.: Audio-Visual Event Recognition in Surveillance Video Sequences. IEEE Transactions on Multimedia 9(2), 257–267 (2007)
5. Dong, Z., Gatica-Perez, D., Bengio, S., McCowan, I.: Semi-supervised adapted HMMs for unusual event detection. In: CVPR, pp. 611–618 (2005)
6. Stauffer, C., Grimson, W.: Adaptive background mixture models for real-time tracking. In: CVPR, vol. 2, pp. 246–252 (1999)
7. Dempster, A., Laird, N., Rubin, D.: Maximum likelihood from incomplete data via the EM algorithm. J. Royal Srar. Soc. 39, 1–38 (1977)
8. Reynolds, D.A., Rose, R.C.: Robust text-independent speaker identification using Gaussian mixture speaker models. IEEE Transactions on Speech and Audio Processing 3(1), 72–83 (1995)
9. Yang, B., Busch, C., de Groot, K., Xu, H., Veldhuis, R.N.J.: Decision Level Fusion of Fingerprint Minutiae Based Pseudonymous Identifiers. In: Hand-Based Biometrics (ICHB), pp. 1–6 (2011)
10. Pearl, J.: Probabilistic Reasoning in Intelligent Systems: Networks of Plausible Inference, pp. 150–197. Morgan Kaufmann, San Mateo (1988)

Interactive Image Segmentation
Based on Grow Cut of Two Scale Graphs

Xiaoqiang Li[1], Jingsong Chen[2], and Huafu Fan[1]

[1] Shool of Computer Engineering and Science, Shanghai University, Shanghai, China
[2] Department of Mathematics and Information Science, Zhoukou Normal University, China

Abstract. This paper proposes a novel interactive image segmentation algorithm based on the Grow Cut of two different scale graphs. Firstly, Watershed algorithm based on color information has been used to partition the image into many different regions which will be considered as the cells of Grow Cut, instead of image pixels. Then a segmentation result can be obtained by using Grow Cut on the aforementioned regions. Finally an automatic edge correction can be used on the segmentation result by Grow Cut of pixel-scale graph. Because the number of nodes and edges for the Grow Cut algorithm is reduced by more than fifty times compared to the pixel based method, the running time of our proposed algorithm is much less than the original Grow Cut. The segmentation performance of our proposed is much better than the original Grow Cut. Experimental results on Berkeley image dataset demonstrated the effectiveness of proposed method.

Keywords: Image segmentation, Grow Cut, Watershed algorithm, Automatic Edge Correction.

1   Introduction

Interactive segmentation has been becoming more and more popular to alleviate the problems inherent to fully automatic segmentation which seems to never be perfect [1]. The goal of interactive segmentation is to extract an object in image or picture from its background with as less user interaction as possible. A user imposes certain hard constrains for segmentation by indicating certain pixels to be part of the object and certain pixels to be part of the background. These hard constrains provide clues on what the user intends to segment, and the rest work is that the image is segmented automatically by computing a global or local optimum among all segmentations based on the hard constrains.

One of the main advantages of interactive segmentation algorithm is that it provides a globally or locally optimal solution for image segmentation when the cost function is clearly defined. Energy minimization is made use of within most recently proposed segmentation frameworks. Level set method [2] is a standard approach to image segmentation, of which an advantage is that almost any energy function can be used, however its local optimum may much depend on initialization. Graph cuts-based energy minimization for image segmentation is introduced by Boykov and Jolly

W. Zhang et al. (Eds.): IFTC 2012, CCIS 331, pp. 90–95, 2012.

[1], gained very popularity because it can incorporate both boundary properties and region properties to get the global optimum solution. In the case of the energy function can be minimized by graph cuts, the graph cuts can obtain better solution [3]. GrabCut [4] and Lazy Snapping [5] are outstanding segmentation methods based on graph cuts. In 2005, Grow Cut is proposed by Vladimir Vezhnevets and Vadim Konouchine [6], which is based on Cellular Automation. The process of the Grow Cut is interactive, as the automaton labels the image, user can observe the segmentation evolution and guide the algorithm with human input where the segmentation is very difficult to compute. Although the segmentation performance of Grow Cut is very well, its most weakness is that the segmentation consumed time is nearly 20 seconds for an image with 321*481. One of our goals is to reduce the consumed time of segmentation of Grow Cut.

The main contribution of this paper is that Grow Cut of two different scale graphs are used to improve the segmentation performance, and to reduce the consumed time of segmentation. Firstly, watershed algorithm based on color information has been made use of to partition the image into a lot of different regions. Then a segmentation result can be obtained by using Grow Cut of region-scale on the aforementioned regions. Finally an automatic edge correction can be used on the segmentation result by Grow Cut of pixel-scale graph.

The remainder of this paper is organized as follows. Pre-segmentation is introduced in section 2, and section 3 describes the theory of the Grow Cut and proposed algorithm. Some experimental results are shown in section 5. The conclusions are given in section 6.

2   Pre-segmentation

The proposed method belongs to region-based segmentation. In order to reducing the running time of segmentation based on Grow Cut, the image is pre-segmented into a lot of small regions including pixels with similar color value, which are considered as the cells of Grow Cut instead of image pixels. Generally the number of nodes and edges for the grow cut algorithm is reduced by more than 50 times compared to the pixel based method. We choose the Watershed algorithm [7] which is based on the color information (RGB color space is used) to get over-segmentation image, which locates good boundaries and preserves small differences inside each small region. The result of watershed algorithm segmentation is shown in Fig 1.

(a)   (b)

Fig. 1. An example of pre-segmentation (a) Original image. (b).Watershed segmentation

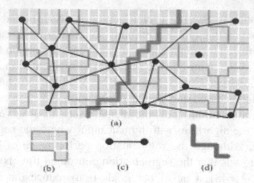

Fig. 2. The improved Grow Cut algorithm works on this graph whose cells are small regions obtained from the watershed segmentation. (a) Segmentation results; (b) Region cell (new neighborhood system); (c) Node and edge of region cell; (d) the last boundary

3   Interactive Segmentation By Improved Grow Cut

3.1   Grow Cut Algorithm

The Grow Cut algorithm is introduced by [6], which is based on the cellular automata theory. A cellular automation is an algorithm discrete in both time and space, which operates on a lattice of sites $\forall p \in P \subset Z^n$ (pixels or voxels in image processing). A cellular automaton is a quad-tuple (Z^n, S, N, δ), where Z^n is the cell space, S is an state set, N is a neighborhood system, and δ is the local state transition function, which defines the rule of calculating the cell's state at $t+1$ time step based on the states of the neighborhood cells at previous time step t, and its typical style is $\delta : S^N \to S$. The common used neighborhood systems N are the von Neumann and Moore neighborhoods:

1) Von Neumann neighborhood

$$N(p) = \{q \in Z^n : \| p - q \|_1 := \sum_{i=1}^{n} |p_i - q_i| = 1\} \tag{1}$$

2) Moore neighborhood

$$N(p) = \{q \in Z^n : \| p - q \|_\infty := \max_{i=1,n} |p_i - q_i| = 1\} \tag{2}$$

The state S_p of the cell p in our case is actually triplet (l_p, θ_p, C_p), where l_p is the label of the current cell p, θ_p is the strength of the current cell p, and C_p is the feature vector. In the original Grow Cut, an image can be considered as a particular configuration state of a cellular automation, where cellular space is defined by the pixels of the image. For every unlabelled pixels of the image p, the initial states for $\forall p \in P$ are set to:

$$l_p = 0, \theta_p = 0, C_p = RGB_p \tag{3}$$

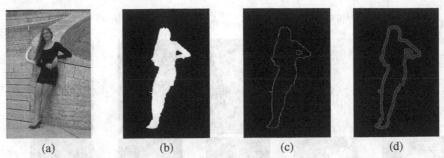

| (a) | (b) | (c) | (d) |

Fig. 3. Segment result of Grow Cut based on watershed algorithm. (a) Original Image; (b) segmentation result of image (a) till step3 of proposed method; (c) the contour of (b); (d) The labeled area (red) and unlabeled area (blue) of the edge correction by using Grow Cut.

When user specify the segmentation seeds by mouse, the seeded cells labels are set accordingly. The initial states of the foreground seed pixels are set to:

$$l_p = 1, \theta_p = 1, C_p = RGB_p \tag{4}$$

The initial states of the background seed pixels are set to:

$$l_p = -1, \theta_p = 1, C_p = RGB_p \tag{5}$$

Where $l_p = 1$ denotes foreground, -1 denotes background. At time step $t+1$, the cell labels l_p^{t+1} and strengths θ_p^{t+1} are updated as algorithm in [6].

3.2 The Proposed Image Segmentation Algorithm

The steps of the proposed segmentation algorithm are described as follow:

1) The user specify the seed by mouse operated brush of white (for object) and blue (for background) color ,and object seed (pixel) set S_O and background seed (pixel) set S_B can be obtained.
2) Watershed algorithm based on color information is used to partition the image into a lot of different regions.
3) The new neighborhood system which is showed in Fig.2 is used, and the regions obtained from the step 2 are the cells of the cellular automata. Then Grow Cut algorithm is performed on this neighborhood system.
4) Automatic edge correction is used on the segmentation result of the step 3 by performing the Grow Cut algorithm.

As show in Fig.3, (a) is an original image and (b) is the segmentation result of step 3 of the improved Grow Cut based on watershed algorithm, the boundary of segmentation result is much roughness. In order to reduce the interactive times of the user, the automatic edge correction is performed. Firstly, we get the contour from the segmentation result of step 3, shown as Fig. 3(c). Then, the pixels whose distance from the contour is less than 15 is considered as unknown region U as shown in Fig. 3(d) the blue region. The pixels whose distance from the contour is less than 30 and more than 15 is the seed region S as shown in Fig. 3(d) the red region. Finally, the Grow Cut algorithm is performed on the region U and S. Because the number of region U and S is much less than the size of the image, the running time of automatic edge correction is very little, which is proven in our experiments.

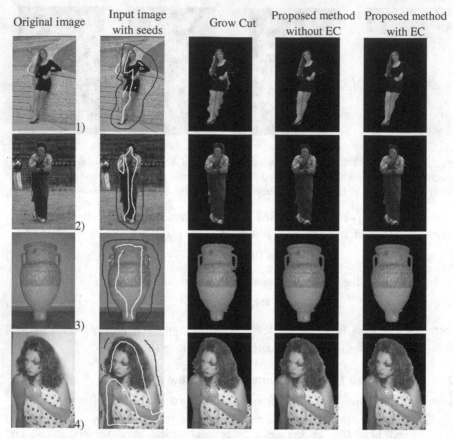

Fig. 4. Examples of segmentation results of different methods   (EC: Edge Correction)

4   Experiments

Images coming from Berkeley database [8] are used in our experiments to verify the effectiveness of the proposed algorithm. Our algorithm is written by VC++ and OpenCV library. The experiments are all finished on the Dell OptiPlex 755. Our proposed approach is compared with the original Grow Cut using the same seeds. Some examples of the segmentation results compared with the two approaches are shown in Fig.4. In second column, blue region denotes seeds of background, white region denotes foreground. In Fig.4, we can find that the segmentation performance of proposed method is much better than the original Grow Cut. The reason is that the proposed method based on watershed algorithm can resolve a problem of original Grow Cut which is easily affected by the local boundary. As show in Fig.4 the result of our proposed method with edge correction is better than the proposed method without edge correction, which means the edge correction works very well .One of our future work is to find a method to solve this problem.

As show in Table 1, the running time of our proposed algorithm on image 1)-4) in Fig.4 is much less than the original Grow Cut. Because watershed method are used to partition image into a lot of small regions, the cells of the proposed Grow Cut are much less than the original Grow Cut, so it cost much less time for cellular automata to become convergence. Form the Table 1, we can find that running time of out proposed method with edge correction is about 0.5 second which are very little.

Table 1. Rrunning time comparison of the Original row Cut and Improved Grow Cut

Image Num.	Original Grow Cut	Proposed method without edge correction	Proposed method with edge correction
1)	18.953s	0.266s	0.516s
2)	18.828s	0.234s	0.547s
3)	13.567s	0.187s	0.515s
4)	14.694s	0.203s	0.469s

5   Conclusion

This paper proposes a novel interactive image segmentation algorithm based on the Grow Cut of two different scale graphs. Watershed algorithm based on color information has been used to partition the image into a lot of different regions which will be the cells of the cellular automata. Then the Grow Cut algorithm is performed on this region-scale graph. Finally edge correction based on Grow Cut of pixel-scale graph is used on the boundary of the segmentation result. Comparative studies with the Grow Cut methods have been done and experimental results demonstrated that the proposed method outperforms Grow Cut method both on running time and correctness of segmentation.

Acknowledgments. This work is supported by Shanghai Natural Science Foundation under Grant No. 10ZR1411700.

References

1. Boykov, Y., Kolmogorov, V.: Interactive graph cuts for optimal boundary and region segmentation of objects in N-D images. In: Proc. of ICCV, pp. 105–112 (2001)
2. Chan, T.F., Vese, L.A.: Active Contours without Edges. IEEE Trans. on Image Processing 10(2), 266–277 (2001)
3. Boykov, Y., Kolmogorov, V.: An experimental comparison of min-cut/max-flow algorithms for energy minimization in vision. IEEE Trans. on PAMI 26(9), 1124–1137 (2004)
4. Rother, C., Kolmogorov, V., Blake, A.: GrabCut-interactive foreground extraction using iterated graph cuts. ACM Trans. on Graphics 23(3), 309–314 (2004)
5. Li, Y., Sun, J., Tang, C.K., Shum, H.: Lazy snapping. In: Proc. of ACM SIGGRAPH, pp. 303–308 (2004)
6. Vezhnevets, V., Konouchine, V.: "Grow-Cut" - Interactive Multi-Label N-D Image Segmentation. In: Proc. Graphicon, pp. 150–156
7. Vincent, L., Soille, P.: Watersheds in digital spaces: an efficient algorithm based on immersion simulations. IEEE Trans. on PAMI 13(6), 583–598 (1991)
8. http://search.microsoft.com/en-us/um/cambridge/projects/visionimagevideoediting/segmentation/grabcut.htm

An Improved Video Retargeting Technique Based on Discontinuous Seam Caving

Yue Chen, Bo Yan*, and Bo Yang

School of Computer Science,
Fudan University, Shanghai, PRC 200433

Abstract. We introduce a new method for video retargeting based on discontinuous seam carving. Existing seam carving based video retargeting method is difficult to maintain spatial and temporal coherence simultaneously. In order to solve this limitation, our proposed method is able to use the optical flow to help keep the temporal coherence. In addition, a new scheme is designed to select the initial seam for video retargeting, which is able to help keep the spatial coherence. Experimental results prove that our proposed method outperforms others in terms of maintaining spatial and temporal coherence significantly.

Keywords: Video retargeting, seam carving, temporal coherence, spatial coherence.

1 Introduction

Recently, with the continuous development of new consumer electronic devices (e.g. mobile phones, notebooks, PDAs), it's increasingly important for video to display on the screens with different resolutions or arbitrary aspect ratios. For this purpose, the performances of the traditional methods, such as letter boxing, cropping or uniform scaling are not satisfactory, which may cause loss or distortion of important details. Video retargeting [1] has played a more and more significant role in order to convert the video to a new target resolution or aspect ratio while preserving the salient content. Recent video retargeting approaches can be classified into two main branches in terms of the essential ideas, on which they are based: warping [2–4] and cropping [5, 6].

Seam carving is a kind of cropping-based technique [7, 8]. Its essential idea is to remove one pixel from every row/column in an image every time, and not to notably cause visual distortion at the same time. When it comes to video retargeting, such a removal, or carving of non-salient regions may cause some degree of distortion or discontinuousness of video content, which would lead to artifacts both temporally and spatially. The artifacts should be reduced by considering the salient content in the target video and enforcing spatial and temporal coherence at the same time. However, spatial and temporal coherence may contradict to each other in some situations. For example, when a salient object moves to a

---

* This work is supported by NSFC (Grant No.: 61073067).

W. Zhang et al. (Eds.): IFTC 2012, CCIS 331, pp. 96–102, 2012.

region where a seam was carved in the previous frame, spatial coherence needs the seam to avoid the object, but temporal coherence requires the seam to stay in its location. As a result, the balance between them is crucial in seam carving based video retargeting. Unfortunately, much less work concentrates on this issue[9] comparing with that of the warping-based video retargeting.

In this paper, we propose a new algorithm for video retargeting based on the seam carving approaches and we enhance those approaches with several novel ideas. We have included the optical flow to achieve the temporal coherence and designed a new scheme to select the initial seam to maintain the spatial coherence. Experimental results show that the performance of vide retargeting can be improved significantly after including our proposed technique.

The rest of this paper is organized as follows. In Section 2, we review current mainstream work on seam carving based video retargeting. In Section 3, we propose our video retargeting algorithm. Then we evaluate the proposed method by simulations and present the results in Section 4. Finally, we draw the conclusion in Section 5.

2   Conventional Methods

Recently, Grundmann *et al.* proposed a discontinuous seam carving algorithm for video retargeting, which resizes a video by sequentially removing seams [9]. This algorithm processes frames sequentially by linearly combing the spatial and temporal coherence costs (S_c and T_c) as well as the saliency (S) cost of removing each pixel in the current frame to one measure M. Then by computing the minimum cost of M with dynamic programming [7], seams are removed or duplicated in each frame to change the width or height of a video.

2.1   Temporal Coherence Measurement

Temporal coherence is an important issue in video retargeting. The optimal temporal coherence criterion replicates the same seam in all frames, which is not necessary and sufficient. In [9], a seam is computed instead in the current frame such that the appearance of the resulting resized frame is similar to the appearance obtained by applying the optimal temporally coherent seam.

Assuming a seam S^i is computed in every $m \times n$ frame $F^i, i \in 1, 2, ..., T$, the previous seam S^{i-1} is reused and applied to the current frame F^i, leading to the most temporally coherent resulting $(m-1) \times n$ frame, R^c. The look-ahead strategy to obtain temporal coherence performs selecting S^i by measuring the temporal coherence cost $T_c(x, y)$ at pixel (x, y) with the help of R^c [9].

$$T_c(x,y) = \sum_{k=0}^{x-1} ||F_{k,y}^i - R_{k,y}^c||^2 + \sum_{k=x+1}^{m-1} ||F_{k,y}^i - R_{k-1,y}^c||^2. \qquad (1)$$

It can be reduced to a per-row difference accumulation for every pixel before any seams are computed.

2.2 Spatial Coherence Measurement

The look-ahead strategy is also applied to the spatial domain by measuring how much spatial error will be introduced after removing a seam[9]. The spatial coherence measure $S_c = S_h + S_v$ is based on variation in the gradient of the intensity in the horizontal and vertical (including diagonal) directions, respectively. S_h only depends on the pixel in question and in some sense adds to its saliency, while S_v defines a spatial transition cost between two pixels in adjacent rows [9].

By generalizing the transition cost S_v to an accumulated spatial transition cost, a pixel is allowed to consider not just its three neighbors in the row above but all pixels in that row, which leads to discontinuous spatial seams[9]. For a pixel (x_b, y) in the bottom row, the summed spatial transition cost to pixel $(x_b, y - 1)$ in the top row (for the case $x_a < x_b$) is [9]:

$$S_v(x_b, x_a, y) = \sum_{k=x_a}^{x_b-1} |G_{k,y}^v - G_{k,y}^d| + \sum_{k=x_a+1}^{x_b} |G_{k,y}^v - G_{k-1,y}^d| \qquad (2)$$

where $G_{k,y}^v = |F_{k,y} - F_{k,y-1}|$ is the vertical gradient magnitude between pixel (k, y) and its top neighbor, while $G_{k,y}^d = |F_{k,y} - F_{k+1,y-1}|$ is its diagonal gradient magnitude with the top right neighbor [9].

3 Our Proposed Improvements

3.1 Temporal Coherence Obtained with Optical Flow

In [9], authors reuse the previous seam S^{i-1} and apply it to the current frame F^i, leading to the most temporally coherent resulting $(m - 1) \times n$ frame, R^c. The look-ahead strategy to obtain temporal coherence performs selecting S^i by measuring the temporal coherence cost $T_c(x, y)$ at pixel (x, y) with the help of R^c [9].

The problem is that the pixels on the previous seam S^{i-1} may not stay at the same place in the current frame because of possible pixel motions, which means the most coherent resulting frame R^c might cause vibration or jittering in the video sequence.

In order to track the pixels on the previous seam S^{i-1}, we introduce optical flow to measure the motions of the pixels and locate the corresponding pixels in the current frame along the optical flow (u, v).

Because only vertical seams are considered in [9], we take videos in which objects move in the horizontal direction as an example. For a pixel $F^{i-1}(x, y)$ on the previous seam S^{i-1}, with (u, v) denoting this pixel's optical flow, its corresponding pixel in the current frame should be $F^i(x + u, y)$, instead of $F^i(x, y)$ in [9]. In this way, with the help of optical flow (u, v) we can obtain the new most temporally coherent resulting $(m-1) \times n$ frame (denoted by $NewR^c(u,v)$). As a result, the new temporal coherent cost $NewT_c(x,y)$ is determined as:

$$NewT_c(x,y) = \sum_{k=0}^{x-1} ||F_{k,y}^i - NewR_{k,y}^c(u,v)||^2 + \sum_{k=x+1}^{m-1} ||F_{k,y}^i - NewR_{k-1,y}^c(u,v)||^2 \tag{3}$$

3.2 Better Initial Seam

The initial seam in the first frame of a retargeted video has a great impact on the following ones. If the first seam is not accurate enough, such as cutting through important objects, in order to obtain temporal coherence, the seams in the following frames will try to stay through the same part of the objects. Consequently, the initial inaccuracy is propagated into the whole video sequence, with deformation of important objects. Even if the initial seam is properly chosen in the first frame, winding through less important regions, foreground objects might move into these regions in the following frame and the current seam will cut through them as a result of the temporal coherence constraints.

Due to the great importance of the initial seam, we need to consider the whole frames of a video sequence to obtain a relatively accurate initial seam. We hope that the importance map of the first frame can reflect the importance information of all the following frames, with the help of which, a better initial seam will be chosen so that seams in the following frames can also avoid important objects even when constrained by the temporal coherence.

In order to solve this problem, we apply the model of "Aligned Importance Map Blending" in [4] to achieve a global importance map for the initial seam. According to [4], the blended importance value at pixel p of frame t is defined as

$$\bar{I}^t(p) = \max_{l=t}^{t+k}\{I^t(p), \delta I^t(p) + (1-\delta)I^l(T_{t \mapsto l}p)\} \tag{4}$$

where I^t denotes a traditional (single-frame) importance map at frame t and k denotes the bounded number of neighboring frames. The contribution of neighboring frames away from frame is mitigated by setting blending factor as $\delta = (l-t)/k$.

The blended importance maps records objects' motion paths by observing their movements within multiple frames, which enables the model to capture motion information observable over a long time period. By marking some background pixels as important, whose corresponding pixels in the neighboring aligned frames are important due to the motion of the moving objects, the blended maps give higher importance values to moving objects and capture salient information in both spatial and temporal context, thus better preserving the aspect ratio of foreground objects.

A blended importance map of the first frame in a retargeted video combines all the important regions in the following frames into a single map. Based on this global importance map, the computed initial seam will be much more accurate globally, avoiding propagating initial inaccuracy or cutting through important objects in the following frames even when constrained by the temporal coherence.

(a)

(b)

Fig. 1. 100th vertical seam in 39th, 49th, 59th, 69th, 79th frames(*from left to right in sequence*) of the retargeted video, *"Totoro"(400*213)*. (a) the original method [9]; (b) our proposed method.

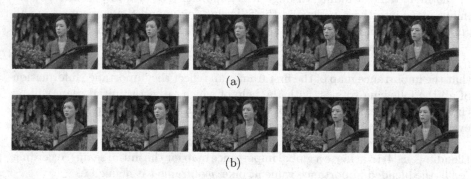

(a)

(b)

Fig. 2. 50th vertical seam in 0th, 3th, 6th, 9th, 12th frames(*from left to right in se-. quence*) of the retargeted video, *"Walking"(400*225)*. (a) the original method [9]; (b) our proposed method.

4   Experimental Results

In this section, we demonstrate our results for video retargeting with the our improved method and compare them with the results of the original method in[9]. Fig. 1 and Fig. 2 show that our approach avoids cutting through important objects (the boy in Fig.1, the woman in Fig.2) in the following frames. While with the original method, seams go through the boy's leg in Fig.1(a) and the woman's shoulder in Fig.2(a), causing deformation in the girls' face and head in Fig.1(a) and in the shoulder of the woman in Fig.2(a).

Fig. 3 and Fig. 4 demonstrate a series of temporally more coherent results with our improved method compared to the original way. Observing the seams in five consecutive frames of the video in Fig. 3(b), we can find that seams in the moving background are tracked closely with our improved method while seams computed with the original method simply stay at almost the same place in Fig.3(a). In Fig.4(a), seams fail to avoid cutting through the flowers because

(a)

(b)

Fig. 3. 50th vertical seam in 40th, 50th, 60th, 70th, 80th frames(*from left to right in sequence*) of the retargeted video, *"Totoro"(400*213)*. (a) the original method [9]; (b) our proposed method.

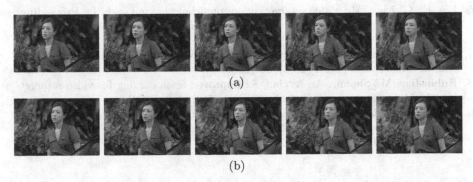

(a)

(b)

Fig. 4. 60th vertical seam in 24th, 25th, 26th, 27th, 28th frames(*from left to right in sequence*) of the retargeted video, *"Walking" (400*225)*. (a) the original method [9]; (b) our proposed method.

of the original temporal coherency constraint while in Fig.4(b) our proposed method is able to track the seam in previous frames and move along.

Therefore, after including these two improvements our improved method can better protect and stress important objects in the video and at the same time obtain more temporally coherent results compared to the original method.

5   Conclusion

In this paper, we have proposed a new video retargeting method based on discontinuous seam carving, which introduces two novel ideas. The first novelty lies in the application of optical flow in measuring the temporal coherence cost, which is able to obtain much better temporal coherence than other methods. The second novelty, which is the design of the new scheme of the initial seam selection, contributes to avoiding cutting the important objects. Experimental results prove that our proposed method outperforms others in terms of maintaining spatial and temporal coherence significantly.

References

1. Shamir, A., Sorkine, O.: Visual media retargeting. In: ACM SIGGRAPH ASIA 2009 Courses, p. 11 (2009)
2. Wolf, L., Guttmann, M., Cohen-Or, D.: Non-homogeneous content-driven video-retargeting. In: IEEE 11th International Conference on Computer Vision, ICCV 2007, pp. 1–6 (October 2007)
3. Yen, T.-C., Tsai, C.-M., Lin, C.-W.: Maintaining temporal coherence in video retargeting using mosaic-guided scaling. IEEE Transactions on Image Processing 20(8), 2339–2351 (2011)
4. Wang, Y., Fu, H., Sorkine, O., Lee, T., Seidel, H.: Motionaware-temporal coherence for video resizing. ACM Transactions on Graphics (TOG) 28(5), 127 (2009)
5. Deselaers, T., Dreuw, P., Ney, H.: Pan, zoom, scan-timecoherent, trained automatic video cropping. In: IEEE Conference on Computer Vision and Pattern Recognition, CVPR 2008, pp. 1–8 (June 2008)
6. Liu, F., Gleicher, M.: Video retargeting: automating pan and scan. In: Proceedings of the 14th Annual ACM International Conference on Multimedia, pp. 241–250 (2006)
7. Avidan, S., Shamir, A.: Seam carving for content-aware image resizing. ACM Transactions on Graphics (TOG) 26(3), 10 (2007)
8. Rubinstein, M., Shamir, A., Avidan, S.: Improved seam carving for video retargeting. ACM Transactions on Graphics (TOG) 27(3), 1–9 (2008)
9. Grundmann, M., Kwatra, V., Han, M., Essa, I.: Discontinuous seam-carving for video retargeting. In: IEEE Conference on Computer Vision and Pattern Recognition, CVPR 2010, pp. 569–576 (2010)

Interactive Object Segmentation
Using Graph Cut and Contour Refinement

Minghua Shen, Lin Zha, Zhi Liu, and Shuhua Luo

School of Communication and Information Engineering,
Shanghai University, Shanghai 200072, China

Abstract. This paper presents an interactive object segmentation approach using graph cut and contour refinement, which can accurately extract any user-interested objects from natural images. Using the user-specified scribbles as the interactive input, the initial object segmentation result is obtained under the framework of graph cut. However, due to the problem of color distribution in some images, in which the color distributions of foreground and background are similar, it is nontrivial to achieve an acceptable segmentation quality using one-shot graph cut. Then, an interactive contour refinement scheme is exploited to correct inaccurate object contours to meet the user's requirement. Experimental results on a variety of images demonstrate the better segmentation performance of our approach.

Keywords: interactive object segmentation, graph cut, contour refinement.

1   Introduction

Object segmentation is a fundamental yet still challenging problem in the field of computer vision and image processing. In general, the color and texture features in a natural image may be complex so that automatic object segmentation is nontrivial. Therefore, interactive segmentation methods, which allow users to provide information regarding the object of interest, have been proposed and are becoming more and more popular.

In the past few years, graph cut based approaches [1-5] have become the most widely used interactive segmentation framework, which extracts the interested objects via max flow algorithm [6]. Since graph cut can involve a wide range of visual cues, a number of recent approaches further extended the original work of Boykov [1-2], and incorporated some regional cues [3] and geodesic distance measures [4] as global constraints into the graph cut framework. In [7], color information and the texture information extracted by SIFT sampling are also used as the energy term of graph cut. In [8], starting from the seeded regions specified on an initial region segmentation result, regions are gradually merged based on the similarity between color histograms of adjacent regions to generate the interested object. In [9], multi-cue dynamic integration is exploited under the framework of conditional random field for object segmentation. However, the aforementioned interactive object segmentation

W. Zhang et al. (Eds.): IFTC 2012, CCIS 331, pp. 103–109, 2012.
© Springer-Verlag Berlin Heidelberg 2012

approaches cannot well handle those images, in which the color distributions of foreground and background are not well separated, and it is difficult to achieve user-satisfied segmentation result.

This paper proposes an interactive object segmentation approach as an extension of the standard graph cut framework. The contour refinement is performed incrementally to obtain a satisfying object segmentation result. The rest of this paper is organized as follows. A brief review of graph cut is presented in Section 2. The proposed interactive object segmentation approach is described in Section 3. Experimental results and comparisons are presented in Section 4, and conclusions are given in Section 5.

2   Graph Cut

Nowadays, graph cut is the mainstream of interactive segmentation algorithms [1-5]. In this section, we provide a brief introduction to graph cut, and describe the details of the corresponding graph construction and the minimum cut that gives the optimal segmentation result.

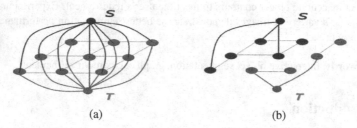

(a)   (b)

Fig. 1. The algorithm of graph cut. (a) graph structure; (b) the cut on the graph.

As shown in Fig. 1(a), an image is represented as an undirected graph $G=<V, E>$, where V is a set of nodes and E is a set of undirected edges connecting these nodes. There are two additional nodes in the graph: an "object" terminal (a source S) and a "background" terminal (a sink T). The set of edges E consists of two types of undirected edges: n-links (neighborhood links) and t-links (terminals links). Let P denotes a set of all pixels in an image, and each pixel $p \in P$ has two t-links, i.e., $\{p, S\}$ and $\{p, T\}$, connecting to each terminal, respectively. Let N denotes the set containing each pair of neighboring pixels $\{p, q\}$, which is called a n-link. Therefore, V and E are defined as follows

$$V = P \cup \{S,T\}. \tag{1}$$

$$E = N \underset{p \in P}{\cup} \{\{p,S\},\{p,T\}\}. \tag{2}$$

Now, the graph G is completely constructed. We draw the segmentation boundary between the object and the background by finding the minimum cut on the graph G as shown in Fig. 1(b). The minimum cut C on G can be computed in polynomial time via algorithm for two terminal graph cut assuming that the edge weights are nonnegative [1].

A cut is formally defined as a subset of edges $C \subset E$, and terminals are separated by this subset on the graph. Graph cut seeks to minimize a cost function with the following form

$$E(A) = \sum_{p \in P} R_p(A_p) + \lambda \sum_{\{p,q\} \in N} B_{\{p,q\}} \cdot \delta(A_p, A_q) \ . \tag{3}$$

In Eq. (3), A is a binary vector of labels which designate pixels to "*obj*" (object) or "*bkg*" (background). $R_p(A_p)$ is a regional cost term based on the label A_p, $B_{\{p,q\}}$ is a boundary cost term for neighboring pixels $\{p, q\}$, and λ is the balancing weight between the region cost term and the boundary cost term.

As shown in Fig. 2, the user draws some scribbles to specify object seeds (white) and background seeds (black), which are termed as hard constraints under the graph cut framework. The object segmentation result is under the influence of these user-specified hard constraints. If users specify some seeds as shown in Fig. 2(b), it is unavoidable that some segmentation errors occur in the object segmentation result as shown in Fig. 2(c). For this reason, in order to obtain an acceptable object segmentation result, it requires users to specify the seeds either by one-shot accurate drawing or repeatedly modification on seeds. However, it may degrade the quality of user experience on interactive segmentation.

(a)   (b)   (c)

Fig. 2. Interactive object segmentation using graph cut. (a) input image; (b) user-specified seeds; (c) object segmentation result.

3   Interactive Object Segmentation Method

The proposed interactive object segmentation approach consists of two stages, i.e., initial segmentation using graph cut with user-specified scribbles, and interactive contour refinement process. Our approach can tolerate relatively poor initial segmentation result, and thus relax restrictions on seeds provided by users. The inaccurate initial result can be improved using the contour refinement method. The following two subsections detail the two stages, respectively.

3.1   Initial Segmentation Using Graph Cut

Based on the hard constraints from the interactive input, pixels are first classified into two sets, i.e, "obj" (object seeds), and "bkg" (background seeds). For each pixel p, its regional cost terms $R_p(obj)$ and $R_p(bkg)$ are assigned with the likelihoods of pixel p belonging to the estimated nonparametric model of object and background, respectively. Specifically, the color distribution of object/background is modeled using the kernel density estimation [10] based nonparametric model, in which Gaussian distribution is selected as the kernel function.

$$f(x) = \frac{1}{N}\sum_{i=1}^{N} K_\sigma(x - x_i) \cdot \tag{4}$$

$$K_\sigma(x) = (\frac{1}{2\pi\sigma^2})^{\frac{1}{2}} e^{-\|x\|^2 / 2\sigma^2}. \tag{5}$$

where x denotes the color feature of each pixel, $x_i \in N$ denotes a seed pixel, and $K_\sigma(x)$ is the kernel function. The weight λ is set to a moderate value, 50, to make a balance between regional cost term and boundary cost term. The bandwidth σ is set to a suitable value, 0.2, in our implementation. Actually, as shown in Fig. 3, the initial segmentation results are usually similar when σ is within the range from 0.05 to 0.4. The max-flow algorithm is exploited to perform the graph cut, and the pixels are labeled as either "obj" or "bkg". However, for the example image in Fig. 2(a), the initial object segmentation result shown in Fig. 2(c) could not be satisfied.

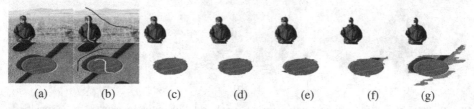

(a)   (b)   (c)   (d)   (e)   (f)   (g)

Fig. 3. Initial segmentation results obtained using different values of bandwidth. (a) input images; (b) user-specified seeds; (c)-(g) results obtained with different values of 0.05, 0.2, 0.4, 1.0 and 1.5, respectively.

3.2   Contour Refinement

On the initial object segmentation result, we draw curves to mark the missing parts of the object and the redundant parts of background, and exploit the following contour refinement process to obtain a more complete and accurate object segmentation result. The rationality of drawing a curve as additional seeds is explained as follows. On the initial segmentation result which contains the missing/redundant parts, the curve can specify the area with segmentation errors, so that we can apply graph cut on the basis of regional processing. For the missing parts of the object, an original rectangle is generated to just cover the drawn curve, and the pixels covered by the drawn curve are used as object seeds. Then, the original rectangle will be enlarged as follows

$$x = x_1 - 0.25 \times h \,|_{h=1.5 \cdot |x_1 - x_2|} . \tag{6}$$

$$y = y_1 - 0.25 \times w \,|_{w=1.5 \cdot |y_1 - y_2|} . \tag{7}$$

where h and w are height and width, respectively, of the enlarged rectangle. (x_1, y_1) and (x_2, y_2) are the start/end pixel of the drawn curve, and (x, y) is the top-left coordinates of the enlarged rectangle.

The pixels covered by the enlarged part, which are the difference between the enlarged rectangle and the original rectangle, are used as the background seeds. Based on the above obtained object seeds and background seeds, uniform sampling is then used to make the number of object seeds and background seeds similar. Finally, the graph cut is performed on the enlarged rectangle to obtain a refined object contour. Similarly, the same process is performed to refine the redundant background regions. An example of contour refinement process is shown in Fig. 4, and we can see that the object can be accurately extracted.

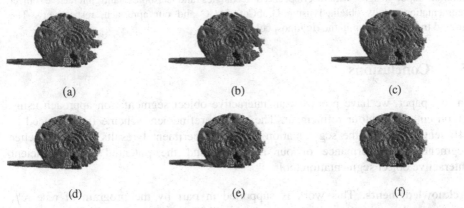

(a)   (b)   (c)

(d)   (e)   (f)

Fig. 4. Illustration of contour refinement process. (a) initial segmentation result; (b)-(e) refinement of missing parts (red) and redundant parts (green); (f) final object segmentation result.

4   Experimental Results

In order to evaluate the segmentation quality of our approach, we use the images provided by Microsoft Research Asia Salient Object Database (MSRASOD) [11] to perform the interactive object segmentation, and make a comparison with GrabCut [3] and iterative adjustable graph cut (IAGC) [5]. Some examples of interactive segmentation results are shown in Fig. 5, in which the input images with user-specified seeds, the interactive object segmentation results obtained using GrabCut, IAGC and our approach, respectively, and the ground truths are shown from left to right. We can observe from Fig. 5 that our approach can segment interested objects with complete regions and smooth boundaries. Our approach can overcome the problem of similar color distribution between object and background, and shows a better segmentation performance than GrabCut and IAGC.

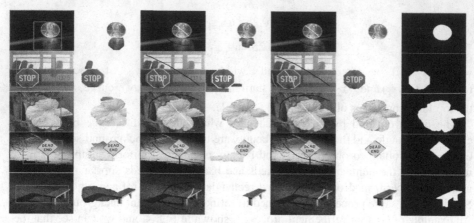

Fig. 5. Segmentation comparison of GrabCut, IAGC and our approach. From the 1st to the 6th column: input images with user-specified rectangles and scribbles, and interactive object segmentation results obtained using GrabCut, IAGC and our approach, respectively. The ground truths are shown in the rightmost column.

5   Conclusions

In this paper, we have proposed an interactive object segmentation approach using graph cut and contour refinement. The contour refinement scheme is introduced to efficiently improve the segmentation quality. Experimental results show the better segmentation performance of our approach, and the potential as an efficient interactive object segmentation tool.

Acknowledgments. This work is supported in part by the program of research, learning and practice for university teachers in Shanghai.

References

1. Boykov, Y., Jolly, M.-P.: Interactive graph cuts for optimal boundary and region segmentation of objects in N-D images. In: Proc. IEEE ICCV, pp. 105–112 (July 2001)
2. Boykov, Y., Funka-Lea, G.: Graph cuts and efficient N-D image segmentation. International Journal of Computer Vision 70(2), 109–131 (2006)
3. Rother, C., Kolmogorov, V., Blake, A.: GrabCut: Interactive foreground extraction using iterated graph cuts. ACM Transactions on Graphics 23, 309–314 (2004)
4. Price, B.L., Morse, B., Cohen, S.: Geodesic graph cut for interactive image segmentation. In: Proc. IEEE CVPR, pp. 3161–3168 (June 2010)
5. Shi, R., Liu, Z., Xue, Y., Zhang, X.: Interactive object segmentation using iterative adjustable graph cut. In: Proc. IEEE VCIP, pp. 1–4 (November 2011)
6. Boykov, Y., Kolmogorov, V.: An experimental comparison of mincut/max-flow algorithms for energy minimization in vision. IEEE Transactions on Pattern Analysis and Machine Intelligence 26(9), 1124–1137 (2004)

7. Tran, T., Vo, P., Le, B.: Combining color and texture for a robust interactive segmentation algorithm. In: Proc. IEEE RIVF, pp. 1–4 (November 2010)
8. Ning, J., Zhang, L., Zhang, D., Wu, C.: Interactive image segmentation by maximal similarity based region merging. Pattern Recognition 43(2), 445–456 (2010)
9. Geng, X., Zhao, J.: Interactive image segmentation with conditional random fields. In: Proc. Int. Conf. Natural Computation, vol. 2, pp. 96–101 (November 2008)
10. Elgammal, A., Duraiswami, R., Harwood, D., Davis, L.S.: Background and foreground modeling using nonparametric kernel density estimation for visual surveillance. Proc. IEEE 90(7), 1151–1163 (2002)
11. Liu, T., Sun, J., Zheng, N., Tang, X., Shum, H.-Y.: Learning to detect a salient object. In: Proc. IEEE CVPR, pp. 1–8 (June 2007)

Generalized Quality Assessment of Blocking Artifacts for Compressed Images

Zhenxing Qian, Wenwen Wang, and Xinpeng Zhang

School of Communication and Information Engineering,
Shanghai University, 200072, Shanghai, China
{zxqian,wwwang,xzhang}@shu.edu.cn

Abstract. Yim and Bovik proposed a referenced quality assessment method named PSNR-B. Base on PSNR, PSNR-B introduced a blocking effect factor (BEF) to measure the blocking effects of the test images, which is more effective for assessing the quality of deblocked images than PSNR. However, PSNR-B ignores the probable blocking artifacts of reference images, and disallows interchange of the test image and the reference. On these aspects, we find PSNR outperforms PSNR-B on assessing the quality of the test images. This paper aims at improving PSNR-B to a generalized metric system for compressed images. We present an improved quality assessment method of blocking artifacts for compressed images. A blocking effect ratio (BER) factor is proposed to evaluate the differences of blocking effects in both the test and the reference images. The proposed method integrates the merits of PSNR and PSNR-B, and Simulations prove the better performances.

Keywords: quality assessment, blocking effect, distortion.

1 Introduction

Quality assessment of digital image is of fundamental importance to image and video processing [1-3]. Some methods such as peak signal-to-noise ratio (PSNR), the structural similarity (SSIM) index [4], have been widely used to determine the quality of images processed in terms of compression, filtering, enhancement, etc. However, researches of assessing blocking artifacts in images are far from enough, which are useful for lossy compression systems of images and videos.

Recently, Yim and Bovik proposed a quality assessment method for deblocked images [5]. They modified the most widely used PSNR metric system to generate a block-sensitive index for assessing qualities of images with blocking artifacts. The new peak signal-to-noise ratio including blocking effects is called PSNR-B. In PSNR-B, the assessment includes two parts, the comparison of calculating the mean square error (MSE) of the both images, and the evaluation of the blocking effect factor (BEF) of the test image. Simulation results show that PSNR-B has better performance than PSNR for the impaired images.

However, in PSNR-B, probable blocking characteristics of the reference images are not considered. Assuming the reference image was once compressed, the referenced assessment for the test image would be imprecise. On this aspect, PSNR

W. Zhang et al. (Eds.): IFTC 2012, CCIS 331, pp. 110–116, 2012.

outperforms PSNR-B. To find a generalized method of quality assessment, we present an improved method for measuring blocking artifacts in compressed images. Instead of using BEF to measure the blocking degree of the test image, we propose a factor of blocking effect ratio (BER) to analyze the blocking differences between both images, and to eliminate the blocking influences of the reference image. As a result, the proposed method has better performances than PSNR-B and PSNR metric systems.

2   Proposed Method

We consider blocking artifacts occur along horizontal and vertical orientations. Denote $\mathbf{x}$ the reference image, and $\mathbf{y}$ the test image, assuming the size of both images is $N_H \times N_V$. Let $\mathcal{H}$ and be the set of horizontal neighboring pixel pairs in the test image, and $\mathcal{V}$ the set of vertical pairs. Let $\mathcal{H}_B \subset \mathcal{H}$ be the set of horizontal neighboring pixel pairs lying across block boundaries. Let $\mathcal{H}_B^C$ be the horizontal neighboring pixel pairs not lying cross boundaries, i.e. $\mathcal{H}_B^C = \mathcal{H} - \mathcal{H}_B$. Similarly, let $\mathcal{V}_B$ be the set of vertical neighboring pixel pairs lying across block boundaries, and $\mathcal{V}_B^C$ the horizontal neighboring pixel pairs not lying cross boundaries, i.e., $\mathcal{V}_B^C = \mathcal{V} - \mathcal{V}_B$.

As was described in PSNR-B, we first calculate the mean boundary pixel squared difference (D_B) and mean nonboundary pixel squared difference (D_B^C) using equation (1) and (2),

$$D_B(\mathbf{y}) = \frac{\sum\limits_{(y_i, y_j) \in \mathcal{H}_B} (y_i - y_j)^2 + \sum\limits_{(y_i, y_j) \in \mathcal{V}_B} (y_i - y_j)^2}{N_{H_B} + N_{V_B}} \tag{1}$$

$$D_B^C(\mathbf{y}) = \frac{\sum\limits_{(y_i, y_j) \in \mathcal{H}_B^C} (y_i - y_j)^2 + \sum\limits_{(y_i, y_j) \in \mathcal{V}_B^C} (y_i - y_j)^2}{N_{H_B^C} + N_{V_B^C}} \tag{2}$$

where (y_i, y_j) is the neighboring pixel pair, and N_{H_B}, $N_{H_B^C}$, N_{V_B}, and $N_{V_B^C}$ are the number of pixel pairs in $\mathcal{H}_B$, $\mathcal{H}_B^C$, $\mathcal{V}_B$, and $\mathcal{V}_B^C$, respectively. If B is the block size, then

$$N_{H_B} = N_V \cdot (\frac{N_H}{B} - 1) \tag{3}$$

$$N_{H_B^C} = N_V \cdot (N_H - 1) - N_{H_B} \tag{4}$$

$$N_{V_B} = N_H \cdot (\frac{N_V}{B} - 1) \tag{5}$$

$$N_{V_B^C} = N_H \cdot (N_V - 1) - N_{V_B} \tag{6}$$

In PSNR-B, the assessment is realized by Equations (7) ~ (9).

$$\text{PSNR - B}(\mathbf{x},\mathbf{y}) = 10\log_{10}\frac{255^2}{\text{MSE}(\mathbf{x},\mathbf{y}) + \text{BEF}(\mathbf{x},\mathbf{y})} \tag{7}$$

$$\text{BEF}(\mathbf{x},\mathbf{y}) = \eta \cdot [D_B(\mathbf{y}) - D_B^C(\mathbf{y})] \tag{8}$$

where η emphasizes the BEF as a function of block size,

$$\eta = \begin{cases} \dfrac{\log_2 B}{\log_2(\min(N_H, N_V))}, & \text{if } D_B(\mathbf{y}) > D_B^C(\mathbf{y}) \\ 0, & \text{otherwise} \end{cases} \tag{9}$$

Different from PSNR-B, we define a factor α for assessing the blocking effects of the reference image $\mathbf{x}$,

$$\alpha = \frac{D_B(\mathbf{x}) + \varepsilon}{D_B^C(\mathbf{x}) + \varepsilon} \tag{10}$$

and a factor β for assessing the blocking effects of the test image $\mathbf{y}$,

$$\beta = \frac{D_B(\mathbf{y}) + \varepsilon}{D_B^C(\mathbf{y}) + \varepsilon} \tag{11}$$

where ε is a positive used to guarantee α and β positive values. As the values of D_B and D_B^C range from 0 to 255^2, blocking artifacts are considered to be inconspicuous when D_B is small. Thus, influences to α and β would be small if we set ε as a small number.

To compare the degree of blocking difference between the reference image and the test image, we further define a factor of blocking effect ratio (BER) as Ψ in (12).

$$\Psi(\mathbf{x},\mathbf{y}) = \left(\frac{\beta}{\alpha}\right)^{\text{sgn}(\beta-\alpha)} \tag{12}$$

where the sgn($\cdot$) is the sign function. The factor BER is larger than or equal to 1, which is used to find the differences of blocking effects between both images. If BER equals 1, both images are the same on the aspect of blocking artifacts.

Finally, the improved metric equation is represented by

$$\text{IPSNR - B}(\mathbf{x},\mathbf{y}) = \left[10\log_{10}\frac{255^2}{\text{MSE}(\mathbf{x},\mathbf{y})}\right] \cdot \left[\frac{1}{\Psi(\mathbf{x},\mathbf{y})}\right]^{1/2} \tag{13}$$

where

$$\text{MSE}(\mathbf{x},\mathbf{y}) = \frac{1}{N}\sum_{i=1}^{N}(x_i - y_i)^2, \quad N = N_H \times N_V \tag{14}$$

The proposed IPSNR-B is a symmetric assessment, for $\mathbf{x}$ and $\mathbf{y}$ are interchangeable. We reduce the PSNR value according to the blocking degree in a multiply way. Thus, the compression errors and blocking artifacts are combined together. We provide an exponent 1/2 to find a balance between PSNR and BER, which comes from experimental trainings.

3   Experiment Results

To evaluate the proposed method, we implemented many experiments of quality assessment for compressed images. Some simulation results are presented here. The improved assessment method IPSNR-B is compared with PSNR and PSNR-B. Sizes of the test images used in simulations are all 512×512. We compress the reference images with different quality factors using JPEG standard in order to generate different degrees of block effects. The coefficient ε is set as 1.

Figure 1 shows the assessment result of the image "*baboon*" using the three assessment methods. The reference image is compressed by JPEG with quality factors from 10 to 90. Results show that IPSNR-B has a larger dynamic range of assessment than PNSR and PSNR-B. The trend of measurements corresponding to different compression degree keeps the same as PSNR and PSNR-B. Figure 2 shows a special reference image with interlaced black and white 8×8 blocks. When we assess the compressed quality of this image using PSNR-B, the metrics have small results and keep unchanged. In fact, little differences exist between the test and the reference which is reflected on IPSNR-B and PSNR assessment. Thus, it is more precise to use the proposed method for this kind of images than PSNR-B.

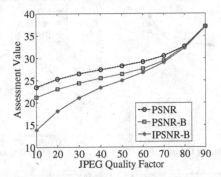

Fig. 1. Assessment results of "baboon" corresponding different degrees of compression

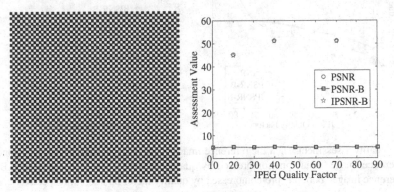

Fig. 2. Assessment of a special image

In PSNR-B, blocking effects of the reference image are ignored when assessing the test image. If the reference image was pre-compressed, the measurement of PSNR-B would be inaccuracy. We designed a group of simulations to verify the metric capability of IPSNR-B. In Fig. 3, we use the pre-compressed reference images "*lena*" and "*baboon*" with the blocking degrees corresponding to the quality factor 85 and 35 for both. Because we used BER for judgment, the trend of IPSNR-B measurements corresponding to quality factors keeps the same as PSNR, which outperforms PSNR-B as the blocking effects of the reference image are not eliminated in PSNR-B.

When we use some filters to deblock the compressed images, perceptual quality of images is enhanced especially for some low bitrate compressed images, which was ignored by PSNR. One purpose of PSNR-B is to find a better capability of assessing deblocked images than PSNR. We also compare the capabilities of PSNR, PSNR-B, and IPSNR-B in experiments. Filters of "3×3 Gaussian" and "3×3 Average" are used for deblocking. Results in Fig. 4 show that the proposed method has the same capability of assessing the deblocked images as PSNR-B, especially when the blocking effects are perceptually severe. Thus, the proposed method overcomes the shortcoming of PSNR for assessing the deblocked images.

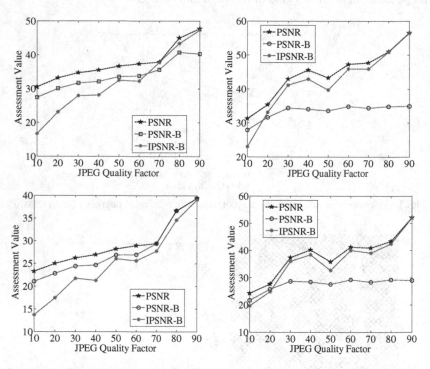

Fig. 3. Quality assessment when the reference image is pre-compressed. Top: corresponding to the reference image "lena" pre-compressed by quality factor 85 and 35, respectively. Bottom: the reference image "baboon" pre-compressed by quality factor 85 and 35, respectively.

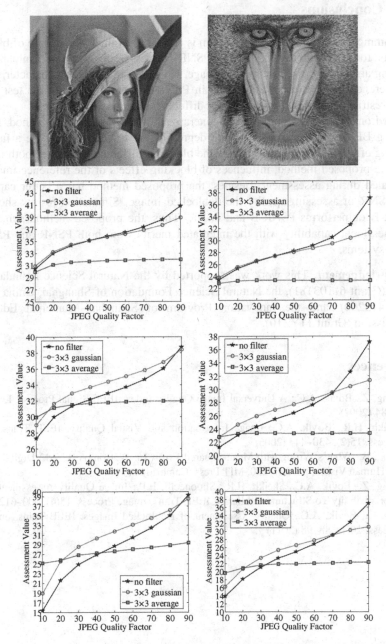

Fig. 4. Assessment of deblocked images with different methods. Left column: for image "lena". Right column: for image "baboon". Methods used from the 2nc row to the bottom for both images: PSNR, PSNR-B, and IPSNR-B.

4   Conclusions

The commonly used PSNR metric system is unable to evaluate the degree of blocking artifacts for the compressed images. PSNR-B presented a way of evaluating the blocking artifacts for the compressed image. However, the blocking characteristics of the reference image are not eliminated in PSNR-B when measuring the test image, which restricts the assessment ability for different images.

Based on PSNR-B, we proposed a generalized quality assessment method. Instead of using BEF to measure the blocking degree of the test image, we use a factor of blocking effect ratio (BER) to analyze the blocking differences between both images. With the proposed method, influences of blocking effects of the reference image are eliminated during assessment. Besides, the proposed method has a better capability than PSNR of assessing quality the deblocked image. Simulation results show that IPSNR-B outperforms PSNR-B and PSNR. Thus, the proposed method generalized the assessment capability with the integrated merits from both PSNR and PSNR-B metric systems.

Acknowledgement. This work was supported by the Natural Science Foundation of China (Grant 61103181), the Natural Science Foundation of Shanghai, China (Grant 11ZR1413200), and the Innovation Program of Shanghai Municipal Education Commission (Grant 11YZ10).

References

1. Wang, Z., Bovik, A.C.: A Universal Image Quality Index. IEEE Signal Process. Lett. 9(3), 81–84 (2002)
2. Sheikh, H.R., Bovik, A.C.: Image Information and Visual Quality. IEEE Trans. Image Process. 15(2), 430–444 (2006)
3. Girod, B.: What's Wrong with Mean-Squared Error. In: Watson, A.B. (ed.) Digital Images and Human Vision, pp. 207–220. MIT Press, Cambridge (1993)
4. Wang, Z., Bovik, A.C., Sheikh, H.R., Simoncelli, E.P.: Image Quality Assessment: From Error Visibility To Structural Similarity. IEEE Trans. Image Process. 13(4), 600–612 (2004)
5. Yim, C., Bovik, A.C.: Quality Assessment of Deblocked Images. IEEE Trans. on Image Process. 20(1), 88–98 (2011)

Visual Comfort Assessment Metric Based on Motion Features in Salient Motion Regions for Stereoscopic 3D Video

Ye Bi and Jun Zhou

Institute of Image Communication and Information Processing
Shanghai Jiao Tong University, Shanghai 200240, China
Shanghai Key Laboratory of Digital Media Processing and Transmissions
Shanghai Jiao Tong University, Shanghai 200240, China

Abstract. Visual comfort assessment for stereoscopic 3D video is of great importance for stereoscopic safety and health issue. In order to investigate visual discomfort induced by motion features in salient motion regions, we propose a visual comfort assessment metric that focuses on pixel-level motion features in salient motion regions. In our framework, we propose the pixel-level motion features extraction method based on point detector, Kanade-Lucas-Tomasi(KLT) feature tracker, and Salient Motion Depth Extraction (SMDE) approach. The motion features are spatially pooled and temporally pooled to predict visual comfort score. Subjective assessments have been conducted to evaluate our proposed visual comfort metric using natural stereoscopic videos. The experiment results have been demonstrated that our proposed visual comfort metric improves the correlation with subjective assessments.

Keywords: visual comfort assessment, point detector, KLT feature tracker, SMDE approach.

1 Introduction

Now the demand for 3D-TV services is stronger, there are more concerns about stereoscopic safety and health issue when viewing stereoscopic 3D (S3D) videos. Current literatures indicate that following factors induce to visual discomfort: vergence-accommodation conflicts, parallax distribution, binocular mismatches, depth inconsistence and so on [1].

In this paper, we aim at investigating visual discomfort induced by motion features in salient motion regions. Previous works have investigated the relationship between visual comfort and motion features in global and local methods. In global method, it utilizes global statistics to predict an overall visual comfort(VC) score. In [2], it exploited the mean and variance of depth pixel values and depth difference values to access overall VC score. In [3], the magnitudes of disparity and motion were utilized to predict overall VC score. In local approach, it applies the attention-based model into VCA framework. It is based on the idea that statistics in salient motion regions play more important role in

W. Zhang et al. (Eds.): IFTC 2012, CCIS 331, pp. 117–124, 2012.
© Springer-Verlag Berlin Heidelberg 2012

VCA framework. In [4], Jung et al. extracted segment-level motion features in salient motion regions. The motion features were spatially pooled and temporally pooled to compute overall VC score.

However, above approaches could arise problems. At first, the global methods may ignore or hidden disparity information and motion features in key regions. Second, local approach in [4] exploited motion magnitudes by block matching method, which led to high computation costs. Such dense optical flow method could not be relatively robust and reliable for motion estimation. Third, perceptually salient motion regions were determined by salient cues and motion cues without taking into consideration of depth context. In most cases, depth context helps to avoid interferences induced into the extraction of salient motion regions.

In this paper, we propose an attention-based model VCA framework that focuses on pixel-level motion features in the extraction of SMDE approach. It's based on idea that motion features in salient motion regions are more likely to play prominent role in VCA framework. To extract pixel-level motion features, we propose method based on point detector, KLT feature tracker, and SMDE approach. The motion features are spatially pooled and temporally pooled to predict overall VC score.

2   Experimental Setup

2.1   Subjective Assessment

In our experiment, subjective assessments were conducted with a 42" polarized stereoscopic monitor (LG-42LS4500) with the resolution 1920 × 1080. Viewers watched stereoscopic stimuli upon wearing polarized glasses. The design of experiments was in line with recommendation of ITU-R BT.500-11 [5]. Fig.1 presents the geometric viewing condition in subjective assessment, where near and far objects are positioned in the binocular disparity of of 1° under the assumption that the interpupillary distance is $65mm$. In detail, the converging angels for the nearest point, the display screen, and the farthest point were 3.42°, 2.42°, 1.42° respectively.

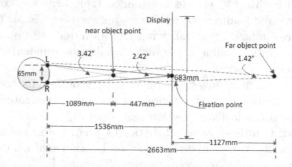

Fig. 1. Geometric viewing condition in subjective assessment

2.2 Visual Comfort Model

In our experiment, we utilize similar VC model proposed in [4] that indicates the relationship between visual comfort and motion features. In detail, $f_x(\cdot)$, $f_y(\cdot)$ and $f_z(\cdot)$ donate VC models for horizontal, vertical and depth directions respectively.

$$f_x(v_x, d) = -1.5ln(v_x + 6.7) - 0.3|d| + 8 \tag{1}$$

$$f_y(v_y, d) = -7.4ln(v_y + 64.8) - 0.8|d| + 36 \tag{2}$$

$$f_z(v_z) = -0.72ln(v_z + 0.27) + 4 \tag{3}$$

where v_x, v_y, v_z denote motion velocities (deg/s) for horizontal, vertical and depth directions respectively; d denotes disparity value (deg) that represents depth position of horizontal and vertical motions.

3 Proposed VCA Framework

Our proposed attention-based model VCA framework consists of four steps: key pixel-level motion feature extraction, spatial pooling strategy, VC score computation and temporal pooling strategy. In Fig.2, it shows the overview of proposed VCA framework.

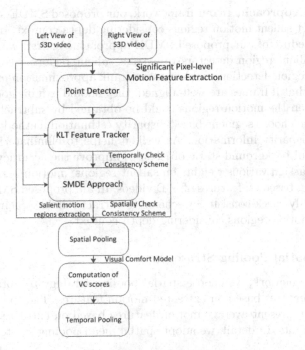

Fig. 2. Overview of our proposed VCA framework

3.1   Key Pixel-Level Motion Feature Extraction

For key pixel-level motion feature extraction method, first we utilize point detector method to search interesting corner points. Second, KLT feature tracker is exploited as temporally check consistency to rule out outlying corner points. Third, we utilize SMDE approach to extract salient motion regions considering depth context. At last, pixel-level motion features are calculated based on reliable tracking corner points in salient motion regions considering depth context.

Point Detector. In our experiment, we investigated KLT detector [6] and SIFT detector [7] as point detector to find out interesting corner points. A desirable quality of interesting corner points meet the definition of being good for tracking. For KLT detector, detected corner points are always good tracking points. For SIFT detector, the SIFT descriptor of detected corner points does provide useful information for tracking.

KLT Feature Detector. In our method, we utilized KLT feature detector [6] as temporally check consistency to assess motion features. When the baseline between camera's optical centres at adjacent frames are widened, the KLT tracker starts to lose tracks of corner points. What's more, compared with block matching method [4], KLT feature detector method is robust and reliable. In addition, its computation cost is much less.

SMDE Approach. In our framework, our proposed SMDE approach is utilized to extract salient motion regions considering depth context. In Fig.3, it presents the procedure of our proposed SMDE approach. At first, we choose frequency-tuned salient region detectors to extract salient regions. Second, we regularize motion region detection problem as low-rank approximation problem. It is based on idea that if frames are well-aligned, they should exhibit good low-rank structure. Then the motion regions could be obtained by subtracting static regions. Third, we choose segment-based disparity estimation method that provides necessary disparity information. As well, it helps to eliminate interferences, such as colorful background static objects, to improve the accuracy of extraction. At last, we assign various weights on salient regions, ,motion regions and depth information based on features of S3D videos. In all, proposed SMDE approach acts as spatially check consistency scheme to extract reliable tracing corner points in salient motion regions considering depth context.

3.2   Spatial Pooling Strategy

In our framework, we choose spatial pooling strategy to obtain spatial pooled motion features based on extracted motion features. The spatial pooled motion features represent average motion features based on extracted reliable tracking corner points. In detail, we adopt spatial mean pooling strategy as follows:

$$m^{(pooled)}(t) = \frac{1}{N} \sum_{k=1}^{N} m^{(k)}(t) \qquad (4)$$

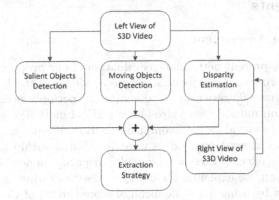

Fig. 3. Framework of our proposed SMDE approach

3.3 VC Score Computation

In our experiment, we investigated two strategies to integrate the VC scores from three motion magnitude components into an overall VC score. The VC scores are computed based on spatial pooled motion features and VC models described 2.2. Due to that VC models are derived as function of average change in angular disparity (deg/s), the unit of motion feature components (pix/s) should be converted into the unit of motion velocity (deg/s). In detail, we investigated the mean integration method and the minimum integration method. The VC score of tth frame is computed as:

$$VC_x(t) = f_x[m_x^{(pooled)}(t), d_x^{(pooled)}(t)] \tag{5}$$

$$VC_y(t) = f_y[m_y^{(pooled)}(t), d_y^{(pooled)}(t)] \tag{6}$$

$$VC_z(t) = f_z[m_z^{(pooled)}] \tag{7}$$

$$VC(t) = mean\{VC_x(t), VC_y(t), VC_z(t)\} \tag{8}$$

$$VC(t) = min\{VC_x(t), VC_y(t), VC_z(t)\} \tag{9}$$

where $mean(\cdot)$, $min(\cdot)$ denotes an average operation and minimal operation of VC scores respectively.

3.4 Temporal Pooling Strategy

In our method, we investigated the temporal mean pooling strategy and temporal median pooling strategy to obtain overall VC scores for S3D videos. In detail, the temporal mean pooling and median pooling are defined as

$$VC^{(mean)} = \frac{1}{N-1} \sum_{t=1}^{N-1} VC(t) \tag{10}$$

$$VC^{(median)} = median\{VC(1), ..., VC(N-1)\} \tag{11}$$

4   Experiments

4.1   Subjective Assessment

In this section, we present performance evaluation of our proposed VCA framework. In our experiment, twenty-one stereoscopic videos in the IVY Lab stereoscopic video database [9] were utilized to analyze its performance. In detail, nine videos have horizon motion, two videos have vertical motion, eight videos have depth motion, and two videos have composite motion. What's more, the binocular disparities of all stereoscopic videos were distributed within the comfortable zone to exclude the effect of excessive binocular disparity on perceived visual discomfort. In addition, we exploited the categorical scales rating method to assess the visual comfort by using five scale mean of score (MOS) of visual comfort(5: very comfortable, 4: comfortable, 3: mildly uncomfortable, 2: uncomfortable, 1: extremely uncomfortable) [5]. Twenty human subjects (fourteen males and six females) with an average of 23.5 participated into our subjective assessment. The viewing conditions were same as described in Sec.2.1.

4.2   Evaluation of VCA Performance

In our experiment, we evaluate our propsed VCA performance based on three popular performance metric. They are respectively Pearson linear correlation coefficient(CC), Spearman rank order correlation coefficient(SROCC) and Root mean square error(RMSE)[10]. In our framework, we investigated VCA performance based on all combinations of point detectors, VC score integration strategies and temporal pooling strategies. Based on performance results tabulated in Fig.4 and Fig.5, the best performance was obtained by KLT point detector,

	Temporal Mean Pooling Strategy			
Point Detector	KLT Detector		SIFT Detector	
Component Score Integration Strategy	Mean Integration	Min Integration	Mean Integration	Min Integration
CC	0.7313	0.8736	0.7761	0.8566
SROCC	0.6780	0.8604	0.7480	**0.9108**
RMSE	0.7314	0.1500	0.7076	0.1510

Fig. 4. proposed VCA performance under temporal mean pooling

	Temporal Median Pooling Strategy			
Point Detector	KLT Detector		SIFT Detector	
Component Score Integration Strategy	Mean Integration	Min Integration	Mean Integration	Min Integration
CC	0.7328	**0.8800**	0.7717	0.8740
SROCC	0.7022	0.8539	0.7885	0.9069
RMSE	0.7387	0.1443	0.7044	**0.1415**

Fig. 5. Proposed VCA performance under temporal median pooling

spatial mean pooling strategy, minimum VC score integration strategy, and temporal median pooling strategy. In our proposed VCA metric, the best CC was 0.8800, the best SROCC was 0.9108, and the best RMSE was 0.1415. The performance results have demonstrated that our proposed VCA method correlates well with subjective assessments.

4.3   VCA Performance Comparison

In order to demonstrate the efficiency of our proposed VCA metric, we try to compare our proposed VCA method with other methods mentioned in Sec.1. Based on performance results tabulated in Fig.6, our proposed VCA method outperforms other approaches in terms of three popular performance metrics CC, SROCC and RMSE. What's more, the scatter plots of MOS versus predicted VC score are presented in Fig.7. The results indicate that predicted VC scores have better correlations with subjective assessments in our proposed VCA framework.

Method	Spatial pooling	Temporal pooling	CC	SROCC	RMSE
Global statistics-based method [2]	Mean	Mean	0.4897	0.6041	0.4876
	Variance	Mean	0.4964	0.6303	0.4350
Global statistics-based method [3]	Ratio	Mean	0.2915	0.4335	0.5645
Local attention-based method [4]	Max	Median	0.6281	0.6708	0.2016
Our proposed VCA method	Mean	Median	0.8800	0.8539	0.1443

Fig. 6. VCA performance comparison

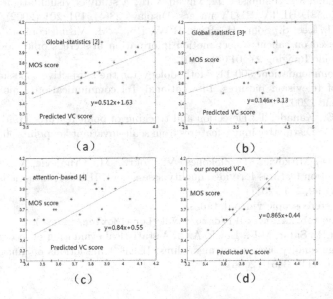

(a)

(b)

(c)

(d)

Fig. 7. Scatter plot of MOS versus predicted VC score (a)global-statistic method in [2], (b)global-statistic method in [3], (c)attention-based method in [4], (d)our proposed VCA method. Each point represents one S3D video.

5   Conclusion

In this paper, we propose attention model-based VCA metric framework that exploits pixel-level motion features in salient motion regions considering depth context. In detail, pixel-level motion features are extracted based on point detector, KLT feature tracker and SMDE approach. Then the extracted motion features are spatial pooled and temporal pooled to predict overall VC score. Based on evaluation performance, the best prediction performance for our proposed VCA method is obtained by KLT point detector, spatial mean pooling, minimum component VC score integration strategy and temporal median pooling strategy. Through comparison, our proposed VCA method outperforms other methods in terms of CC, SROCC and RMSE.

Acknowledgement. The work for this paper was supported by MOST under Contact 2011BAH08B01, and Science and Technology Commission of Shanghai Municipality grant under Contact 10511501102.

References

1. Tam, W.J., Speranza, F., Yano, S., Shimono, K.: Ono: Stereoscopic 3D-TV: Visual Comfort. IEEE Transactions on Broadcasting 99, 1–1 (2011)
2. Choi, J., Kim, D., Ham, B., Choi, S., Sohn, K.: Visual fatigue evaluation and enhancement for 2D-plus-depth video. In: 2010 17th IEEE International Conference on Image Processing (ICIP), pp. 2981–2984 (2010)
3. Yano, S., Ide, S., Mitsuhashi, T., Thwaites, H.: A study of visual fatigue and visual comfort for 3D HDTV/HDTV images. Displays 23(4), 191–201 (2002)
4. Jung, Y.J., Lee, S., Sohn, H., Park, H.W., Ro, Y.M.: Visual comfort assessment metric based on salient object motion information in stereoscopic video. Journal of Electronic Imaging 21, 011008 (2012)
5. ITU Recommendation. 500-11, Methodology for the subjective assessment of the quality of television pictures, International Telecommunication Union, Geneva, Switzerland (2002)
6. Tomasi, C., Kanade, T.: Detection and tracking of point features (1991)
7. Lowe, D.G.: Distinctive image features from scale-invariant keypoints 60(2), 91–110 (2004)
8. Culibrk, D., Mirkovic, M., Zlokolica, V., Pokric, M., Crnojevic, V., Kukolj, D.: Salient motion features for video quality assessment. IEEE Transactions on Image Processing 99, 1–1 (2011)
9. IVY Lab stereoscopic video database, http://ivylab.kaist.ac.kr/demo/ivy3D-LocalMotion/index.htm
10. Sheikh, H.R., Sabir, M.F., Bovik, A.C.: A statistical evaluation of recent full reference image quality assessment algorithms. IEEE Transactions on Image Processing 15(11), 3440–3451 (2006)

A Comparison of Testing Metrics between 3D LCD TV and 3D PDP TV*

Jing Zhang**, Sumei Li, Lili Shen**, and Chunping Hou

School of Electronic and Information Engineering, Tianjin University,
300072 Tianjin, China
sll@tju.edu.cn, srty1989@163.com

Abstract. 3D display technologies offer attractive solutions for enriching the multimedia experience. However, both characterization and comparison of 3D displays have been challenging when displays with similar specifications may appear quite different. This paper reviews and compares a series of measurement methods of luminance, turn-off ratio, contrast, cross-talk, angle cross-talk and some color measurements in various stereoscopic displays, including: LCDs with active shutter glasses, LCDs with polarized glasses and PDPs with polarized glasses.

Keywords: 3DTV, Testing metrics, LCD, PDP.

1   Introduction

With the rapid expansion of 3D market, 3D standard seems more and more necessary to 3D industry. China, the United States, Japan and Korea are establishing standard according to their own national conditions. Nowadays, each union and organization in the global has formulated some related standard system in the basis of their situation. So this paper provides an overview of present standard of testing stereoscopic 3D displays, including a review of differences of 3D display type and measuring methods of different items. Finally, testing results of different display device are discussed and compared.

2   Background

Auto stereoscopic 3DTV is more comfortable than glasses-style 3DTV. However, the technology of 3DTV with active shutter eye-glasses or polarized eye-glasses display is more mature, and the display is better. So in this paper, we choose two latest 3DTV types, active shutter eye-glass type and passive eye-glass type, to be tested. Passive 3DTVs are all LCD TVs and active 3DTVs can be both LCD and PDP TVs.

---

* These works were supported in part by NSFC (60932007), the National High Technology Research and Development Program of China (2012AA011505, 2012BAC13B05).
** Corresponding author.

W. Zhang et al. (Eds.): IFTC 2012, CCIS 331, pp. 125–132, 2012.
© Springer-Verlag Berlin Heidelberg 2012

Liquid Crystal Display (or LCD) refers to a type of screen that is comprised of a number of pixels that are filled with liquid crystals, which are then displayed in front of a particular light source. Plasma Display Panel (or PDP) refers to a type of flat paneled screen. Its composition is a bit more complex than that of an LCD screen. The gas in cells within the panel becomes plasma via electricity, which then emits ultraviolet light, and turns into a light that is visible to the average person.

Active Shutter technology displays one image to your left eye and one image to your right eye. Since the effective frame rate is halved, 3D HDTVs need to double the refresh rate of HDTVs. Passive (or Polarized) Glasses is that the display shows two overlapping images and the glasses have polarized lenses. Each lens is polarized so that it can see only one of the two overlapping images.

3   Test Method and Results

In this paper, 20 types of 3DTVs were tested for some important items for 3D standard [1], such as luminance, turn-off ratio, contrast, cross-talk, angle cross-talk and some color measurements. After a number of experiments, we choose three typical types of displays for discussing. The first type is 50" PDP with active shutter glasses. The second type is 42" LCD with polarized glasses. The last type is 46" LCD with active shutter glasses. In this paper we use PDP-50-SG, LCD-46-SG and LCD-42-PR to represent these three types of displays.

3.1   3D Luminance

The 3D luminance measurements [2] [3] were tested by CA-2000 instrument which is a kind of two dimensional color analyzer. At the beginning of test, the display type is set to 3D mode. The test pattern for each view was full screen of homogenous black or square white window, of which side length is a half of screen height. The measured view combinations were white/white, black/white and white/black.

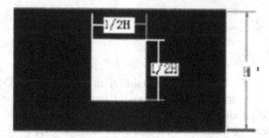

Fig. 1. This is one of the test patterns for measuring luminance. The other pattern is full screen black.

The Equation (1) was used for calculating the maximum luminance difference of left channel:

$$L_{3D_L} = L_{L_{WW}} - L_{L_{BW}} .$$ (1)

Where L_{3D_L} represents the luminance of left eye channel, $L_{L_{WW}}$ represents the luminance at the center with both channels being white window when left glass was putting behind the luminance meter, $L_{L_{BW}}$ represents the luminance at the center of the screen with left channel being full screen black and right channel being square white window when left glass was put behind the luminance meter. And so it is with the right channel.

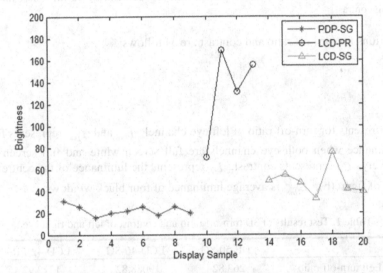

Fig. 2. Test results of 3D luminance of left and right eye channel. Horizontal axis represents different display samples, 1 to 7 are PDP-SG, 10 to 13 are LCD-PR and 14 to 20 are LCD-SG. Vertical axis represents luminance.

Figure 2 is luminance results of 20 samples. The test data of 3D luminance show that PDP-SG display has a lowest luminance about 17nits to 30nits. The next is LCD-SG, the luminance is about 30nits to 80nit. The luminance of LCD-PR is the highest, about 70nits to 170nits. So we can conclude that LCD display with polarized glasses has the best transmission of light.

3.2   3D Turn-Off Ratio and Contrast

The test pattern used for measuring turn-off ratio was full screen of homogenous either black or white for each view. Figure 3 (b) shows the test pattern for measuring contrast [4] [5]. The turn-off ratio and contrast measurements were done with the same CA-2000 instrument as was used for the luminance.

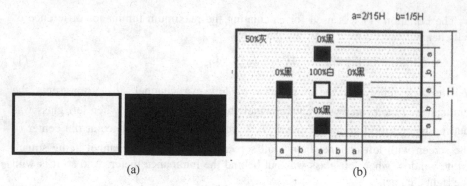

(a)   (b)

Fig. 3. Figure (a) is test images for measuring turn-off ratio and figure (b) is test image for measuring contrast

Equations for turn-off ratio and contrast are as follows:

$$CR_{3DL} = \frac{L_{Lww}}{L_{Lbb}}.$$ (2)

$$C_r = \frac{L_0}{L_{bw}}.$$ (3)

CR_{3DL} represents for turn-off ratio of left eye channel. L_{Lww} and L_{Lbb} represents for left eye luminance when both eye channels are full screen white and full screen black respectively. C_r represents contrast, L_0 represents the luminance of the centre white window of figure(b), L_{Lbw} is average luminance of four black windows.

Table 1. Test results of 3D turn-off ratio and contrast of left and right eye

	PDP-50-SG	LCD-46-SG	LCD-42-PR
Left turn-off ratio	263.82	9088.82	1712.92
Right turn-off ratio	257.09	7043.97	1716.20
Left eye contrast	85.18	193.54	238.61
Right eye contrast	73.48	146.83	226.18

Table 1 is test results of 3D turn-off ratio and contrast of the 3 of 20 samples. As we know, contrast is used for compare the difference between maximum luminance and minimum luminance on a screen. The turn-off ratio is similar to contrast. So according to a comprehensive evaluating, we conclude that PDP-SG has a minimum contrast and turn-off ratio. As a result, the luminance range of this kind of displays is the smallest, and LCD-SG and LCD-PR relatively large, especially LCD-SG.

3.3   Crosstalk

There are several definitions for the term "crosstalk" [6] [7] with respect to stereoscopic displays. In this paper, we study crosstalk that can be physically measured, which is independent of the human visual system. Figure 4 is the test pattern for crosstalk.

The principle of stereoscopic display is that making left and right eye to obtain different images, and form a virtual three-dimensional image in the human brain. So the left eye can only see the left eye image on the three-dimensional display, while the right eye can only see the right eye image. However, due to technical reasons, the three-dimensional images cannot fully meet the above requirements, resulting in the crosstalk of the left and right eye. Cross-interference indicator of left and right eye is used to measure left and right eye crosstalk level.

Because brightness of the images in stereoscopic display is not only a binary black and white, but contains middle gray. The viewer will see the crosstalk in middle gray level. Moreover, the response speed of black/white signal and middle gray signals are different, so the crosstalk of black/white and middle gray are different. Thus, this paper adds middle grayscale to test image crosstalk.

The Equation (4) [8] was used for calculating the crosstalk:

$$X_{Gi,RtoL,m-l} = \frac{L_{Li,l-m} - L_{Li,l-l}}{L_{Li,100\%-100\%} - L_{Li,0\%-0\%}} \times 100\% \quad . \tag{4}$$

Where $L_{Li,l-m}$ is the luminance of the left view when the gray level of left view is 'l' and the gray level of right view is 'm', 'l' and 'm' are 0%, 25%, 50%, 75%, 100% gray level. $L_{Li,0\%-0\%}$ is the luminance of the left view when the left view is white and the right view is white, $L_{Li,100\%-100\%}$ is the luminance of the left view when the left view is black and the right view is black.

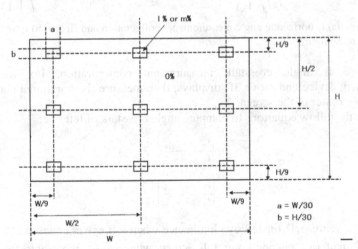

Fig. 4. This figure is the test pattern of measuring crosstalk, choose nine square on the settled position from the screen, positions were showed on the figure

Table 2. Crosstalk of three sample displays

	PDP-50-SG			LCD-46-SG			LCD-42-PR		
	Ave.	Max.	S.D.	Ave.	Max.	S.D.	Ave.	Max.	S.D.
Left-Glass	0.6	0.7	0.04	3.9	4.7	0.36	0.8	1.3	0.23
Right-Glass	0.6	0.7	0.03	4.2	5.0	0.45	0.8	1.2	0.18

Table 2 gives the average, maximum and standard deviation of the crosstalk value .This table shows that PDP displays have a better function of isolate light. As for LCD, displays with active shutter technology have a lower crosstalk than those with polarized technology.

3.4   Angle Crosstalk

The test pattern for measuring angle crosstalk is just full black and white screen.

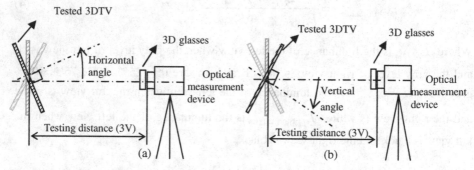

Fig. 5. Figure (a) is horizontal angle measurement configuration and figure (b) is vertical angle measurement configuration

Figure 5 is angle crosstalk measurement configuration. Fix the optical measurement device and move 3D displays, then measure the horizontal and vertical angle on the center of the screen.

We use the follow equations to compute angle crosstalk of left eye:

$$X_{L,W\text{-}B} = \left| \frac{L_{L,BW} - L_{L,BB}}{L_{L,WW} - L_{L,BB}} \right| . \tag{5}$$

$$X_{L,B\text{-}W} = \left| \frac{L_{L,WB} - L_{L,WW}}{L_{L,WW} - L_{L,BB}} \right| . \tag{6}$$

Where $L_{L,BW}$ represents for left eye luminance when left eye channels are full screen black and right eye channels are full screen white, $L_{L,WB}$ represents for left eye luminance when left eye channels are full screen white and right eye channels are full screen black, $L_{L,WW}$ and $L_{L,BB}$ represents for left eye luminance when both eye channels are full screen white and full screen black respectively. The right eye angle crosstalk is the same to the left eye.

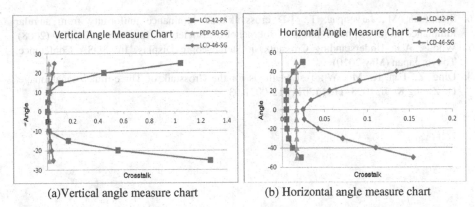

(a) Vertical angle measure chart   (b) Horizontal angle measure chart

Fig. 6. Figure (a) is vertical angle measure chart and figure (b) is horizontal angle measure chart. Horizontal axis represent crosstalk and vertical axis represent measure angle.

Angle crosstalk is crosstalk measured in different angle. It represents the watching extent of angle size of 3D screen, including vertical angle and horizontal angle. From the two charts in figure 6 we found that PDP has a less effect of a large watching angle both vertical and horizontal angle. For LCD screen, there is a huge effect of vertical angle on active shutter technology and a huge effect of horizontal angle on polarized technology.

4   Conclusions

In this paper, we summarize the characteristics of different display type of 3D TV. LCD display has a relatively higher luminance compared with the PDP display. The light transmittance of polarized glasses is better than that of the shutter glasses. Contrast of LCD is much larger than that of PDP screen. Crosstalk of LCD screen with active shutter glasses is much more serious. For PDP there is less effect of a large watching angle both vertical and horizontal angle, while for LCD screen, the effect is huge.

References

1. Abileah, A.: 3D Displays –Technologies &Testing Methods. 2011 Planar Systems, Inc. (2011)
2. Salmimaa, M.: Optical Characterization and Measurements of Auto stereoscopic 3D Displays. In: Proc. of SPIE, vol. 7001, pp. 700102–700108
3. Jarvenpaa, T., Salmimaa, M.: Optical characterization methods for autostereoscopic 3D displays. Eurodisplay (2007)
4. Mai, Z.: Contrast Effect On 3D and 2D Video Perception. In: 2011 Third International Workshop on Quality of Multimedia Experience (2011)
5. ITU-R Recommendation BT.709-5: Parameter values for the HDTV standards for production and international programme exchange

6. Salmimaa, M., Jarvenpaa, T.: 3-D crosstalk and luminance uniformity from angular luminance profiles of multiview auto. Journal of the Society for Information Display (2008)
7. Woods, A.J.: Understanding Crosstalk in Stereoscopic Display. In: 3DSA Conference, Tokyo, Japan (May 2010)
8. Ding, Z., Fan, K., Mo, W.: Test Methods for the Crosstalk of Three-dimensional Image. Da Zhong Ke Ji, 1008–1151 (2011) 12-0021-03

Primary Quality Factor Estimation in Double Compressed JPEG Images Using Quantization Error

Yang Shuang and Fang Zhen

School of Communication and Information Engineering, Shanghai University,
Shanghai 200072, China
yangshuang@shu.edu.cn, zhfang@staff.shu.edu.cn

Abstract. In this paper, we propose a new method to estimate the primary quality factor of double JPEG compressed image using quantization error. The method includes three steps: requantize DCT coefficients with a set of possible quantization matrixes, compute *NMSQE* (normalized mean square quantization error), and find the position of the smallest local minimum. Experimental results show that this method can estimate the primary quality factor effectively.

Keywords: double-compression, image forensics, JPEG, quantization error, quality factor.

1   Introduction

With the wide use of image processing software like Photoshop, it is getting easier to manipulate image content without leaving any visual traces. Verifying the authenticity of image content has become increasingly important. JPEG [1] is the most used image format, tampered images are often JPEG compressed. Therefore, analyzing this type of image is useful to image forensics.

A tampered JPEG image may be resaved as BMP or JPEG format. Some studies [2]-[4] have been done to identify whether a bitmap was JPEG compressed before and estimate the corresponding quantization table. On the other hand, the work of [5]-[10] explored the detection of recompression in JPEG image. Estimating the primary compression parameters [11], [12] is helpful to further decide if a recompressed image was tampered or even locate the forged region.

Many studies have been done on the estimation of primary compression parameters. Based on some characteristic features of DCT histograms due to double compression, Lukáš *et al.* [14] presented three different approaches to estimate primary quantization matrix from double JPEG compressed images, the most successful one is based on Neural Network classifier. In most JPEG compression schemes, a quantization matrix is dependent on a quality factor. Pevný *et al.* [15] focused on the estimation of primary quality factor by using SVM classifier with feature vectors formed by histograms of low-frequency DCT coefficients, and

W. Zhang et al. (Eds.): IFTC 2012, CCIS 331, pp. 133–139, 2012.

archived a higher accuracy. However, the previous two methods need to train a classifier prior to detection, so the classify results may be affected by the training sample selection.

In this paper, we propose a simple method to estimate the primary quality factor based on quantization error in double JPEG compressed images. The rest of this paper is organized as follows. In Section 2, we analyze the quantization error introduced by JPEG compression. Section 3 describes details of the proposed method. Experimental results and discussions are showed in Section 4. Section 5 concludes the paper and discusses the future work.

2   Quantization Error of JPEG Compression

To compress a gray image, there are three main steps: divide it into disjoint 8x8 pixels blocks and compute the DCT coefficients, uniformly quantize them with a quantization matrix, entropy encode the quantized coefficients. If X_{ij} is the DCT coefficient in the position (i, j), Q_{ij} is the quantization step. The quantized value is computed as follows:

$$X_{ij} = round\,(X_{ij} / Q_{ij})\,. \tag{1}$$

To decompress a JPEG image, the steps are: entropy decode, dequantize the DCT coefficients, and compute the inverse DCT (IDCT) coefficients of every block and round them to integers. In most JPEG compression schemes, the quantization matrix depends on a quality factor (QF). The range of quality factor is [1, 2, ... , 100]. Details of computing quantization matrix based on quality factor can be found in [4].

Quantization error happens due to the rounding of quantization, and it's dependent on quantization step. For a one dimension random signal x, quantize it with step q_1 and dequantize it, we get $x_1 = [x/q_1]*q_1$. The quantization error is $e_1 = x_1 - x$, and its range is $(-q_1/2, q_1/2]$.

If we requantize x with step q_2 and dequantize it, we get $x_2 = [x_1/q_2]*q_2$. The quantization error is $e_2 = x_2 - x_1$, and its range is $(-q_2/2, q_2/2]$. If we normalize the quantization error e_1 and e_2 by divide the quantization step respectively and get the square values, we can get $NSQE = (e/q)^2$, and its range is [0, 0.25]. Therefore, we can analyze quantization error of double compressed image in a certain interval.

Hany Farid [16] made use of quantization error to identify the forged region in tampered JPEG images. In the next section, we'll describe how to estimate the primary quantization matrix using quantization error.

3   Primary Quality Factor Estimation

For a one dimension random signal x with length of 1000, quantize it with $q_1 = 17$, we get x_1. Requantize it with q_2 in the range of [1, 30], we get x_2. Compute normalized mean square quantization error ($NMSQE$, and $k = 2$) based on Eq.2:

$$NMSQE = mean \ ((x_k - x_{k-1})/q_k)^2. \tag{2}$$

In Eq.2, k represents the total quantization times of x. We can see in Fig.1 (a) that when $q_2 = q_1$, $NMSQE$ is zero and is minimum with the exception of $q_2 = 1$ (i.e., no quantization).

Meanwhile, quantize x with $q_1 = 23$, followed by $q_2 = 17$, we get x_2. Requantize it with q_3 in the range of [1, 30], we get x_3. Compute $NMSQE$ ($k = 3$) based on Eq.2. As showed in Fig. 1(b), when $q_3 = q_2$, $NMSQE$ is zero and is minimum. When $q_3 = q_1$, $NMSQE$ is a local minimum and is smaller than other local minimums in the range of $(q_2, 30]$. The result stands as long as $q_2 < q_1$. By finding the position of the smallest local minimum in the range of $(q_2, 30]$, we can estimate q_1.

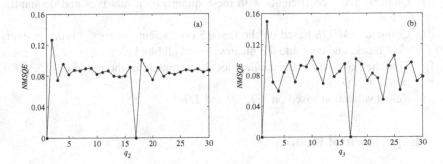

Fig. 1. NMSQE of different requatization step: (a) $q_1 = 17$. When $q_2 = q_1$, there is a minimum. (b) $q_1 = 23$, $q_2 = 17$. When $q_3 = q_2$, there is a minimum; when $q_3 = q_1$, there is a local minimum.

To extend to double JPEG compressed images ($QF_1 < QF_2$), we extract DCT coefficients and requantization them with quantization matrixes based on QF_3 in the range of [15, 90]. As most high frequencies coefficients are rounded to zero, we choose to compute $NMSQE$ ($k = 3$) of the first 15 coefficients in zigzag order in every 8×8 block based on Eq.3 for every QF_3, and compute the mean value of all blocks.

$$NMSQE = mean \left(\sum_{ij}^{15} \left(\left(X_{ij}^k - X_{ij}^{k-1} \right) / Q_{ij}^k \right)^2 \right). \tag{3}$$

In Eq.3, k represents the total quantization times of original DCT coefficients; ij represents the (i, j) position of an 8×8 DCT coefficients block; X_{ij}^{k-1} and X_{ij}^k represent a DCT coefficient before and after requantization respectively; Q_{ij}^k represents the requantization step.

When $QF_3 = QF_1$, $NMSQE$ is a local minimum and is smaller than other local minimums in the range of [15, QF_2). By finding position of the smallest local minimum in the range of [15, QF_2), we can estimate QF_1. In real cases, QF_2 is not known, but we can get the quantization matrix of recompression by reading the file header and compute the most possible QF_2.

Sometimes, other than the estimation value (EST_1), there is a local minimum (EST_2) whose value (V_2) is greater but very close with the estimation value (V_1), and

EST_1 is smaller than EST_2. By observing the experiment results, we found that if V_2 is greater than a threshold and the distance between EST_2 and EST_1 is far enough, EST_2 is the real QF_1, so the estimator fails in this situation. By setting VD as the difference between V_1 and V_2, TD as the difference between EST_2 and EST_1, TH as the threshold, we can improve the result by extra validation.

Based on the researches above, we can conclude the steps of the proposed method to estimate the primary quality factor of a double JPEG compressed image as follows:

a) Extract DCT coefficients and quantization matrix of the luminance channel.
b) Compute the most possible quality factor based on the quantization matrix, mark it as QF_2.
c) Compute all the quantization matrixes with QF_3 in the range of [15, QF_2).
d) Quantize DCT coefficients with these quantization matrixes and dequantize them.
e) Compute $NMSQE$ based on the first 15 coefficients in zigzag order in every 8x8 block, and compute the mean value of all blocks.
f) Find the position of the smallest local minimums in the range of [15, QF_2), mark it as $QF1$.
g) Result validation based on VD, TD and TH.

4   Experimental Results

The experimental images are all from UCID [17] database. We random select 100 images with size of 512×384. These uncompressed color images are first converted to grayscale and saved with QF_1, and then resaved with QF_2. The JPEG compress procedure is archived with the Matlab toolbox. QF_2 ranges from 40 to 90 in increments of 5, and $QF_2 - QF_1$ (the difference between QF_1 and QF_2, $QF_1<QF_2$) ranges from 10 to 25 in increments of 5. We get 4400 images totally. The default value of VD is 0.0005, TD is 5, and TH is 0.004. If the estimation value equals to real QF_1, we mark it right, else we'll mark it wrong.

Table 1 shows the results in different $QF_2 - QF_1$ and QF_1 cases, the total average accuracy is 98.55%. When many quantization steps of QF_1 and QF_2 have big common dividers, more local minimums appear and make it hard to find the right QF_1. The result validation (step g in Section 3) can help to improve the accuracy effectively.

Table 1. The average accuracy of QF_1 estimation in different $QF_2 - QF_1$ and QF_1 cases

QF_2 - QF_1	QF_2											
	40	45	50	55	60	65	70	75	80	85	90	average
10	0.96	0.99	1	1	1	1	0.99	1	1	1	1	0.9946
15	0.89	0.98	0.95	0.97	0.99	1	1	1	1	1	1	0.98
20	1	1	1	0.92	0.96	0.96	1	0.99	1	1	1	0.9846
25	0.83	1	1	0.98	1	1	1	1	1	1	1	0.9828
average	0.92	0.9925	0.9875	0.9675	0.9875	0.99	0.9975	0.9975	1	1	1	**0.9855**

Remark 1. For $QF_1 = 50$, the estimation value can be 49, 50 or 51. We consider them as the same, because the first 15 quantization steps of these three quality factors are the same.

To analyze the influence of image size on the estimation accuracy, the images for experiment are center-cropped into blocks with sizes ranging from 256x256 to 16x16. Fig.3 (a) shows the results in different QF_2 - QF_1 cases, and every dot in the figure represents the average estimation accuracy of 1100 images. When the image size is decreased to 16×16, the average accuracy can still reach to 71.55%.

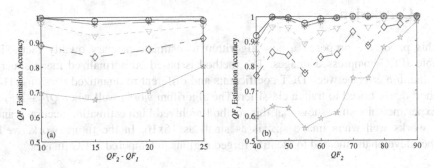

Fig. 2. (a) The average accuracy of QF_1 estimation in different QF_2 - QF_1 cases. (b) The average accuracy of QF_1 estimation in different QF_2 cases.

Fig.3 (b) shows the results of different QF_2 cases, and every dot in the figure represents the average estimation accuracy of 400 images. When image size is big, the accuracy is high and stable in most QF_2 cases, but the accuracy falls with QF_2 when image size is small, especially when $QF_2 = 40$ or 55. This is because *NMSQE* of different QF_3 may be more close to each other as QF_2 drops, and it's more obvious for small size images. So the estimation result is a value around the real QF_1. To improve the result, research on relationship between individual quantization steps of QF_1 and QF_2 is needed.

The algorithm in [15] can also estimate QF_1 for double-compressed images. Results of QF_1 estimation in the range of [63, 98] for images whose QF_2 is 75 or 80 were showed in Fig.6 of [15], and high accuracy was archived in most cases. We test our algorithm for the same QF_1 and QF_2 on 100 images, the results are showed in Table 2.

Table 2. The average accuracy of QF_1 estimation when QF_2 is 75 or 80

QF_2	QF_1																
	63	64	65	66	67	68	69	70	71	72	73	74	75	76	77	78	79
75	0.99	1	1	1	1	1	1	0.02	0	0	0	0	\	\	\	\	\
80	1	1	1	0.98	1	1	1	1	1	1	1	1	1	0	0	0	0

Remark 2. "\" *represents the method cannot work in this case. For QF₁ = 74, the estimation value can be 74 or 75, because the first 15 quantization steps of these two quality factors are the same.*

As showed in Table 2, the proposed method works well when $QF_2 - QF_1 > 5$, results are competitive with [15]. When the difference gets smaller, our algorithm cannot work effectively, this is because most quantization steps of QF_2 and QF_1 are equal or very close.

5   Conclusion

In this paper, we proposed a new algorithm to estimate primary quality factor in double JPEG compressed images. The method is based on normalized mean square quantization error between DCT coefficients and different re-quantized versions. The method doesn't need to train a classifier. The algorithm works well when $QF_2 - QF_1 > 5$. Experimental results show that this method archived high estimation accuracy and still works well when image size is as small as 16x16. In the future work, we'll further develop the method to identify forged regions in tampered JPEG images.

References

1. Wallace, G.K.: The JPEG still picture compression standard. IEEE Transactions on Consumer Electronics 38(1), xviii–xxxiv(1992)
2. Fan, Z., de Queiroz, R.L.: Identification of bitmap compression history: JPEG detection and quantizer estimation. IEEE Transactions on Image Processing 12(2), 230–235 (2003)
3. Neelamani, R., de Queiroz, R., Fan, Z., Dash, S., Baraniuk, R.G.: JPEG compression history estimation for color images. IEEE Transactions on Image Processing 15(6), 1365–1378 (2006)
4. Luo, W., Huang, J., Qiu, G.: JPEG Error Analysis and Its Applications to Digital Image Forensics. IEEE Transactions on Information Forensics and Security 5(3), 480–491 (2010)
5. Lin, G.S., Chang, M.K., Chen, Y.L.: A Passive-Blind Forgery Detection Scheme Based on Content-Adaptive Quantization Table Estimation. IEEE Transactions on Circuits and Systems for Video Technology 21(4), 421–434 (2011)
6. Popescu, A.C.: Statistical Tools for Digital Image Forensics. Ph. D., Department of Computer Science, Dartmouth College, Hanover, NH (2004)
7. Popescu, A.C., Farid, H.: Statistical Tools for Digital Forensics. In: Fridrich, J. (ed.) IH 2004. LNCS, vol. 3200, pp. 128–147. Springer, Heidelberg (2004)
8. Li, B., Shi, Y.Q., Huang, J.: Detecting double compressed JPEG images by using mode based first digit features. In: Proc. IEEE Int. Workshop on Multimedia Signal Processing, Cairns, Queensland, Australia (2008)
9. Fu, D., Shi, Y.Q., Su, W.: A generalized Benford's law for JPEG coefficients and its applications in image forensics. In: Proc. SPIE, Security, Steganography and Watermarking of Multimedia Contents IX, San Jose, CA (2007)
10. Chen, C., Shi, Y.Q., Su, W.: A marching learning based scheme for double JPEG compression detection. In: Proc. IEEE Int. Conf. Pattern Recognition, Tampa, FL (2008)

11. Huang, F., Huang, J., Shi, Y.Q.: Detecting Double JPEG Compression With the Same Quantization Matrix. IEEE Transactions on Information Forensics and Security 5(4), 848–856 (2010)

12. Ye, S., Sun, Q., Chang, E.C.: Detecting Digital Image Forgeries by Measuring Inconsistencies of Blocking Artifact. In: IEEE International Conference on Multimedia and Expo, pp. 12–15 (2007)

13. Lin, Z., He, J., Tang, X., Tang, C.K.: Fast, automatic and finegrained tampered JPEG image detection via DCT coefficient analysis. Pattern Recognit. 42, 2492–2501 (2009)

14. Lukáš, J., Fridrich, J.: Estimation of primary quantization matrix in double compressed JPEG images. In: Proc. Digital Forensic Research Workshop, Cleveland, OH (2003)

15. Pevný, T., Fridrich, J.: Detection of Double-Compression in JPEG Images for Applications in Steganography. IEEE Transactions on Information Forensics and Security 3(2), 247–258 (2008)

16. Farid, H.: Exposing Digital Forgeries from JPEG Ghosts. IEEE Transactions on Information Forensics and Security 4(1), 154–160 (2009)

17. Schaefer, G., Stich, M.: UCID - An Uncompressed Colour Image Database. In: Proc. SPIE, Storage and Retrieval Methods and Applications for Multimedia 2004, San Jose, USA, pp. 472–480 (2004)

Measurement Algorithm for Image Structure Noise on Hardcopy

Cheng xia[1,2], Tsuyoshi Saito[2], and Li Song[1]

[1] Department of Electrical Engineering, Shanghai Jiao Tong University
[2] Fuji Xerox Co., Ltd
xiacheng1988@gmail.com,
tsuyoshi.saito@fujixerox.co.jp, song_li@sjtu.edu.cn

Abstract. Image structure noise sometimes is a key factor influencing the image quality of hardcopies and widely exists in presswork using halftone technology. This paper describes an algorithm for measuring image structure noise, including moiré and screen dot effect. In order to objectively meter the degree of structure noise, L^* spectrum of colorful flat-area patch is mainly utilized to represent the structure noise of images, according to the subtraction principle and frequency prediction algorithm of moiré. With human evaluation and rating, a linear model of structure noise is regressed by moiré index and screen dot index. Finally the high correlation between human rating and metrics proves the effectiveness of the model.

Keywords: Image Quality, Hardcopy, Image Structure Noise, Moiré, Screen.

1 Introduction

Hardcopies are easily subject to a wide variety of image structure noise if half toning technology is used. Halftone is a kind of reprographic technique that simulates continuous tone imagery and widely used in commercial printing market. Conventionally, one of digital half toning, amplitude modulation (AM) [1], changes the dot coverage percent to realize the tone reproduction. However this process will lower down the resolution of hardcopy and cause screen dot. Furthermore, when full-color image is printed by superimposition of halftone screens with certain angles, an excessively visible pattern occurs, which is named as moiré or rosette, see Fig.1. In AM printing, the level of gradation is realized by input coverage (Cin) of toner or ink. The mixture of three colors, cyan, magenta, and yellow with same Cin, will produce a kind of color close to black, named as $3C$ in this paper.

As a serious problem, moiré prediction and prevention has been studied in geometrical view for many years. O.Bryngdahl had described the characteristics of superposed patterns in optics [2] in 1975. D.Kermisch and P.G. Roetling proposed Fourier spectrum analysis for periodic images like halftone images in 1974[3]. Based on the former theories, H.R.Kang founded screen-angle-based geometric and spectral model for moiré phenomenon in his book Digital color Halftoning [4]. In this paper,

W. Zhang et al. (Eds.): IFTC 2012, CCIS 331, pp. 140–147, 2012.

based on H.R.Kang's theory, the moiré prediction on lightness spectrum is carried out to locate moiré component on lightness spectrum after the subtraction process.

To measure the impact of moiré and screen dot, a patch-based method is proposed. Firstly a color pattern with different square patches is printed with the target images; see Fig.3.2 (b). Secondly, the images and patches are separately measured by human and machine. Finally, a model is built within human's scores and machine's metrics.

Because moiré is much more visible than screen dot, it occupies the main work. Both of them are investigated in frequency domain by Fourier transformation. Moiré detection principle is mainly based on the spectral subtraction of $3C$ and magenta patches and integration. Furthermore, the screen dot can be quantified by integration on modulation frequency span from $3C$'s lightness spectrum. By that way, the psychometric response for image structure noise can be mapped into different frequency parts in lightness spectrum.

By both indexes of moiré and screen dot, a linear model of structure noise is built based on 47 samples and checked by 10-fold cross validation.

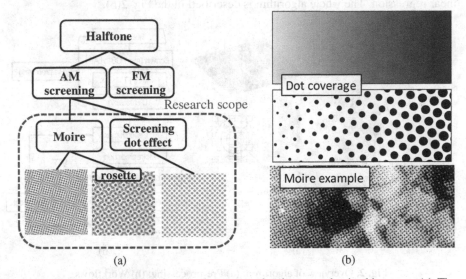

(a)   (b)

Fig. 1. Background illustration of research scope and noise examples in this paper: (a) The relationship between two kinds of image structure noise and halftone technology; (b) Examples for how dot coverage changes with the tone and the moiré phenomenon on a flower picture when mixed with multi color toner

2   Overview of Measurement Algorithm

In this paper, the flat area color patch of hardcopy in Fig.2 (a) is used as the materials for measurement. Each patch is 33x33 mm^2 sized with only one color. After transferring from RGB to CIE-LAB space and extracting the $L*$ value, the 2D $L*$ value is transformed to spatial frequency domain by FFT. Then the 1D $L*$ spectrum is carried out by one dimensionalization process. From the 1D $L*$ spectrum, if direct current (DC) part is removed, the noise of this single color patch is left.

$$L^* = \alpha * Cin + \beta \ . \tag{1}$$

$$Noise_{L^*}(d) = \alpha * Cin * \sum_{n=1}^{\infty} A_n \sin(n\omega d + \varphi_n) \ . \tag{2}$$

The above formulas illustrate the relationship between L^* and Cin and the expression of noise. Literally all the research in this paper is based on this noise spectrum. The spectrum should firstly go through a visual transfer function (VTF) which simulates the frequency response of human visual system. Its parameter is optimized based on P. Dooley and R.Shaw's work [5]:

$$VTF(f) = 5.05 * (e^{-0.422f} - e^{-0.707f}) \ . \tag{3}$$

Then different parts in the spectrum are separately calculated into moiré index and screen dot index. Last step is using a model to combine the two features together by linear regression. The whole algorithm is described in the Fig. 2(b).

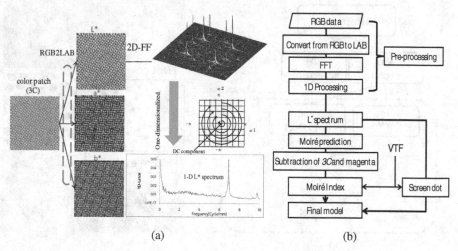

Fig. 2. Overview of algorithm: (a) Pre-processing; (b) Workflows

3   Moiré and Screen Dot Quantization

Lots of experiments tell us that $3C$ patch contain moiré and screen dot phenomenon but in magenta patch only exists screen dot. That inspires us that the spectral subtraction between $3C$ and magenta patch will leave moiré noise part only. However, the differential spectrum not only contains moiré component, but also suffers from Gaussian noise and screen dot residual, which arise the need for selective calculation on predicted moiré frequency span. So there come two problems: how to predict the frequency position which represents moiré; how to use subtraction with suitable $Cins$.

3.1   Moiré Frequency Predictions

In Fig.3.1 (a), magenta patch has 45° screen angle. If transformed to 2D frequency domain, the angle of real part or imaginary part will still be 45°. Practically, the largest value in the frequency domain must be located in the modulation frequency, see Fig.3.1 (b). So by maximum searching on the spectrum, the angle and modulation frequency can be measured. Then it is easy to get the same information from other color, like cyan and yellow.

In H.R.Kang's work, moiré producing mechanism between gratings has been explained by screen vectors. In his theory, if the sum of every frequency vector is not zero, the interference of them will cause moiré. In figure 3.1(c), there are cyan and magenta frequency vector there. If the modulation frequency is 5.23 cycles/mm, by vector operation, the modulus of moiré frequency is determined as f=2.7.

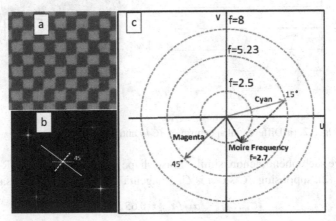

Fig. 3.1. (a) Magenta screen dot (b) 2D frequency domain of magenta (c) moiré producing mechanism (use magenta and cyan as example)

Suppose F is modulation frequency, θ is screen angle, vector of one color is:

$$V = (F * \cos\theta, F * \sin\theta). \tag{4}$$

In *3C* patches, C, M, Y colors are superposed with each other. Compared with cyan and magenta, yellow has extreme low impact in human eye. Therefore, only cyan and magenta are taken into consideration. Then the predicted moiré frequency is:

Table 3.1. Moiré frequency prediction result

C: 15° M: 45°	Modulation frequency span: 4.23-6.23 cycle/mm
$\|V_c + V_m\|$	Moiré frequency span: 2.19-3.23 cycle/mm

3.2   Subtraction Rule between *3C* and Magenta Patches

In comparing the $L*$ spectrum between magenta and *3C* patches, the obvious difference happens in predicted moiré frequency; see in Fig.3.2 (a).

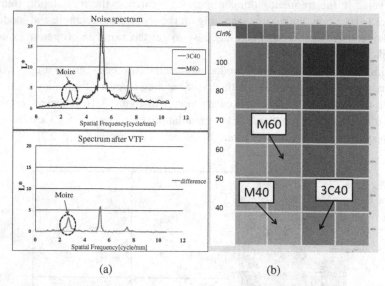

(a)   (b)

Fig. 3.2. (a)Differential specturm of *3C40* and *M60* (b) patterns for testing

To realize such phenomenon, similar noise shape should be achieved. Referring formula (1) (2), supposing *3C*'s *Cin* is C_{3c}, magenta's is C_M, they should satisfy:

$$\|C_{3c}/C_M\| = \|\alpha_M/\alpha_{3c}\| \approx 0.65 . \tag{5}$$

In this case, considering moiré in *3C40* (*3C* at *Cin*=40%) is more visible than in other *3C* patches, the *3C40* patch is selected while the coverage of magenta patch should be 61.5%. So *M60* should be selected for subtraction.

3.3   Moiré and Screen Dot Effect Calculation

M_1 and M_2 are predicted frequency span predicted. On the differential spectrum, moiré index can be calculated by integrating $L*$ value from M_1 to M_2:

$$MoireIndex = \int_{M_1}^{M_2} Diff(f)*VTF(f)df . \tag{6}$$

Screen dot should be accounted on 3C40's spectrum, integrated from $F-1$ to $F+1$; see in Fig. 3.3(b). Before modulated by F, more than 90% energy gathers in $f = [-1\ 1]$. So after carried to F, the interval keeps from $F-1$ to $F+1$. The equation is:

$$ScreenDot = \int_{F-1}^{F+1} 3C(f)*VTF(f)df . \tag{7}$$

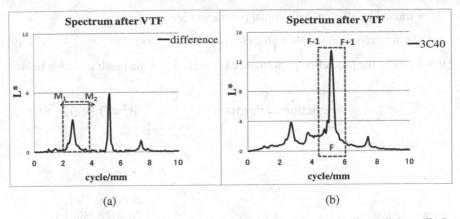

(a)   (b)

Fig. 3.3. (a) Integration begins from M_1 to M_2 (b) Integration begins form $(F-1)$ to $(F+1)$

4   Model for Image Structure

There are 47 A4-sized test samples from different commercial use market printers varying in screen line resolution and other noise. Image structure noise degree from G0 to G4 is given by each tester. Every image is evaluated by 10 testers and its result should pass through T-test.

Table 4.1. Psychometric scaling for image structure noise

Grade	description
G0	Imperceptible
G1	Perceptible, but not annoying
G2	Slightly annoying
G3	Annoying
G4	Very annoying

A linear model is used to calculate structure noise index to predict the human rating above. Suppose:

$$StructureNoise = \alpha * MoireIndex + \beta * ScreenDot + \gamma \quad . \qquad (8)$$

On the 47 dataset, 10-fold cross validation is used. In this case, at each round, 42 samples are used for training and 5 are left for validation, coefficient of determination R^2 is recorded in table 4.2.

Table 4.2. 10-fold cross validation (T: training set; V: validation set)

	1	2	3	4	5	6	7	8	9	10	Avg.
T	0.97	0.97	0.97	0.98	0.97	0.97	0.97	0.92	0.97	0.97	0.966
V	0.97	0.94	0.96	0.94	0.84	0.98	0.94	0.97	0.99	0.95	0.948

After trained by all data, the optimal parameters are:

$$StructureNoise \approx 0.0046 * MoireIndex + 0.034 * ScreenDot \quad . \tag{9}$$

By this formula, the prediction performance is checked and the result is shown below.

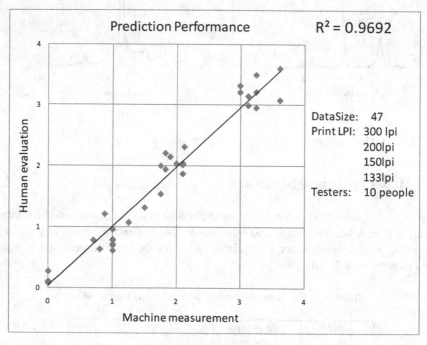

Fig. 4. Prediction performance

5   Conclusion

This study focuses on moiré and screen dot measurement. Especially for moiré, spectral subtraction between $3C$ and magenta patches and an angle-based prediction algorithm are used to carry out integration on differential spectrum. By the optimized VTF, the linear model, which reaches high correlation with human rating score, is acquired.

Acknowledgments. The right of this paper belongs to Fuji Xerox Co., Ltd and Shanghai Digital Media Processing and Transmission Lab. Sponsorship No.: STCSM (12DZ2272600).

References

1. Itoh, T., Sakatani, K.: Noise evaluation metric derived from digital AM halftone image analysis. Journal of Imaging Science and Technology, 133–119 (1999)
2. Bryngdahl, O.: Characteristics of superposed patterns in optics. Journal of the Optical Society of America, 87–94 (1976)

3. Kermisch, D., Roetling, P.G.: Fourier spectrum of halftone images. Journal of the optical society of America 65(6), 716–723 (1975)
4. Kang, H.R.: Digital Color Halftonin. SPIE Press (1999)
5. Dooley, R.P., Shaw, R.: Noise perception in Electrophotography. Journal of Applied Photographic Engineering, 190–196 (1979)

Reduced Reference Image Quality Assessment Based on Image Statistics in Pixel Domain

Xiaolin Chen, Shibao Zheng, and Rui Zhang

Institute of Image Communication and Information Processing
Shanghai Key Laboratory of Digital Media Processing and Transmissions
Shanghai Jiao Tong University, Shanghai, China 200240
xiaolin.chen317@gmail.com, {sbzh,zhang_rui}@sjtu.edu.cn

Abstract. In this paper, we propose a new reduced reference image quality assessment (RR IQA) algorithm based on the image statistics. The image statistics is modeled in pixel domain, which is based on the gradient distribution of image. Compared with frequency domain coefficients, gradients are more easily calculated. The change of statistics in the gradient domain is measured to evaluate image distortion. To solve this problem, we fit the marginal distribution of image gradients to the integrated Weibull distribution locally. Then the estimated model parameters are extracted as the quality feature. We further propose a new RR IQA metric by quantifying the similarity between the original and the distorted quality features. Experimental results show that the proposed metric outperforms the well known RR IQA metric and has a comparable performance with the widely used full reference IQA metric Peak Signal to Noise Ratio (PSNR).

Keywords: Reduced reference image quality assessment, Statistical image modeling, Integrated Weibull distribution.

1 Introduction

Image quality assessment (IQA) is an important problem for a variety of real world applications, including image compression, communication, printing, display and restoration[1]. The most accurate means of assessing image quality is subjective evaluation. However, subjective testing is not only expensive and time-consuming, but also unable to be incorporated into the automatic image system. Therefore, it is desirable to design objective quality metrics which can automatically assess the quality of images in agreement with subjective scores.

The existing IQA methods can be classified into three categories according to how much information about the reference image is employed: full reference (FR) methods, reduced reference (RR) methods, and no reference (NR) methods, where full, partial, and no information of reference images is available, respectively. In this paper, we focus on the design of an RR IQA algorithm. The partial information about the reference image(i.e the original image) is a set of RR quality feature.

W. Zhang et al. (Eds.): IFTC 2012, CCIS 331, pp. 148–155, 2012.

RR IQA is a relatively new research topic, as compared with FR and NR assessment methods. It have also been considered as one of the important issues for future directions. RR quality measures provide a useful solution that delivers a compromise between FR and NR method. It supplies a practically useful and convenient tool in applications such as real-time multimedia communication networks. In such case, the original image/video data can not be access at the receiver side, RR quality measures can be employed to monitor image quality degradations and thus to adjust the network parameters.

Various RR IQA algorithms have been proposed in the literature. In early works, most of the RR methods are developed for specific application environments. When the distortion type is known, image features may be defined that are particularly useful to quantify typical artifacts [2,3]. Based on modeling the human visual system, RR IQA methods could potentially be extended for general purpose [12,13]. However, these methods can only be applied to assess JPEG and JPEG2000 compressed images. Two general-purpose RR IQA methods using natural scene statistics are purposed in [8] and [6]. Within these works, the image is transformed into a wavelet domain and a divisive normalization domain, respectively. Then the marginal distributions of sub-bands coefficients are summarized by statistical model. Finally they compute the distance between the distribution of the reference and distorted images as the image quality score. However, the computation complexity of these two methods is high, as they need domain transform. In this paper, we aim to search for a more simple but efficient model to fit the nature image quality.

Many studying results show that human eyes are very sensitive to the edge and contour information of an image [4]. Based on this, many gradient-based FR IQA method have been proposed [5]. They create gradient map of the reference and distorted image, then compare the difference between these two maps. While in the development of RR method, since the gradient map of the reference image can not be achieved at the receiver side, we use a statistical model to fit the distribution of gradient map. We believe that the degradation of image will result in the change of gradient distribution and the perceptual image distortion is highly correlated with this change.

In this paper, to determine the image quality, we first use the Gaussian derivative filter to obtain the information about gradient distribution. Then we fit the marginal distribution of filter response to the integrated Weibull distribution locally. We estimate the fitting parameters as the quality feature. We further propose a new RR IQA metric by quantifying the similarity between the original and the distorted quality features. Experimental results show that the proposed metric outperforms the well known RR IQA metric and has a comparative performance with PSNR.

The rest of the paper is organized as follows. In section 2, we focus on presenting the details of extracting quality features from image and the proposed quality metric. Section 3 presents the experimental results and discussion. Finally, section 4 draws the conclusion.

2 The Proposed RR IQA Method

2.1 Image Statistics

Statistical modeling of the image is of particular importance in the development of RR IQA methods. Based on the statistical model, we can extract the RR quality feature with low data rate, and is applicable to a wide range of distortion types. In this paper, we will modeling the image statistics in pixel domain. The proposed RR IQA metric is based on the gradient distribution of image. Compared with frequency domain coefficients, gradients are more easily calculated. Moreover, it is observed that the degradation of image will result in the change of gradient histogram of image and such variation is highly correlated with perceived image quality. Since the marginal distribution can summarize the gradient histogram of image efficiently, we will use the image statistical model to fit it.

The gradient magnitude distribution of natural images is proved to follow the integrated Weibull distribution, both when looking at global statistics as well as when considering local patches [7]. We first use the Gaussian derivative filter to obtain the information about gradient distribution. Then we fit the marginal distribution of filter response to the integrated Weibull distribution locally. In our method, the gradient distribution is calculated in vertical and horizontal directions separately.

The two parameters integrated Weibull probability distribution function (PDF) is given by [7]:

$$p(x) = \frac{\gamma}{2\gamma^{\frac{1}{\gamma}} \beta \Gamma(\frac{1}{\gamma})} \exp(-\frac{1}{\gamma} \left| \frac{x}{\beta} \right|^{\gamma}) \tag{1}$$

where x is the Gaussian derivative filter response, $\gamma > 0$ is the shape parameter and $\beta > 0$ is the scale parameter of the distribution. $\Gamma(\cdot)$ is the Gamma function,

$$\Gamma(x) = \int_0^{\infty} t^{x-1} \exp(-t) dt \tag{2}$$

The parameter β denotes the width of the distribution and the parameter γ represents the peakness of the distribution.

2.2 RR Feature Extraction

The appropriate RR features are desirable to be sensitive to image distortion. For a noise contaminated image, the shape of its gradient histogram will be changed compared with the one of the original image. When we fit the gradient histogram with image statistic model, the parameters of the fitting model can be employed as RR feature. Given an reference image and the distorted one, we believe the difference between the parameters of the two images are correlated with image quality degradation.

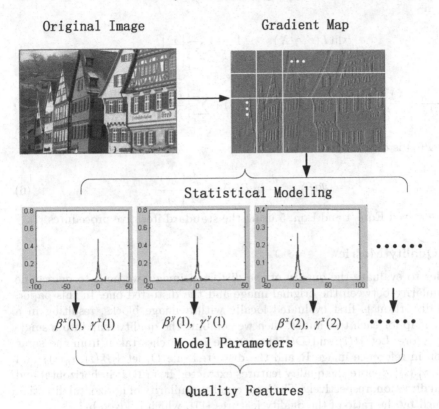

Fig. 1. The framework of RR feature extraction. For statistical modeling, we use the integrated Weibull distribution (the black curve) to fit the histogram (the red curve) of gradient for each block. $\beta^x(1)$ and $\gamma^x(1)$ means the scale and shape parameter estimated from the first block of image in horizontal direction respectively.

The diagram of feature extraction is explained in Fig. 1. First, the input image is divided into blocks, then we fit the marginal distribution of filter response to the integrated Weibull distribution for each patch. Finally, model parameters β and γ are extracted as the the RR quality feature. Note that for each patch, we extract a 4-dimensional feature vector, as the gradient distribution is calculated in vertical and horizontal directions separately.

The model parameters can be estimated with the Maximum Likelihood Estimation (MLE) technique [7]. Given all the gradients for each patch $\{X = x_1, x_2, ..., x_n\}$, the log-likelihood function is:

$$\ln L(\beta, \gamma | X) = \ln n + \frac{\gamma - 1}{\gamma} \ln \gamma - \ln 2 - \ln \beta - \ln \Gamma\left(\frac{1}{\gamma}\right) - \frac{1}{\gamma} \sum_{i=1}^{n} \left|\frac{x_i}{\beta}\right|^{\gamma} \quad (3)$$

If this function is differentiable, maximum likelihood estimation $\hat{\beta}$ and $\hat{\gamma}$ must satisfy the following differential equations:

$$\frac{\partial \ln L(\beta, \gamma | X)}{\partial \beta} = -\frac{1}{\beta} + \frac{1}{\beta} \sum_{i=1}^{n} \left| \frac{x_i}{\beta} \right|^{\gamma} = 0 \tag{4}$$

$$\frac{\partial \ln L(\beta, \gamma | X)}{\partial \gamma} = \frac{1}{\gamma^2} \left(\gamma - 1 + \Psi\left(\frac{1}{\gamma}\right) + \ln(\gamma) + \sum_{i=1}^{n} \left| \frac{x_i}{\beta} \right|^{\gamma} \right) - \frac{1}{\gamma} \sum_{i=1}^{n} \left| \frac{x_i}{\beta} \right|^{\gamma} \ln \left| \frac{x_i}{\beta} \right| = 0 \tag{5}$$

where $\Psi(\gamma)$ is diggamma function

$$\Psi(\gamma) = \frac{d}{d\gamma} \ln \Gamma(\gamma) = \frac{\frac{d}{d\gamma} \Gamma(\gamma)}{\Gamma(\gamma)} \tag{6}$$

here we solved Eqn. 4 and Eqn. 5 using the standard iterative procedures [7].

2.3 Quality Metric

In order to evaluate the quality of the distorted image, we need to determine the similarity between the original image and the distorted one. In this paper, image distortion is first evaluated locally within image blocks, resulting in a quality map for each test image, then we combine the quality map into a single quality score. Let $\mathbf{R}(i)$ and $\mathbf{D}(i)$ denote the ith patches taken from the same location in reference image $\mathbf{R}$ and the distorted one $\mathbf{D}$, let $\{\beta_R^x(i), \gamma_R^x(i)\}$ and $\{\beta_R^y(i), \gamma_R^y(i)\}$ denote the quality features extracted from $\mathbf{R}(i)$ in horizontal and vertical direction, respectively. The local quality similarity of horizontal direction is defined by the ratio of the quality features [11], which is given by:

$$D^x(i) = \sqrt{\frac{\min(\beta_R^x(i), \beta_D^x(i))}{\max(\beta_R^x(i), \beta_D^x(i))} \frac{\min(\gamma_R^x(i), \gamma_D^x(i))}{\max(\gamma_R^x(i), \gamma_D^x(i))}} \tag{7}$$

For vertical direction, we define the same quality similarity $D^y(i)$ as the horizontal direction.

Now we can define the overall quality similarity with horizontal and vertical direction as:

$$D^x = \frac{\sum_{i=1}^{L} w^x(i) D^x(i)}{\sum_{i=1}^{L} w^x(i)} \tag{8}$$

$$D^y = \frac{\sum_{i=1}^{L} w^y(i) D^y(i)}{\sum_{i=1}^{L} w^y(i)} \tag{9}$$

where L is block number, $w^x(i)$ and $w^y(i)$ are the relative weights of different blocks, and $w^x(i) = w^y(i) = 1/L$ in this paper.

Finally, assuming the vertical and horizontal similarities to be of the same importance, and they are statistically independent of each other, so the overall quality of the test image is given by:

$$D = D^x \cdot D^y \tag{10}$$

3   Experimental Results

3.1   Database

We test our approach on the LIVE Image Quality assessment Database Release 2 made available by University of Texas [9]. This database contains a total of 982 distorted images which are developed from 29 high resolution color images which are quite representative in the content, structure, and lighting condition. The distortion types are: JPEG2000 compression, JPEG compression , white noise, Gaussian blur, and Fastfading (i.e., the transmission errors in the JPEG2000 bit stream using a fast-fading channel model, FF). The database also contains the subjective evaluation result [i.e., the degradation mean opinion scores (DMOS)] for each image which is obtained by psychometric tests.

3.2   Methodology

To verify the validity and usefulness of the proposed method, the experiments are performed by the following procedure [10]:

Step 1: As suggested by VQEG [10], before validation, objective scores obtained from the IQA algorithms are nonlinearly mapped with a logistic function. The logistic fitting function is shown as follow:

$$Quality(x) = \frac{\lambda_1 - \lambda_2}{1 + \exp\left[-(x - \lambda_3)/\lambda_4\right]} + \lambda_2 \tag{11}$$

where x being the input score obtained from the objective IQA metric, $Quality(x)$ is the mapped score. $\lambda_1, ..., \lambda_4$ are free parameters to be determined during the curve fitting process.

Step 2: After the nonlinear regression, four popular statistical metrics are used to measure the performance of these models. For each model, we compute the correlation coefficient (CC), Spearman Rank Order Correlation coefficient (SROCC), Root Mean Square Error (RMSE) and Mean Absolute Error (MAE) between the mapped score and the subjective DMOS scores. For the metrics of CC and SROCC, larger values mean the corresponding IQA algorithm has better accuracy (perfect match=1). On the contrary, smaller values in MAE and RMSE mean better performance (perfect match=0).

3.3   Results and Discussion

We compare the performance of the proposed method against Wang [8] and PSNR, which is the most widely used full-reference IQA measure. Our method is performed with the following parameter configuration: $\sigma = 1$ for Gaussian derivative filter, each image is divided into non-overlapping 30×30 blocks, so the block number L varies with image resolution.

Table 1 shows the simulation results of our proposed method (M1) and other IQA ones for all distorted images in the LIVE dataset. It can be seen that our method outperforms the Wang's method under all of the performance measures.

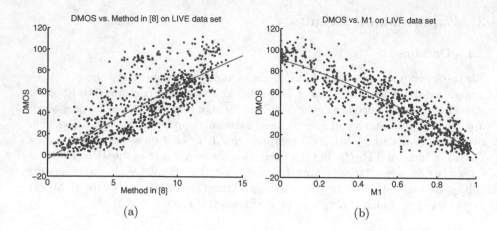

Fig. 2. Scatter plots for the objective quality measures versus DMOS for 982 distorted images in LIVE dataset. (a) method proposed in [8], (b) M1 method.

Table 1. Performance comparison of image quality assessment models on LIVE dataset

Model&Measures	CC	SROCC	RMSE	MAE
Wang *et al.*[8] (RR)	0.846	0.861	16.699	12.225
M1 (RR)	0.923	0.935	12.011	8.668
PSNR (FR)	0.924	0.937	11.996	8.372

Table 1 also shows our method has a comparable performance with the full-reference PSNR measure. Note that PSNR requires full access to the original image, and we extract a 4-dimensional feature vector for each 30×30 image patch, the data rate is much lower than PSNR. Fig. 2 shows the scatter plots of DMOS versus the predicted score by our method and Wang's [8]. It is clear that our method is more consistent with the subjective measure. The reason for the performance improvement is that we use a more accurate fitting model, Furthermore, we also define suitable distances of two quality features.

4   Conclusion

In this paper we propose a pixel domain image statistics based reduced reference image quality assessment method. The premise of this approach is that the degradation of image will result in the change of gradient histogram of image and such variation is highly correlated with perceived image quality. Operationally, we use the integrated Weibull distribution to fit the marginal distribution of gradient histogram, and estimate the fitting parameter as the quality feature.

We also define the similarity between two quality features for evaluating image quality. Experimental results show that the proposed metric outperforms the well known RR IQA metric and has a comparable performance with the full reference IQA metric PSNR.

Acknowledgments. This work was supported by NSFC (61171172, 61071155).

References

1. Wang, Z., Bovik, A.: Modern image quality assessment. Morgan & Claypool (2006)
2. Gunawan, I.P., Ghanbari, M.: Reduced-reference picture quality estimation by using local harmonic amplitude information. In: Proc. London Communication Symposium, pp. 137–140 (September 2003)
3. Kusuma, T.M., Zepernick, H.J.: A reduced-reference perceptual quality metric for in-service image quality assessment. In: Proc. Joint First Workshop on Mobile Future and Symposium on Trends in Communications, pp. 71–74 (October 2003)
4. Elder, J., Zucker, S.W.: Evidence for boundary-specific grouping in human vision. Vision Research 38(1), 143–152 (1998)
5. Chen, G., Yang, C.L., Xie, S.: Gradient-based structural similarity for image quality assessment. In: IEEE International Conference on Image Processing, Atlanta, USA, pp. 2929–2932 (October 2006)
6. Li, Q., Wang, Z.: Reduced-reference image quality assessment using divisive normalization-based image representation. IEEE Journal of Selected Topics in Signal Processing 3(2), 202–211 (2009)
7. Yanulevskaya, V., Geusebroek, J.: Salient region detection from natural image statistics. In: Proc. the Fourteenth Annual Conference of the Advanced School for Computing and Imaging, Heijen, The Netherlands, pp. 389–395 (June 2008)
8. Wang, Z., Wu, G.X., Sheikh, H.R., Simoncelli, E.P., Yang, E.H., Bovik, A.C.: Quality-aware images. IEEE Transactions on Image Processing 15(6), 1680–1689 (2006)
9. Sheikh, H., Wang, Z., Cormack, L., Bovik, A.: Live image quality assessment database release 2, http://live.ece.utexas.edu/research/quality
10. VQEG, Final report from the video quality experts group on the validation of objective models of video quality assessment, phase II (2003), http://www.vqeg.org
11. van Gemert, J., Geusebroek, J., Veenman, C., Snoek, C., Smeulders, A.: Robust scene categorization by learning image statistics in context. In: Proc. CVPR Workshop on Semantic Learning Applications in Multimedia, p. 105 (June 2006)
12. Carnec, M., Le Callet, P., Barba, D.: An image quality assessment method based on perception of structural information. In: Proc. IEEE International Conference on Image Processing, Barcelona, Catalonia, Spain, pp. 185–188 (September 2003)
13. Carnec, M., Le Callet, P., Barba, D.: Visual features for image quality assessment with reduced reference. In: Proc. IEEE International Conference on Image Processing, Genoa, Italy, pp. 421–424 (September 2005)

Text Detection from Natural Scene Images Using Scale Space Model

Qiaoyu Sun[1,2] and Yue Lu[1]

[1] Department of Computer Science and Technology, East China Normal University,
Shanghai 200241, China
[2] Department of Electronic Engineering, Huaihai Institute of Technology,
Jiangsu 222005, China
ylu@cs.ecnu.edu.cn

Abstract. A scale space based approach is proposed to detect text from natural scene images with complicated background. An edge map containing the edge information of four directions is obtained by Sobel operators. Character areas are detected by connected components analysis and are merged into candidate text regions. We construct a N-level scale space model and compute spatial responses to the Laplacian-of- Gaussian operator at these scale levels. The distribution of some strongest responses obtained from scale space model is employed to verify whether a candidate is a true text region or not. The experimental results demonstrate that the proposed method is able to effectively filter the nontext regions and locate text regions in natural scene images with complicated background.

Keywords: Text Detection, Edge Detection, Connected Components Analysis, Scale Space, Laplacian-of-Gaussian operator.

1 Introduction

Text contained in natural scene images have significant and detail information about the scenes. Automatic text detection is an important procedure prior to character recognition. The use of cameras has greatly facilitated document acquisition and has enabled human interaction with any type of documents. The capability of capturing nonpaper document images such as scene text has promoted potential applications such as license plate recognition, road sign recognition, digital note taking, document archiving and wearable computing [1]. However, variations due to textual differences in sizes, styles, orientations, alignments, as well as image contrasts, make automatic text extraction extremely challenging. Moreover, natural scene images usually suffer from low resolution and low quality, perspective distortion and complicated background.

Research has been done in text extraction and location. Existing methods can be classified into two categories. The first is region based methods, which first generate connected components from images and then identify text components according to some geometrical constraints [2]. The second is texture based methods, which use texture analysis algorithms such as Gabor filter, DCT transform, Wavelet decomposition to detect text regions [3]. Sometimes these methods are combined for achieving better performance.

W. Zhang et al. (Eds.): IFTC 2012, CCIS 331, pp. 156–161, 2012.

In this paper, we employ the connected components analysis (CCA) on the edge map to detect the candidate text regions and apply the scale space model to verify the candidate text regions.

2 Methodology

Sobel edge detectors are first applied to obtain the edge map of an input image. The CCA method is employed to detect potential character areas of the image. A N-level scale space model is constructed and the spatial responses to the Laplacian-of-Gaussian operator over these scales are computed. The distribution of the strongest responses is used to verify the candidate text regions.

2.1 The Strongest Responses to Laplacian-of-Gaussian Operator in Scale Space

Lindeberg proposed a general methodology for scale selection by detecting local maxima in feature responses over scales [4]. The scale-space representation of an image is generated by smoothing the image using a set of Gaussian kernels with different variances t as

$$L(x, y; t) = f(x, y) * g(x, y; t) \tag{1}$$

where $f(x, y)$ is the original image and $g(x, y; t)$ is the Gaussian kernel

$$g(x, y; t) = \frac{1}{2\pi t} e^{\frac{-\|x^2 + y^2\|}{2t}} \tag{2}$$

Therefore, the normalized derivatives are equal in the two domains, provided that the scale parameters and the spatial positions are matched. Moreover, the scale t_{max} at which the Laplacian-of-Gaussian (LOG) $t(L_{xx} + L_{yy})$ attains a maximum is related to the characteristic size of the blob. The so-called "interesting points" are the local extremum of LOG with respect to both the spatial co-ordinates and the scale parameter. Moreover, they may indicate other shapes of objects (such as the square, the ellipse, the bar, etc..), as well as endpoints of strokes which present local extremas on certain scales.

Fig. 1. The strongest spatial responses to the LOG operator of the images

Fig. 1 shows the results of detecting scale-space extrema to the LOG for each image. Fig. 1(a) and Fig. 1(b) contain a English word and two Chinese characters, respectively. Each scale-space maximum has been graphically illustrated by a "+" centered at the point at which the spatial maximum is assumed and with the size determined such that the length is proportional to the scale at which the maximum over scales is assumed. To make it clearer, a threshold on the maximum normalized response has been selected such that only about 40 crosses having the maximum normalized responses remain. We can find from Fig. 1 that most of the strongest spatial responses locate at the intersection points or the ending points of the strokes for both English and Chinese characters. Meanwhile, the strongest spatial responses appear on the same scale whose corresponding characteristic size is approximately equal to the width of the strokes.

The LOG filter can be well approximated with Difference-of-Gaussian (DOG) filter, which is the difference of two centered Gaussians $g(x, y; t_1) - g(x, y; t_2)$ with scales related by $\sqrt{t_1/t_2} = \alpha = 1.6$ [5].

We construct a scale space model with N levels. The DOG operator of the pixel (x, y) at the ith level is

$$DOG(x, y; t_i) = \frac{1}{2\pi t_i/\alpha} e^{\frac{-\|x+y\|^2}{2t_i/\alpha}} - \frac{1}{2\pi t_i \alpha} e^{\frac{-\|x+y\|^2}{2t_i \alpha}} \qquad (3)$$

where t_i is the scale parameter, $i = 0, 1, 2, ..., N$.

If the response value of the point is greater than a given threshold, it will be regarded as a Strongest Response (SR). The threshold is empirically set as 0.4 times of the local extremum in our experiments.

2.2 Text Regions Detection and Verification

The CCA method is applied to detect each region with strong edges in the edge map, which will act as the text candidates for further processing. We obtain the edge map by combining Sobel operators with models in four directions (horizontal, vertical, up-right and up-left).

The connected components detected from the edge map may be characters themselves or part of them, of course, or background. Some connected components may be merged according to their positional relation. The obtained candidate text region may contain a whole character, a word or a text line.

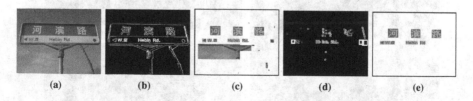

Fig. 2. Example of text extraction using the proposed method. (a) Original image, (b) Edge map, (c) Text detection result with CCA, (d) The SRs with the corresponding scales, (e) Final detection result.

As stated above, the SRs are capable of representing the strokes of characters, and their response values may indicate the stroke widths. We apply the SRs to verify the candidate text regions obtained by the CCA method.

For each candidate text region, it may be a true text region if it satisfies the follow conditions:

1. The number of SRs in the text region should be larger than the ratio of the width and the height of the region.

2. The scale corresponding to the SR should be corresponding to the stroke width of the region.

3. The area of the minimum enclosing rectangle consisting of the SRs is larger than half of the area of the region.

Fig. 2 shows the procedure of the method. In Fig. 2(b), the edge map contains almost all stroke information of characters without distinguishing the strong edge information of text from that of the background. Fig. 2(c) indicates the preliminary result using CCA. Fig. 2(d) shows the SRs by squares centered at the point at which the SRs are assumed and with the sizes being proportional to the corresponding scales. We can find that the SRs can accurately describe endpoints of the character strokes and correspond with the stroke widths. In the meantime, they are efficient in filtering out many false text regions which present the strong edge property in the edge map. The non text regions contained in Fig. 2(e) are filtered out because their responses are not strong enough.

3 Experimental Results

To test the validity of the proposed method, we constructed a dataset of images captured from natural scene by mobile phone cameras. The dataset named ECNU-CCG includes 300 images. The images contain either Chinese text or English text, or both. In addition, 249 images from the dataset of ICDAR 2003 Robust Reading and Text Locating Competition (ICDAR 2003) are also tested in this study for comparison.

We employ the performance measure which was recently proposed by Shivakumara et al. [6]. They evaluated the performance at the block level, which is a common granularity level in many literatures. Three performance measures, precision (P), recall (R) and f-measure (F), were defined similarly to the measures which were employed to evaluate text location performance in competition of ICDAR 2003 and 2005. They also included misdetection (MDR) as a performance measure and provided discussion on partial detection to ensure a fair comparative study.

Table 1 shows the efficiency of the proposed method on the ECNU-CCG dataset. The method without the scale space (SS) model achieves the highest recall results but rather low precision. On the other hand, the application of SS improves the precision from 0.44 to 0.91, but with about 10 percents decrease of the recall results. The f-measure of the method with SS is higher than that without SS, while its MDR increases slightly. For comparison, in Table 1, we also provide the performance of our earlier work in [7]. The proposed method with SS achieves the highest precision, which benefits from the fact that the application of SS removes non-text objects. Even though the recall decreases, the f-measure of the proposed method with SS is still the highest. This confirms the efficiency of the SS.

Table 1. Performance comparison of without/with SS

Method	P	R	F	MDR
Without SS	0.44	**0.95**	0.60	**0.07**
With SS	**0.91**	0.85	**0.88**	0.11
method of [7]	0.60	0.91	0.72	**0.07**

Table 2. Performance comparison on ICDAR 2003 dataset

Method	P	R	F	MDR
Our method	**0.82**	0.62	0.71	0.13
method of [7]	0.42	0.80	0.55	**0.11**
method of [6]	0.76	**0.86**	**0.81**	0.13

We also test the proposed method on the commonly-used dataset provided by ICDAR 2003 Robust Reading Competition. The performance of our earlier method [7] and the recently reported work [6] is also shown in Table 2. Compared to other methods, the proposed one with SS achieves the highest precision on the ICDAR 2003 dataset as well. However, the application of SS may filter some text regions by mistake, which results in lower performance of the recall. The f-measure of the proposed method is lower than that of [6]. The reason may be that the proposed method attempts to deal with not only English but also Chinese texts.

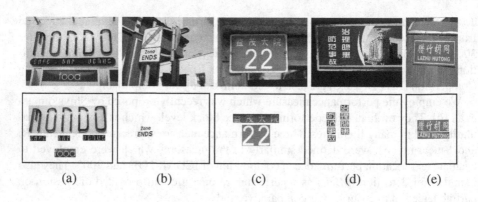

(a)   (b)   (c)   (d)   (e)

Fig. 3. Location results of some typical images

Fig. 3 shows the experimental results of some typical images achieved by the proposed method. Fig. 3(a)-(b) and Fig. 3(c)-(e) are text location results of images in ICDAR 2003 and ECNU-CCG, respectively. It can be seen that our proposed method is able to locate the accurate boundaries of the text regions and is effective in detecting text regions with different fonts, sizes (Fig. 3(a)), space alignments (Fig. 3(d)), and background complexity. The proposed method is robust to the images with perspective distortion or skewed text as shown in Fig. 3(b)and Fig. 3(e).It also can detect the text with uneven illumination in Fig. 3(c).

4   Conclusion

We have proposed a method to locate the text from natural scene images. A N- level scale space model is built to compute the SRs to LOG operator because they can accurately locate the character strokes and describe their widths. Edge detection is employed to get the four-direction edge information in yielding the edge map. The character areas can then be detected by CCA from the edge map. The candidate text regions are obtained by merging these character areas. The SRs are used to verify the candidate text regions. The results with various kinds of the natural scene images show that the proposed method is effective in distinguishing the text regions from the images and is robust for font, size, language, space alignment, and background complexity. It is also capable of correctly detecting the perspective or skewed text of images.

References

1. Kasar, T., Kumar, J., Ramakrishnan, A.: Font and background color independent text binarization. In: 2nd International Workshop on Camera Based Document Analysis and Recognition, pp. 3–9 (2007)
2. Kim, K.C., Byun, H.R., et al.: Scene Text Extraction using Focus of Mobile Camera. In: 10th International Conference on Document Analysis and Recognition, pp. 166–170. IEEE Press, Barcelona (2009)
3. Zhang, J., Kasturi, R.: Text Detection Using Edge Gradient and Graph Spectrum. In: 20th International Conference on Pattern Recognition, pp. 3979–3982. IEEE Press, Istanbul (2010)
4. Lindeberg, T.: Feature detection with automatic scale selection. Int. J. of Comput. Vision 30, 79–116 (1998)
5. Collins, R.: Mean-shift blob tracking through scale space. In: IEEE Computer Society Conference on Computer Vision and Pattern Recognition, pp. 234–240. IEEE Press, Pittsburgh (2003)
6. Shivakumara, P., Phan, T.Q., Tan, C.L.: A Laplacian Approach to Multi-Oriented Text Detection in Video. IEEE Trans. Pattern Anal. Mach. Intell. 33, 412–419 (2010)
7. Sun, Q., Lu, Y., Sun, S.: A Visual Attention Based Approach to Text Extraction. In: Proceedings of International Conference on Pattern Recognition, pp. 3991–3995. IEEE Press, Istanbul (2010)

Text-Independent Writer Identification Using Texture Feature

Dongli Wang, Ying Wen, and Yue Lu

Department of Computer Science and Technology
East China Normal University, Shanghai 200241, China

Abstract. This paper proposes an efficient method based on texture feature for text-independent writer identification. In order to extract texture feature, we use the modified 2-D Gabor filter, which can decompose the image into sub-bands with different frequencies and orientations. Nearest neighbor classifier based on weighted chi-square distance is utilized in classification. The experiments on a database containing 203 writers of address images demonstrate that the performance of our modified 2-D Gabor filter is better than that of the traditional 2-D Gabor filter and our proposed method achieves promising results.

Keywords: writer identification, modified 2-D Gabor filter, weighted chi-square distance.

1 Introduction

Automatic handwriting based writer identification constitutes an important active research area in the computer vision and pattern recognition and is receiving growing interest from both academia and industry [1]. Writer identification methods fall into two broad categories: text-dependent methods and text-independent methods. The main difference between them is that the former require the writers to write the same fixed text and only compare the same character, such as the character shape, stroke and other characteristics. Contrastively, in text-independent methods any text with different characters may be used to extract writing style features, such as texture, contour, gradient and so on. These methods can be classified into on-line (also called dynamic), where the information on the writing order and dynamics of the writing process is available, and off-line (also called static), where only a scanned image of handwriting is available, and thus much dynamic information of writing process is lost.

Recently, different approaches for off-line text independent writer identification have been proposed. Said et al. [1] treat each writer's handwriting as a different texture using multi-channel Gabor filtering and gray-scale co-occurrence matrices. Bulacu et al. [2] evaluate the performance of edge-based directional probability distributions as features in writer identification. The HMM is used to obtain the output log-likelihood scores to identify the writer on separate text lines of variable content in [3]. Schlapbach et al. [4] build a Gaussian mixture models to model an individual's handwriting. Schomaker et al. [5] present a new approach to compute the

W. Zhang et al. (Eds.): IFTC 2012, CCIS 331, pp. 162–168, 2012.

probability-density functions of the common connected-component shapes from the codebook by clustering. In order to improve the accuracy and enhance the robustness, combing multiple features is adopted for writer identification in [6]. Our research which focuses on the off-line text independent writer identification, presents a modified method based on 2-D Gabor filter.

The remainder of the paper is structured as follows. Feature extraction is introduced in details in Section 2. Section 3 describes writer identification. Experimental results and correspondence analysis follow in Section 4. Finally in Section 5, we draw conclusions from this work.

2   Feature Extraction

For the purpose of texture feature extraction, the input documents need to be normalized to create a uniform block of text. Some studies have discussed pre-processing [1, 7]. The steps adopted for pre-processing are as follows: firstly, removing the noises in the handwriting image; secondly, separating the single character using the connected unit method; thirdly, normalizing each character into a same size; finally, creating the texture image by text padding. We also use the same method to obtain the preprocessed image. Figure 1 shows an original handwriting image and the normalized binary image.

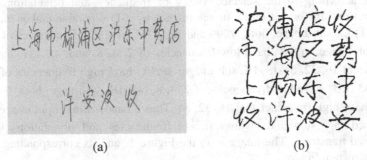

(a)   (b)

Fig. 1. (a) The original handwriting image. It may contain different spaces between characters. (b) The normalized binary image. Its size is 256×256 pixels. It contains 16 Chinese characters with size 64×64 pixels.

2.1   The Traditional 2-D Gabor Filter

The multi-channel Gabor filtering approach has been verified to be practically useful for analyzing textured images [8]. An input image $I(x,y), x, y \in \Omega$ (Ω - the set of image points), is convolved with a 2-D Gabor function $g(x,y), x, y \in \Omega$, to obtain a Gabor feature image $f(x,y)$ as follows:

$$f(x,y) = \iint I(\delta,\varphi) g(x-\delta, y-\varphi) d\delta d\varphi. \tag{1}$$

The computational models of the 2-D Gabor filters are (h_e and h_o denote the even- and odd- symmetrical Gabor filters respectively):

$$h_e(x,y;f,\theta) = g(x,y) \cdot \cos\left[2\pi f\left(x\cos\theta + y\sin\theta\right)\right],$$
$$h_o(x,y;f,\theta) = g(x,y) \cdot \sin\left[2\pi f\left(x\cos\theta + y\sin\theta\right)\right], \tag{2}$$

where

$$g(x,y) = e^{\sqrt[1]{\frac{1}{2}\left[(x^2+y^2)/\sigma^2\right]}}. \tag{3}$$

Texture characteristics can be extracted from different frequencies and directions by altering the value of f and θ which are the radial frequency and orientation that define the location of the channel in the frequency plane. Using frequencies of 2, 4, 8, 16, 32, 64 cycles/degree and $\theta = 0°, 45°, 90°, 135°$, the traditional 2-D Gabor filter gives a total of 24 output images. The feature vector is the mean and variance of each output image. Therefore, 48 features per input image are calculated. The traditional 2-D Gabor filter convolutes the whole image for each orientation and each frequency, thus one of the most serious disadvantages is the high computational cost.

2.2   The Modified 2-D Gabor Filter

Compared with the traditional 2-D Gabor filter, we propose a modified method based on 2-D Gabor filter. The modified 2-D Gabor filter can decompose the image into sub-bands according to the selected values of frequency and orientation. For an image, we can transform it into four sub-images by 2-D separable Gabor transform, namely: (1) LL sub-image: both $0°, 90°$ and $45°, 135°$ have low frequencies of 2, 4, 8. (2) LH sub-image: $0°, 90°$ have low frequencies of 2, 4, 8, and $45°, 135°$ have high frequencies of 16, 32, 64. (3) HL sub-image: $0°, 90°$ have high frequencies of 16, 32, 64, and $45°, 135°$ have low frequencies of 2, 4, 8. (4) HH sub-image: both $0°, 90°$ and $45°, 135°$ have high frequencies of 16, 32, 64. Thus a handwriting input image can be decomposed into sub-bands with different frequencies and orientations via 2-D Gabor-based transform. The image is in the Figure 1, and its corresponding filtered image is shown in Figure 2.

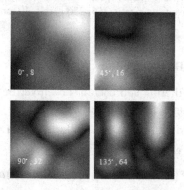

Fig. 2. The corresponding filtered image. It is divided into four sub-images by 2-D separable wavelet transform in direction $0°, 45°, 90°, 135°$ and the central frequency is set in 8, 16, 32, 64.

The modified 2-D Gabor filter gives a total of 48 output images. The feature vector is the mean and variance of each output image. Therefore, a total of 96 features are extracted from a given image. The flowchart of texture feature extraction in our modified 2-D Gabor filter is given in Figure 3.

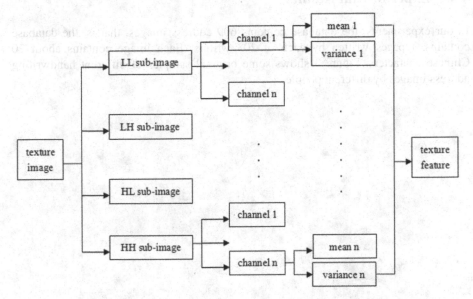

Fig. 3. The flowchart of texture feature extraction in our modified 2-D Gabor filter

Though the traditional 2-D Gabor filter is effective in text-independent writer identification, it has the high computational cost. Compared with the traditional 2-D Gabor filter, we only need to extract features from specified sub-bands but not from the whole handwriting image, thus calculational cost is substantially reduced.

3   Writer Identification

After the handwriting samples have been represented by their respective feature vectors, an appropriate distance measure is necessary for computing the similarity between the feature vectors. We use a number of distance measures, which include: Euclidean, weighted Euclidean, chi-square, weighted chi-square and weighted Manhattan. Since weighted chi-square distance performs the best results in our evaluations, it is adopted and is defined as follow:

$$wcd(s,t) = \sum_{i=1}^{N} \frac{(s_i - t_i)^2}{\sigma_i(s_i + t_i)} \tag{4}$$

Where s_i is the *ith* feature of the unknown input sample s, t_i is the *ith* feature of writer t from the reference database, σ_i is the standard deviation of the *ith* feature from all of the reference samples, N denotes the total number of feature vectors extracted from a single sample.

4   Experimental Results

In our experiments, the database contains 609 address images, that is, the database contains 3 pages written by each of 203 writers. Each image contains about 20 Chinese characters. Figure 4 shows some original samples of different handwriting address images by different people.

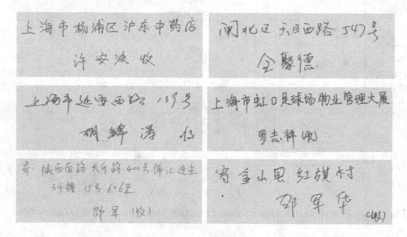

Fig. 4. The original samples of different handwriting address images are written by 6 different people

We evaluate the efficiency of the method using both leave-one-out and three-fold cross validations. Table 1 shows the performance of the traditional 2-D Gabor filter and our modified 2-D Gabor filter.

Table 1. Experimental results

method	3-fold cross validation				leave-one-out validation			
	Top_1	Top_3	Top_5	Top_10	Top_1	Top_3	Top_5	Top_10
traditional 2-D Gabor filter	68.3	79.8	89.2	93.5	61.6	76.6	85.0	91.6
	76.1	86.5	91.8	100	75.0	86.5	90.3	100
	70.5	93.1	94.2	98.0	69.2	92.3	94.2	96.1
modified 2-D Gabor filter	85.0	91.6	95.0	95.0	83.3	91.6	95.0	95.0
	90.3	92.3	94.2	98.0	82.6	92.3	94.2	94.2
	84.6	98.0	100	100	86.5	88.4	94.2	100

It is evident that the preferred identification performance of our modified 2-D Gabor filter is better than that of the traditional 2-D Gabor filter. The best correct identification rate of Top-1 candidates achieves 90.3% in our modified method, while the traditional 2-D Gabor filter on our experimental database yielding the best performance is 76.1% Top-1.

We also present a comparison of the performance of the recent methods on the different data set in Table 2. The comparison demonstrates our proposed method achieves promising results with potential applications in writer identification.

Table 2. Comparison of writer identification methods on the different database

Method	Database	Writers	Samples/writer	Performance
Schlapbach et al. [4]	IAM	100	5/4	98.46%
Siddiqi et al. [9]	IAM	650	2	86%
Golnaz et al. [10]	Farsi	180	2	92.7%
Our proposed method	IAM	650	2	· 90.7%
Our proposed method	Farsi	240	2	92.9%

5   Conclusion

In this paper, we propose an effective technique using the modified 2-D Gabor filter to improve the accuracy and enhance the robustness for off-line text independent automatic writer identification. The proposed method not only successfully avoids the intensive computational cost, but also whose performance is better than that of the traditional 2-D Gabor filter and achieves promising results with potential applications in writer identification.

References

1. Said, H.E.S., Tan, T., Baker, K.: Personal Identification Based on Handwriting. Pattern Recognition 33, 149–160 (2000)
2. Bulacu, M., Schomaker, L., Vuurpijl, L.: Writer Identification Using Edge-Based Directional Features. In: 7th International Conference on Document Analysis and Recognition, pp. 937–941 (2003)
3. Schlapbach, A., Bunke, H.: Off-line Handwriting Identification Using HMM Based Recognizers. In: 17th International Conference on Pattern Recognition, pp. 654–658 (2004)
4. Schlapbach, A., Bunke, H.: Off-line Writer Identification Using Gaussian Mixture Models. In: 18th International Conference on Pattern Recognition, pp. 992–995 (2006)
5. Schomaker, L., Franke, K., Bulacu, M.: Using Codebooks of Fragmented Connected-Component Contours in Forensic and Historic Writer Identification. Pattern Recognition Letters 28, 719–727 (2007)
6. Zois, E.N., Anastassopousls, V.: Fusion of Correlated Decisions for Writer Verification. Pattern Recognition 34, 47–61 (2001)

7. Shahabinejad, F., Rahmati, M.: A New Method for Writer Identification and Verification Based on Farsi/Arabic Handwritten Texts. In: 9th International Conference on Document Analysis and Recognition, pp. 829–833 (2007)
8. Jain, A.K., Farrokhnia, F.: Unsupervised Texture Segmentation Using Gabor Filters. Pattern Recognition 24, 1167–1186 (1991)
9. Siddiqi, I., Vincent, N.: A Set of Chain Code Based Features for Writer Recognition. In: 10th International Conference on Document Analysis and Recognition, pp. 981–985 (2009)
10. Golnaz, G., Safabakhsh, R.: An Efficient Method for Offline Text Independent Writer. In: 20th International Conference on Pattern Recognition, pp. 1245–1248 (2010)

Segmentation of Overlapped and Touching Handwritten Chinese Strings

Lei Ai[1], Shujing Lu[1,2], Ying Wen[1], and Yue Lu[1,2]

[1] Department of Computer Science and Technology
East China Normal University, Shanghai 200241, China
[2] ECNU-SRI Joint Lab for Pattern Analysis and Intelligent System
Shanghai Research Institute of China Post, Shanghai 200062, China
alei@shu.edu.cn

Abstract. In this paper, we present segmentation of handwritten Chinese strings in presence of overlapped and touching characters. A contour tracing based method is proposed to segment the overlapped characters. To segment touching characters, a corner point analysis method is carried out to identify the cutting positions. Experimental results on 564 Chinese character strings captured from postal mail pieces show the effectiveness of the proposed methods on the segmentation of handwritten Chinese character strings.

Keywords: Character Segmentation, Handwritten Chinese characters, Contour tracing, Overlapped characters, Touching characters.

1   Introduction

Offline handwritten Chinese characters recognition is a challenging problem in the field of pattern recognition. Correct segmentation of handwritten Chinese character string is crucial to recognition. However, correct segmentation is a difficult problem because of the overlapped characters and touching characters in the handwritten Chinese character strings. Methods of segmenting handwritten Chinese strings can be mainly categorized into two strategies: geometrical feature analysis and recognition-based methods (over-segmentation and merging strategy)[1-4]. In the first strategy, some algorithms have been carried out to generate segmentation path, such as connected components analysis[1], background thinning approach[5, 6] and Viterbi algorithm[6]. Some of them are integrated into the recognition-based methods for achieving better performance.

In this paper, we proposed two character segmentation methods for overlapped characters and touching characters respectively. For overlapped characters, the

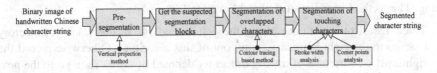

Fig. 1. Block diagram of Segmentation

W. Zhang et al. (Eds.): IFTC 2012, CCIS 331, pp. 169–174, 2012.
© Springer-Verlag Berlin Heidelberg 2012

segmentation paths are generated by tracing the contours of stroke in the dynamical suspected region. The experiment results show the contour tracing method needs few candidates to generate a segmentation path. To segment touching characters, the cutting position is identified by two methods. The first one is based on the stroke width analysis[2]. The other one is based on the corner point analysis. In experiment, the corner point analysis method improves the performance of the segmentation. The block diagram of string segmentation is shown in Fig. 1.

2   Segmentation

In the pre-segmentation step, a character string is split into primitive segmentation blocks based on its vertical projection. Then three parameters are obtained: the average width of characters, the stroke width and the average ratio of height to width of characters, denoted as Wm, Ws and Rhw respectively.

When $w > \alpha_1 \cdot Wm$ and $h/w < \alpha_2 \cdot Rhw$, the segmentation block is a potential overlapped or touching pattern. w and h are the block width and height. The coefficients α_1 and α_2 are determined by experience. Before splitting a segmentation block, the suspected region of this block, denoted by $< lx, rx >$, should be detected, where the overlapped or touching position may exist. Assuming nc and Lx denote the number of characters contained in the segmentation block and the left x-coordinate value of the segmentation block respectively, then lx and rx are calculated as:

$$lx = Lx + \theta \cdot w / nc .\tag{1}$$

$$rx = Lx + (2 - \theta) \cdot w / nc .\tag{2}$$

where θ is the parameter to control the size of suspected region.

2.1   Segmentation of Overlapped Characters

Contour tracing method is applied to split the overlapped Chinese characters. This method generates a pair of nonlinear paths for each segmentation block which contain overlapped characters. These two splitting paths, the left path and the right path, belong to the left part and the right part of the split block respectively.

The suspected region $< lx, rx >$ presents dynamical change with implementation of the method. The two vertical lines corresponding to lx and rx are used to be the left boundary and the right boundary respectively. The traced contours must be in the suspected region. And the bottom of each boundary is the start point of contour tracing. The method is an iterative algorithm as follows:

a.   Trace the stroke contours along the left boundary. If the tracing trajectory reaches to the right boundary, jump out of this algorithm. Otherwise record the rightmost x-coordinate of tracing trajectory denoted by lpx. Then go to the next step. This step is shown in Fig. 2(a). The whole tracing trajectory is the left path.

b.   Update rx: $rx = lpx + \Delta_1.$ (3)

where Δ_1 is a small offset and not greater than Ws. Trace the stroke contours along the updated right boundary to get the right path and record leftmost x-coordinate of the right path denoted by rpx. Then go to the next step. This step is shown in Fig. 2(b).

c.   Update lx: $lx = rpx - \Delta_1.$ (4)

Trace the stroke contours along the updated left boundary to get the more precise left path. Then go to the next step. This step is shown in Fig. 2(c).

d.   Compute the score of the generated path pair:

$$\text{score of path pair} = \omega_1 \cdot (lpx - rpx) + \omega_2 \cdot \min(\mid lx - mx \mid, \mid rx - mx \mid). \quad (5)$$

where $mx = Lx + w / nc$, ω_1 and ω_2 are two weights. If the score of this path pair is smaller than that of previous pair or there is no previous pair, store this pair and abandon previous one simultaneously. Otherwise, keep going. Then go to the next step.

e.   Update lx and rx simultaneously:

$$lx = lpx + \Delta_2. \quad (6)$$

$$rx = Lx + (2 - \theta) \cdot w / nc. \quad (7)$$

where Δ_2 is a step size bigger than Ws. Then go back to step a.

An example is shown in Fig. 2. The result of first iteration is shown in Fig. 2(c). Fig. 2(d) is the final result. If there are no splitting paths generated, this segmentation block has a touching problem.

Fig. 2. An example of contour tracing

2.2   Segmentation of Touching Characters

Ikeda et al. proposed a stroke width analysis method to segment the touching characters[2]. However, it can't effectively deal with the complex touching problem. In order to overcome the shortcoming of the stroke width analysis method, we proposed another method based on corner point analysis. This method is used after the touching characters segmented by the stroke width analysis method.

All the corner points used in the corner point analysis are extracted from the traced stroke contours. To detect the corner points on the stroke contours, a corner point extraction algorithm is proposed firstly.

Corner Point Extraction. Before detecting the points, the stroke contours are traced and stored. Then a $(2Ws + 1) \times (2Ws + 1)$ template is used to detect corner points

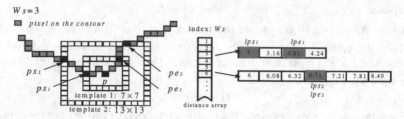

Fig. 3. Corner point extraction

along the contours. Then another $(4Ws+1)\times(4Ws+1)$ template is used to filter the corner points. The algorithm to detect a point p is as follows:

a. Search along the contour to get the two points ps_1 and pe_1, which are on the $(2Ws+1)\times(2Ws+1)$ template.

b. Search through Ws in the distance array to get the two distances from ps_1 to p (denoted as lps_1) and from pe_1 to p (denoted as lpe_1).

c. If $(\overrightarrow{ps_1-p})\cdot(\overrightarrow{pe_1-p})\geq COS\cdot lps_1\cdot lpe_1$, change the template size to $(4Ws+1)\times(4Ws+1)$. Otherwise, p is not a corner points and jump out of this algorithm. COS is the cosine threshold.

d. Search along the contour to get the two points ps_2 and pe_2, which are on the bigger template.

e. Search through Ws in the distance array to get the two distances from ps_2 to p (denoted as lps_2) and from pe_2 to p (denoted as lpe_2).

f. If $(\overrightarrow{ps_2-p})\cdot(\overrightarrow{pe_2-p})\geq COS\cdot lps_2\cdot lpe_2$, this point p is regarded as a corner point.

These steps are shown in Fig. 3. Corner points often appear in groups on the contour. So the point in the middle of a group is chosen to be the final corner point.

Cutting by Corner Point Analysis. For a suspected region $<lx,rx>$, the contours which connect the left boundary (lx) and the right boundary (rx) are used to extract corner points. These contours are divided into two types: the lower contour which is the lower edge of the stroke and the upper contour corresponding to the upper edge of the stroke. According to the contour type, the corner points, extracted by the above method, also fall into two classes: lower corner point and upper corner point. The blue solid squares and the grey solid squares in Fig. 4(a) denote the lower corner points and the upper points respectively.

Not all corner points are used to generate the cutting position candidates. A corner point p is kept if it satisfies one of the following two conditions:

(1) $(\overrightarrow{ps_1-p})\times(\overrightarrow{pe_1-p})>0$ and p is a lower corner point

(2) $(\overrightarrow{ps_1-p})\times(\overrightarrow{pe_1-p})<0$ and p is an upper corner point

Fig. 4(b) shows the reserved corner points.

A cutting position candidate is a corner point pair which consists of an upper corner point and a lower corner point closest to the upper one. If a corner point can't get the closest partner, the vertical cutting position which starts from this corner point is also a candidate. Fig. 4(c) shows the cutting position candidates. Let cfc denote the cutting position candidate. Then the cutting position is defined as:

$$\arg\min_{cfc}(\beta_1 \cdot clen / Ws + \beta_2 \cdot cdis / Wm) . \tag{8}$$

where $clen$ is the length of the candidate and $cdis$ is the distance from the middle of the candidate to the vertical line at $Lx + w / nc$. β_1 and β_2 are weights. By tracing contour after cutting, two splitting paths are generated as the Fig. 4(d) shows.

(a)   (b)   (c)   (d)

Fig. 4. Corner point analysis

3   Experiments and Results

564 handwritten Chinese character strings, consisting of 5066 Chinese characters, are used in our experiment, which are captured from the Chinese postal mail pieces. Each string contains overlapped and/or touching characters. There are 1011 overlapped and 1057 touching characters in these strings. Some characters are both overlapped and touching characters. The sum of overlapped characters and touching characters is 1964. The results of experiment are shown in Table 1. R1 is the correct rate of individual character without corner point analysis. R2 is the correct rate of individual character with corner point analysis. The results show the corner point analysis improves the segmentation performance, especially in segmenting the touching characters.

Table 1. Experiments on 564 strings

	All characters	Overlapped characters	Touching characters	Overlapped characters and touching characters
#Charaters	5066	1011	1057	1964
R1(%)	81.60%	—	58.94%	71.95%
R2(%)	85.81%	84.67%	74.93%	80.55%

We also use 814 overlapped characters to evaluate the performance of the contour tracing method. The correct rate of segmentation path pair R_c and the valid rate of segmentation path pair R_v are defined as follows:

$$R_c = N_c / N_t . \tag{9}$$

$$R_v = N_c / N_g . \tag{10}$$

where N_c is the number of correct segmentation path pairs, N_t is the number of true segmentation path pairs and N_g is the number of all generated segmentation path pairs including the abandoned path pairs by the contour tracing method. In this experiment, $N_c = 387$, $N_t = 427$, $N_g = 529$. According to formula (9) and (10), 90.63% ($R_c = 90.63\%$) segmentation path pairs are correct and 73.16% ($R_v = 73.16\%$) segmentation path pairs are valid. In addition, 8.2% (35) segmentation path pair are wrongly abandoned by the contour tracing method and it just needs 1.24 ($N_g / N_t = 1.24$) candidates to generate a segmentation path pair on average.

Some segmentation examples of Chinese handwritten character strings are shown in Fig. 5.

Fig. 5. Examples of segmentation

4   Conclusion

In this paper, two character segmentation methods are proposed for segmenting overlapped and touching Chinese characters respectively. The experiment result shows that the proposed methods are very effective in the segmentation of handwritten Chinese strings. In future work, we will use the recognition results to improve the accuracy rate of segmentation.

References

1. Liu, C.-L., Koga, M., Fujisawa, H.: Lexicon-driven segmentation and recognition of handwritten character strings for Japanese address reading. IEEE Transactions on Pattern Analysis and Machine Intelligence 24(11), 1425–1437 (2002)
2. Ikeda, H., et al.: A recognition method for touching Japanese handwritten characters. In: Proceedings of the Fifth International Conference on Document Analysis and Recognition (ICDAR), pp. 641–644 (1999)
3. Fu, Q., et al.: A Novel Segmentation and Recognition Algorithm for Chinese Handwritten Address Character Strings. In: 18th International Conference on Pattern Recognition (ICPR), pp. 974–977 (2006)
4. Wang, Q.-F., Ying, F., Liu, C.-L.: Improving Handewritten Chinese Text Recognition by Confidence Transformation. In: Proceedings of the 11th International Conference on Document Analysis and Recognition (ICDAR), pp. 518–522 (2011)
5. Zhao, S., et al.: Two-stage segmentation of unconstrained handwritten Chinese characters. Pattern Recognition 36(1), 145–156 (2003)
6. Liang, Z., Shi, P.: A metasynthetic approach for segmenting handwritten Chinese character strings. Pattern Recognition Letters 26(10), 1498–1511 (2005)

Word Detecting in Document Image
Based on Two-Stage Model

Xiujuan Li[1], Zhimin Huang[2], Ying Wen[1], and Yue Lu[1]

[1] Department of Computer Science and Technology
East China Normal University, Shanghai 200241, China
[2] The Third Research Institute of the Ministry of Public Security
Shanghai 200031, China

Abstract. This paper proposes a word detecting method for document image using character models and word models to evaluate the features of single-character and between-character. First, the text line is segmented into several fragments. Second, the candidate character, which is generated by merging some consecutive fragments, will be identified to be the right one if it conforms to the query word character models. Third, the path search strategy is used to search the candidate words constructed with candidate characters. The word model is used to identify the matching cost. Our experimental results on a dataset of document images demonstrate the effectiveness of the proposed method.

Keywords: Word Detecting, Word Model, Character Model.

1 Introduction

Recently, people have paid more attention to handwritten document retrieval. Word detecting in document is a challenging work in this task [1][2][3]. The fully automatic recognition of handwritten text is an imperfect field. The retrieval of handwritten documents still needs more research efforts to handle the difficulty of layout analysis, character/word segmentation, and variability of writing styles [2], especially on the classifier training. Under these conditions, word detecting is proposed for retrieving words from document images [1].

The techniquewhich measures the similarity of the candidate word and the query wordis important for query word detecting. Existing methods can be classified into two categories, template-based method and training method. For the first method, the holistic gradient-based binary features (GSC) [4] and the dynamic programming (DP) [2] are commonly used to measure the best match. The second one trains models for scoring candidate patterns. Traditional methods require a lot of effort to train the character model [5] and word model [6]. Both of the methods have their limits.

Word detecting using character segmentation and recognition candidates is effective in Japanese document retrieval [7]. We use a similar method, but we pay more attention to measure the similarity of the candidate models and the query word models. In our method, we train models for the query word at first. Then,

W. Zhang et al. (Eds.): IFTC 2012, CCIS 331, pp. 175–181, 2012.
© Springer-Verlag Berlin Heidelberg 2012

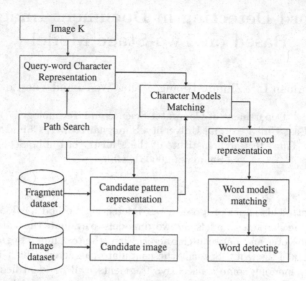

Fig. 1. Flowchart of the proposed word detecting system

for each candidate word, we get the candidate patterns from the exacted primitive fragments and match them with the query-word character in the character models matching phase. According to the searching cost, we take the n-best list and locate the $Top - n$ word in each candidate list. Fig.1 provides the flowchart of the proposed system.

2   System Overview

In our work, we describe the text line as a sequence of primitive fragments ordered from left to right $I = \{I_1, ..., I_m\}$. To get the primitive fragments, we merge the consecutive fragments which have a certain level of overlap horizontally [8] and judge each fragment for forced splitting after contour analysis. To align with a candidate word $T = \{C_1...C_n\}, (n \leq m)$, we define the detecting pattern as a correspondence between candidate character and the sequence of primitive fragments:

$$A = (C_1, I_1...I_{k_1-1}), ...(C_i, I_{j-k_i-1}...I_j), ...(C_n, I_p...I_m) \qquad (1)$$

where a candidate pattern $C_i = I_{j-k_i-1}...I_j$ is matched with query-word character KC_i which is selected from the sequences of query word primitive fragments. We allow a candidate pattern to be formed by at most 4 primitive fragments $(1 \leq k_i \leq 4)$.

Each possible candidate word corresponds to a path measured by DP using a path search algorithm [8] for efficient search of candidate word from candidate primitive fragments. Fig. 2(left) shows how to detect a query word

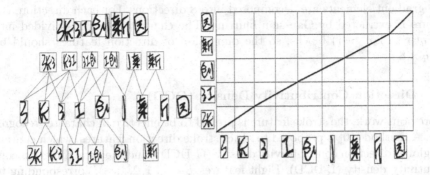

Fig. 2. Primitive fragments generating(left),path search to locate "张江创新园"(right)

"张江创新园"from sequence of candidate primitive fragments. The first character "张"is located as a seed node at first. Other characters are searched according to the seed (Fig. 2(right)). To get the corresponding candidate pattern, we define our matching conditions as:

$$g(A) = \&D_D\&D_G\&D_L \tag{2}$$

where D_D, D_G and D_L are the corresponding costs of direction features, G-DCD and L-DCD in character model matching phase, respectively.

To search for the best match, each path is evaluated by a cost function. Inspired by [7], we define the searching cost as a weighted sum:

$$g(A) = \sum_{h=0}^{4} \lambda_h \cdot F_h \tag{3}$$

where $\lambda_h(h = 0, ..., k)$ and $F_0, ..., F_h$ are weight coefficients and word model matching costs. Based on weighted sum, the $top-n$ candidate words are available.

3   Character Model

In this stage, we propose a serial of single-character features to describe candidate patterns and query-word characters.

3.1   Direction Feature

The gradient direction histogram feature [1][4] is popular in character processing. First, we get the normalization-cooperated gradient vector d. Then, standard directions are defined and d is decomposed into two vectors with coefficients l_1 and l_2, here e_1 and e_2 are unit vectors. Finally, the corresponding standard direction coefficient is added in each block.

$$d = l_1e_1 + l_2e_2 \tag{4}$$

The gradient elements are decomposed into 8 directions. For each direction, the feature is extracted by Gaussian blurring. The character image is divided into $p \times q(p > 1, q > 1)$ blocks, so the dimension of direction features should be $p \times q \times 8$.

3.2 Direction Contributivity Density (DCD)

In previous work, the stroke feature is proved to be effective in character recognition. A method [10] is proposed to exact stroke direction features, which contain the global direction contributivity density (G-DCD), and the local direction contributivity density (L-DCD). Eight features $L_i(i = 1, 2, ..., 8)$, corresponding to $0°, 45°, 90°, 135°, 180°, 225°, 270°$ and $315°$, indicate eight distances between the pixel on a stroke and eight directional edges of the stoke. Normalization of d_i is defined as

$$d_i = \frac{L_i + L_{i+4}}{\sqrt{\sum_{i=1}^{4}(L_i + L_{i+4})}}, i = 1, 2, 3, 4 \tag{5}$$

Then a quaternion $D = (d_1, d_2, d_3, d_4)$ for each pixel on stroke is calculated. The G-DCD feature indicates the direction features D for all crosspoints. We divide the features into r parts and values of each part is added. The character image is segmented into $p \times q$ blocks, and L-DCD feature is the sum of the direction features for each block. It reflects the local structure of the character.

4 Word Model

To identify if the candidate word consisting of candidate patterns matches with query word, we construct word models to measure between-character features.

4.1 Penetrated Feature

The input image is scaned horizontally, and the locations of the turning pixels between character and background are recorded in binary digital images. We could get two signals: the horizontal distance to left-most pixel and the sum of turning pixels [10]. For the first one, a maximum value (MAX) is defined as the largest number of transitions. If the number of the recorded transition pixels (i.e. n) is less than MAX, then the remaining MAX-n transitions would be assigned values of 0. Otherwise, drop the extra ones. For other directions, i.e. $45°$, $90°$, and $135°$, we use the same method.

4.2 Modified Direction Feature (MDF)

Transition information is commonly applied in handwritten text processing [9], a technique which contained this information is called Modified direction feature extraction. For MDF, the collinear direction vectors are normalized to one standard direction. First, we mark out the direction of the character [9]. Then,

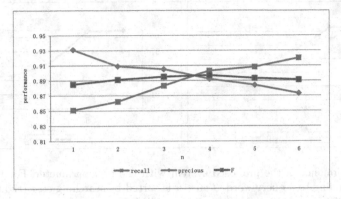

Fig. 3. Performance of proposed word detecting system with different parameters

location transitions (LTs) and Direction Transition (DTs) features according to the direction of transition pixel are obtained. Finally, a local averaging process is applied to the LT and DT values obtained in four traversal directions to reduce the feature vector size.

5   Experimental Results

In our work, the performance of the word detecting method is tested on a dataset constructed with 10002 images of different grays, sizes, skews and noise levels . They are captured from real-life letters. In the dataset, 240 pieces with candidate patterns match with 21 different query words. For each query word $K_i(i \leq 21)$, corresponding to a relevant match list $\hat{K}_i(i \leq 21)$, we take one image from each of 21 lists for training the query word model and others (more than 3) for testing. We count $Top - n$ images for every match list. The candidate word, which is from the query word writer and has the same text as the query word, is defined as the correct search in our system.

The performance is defined by *recall, precision* and $F - score$ as:

$$recall = \frac{cdw}{tw}, precision = \frac{cdw}{dw}, F = \frac{2}{\frac{1}{recall} + \frac{1}{precision}} \qquad (6)$$

where cdw indicates the sum of correct detected words, tw means the sum of the truth words, and dw describes the sum of detected words.

We show the detecting performance when adjusting different parameters (Fig.3), from which we can see that *recall* is inversely proportional to *precision*. F, which integrates *recall* and *precision*, almost stays the same and reflects the performance of the overall system. It proves our system's relatively stable.

Given the best parameter (*recall* is 0.903, *precision* is 0.892, F is 0.897, they have the best performance in the Fig.3), performance index of the system is measured in the following way. First, we take the n-best list in accordance with

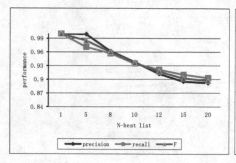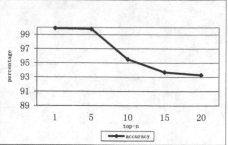

Fig. 4. Performance of the proposed system with the best parameter. For the match list corresponding to a query word, $Top - n$ is sorted by searching cost (right). For all lists, n-best list is sorted by *precision* and *recall* (left).

the performance of candidate word list for each query word. Experimental result for n-best list is shown in Fig.4(left), where N is the number of the list. Second, we sort the candidate word according to the searching cost in each candidate list and locate the $Top - n$ candidate word. The performance of our system in terms of $Top - n$ accuracy is shown in Fig.4(right). The high accuracy of $Top - n(n \leq 5)$ means the incorrect almost at the end of the list, where n denotes the location in the candidate list.

Table 1. The performance comparison of the state-of-the-art methods and the proposed method

method	precision	recall	F
Rodriguez J. and Perronnin F.[3]	0.883	0.789	0.833
Huang L. et al.[1]	0.871	0.893	0.882
the proposed method	0.892	0.903	0.897

Since there are many works for word detecting in recent years, we compared the proposed system with method using gradient histogram features [3] and method using statistical model [1]. The performance for the different methods are shown in Table 1. It can be appreciated that the proposed method gives better performance than the other two methods.

6   Conclusions

Word retrieval has recently attracted a lot of attention. In this paper, we focus on a word detecting method that employs character models and word models. The similarity between the query words and every candidate word is measured by integrating single-character feature and between-character feature. Our method achieves high performance in experiments.

References

1. Huang, L., Yin, F., Chen, Q.H., Liu, C.L.: Keyword Spotting in Offline Chinese Handwritten Documents using a Statistical Model. In: 11th International Conference on Document Analysis and Recognition, Beijing, pp. 78–82 (2011)
2. Yin, F., Wang, Q.F., Liu, C.L.: Integrating Geometric Context for Text Alignment of Handwritten Chinese Documents. In: 12th International Conference on Frontier in Handwriting Recognition, Kolkata, pp. 7–12 (2010)
3. Rodriguez, J., Perronnin, F.: Local Gradient Histogram Features for Word Spotting in Unconstrained Handwritten Documents. In: 11th International Conference on Frontier in Handwriting Recognition, Montreal, pp. 7–12 (2008)
4. Liu, C.L.: Normalization-Cooperated Gradient Feature Extraction for Handwritten Character Recognition. IEEE Trans. Pattern Anal. Mach. Intell. 29(8), 1465–1469 (2007)
5. Zhang, B., Sargur, S., Huang, C.: Word Image Retrieval using Binary Features. In: 11th Document Recognition and Retrieval, California, pp. 45–53 (2004)
6. Chan, J., Ziftci, C., Forsyth, D.: Searching Off-line Arabic Documents. In: 22th IEEE Computer Society Conference on Computer Vision and Pattern Recognition, New York, pp. 1455–1462 (2006)
7. Oda, H., Kitadai, A., Onuma, M., Nakagawa, M.: A Search Method for On-line Handwritten Text employing Writingbox-free Handwriting Recognition. In: 9th International Conference on Frontier in Handwriting Recognition, Tokyo, pp. 545–550 (2004)
8. Liu, C.L., Sako, H., Fujisawa, H.: Effects of Model Structures and Training Regimes on Integrated Segmentation and Recognition of Handwritten Numeral Strings. IEEE Trans. Pattern Anal. Mach. Intell. 26(11), 1395–1407 (2004)
9. Blumenstein, M., Liu, X.Y., Verma, B.: An Investigation of the Modified Direction Feature for Cursive Character Recognition. Pattern Recognition 40(2), 376–388 (2007)
10. Wen, Y., Lu, Y., Yan, J.Q., Zhou, Z.Y., von Deneen, K.M., Shi, P.F.: An Algorithm for License Plate Recognition applied to Intelligent Transportation System. IEEE Trans. Intelligent Transportation Systms 12(3), 830–845 (2011)

Competing Model Based Tone Evaluation
for Mandarin Speech

Yang Qu[1], Yue Lu[1], Patrick S.P. Wang[1,2], and Xin He[3]

[1] Department of Computer Science and Technology
East China Normal University, Shanghai 200241, China
[2] College of Computer and Information Science
Northeastern University, Boston, MA 02115, USA
[3] Motorola China Research Center, Shanghai, China

Abstract. Tone is a distinctive feature in Mandarin. This paper describes an attempt to automate the tone evaluation for continuous Mandarin speech. An HMM forced alignment based tone model is used to get tone score for Mandarin syllables. The competing model based approach is introduced to get tonal syllable score. Especially, we generate the syllable-based competing models by using the simplified linguistic knowledge based initial/final net. For the purpose of getting more objective tone evaluation, we integrate tonal syllable score and tone score together to acquire the overall tone scoring results. The experimental results demonstrate that this proposed competing models based method gives an accurate tone evaluation.

Keywords: Tone evaluation, Competing models, Linguistic knowledge, speech recognition.

1 Introduction

Tone plays a vital role in speech recognition of tonal languages. In Mandarin, each character is associated with one out of five possible tones. In previous work, many researchers have investigated on automatic pronunciation quality assessment by speech recognition techniques [1], [2]. In Mandarin, research and development of speech recognition have been conducted for nearly two decades [3], [4], [5], [6]. Among them, an approach based on the ranking among all competing biphone models was used to measure confidence in pronunciation evaluation [6].

In this paper, the simplified linguistic knowledge based initial/final net is proposed to generate syllable-based competing models. And the competing models based approach is introduced in our system to get tone evaluation. Particularly, the tonal syllable score is obtained by using tonal syllable competing models, and the tone score is computed by using tone competing models.

The remainder of the paper is organized as follows. In section 2, we discuss the proposed method in detail. Experimental results are presented in Section 3, followed by conclusions in Section 4.

W. Zhang et al. (Eds.): IFTC 2012, CCIS 331, pp. 182–188, 2012.
© Springer-Verlag Berlin Heidelberg 2012

2   The Proposed Approach

We propose an approach, which uses the competing models based tone assessment to improve the performance of tone evaluation system for Mandarin speech.

2.1   System Architecture Description

The architecture of our tone evaluation system is shown in Fig. 1. 39-dimensional MFCC features are used for segmentation. The competing models based approach is introduced to get objective tone evaluation results. The overall tone score is obtained by combining tonal syllable score and tone score. Especially, the tonal syllable score is obtained by using tonal syllable competing models, and the tone score is computed by using tone competing models.

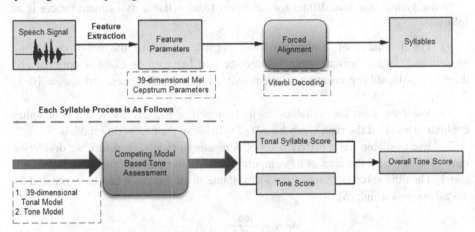

Fig. 1. Architecture of our tone evaluation system

2.2   Forced Alignment Based Tone Model

In this paper, we partition training samples into 5 tonal classes, the high flat (tone 1), the low rising (tone 2), the high low rising (tone 3), the high falling (tone 4), and the neutral tone (tone 0). For all the utterances, we employ SMDSF method [7] to extract pitch features, which are 4-dimension, five tone triphone features. Before training the model, each training utterance needs to be segmented into several syllables by using HMM forced alignment. The acoustic model for the forced alignment is based on context-dependent triphone modeling, and the model is a 39-dimension MFCC tonal model. After forced alignment, the segmental results are used as parameters in training our tone model.

2.3   Competing Model Based Tone Evaluation

With the purpose of getting objective tone evaluation, we use a relative measure based on competing models. Basically, the whole evaluation procedure contains two parts: tonal syllable evaluation and tone evaluation.

As shown in Fig. 2, the parallel network composes our proposed tonal syllable competing network, which includes initial network, final network and tone network.

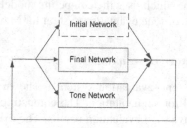

Fig. 2. Architecture of tonal syllable competing network

In the system, the initial/final format based tonal syllable assessment proceeds as follows:

1) For a syllable of "(initial) + final" format, we define the set of competing models as "(initial)*+final*+tone*"where the part between brackets is optional and the * is a wildcard representing all the possible initials/finals/tones, and tone = {0, 1, 2, 3, 4}.

2) We then send the syllables to the competing models for a log probability evaluation and find the rank (zero-based) of syllable in the competing models.

3) Each syllable has a different set of competing models; therefore we divide the rank of syllable by the size of its competing models to obtain a rank ratio between 0 and 1. Then the syllable score of the i-th syllable in an utterance can be expressed by the following formula[6]:

$$Score_i = \frac{100}{1+\left|\frac{r_i}{a}\right|^b} \tag{1}$$

Where r_i is the rank ratio of the i-th syllable, and a and b are the tunable parameters of this scoring function.

2.4   Simplified Linguistic Knowledge-Based Initial/Final Net

A Mandarin syllable has either a structure form of CV (Consonant-Vowel or initial-final) or a single structure form of V (Vowel). Fig. 3(a) shows the full initial/final net of Mandarin syllable, where the total number of initials and finals are, respectively, 21 and 37. According to the definition of competing models described in section 2.3, using full initial/final net will generate large numbers of competing models. Since the total number of initials, finals and tones are, respectively, 21, 37 and 5, each syllable has 21*37*5 competing models at most. Accordingly, the simplified net is introduced to form legal competing models. Fig. 3(b) lists the simplified initial/final net based on the linguistic knowledge of Mandarin pronunciation.

Take the phrase "斗争"(it means fight or struggle) for example, it can be pronounced as "dou4 zheng1". For the first word "dou4", initial "d" is in the second initial net "d, t, g, h, k", while final "ou" is in the first final net "en, eng, iong, ong, ou, u, uen" and the second final net "ao, e, o, ou, u, uo". Therefore, the competing models of "dou4" can be represented in the form as "initial from initial net 1 + final from final net 1 and final net 2 + tone".

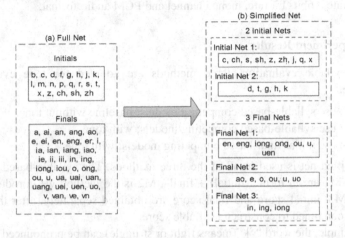

Fig. 3. Mandarin syllable competing network: *(a)* full initial/final net; *(b)* simplified linguistic knowledge-based initial/final net

2.5   Tone Evaluation

In tone evaluation, we employ the forced alignment based tone model to extract pitch features of a given utterance, and send each syllable into five tone competing models for a log probability evaluation and find the tone rank (zero-based) of syllable in the competing models. In like manner, the tone competing models is defined as "initial+final+tone*" where the initial/final is constant and the * is a wildcard representing all the possible tones. Similarly, formula (1) is brought to compute the i-th correct tone score.

After previous two evaluations, we have obtained two scores. The overall tone scoring function is designed as a weighted average of two scores:

$$Score_{overall} = w_1 \cdot Score_{tonalsyllable} + w_2 \cdot Score_{tone} \tag{2}$$

Where w_1 and w_2 are the tunable parameters, and $w_1 + w_2 = 1$.

3   Experiments

3.1   Speech Database

The speech corpus used in the experiments is the Mandarin Database collected under 863 Project (863 Database), which is a speaker-independent, large vocabulary, continuously read Mandarin Chinese speech database [8]. The text material is selected from the Chinese newspaper "People's Daily", telescripts and dictionaries. The corpus covers 2185 sentences and 388 phrases. The database is recorded by 80 speakers, which include 40 males and 40 females, and each speaker read 520 utterances. 60 speakers (30 males and 30 females)' records are used as training set and the rest are used as testing set. Speeches of the 863 Database are in the format of 8000 Hz sampling rate, 16bits bit rate, mono channel and PCM audio format.

3.2   Experiment Results

In tonal syllable evaluation, three methods are adopted for tone evaluation in comparing.

1) M1: use syllable-based competing models; baseline without tone.
2) M2: use syllable-based competing models; with tone.
3) M3: use initial/final-based competing models; with tone.

The simplified net is used in all of the three methods. The syllable-based competing models of M1 are in form "(initial) + final". M2 is the method we introduced in this paper. In M3, initial score and final score are obtained separately, after that the two scores are combined to construct a syllable score.

For example, the word "斗"(means fight or struggle) can be pronounced as "dou4". In our experiment, we compared the three methods, and in each method we read "dou4" as "dou4", "dou1", "dou3", "tou4", "yi1", respectively. Table 1 gives the number of competing models of three methods. Table 2 shows the tonal syllable scores attained by using three methods. In M1 and M2, formula (1) is used to calculate the tonal syllable score. Similarly, formula (1) is applied in M3 to get the i-th correct initial score and the i-th correct final score. Then the syllable scores are computed by initial and final scores. Since tone is considered in M2 and the number of competing models getting from M2 is larger than that from M1 and M3, tonal syllable scores acquire from M2 are more objective.

Table 3 shows the tone ranks and corresponding tone scores of "dou4", and combines the preceding syllable scores from M2 to obtain the overall scores. The results of combination method are better than that of using only competing models method. For the wrong pronunciation "dou1", "dou3", "tou4" and "yi1", the combination method gives a lower score than only competing models method.

Moreover, in order to get more intuitive results, we use the 863 Database to test the performance of the proposed method. The test set includes 4 male utterances data and 4 female utterances data. There are 800 sentences, 9692 syllables in all. Table 4 gives the tone recognition results of syllables. The first line lists the results of the decision tree based approach reported in [9], and its recognition accuracy is 66.3%. By using combination method, the TER of syllables is 16.08%. TER of only using tone models is 33.59%, and the TER of only using competing models is 16.11%.

Table 1. The number of Competing Models of "dou4" by three methods

Method	Competing Models
M1	29 (Syllable)
M2	102 (Tonal Syllable)
M3	4 (initial); 21 (final).

Table 2. Tonal syllable score of "dou4" by three methods

Pronunciation	M1	M2	M3
dou4	100	100	89.55
dou1	98.13	96.98	87.69
dou3	59.35	55.14	58
tou4	28.44	31.62	33.38
yi1	32.28	29.42	55.05

Table 3. Tone evaluation results of "dou4"

	Competing Models Method			Combination Method (Tone model +Competing Model)		
	rank	Tone	Overall Score	rank	Tone Score	Overall Score
dou4	2	60.98	80.49	0	100	100
dou1	2	60.98	78.98	3	40.98	68.98
dou3	1	86.21	70.68	3	40.98	48.06
tou4	2	60.98	46.3	1	86.21	58.92
yi1	3	40.98	35.2	4	28.09	28.76

Table 4. Tone error rate (TER) for three methods

	TER
Approach in (Cao et al., 2004)	33.7%
Tone Model	33.59%
Competing Model	16.11%
Combination Method (Tone Model + Competing Model)	16.08%

4 Conclusions

In this paper, we propose a competing model based approach to attain objective tone evaluation for Mandarin speech. Experiments have shown that the combination approach of using forced alignment based tone model with competing models based tone assessment is able to gain better performance in tone evaluation. By using this combination measure, the tone assessment result is more objective than using only competing models.

References

1. Molina, C., Yoma, N.B., et al.: ASR Based Pronunciation Evaluation with Automatically Generated Competing Vocabulary and Classifier Fusion. Speech Communication 51(6), 485–498 (2009)

2. Nair, N.U., Sreenivas, T.V.: Joint Evaluation of Multiple Speech Patterns for Speech Recognition and Training. Computer Speech and Language 24(2), 307–340 (2010)
3. Ni, C.J., Liu, W.J., et al.: Prosody Dependent Mandarin Speech Recognition. In: IJCNN, San Jose, CA, pp. 197–201 (2011)
4. Lin, C.K., Lee, L.S.: Improved Features and Models for Detecting Edit Disfluencies in Transcribing Spontaneous Mandarin Speech. IEEE Trans. Audio, Speech, Lang. Process. 17(7), 1263–1278 (2009)
5. Zhu, M., Fu, Q.J., et al.: Mandarin Chinese Speech Recognition by Pediatric Cochlear Implant Users. Int. J. Pediatr. Otorhi. 75(6), 793–800 (2011)
6. Chen, J.C., Jang, J.S.R.: Automatic Pronunciation Assessment for Mandarin Chinese: Approaches and System Overview. IJCLCLP 12(4), 443–458 (2007)
7. Liu, J., Zheng, T.F., Deng, J., et al.: Real-time Pitch Tracking Based on Combined Smdsf. In: Proc. INTERSPEECH, Lisbon, Portugal (2005)
8. Zu, Y.Q.: The Text Design for Continuous Speech Database of Standard Chinese. Acta Acustica 24(3), 236–247 (1999) (in Chinese)
9. Cao, Y., Huang, T.Y., et al.: A Stochastically-based Study on Chinese Tone Patterns in Continuous Speech. Acta Automatic Sinica 30(2), 191–198 (2004) (in Chinese)

Line-Type Moving Object Detection for Sonar Images[*]

Qiuyu Zhu, Yichun Li, and Yilong Jiang

School of Communication and Information Engineering, Shanghai University,
Yanchang Road 149, 200072 Shanghai, China
zhuqiuyu@staff.shu.edu.cn, athrun_asuka@yahoo.com.cn,
jiangyilong8975@sina.com

Abstract. This paper proposes a novel solution to process sonar images. It uses intensity Hough transformation to find out line-type moving objects in B-mode images of sonar. Considering that objects in sonar B-mode images always have enough values of intensity and are shown as local peaks, mathematical morphology is adopted to restrain noises, and extract the peaks. The intensity images are involved, which are different from the binary images used by standard Hough transformation. Intensity accumulation is performed in accumulation space. Line-type moving objects are discovered when the accumulation exceeds the preset threshold. The approach is suitable for a variety of underwater environments due to the independence on the model of reverberation. The experimental result illustrates the effectiveness and robustness of the novel solution.

Keywords: mathematical morphology, intensity Hough transformation, object detection, sonar image.

1 Introduction

In recent years sonar detection technology has developed rapidly. People have been able to successfully finish a series of tasks such as navigation, ranging, acoustic communication and underwater positioning with sonar. Sonar images play as the data information carriers, so the imaging quality is directly related to the accuracy of the subsequent processings, like underwater object detection, tracking and behavior analysis, and also related to the construction of underwater environment monitoring systems using computer vision in the future.

Although sonar images, same as optical images, in essence are plane or spatial distributions of energy, because of the unique transmission characteristics of the sound and underwater acoustic channels, sonar images are in many aspects different from optical images. Prevailing image processing technology cannot be applied directly to acoustic image processing. Underwater topography and geology, sound waves produced by working marine equipments, bad movement stability of sonar

---

[*] This work was supported by the Development Foundation of Shanghai Municipal Commission of Science and Technology (11dz1205902), and the Leading Academic Discipline Project of Shanghai Municipal Education Commission (J50104).

W. Zhang et al. (Eds.): IFTC 2012, CCIS 331, pp. 189–196, 2012.
© Springer-Verlag Berlin Heidelberg 2012

carriers, and many other factors can make sonar work in strong reverberation fields, which induces the phenomenon that the images often have great noises and low contrast, deteriorating edges. Therefore the images have poor quality. Small targets are often submerged by interferences while artifacts appear frequently[1].

In order to eliminate fundamentally the underwater reverberation, and guarantee the accuracy of underwater object detection, many researchers have made great efforts to model the ocean reverberation[2, 3].Under the support of U.S. Office of Naval Research, Reverberation Modeling Workshop summarized several models, put forward appropriate reference models corresponding to some typical environments[4]. However, considering the complexity and variability of the water, large amounts of model parameter adjustments are involved so that generality, computing and accuracy may be hard to be ensured all. Hence post-processing the sonar images under the environmental reverberation directly, or avoidance noises in acoustic imaging course are also good ways. Firoiu[5] had put forward a new type of wavelet transformation-HWT. With the excellent performance of translation invariance of HWT, the speckles in the sonar images could be cleared. Combined with bishrink filter for repairing outlines, the approach improved the image contrast greatly. Liang[6] integrated null-forming weights with Bartlett beam-forming technology, only grabbed maximum output power in the target's direction. The method was exclusive from multipath noises. Leier and Zoubir[7] used synthetic an aperture sonar to realize high resolution image reconstruction. The ratio of energy to the reference echo was introduced for evaluating compensation in the process of the motion compensation to low resolution images. The largest continuous echo whose ratio was within the scope expected was got to reconstruct the high resolution focused images. Yang[8] considered the multiplying characteristics of the speckle noise. Multilevel median filter and rough set weighted mean filter which both preserved edges well were combined with homomorphic transformation. The image noise effect was effectively suppressed.

Moving targets exist in the form of lines in multi-beam sonar B-mode images. Owing to the presence of the surrounding reverberation, it is rather difficult to detect targets' trajectories. In view of this situation, this paper proposes an approach to realize sonar image line-type moving objects detection by using intensity Hough transformation. Mathematical morphology is involved to inhibit reverberation interference at the same time extracting local gray-scale peaks of the images. Afterwards intensity Hough transformation is performed in order to detect line-type moving targets. The method is not dependent on reverberation model, and suitable to be used in all kinds of water environment. The experimental results demonstrate that the theoretical analysis is rational and the proposed method is valid.

2   Line-Type Moving Objects Detection by Intensity Hough Transformation for Sonar Images

The representation of the multi-beam sonar B-mode image is a distance-time-intensity 2D image. The image consists of the bar sub-images ordered by the angles of receiving elements as shown in Fig. 1.

Accordingly, trajectories of the objects exist as continuous lines. Further ones of the moving targets are shown as straight lines with certain sloping degrees. Figuring out the sloping lines in the image means line-type moving objects detection. Hough transformation and its improved form are common and effective ways of line detection. The reverberation of the sonar image deteriorates the binary edge image involved in standard Hough transformation which is full of the edges belonging to noises. Restraining reverberation and strengthening the information of linear targets is related to actual detection effects. The algorithm proposed in this paper according to the image characteristics, through the following two steps: (1) mathematical morphology pre-processing, (2) intensity Hough transformation, realizes line-type moving objects detection.

Fig. 1. A multi-beam sonar B-mode image

2.1 Mathematical Morphology Pre-processing

Close Operation. We know that close operation in morphological operation can make up for interior small holes and gaps of objects, and connect neighboring objects. Noises in sonar B-mode images exist in the form of clouds of points. At the same time tracks of targets are always fractured. Using close operation at first may change the form of the reverberation from clouds into blocks, which the distribution of the noises appears smoothly so that lines of the targets around the noises can be obvious. Also, close operation carries out linking with these lines properly. As a result, connectivity of moving objects is assured. In practice, to improve the ability of filling and connection, the operation adopted in this paper is:

$$f \bullet \bullet b = (f \oplus b \oplus b) \otimes b \otimes b. \tag{1}$$

where $\oplus$ stands for dilation, $\otimes$ is erosion operator. The large close operation as (1) with the processing of "dilation-dilation-erosion-erosion" improves the fitness of pre-processing and robustness under great reverberation.

Top-Hat Transformation. Top-hat transformation is a kind of image processing method in the field of mathematical morphology. It is an effective image detection and enhancement measure, as is often used for images with uneven background illumination. It can be achieved by combination of open operation and input images. The expression of top-hat transformation is:

$$f_{top}(x, y) = f(x, y) - f \circ b(x, y) \tag{2}$$

where $f(x, y)$ is the input image, $f \circ b(x, y)$ is the result of open operation. Through Top-hat transformation can compensate the phenomenon that intensities of local backgrounds vary dramatically due to reverberation. The output image of top-hat transformation has great contrast between targets and backgrounds, guaranteeing performance of detection.

Considering the experiences of finding out moving targets in sonar B-mode images with naked eyes, we notice that the targets always show certain intensities that are local peaks around as well. In view of the above prior knowledge, top-hat transformation has ability to point out the peaks instead of naked eyes. Top-hat transformation following close operation will ignore relatively uniform blocks of noise areas, and extract trajectories rightly.

2.2   Intensity Hough Transformation

Standard Hough transformation usually contains the following step: 1) Points in the images that has finished edge detection and binarization (labeled as B) should be mapped into parameter space. 2) Evidence accumulation is done by the rule of binary accumulation. 3) Local peaks are found out. Parameters corresponding to these peaks are confirmed. Line could be detected by the parameter backward. The procedure is shown in Fig. 2.

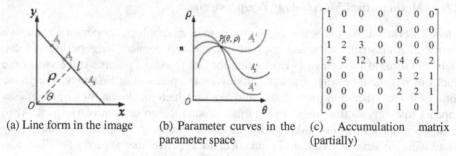

(a) Line form in the image   (b) Parameter curves in the   (c)   Accumulation   matrix
                                parameter space   (partially)

Fig. 2. Use standard Hough Transformation to detect lines

It is obvious that all the points belonging to the same line in the image will become several curves that cross at a certain position in the parameter space after Hough transformation. The curves display radiating, as shown in Fig. 2(b). It is the distribution of the curves that lead to the butterfly distribution around the peaks in the parameter space under the rule of binary accumulation. The meaning is that the values in the accumulation matrix turn to decrease gradually around the peaks. The problem lies on the point that the values near the peaks are quite close to the peaks, as shown in Fig. 2(c).It makes threshold setting and peak extracting more difficult. Moreover, noises will let the problem more troublesome. To deal with such situation, an improving scheme of Hough transformation, intensity Hough transformation, is given in this paper on the basis of analyzing characteristics of sonar B-mode images.

Segmentation of Bar Regions. Multi-beam imaging sonar B-mode image is a distance-time-intensity 2D image. Signal impulses are launched at a fixed time interval in a period of time. Then divided by the received angles of the sonar, the received echoes of each angle are recorded, composing the echo bar image of each angle. All the echo bar images constitute the whole B-mode image. Since the echo bar images are independent with each other, it is obviously appropriate to deal with the whole picture for linear detection. Several artificial lines spanning two or more bar regions will be found wrongly. Therefore, according to the number of the angles K, we divide off the bar regions one by one to avoid the interference among them. This method benefits improvement of speed and robustness as well through limiting accumulate space.

Intensity Accumulation. Facing the shortcoming of binary accumulation of standard Hough transformation, many scholars [9,10] put forward several solutions. The general thoughts are either analysis of distributions in parameter space or optimization of accumulating data. The latter replaces binary accumulation with weight accumulation, highlighting the peaks. However, input images needed in both approaches above are mostly binary edge images. It is especially in sonar images that the greater intensities of the edges are, the more probably they belong to a straight line in view of the prior knowledge about travelling object detection with naked eyes. Abnegating intensities means abnegating the most original weight factor. Hence in this paper intensity accumulation is utilized.

$f_{top}(x, y)$ represents the intensity image after mathematical morphology pre-processing. $T_i(x, y)(i = 1,\ldots K)$ are the sub-images after segmentation of the bar regions of the intensity image whose sizes are all $M \times N$. The corresponding accumulation function can be expressed as:

$$V_i(H_{\rho,\theta} \mid T_i(x, y)) = \sum_{x=1}^{N} \sum_{y=1}^{M} S_i(\rho,\theta) \qquad (3)$$

where weight function is:

$$S_i(\rho,\theta) = \begin{cases} T_i(x, y), (x\cos\theta + y\sin\theta, \theta) \in H_{\rho,\theta} \\ 0, (x\cos\theta + y\sin\theta, \theta) \notin H_{\rho,\theta} \end{cases}, \theta \in (\theta_{down}, \theta_{up}), \rho \in (1, sqrt(M^2 + N^2)) \qquad (4)$$

where $H_{\rho,\theta}$ stands for the point in parameter space whose coordinate is (ρ,θ). Voting and accumulation is done by the intensities of all the points whose curves in parameter space pass (ρ,θ) according to (3),(4). If the accumulation value of $V_i(H_{\rho,\theta} \mid T_i(x, y))$ exceeds preset threshold Th, a line exists in the area which $H_{\rho,\theta}$ corresponds to under Cartesian coordinates. In addition, noises appear in the form of 0-degree or near 90-degree outlines of blocks. The trajectories of expected moving targets have certain slopes (Still targets' slope is 0 degree). Thereby upper and lower bounds of the angle θ are introduced in this paper, expressed as θ_{up} and θ_{down} separately. By the bounds, outlines of noises and still targets can be ignored. At the same time, computation of parameter and accumulation space will be reduced.

3   Experimental Results

To verify the effectiveness of the algorithm, functions expected are realized with C++ development language in the Microsoft Visual 2008 C++ environment, combined with open source computer vision library OpenCV. The sonar B-mode image ready for processing is shown as Fig. 1. Fig. 1 comes from the dataset of sonar images provided by Mogan Mountain Lake Test Station. The central part of Fig. 1 contains a number of moving targets captured by the sonar. Unfortunately moving targets are also accompanied by reverberation. Firstly morphological pre-processing is performed by two dilations and two erosions. The result after the operation is shown in Fig. 3(a).The clouds of the noises merge into blocks while information of moving objects is still well reserved. Then next morphology pre-processing step, top-hat transformation, is done, whose effect is shown in Fig. 3(b). After the transformation, reverberation turns into rectangle outlines from blocks. Internal parts of the noises throughout the image are eliminated greatly. It makes the targets surrounded by reverberation more distinct while harsh background is inhibited enough. Afterwards, the whole image (378×840) is divided into 24 sub-images with size of 378×35 pixels each. At last intensity Hough transformation is carried out through intensity accumulation in parameter space according to bar regions. Fig. 3(c) is the output image after intensity Hough transformation. In this process, in order to balance the sensitivity to targets and the judgments of the smallest moving objects accepted, after a lot of testing, accumulation threshold Th is finally set to 260. Upper and lower bounds of the angle(θ_{up} , θ_{down}) are respectively set to 60 degrees and 10 degrees, to avoid the environment noises left and still targets. It takes 0.327 (sec) for conducting the algorithm on a PC with an Intel Core i3 CPU at 2.27GHz. The computing speed of about 3 (frame/s) meets the need of real-time sonar systems.

To assess intensity Hough transformation under challenging conditions, the ground truth of another sonar image from the dataset is labeled and quantitative comparison between intensity Hough transformation and standard Hough transformation is made. Fig. 4 shows the ground truth and the results of both algorithms. The local regions of the image where line-type objects appear are displayed. The method proposed in this paper could cover all the moving objects correctly even if multi-targets exist in the image while standard Hough transformation misses some targets. Other prevailing algorithms like Radon transformation could not reach the accuracy of intensity Hough transformation also.

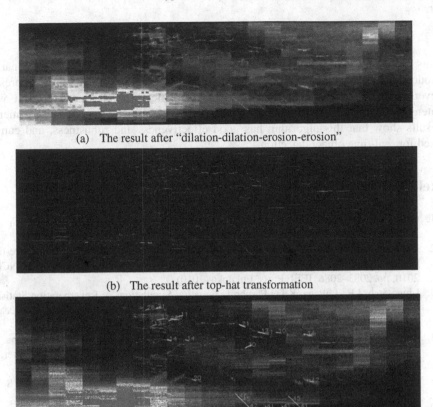

(a)   The result after "dilation-dilation-erosion-erosion"

(b)   The result after top-hat transformation

(c)   Trajectories of moving targets after intensity Hough transformation

Fig. 3. Using intensity Hough transformation to realize moving object detection for a sonar B-mode image

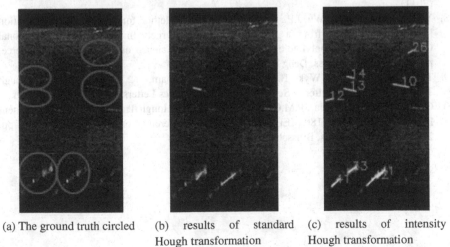

(a) The ground truth circled   (b)   results   of   standard   Hough transformation   (c)   results   of   intensity   Hough transformation

Fig. 4. Assessment of intensity Hough transformation for sonar B-mode images

4   Conclusion

This paper puts forward an approach to detect line-type moving objects for sonar B-mode images. Mathematical morphological operation effectively suppresses reverberation and extracts local peaks of intensities. Hough transformation with intensity accumulation is done to detect line-type moving targets. Experimental results show that this algorithm has good effectiveness and robustness, and can be used for real-time object detection.

References

1. Greco, M., Stinco, P., Gini, F.: Identification and Analysis of Sea Radar Clutter Spikes. IET Radar, Sonar & Navigation 4, 239–250 (2010)
2. Huang, J.G., Cui, X.D., Wang, R.H.: Modeling and Simulation of Space-time Reverberation for Active Sonar Array. In: 2010 IEEE Region 10 Conference, TENCON 2010, pp. 2083–2086. IEEE Press, Fukuoka (2010)
3. Lingevitch, J.F., LePage, K.D.: Parabolic Equation Simulations of Reverberation Statistics From Non-Gaussian-Distributed Bottom Roughness. IEEE Journal of Oceanic Engineering 35, 199–208 (2010)
4. Thorsos, E.I., Perkins, J.S.: Overview of the Reverberation Modeling Workshops. In: Proceedings of the International Symposium on Underwater Reverberation and Clutter, La Spezia, pp. 3–22 (2008)
5. Firoiu, I., Nafornita, C., Isar, D., Isar, A.: Bayesian Hyperanalytic Denoising of Sonar Images. Geoscience and Remote Sensing Letters 8, 1065–1069 (2011)
6. Liang, G.L., Liu, K., Lin, W.S.: A New Beam-forming Algorithm Based on Flank Acoustic Vector-sensor Array Sonar. In: 2009 International Conference on Wireless Communications & Signal Processing, pp. 1–5. IEEE Press, Nanjing (2009)
7. Leier, S., Zoubir, A.M.: Quality Assessment of Synthetic Aperture Sonar Images Based on a Single Ping Reference. In: OCEANS 2011 IEEE-Spain, pp. 1–4. IEEE Press, Santander (2011)
8. Yang, H.W., Li, X.L., Wu, J.P., Guo, H.T.: Complex Method for Speckle Noise Reduction in the Sonar Image from a Small Underwater Target. In: 2011 2nd International Conference on Artificial Intelligence, Management Science and Electronic Commerce, pp. 254–256. IEEE Press, Deng Leng (2011)
9. Tu, C., Du, S., van Wyk, B.J., Djouani, K., Hamam, Y.: High Resolution Hough Transform based on Butterfly Self-Similarity. Electronics Letters 47, 1360–1361 (2011)
10. Guerreiro, R.F.C., Aguiar, P.M.Q.: Incremental Local Hough Transform for Line Segment Extraction. In: 2011 18th IEEE International Conference on Image Processing, pp. 2841–2844. IEEE Press, Brussels (2011)

Spatial Detection of Line Scratch
Based on Histogram

Xi Hu, Xiaokang Yang, and Li Chen

Shanghai Key Labs of Digital Media Processing and Communication,
Shanghai Jiao Tong University, Shanghai, China
{hed279,xkyang,hilichen}@sjtu.edu.cn

Abstract. This paper presents a histogram degradation model of line
scratch. The degradation of line scratch results in compression of its
column's histogram, which can be expressed by histogram's key features. Based on the histogram model, a histogram-based approach of
line scratch detection is proposed. By combining the scratch histogram
model and a serious of constraints such as *Weber's Law*, width selection
and symmetry selection, the proposed algorithm performs well automatically. The experimental results show that the proposed algorithm work
better in terms of false alarms rejection with low computing complexity.

Keywords: line scratch, detection, histogram.

1 Introduction

In the last few years, digital film restoration has attracted increasing attention.
Kinds of degradation, such as dust spots, scratches and abrasions, heavily affect
old-film's visual effects -see [2], [4], [5]. For the sake of preservation the art value
of old movies, many computer-aid algorithms have been adopted to restore the
defects. The main goal of restoration is to gain a better visual effect with a low
computation complexity and the least modification of good original image information. In this paper we will focus on spatial(one frame at a time) line scratch
detection. Scratches consist of long, vertical lines of bright or dark intensity, oriented more or less vertically over much the image (up to 5% of the film width),
with width from about 3 to 10 pixels[6][7]. They are caused by the abrasion of
the film material during its transport or in the developing process [1],[2],[4],[5].

Generally speaking, scratches in most old films have the features and classification as TABLE-1, which are very helpful to our further work.

In [4] and [5], scratch degradation problem is dealt with by means of a temporal representation, i.e., using all frames of the degraded sequence. The detection
phase is characterized by performing the Radon's transform and the combination of the Kalman 's filter and the Hough transform. In [1] and [2], *Kokaram*
proposed a spatial model which is based on the Hough transform on the image
previously vertically sub-sampled and horizontally median filtered. Then it employs a bayesian refinement strategy to find scratches, looking at the marginal
distribution of their brightness. And in [7], *V.Bruni* generalized *Kokaram* 's

W. Zhang et al. (Eds.): IFTC 2012, CCIS 331, pp. 197–204, 2012.

Table 1. Type of Scratch

Kind of Scratch	Description
Static Scratch	Present at the same position on consecutive frames
Moving Scratch	Can change positions during sequence
Principal Scratch	Lying on more than 95% the image height
Secondary Scratch	The others
Alone Scratch	Without any other scratch nearby it
Not-alone Scratch	With other scratch nearby it
Positive Scratch	Dark intensity
Negative Scratch	Light intensity

theory into a damped sinusoid model and adopted *Weber's Law* to determine threshold for the first time.

In recent years, researchers have used wavelet[8], canny operator[9], shape filter[10] and some other tools to deal with spatial scratch detection. However, they were still puzzled by false retrieval and long elapsed time. False retrievals have been faced by most spatial scratch detection especially those who employ wavelet in frequency domain. Moreover, filter algorithms remove some vertical edges which drive visual effect worse. Other spatial approaches like template matching perform well for some frames, but cost too much time.

Although can be dealt with by some temporal approaches, false drop remain hard problems for spatial detectors. From this perspective, we would like to present a novel spatial scratch detection approach which performs relatively high detect rate while some resistance of false retrieval with less computation complexity. In this paper, we generalize a degradation model of scratch's histogram and further propose a new scratch detecting method. The proposed approach performs: i) completely automatic, ii) better at distinguishing between real scratches and false alarms and finally iii) very fast, i.e., it has an complexity $O(N)$, where N is the input image's number of columns.

2   Scratch Histogram Degradation Model

As is well known, histogram represents some statistical characteristics of the image. Since histogram's intensity level whose probability value is zero does not make sense, histogram $\mathbf{H}$ can be represented by a $2 \times K$ matrix as follows

$$\mathbf{H} = \begin{pmatrix} h_1 \ ... \ h_K \\ p_1 \ ... \ p_K \end{pmatrix} = \begin{pmatrix} \mathbf{h} \\ \mathbf{p} \end{pmatrix} \tag{1}$$

where K is the number of intensity level whose probability value is non-zero. $\mathbf{h} \in R^K$ represented the total K intensity levels with the corresponding probability vector $\mathbf{p} \in R^K$ in the histogram. The distance between adjacent intensity levels whose probability value are non-zero is $s_k = h_k - h_{k-1}$, $k = 2, ..., K, s_1 = h_1$.

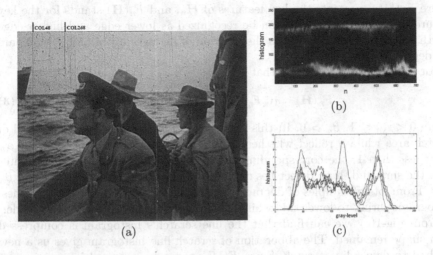

Fig. 1. ((a)The 700 × 576 8-b image of the 1st frame of Star sequence. (b)The corresponding column histogram $\mathbf{H}_{1,...,N}$. (c).Comparison between scratch line's histogram and nearby columns'.

In order to exploit the model, we consider an input image with size $M \times N$, where $M, N \in \mathcal{N}$. For nth image column, its histogram corresponds to $\mathbf{H_n}$. Then we have a column histogram sequence $\mathbf{H}_{1,...,N}$. Now assume that $\mathbf{H}_{1,...,N}$ is the clean image's column histogram sequence, $\tilde{\mathbf{H}}_{1,...,N}$ represents the degraded column histogram sequence. Based on the consistency of image data, $\mathbf{H_n}$ should be similar with its neighbors. $\tilde{\mathbf{H}}_\mathbf{n}$, if is a line scratch, will be outstanding from the others. See Fig-1(c), col 48 of *Star* is a line scratch lying on more than 95% of image height. The red curve is the scratch's histogram and the black curves are nearby columns' histograms. It is noticed that scratch's histogram is obviously different with the histograms nearby. Another important point is that the degraded histogram remains its shape. Besides *Star*, many experimental observations also back up the assumption that histogram degradation does not change original histogram shape. The phenomenon indicates that the degraded area still holds some information which can be used in restoration. This may come from the fact that grains or dusts which resulted in scratch did not completely remove the film layers. After film-to-tape and A-D transformation, the information carried by the remained layers is too little to be seen, which is the reason why scratch looks dark or light.

Based on the analysis above, we can simplify the expression of histogram with some key features because of the invariability of shape.

$$F_n(\mathbf{H}) = \begin{pmatrix} h_{1n} \\ h_{Kn} \\ p_n \end{pmatrix}, \tilde{F}_n(\mathbf{H}) = \begin{pmatrix} \tilde{h}_{1n} \\ \tilde{h}_{Kn} \\ \tilde{p}_n \end{pmatrix}, n = 1, ..., N \qquad (2)$$

where $\tilde{F}_n(\mathbf{H})$ represents the key features of $\tilde{\mathbf{H}}_{\mathbf{n}}$, and $F_n(\mathbf{H})$ stands for the key features of $\mathbf{H}_{\mathbf{n}}$. h_{1n} and h_{Kn} can be recognized as lower edge and higher edge of nth column's histogram, p_n is the position of histogram peak.$\tilde{h}_{1n}, \tilde{h}_{Kn}, \tilde{p}_n$ are the degraded ones.

For each $n \in [1, N]$, $\exists \alpha_n, \beta_n$ that

$$\tilde{F}_n(\mathbf{H}) = \alpha_n F_n(\mathbf{H}) + \beta_n, n = 1, ..., N \tag{3}$$

where $0 < \alpha_n \le 1$, $\beta_n > 0$. In this equation, α indicates the degraded level of scratch area while β reflect whether the line scratch is dark or light. If the α_n is far less than 1, the corresponding image column will look darker or lighter than the surround. If no defect lies on nth column, α_n will be equal to 1 and β_n be 0. From lots of samples of degraded film image, we find that dark scratches' histograms shrink to lower side while light scratches' shrink to the higher side.

From Fig-1(c), we can find that the line scratch's histogram is compressed with shape remained. The abberation of scratch line histogram gives us a new method to detect line scratch. Since $F(\mathbf{H})$ cannot be acquired in practice, we use local average $\overline{F}(\mathbf{H})$ instead.

Solve the equation (3),

$$\alpha_n = \frac{\tilde{h}_{Kn} - \tilde{h}_{1n}}{\overline{h}_{Kn} - \overline{h}_{1n}}, \beta_n = \tilde{h}_{1n} - \overline{h}_{1n} \frac{\tilde{h}_{Kn} - \tilde{h}_{1n}}{\overline{h}_{Kn} - \overline{h}_{1n}}, n = 1, ..., N \tag{4}$$

For column histogram sequence $\tilde{\mathbf{H}}_{1,...,\mathbf{N}}$, α is a vector as $\boldsymbol{\alpha} = \{\alpha_1, ..., \alpha_N\}$.

3   Proposed Algorithm of Scratch Detection

According to $\boldsymbol{\alpha}$, we are able to locate line scratches after several steps of constraints and criterion.

At first, for each column histogram $\tilde{\mathbf{H}}_{\mathbf{n}}$, find the lowest and highest intensity level whose probability value is non-zero. But taking noise and other defects into consideration, we usually set a threshold little higher than zero in practice. Then compute the local average $\overline{h_1}$ and $\overline{h_K}$. According to (4), $\boldsymbol{\alpha}$ can be figured out.

The second step contains width selection and symmetry selection. Width selection is to select local minima with adjacent maxima's distance in the range of 3 to 10 pixels. Symmetry selection requires the local minima locates at the approximate center of a scratch. See Fig-2(b), c is a candidate local minima and b_1, b_2 are the adjacent local maxima whose α must not be less than one. b_1 and b_2 are viewed as the scratch edges in order to get the width. A potential scratch should satisfy the width and symmetric shape constraints that $c \in [\frac{2b_1 + b_2}{3}, \frac{b_1 + 2b_2}{3}]$.

In the third step, the well known *Weber's Law* is employed, which helps us determine whether a possible scratch can be perceivable on the image. In other word we can determine the best threshold to detect real scratches, applying the *Weber's law*. According to *Weber's law* [11], an object of luminance f_0 is noticeable on a surround of luminance f_s if $\frac{|f_s - f_0|}{f_0} \ge 0.02$. In our case, α is the proportion of degraded intensity level to un-degraded intensity level which is approximately equal to surround intensity level. For a candidate scratch, weber's law is applied as follows:

$$\int_{b_1}^{b_2} \alpha_n dn \le 0.98(b_2 - b_1) \tag{5}$$

Besides employing *Weber's Law* to determine local threshold, we still have a global threshold α_{th}, where α_{th} is the average of all minima of α. For a candidate scratch, its center degrade rate α_c should less than the global threshold.

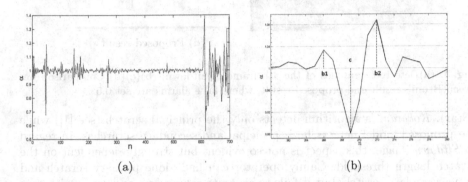

(a)   (b)

Fig. 2. (a)α of Star. Red points are candidate position of scratches, green ones are final results. (b)Detail of α surrounding a scratch. c is the center of scratch, b_1 and b_2 are boundaries.

4   Experimental Results

We have tested proposed algorithm on many frames. In this section, we will show the results on 4 typical images: *Sitdown, Star, Knight* and *Worker's Love.*(Fig-3)

Comparison of our result with some other spatial detection algorithms is shown in Table-2. It is evident that our algorithm has a better performance in decreasing the false detect rate, although it sacrifice some effectiveness. *Kokaram* 's technique loses secondary scratches because of the minimum length threshold for a detectable scratch. The same drawback is in [8], [9]. For example in

Table 2. Comparison Between State of Art Model And The Proposed One. We Outline That True Scratches Are The Ones Perceived By A Sample Of 10 Observers. The Number Of False Alarms Has Been Put In Brackets.

	Sitdown	Star	Knight	Worker's Love
Ground Truth	17	18	1	33
Kokaram's Model	9(1)	1	1	1
Bruni's Model	8(4)	13(8)	1	21(4)
Canny Operator	6(2)	2	1	3
Proposed	10	6	1	18

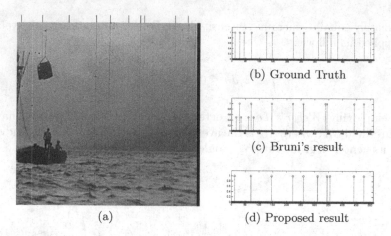

(a)

(b) Ground Truth

(c) Bruni's result

(d) Proposed result

Fig. 3. (a)Detected scratches of the 8th frame of Sitdown; (b)(c)(d) Comparison between Bruni's result and proposed result, where false alarms are set 0.5

(Star), *Kokaram* 's algorithm detects only the principal scratch (see [1]) while the proposed model detects both principal and secondary scratches. In regard to *Sitdown* image, this aspect is not so evident but strongly dependent on the scratch length threshold. Canny operator can find alone primary scratch and some secondary scratch, but it fails to separate some edges and ropes with true line scratches. *V.Bruni*'s model [7]is most effective because it detects most perceivable scratches, however it results in many false alarms. Her model has been widely used for long time but it also detects many invisible "scratches". With such false detection, real image information will be lost after scratch removal algorithm.

Inspired by *V.Bruni*'s generalized model, proposed algorithm employs *Weber's Law* to strengthen effectiveness. Besides, width selection and symmetry selection help to avoid false alarm. And experimental results also proved that these selection succeeded to lower the false rate. Our algorithm is not so sensitive to some not-alone secondary scratch. For secondary scratch, our basic assumption that histogram of scratch column holds its shape might not be completely correct. Note that, (3) is correct only for part of the histogram caused by the fact that secondary scratches do not lie on most part of image, thus making column histogram not maintain its shape. In such cases, a band-filter might be used in order to keep the model correct by swapping the un-degraded part.

Finally, in regard to the computational effort, complexity of computing column histogram is $O(MN)$ and α computation costs $O(256N)$, for 8-bit image. We notice that column histogram's computation is the most time-consuming part. Due to column's independency of each other, this part can be accelerated by parallel algorithm. Computing α takes less time than histogram computation. In average, the complexity is about $O(N)$. The rest operations of proposed algorithm take $O(N)$ because our detector completely performs on 1-D signal α vector, which can save lots of time. *Kokaram* 's technique complexity is $O(MNk) + O(N^2k^2)$ where k is the size of the accumulator array used in

Fig. 4. Some experiment results. (a) Sitdown, (b) Knight, (c) Star (d) Worker's Love.
Lines on top row indicate the detection results.

the Hough Transform[7]. *V.Bruni*'s algorithm complexity is $O(MN) + O(N)$.
In terms of computation complexity, proposed algorithm takes same time as
V.Bruni's model but much faster than *Kokaram* 's technique and other spatial
algorithms like OWE and Canny operator.

5   Conclusion

We have proposed a new degradation model of column histogram along with
a spatial scratch detection algorithm. The proposed model recognizes scratch
degradation as histogram's compression. The new algorithm decreases false retrieval rate, while maintaining efficiency and rapidity. The degradation model of
scratch's histogram might also be used in scratch removal. Integration of image
enhancement methods and traditional region filling algorithms may be applied
to restore scratches in the future.

Acknowledgement. This paper was supported by NSFC (61025005, 60932006, 61001145), SRFDP (20090073110022), CPSF (20100480603), SPSF (11R21414200), 111 Project (B07022).

References

1. Kokaram, A.C.: Detection and removal of line scratches in degraded motion picture sequences. In: Proc. Signal Processing VIII, September 5-8, vol. 1 (1996)
2. Kokaram, A.C.: Motion Picture Restoration: Digital Algorithms for Artifact Suppression in Degraded Motion Picture Film and Video. Springer, Berlin (1998)
3. http://www.mee.tcd.ie/~ack/cd/lines/lines.htm
4. Joyeux, L., Buisson, O., Besserer, B., Boukir, S.: Detection and removal of line scratches in motion picture films. In: Proc. CVPR 1999, Fort Collins, CO (1999)
5. Joyeux, L., Boukir, S., Besserer, B.: Film line scratch removal using kalman filtering and bayesian restoration. In: Proc. WACV 2000, Palm Springs, CA (2000)
6. Schallauer, P., Pinz, A., Haas, W.: Automatic restoration algorithms for 35 mm film. VIDERE: J. Comput. Vis. Res 1(3) (1999)
7. Bruni, V., Vitulano, D.: A Generalized Model for Scratch Detection. IEEE Transactions on Image Processing 13 (2004)
8. Xu, J., Zhai, G.: An OWE-based Algorithm for Line Scratches Restoration in Old Movies. In: ISCAS 2007 (2007)
9. Zeng, Q., Ding, Y.: Scratch Line Detection and Restoration Based on Canny Operator. In: Asia-Pacific Conference on Information Processing 2009 (2009)
10. Kim, K.-T., Kim, E.Y.: Automatic Film Line Scratch Removal System based on Spatial Information. In: ISCE 2007, Irving, TX (2007)
11. Jain, A.K.: Fundamentals of Digital Signal Processing. Prentice-Hall, Englewood Cliffs (1989)

An Efficient Isolation Method for Contextual Object Detection

Yukun Zhu, Jun Zhu, and Rui Zhang

Insititute of Image Communication and Information Processing
Shanghai Jiao Tong University
{xiphilute,junnyzhu,zhang_rui}@sjtu.edu.cn

Abstract. Recent object detection systems utilize contextual information to boost recognition performance. A state-of-the-art contextual object detection method [7] adopts a structural model with greedy forward search inference algorithm. In this paper, we propose an isolation method for contextual object detection. It decomposes a complicated structural learning problem into several "local" ones, which can be efficiently solved by standard SVMs, to boost the speed of training and inference processes. Moreover, such isolation can readily deal with additional real-valued features to further improve the performance. The experimental results on PASCAL VOC 2007 dataset demonstrate the superiority of our method relative to other state-of-the-art ones both in computational cost and detection accuracy.

Keywords: contextual object detection, isolation, structural model, SSVM.

1   Introduction

In literatures of object detection, most methods extract appearance features (e.g., HOG [2]), train a local model [2][3][4] with labeled bounding-boxes, and perform sliding-window detection process over multiple scale and positions for testing images. However, for this challenge task, using only local visual cues tends to be failure, and a host of works [5][6][7] suggest exploiting contextual information between object detections to further improve the performance.For example, a tree-based model, which automatically builds up the contextual relationship within related classes [5], and [6], where the results of image classification are used as context. Meanwhile, [7] is also a practical approach, where a fixed set of spatial types are defined with respect to the category and relative position of detection windows.

[7] shows a state-of-the-art performance in VOC 2007 dataset. In this scenario, a structural model is adopted to exploit the contextual information through pair-wise spatial layout features.Although the structural model in [7] can effectively utilize context information, straightforward inference might be intractable due to an exponentially large solution space would be considered.The training of structural model adopts StructuralSVM (SSVM) [8][9], it could also become slow when large qualities of samples are presented. In practice, some approximate method (e.g. greedy

W. Zhang et al. (Eds.): IFTC 2012, CCIS 331, pp. 205–211, 2012.

forward search [7] or loopy belief propagation) is introduced to achieve tractable inference.However, the greedy forward search method can only find a local optimum solution in general, and bad initialization tends to lead it to some unexpected results. Besides, the structural model itself might also place some constraintson the usage with more flexible form of spatial features.

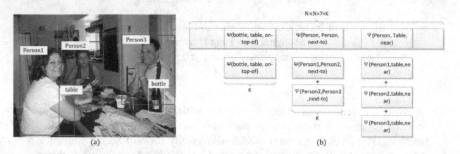

Fig. 1. (a) Detection windows in a sample image; (b) The structure of spatial feature. Note that the length of total feature is N×N×7×K. For each triplet, the feature vector is of length K.

In this paper, we develop an isolation method to simplify the problem into many sub problems based on certain estimation of spatial feature. With proper prior information, such estimation can be close to its real value. In addition, such isolation method can also render a higher flexibility in the representational forms of spatial feature, thus more useful information can be considered. We experiment the proposed methods by VOC 2007 dataset, and demonstrate its superiority in computational cost and detection performance relative to state-of-the-art object detection scheme [7].The contributions of this paper are summarized as follows: 1) we propose an efficient isolation method on multi-class object detection, which provides availability to consider more flexible real-valued features of context information; 2) It can achieve state-of-the-art performancewith standard SVMsas on VOC 2007 dataset.

The rest of the paper is organized as follows: Section 2 sets up the structural model to represent the spatial contexts, and the isolation method is proposed in Section 3. Corresponding learning method is discussed in Section 4 and experimental results are shown in Section 5. Finally, we conclude this paper in Section 6.

2   Model

Assuming there are$N$ candidate object classes to be detected, as in [7], we first train a local detector for each class and detect any potential object instances (with detection windows) for a given image. Thus, an image could be represented as a set of scored detection windows $X = \{x_1, x_2, \ldots \ldots x_M\}$, where each detection window $x_i$is represented by its location d_i, class labelc_i and confidence score s_i output by corresponding local detector. Accordingly, there is a label set for this image, denoted by$Y = \{y_1, y_2, \ldots \ldots, y_M\}$, where $y_i$represents the class label of x_i. As in [7], we consider a window to be one foreground class or background, namely $y_i \in \{0, c_i\}$. We use 0 to denote the background class.Given X and Y , the total score of labeling Yfor image X is computed as:

$$S(X,Y) = \omega_s \underset{i,j \neq i}{\mathfrak{F}} \left[\varphi(y_i, y_j, x_i, x_j) \right] + \omega_a \sum_i \phi(x_i, y_i) \tag{1}$$

where for every $0 < i \leq M$, $\varphi(y_i, y_j, x_i, x_j)$represents the spatial feature between the ith window x_i, which is called current window and another windowx_j, called reference window. In our model, $\varphi(y_i, y_j, x_i, x_j)$ is a kind of mapping from the triple$\{y_i, y_j, t(x_i, x_j)\}$ to a feature vector of length K, where $t(x_i, x_j)$ is the spatial type between x_i and x_j. In this paper, we adopt 7 spatial types as in [7], including above, below, on top of, next-to, near, far and overlap.$\mathfrak{F}$represents a pooling operation forgathering spatial features of all potential windows to form an unified feature descriptor for the image.E.g., it can be obtained by summation or maximization over those features.$\phi(x_i, y_i)$ represents a feature vector composed of the detection scores given by local model. In this paper, we use a linear model to calculate the final score, thus a weight vector ω_s is used to represent the weight for spatial relationship, while ω_a for local part.

3 Inference

Our target is to find the best labeling Y^* of image X. However, the learning of weight vector ω_s andω_a, as well as the inference of $\text{argmax}_Y S(X,Y)$ are generally intractable due to an exponential number of states need to be considered. To achieve tractable inference, [7] proposed an approximate greedy forward search algorithm, which iterativelysearches and instances the non-instancedwindow with maximum gain based on former iterations.Another problem is the operation $\mathfrak{F}$. Since each triplewill be mapped into a feature vector of length K, a common practice of $\mathfrak{F}$ is to sum the vector of every combination of current windowclass, reference window class and spatial type. See Fig.1.(b) as an example. However, this operation is not applicable to some features such as aspect ratio and overlap percentage.Under this constraint, we choose K=1 and the vector will be 1 if $y_i \cdot y_j \neq 0$, and the vector will be 0 otherwise.

In this paper, wepropose a method to isolatethose detection windows by estimating the label values of reference windows. For a current window x_i, we substitute the label of its each reference window y_j by $\tilde{y}_j$. With the sum pooling operation, the score of a solution Y could be obtainedas follows:

$$\begin{aligned} \tilde{S}(X,Y) &= \omega_s \sum_{i \leq M} \sum_{j \neq i} \varphi(y_i, y_j, x_i, x_j | y_j = \tilde{y}_j) + \omega_a \sum_{0 < i \leq M} \phi(x_i, y_i) \\ &= \sum_{i \leq M} [\omega_s, \omega_a] \left[\sum_{j \neq i} \varphi(y_i, y_j, x_i, x_j | y_j = \tilde{y}_j), \phi(x_i, y_i) \right]' \end{aligned} \tag{2}$$

Thus the original structured inference problem $\arg \max_Y S(X,Y)$ can be transformed to M separated sub-problems, which can be easily solved by matrix multiplication. Note that each sub-problem is isolated with others, and the value of y_i could be either

0 or y_i. If $\tilde{y}_j = y_j$, the solution $\text{argmax}_Y \tilde{S}(X, Y)$ will be exactly that of $\text{argmax}_Y S(X, Y)$. Meanwhile, since $\varphi(y_i, y_j, x_i, x_j)$ sums up the value of the same triples, we can separate i into N groups by its category, thus for each category, the length of spatial feature is N×7×K. In this scenario, each sub-problem can be described as equation(3).

Now we will show how to find a proper estimation of y_j without calculating the value

$$s(x_i, y_i) = \sum_{j \neq i} \omega_{s,c_i} \varphi(y_i, y_j, x_i, x_j | y_j = \tilde{y}_j) + \omega_{a,c_i} \phi(x_i, y_i) \tag{3}$$

of y_j itself. A thresholding-based method can be used to get an approximate value $\tilde{y}_j$ by $\{y_j = c_j | s_j > thr\}$, where thr is thevalue of threshold. A relative smaller threshold could allow for more contextual information, while it has the risk of introducing more noises. For the case that local models provide more accurate detection results over the threshold, our method will obtain a solution closer to the optimal labeling Y.

Another method based on max pooling is caused by the structure of spatial feature. In the thresholding-based method, we will sum the spatial feature for all triples of the same value. But in the max-pooling-based method, for all triples with the same value, we only consider the one with maximum value of s_j. Besides the efficiency of the proposed isolation method, it can also facilitate the usage of more flexible features through the maximization operation. Note that to each sub problem, the spatial feature regarding the class of current window, the class of reference window and the spatial type, will consider only one triplet. Thus, some other spatial context features, such as the percentage of overlapping degree and the relative aspect ratio between detection windows, can be appropriately considered by our model. Meanwhile, those context features help to improve detection performance in the end.

4   Learning

For both the thresholding-based method and maximization-based method, the learning problem can be formulated as follows:

$$\underset{w,\varepsilon}{argmin} \frac{1}{2} |\omega|^2 + C \sum_{i=1}^{n} \varepsilon_i \tag{3}$$

$$s.t. \ sgn(y_i, y_i^{\#})(\omega \cdot F_i') \geq 1 - \varepsilon_i$$

where $\omega = [\omega_{s,c}, \omega_{a,c}]$ in (3) and $F_i = \left[\sum \varphi\left(y_i, y_j, x_i, x_j | y_j = \tilde{y}_j\right), \phi(d_i, y_i) \right]$. $sgn(y_i, y_i^{\#})$ is the sign function which takes +1 ify_i equals to the groundtruth value$y_i^{\#}$ and -1 otherwise. We observe that it is a standard linear SVM problem [10], which can be solved by any off-the-shelf SVM implementation in practice.

5   Result

We evaluate our method on VOC 2007 dataset. The dataset contains 5000 images for training and validation, while 5000 images for testing. There are 20 object classes to be considered in total. The name for each class is illustrated in Table 1. In this paper, we consider the ordinary objects and those labeled with 'truncated'. The dataset is quite challenging due to that the objects are vary in size, pose, illumination, etc. Similar as object detection literatures [3][4][7], we adopt average precision (AP) as the performance measurement for detection results.

We use deformable, part-based model [4] to train the local model for the objects in the image. This local model produces state-of-the-art result in the VOC 2007 dataset. Moreover, we use the public available code for contextual model in [7] as a baseline.

For the thresholding-based method, the length of spatial feature is N×7. We sum the feature vector of triples with the same current window class, reference window class and spatial type, and then join them together. In terms of max-pooling-based method, we first build a N×7 spatial feature by maximization, then added the relative aspect ratio and overlap percentage between reference window and current window, together with the confidence of reference window. Thus a feature with length of N×7×4 is used. The model for each class is trained by LibSVM with RBF kernel [10]. With additional information, our max-pooling-based method achieves the best performance over all classes. The per-class APis shown in Table 1. More detailed comparisons of quantitative and qualitative resultsare shown in Fig.3.

Table 1. AP scores for each class on VOC 2007 dataset.The result of local detector [4] is shown inthe first row, while the baseline [7] is in the second row. Our max-pooling-basedisolation method with additional information is shown in 3rd row, and it is clear to see the improvements of detection results for most object classes.

Class	aeroplane	bicycle	bird	boat	bottle	bus	car	cat	chair	cow
[4]	0.621	0.831	0.067	0.436	0.568	0.732	0.711	0.289	0.329	0.522
[7]	0.616	0.823	0.091	**0.491**	0.606	0.687	0.737	0.318	0.343	**0.584**
Isolation	**0.640**	**0.860**	**0.100**	0.412	**0.625**	**0.691**	**0.751**	**0.356**	**0.346**	0.542

Class	diningtable	dog	horse	motorbike	person	pottedplant	sheep	sofa	train	tvmonitor
[4]	0.561	0.072	0.745	0.690	0.586	0.150	**0.458**	0.674	0.608	0.722
[7]	**0.588**	0.088	0.755	0.720	0.584	0.135	0.405	**0.693**	0.619	**0.744**
Isolation	0.575	**0.127**	**0.760**	**0.721**	**0.625**	**0.159**	0.434	0.621	**0.623**	0.730

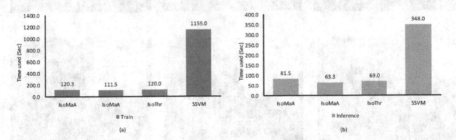

Fig. 2. (a) The comparison of time used for training in *SSVM*[7], our thresholding-based method *IsoThr*, our max-pooling-based method with/without additional information *IsoMa* and *IsoMaA*;(b) Time used for inference in *SSVM*, *IsoThr*, *IsoMa* and *IsoMaA*. We can see our method takes much less run-timethan that of [7].

From Table 1, we can observe significant gain in AP for most classes when using the isolation method with additional spatial information. The computational complexity of our methods is comparatively lower, and even with additional information, it is still faster than applying SSVM[7] to optimize the structural model. With a computer of dual-core 2.53GHz CPU and 4GB memory, the average time for training and inference stages are shown in Fig 2.

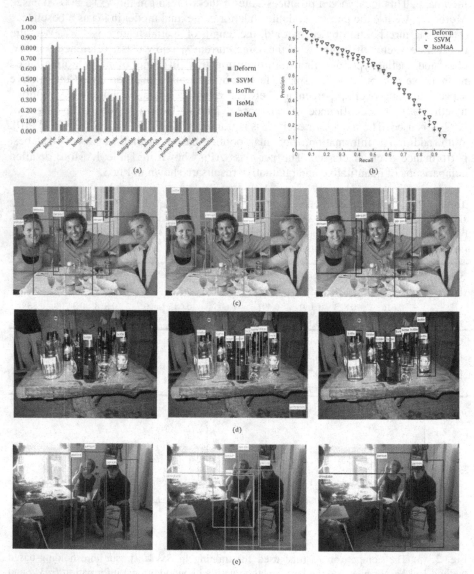

Fig. 3.(a) The comparison of AP for *deform*[4], *SSVM*[7] and our thresholding-based method *IsoThr*, max-pooling-based method with/without additional information *IsoMa* and *IsoMaA*;(b) PR curve for object class person; (c)(d)(e) detection result by [4], [7] and our method *IsoMaA*

6   Conclusion

In this paper, we present a novel isolation method present a novel isolation method spatial context relationship for multi-class object detection. Based on prior assumption about the contextual relationship, it can effectively reduce the computational complexity compared to the structural-SVM-based methods in literature. Besides, it can also readily use more spatial features to improve detection performance further.

Acknowledgement. This work is supported by NSFC (61071155) and STCSM (12DZ2272600).

References

1. Everingham, M., Van Gool, L., Williams, C.K.I., Winn, J., Zisserman, A.: The pascal visual object classes (voc) challenge. International Journal of Computer Vision 88 (2010)
2. Dalal, N., Triggs, B.: Histograms of oriented gradients for human detection. In: CVPR (2005)
3. Felzenszwalb, P., McAllester, D., Ramanan, D.: A discriminatively trained, multi-scale, deformable part model. In: CVPR (2008)
4. Felzenszwalb, P., Girshick, R., McAllester, D., Ramanan, D.: Object detection with discriminatively trained part-based models. Pattern Analysis and Machine Intelligence (2010)
5. Choi, M.J., Torralba, A., Willsky, A.: A tree-based context model for object recognition. Pattern Analysis and Machine Intelligence (2012)
6. Song, Z., Chen, Q., Huang, Z., Hua, Y., Yan, S.: Contextualizing object detection and classification. In: Computer Vision and Pattern Recognition (2011)
7. Desai, C., Ramanan, D., Fowlkes, C.: Discriminative models for multi-class object layout. In: IEEE 12th International Conference on Computer Vision (2009)
8. Finley, T., Joachims, T.: Training structural svms when exact inference is intractable. In: Proceedings of the 25th International Conference on Machine Learning (2008)
9. Joachims, T., Finley, T., Yu, C.: Cutting-plane training of structural svms. Machine Learning 77 (2009)
10. Chang, C.C., Lin, C.J.: LIBSVM: a library for support vector machines. ACM Transactions on Intelligent Systems and Technology (2011)

A Novel and Adaptive Method for Image Search Reranking

Hong Lu*, Guobao Jiang, Zhuohong Cai, and Xiangyang Xue

Shanghai Key Lab of Intelligent Information Processing
School of Computer Science
Fudan University, Shanghai, China
honglu@fudan.edu.cn

Abstract. In this paper, we propose a novel and adaptive method for image search reranking. We firstly evaluate different visual features based on the results of image classification on object and scene separately. And visual features are chosen adaptively to rerank the initial image search result. For a given query, it can be classified into either object or scene using the trained classifier on text features. Then, low-level visual features are adaptively selected and fused for image search reranking. Experimental results on large scale image dataset of WebQueries demonstrate the efficacy of the proposed method.

Keywords: Image search reranking, adaptive feature selection and fusion, object and scene.

1 Introduction

As more and more images with user free tags are appearing on the Internet, it is necessary to help a user to effectively obtain the real relevant images when the user submit a query. Most image search engines normally return images for one query based on associated texts. And, the search results may contains some unrelated images. So, many image reranking methods based on visual features occur in recent years, which aims to improve the image search result [1].

There are some different characteristics between object and scene on observation. For object, Alexe *et al.* [2] argue that any object has at least one of three distinctive characteristics: (a) a well-defined closed boundary in space; (b) a different appearance from their surroundings; (c) sometimes it is unique within the image and stands out as salient. And in [3,4], some image properties such as openness, expansion, ruggedness, verticalness, which is to describe scene content, are computed and used. It can be found that object and scene perception has different processes, different features or different feature fusion. So, in this paper, we choose different features to rerank the initial search result for object and scene.

Before use low-level visual features for reranking, we evaluate the performance of different visual features. In this paper, the features we considered include

---

* Corresponding author.

W. Zhang et al. (Eds.): IFTC 2012, CCIS 331, pp. 212–218, 2012.

color features: CAC (color auto-correlogram), CCV (color coherence vector), CLD (color layout descriptor), CSD (color structure descriptor), SCD (scalable color descriptor), texture features: EHD (edge histogram descriptor), HT (homogeneous texture) [5], and other features: SIFT (Scale invariant feature transform) [6], HoG (Histograms of oriented gradients) [7], GIST [3]. We choose the optimal feature and determine the feature fusion method from each feature subset based on classification results for reranking.

For a given query, it is classified into either object or scene using the trained classifier on textual features. And low-level visual features are adaptively selected and fused for reranking. Fig. 1 shows the flowchart of our proposed reranking method.

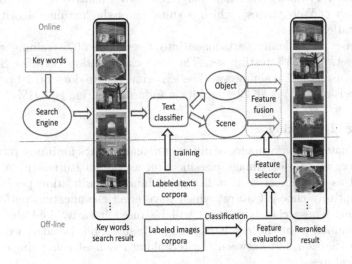

Fig. 1. Proposed re-ranking model based on adaptive feature selection and fusion

The rest of the paper is organized as follows. In section 2, we discuss our proposed model. Experimental results and some discussions on image search reranking are given in Section 3. And we conclude our work in Section 4.

2 Adaptive Re-ranking Model

In this section, we describe the proposed reranking model which is illustrated in Fig. 1. It includes two parts: off-line model training and online reranking.

During off-line stage, the text classifier is trained using the textual features of images. Meanwhile, visual features are evaluated from the results of image classification on object or scene.

During the online phase, the user submits a query to the search engine, and then the query will be automatically classified into either object or scene using the trained classifier. Next, the search engine will select adaptive visual features based on off-line feature evaluation results, and then the search engine reranks the search results based on the selected visual features and the fused features. Finally, the search engine returns the reranking results to the users.

2.1 Text Classification

In order to automatically classify the query into either object or scene, we need to train a text classifier off-line. In this work, we adopt query-relative textual features for text classification: the concept, the text surrounding the image, the web page's title, the image's alternative text [8]. Those information are closely related to query and can be easily obtained.

Prior to the text classification, we extract BoW (bag of words) of textual feature from every document (each image refers to a relative textual document in the dataset of WebQueries), which is suitable for the learning algorithm and the classification task.

The dataset is randomly partitioned into 3 sets, i.e., 50% training set, 25% validation set, and 25% testing set. The text classification classifier SVM1 is modeled by using 50% training set. The experiments are done on 10 runs. The average precision (AP) is 86.23% and its standard deviation is 3.41%.

2.2 Image Reranking

How to evaluate the performance of different visual features for image reranking? In this work, we consider image classification as the measurement. A feature is regarded as discriminative if it has good image classification performance. So, we adaptively choose features which have good classification performance for reranking. Those chosen features will be fused linearly. And the weights are also obtained from the result of image classification. Besides, we make a comparison (Section 3.2) between the reranking result of using single feature and fused features.

As indicate in [1], most image search engines, such as Google, Yahoo, Bing, have good performance at the top several images. So, in this paper, we assume that the top 5 images which are returned by a specific engine for a query are query-relative images (QRIs). These images are represented as the exemplar [9].

Fig. 2 shows how to calculate the distance between the n-th image and the exemplar using the m-th feature. Finally, the initial search results are reranked based on the score of images, which is defined as follows.

$$Score_n = \frac{1}{\sum_{m=1}^{M} w_m d_{mn}} \tag{1}$$

where, d_{mn} represents the distance between the n-th image and the exemplar using the m-th feature, w_m the weight of the m-th feature, M the number of fused features. w_m is determined from the classification results, which is obtained as follows.

$$w_m = \frac{mAP_m}{\sum_{i=1}^{M} mAP_i} \tag{2}$$

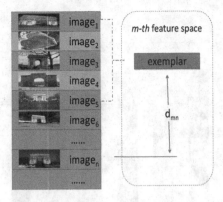

Fig. 2. The distance between the n-th image and the exemplar using the m-th feature

where mAP_i means the mean average precision of classification for object or scene using the i-th feature and M represents the number of fused features.

3 Experimental Results and Analysis

In this section, we evaluate the proposed adaptive method for image reranking. And, we use a public dataset so that we can easily make a comparison of our proposed method with previous related work such as [8].

3.1 Feature Evaluation and Selection

We conduct our experiments on WebQueries[1], which was first introduced in [8]. It contains 71,478 images retrieved from a web search engine using 353 different web queries. For each query, the dataset includes the original textual query, the top-ranked images found by the web search engine, and an annotation file for each image by human labeling. And for each query, $300 \sim 500$ images on the top of text queried ranking list are got for further reranking.

To illustrate detail evaluation and make comparison, we group concepts into several sets as follows [8].

- Low Precision (LP): 25 queries where the search engine performs worst, e.g. 'will smill', 'rugby pitch', 'bass guitar', 'mont blanc', 'jack black'.
- High Precision (HP): 25 queries where the search engine performs best, e.g. 'batman', 'aerial photography', 'shrek', 'pantheon rome', 'brazil flag'.
- Search Engine Poor (SEP): 25 queries where the search engine improves least over random ordering of the query set, e.g. 'clipart', 'cloud', 'flag', 'car'.
- Search Engine Good (SEG): 25 queries where the search engine improves most over random ordering of the query set, e.g. 'rugby pitch', 'tennis court', 'golf course', 'ben stiller', 'dustin hoffman'.

---

[1] http://lear.inrialpes.fr/pubs/2010/KAVJ10/

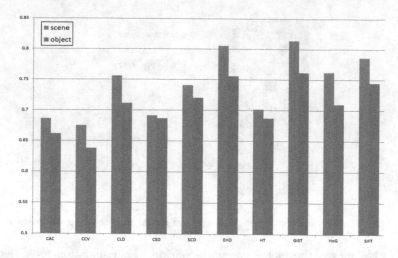

Fig. 3. The mean average precision (mAP) of classification results

Fig. 3 shows the results of classification which are used to measure the discriminability of visual features. It can be observed that SCD and CLD are the discriminative color features for object and scene, respectively. However, EHD is the discriminative texture feature for both object and scene. From this figure, we know which color feature and texture feature should be chosen for reranking. In order to specifically describe the reranking results, we group visual features into following two sets.

- Object Features (OFs): SCD, EHD, HoG, GIST, SIFT.
- Scene Features (SFs): CLD, EHD, HoG, GIST, SIFT.

According to our proposed reranking model (Fig. 1), we know that when users submit a new query to a specific search engine, the search engine will classify the query into either object or scene using the trained text classifier. Then, we choose OFs to re-rank the initial rank result for the class of object and SFs to re-rank the initial rank result for the class of scene.

3.2   Reranking Results

Table 1 shows the reranking results comparing with that of in [8]. From this table, it can be observed that as follows.

- Overall, our method obtians about 5.82% and 7.38% relative improvements compared with the text-based image search engine.
- Reranking result keeps consistent with the classification evaluation when using single feature. And the best performance on single feature is achieved when using the following features: CSD, SCD, EHD, HoG, GIST, SIFT.

- Adaptive feature selection and fusion (OFs and SFs) can achieve better performance than that of single feature'. The reason lies that the selected low-level visual features are relatively complementary.
- Although we use only visual features, our proposed method can obtain better or comparable reranking performance compared with [8].
- Overall, our method obtains about 5.82% (object) and 7.38% (scene) relative improvements compared with the text-based image search engine.

Table 1. Reranking results on WebQueries

mAP×100	Overall	LP	HP	SEP	SEG
Search engine (object/scene)	49.59/44.93	16.27/21.92	80.52/81.84	73.96/79.68	47.07/57.06
Best result (visual features only) [8]	64.9	24.1	91.0	71.9	58.4
Color feature:CAC (object/scene)	49.3/46.0	15.3/16.0	85.0/84.4	80.1/84.1	48.0/57.1
Color feature:CCV (object/scene)	49.2/46.8	14.8/16.3	85.3/82.6	77.3/83.6	51.1/56.9
Color feature:CLD (object/scene)	51.0/49.4	19.6/22.5	85.1/86.5	79.4/86.6	52.1/57.0
Color feature:CSD (object/scene)	**55.6**/49.6	18.3/**24.0**	87.5/83.0	79.4/83.3	55.7/52.7
Color feature:SCD (object/scene)	54.1/49.2	**21.2**/23.3	86.7/85.2	**83.7**/84.6	54.2/58.2
Texture feature:EHD (object/scene)	53.9/49.5	18.3/20.3	**88.0**/88.2	79.3/89.0	57.2/63.0
Texture feature:HT (object/scene)	51.8/48.6	17.4/21.7	85.6/85.3	79.5/84.7	53.3/64.9
HoG (object/scene)	49.3/49.2	17.3/19.6	84.9/89.0	76.5/89.0	55.6/**67.4**
GIST (object/scene)	52.7/**50.5**	18.2/22.5	85.8/**90.1**	76.8/**89.3**	**57.8**/64.8
SIFT (object/scene)	50.4/45.9	17.1/21.2	81.8/79.1	79.4/80.2	47.3/51.6
Feature fusion: (OFs/SFs)	**55.41**/**52.31**	19.14/**25.62**	87.11/**91.41**	81.45/**91.40**	53.30/59.49

4 Conclusions

In this paper, we propose a novel and adaptive method for image search reranking, which adaptively choose low-level visual features and fuse the selected features on object and scene. The selected features include color, texture, scene, and local features and are complementary. Experimental results on a public large-scale dataset of WebQueries show that our proposed method can obtain promising reranking results.

Acknowledgements. This work is supported in part by 973 Program (Project No. 2010CB327900), Natural Science Foundation of China (No. 61170094), Shanghai Committee of Science and Technology, China. Grant No. 11ZR1403400, and National High Technology Research and Development Program of China (No. 2011AA100701).

References

1. Yang, L., Hanjalic, A.: Supervised reranking for web image search. In: Proc. ACM Multimedia Conf., pp. 183–192 (2010)
2. Alexe, B., Deselaers, T., Ferrari, V.: What is an object? In: Proc. IEEE Int'l Conf. Computer Vision and Pattern Recognition, pp. 73–80 (2010)
3. Oliva, A., Torralba, A.: Modeling the shape of the scene: A holistic representation of the spatial envelop. Int'l J. Computer Vision 42(3), 145–175 (2001)

4. Oliva, A., Torralba, A.: Scene-Centered Description from Spatial Envelope Properties. In: Bülthoff, H.H., Lee, S.-W., Poggio, T., Wallraven, C. (eds.) BMCV 2002. LNCS, vol. 2525, pp. 263–272. Springer, Heidelberg (2002)
5. Text of ISO/IEC 15938-3/FCD Information Technology - Multimedia Content Description Interface - Part 3 Visual, Internation Organization for Standardization, vol. ISO/IEC JTC1/SC29/WG11/N4062 (March 2001)
6. Lowe, D.G.: Distinctive image features from scale-invariant keypoints. Int'l J. Computer Vision 60(2), 91–110 (2004)
7. Dalal, N., Triggs, B.: Histograms of oriented gradients for human detection. In: Proc. IEEE Int'l Conf. Computer Vision and Pattern Recognition, vol. 1, pp. 886–893 (2005)
8. Krapac, J., Allan, M., Verbeek, J., Jurie, F.: Improving web image search results using query-relative classifiers. In: Proc. IEEE Int'l Conf. Computer Vision and Pattern Recognition, pp. 1094–1101 (2010)
9. Chum, O., Zisserman, A.: An exemplar model for learning object classes. In: Proc. IEEE Int'l Conf. Computer Vision and Pattern Recognition, pp. 1–8 (2007)

Video Structured Description—Vitalization Techniques for the Surveillance Video Data

Lin Mei[1], Xuan Cai[1,2], Hongzhou Zhang[3], Chuanping Hu[1], and Li Qi[1]

[1] The 3rd Research Institute of Ministry of Public Security, Shanghai 201204, China
[2] School of Computer Science, Fudan University, Shanghai 201204, China
[3] Chinese People's Public Security, Beijing 100038, China
l_mei72@hotmail.com, caixuanfire@126.com, zhang.hongzhou@gmail.com,
cphu@vip.sina.com

Abstract. Video structured description was proposed for video surveillance system in this paper, and a prototype system was also introduced. As a novel video data vitalization technique, it employs knowledge model of certain surveillance scenario and image/video understanding to distill visual knowledge from video. Benefit from knowledge modeling, visual information distilled by the proposed method could be accessed by other information systems much easier than before. A technical overview was given and some key characteristics were also discussed.

Keywords: video structured description, vitalization, computer vision.

1 Introduction

As is well-known to all, the "Smart City" relies on the new information technology. By the methods of the internet and internet of things, we can monitor all kinds of components dynamically and get the important data. Analyzing and integrating those data, we have a better and deeper perception to our living environment and have a more complete and accurate regulation and control to our cities. It enables each component of our cities to work together more efficiently and conveniently such as economy, transportation, communications, education, environment, energy, security, management, service, culture, medical care and so on. Thus, all of these progresses will improve the quality of our lives and the whole environment of our city, and enhance the relationship between us and our cities.

The development of the "Smart City" requires more comprehensive data, more extensive communications, more harmonious human-computer interactions and more powerful intelligence. It also needs a unified framework of standards. Nowadays, it is undoubted that the data has become a type of strategic resources and the "Smart City" is a classical family of the dense data. It is a certain trend to the development of the "Smart City" to maximize the use of the data and mine the information the data obtained more intelligently. One of the methods of developing the "Smart City" is to establish a unified and comprehensive system of standards on the technology, build a framework which is the government-oriented, business-oriented and individual-oriented, and has a dynamic sensing

W. Zhang et al. (Eds.): IFTC 2012, CCIS 331, pp. 219–227, 2012.

network for collecting data and a dynamic data center and uses the technique of data vitalization. The video surveillance system is one of the most important components of the security and emergency systems of the "Smart City". It aims to build a system coving the whole city. This system can supply a platform with the unified command and cooperative work in both the peacetime and the wartime. It can integrate and share the information to guarantee the safety and harmony of the city. About 30 years ago, the video surveillance system was applied in many fields including security, industries and business in China. So far, the video surveillance network built by the public security departments is the most extensive and representative video surveillance network. It is always used to preserve society stable, fight against crime and serve for the people. Thus, all the governments at different levels attach great importance to the construction of the video surveillance systems. Recently, the police have carried out systematic and large-scale video surveillance networks sponsored by some policies such as the "Green City", the "3111" project and so on.

The video surveillance system has played an important role in the police affairs in the society managing, the case detecting, information collecting. It has become an essential technical method in the police. The Ministry of Public Security is going to build a national connected network of video surveillance system. However, there are still some difficulties and restrictions for the further applications of video surveillance system. Roughly, they contain the following aspects:

1. There is a contradiction between the mass redundant information and the weak ability of retrieving the useful information in the system. Even though we compress the video surveillance data, there is a lot of useless information. For example, a medium-sized city has about 30 million surveillance cameras. If a standard-definition video camera produces data 10MB/s after compression, then the video surveillance system will yield the data 3TB/s totally. Commonly, not only the data is redundant but also it takes much time to process the data. Facing the rich video data, we lack good automatic processing methods and the system's processing capacity is very limited. Therefore, so many people have to cost much time to watch and check the video once there are some abnormal events somewhere.

2. The isolated surveillance video data results in the difficulty of the integration and interaction the resource. First, the contradiction between the mass video data and the limited bandwidth of the data-sharing channels yields some hard problems. Secondly, there are difficulties to integrate the police information systems and interoperate the resource currently. After gathering and sharing information initially, it is an inevitable trend to integrate and interoperate the resource. It needs co-work and share in different information systems, i.e., interoperability. The interoperability requires that the systems can communicate with each other by the data formats, the communication protocols and the description interfaces. Then it results in the data vitalization in the heterogeneous networks. Moreover, the exchange of data among the systems leads to co-work semantically.

3. There is a contradiction between the mass data and the limited storage in the video surveillance system. The total storage of thousands of video surveillance systems will be extreme huge. It usually costs about 5-10 million RMB to build a typical video surveillance center, whose storage capacity attains on the PB level at least. All the same, this center maintains the video at most 30 days. Obviously, we have no idea to decide whether a video should be deleted or preserved. Thus, it does not satisfy the practical work of the police.

4. There is no accurate and efficient method to retrieve the specific video. Thus, we have to employ many people to check all the videos. This approach is not only brute-force and time-consuming but also cannot guarantee the accuracy of the retrieval.

5. There is no unified standard and criterion for the applications of video surveillance in the police. Naturally, it cannot guide the system of the video surveillance well.

2 Related Work

For the private video network of the MPS, the application requirement of the police is that the video surveillance system can be regarded as an information resource and integrate with other information resource about the police affairs to supply the information for the practical work of the police.

To satisfy the above requirements, we have to make a breakthrough in many techniques including modeling and administrating the knowledge on the application of the surveillance, understanding and describing the surveillance video, storing the video and the corresponding description data, and the creating the software environment [15] based on SOAService-Oriented Architectureby the technique of the semantic Internet. In other words, the techniques involved in the construction of the sensing system of semantic contains machine vision [4, 5], image understanding [10, 11, 20], Semantic Web, software services, the development of the special equipment.

The techniques of machine vision [7-9, 24, 18] and images understanding [26, 3, 6, 23, 13] are very significant to anti-terrorism and domestic safety. Since the 11/9 disaster especially, the intelligent technique of the surveillance video understanding [16, 1, 25] has become a hot research topic. Many governments have investigated so much in many aspects including the policy, legislation, economy and applications. It has promoted the understanding technique of intelligent video surveillance. Now, the research of these techniques has become a national security strategy. The UK and USA have begun to the research work and achieved many advanced progresses. For instance, the Defense Advanced Research Projects Agency (DARPA) of USA has funded or initiated a number of related projects such as AVS project (Airborne Video Surveillance, 1998-2002), which mainly addressed on how to register, analyze and detect the stationary or moving objects accurately, and how to monitor the multiple objects simultaneously and the events in the different space.

The program HID (Human Identification at a Distance, 2000) focused on long-range human detection, classification and identification using multi-mode control techniques. Then it can enhance the protection of the sensitive environment. The program ADVISOR (Annotated Digital Video for Intelligent Surveillance and Optimized Retrieval) in the UK can estimate the density and movement of the population of the metro, analyze the behaviors of persons or groups and predict the potential dangers according to the video data. Now, some companies such as IBM, Microsoft are introducing the technique of the gesture recognition into the video surveillance in the metro station. It can tell us some abnormal events such as overcrowding, fighting, and leaving the unknown bags.

The technique of the semantic web is one of the hot research topics in the next generation of Internet. Although we have started the research on the Semantic Web in recent years, there are few theoretical study and applications of the semantic web. Most current jobs neglect the architectures, methods, principles and strategies on the Semantic Web. Thus, there is less study on constructing ontology. The concept of the Semantic Web is proposed by Berners-Lee, who is the chairman of the World Wide Web Consortium (W3C) in 1998. In his view, the Semantic Web is not independent web but an extension of the current web in which the information is well-defined and convenient to cooperate between human and machines. Moreover, he also presented a road map for building the Semantic Web. In this architecture, three core techniques are involved in on the Semantic Web, i.e. XML (eXtensible Markup Language), Resource Description Framework RDF (Resource Description Framework) and body (Ontology).

3   Video Structured Description

The technique of video structured description addresses generating the text on the surveillance video understood by both human and computer by the information methods such as space-time segmentation, feature extraction and objects recognition and so on. The technique of data vitalization [2] is one of the key techniques in the "Smart City". It describes the process of abstracting disparate data sources (databases, applications, file repositories, websites, data services vendors, etc.) through a single data access layer which may be any of several data access mechanisms. This abstraction enables data access clients to target a single data access layer, serialization, format, structure, etc., rather than making each client tool handle multiples of any or all of these.

Since there are different accesses to data of the city from the dimensions, sources to types, the traditional organizing and managing techniques of the data cannot smooth the new problems. It is necessary to describe the correlation information implied by the original data efficiently. Thus, we need a description language of the heterogeneous data. Based on a unified and comprehensive description language for the heterogeneous data and the other related data, we will construct a multi-granularity mapping from the underlying features of the massive heterogeneous data to the high-level semantics of the cross-media data. This helps to form a more complete understanding and cognitive methodology.

The data on "Smart City" collected contains the descriptions of the content and semantic knowledge. Although the information of data has been used fully, the related information is often ignored. We need the technique of semantics perception of the mass data to recognize, reconstruct and manage semantic knowledge. Since the new data is constantly changing, the new semantic relationships must be created, too.

3.1 Video Understanding for the Applications of Police Affairs

In this project, we will aim at solving the key problem which concerns the process of the video data, extraction of the information and the representation of the content of the surveillance video. As is shown in Figure 1, our project follows the main idea and the description model of the video structured description, propose the advanced algorithm for creating the abstract of the surveillance video, recognizing characters and the types of the vehicles, understanding the behaviors of the monitored objects and scenes in the applications of the police. Then it is able to improve the practicality, reliability and efficiency of the surveillance video furthermore. We will study how to extract the features of the people, vehicles, objects, behaviors, events and get the corresponding concepts. Finally, we use the results obtained to form the ontology on the knowledge of the police affairs.

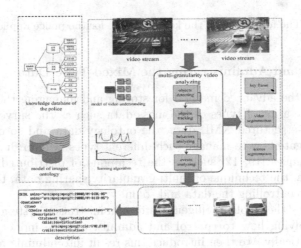

Fig. 1. The framework of the video understanding in typical applications of the police

3.2 Perception of Video Semantics and Design on Knowledge Databases of Service Systems and Databases

This project aims at supporting the applications of the surveillance video in the police affairs. We will build a unified database for registering all kinds of meta-data. It will help to realize the interoperations of different types of meta-data.

For the problems including lack of management of knowledge and interoperation among the heterogeneous data in the applications of the police affairs, we will study the technique of the video semantics and the approaches on extracting the knowledge. It will help to build the knowledge database of the applications in the specific field. In addition, we will develop the web-oriented software for the knowledge services and administration to realize the automatic management and evolution of the knowledge as is exhibited in Figure 2.

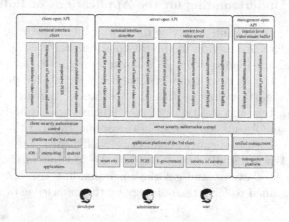

Fig. 2. The framework of the key technique for the police application

3.3   Storing and Administrating the Mixed-Type Data

We will study the advanced method for storing and managing the mixed-type data. There are a lot of types of the mass data such as the surveillance video data, the semi-structured XML data, the ontology data and so on. Thus, we have to investigate how to manage such different types of data. It must involve so many techniques [19, 12] such as the technique of distributed storing and processing data, the technique of multi-granularity sharing data, the technique of visiting and controlling the data and so on.

After finishing the whole intelligent traffic administration system, this project will go on studying how to control and administrate the indoor surveillance system automatically. We then introduce this result into administration system of a prison and reduce the cost for monitoring all the screens.

We will construct the intelligent surveillance system for the outside of the prison based on the indoor surveillance system. This system uses some tools for locating outside and the structured description information of video semantics to track some special objects in the crowd dynamically. We will study the features about the incident of violence, the suspicious incident and the colony events and construct the semantic database for the special fields and establish an efficient system for the police affairs and protection.

4   Application

This work will extract the structured information of people and vehicles on the main roads in the experimental cities. After building the traffic environment semantic model and the knowledge databases for police affairs and the semantic searching model about time, space and objects monitored, we will compute the important information such as the number of the people and vehicles, densities of people and vehicles and the load ratio. According to the statistics data of traffic surveillance and external GIS, we will mine the data deeply and administrate the cards of vehicles, traffic events and schedule. This will supply the support for the rapid and precise traffic administration and schedule.

Meantime, by integrating with the data network of traffic command centre, GIS data, knowledge databases of police affairs, we can design and establish the opening serving group of the intelligent traffic surveillance. We will use the descriptions from the semantic model based on the knowledge databases of the police affairs and the description methods to predict, mine, auto-alarm and distribute the typical abnormal traffic incident such as the heavy traffic jams. Researching the synchronous platform based on the applications of police and sending the alarm message to the call centers such as 110, 119 and 120 according to the current environment, it is convenient to prepare and control the emergent accident to the police.

All the applications involved are as follows:

1. Build the of the semantic knowledge databases about the intelligent traffic based on the structured semantic model of video description for the field of traffic.
2. Based on the created knowledge database, we will compute some important information including the number of people and vehicles, distributions and densities of people and vehicles.
3. Study the information distribution about the people and vehicles. Based on the distribution models and GIS, we will analyze the condition of the roads efficiently and supply the real-time traffic data for the traffic schedule system.
4. Study the real-time charging methods of the information distribution, subscription, synchronism and service. Build the interfaces to work cooperatively for different traffic surveillance systems.
5. Study the techniques based on the traffic semantic knowledge databases and the models of video structured description for the abnormal traffic events checking and information mining. Study the techniques based on the semantic model of the video structured description to alarm jointly and make decisions intelligently for the abnormal traffic events.
6. Study the patterns and coded formats in the current video surveillance system. Implement the protocols in the current video and the patterns and schemes of the video surveillance.
7. Study the associating and analyzing techniques based on video semantic databases and police affairs. By the model of semantic databases, we will implement the analysis of the space-time relations and efficient retrieval based on the features of the traffic events.

8. In order to facilitate the scan and searching and improve the efficiency of the decisions, we will study the visual technique of the key content about specific events in the video structured description and relations.

5   Conclusions and Future Work

In this paper, we presented a new technique for video surveillance system-video structured description. This technique is also a novel video data vitalization technique. It uses a knowledge model of certain surveillance scenario and image/video understanding to attain related knowledge from video. Moreover, the knowledge obtained could be accessed much more conveniently by other information systems than before. Finally, we introduced a prototype system and put it into the practice. In future, we will go on studying how to control and administrate the indoor surveillance system more automatically, more quickly, more accurately and more intelligently. We will extend this technique to the outside system.

Acknowledgments. This work was supported by the China Postdoctoral Science Foundation (No.2011M500732). The authors would like to thank the anonymous reviewers and all the members of the third research institute of ministry of public security.

References

1. Dean, J., Ghemawat, S.: MapReduce: Simplified Data Processing on Large Clusters, in. In: Proceedings of the 6th conference on Symposium on Operating Systems Design and Implementation, pp. 1–13 (2004)
2. Deng, J., Dong, W., Socher, R., Li, L., Li, K., Li, F.: ImageNet: A Large-Scale Hierarchical Image Database. In: Computer Vision and Pattern Recognition, CVPR (2009)
3. Jeon, J., Lavrenko, V., Manmatha, R.: Automatic Image Annotation and Retrieval using cross-media Relevance Models. In: Proceedings of the 26th Annual International ACM SIGIR Conference on Research and Development Information Retrieval, pp. 119–126 (2003)
4. Jeon, J., Manmatha, R.: Using Maximum Entropy for Automatic Image Annotation. In: Proc. CIVR, pp. 24–32 (2004)
5. Jinm, R., Chai, J.Y.: L. Si Effetive Automatic Image Annotation via Coherent Language Model and Active Learning. In: Proceedings of the 12th Annual ACM International Conference on Multimedia, pp. 892–899 (2004)
6. Lavrenko, V., Manmatha, R., Jeon, J.: A Model for Learning the Semantics of Pictures. In: NIPS (2003)
7. Li, L., Li, F.: What, Where and Who? Classifying Event by Scene and Object Recognition. In: IEEE International Conference in Computer Vision, ICCV (2007)
8. Li, L., Su, H., Lin, Y., Li, F.: Objects as Attributes for Scene Classification. In: Proceedings of the 12th European Conference of Computer Vision, ECCV (2010)
9. Li, F., Perona, P.: A Bayesian Hierarchical Model for Learning Natural Scene Categories. In: Proceedings of ICCV 2005 (2005)

10. Li, J., Wang, J.: Automatic Linguistic Indexing of Pictures by a Statistical Modeling Approach. IEEE Transaction on Pattern Analysis and Machine Intelligence 25(10) (2003)
11. Liu, Y., Wu, F., Zhang, Z., Zhuang, Y., Ya, S.: Sparse Representation using Nonnegative Curds and Whey. In: CVPR 2010, pp. 3578-3585 (2010)
12. Liu, M., Yu, D., Zhang, Q., et al.: Network Security Situation Assessment Based on Data Fusion. In: 2008 Workshop on Knowledge Discovery and Data Mining (2008)
13. Lowe, D.G.: Fitting Parameterized Three-dimensional Models to Images. IEEE Transactions on Pattern Analysis and Machine Intelligence 13(5), 441–450 (1991)
14. Metzler, R.D., Metzler, D., Manmatha, R.: An Inference Network approach to Image. In: Proceedings of the International Conference on Image and Video Retrieval, pp. 42–50 (2004)
15. Papadias, D., Kalnis, P., Zhang, J., Tao, Y.: Efficient OLAP operations in spatial data warehouses. In: Advances in Spatial and Temporal Databases, pp. 443–459 (2001)
16. Sivic, J., Russell, B.C., Efros, A.A., Zisserman, A., Freeman, W.T.: Discovering Object Categories in Image Collections. In: Proceedings of IEEE International Conference on Computer Vision and Pattern Recognition (2005)
17. Savarese, S., Winn, J., Criminisi, A.: Discriminative Object Class of Appearance and Shape by Correlations. In: Proceeding of IEEE International Conference on Computer Vision and Pattern Recognition, pp. 2033–2040 (2006)
18. Smeulders, A.W.M., Worring, M., Santini, S., Gupta, A., Jain, R.: Content-based Image Retrieval at the End of the Early Years. IEEE Transactions on Pattern Analysis and Machine Intelligence 22(12), 1349–1379 (2000)
19. Wang, H., Lai, J., Ying, L.: Network Security Situation Awareness Based on Heterogeneous Multi-Sensor Data Fusion and Neural Network. In: Second International Multisymposium on Computer and Computational Sciences (2007)
20. Wu, L., Li, M., Li, Z., Ma, W., Yu, N.: Visual Language Modeling for Image Classification. In: Proceedings of 9th ACM SIGMM International Workshop on Multimedia Information Retrieval (2007)
21. Xi, W., Fox, E.A., Fan, W., Zhang, B., Chen, Z., Yan, J., Zhuang, D.: SimFusion: Measureing Similarity using Unified Relationship Matrix. In: SIGIR 2005, pp. 130–137 (2005)
22. Yang, J., Li, Q., Zhuang, Y.: Towards Data-Adaptive and User-Adaptive Image Retrieval by Peer Indexing. International Journal of Computer Vision 56(1/3), 47–63 (2004)
23. Yavlinsky, A., Schofield, E., Ruger, S.: Automated Image Annotation using Global Features and Robust Nonparametric Density Estimation. In: Proceedings of the International Conference on Image and Video Retrieval, pp. 507–517 (2005)
24. Yuan, J., Wu, Y., Yang, M.: Discovery of Collection Patterns: from Visual Words to Visual Phrases. In: Proceedings of IEEE International Conference on Computer Vision and Pattern Recognition (2007)
25. Zhang, X., Luo, W., Chen, L., Ni, L.M.: Data Vitalization: A New Paradigm for Large-Scale Dataset Analysis, in. In: Proceedings of the 2010 IEEE Sixteenth International Conference on Parallel and Distributed Systems (2010)
26. Zhu, S., Mumford, D.: A Stochastic Grammar of Images. Foundations and Trends in Computer Graphics and Vision 2(4), 259–362 (2006)

Vehicle Trajectory Description for Traffic Events Detection

Chao Yu[1,*], Chongyang Zhang[1,2], Guang Tian[3], and Longfei Liang[3]

[1] Institute of Image Communication and Network Engineering,
Shanghai Jiao Tong University, Shanghai 200240, China
[2] Shanghai Key Labs of Digital Media Processing and Transmission,
Shanghai 200240, China
[3] Bocom Smart Network Technologies Inc., Shanghai 200233, China

Abstract. The trajectory of moving object is a significant feature for events detection in intelligent video surveillance. In this paper, a novel method of trajectory description is proposed to establish the semantic model for automatic traffic violation events detection. Firstly, using polynomial fitting, we classify a trajectory into two shapes: straight line and parabola, which is used to determine the vehicle's route type: straight, left/right-turn, or U-turn. In the meantime, a region description scheme is also developed to explore the path that one vehicle has passed through, which can be taken as the evidence for traffic event decision. Experiments results showed that the proposed scheme was more efficient and more accurate than the traditional MPEG-7 method.

Keywords: trajectory, regions, traffic events.

1 Introduction

Intelligence video surveillance has made considerable progress these years, making it possible to detect traffic violation events automatically. The trajectory of a vehicle is a significant feature that could be utilized for activity analyzing and event detection.

Many algorithms and methods have been implemented to extract trajectory information. Ying Zhang *et al* utilize region information to describe the path that a vehicle has passed through [1]. Akio Yamada *et al* build a mathematical method in MPEG-7 to fit the points on a trajectory to a polynomial [2]. Melo, J. *et al* employ clustering method to process the trajectories [3]. As for trajectory classification, Bashir, F *et al* use Hidden Markov Model [4], Weiming Hu *et al* use self-organized Neural Network [5].

The method mentioned in [1] couldn't describe the geometric shape of the trajectory and the type of the route, which will result in the inconvenience in classifying the trajectories. The description for trajectory mentioned in [2] only

---

* This work was supported by the NSF of China under grant No.61001147, No.61171172, the China National Key Technology R&D Program under grants No. 2012BAH07B01, and by the STCSM of Shanghai under grant No.12DZ2272600.

W. Zhang et al. (Eds.): IFTC 2012, CCIS 331, pp. 228–235, 2012.

indicated the information on trajectory shape, and the lack of route information makes it impossible to detect traffic violation events directly. Clustering in [3] needs some trajectories to be predefined, whose rationality will also have to be taken into consideration, involving some undesired workload. Regarding classification, the methods mentioned in [4] and [5] are complicated and complex in calculation.

In this paper, a novel method of trajectory description is proposed. The description for a vehicle trajectory has two aspects, one is route type, and the other is region-based path information. Using polynomial fitting, a trajectory can be classified into two shapes: straight line and parabola, which are then used to determine the vehicle's driving route type: straight, left/right-turn and turn-around (or U-turn). The other aspect is region-based path information, which includes the regions that a vehicle has passed through. The result of route type classification, path information, and other traffic information such as the state of traffic light, are combined to model the traffic event detection.

The rest of the paper is organized as follows. Section 2 describes the process of trajectory fitting and route type classification. Section 3 presents a description of region-based path information and the construction of trajectory vectors. Section 4 gives the semantic model for events detection, and it also presents the related experiments results. Finally, the conclusions are drawn in Section 5.

2   Trajectory Shape Fitting and Route Type Classification

2.1   Basic Idea

Features of moving objects are narrated in MPEG-7. The features have several significant components, among which motion trajectory is a significant aspect. In MPEG-7, two polynomials are put forward to fit a certain trajectory, as is shown in formulas (1) and (2). For vehicles at intersections, however, the shape of their trajectories could be either straight lines or parabolas. Consequently, the polynomial in formula (2) is adopted in the process of fitting a certain trajectory.

In surveillance system, most of the cameras are deployed at traffic intersections, and Fig.1(a) is a typical intersection with three lanes for each direction. In Fig.1(a), the routes that vehicles pass through can be classified into three categories, i.e. straight, left/right- turn and U-turn, as is illustrated in Fig.1(b).

Using polynomial fitting, the trajectory shape and the corresponding polynomial information could be gathered, which is then employed to classify the route to a certain type (shown in Fig.1(b)).

$$y = ax + b \tag{1}$$

$$y = ax^2 + bx + c \tag{2}$$

2.2   Classification of Trajectories in Surveillance Videos

Temporal interpolation is introduced as the fitting algorithm in MPEG-7. In this algorithm, the interpolation interval is initialized with the first two points on the trajectory, which are defined as start point and end point respectively. The interpolation is then widened to include one point at a time to be the end point of the interval. When the maximum approximation error, defined in (5), becomes larger than a given threshold, the previous interval is terminated. A new start point is added and a new interpolation interval is started with the new start point and the immediately following point which is the new end point. This procedure is iterated until all points have been processed. There exists several variables used in this algorithm, denote the coordinate of the point derived from trajectory as $p(x_i, y_i)$, where i is frame number. For an interpolation interval, the start position and end position is denoted by $p_{start}(x_{start}, y_{start})$ and $p_{end}(x_{end}, y_{end})$, where *start* and *end* represent the start frame number and end frame number of the interpolation interval. $y(x)$ is the interpolation function using formula (2). $y(x)$ can be derived using least squares. In this case, $y(x)$ is calculated to minimize (3) [2].

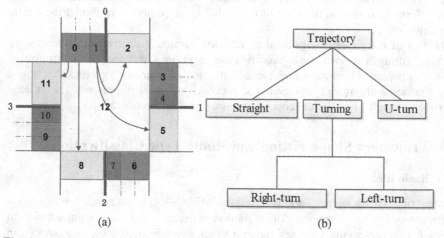

(a)   (b)

Fig. 1. (a) A typical three-lane intersection. The intersection could be divided into 13 regions, in which, 0, 3, 6 and 9 allow vehicles to go straight and turn right;1, 4, 7, 10 allow vehicles to turn left and make a U-turn, 2, 5, 8, 11 are the entries, and 12 is the central region that vehicles pass through.(b) The classifications of trajectories in surveillance videos.

$$\sum_{i=start}^{end} |y_i - y(x_i)|^2 \tag{3}$$

Define T to be the threshold and approximation error e_i is defined in (4).

$$e_i = y_i - y(x_i), \quad i = start, start+1, ..., end \tag{4}$$

And the maximum approximation error e_{MAX} is defined in (5).

$$e_{MAX} = MAX\{e_i\}, \quad i = start, start+1, ..., end \tag{5}$$

The following are the steps of the algorithm [2].

1. Initialization: Set $x_{start}=x_1$, $x_{end}=x_2$, where subscripts 1 and 2 represent the first and the second frame. .

2. Interpolation Calculation: Calculate interpolation function $y(x)$ using least squares to minimize (3).

3. Interpolation Evaluation: Compute the maximum approximation error e_{MAX}, If $e_{MAX} > T$, go to Step 4. Otherwise, go to Step 5.

4. Key Point Insertion: Accept $y(x)$ and set $x_{start} = x_{end-1}$.

5. Increment and Termination: If x_{end} is the end of the whole interval, terminate the procedure. Otherwise, set $x_{end} = x_{end+1}$ and go to Step 2.

Through the above algorithm, one or more polynomials could be fitted from the coordinates of a certain trajectory. There exists one problem that different thresholds may cause different polynomial numbers for a certain trajectory. In this work, a method called double-fitting is adopted to overcome this deficiency.

In the proposed double-fitting method, a pair of thresholds is given: a larger threshold and a relatively smaller one. Using the larger threshold, we may get the overall shape of the trajectory, which could be straight lines or parabolas; with the smaller threshold, the direction information about the trajectory could be extracted. Afterwards, a comprehensive classification is implemented to acquire the route type, which could be straight, left/right-turn or U-turn. And the flow chart is depicted in Fig.2, where θ_{in} describes the direction that a vehicle bear up for at the start point, and θ_{out} describes the direction that a vehicle is heading to at the end of its route.

After double-fitting, with trajectory shape and the value of θ_{in} and θ_{out}, the route of a certain vehicle could be classified into one of the types listed in Fig.1(b).

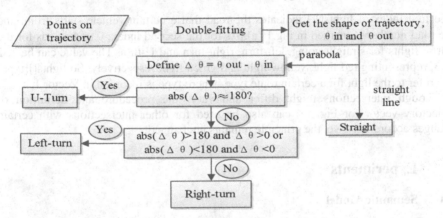

Fig. 2. The flow chart of trajectory classification

3   Region-Based Path Description and Trajectory Vectors Construction

Some mathematical methods for trajectory processing are included in the previous section. This method, however, could only inform the route type, making it less convenient detecting traffic events. Yet, with the help of regions, some traffic violation events are less complicated to be identified, making region-based path information another significant trajectory descriptor.

Region-based path information includes two aspects, one is the property of a certain region, which is defined as the driving direction that it permits, and the other is the regions that a vehicle has passed through. Regarding a typical 4-leg intersection as is shown in Fig.1(a), it has four exits and four entries. So the property of a certain lane could be straight, left-turn, right-turn, U-turn or their combination. The intersection in Fig.1(a) is divided into 13 regions according to their properties, denoted as 0 to 12. This division is definitely an example of dividing the roads into regions, for other different intersections, the division might vary, but the implementation could be operated likewise. Based on this division, the movement of a certain vehicle can be described with a start region, a midway region and an end region, where all the regions have their own properties. Define trajectory vector1 in (6).

$$Vector1 = \{type, \ region[3]\} \tag{6}$$

In Vector1, type can be 0, 1, 2 or 3, standing for straight, left-turn, right-turn and U-turn respectively. Consequently, the value could be derived from route type as is mentioned previously. As for region[], region[0] is the start region, region[1] is the midway region, and region[2] is the end region. So if a vehicle drives straight from region 0 to region 8 via region 12, Vector1 should be {0, 0, 12, 8}.

Generally speaking, traffic violation might happen where there are red lights. So the state of traffic lights is introduced to detect traffic violation detection, and trajectory vector2 is defined in (7).

$$Vector2 = \{lights[4][4]\} \tag{7}$$

The first index of lights[][] indicates the road that a certain vehicle starts from, and the road number is marked in Fig.1 (a). As for the second index, 0 to 4 stands for the traffic lights for straight-going, left-turn, right-turn and U-turn. The value can be 1, 2 or 3, representing red light, yellow light and green light respectively. So lights[][type] can refer to the light for a certain route type, where type is recorded in Vector 1.

Though intersections might differ and vary, the procedure and definition of trajectory vector for Fig.1(a) can also be used for other intersections with certain changes accordingly, yet the principle remains unchanged.

4   Experiments

4.1   Semantic Model

The previous sections narrated the description of a trajectory from two aspects. And with trajectory vectors and the property of each region, some general traffic violations like running red lights and driving violations could be detected.

As for the detection of running red lights, the route type and the state of traffic lights are to be utilized. For a vehicle with a certain route type, if the light is red for this route type then it could be inferred that running red lights has occurred.

And for driving violation, the property of the start region and the route type are used. If the route type is not included in the property of its start region, i.e. certain route type is prohibited, then it could be inferred that the vehicle has committed driving violation.

Take left-turn violation as an example to illustrate the establishment of the semantic model for traffic events detection. Left-turn violation might happen when the left-turn light is red or the region from which a vehicle turns left prohibits left-turn.

As for the first condition, running left-turn red light could be expressed as (8)

$$\{type == left\} \ \& \ \{lights[roadNum][left] == red\} \tag{8}$$

In (8), *type* and *lights* have been extracted and recorded in trajectory vector1 and trajectory vector2, and roadNum refers to the road from which a vehicle starts its driving, and the value is 0, 1, 2, 3 in Fig.1 (a) and it might differ in number and value for other intersections.

And the second condition can be expressed as (9).

$$\{type == left\} \ \& \ \{left \not\subset region \ property\} \tag{9}$$

In (9), type is recorded in trajectory vector1, and the region property could be recorded according to different intersections. So if left is not included in region property, then left-turn is prohibited.

So with (8) and (9) left-turn violation could be judged by (10)

$$\{type == left\} \ \& \ \{\{left \not\subset region \ property\} \ \| \ \{lights[roadNum][left] == red\}\} \tag{10}$$

Besides left-turn, the semantic models for the detection of other driving violations are listed in Table 1.

Table 1. The semantic model for traffic violation detection

Event Type	Semantic Model
Right-turn Violation	$\{type == right\} \ \& \ \{\{right \not\subset region \ property\}$ $\| \ \{lights[roadNum][right] == red\}\}$
Straight Violation	$\{type == straight\} \ \& \ \{\{straight \not\subset region \ property\}$ $\| \ \{lights[roadNum][straight] == red\}\}$
U-turn Violation	$\{type == U\text{-}turn\} \ \& \ \{\{U\text{-}turn \not\subset region \ property\}$ $\| \ \{lights[roadNum][U\text{-}turn] == red\}\}$

4.2 Experiment Results

The experiments tested the algorithm on a total of 76 legal vehicles and 66 violation vehicles. The result is twofold, on the one hand, the accuracy of this algorithm for route type detection is tested, and on the other hand, the accuracy of the semantic model for traffic violation events detection is verified.

The intersections used in this experiment have been divided into 8 regions. Region 3, 6 and 8 are three entries. The properties of the entries are as follows. Region1: straight, region2: left-turn, region 4: right-turn and straight, region5: left-turn and straight. In Fig.3, an example of the process and trajectory of a left-turning car is depicted. And two examples of left-turn violation cars are illustrated in Fig.4(a) and Fig.4(b). The result of route type detection is shown in Table 2. And the result of traffic violation detection is shown in Table 3.

From the experiment results, though there exist some failures, the algorithm could provide good accuracy. Route type detection involves the double-fitting algorithm alone, and failures would occur when the trajectory contains too many points that have identical x value. As for violation detection, region-based path information and the state of traffic lights are also to be concerned and the failures are primarily caused by incorrect region information and traffic lights information. Due to the position of the camera, the centroid of a vehicle on a certain lane might be in another region, causing incorrect region information. The traffic light might change from green to red after a legal turn, yet the red light is recorded as lights information, which is incorrect. The trajectories are manually labeled in order to test the proposed method. In practice, the accuracy might drop according to different tracking algorithms.

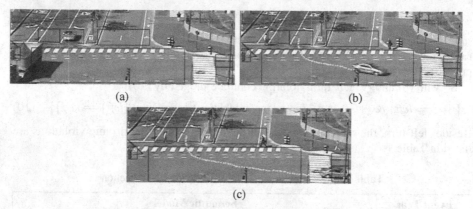

Fig. 3. An example of a left-turning vehicle. (a) Start (b) Midway (c) End.

Fig. 4. Example of left-turn violation detection. (a) Running red lights (b) Left-turn from a region without left-turn property.

Table 2. Result of Route Type Detection

Route Type	Total	Detected	Accuracy
Left-turn	18	17	95%
Right-turn	21	20	95%
U-turn	12	11	92%
Straight	25	23	92%

Table 3. Result of Traffic Violation Events Detection

Event Type	Total	Detected	Accuracy
Left-turn Violation	16	15	94%
Right-turn Violation	18	16	89%
U-turn Violation	12	11	92%
Straight Violation	20	19	95%

5   Conclusion

A novel method of trajectory description is proposed in this work to establish the semantic model for automatic traffic violation events detection. The trajectories of vehicles are extracted and classified into two shapes, and double-fitting is operated to get the route type. The regions with certain properties that a vehicle passes have been extracted as well. The method combines both mathematical and region-based path information of the trajectory, and the test results showed it can achieve good detection accuracy and efficiency.

References

1. Zhang, Y., Wang, S., Ding, X.: Traffic Flow Surveillance System for Urban Intersections. In: International Conference on MultiMedia and Information Technology, pp. 405–408. IEEE Press, Three Gorges (2008)
2. Yamada, A., Pickering, M., Jeannin, S., Cieplinski, L., Ohm, J.R.: MPEG-7 Visual part of Experimentation Model Version 8.1., pp. 17–19, 59–60 (2001)
3. Melo, J., Naftel, A., Bernardino, A., Santos-Victor, J.: Detection and classification of high-way lanes using vehicle motion trajectories. IEEE Transactions on Intelligent Transportation Systems, 188–200 (2006)
4. Bashir, F., Khokhar, A., Schonfeld, D.: Automatic object trajectory-based motion recognit-ion using gaussian mixture models. In: IEEE International Conference on Multimedia and Expo, pp. 1532–1535 (2005)
5. Hu, W., Xie, D., Tan, T.: A hierarchical self-organizing approach for Learning the patterns of motion trajectories. IEEE Transactions on Neural Networks, 135–144 (2004)
6. Pan, Q., Cheng, Y., Yang, T., Pan, Q., Zhao, C.: Automatic Validating and Clustering Method for Trajectories of Moving Objects in Real Scene. Application Research of Computers 24(4), 158–160 (2007)
7. Lee, K.K., Xu, Y.: Boundary modeling in human walking trajectory analysis for surveillance. In: Proceedings of the 2004 IEEE International Conference on Robotics and Automation, vol. 5, pp. 5201–5205 (2004)
8. Yang, J., Wang, R.: Video Image Analysis Technologies for Smart Traffic Surveillance. Video Engineering, 74–77 (2006)
9. Veeraraghavan, H., Masoud, O., Papanikolopoulos, N.P.: Computer Vision Algorithms for Intersection Monitoring. IEEE Transactions on Intelligent Transportantion System 4(2), 78–79 (2003)
10. Kamijo, S., Matsushita, Y., Ikeuchi, K., Sakauchi, M.: Traffic monitoring and accident detection at intersections. IEEE Transactions on Intelligent Transportantion System 1(2), 108–118 (2000)
11. Piciarelli, C., Micheloni, C., Foresti, G.L.: Trajectory-Based Anomalous Event Detection. IEEE Transactions on Circuits and Systems for Video Technology 18(11), 1544–1554 (2008)

An Automatic TV LOGO Detecting Method

Tao Fan, Jianhua Peng, Haiwu Zhao, and Guozhong Wang

School of Communication and Information Engineering,
Shanghai University
fantao@shu.edu.cn

Abstract. This paper outlines a simple and practical technique for detecting logos characterizing a broadcast station in TV Programme. Traditional detecting algorithms such as feature extraction and template matching has been applied in many applications. However the limitation of these method cannot recognize the transparent logo effectively. More sophisticated learning-based methods have been address these issues, but they typically involve very high computational complexity. We present an automatic TV logo detection method based statistical property of video sequences. Different other approaches, a transparency factor is introduced firstly in this paper. It is a symbol that responses the level of TV logo transparency and indispensability as a part of the logo information. Combined with the statistical property of video sequences, the logo information can be obtained and detected clearly. Experimental results show that the proposed method not only simple, but gives performs well.

Keywords: TV logo detection, statistical property, transparency.

1 Introduction

Television (TV) logos usually claim the video content ownership. These logos can be considered as the identification of TV stations and plays an irreplaceable role in copyright authentication [1]. However, Some Broadcast stations may reuse TV Programme like sports Programme or news originally produced by another station. In order to avoid the issue of copyright, they often seek to remove the TV logo and to replace it by their own logo. So it is vitally important to detect the logo information accurately and fast. As an indispensable part of one TV content analysis system, our study just intents to make use of TV Programme information to detect the TV logo fast and efficiently.

TV logo detection is one of an oldest and also most important research topic in digital TV application. Commonly used detecting algorithms include feature extraction [2] and template matching [3]. However, logo region artifacts like blurring or zigzag of edges may occur when these schemes are used. A more critical problem cannot be solved via these approaches when the logo is transparent. In order to solve these approaches, alternative algorithms have been proposed into categories of 1)Markov Random Fields based [4] 2) Semi-supervised learning based [5] 3) temporal-spatial segmentation based [6]. The underlying approach in these algorithms is to extract TV logo using machine learning. These approaches

W. Zhang et al. (Eds.): IFTC 2012, CCIS 331, pp. 236–243, 2012.
© Springer-Verlag Berlin Heidelberg 2012

can improve the performance; however, the extraction of logo information may have long and complex training requirements.

To address this, an automatic TV logo detected method was proposed in this paper. Different from other approaches, a transparency factor was introduced firstly. As an important part of logo information, the value of it can be obtained firstly based on the statistical property of video sequence. By means of this, we can easily distinguish whether the logo is transparent or not. After that a template of logo which includes the position and shape information is got via some priori knowledge and statistical property of the video sequence. Finally, using obtained template the logo can be detected accurately.

The paper is organized as follows. Section 2 describes the proposed approach and method for TV logo detection automatically in detail. Section 3 provides experimental results and some details of the implementation. Conclusions and future work are presented in Section 4.

2 Proposed Algorithm

2.1 Overview of the Algorithm

Like many other detecting algorithms, the proposed algorithm for automatic logo removal requires two steps: First the logo temple is constructed and then the logo is detected. However, different from other methods, the transparency factor is introduced in this paper which can measure the transparency level of the TV logo. Then the statistical property of the TV sequences can be utilized to obtain the transparency factor and the logo temple which can fast and effectively extract and remove the logo of video.

Assuming that $\hat{P}(x, y)$ is the pixel of the frame after superimposing the logo, L represent the logo pixel and $P(x, y)$ indicate the pixel of original frame without overlaying logo pixel. The prominent mathematical model for composition of video and logo can be slightly modified in the presence of TV logo, as Equation 1:

$$\hat{P}(x, y) = (1 - \alpha) \cdot L(x, y) + \alpha \cdot P(x, y) \tag{1}$$

Where, the α is the logo transparency which changed from 0 to 1. If α equals zero that the logo is not transparent. Reversely α is one shows that it doesn't have logo in the video. Supposing that there have n frames in the TV sequences, let $\hat{p}_i(x, y)$ and $p_i(x, y)$ be the value at the same position in frame i after and before superimposing logo. Put $\hat{p}_i$ and p_i into formula 1, it can be easy seen that the systems of equations are obtained including n equations but $n+2$ unknowns. As we all know, it is unsolvable for this that the unknowns are larger than the equations. Moreover, it is very difficult to judge which position have superposed logo or not. These are the key issues to address as below.

According to the equation 1, if the range of $P(x, y)$ is on Interval $[P_{min}, P_{max}]$, the value of pixel after superimposing logo will be in the range of $(1 - \alpha) \cdot L + \alpha \cdot P_{min}$ to $(1 - \alpha) \cdot L + \alpha \cdot P_{max}$. The α and L are constant because the pixels of logo in one sequence is immovable. It will lead to narrow the range of pixel in the logo region. Moreover, the value after overlapping the logo with before is linear relation when the α and L are inalterability. In other word, if the $P(x, y)$ got the maximum or minimum, the $\hat{P}(x, y)$ also gain the maximum or minimum correspondingly. The logo value L and its transparency can be obtained through solving the system of equations with two equations in every position, as follows:

$$\begin{cases} \hat{P}_{min} = (1 - \alpha) \cdot L + \alpha \cdot P_{min} \\ \hat{P}_{max} = (1 - \alpha) \cdot L + \alpha \cdot P_{max} \end{cases} \tag{2}$$

Where, $\hat{P}_{min}$ and $\hat{P}_{max}$ are the minimum and maximum pixel after superimposing logo, and P_{min} and P_{max} are the minimum and maximum pixel value before superimposing logo. From Equation 2, the transparency of the position can be computed clearly as below:

$$\alpha = \frac{\hat{P}_{max} - \hat{P}_{min}}{P_{max} - P_{min}} \tag{3}$$

From the Equation 3, it is obvious that if a pixel doesn't overlap TV logo α equals one, and vice versa. Substitute Equation 3 into Equation 2, we can obtain:

$$L = \frac{P_{max} \cdot \hat{P}_{min} - P_{min} \cdot \hat{P}_{max}}{P_{max} - P_{min} - \hat{P}_{max} + \hat{P}_{min}} \tag{4}$$

Obviously, the $\hat{P}_{max}$ and $\hat{P}_{min}$ can be easily obtained through adding up pixels of the same position in all frames. However, the P_{max} and P_{min} cannot be get in the same way, just because it is impossible to know the video before superimposing TV logo in practical applications. Fortunately, some priori knowledge can be obtained in the statistical meaning. As we all know, dynamic change and high correlation in temporal and spatial domain are two significant characteristics for video sequence. With the objects movement or background changes, the regions with maximum or minimum will make the other region as the same value. That is to say the range of pixel value in every position would be same before overlapping the TV logo if the number of frames is large enough. Obviously, the ranges of pixel in adjacent positions are more approximate. So these features can be utilized to estimate the pixel values before superimposing the TV logo. What's more, there are many parts without logo in the real TV logo sequences, the P_{max} and P_{min} can be estimated from the $\hat{P}_{max}$ and $\hat{P}_{min}$ in whole position. Whereas, if statistical time is not longer enough or the video has the static background, some dissatisfied results will appear. In fact, it is an extreme cases in the digital TV application.

In actual fact, the video programme usually has been changed during the coding and decoding, so the logo is not absolutely invariable at all. In order to address this issue, two values of α are set to judge whether one position is overlapped by logo or not and whether the logo is transparent. Furthermore, the non-transparent logo pixel is updated by the formula as follow:

$$L = \frac{\hat{p}_{max} + \hat{p}_{min}}{2} \tag{5}$$

2.2   TV Logo Mark Construction

In order to obtain TV logo information exactly, complex training process is inevitable in the traditional methods. Actually, due to the high coherence in temporal and spatial of video, we can use the statistical information of video to achieve the target. As we mentioned before, a transparent brought in this algorithm combined with the statistical characteristic of video would solve the issue fast and effectively. The steps our algorithm are:

Step 1. The pretreatment of the TV sequence. This method mainly aims at the detection of static TV logo used by most TV station. The logos usually are embedded at top right or top left corner. In order to reduce the computing complexity, we extract the region including logo which resolution is 208×128 firstly. in addition, the video sequence is made up three color components. In this paper, one component is illustrated mainly and anther color components is similar.

Step 2. The initialization of algorithm. Set the initial training sample size and the threshold T_1 to judge whether the logo pixel is or not. For the sake of obtaining exact results, training sample size may be as large as possible. In order to calculate briefly, we distill the number of 800 frames as the samples. In term of the threshold T_1, 0.6 is set firstly.

Step 3. Counting $\hat{p}_{min}$ and $\hat{p}_{max}$ as section 2.1 described. Firstly, we extract the pixel value of the n frames of the TV logo sequence in the same position to composite a data stream which set from large to small order. It means that the minimum one indicate $\hat{p}_{min}$ and the maximum stand for $\hat{p}_{max}$.

Step 4. Judgment of logo position. As front section described, the value range of every position in the video are uniform. P_{min} and P_{max} can be estimated from the positions which not overlapped the logo. As described above, it will narrow when the logo superimposes onto video frames. We establish a threshold T_1 to decide which pixel superimposes the logo. In fact, owing to the influence of encoding and decoding the value of P_{min} and P_{max} are not completely equivalent in every position. The threshold T_1 have another function to limit this influence. In most cases the some priori knowledge of the TV logo can be used to set the value of T_1. After that we can get an important logo mark information which includes the position and shape of the TV logo. It can be obtained as follows:

$$mark(x,y) = \begin{cases} 1; & if(\frac{\hat{P}_{max}-\hat{P}_{min}}{P_{max}-P_{min}} \leq T_1) \\ 0; & else \end{cases} . \tag{6}$$

From the Equation 6, the $mark(x, y)$ equals one shows that this position overlaps logo and P_{max} and P_{min} of this position are replaced by the $\hat{p}_{max}$ and $\hat{p}_{min}$ which position doesn't overlap logo($mark(x, y)$=0).

2.3   TV Logo Detection and Elimination

Considering mainly the static logo detection, the region of logos has the same location in every frame. This paper underlines the efficient logo detection approach to make for the application of some postprocessing in multimedia non-linear editing system such as TV logo elimination, TV logo replacement and so on. According to the result of logo temple what we mentioned above, the algorithm of logo detection depict detailedly as below:

Step 1. Input the testing frame. Extract the same region pixels as the logo mark to be the set of testing samples.

Step 2. Computing the transparency of the logo. According to the described above, the the transparency of the logo can be obtained as Equation 3. It is an important information as part of logo detected which can help us to do the follow-up work such us logo removing.

Step 3. The TV logo detection. The $mark(x, y)$ obtained above is used to judge whether the position overlaps logo or not. If $mark(x, y)$ equals zero, we let $L(x, y)$ to be zero which manifests the position doesn't contain the logo, otherwise, we obtain the logo value from equation 4 .

Step 4. TV logo update. In some application, the logo is not always transparent. It is necessary that the algorithm may have the ability to distinguish automatically the which logo is transparent. The biggest characteristic of our approach bring in a transparent factor which can measure the level of transparency. From step 2, the value of the transparency can be obtained. Generally, when α equals zero, the position has non-transparent logo pixel. However, owing to the process of the coding and decoding, the logo is not absolutely invariable at all. A threshold T_2 is used to manage this process. Concrete equation of this update is as follows:

$$L(x, y) = \begin{cases} \frac{\hat{p}_{max}(x,y)+\hat{p}_{min}(x,y)}{2}; & if(\alpha \leq T_2) \\ L(x, y); & else \end{cases}. \tag{7}$$

3   Experimental Results and Analysis

In this section, we conduct two experiments: one is a verification to illustrate the efficiency of the transparent and opaque logo based on our method. The other is a confirmation that the algorithm is suit for a large scale TV sequences which have different transparent logo. All the experiments are carried out on a PC with Core i5 2.5GHz CPU and 4GB memory.

In order to test the validity of our method two group data set are carried out in our system. Group one is to detect the logo of Channel Young and the Hunan Tv (as shown in Fig.1) which have different features that one is transparent logo (in Fig.1a) and the other is opacity (in Fig.1b). Group two is to detect the logo information from the three different videos (as shown in Fig.2). All the videos analyzed have 1000 frames and the color space of them are raw YUV sampled 4:2:0.

Firstly, using the method we proposed above, we detect the transparent TV logo of Channel Young and the opacity TV logo of Hunan TV. The results of detection can be seen from Fig.3. Fig .3a and Fig.3b are the minimum and maximum value in statistical sample. It is clear that the TV logo region's pixel changed less than the background's, which verifies the exactness of theory we discuss above. Fig.3c is the temple of the logo. Fig.3d shows the TV logo detected using proposed method, and the results give a well performance expectantly. Fig.3h is the detected result of the transparent TV logo. It is excited that we also obtain a better outcome in subjective quality.

As shown in Fig.4, the results of detection also get good effect. It indicates that the method proposed have well commonality in terms of different transparent TV logos. From the above, the method proposed can detect adaptively most static TV logos whatever the logo is transparency or not.

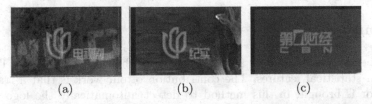

Fig. 1. The group one texting data set:(a)The transparent logo of Channel Young;(b)The opaque logo of hunan TV

Fig. 2. The group two texting data set:the channels having different transparency (a)TV drama channel;(b)Documentary Channel;(c)China Business Network

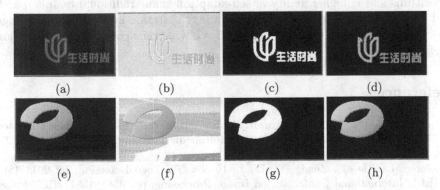

Fig. 3. The experimental results of Group 1 :(a) the minimum value of Channel Young sequence; (b) the maximum value of Channel Young sequence; (c) the temple of Channel Young logo; (d) the final detection result of Channel Young logo;(e)the minimum value of hunan TV;(f)the maximum value of hunan TV;(g)the temple of hunan TV;(h)the final detection result of hunan TV logo

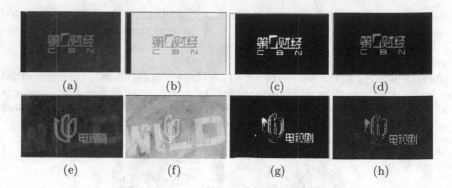

Fig. 4. The experimental results of Group 2: (a) the minimum value of China Business Network sequence; (b) the maximum value of China Business Network sequence; (c) the temple of China Business Network logo; (d) the final detection result of China Business Network logo;(e)the minimum value of TV drama channel sequence;(f)the maximum value of TV drama channel sequence;(g)the temple of TV drama channel;(h)the final detection result of TV drama channel logo

4   Conclusion

This paper proposes a simple and effective algorithm to extract static TV logo based on statistical features. The contribution of our work is that a transparent factor is brought in this method to detect automatically the logo region. Combined with the statistical law of TV sequences, the approach delivers a high performance. It produces significantly fewer counts than other high performance algorithms and is higher ability of self-adaption than traditional temple march and feature extraction. Given the growth in TV station systems requiring logo processing, we believe that this method has a wide range of possible application environments.

References

1. Soysal, M., Ates, T.K., Saracoglu, A., Aydin Alatan, A.: A fast method for animated TV logo detection. In: Content-Based Multimedia Indexing, CBMI 2008, pp. 236–241. IEEE Press, New York (2008)
2. Zhang, L., Xia, T., Zhang, Y., Li, J.: Hollow TV Logo Detection. In: 2011 18th IEEE International Conference on Image Processing, pp. 3581–3584. IEEE Press, New York (2011)
3. Ozay, N., Sankur, B.: Automatic TV Logo Detection and Classification in Broadcast Videos. In: 17th European Signal Processing Conference (EUSIPCO 2009), Glasgow, Scotland, pp. 839–843 (2009)

4. Meisinger, K., Troeger, T., Zeller, M., Kaup, A.: Automatic TV Logo Removal Using Statistical Based Logo Detection and Frequency Selective Inpainting. In: Proc. European Signal Processing Conference 2005 (September 2005)
5. Xiao, G., Dong, Y., Liu, Z., Wang, H.: Supervised TV Logo Detection Based on SVMS. In: Proceedings of IC-NIDC 2010, pp. 174–178. IEEE Press, New York (2010)
6. Co'zar, J.R., Guil, N., Gonzalez-Linares, J.M., Zapata, E.L.: Video Cataloging Based on Robust Logotype Detection. In: 2006 IEEE International Conference on Image Processing, pp. 3217–3220. IEEE Press, New York (2006)

Quantization Matrix Coding for High Efficiency Video Coding

Yijun Mo[1], Jiaji Xiong[1], Jianwen Chen[2], and Feng Xu[2]

[1] Huazhong University of Science and Technology,
Department of Electronic Information, Wuhan, Hubei, 430074, China
[2] University of California, Los Angeles
Department Electrical Engineering, Los Angeles, CA, 90095, USA
moyj@hust.edu.cn, xiongjiaji@smail.hust.edu.cn, jianwen.chen@ieee.org,
xu-feng@live.com

Abstract. Quantization matrix (QM) has been adopted in image coding standards such as JPEG and JPEG-2000, as well as in video standards such as MPEG2, MPEG4 and H.264/AVC. QM can improve the subjective quality through frequency weighting on different frequency coefficients. In the latest high efficiency video coding (HEVC) standard, the quantization block sizes can go up to 32x32. To apply the frequency weighting techniques to HEVC, it needs multiple sizes (4x4, 8x8, 16x16 and 32x32) QMs. The bits to signal the multiple matrices will result in a huge overhead. In this paper, a predictive coding method for the quantization matrix is proposed. The bits consumption for QMs can be reduced significantly. Experimental results show that the proposed method is 28x times efficient (96.4% bit saving) than the quantization matrix compression method used in H.264/AVC. Moreover, the proposed method will only introduce negligible complexity on encoder and decoder.

Keywords: Quantization matrix, HEVC, Video Coding, Predictive Coding.

1 Introduction

The well-known spatial frequency sensitivity of the human visual system(HVS) [1][2], has been a key driver behind many aspects of the design of modern image and video coding algorithms and standards including JPEG, MPEG2, H.264/AVC High Profile [3] and the ongoing HEVC.

Fig.1 illustrates how quantization matrix is used in video encoding process.The quantization matrix used in MPEG2 is an 8x8 matrix. In H.264/AVC, the quantization matrix block size includes both 4x4 and 8x8. These QMs are encoded in SPS (sequence parameter set) and PPS (picture parameters set) as illustrated in Fig.2. The compressed method in H.264/AVC method is Differential Pulse Code Modulation (DPCM). Although the compression ratio of QMs is not very high, it will not affect the whole coding efficiency because just a few QMs need to be encoded into bitstream.

W. Zhang et al. (Eds.): IFTC 2012, CCIS 331, pp. 244–249, 2012.
© Springer-Verlag Berlin Heidelberg 2012

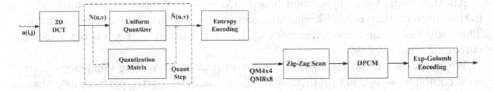

Fig. 1. QM in video encoding   **Fig. 2.** QM coding method in H.264/AVC

In H.264/AVC High Profile, 4x4 block size and 8x8 block size are used. Six QMs for 4x4 block size (i.e. separate matrix for intra/inter coding and Y/Cb/Cr components) and two QMs for 8x8 block size (i.e. separate matrix for intra/inter Y component), so only eight quantization matrices need to be encoded into bitstream. But in HEVC[4], the block size that used for transform and quantization increases to 32x32, QMs with the size of 4x4, 8x8, 16x16, 32x32 should be encoded in the bitstream. For each block size, intra/inter prediction types and Y/Cb/Cr color components need different quantization matrix. In total 24 quantization matrices (separate matrices for 4x4, 8x8, 16x16 and 32x32 four block sizes, intra/inter and Y, U, V components) should be encoded [5]. The number of matrices coefficients of larger blocks is (16x16 + 32x32) x 2 x 3=7680, which need to be coded and stored in picture parameter sets. For each coefficient, it has a range from 0 to 255 (8bits) resulting 60k (7680 x 8) bits in total for each video frame. It is not a huge size data, but compared with the coding bits for one frame, which typically has a size of 50k~500k for HD video frame, the overhead is too large. The QMs data size is about 40 times larger than that of H.264/AVC. In H.264/AVC, QM is coded by differential pulse code modulation (DPCM). It was reported that such an overhead could be roughly 10x of that of AVC if the QMs are coded directly by AVC's method. Therefore efficient coding method of quantization matrix is required in HEVC.

The rest of the paper is organized as follows. In Section 2, the QMs in HEVC are introduced. In section 3, the proposed QM coding algorithm is presented in detail. Experimental results and discussions are given in Section 4. Section 5 presents conclusions.

2 Quantization Matrix Coding in HEVC

This is a new coding problem coming out with HEVC standard. Several approaches have been proposed to improve the QM compressing ratio such as down-sampling method and QM prediction method [5][6]. [5] proposed a down-sampling method. The first step is down-sampling the large size QM into small size one. For example, 32x32 block size is down-sampled to 16x16. Then 135 degree symmetry processing and 45 degree symmetry processing is done to the matrix. At last, the remaining coefficients are compressed by AVC method. This algorithm can provide a better compression ratio but its error between the origin and reconstructed QM coefficients can reach to 7.27 in average. Down-sampling makes it a lossy encoding method.

Another approach is prediction based QM coding algorithm. The basic idea is that current matrix coefficients are predicted from previously coded matrix. Then residual error between current QM and predicted QM is encoded using entropy coding.

We proposed an algorithm that further improves the coding efficiency based on a combined weighting prediction which can achieve better performance than the other methods.

3   Proposed Algorithm

3.1   QM Encoding Scheme

In H.264/AVC, the temporal correlation between different quantization matrix is ignored when conduct the encoding. Actually, for general video sequences, the temporally adjacent video frames always have similar content and continuously changing background. When frequency weighting methods are applied, the QMs for these frames are also similar with little difference on the coefficients. This temporal correlation should be exploited. Based on this, we propose a prediction based QM coding algorithm, in which the previous encoded QMs are used as references.

The proposed algorithm is illustrated in Fig.3. It is composed of two steps. The first step is to predict QM coefficients using coded QMs. There are four prediction modes can be used and the best one mode will be selected for each QM encoding. The second step involves DPCM and run-length coding to encode the residual error of prediction. At last, exp-golomb coding is applied.

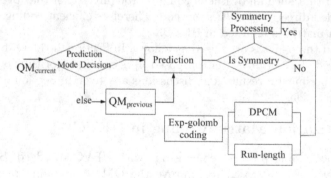

Fig. 3. Proposed QM encoding method

3.2   Prediction Mode

To improve the coding efficiency, four types prediction modes are used. The four modes cover most of the cases of QM prediction and make the proposed encoding scheme more flexible. For example, if a video sequence only contains one set of quantization matrices, namely the sequence uses the same 24 quantization matrices for all frames, up/down-sampling mode would be the best and only choice, since there is no temporally neighboring QM available.

For video encoders, the quantization parameters (QP) and picture types will change when a scene cut occurs. QM coefficients should also be updated accordingly. QM may change adaptively in the GOP level or frame level. There has evidence indicates that if the QM can be updated in MB level, the coding performance can be further improved [7]. This dynamic QM updating make it very important for an accurate QM prediction. And the frequency of QM updating will determine how significant the QM coding will be in the whole HEVC coding scheme.

In the paper, we propose to use predictive methods for QM prediction. The quantization matrix prediction method can be formulated as following,

$$QMcp = \alpha_1 QMp1 + \alpha_2 QMp2 \tag{1}$$

In which QMcp is the predicted quantization matrix of current QM, QMp1 and QMp2 are two referenced QMs. α_1, α_2 are the weighting factors of the references.

We use the followed formulation to adaptively decide the value of α_1 and α_2. $Average\{QMcp_{coeff}(1..N)\}$ represent the average value of the current QM's coefficients. $Average\{QMp1_{coeff}(1..N)\}$ represent the average value of the previous QM's coefficients. N is the number of QM's coefficients.

$$\alpha_1 = \frac{Average\{QMcp_{coeff}(1..N)\}}{Average\{QMp1_{coeff}(1..N)\}}/2 \tag{2}$$

$$\alpha_2 = \frac{Average\{QMcp_{coeff}(1..N)\}}{Average\{QMp2_{coeff}(1..N)\}}/2 \tag{3}$$

The QM prediction modes can be explained in the following difference cases.

1. QM forward/backward prediction: The reference QMs are from the forward/backward frames;

2. QM bi-direction prediction: Some reference QMs are obtained from the previous frames and other reference QMs are obtained from the subsequent frames.

3. QM joint intra/inter prediction: The reference QMs can be selected from intra QMs or inter QMs;

4. QM up-sampling or down-sampling: The reference QMs can obtained by up-sampling or down-sampling from the QMs with different size.

A sum of absolute different (SAD) based approach is used to decide which prediction mode will be used. The SAD of QM under each prediction mode is calculated, then the mode with the smallest SAD will be selected as the best prediction mode. The SAD-based method is very efficient with very low complexity.

3.3 Residual Coding

If the matrix is symmetry, symmetry processing is done which means only half of the coefficients need to be encoded. To decide to use DPCM or run-length, the residual is coded by twice with DPCM and run-lenth respectively. From the total bits of final encoded QM, we choose the better approach.

4   Experiment Results

To test our encoding method, two test conditions are tested: (1) QMs update at frame level, and only one kind of the size such as 8x8 or 16x16 is refreshed every frame. (2) QMs update at GOP level, and all the 24 QMs is different from GOP to GOP. Texture difference between adjacent frames will not be very large, so the QMs will not change much from the previous one. But if QMs are updated by GOP, it will probably change a lot because of the inconsecutive content in different GOPs.

In each test condition, we test several QM encoding methods including AVC method, sony(prediction) method, TI (downsampling) method and the proposed method. All of them are tested in HEVC Test Model-HM4.0 provided by JCT-VC. All sequences are encoded by the random access anchor. In HEVC's core experiment, it offers eight sets of quantization matrices and we use them as the experiment material [8] [9].

Table 1. QM updates at frame level

	average bits	average error
AVC	28037	0
SONY	1821	0
TI	2589	7.25
Our Algorithm	820	0

Table 2. QM updates at GOP level

	average bits	average error
AVC	10479	0
SONY	524	0
TI	735	9.50
Our Algorithm	442	0

Table 1 and Table 2 show the average bits of one set of QMs. One set contains 24 matrices includes 4x4, 8x8, 16x16, 32x32 with inter Y/Cb/Cr and intra Y/Cb/Cr. Our method is a lossless encoding algorithm. Test results show in both of the conditions, our method can achieve the best coding efficiency with zero average error.

Table 3. QM bits ratio(GOP update)

	AVC	SONY	TI	Our
classA	19.9%	1.3%	1.8%	0.6%
classB	29.5%	1.9%	2.7%	0.9%
classC	48.2%	3.1%	4.5%	1.4%
classD	53.2%	3.5%	4.9%	1.6%
Average	37.7%	2.5%	3.5%	1.1%

Table 4. QM bits ratio(frame update)

	AVC	SONY	TI	Our
classA	62.0%	3.1%	4.3%	2.6%
classB	88.2%	4.4%	6.2%	3.7%
classC	145.4%	7.3%	10.2%	6.1%
classD	160.3%	8.0%	11.2%	6.8%
Average	114.0%	5.7%	7.9%	4.8%

Table 3 and Table 4 shows the impact of the proposed method in the entire bitstream. These two tables list the average ratio of the generated bits for matrix coefficients in the whole bitstream. For each video type classified in [10] is tested. These are the standard test sequences for HEVC coding performance evaluation. ClassA represents the video sequence with the resolution of 2560x1600, ClassB is 1920x1080, ClassC is 832x480 and ClassD is 416x240. It is noticed that the overhead of QM in the bitstream decrease significantly from 37.7% to 1.1% under GOP update condition and decrease from 114.0% to 4.8% under frame update condition.

Experiments on HM4.0 show that less than 1% encoding time is increased.

5 Conclusions

This paper proposes a novel QM coding approach for HEVC video standard. High coding efficiency is achieved by use of the temporal correlation among QMs and multiple QM prediction modes. The encoding complexity increasing can be neglected. QM is a tool to improve subjective quality but could lead to a big overhead when used in HEVC. If our QM coding algorithm is applied to HEVC, QM will be a practical tool for subjective quality control at frame or GOP level because the overhead is much reduced.

References

1. Mannos, J.L., Sankrison, D.J.: The effect of a visual fidelity criterion on the encoding of images. IEEE Trans. Inform. Theory 20, 525–536 (1974)
2. Ciptpraset, B., Rao, K.R.: Human visual weighted progressive image transmission. In: International Conference on Commun. Systems, Singapore, pp. 195–197 (1987)
3. Thomas, W., Gary, S., Gisle, B., Ajay, L.: Overview of the H.264/AVC Video Coding Standard. IEEE Transactions on Circuits and Systems for Video Technology 13, 560–576 (2003)
4. Andersson, K., Fuldseth, A., Bjontegaard, G., et al.: High Performance, Low Complexity Video Coding and the Emerging HEVC Standard. IEEE Transactions on Circuits and Systems for Video Technology 20, 1688–1697 (2010)
5. Zhou, M.H., Sze, V.: Compact representation of quantization matrices for HEVC. ISO/IEC JTC1/SC29/WG11, JCTVC-D024, Daegu, Korea (2011)
6. Tanaka, J., Morigami, Y., Suzuki, T., Shinagawa, K.: Enhancement of quantization matrix coding for HEVC. ISO/IEC JTC1/SC29/WG11, JCTVC-F475, Torino, Italy (2011)
7. Chen, J.W., Zheng, J.H., He, Y.: Macroblock-Level Adaptive Frequency Weighting for Perceptual Video Coding. IEEE Transactions on Consumer Electronics 53, 775–781 (2007)
8. Sato, S., Budagavi, M., Coban, M., Aoki, H., Li, X.: Description of Core Experiment 4: Quantization. ISO/IEC JTC1/SC29/WG11, JCTVC-G1204, Geneva, Switzerland (2011)
9. Tabatabai, A., Haque, M., Morigami, Y.: HVS Model based Default Quantization Matrices. ISO/IEC JTC1/SC29/WG11, JCTVC-G880, Geneva, Switzerland (2011)
10. Bossen, F.: Common test conditions and software reference configurations. ISO/IEC JTC1/SC29/WG11, JCTVC-B300, Geneva, Switzerland (2010)

A Framework of Building Complexity Scalable and Cost-Effective Algorithms for HEVC[*]

Huang Li[1], Jiyuan Lu[1,2], and Hongyang Chao[1,**]

[1] School of Software & School of Info. Sci. and Tech., Sun Yat-sen University, China
[2] Department of Computer Science, Guangdong University of Finance, China
isschhy@mail.sysu.edu.cn

Abstract. More and more inter-frame technologies are adopted in the latest video coding standard HEVC in the aim of improving coding efficiency, which also greatly increase the encoder complexity as well. For application scenarios with constrained and varying computing resources, e.g. portable devices or real-time visual communications, degradation on rate-distortion (R-D) performance is inevitable. How to maximize the R-D performance with constrained and varying computing resources is our main concern. In this paper, we will provide a new approach of building a complexity scalable and cost-effective framework consisting of three hierarchical levels.

Keywords: video coding, complexity scalable, cost-effective, HEVC.

1 Introduction

From the initial H.261 to the emerging High Efficiency Video Coding (HEVC) standard, video coding technology has come a long way on coding efficiency, which is measured by rate-distortion (R-D) performance. Each step of improvement on R-D performance is at the cost of increasing computing complexity. The newer standards always improve coding efficiency by adopting more complex inter-frame technologies which in turn greatly increase computational costs at the same time. However, in many application scenarios, available computational resources for encoder are constrained and varying, especially for portable devices or real-time visual communication. Moreover, different devices are likely to have different computing capacities. Even for the same device, the available computing capacities for video encoder varies from time to time because of multitasking. When computational resources are not enough to apply all the optional coding technologies, coding efficiency, i.e. R-D performance, will be reduced.

Our goal of this paper is to develop algorithms which may maximize the R-D performance while computational resources are constrained and varying, where two main problems arise. The first one is how to adaptively fit the encoder to the

---

[*] This work was partially supported by NSF of China under Grant 61173081 and Guangdong Natural Science Foundation, P.R. China, under Grant S2011020001215.
[**] Corresponding author.

W. Zhang et al. (Eds.): IFTC 2012, CCIS 331, pp. 250–257, 2012.

environment (or device) of varying computational resources. The second one is how to minimize the degradation on R-D performance with a specific constraint on computational resources.

There have been a lots of research works done on complexity control for the state-of-the-art coding standard H.264. Most of these were managed to develop fast algorithms for a specific inter-frame technology, such as multi-mode decision, motion estimation (ME), etc [1-5]. However, few of them are able to answer above questions at the same time. For example, He *et al.* try to control the complexity by employing a power-rate-distortion (P-R-D) model [6]. But many parameters are needed to describe the P-R-D relationship, which introduce significant overhead. In [7,8], Liang et al. propose a greedy ME, zero quantized macro-block (MB) early detection and frame rate adjusting algorithms in order to start the coding from the highest complexity level to a lower one, but these algorithms is hard to meet arbitrary computational complexity constraint. The work in [9] may achieve arbitrary computational complexity by setting the proportion of MBs coded with the SKIP mode. However it leads to significant degradation on R-D performance. The work in [10] control the encoder complexity by employing complexity configurable mode decision or motion estimation, but these schemes put more emphasis on complexity control and neglect to minimize the degradation of R-D performance.

Differing from previous works, we find a new approach to maximize the R-D performance under constrained and varying computational resources: cost-performance rankings for all the combinations among all optional inter-frame technologies and steps. Based on this idea, we propose in this paper a video coding framework with two features: complexity scalability and cost-effectiveness. As shown in Fig 1, complexity scalability enables the encoder to fit to the varying constraint on computational resources, while cost-effectiveness guarantees that the encoder can maximize the R-D performance at the same time.

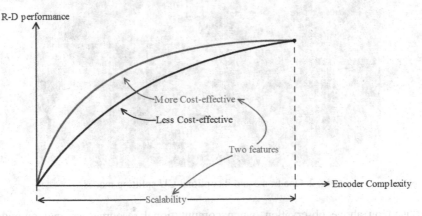

Fig. 1. Two features of the proposed framework

Although the basic concept above is easy to understand, it is hard to implement. The main contribution of this paper is to propose a framework to develop algorithms with above two features. The rest of the paper is organized as follows. In section 2, we describe the proposed framework in detail. Some contributions on implementing the framework is elucidated in section 3. Finally we conclude this paper in section 4.

2   Framework of Complexity Scalable and Cost-Effective Algorithms

As we know, HEVC is still utilizing a hybrid block-based motion compensation/DCT transform architecture. The basic unit for compression in HEVC is termed 'coding unit' (CU), which is analogous to 'macro-block' (MB) in H.264, etc. Similar to other existing standards, all inter-frame technologies adopted in HEVC are optional in encoder, such as motion estimation, multi-mode decision and so on. Whether using these technologies in encoder or not would not violate the criterion of bit-stream, but would have big impact on both R-D performance and encoder complexity.

In addition, we have following two observations according to our experiments: the first is that the same inter-frame technology costs and benefits differently from different CUs (or MBs) based on their contents; and the second is that the same CU also gets different benefits if different methods applied. For example, Fig. 2 shows one frame of the HEVC test sequence and its optimal CU splitting modes. The first observation is, for the multi-mode decision technology, the CU with blue border benefits more than the CU with red border; and the second one is, for the same CU with red border, motion estimation improves more R-D performance than multi-mode decision.

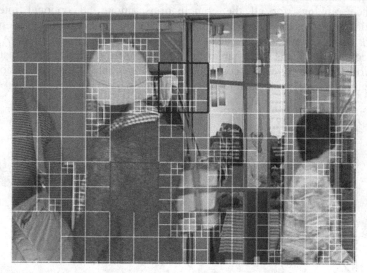

Fig. 2. One frame and its optimal CU splitting modes

Based on above observation, when computational resources are not enough to carry out all the optional inter-frame technologies and all CUs, it is wiser to firstly apply those improving most on R-D performance and costing least on computation, which are referred to as having best cost-performance ratio. Therefore, the two features of the proposed framework can be simultaneously accomplished by performing cost-performance ranking for all the combinations of all optional inter-frame technologies and all CUs in HEVC. However, it's hard or impractical to rank all the optional inter-frame technologies with all CUs in advance because it is too complicated to build a mathematical model to describe the relationships among all the options. Thus we simplify our idea by decomposing the framework into three hierarchical levels: sequence level, frame level and coding unit (CU) level. We only perform cost-performance rankings for the technologies or CUs at the same level. Here are the main thoughts.

Sequence Level. As we know, there are many inter-frame compression technologies in HEVC, including multiple reference frames, mode decision and motion estimation etc. At sequence level, we intend to rank these technologies, for each frame, according to their cost-performance ratios. The one with better cost-performance ratios should be firstly applied in current frame. When computational resources are inadequate, we only perform those technologies with better cost-performance ratios.

Frame Level. At this level, we try to rank all the CUs in current frame, for a given technology, according to their cost-performance ratios. When computational resources are constrained. When applying certain technology to current frame, we allocate more resources to those CUs with better cost-performance ratios, which is different from [10]. [10] once equally allocate the computational resources among the CUs inside one frame. But it's evident that different CUs are likely to have difference R-D gains for certain inter-frame technology. An example is shown in Fig. 3. The left half of Fig. 3 is the current frame to be encoded. The right half is the residual of inter prediction with digits indicating the R-D gains of motion estimation in descending order (i.e. smaller numbers indicates larger R-D gains for inter prediction).

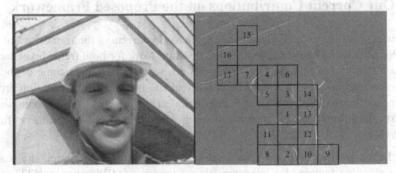

Fig. 3. The order of R-D gains for CUs in one frame

CU Level. How to apply a given inter-frame technology to a CU (HEVC) or MB (H.264, etc.) is one of the most important tasks for video compression, as well as for this framework. Therefore, we try to develop complexity scalable and cost-effective algorithms for the most time-consuming modules in CU compression at CU level. Not only are these algorithms required to be scalable on computational complexity, but also they achieve relatively best R-D performance at any given complexity constraint. For better elucidation of the desired algorithms, an exemplar is shown in Fig. 4. We assume that X and Y are two different algorithms with the R-D cost vs. computational cost curves shown in Fig. 4. Algorithm X and Y has the same R-D performance at a computational cost A or B, but for an arbitrary computational cost constraint C between A and B, algorithm Y always outperform X. Our goal here is to develop an algorithm like Y that is cost-effective at an arbitrary computational cost at CU level, since the allocated resources are not guaranteed to be enough to perform all the steps to reach target B in certain algorithm.

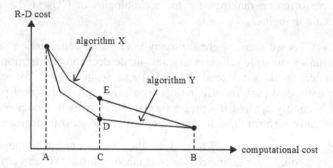

Fig. 4. The relation between R-D cost and computational cost

We have already make a contribution to implementing the proposed framework at frame level and CU (MB) level on the standard H.264, which will be described in next section. All these work can be easily extended to HEVC because it shares almost the same coding architecture with H.264.

3   Our Current Contributions on the Proposed Framework

In previous section, we have elucidated our ideas on designing the framework at each level. We actually have already done some research work for both frame level and CU level based on above framework. In this section, we will introduce some of them as the proof of the concept. It should be noted that the methods in this section are just some approaches to implement our framework described in Section 2. Theoretically, any fast algorithms can be combined with this framework to achieve further improvement.

Frame Level. At this level, we have developed an algorithm with complexity scalable and cost-effective features for integer motion estimation (ME) technology[11], which adjusts its complexity by adaptively setting the number of MBs on which integer motion estimation should perform. More specifically, we firstly rank MBs in the same frame according to their cost-performance priorities which were predicted by our proposed distortion and computational complexity model. Then the complexity of integer ME would be adjusted adaptively by setting the number of MBs on which integer ME should perform, based on the available computing resources for the frame. An ordinary differential equation is being used to describe the relation between the parameter and the computational complexity of our algorithm. And we give an efficient technique to adjust the parameter of the algorithm to meet any computational complexity constraints. According to our experimental results, the proposed algorithm precisely controls the complexity of motion estimation and reaches the best R-D performance compared with all other methods. It is worth emphasizing that the proposed algorithm dose not involved any details of the integer ME process, thus it can be combined with all of existing fast integer ME schemes to achieve even better results.

CU Level. For the existing standard H.264, we have developed a scalable and cost-effective algorithm for fractional-pixel ME at CU (MB) level, which can stop at any step while still achieving a relatively best R-D performance by that time [12]. A special search order in the refinement search pattern has been first introduced to accomplish those features. The search order is in accordance with the search points' cost-performance ratios in descending order. That is to say, among those points in the refinement search pattern, the one with better cost-performance ratio will be searched earlier. The cost-performance ratio of a search point is define as follow: The 'cost' indicates the computational cost of generating fractional pixels for this search position, which can be inferred by the interpolation process defined in the standard; the 'performance' means the probabilities of certain search position to be the optimal match point, which can be obtained in advance by observing the distribution of the best match point in some training sequences. With a refinement search order in accordance with the cost-performance ratios, whenever the procedure of the fractional motion estimation process stopped, we would be expected to maximize the R-D gain by that time.

We have migrated this work to the upcoming video standard HEVC. We implement an improved version of above fractional-pixel motion estimation algorithm basing on HEVC test model 4.0 (HM-4.0). The test sequences are the 20 official test sequences for HEVC in [13]. QP is 32 and the coding structure is IPPP. The experiment results are shown in Fig. 5. Full search (FS) is the default algorithm for fractional-pixel motion estimation in HEVC encoder; CBFPS is the state-of-the-art scheme proposed in [14]; RFSME is the algorithm proposed in [15]. The mean R-D cost is the mean SATD for each pixel. Smaller SATD means better R-D performance. The experiment result shown in Fig. 5. It's obvious that the proposed algorithm outperforms the other ones at an arbitrary constrain on computational complexity.

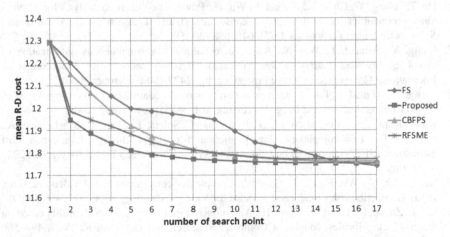

Fig. 5. The performance comparison between the proposed fractional-pixel motion estimation algorithm and other existed fast algorithms

4   Conclusion

In this paper, in the aim of maximizing R-D performance with constrained and varying computing resources, we have presented our ideas on the framework of designing a complexity scalable and cost-effective algorithm for video coding standards, especially for HEVC. In each level of the framework, cost-performance rankings are performed and more computational resources will be allocated to those parts with better cost-performance ratios. With this complexity scalable framework, not only is the encoder able to fit the constrained or varying computational resources, but also it can achieves a relatively best R-D performance. Based on this framework, we illustrate some research results on both frame level and CU level for HEVC, which will be out in detail soon.

References

1. Ri, S.H., Vatis, Y., Ostermann, J.: Fast inter-mode decision in an H.264/AVC encoder using mode and lagrangian cost correlation. IEEE Transactions on Circuits and Systems for Video Technology 19(2), 302–306 (2009)
2. Vatis, Y., Lu, L., Jagmohan, A.: Inter mode selection for H.264/AVC using time-efficient learning-theoretic algorithms. In: Proceedings of International Conference on Image Processing, pp. 3413–3416 (November 2009)
3. Shen, L., Liu, Z., Zhang, Z., Shi, X.: Fast inter mode decision using spatial property of motion field. IEEE Transactions on Multimedia 10(6), 1208–1214 (2008)
4. Zeng, H., Cai, C., Ma, K.K.: Fast mode decision for H.264/AVC based on macroblock motion activity. IEEE Transactions on Circuits and Systems for Video Technology 19(4), 491–499 (2009)
5. Lee, J.Y., Jun, D.S., Park, H.W.: An efficient and fast mode decision method for inter slice of H.264/AVC. In: Proceedings of International Conference on Image Processing, pp. 3405–3408 (November 2009)
6. He, Z., Liang, Y., Chen, L., Ahmad, I., Wu, D.: Power-rate-distortion analysis for wireless video communication under energy constraints. IEEE Transactions on Circuits and Systems for Video Technology 15(5), 645–658 (2005)
7. Liang, Y., Ahmad, I., Wei, X.: Adaptive techniques for simultaneous optimization of visual quality and battery power in video encoding sensors. In: Proceedings of International Conference on Image Processing, pp. 2477–2480 (October 2006)
8. Liang, Y., Ahmad, I., Luo, J.: Joint power and distortion control in video coding. In: SPIE Video Communications and Image Processing, vol. 5685, pp. 885–895 (2005)
9. Kannangara, C.S., Richardson, I.E.G., Bystrom, M., Solera, J., Zhao, Y., MacLennan, A., Cooney, R.: Low-complexity skip prediction for H.264 through Lagrangian cost estimation. IEEE Transactions on Circuits and Systems for Video Technology 16(2), 202–208 (2006)
10. Su, L., Lu, Y., Wu, F., Li, S., Gao, W.: Complexity-constrained H.264 video encoding. IEEE Transactions on Circuits and Systems for Video Technology 19(4), 477–490 (2009)
11. Lu, J., Zhang, P., Duan, X., Chao, H.: An optimized motion estimation algorithm based on macro-block priorities. Journal of Computer Research and Development 48(3), 494–500 (2011)

12. Lu, J., Zhang, P., Chao, H., Fisher, P.S.: On combining fractional-pixel interpolation and motion estimation: a cost-effective approach. IEEE Transactions on Circuits and Systems for Video Technology 21(6), 717–728 (2011)
13. Bossen, F.: Common test conditions and software reference configurations. Document of Joint Collaborative Team on Video Coding, JCTVC-F900 (2011)
14. Chen, Z., Xu, J., He, Y., Zheng, J.: Fast integer-PEL and fractional-PEL motion estimation for H.264/AVC. Journal of Visual Communication and Image Representation 17(2), 264–290 (2006)
15. Lin, W., Panusopone, K., Baylon, D.M., Sun, M.-T., Chen, Z., Li, H.: A fast sub-pixel motion estimation algorithm for H.264/AVC video coding. IEEE Transactions on Circuits and Systems for Video Technology 21(2), 237–242 (2011)

Deblocking Filtering Based on View Correlation for Multiview Video Decoding

Yongfang Wang[1], Wei Zhang[2], Ping An[1], and Zhaoyang Zhang[1]

[1] School of Communication and Information Engineering, Shanghai University,
Shanghai, China
[2] Department of Electronics and Information Engineering, Huazhong University of Science
and Technology, Hubei, 430074, China
{yfw,anping,zyzhang}@shu.edu.cn, weizhang1216@hotmail.com

Abstract. A well-designed deblocking filtering scheme should make tradeoff between both coding efficiency and coding complexity. However, the existing multiview video deblocking filtering algorithm has adopted H.264 deblocking scheme to improve the video quality with high coding complexity without consideration the view correlation. In this paper, we propose a low complexity deblocking filtering algorithm based on motion skip mode. It makes use of view correlation to simplify the BS of an MB computation time when the coded macroblock is in motion skip mode. Experimental results show that the proposed algorithm can achieve decoding time saving significantly without any perceptual quality loss in comparison to the deblocking filtering in JMVC.

Keywords: Deblocking filtering, multiview video coding, motion skip mode.

1 Introduction

The mutiview video coding (MVC) standard [1], as an extension profile of H.264/AVC, draws more and more attention for its high compression ratio and free-viewpoint support. The deblocking filtering (DF) method for MVC [1] has adopted the H.264/AVC DF method to reduce the presence of blocking artifacts in decoded video frame, however, it resulted in increased computational complexity, which takes one third of decoder complexity in only single view video coding [2].Therefore the low complexity DF designs are needed for MVC.

Several methods have been proposed to improve the DF efficiency for MVC. SeungHo Shin et al.[3] proposed the novel DF based on variable block sizes and the human visual system for stereoscopic video, which could save more than 20% of the entire filtering time without a loss of visual quality. A DF method for MVC [4] was proposed to improve subjective picture quality by diminishing blocking artifacts caused by illumination compensation. In [5], we proposed an efficient DF method to improve chroma PSNR in a low rate for MVC. However, few literatures have been reported related with the decreasing computational complexity of the DF algorithm for MVC. Although the previous methods related to the decreasing computational

W. Zhang et al. (Eds.): IFTC 2012, CCIS 331, pp. 258–263, 2012.

complexity of the DF for H.264 [6-8] can be applied to MVC to speedup the DF, they were developed for single view video coding without considering multiview video coding characteristic. In the paper, we propose a low complexity DF algorithm in consideration of view correlation, which can skip the BS computation of many MBs and directly copy BS values from the corresponding reference MB in neighbor view when the current MB is in the motion skip coding mode, thus the whole time consumption of DF is reduced observably. Our algorithm significantly reduces the debloking filtering complexity while keeping the similar subjective quality compared with the conventional algorithm.

2   Proposed Deblocking Filtering Algorithm for MVC

Since the motion of neighboring views are highly correlated, motion skip coding is proposed in [9] to reuse motion information of corresponding MB in previously coded inter-view pictures. The corresponding MB is inferred by the global disparity between current view and reference view. If the motion skip mode is used, the BS value of an MB in current view will be similar to that of the corresponding MB in neighbor view. Whereas the main cause of high computational complexity is heavy conditional processing at block edge and pixel level for BS computation in H.264 deblocking filter [7].To improve the speed of computing BS, the BS of an MB in current view may be directly copied from the corresponding MB in neighbor view, thus some of the BS computation may be skipped.

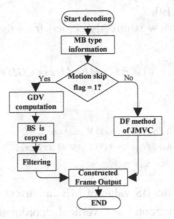

Fig. 1. Flowchart of the proposed deblocking filtering algorithm

Based on the above analysis, we propose a simple method of copying the BS of the DF in order to effectively reduce the BS computation time based on motion skip coding. Firstly, we use the motion skip coding at coding mode and analyze the MB coding mode at encoder, Secondly, the information of MB coding type is transferred to the decoder using flag information, which motion_skip_flag equals to 1 indicates that the coded MB is in motion skip mode and motion_skip_flag equals to 0 indicates that the coded MB is not in motion skip mode. Finally, we reduce DF complexity based on the MB motion skip coding information at decode.

The flowchart of the proposed DF algorithm at decoder is shown in Fig.1.

The proposed approach is processed as follows.

Step 1. Start decoding the MB coding type information at decoder. If motion_skip_flag =1, go to step2, otherwise go to step5.

Step 2. When the MB coding type information is motion skip mode, the global disparity vector (GDV) between two views is applied to find the corresponding MB position in the picture of reference view. The GDV for motion skip mode [9] that derivates GDV in MB-based unit from neighbor view already decoded is utilized in the proposed method and obtained by the full search frame matching with 8*8 sized block between reference view and current view in (1) and (2)

$$GDV = \operatorname*{arg\,min}_{-SR \le x, y \le SR} \{MAD(8 \times x, 8 \times y)\} \tag{1}$$

$$MAD(x, y) = \frac{1}{(h-y)(w-x)} \sum_{i=0}^{w-x-1} \sum_{j=0}^{h-y-1} |fr(i+x, j+y) - fc(i, j)| \tag{2}$$

where fr and fc are the inter-view reference frame and current frame. w and h are the width and height of frame. i and j represent horizontal and vertical coordinates for image pixels, respectively. SR is the search range with precision of 8*8 block size. For anchor pictures, the GDV is calculated using the method described above. For non-anchor pictures, the GDV can be interpolated using the $GDVs$ from the two neighboring anchor pictures [9].

Step 3. The BS of current view is directly copied from the corresponding reference MB of neighbor view in (3).

$$BS_c (MbAddress, x, y) = BS_r (MbAddress + GDV, x, y) \tag{3}$$

Subjective to

$$\begin{cases} 0 \le MbAddress_x + GDV_i \le MaxCol; \\ 0 \le MbAddress_y + GDV_j \le MaxLine; \\ 0 \le x \le 3; 0 \le y \le 3; \end{cases} \tag{4}$$

where $BS_c()$ and $BS_r()$ are the BS value of MB in current view and reference view, respectively. x and y are horizontal and vertical coordinates boundary of 4×4 left-upper luna block of the current MB, respectively. GDV_i and GDV_j denote horizontal and vertical of GDV for MB, respectively. $MbAddress$ denotes the position of the MB. $MbAddr_x$ and $MbAddr_y$ denote horizontal and vertical position of the MB, respectively. $MaxCol$ and $MaxLine$ denote MB numbers in horizontal and vertical coordinates in frame, respectively.

Step 4. The BS value is obtained, the corresponding filtering is performed, then go to step6.
Step 5. The DF is adopted by the conventional DF method of JMVC.
Step 6. Go to Step1 and proceed with next MB.

3   Experimental Results

The experiments are conducted using a 3-GHz Intel Pentium 4 processor with 512M memory. We compared the performance of the proposed algorithm with the conventional deblocking fitering method in JMVC8.2 [10]. The employed three sequences are Ballroom, Exit and Race1. The three views (view0,view1,view7) for Ballroom and the three views (view0,view1,view2) for Exit and Race1 are used to simulate as I-view, B-view and P-view. In all tests, the DF is turned on. Temporal length of a GOP is 8, the search ranges for disparity estimation and motion estimation are ± 64, and the quantization parameter (QP) is with 30, 33, 36, 39 and 42.

Table 1 illustrates the coding efficiency and complexity comparison results under different QP for three sequences between the proposed algorithm and the DF method in JMVC8.2. Complexity is measured with consumed coding time. It can be seen from Table1 that the proposed algorithm can greatly reduce the BS computation time, and lead to the DF time saving with only a negligible loss of PSNR for all sequences. An average 18% filtering time saving is achieved compared with the DF method in JMVC8.2 for three sequences, with maximum of 37% for Ballroom, whereas the loss of coding efficiency is negligible for the proposed algorithm, providing an average PSNR loss of about 0.0136dB. Since the Ballroom sequence has a slow movement with complex texture information, the proposed algorithm shows better results providing about 26% deblocking time saving with negligible loss of objective quality. For the Exit sequence, our algorithm is also obvious because the sequence shows a large area with static background. On the other hand, Race1 sequence is as of fast movement, the DF time saving is around 7–14% and much less than the saving of other two sequences. From Table 1, we can also see that P view has much more DF time saving than B view, it is because that the B-view will take more time to pre-judge BS values than P-view. Fig.2 shows the subjective comparison of the decoded images for the Ballroom It can be seen that the perceptual quality of the proposed method is almost same of the conventional DF for MVC.

Fig. 2. The 30th decoded frame of the P-view in the ballroom sequence (QP:39):the proposed deblocking filtering method (left) and the JMVC deblocking filtering method (right)

Table 1. Performance Evaluation for "Ballroom" "Exit" "Race1" sequence

Sequences (resolution)		BasicQP	Bs time saving(%)	DF saving(%)	PSNR degradation(dB)
Ballroom 640×480	P Slice	30	48%	32%	0.0174
		33	50%	37%	0.0312
		36	42%	21%	0.0202
		39	40%	23%	0.0205
		42	54%	33%	0.0192
	B Slice	30	42%	24%	0.0134
		33	32%	23%	0.0125
		36	30%	20%	0.0129
		39	42%	19%	0.0136
		42	36%	21%	0.0121
Exit 640×480	P Slice	30	27%	20%	0.0152
		33	33%	22%	0.0169
		36	32%	22%	0.0196
		39	25%	20%	0.0195
		42	35%	23%	0.0208
	B Slice	30	23%	15%	0.0091
		33	31%	22%	0.0078
		36	28%	17%	0.0101
		39	21%	18%	0.0100
		42	32%	20%	0.0121
Race1 640×480	P Slice	30	21%	12%	0.0125
		33	23%	13%	0.0111
		36	23%	14%	0.0105
		39	15%	12%	0.0110
		42	17%	9%	0.0118
	B Slice	30	14%	6%	0.0067
		33	17%	8%	0.0077
		36	20%	8%	0.0063
		39	12%	11%	0.0101
		42	14%	7%	0.0067
Average			29%	18%	0.0136

4   Conclusion

The paper has presented a low complexity DF algorithm based on motion skip coding mode by exploiting view correlation for MVC, which can skip the BS computation of many MBs and be directly copied BS value from the corresponding reference MB in neighbor view. Experimental results showed that the proposed scheme can significantly reduce DF complexity of MVC with negligible quality degradation.

Acknowledgment. This work was supported by Natural Science Foundation of China under Grant No.60972137 and 61174182, 61172096, and Key Project of National Science Foundation of China under Grant No.60832003.

References

1. ISO/IEC/JTC1/SC29/WG11, Multiview coding using AVC, Bangkok, Thailand (January 2006)
2. Horowitz, M., Joch, A., Kossentini, F.: H.264/AVC Basline Profile Decoder Complexity Analysis. IEEE Trans. Circ. and Syst. Video Technol. 13, 704–716 (2003)
3. Shin, S., Chai, Y., Kim, T.: Fast Deblocking Filter for Stereoscopic Video Coding in Mobile Broadcasting. IEEE Transactions on Consumer Electronics 57(2), 811–816 (2011)
4. Park, G.H., Park, M.W., Lim, S.-C., Shim, W.S., Lee, Y.-L.: Deblocking Filtering for Illumination Compensation in Multiview Video Coding. IEEE Transactions on Circuits and Systems for Video Technology 18(10), 1457–1460 (2008)
5. Fu, Y., Wang, Y., Zhang, Z.: "An efficient deblocking filtering algorithm in multi-view video coding. In: 2010 International Conference on Audio Language and Image Processing, ICALIP 2010, pp. 329–332 (2010)
6. Pieters, B., Hollemeersch, C., De Cock, J., Lambert, P., De Neve, W., Van de Walle, R.: Parallel Deblocking Filtering in MPEG-4 AVC/H.264 on Massively-Parallel Architectures. IEEE Transactions on Circuits and Systems for Video Technology 21(1), 96–100 (2011)
7. Lou, J., Jagmohan, A., He, D., Lu, L., Sun, M.-T.: H.264 Deblocking Speedup. IEEE Transactions on Circuits and Systems For Video Technology 19(8), 1178–1182 (2009)
8. Chung, H.-C., Chen, Z.-Y., Chang, P.-C.: Low Power Architecture Design and Hardware Implementations of Deblocking Filter in H.264/AVC. IEEE Transactions on Consumer Electronics 57(2), 713–719 (2011)
9. Koo, H.-S., Jeon, Y.-J., Jeon, B.-M.: MVC Motion Skip Mode. In: ITU-T and ISO/IEC JTC1, JVT-W081, San Jose, California, USA (April 2006)
10. Joint Video Team of ISO/IEC MPEG and ITU-T VCEG, WD1 Reference Software for MVC. ISO/IECJTC1/SC29/WG11 and ITU-T SG16 Q.6 JVT-AA212 (April 2008)

Compressive Sensing Image Coding with Perceptual Weighting Measuring Matrix

Yundong Song[2], Yongfang Wang[1,2], Xiwu Shang[2], and Zhaoyang Zhang[1,2]

[1] Key Lab. of Advanced Display and System Application, Ministry of Education,
Shanghai University, Shanghai, 200072, China
[2] School of Communication and Information Engineering, Shanghai University,
Shanghai, 200072, China
{yfw,orient,zyzhang}@shu.edu.cn, dxsxw@126.com

Abstract. Compressive sensing is a new technology, which combines data sampling with compressing. Many applications of compressive sensing in image processing and computer vision are being explored. In this paper, we propose a compressive sensing image coding scheme with weighting measuring matrix based on just noticeable distortion, where image coefficients have been adaptively weighted according to their different visual significances. Simulation results demonstrate that the proposed method can greatly improve the quality of the reconstructed image compared with the existing algorithm.

Keywords: Compressive Sensing, Just noticeable distortion model, Measuring Matrix, Weighting Function.

1 Introduction

With the development of information society, the multimedia technology and wireless communication technology have gained popularity in our daily life. We will face the pressure of mass data when they are sampled, transmitted and stored. In conventional data sampling and compressing system, natural signals are sampled according to Shannon sampling theory: twice of the signal bandwidth challenges our existing hardware and software equipments. Compressive sensing breaks the sampling frequency limit based on Nyquist's theory [1]. Now the practice has proved that we can reconstruct the original message with lesser signals.

Compressive sensing (CS) indicates that we can measure to get the compression form of original signals with a matrix that is irrelevant with transformed base. It is entirely possible to recover desired signal by solving optimization problem in receiver, because these small amounts of measuring signals carries all the needed information of original signal. Owing to the simple operation of sensor measuring, which only involves projecting signals from high dimensional space to low dimension, the sensor can consume low energy and compute simply.

Researchers have made considerable progress in applications and algorithms of compressive sensing recently. The authors in [2] have proposed block 2D-DCT CS, which can reconstruct original signals perfectly besides lower complexity than

W. Zhang et al. (Eds.): IFTC 2012, CCIS 331, pp. 264–270, 2012.

1D-DCT CS. A new measuring matrix——CHT has proposed to recover signals with less measurements in [3]. [4] presented block CS with DWT reduces not only complexity, but also memory space through OMP algorithm. A weighting measuring matrix based on JPEG quantization table is proposed in [5] to improve compressive sensing reconstructed image quality, which took matrix multiplication of weighting matrix and measuring matrix as new measuring matrix. Authors in [6] propose a weighting Equ.(1),

$$w(i, j) = 1 + 1/(1 + (i + j)/q) \tag{1}$$

which is the same size as the image (i, j refer to the row and column number of the whole image, q refers to a constant).

The paper studies measuring matrix of compressive sensing image coding, and proposes a reconstructing algorithm based on JND weighting function. Extensive experiments demonstrate that the proposed algorithm can improve the quality of reconstructed image greatly.

2   Overview of Compressive Sensing

In compressive sensing framework, when the signals are sparse or compressible, that is, they have a sparse representation under some linear transformation, a small number of random projections of the signal contains sufficient information for exact reconstruction. Three core problems are involved in compressive sensing [1][7]: signal sparsity, the design of measuring matrix and reconstructing algorithm. First of all, we suppose that the signal $X \in R^N$ is sparse under a orthogonal base or tight frame ψ (conversion coefficient $\Theta = \psi^T X$, Θ is equivalent or approximation spare representation); then, we design a $M \times N$ dimensional measuring matrix Θ which is steady and irrelevant with transformed base for measuring Θ to get measuring data $Y = \Phi\Theta = \Phi\varphi^T X$; solving precision or approximation for X by computing optimization under the meaning of 0-norm: $\min \left\| \psi^T X \right\|_0 \text{s.}t\, \Phi\Psi^T X = Y$ [7] at last. Considering the study of compressive sensing, domestic and overseas experts are mainly aimed at these three parts.

The sparsity of signals is a precondition for the application of CS. Most natural signals are not sparse, but we can make them be sparse representation through transforming. That is to say, the signal can also apply CS when it is compressive. Common sparse transforms embrace DCT、DWT、DFT、Walsh transform and so on.

To some extent, reconstructing algorithm of CS is to solve an underdetermined system of equations, which means reconstructing original signal from low dimension to high dimension. The application of CS from theory to engineering practice is significantly affected by reconstructing quality. Reconstruction is a non-linear process, therefore finding the most sparse signal coefficient is a must, which is a problem to solve a min 0-norm. Currently orthogonal matching pursuit (OMP) algorithm is an excellent method and also needs more study.

3   The Proposed Algorithm with Perceptual Measuring Matrix

3.1   JND Model

JND model refers to the minimum perceivable distortion based on physiology and psychology, that is the minimum distortion that human eye can perceive. The size of JND value reflects the visual redundancy in image and video. At present, JND model is the most effective method to feature visual redundancy. The main factors affecting JND model include brightness adaptive characteristics, contrast sensitivity function, texture masking effect, smooth pursuit eye movement and so on. JND model provides a screen for visual redundancy information through computing a varying noise threshold that human eye cannot perceive.

At the moment, JND model is widely applied to preprocessing, bit rate control, motion estimation and quantization table—making. There are two research directions about JND model: pixel domain JND model and transform domain such as DCT domain and wavelet domain. The paper adopts the JND model proposed in [8].

3.2   Weighting Measuring Matrix Based on JND

Measuring matrix plays an important role in data sampling and reconstructing, and its performance will greatly affect the quality of reconstructing image. The design of measuring matrix is based on Restricted Isometry Principle (RIP) [9], which is equivalent to irrelevancies between measuring matrix Φ and sparse base Ψ . Under the guidance of RIP, there are random and definitive measuring matrices being adopted. Now random Gaussian matrix, random Fourier matrix and random Bernoulli matrix are widely used for measuring matrix. Because of its irrelevance with any sparse signal, we can measure less in sampling and get good result. However, it is difficult to realize in hardware for their large storage space and high computation complexity.

On account of the properties of image processing based on compressive sensing, In the paper, we design a weighting measuring matrix in accordance with different importance to reconstructing quality of different frequency coefficients based on JND.

In order to achieve better reconstructed image, we expected that the low frequency coefficients would be larger weighted while high frequency coefficients be smaller weighted when we take into account the sensitivities of the human visual systems. At the same time, JND threshold reflects the the sensitivities of the human visual systems. Therefore, we proposed a new weighting measuring matrix based on JND model, the weighting function of the weighting measuring matrix is defined as follows,

$$w(i, j) = 1 + k/jnd'$$

(2)

where k is empirical value, jnd is threshold of JND, i, j refer to the row and column number of the whole image. It is obvious from Equ.(2) that the function value $w(i,j)$ decreases with the increase of JND. Corresponding to DCT coefficients, we can see that low frequency coefficients get a bigger weight, while high frequency coefficients get a smaller weight, which corresponds with the properties of human visual system.

3.3   System Description of the Proposed Algorithm

The flowchart of the proposed algorithm is shown in Fig.1. The proposed approach is processed as follows.

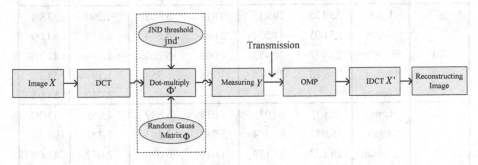

Fig. 1. The flowchart of the proposed algorithm

1) Sparse transform on original image with 8*8 block DCT to get DCT sparse coefficients X ;

2) To compute the JND threshold jnd in DCT domain;

3) To generate a Gaussian random matrix Φ ;

4) Capturing M rows of JND threshold to get a $M \times N$ weighting function jnd' ;

5) Doing dot multiplication with jnd' and Φ to get a new measuring matrix Φ' ;

6) Measuring DCT coefficients of the image with Φ' to get measuring data Y ;

7) Reconstructing the measuring data Y to get X' through OMP algorithm;

8) Doing block DCT inverse transform on X' to recover image.

4   Experimental Results

In simulation, a fairly general set of test images was used in our comparative study, including Lena, Organ, Foreman and Caman (Cameraman). We choose Gaussian random matrix as measuring matrix (error range 2%). K in weighting function is empirically set to 10; we compared our proposed algorithm with the algorithm in [10], and complexity is measured with consumed decoding time.

Table 1 illustrates the coding efficiency and complexity comparison results under different sampling number for four test images between the proposed algorithm and [10]. It can be seen from Table 1 that the proposed algorithm can achieve better reconstructing quality than the algorithm in [10], while it would consume more time. With the increase of sampling number, we can achieve better image quality.

Fig.2 and Fig.3 show the subjective comparison of the decoded images. For Fig.2, the quality of the proposed algorithm in Fig.2 (b) is much better than that [10] in Fig.2 (a), but the quality effect is not obvious in Fig.3. It is because the gain of the PSNR is 6.173db in Fig.2, whereas the gain of PSNR in Fig.3 is only 1.338db. It is concluded that the quality improvement is different by extent for different images, mainly due to the different details of the image, space redundancy and so on.

Table 1. The results of measuring matrix weighted before and after

Number/ M	Test Image	PSNR/dB		OMP time/s		△PSNR /db	△T/T× 100%
		[10]	Proposed	[10]	Proposed		
80	Lena	25.125	29.415	4.411	5.863	4.290	32.9%
	Organ	35.005	41.521	2.646	4.843	6.516	83.0%
	Foreman	23.457	26.453	4.065	5.800	2.996	42.7%
	Caman	24.718	25.915	3.756	5.754	1.197	53.2%
	Average	——	——	——	——	3.750	53.0%
85	Lena	25.973	30.038	5.019	6.689	4.065	33.3%
	Organ	36.952	44.284	2.742	5.383	7.332	96.3%
	Foreman	25.127	27.179	4.648	6.676	2.052	43.6%
	Caman	25.814	26.813	4.149	6.633	0.999	59.9%
	Average	——	——	——	——	3.612	58.3%
90	Lena	28.281	32.483	5.425	7.138	4.202	31.6%
	Organ	38.789	46.968	3.061	6.193	8.179	102.3%
	Foreman	26.491	28.727	5.163	7.180	2.236	39.1%
	Caman	27.194	28.532	4.472	7.351	1.338	64.4%
	Average	——	——	——	——	3.989	59.4%
95	Lena	29.149	34.125	6.020	8.067	4.976	34.0%
	Organ	40.619	52.471	3.144	7.033	11.852	123.7%
	Foreman	28.581	29.188	5.471	8.364	0.607	52.9%
	Caman	27.641	30.047	4.921	8.137	2.406	65.4%
	Average	——	——	——	——	4.960	69.0%
100	Lena	30.726	36.899	6.162	8.711	6.173	41.4%
	Organ	44.053	52.964	3.246	7.918	8.911	143.9%
	Foreman	28.306	31.928	5.998	9.144	3.622	52.5%
	Caman	29.750	30.600	5.192	9.127	0.850	75.8%
	Average	——	——	——	——	4.889	78.4%
Average		——	——	——	——	4.24	48.1%

Furthermore, the experiments also reveal that we can recover original signals from a small amount of data, which means compression. Compressive sensing can realize this effect, because every sparse DCT coefficient has global information of the original image.

(a) [10]	(b) Proposed	(c) Original

Fig. 2. Lena (weighted before and after, sampling number M=100)

(a) [10]	(b) Proposed	(c) Original

Fig. 3. Cameraman (weighted before and after, sampling number M=90)

5   Conclusion

In the paper, we have presented a new perceptual measuring matrix based on JND for compressive sensing image coding considering of visual perception. Simulation results show that the proposed algorithm improves reconstructed image quality greatly, although it resulted in increased computational complexity. More work is needed to reduce the computation time of image recovery for real-time applications in future.

Acknowledgment. This work was supported by Natural Science Foundation of China under Grant No.60972137 and Key Project of National Science Foundation of China under Grant No.60832003.

References

1. Donoho, D.L.: Compressed sensing. IEEE Trans Inform. Theory 52(4), 1289–1306 (2006)
2. Bai, H.H., Wang, A.H., Zhang, M.M.: Compressive Sensing for DCT Image. In: 2010 International Conference on Computational Aspects of Social Networks, Taiyuan, pp. 378–381 (2010)

3. Kumar, N.R., Wei, X., Soar, J.: A Novel Image Compressive Sensing Method Based on Complex Measurements. In: 2011 International Conference on Digital Image Computing: Techniques and Applications, Toowoomba, pp. 175–179 (2011)
4. Sermwuthisarn, P., Auethavekiat, S., Patanavijit, V.: A fast image recovery using compressive sensing technique with block based Orthogonal Matching Pursuit. In: 2009 International Symposium on Intelligent Signal Processing and Communication Systems, Kanazawa, pp. 212–215 (2009)
5. Yang, Y., Au, O.C., Fang, L., Wen, X., Tang, W.R.: Perceptual compressive sensing for image signals. In: 2009 IEEE International Conference on Multimedia and Expo, New York, pp. 89–92 (2009)
6. Li, Y.H.: Improved model of image block compressed sensing. Computer Engineering and Applications 47(25), 186–189 (2011)
7. Tralic, D., Grgic, S.: Signal Reconstruction via Compressive Sensing. In: 53rd International Symposium ELMAR 2011, Zadar, pp. 14–16 (2011)
8. Wei, Z.Y., Ngan, K.N.: Spatio-Temporal Just Noticeable Distortion Profile for Grey Scale Image/Video in DCT Domain. IEEE Transactions on Circuits and Systems for Video Technology 19(3), 337–346 (2009)
9. Candes, E.J., Tao, T.: Decoding by Linear Programming. IEEE Transactions on Information Theory 51(12), 4203–4215 (2005)
10. Lu, G.: Block Compressed Sensing of Natural Image. In: 15th International Conference on Digital Signal Processing, Cardiff, pp. 403–406 (2007)

Error Concealment for Whole Frame Loss in HEVC

Chang Liu[1,2], Ran Ma[1,2], and Zhaoyang Zhang[1,2]

[1] School of Communication and Information Engineering, Shanghai University,
Shanghai 200072, China
[2] Key Laboratory of Advanced Displays and System Application, Ministry of Education,
Shanghai 200072, China
{liuchang1986,maran}@shu.edu.cn

Abstract. The next-generation video coding standard, called High Efficiency Video Coding (HEVC), obtains high efficiency compression by using variable size coding block based on quad-tree structure. However, when HEVC stream is transmitted through the network, the burst loss of data packet may lead to the loss of the whole frame. By analysis of the texture features of video, motion vector (MV) extrapolation based on variable size coding blocks is proposed in this paper to recovery the lost frame fast and effectively. Experimental results show that the proposed method can reduce computational complexity effectively, compared to traditional error conceal algorithms in case of the similar PSNR.

Keywords: HEVC, error concealment, motion vector extrapolation, whole frame loss.

1 Introduction

Recently, ISO-IEC/MPEG and ITU-T/VCEG have formed the Joint Collaborative Team on Video Coding (JCT-VC). The JCT-VC group is aiming to develop the next generation video coding standard, called HEVC. Hybrid prediction coding scheme used in HEVC is similar to H.264/AVC. The difference between them is that the maximal block size of HEVC can be expanded to 64×64[1], while only 16×16 for H.264/AVC. Besides, HEVC utilizes quad-tree coding structure and flexible block segmentation [2].

However, video packets may be damaged or lost due to the unreliability of the communication channel. In low bit-rate video transmission, one packet loss often results in whole frame loss. HEVC still uses inter prediction encoding framework, so error propagation largely impacts the constructed quality of subsequent frames. Therefore, it is particularly important to conceal error in the decoder.

In this paper, we propose a new motion vector extrapolation based on variable size block, which can conceal error of HEVC frames fast and effectively. The rest of the paper is organized as follows: Part 2 describes the existing error concealment (EC) algorithm, Part 3 proposes our EC algorithm, experimental results are presented in Part 4, and a conclusion is given in Part 5.

W. Zhang et al. (Eds.): IFTC 2012, CCIS 331, pp. 271–277, 2012.
© Springer-Verlag Berlin Heidelberg 2012

2   Motion Vector Extrapolation

When whole frame loss occurs during transmission, it means no adjacent pixels can be used for EC. Many frame loss EC methods have been proposed. Frame copy (FC) [3], for example, is the simplest way, which copies the pixels of previous frame to current frame. FC is only suitable for slow movement in frames. Classic concealment method for the whole frame loss is motion vector extrapolation (MVE) [4].

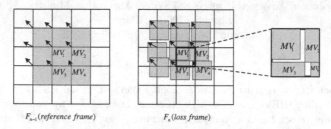

F_{n-1} (reference frame) F_n (loss frame)

Fig. 1. Motion vector extrapolation

In MVE, the objects in frames are assumed to make linear motion. Shown in Fig. 1, F_n denotes the lost frame, and F_{n-1} is its reference frame. Four blocks in F_{n-1} are extrapolated onto one lost block in F_n by using their MVs, called MV_1, MV_2, MV_3 and MV_4 respectively (see Fig.1). The lost block in F_n, which is depicted as a bold-lined square in Fig.1, overlaps with these extrapolated blocks. The MV of the lost block is predicted by a weighted average of the MVs of all the extrapolated blocks, and is characterized by Equation (1).

$$MV = \frac{\sum_{k=1}^{N} MV_k \times \omega_k}{\sum_{k=1}^{N} \omega_k} \tag{1}$$

Where the weighting factor ω_k indicates the number of pixels in the overlapping area and N denotes the number of the overlapping blocks.

In MVE, fixed-size block is processed as the basic unit for EC. The weighted average method can cause artifacts. Besides, for HD video, error concealment with small fixed-size block will increase computational complexity largely. If used directly in HD video, it achieves either unsatisfying reconstructed quality or high computational complexity. So motion vector extrapolation based on the variable size blocks is described in Part 3, which can conceal damaged frames fast and effectively.

3   Proposed Algorithm

Traditional error concealment for whole frame loss is mainly based on fixed-size blocks, and the lost blocks are generally processed with small size 4 × 4 or 8 × 8 pixels. The texture features of the image and strong time-domain correlation between video sequences are ignored to some extent. HEVC is typically designed for high resolution video content, so EC with small fixed-size blocks will largely increase computational complexity, which is not applied to the real-time communication.

3.1   Decision for Block Size in Lost Frame

In HEVC, blocks with different sizes can be combined in various ways. The encoder decides on the quad-tree structure in a rate-distortion optimized fashion. Usually, the smooth areas in frames are mainly coded with blocks of size 32 × 32 or 64 × 64 pixels. As expected, the areas with higher motion and detailed texture are coded using smaller blocks, such as 16×16 or 8×8[5]. One lost frame in HEVC means that all blocks with different sizes will be lost. If all the blocks in the lost frame are regarded as the same large-size blocks to be concealed, the computational complexity of EC might be reduced. But it is not inadvisable to replace small blocks with large blocks that might ignore some details in HD video.. Therefore, the correlation of motion vectors is proposed to decide whether large block will be divided into smaller blocks or not.

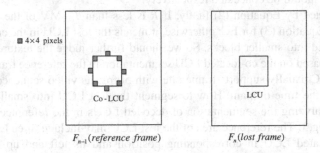

Fig. 2. Analysis of correlation between frames

Giving the example of large coding unit (LCU), as shown in Fig.2, the correlation of MVs, which come from co-located LCU (Co-LCU in Fig.2) and its neighboring ones, is discussed. In order to reduce computational complexity, four MVs of 4×4 pixels from bi-diagonal and four MVs of 4×4 pixels from its neighboring LCUs are chosen for the calculation of temporal correlation. The following Equation (2) characterizes the relation between the temporal correlation and the MVs.

$$R = \frac{1}{28} \times \sum_{k=1}^{M-1} \sum_{j=k+1}^{M} \left\| V_k - V_j \right\| \tag{2}$$

Where M denotes the number of the chosen MVs, V_k and V_j denotes any two MVs from different locations, R indicates the correlation of MVs. Actually, Equation (2) is also applied to block size with 32×32 or 16×16. The higher value of R means larger difference among MVs, so it is necessary to divide large block into smaller blocks. Conversely, the lower value of R means that motion regions are smooth and large block is used as the basic processing unit. Thus, a threshold value T_0 should be set to decide the lost block in F_n will be divided or not. After many experiments to different test sequences, we find out that the accurate decision to divide or not is made when T_0 is set to 0.55 no matter how size the lost block is.

Generally, LCUs correspond to static background areas or motion regions with simple texture, and movement continuity among frames is strong. So it is not necessary for LCUs to extrapolate MVs. The average value of all candidate MVs is used as the compensated MV of the lost LCU. The mean of MVs can be obtained by Equation (3), which can be with much lower complexity.

$$MV = \frac{1}{N} \sum_{k=1}^{N} V_k \qquad (3)$$

Where N denotes the number of all candidate MVs, V_k denotes any candidate MV.

3.2   Error Concealment Based on Variable Size Block

In HEVC, LCU is both the basic coding unit and the concealing unit. Concealing the whole frame loss means concealment of all LCUs in the lost frame. So every LCU in the lost frame should be concealed respectively.

R is computed by Equation (2) firstly. If R is less than T_0, MV of the lost LCU is estimated by Equation (3) for EC; otherwise, it means the lost LCU in the current frame must be divided into smaller blocks. So we should further judge the texture features of the lost LCU based on the co-located LCU segmentation in the reference frame.

Since HEVC usually supports frame rate with 50fps, its video sequence has strong correlation in the time domain. How to segment the lost LCU into smaller blocks is decided by analyzing the segmentation of decoded LCUs in the reference frame F_{n-1}, as shown in Fig.3. The reference area of the lost LCU may include three LCUs, which are the co-located LCU in corresponding position and its left and up ones in the reference frame. Strong correlation in the time domain determines that texture information and motion information of the lost smaller blocks have certain continuity with the three LCUs in the reference area. Furthermore, the degree of the lost LCU segmentation, called depth, can reflect the texture and motion information to some extent. The depth of the lost LCU denotes the smallest depth of the three LCUs in the reference areas. The depth is important to decide the size of the lost blocks. HEVC can support block size with $2^{6-depth} \times 2^{6-depth}$ (depth=0, 1, 2, 3, 4). In particular, when depth is zero, it means the block size is 64×64, which corresponds to LCU.

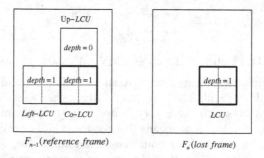

F_{n-1}(reference frame) F_n(lost frame)

Fig. 3. Analysis of motion and texture correlation between frames

When the depth in the reference area is equal to 1, the texture of lost LCU is considered as smooth, and the LCU is divided into four blocks with size 32×32. In this case, Equation (1) is usually used to conceal each error block. Specially, for the areas without overlapping blocks, the MV of corresponding position block in the reference frame is selected directly as the MV of the missing block for EC.

When the depth in the reference area is greater than 1, the texture of lost LCU is complex. The lost LCU might include many smaller blocks with different sizes, Fig.4 shows an example of LCU encoded with different sizes. It is most difficult to infer the size of every block accurately.

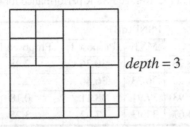

$depth = 3$

Fig. 4. LCU encoded with different sizes

In this case, the LCU is divided into many blocks with size 16 rather than 8, which can get lower complexity. However, if existed 8×8 pixels are merged into 16×16 pixels, some details may be damaged, which influence the quality of reconstructed video. So for each 16×16 pixels, we still need to judge whether it should be divided into smaller blocks, as described follows:

Regard 16×16 as basic unit for all MVs in overlapping area. Equation (2) is still used to judge the temporal correlation. If R is lesser than T_0, Equation (3) is used to conceal error block; otherwise, regard 8×8 as basic unit. Equation (1) is used to conceal each error block. Note, for the block coded with intra mode in reference frame, its motion vector is replaced by neighboring MV.

From above method, the size of missing block can be adaptively adjusted according to texture and motion information. So, larger blocks can be used to describe smooth regions and smaller blocks to describe detailed regions, which can avoid high computational complexity caused by fixed-size block and improve decoding efficiency. This method can make for the development of real-time HD video.

4   Experimental Results

Our experiment is based on HEVC reference software HM6.0[6]. The group of picture is set to 8, the frame rate is set to 50fps, and quantization parameter is set to 32.Here, we use HEVC RTP loss model proposed in JCTVC-H0072 [7]to simulate the packet loss. There is one assumption in our experiment: only the P frame loss occurs, which can assure low-delay. As for B frame loss, our method can also be applied. For this situation, previous P frames and subsequent P frames can both be used for EC.

Four different sequences, namely BasketballDrill (832×480), Vidyo4 (1280×720), KristenAndSara (1280×720) and Cafe (1920×1080), are tested. Under the same condition, we also implement FC method in HM6.0 and MVE algorithm in H.264, which are used to compare with our proposed method. Table 1 summarizes the experimental results of different sequences with packet loss rate of 10%. Compared with FC method, our method can achieve about 1.67dB in average for four sequences. Compared with MVE method, our method is roughly equivalent to the reconstruction quality of MVE algorithm.

Table 1. Comparison of the average PSNR performance for different sequences

Sequences	PSNR(dB)			Gain(dB)	
	FC	MVE	Proposed	Proposed-FC	Proposed-MVE
BasketballDrill	28.28	30.08	30.76	2.48	0.68
Vidyo4	34.26	36.23	36.46	2.20	0.23
KristenAndSara	37.93	37.91	38.11	0.18	0.20
Cafe	34.67	37.93	37.92	3.25	-0.01

Table 2 summarizes the decoding time with three different methods. The decoding time of our propose method is very close to FC. Compared with MVE method, the proposed method reduces about 38.5% in average, which greatly decreases computational complexity, and basically guarantees the real-time reconstruction of high-definition video.

Table 2. Comparison of computational complexity for different sequences

Sequences	Time(sec)			Reduced Time(%)
	FC	MVE	Proposed	Proposed-MVE
BasketballDrill	45.67	64.47	47.00	27.0%
Vidyo4	58.23	100.75	59.14	41.3%
KrisenAndSara	54.88	98.03	56.14	42.7%
Cafe	114.23	206.55	117.97	42.9%

5   Conclusion

For HD video, the large resolution determines that it leads to higher complexity by using motion vector extrapolation based on 4 × 4 block or pixel-based. In this paper, firstly, by analyzing the texture and motion information of the missing blocks, strong correlations between the time-domain are used to judge variable size blocks. Then, the regions with simple texture are concealed quickly. Finally, error concealment method based on variable size motion vector extrapolation is proposed, which can greatly reduces the complexity while guaranteeing better reconstruction quality.

References

1. McCann, K., Han, W.-J., Kim, I.-K., et al.: Video Coding Technology Proposal by Samsung (and BBC) (Online). In: JCTVC-A124, Dresden, Germany, April 15–23 (2010)
2. Zheng, X., Yu, H.: Flexible macroblock partition for inter-frame coding. In: JCTVC Contribution JCTVC-A029, Dresden, Germany (April 2010)
3. ITU-T, Draft Recommendation H.263 Video Coding for Narrow Telecommunication Channels at below 64kbit/s (1995)
4. Peng, Q., Yang, T., Zhu, C.: Block-based temporal error concealment for video packet using motion vector extrapolation. In: Proceedings of IEEE International Conference on Communications, Circuits and Systems and West Sino Expositions, pp. 10–14 (2002)
5. Ugur, K., Andersson, K., et al.: High performance, low complexity video coding and the emerging HEVC standard. IEEE Trans. Circuits Syst. Video Technol. 20(12), 1688–1697 (2010)
6. https://hevc.hhi.fraunhofer.de/svn/svn_HEVCSoftware/tags/HM-6.0/svn_HEVCSoftware-Revision2476:/tags/HM-6.0
7. Wenger, S.: NAL Unit Loss Software. JCT-VC Document, JCTVCH0072 (February 2012)

Error Concealment for B-View in Multi-View Video

Ran Ma[1,2], Deyang Liu[1,2], Liang Liang[1,2], and Ping An[1,2]

[1] School of Communication and Information Engineering, Shanghai University,
Shanghai 200072, China
[2] Key Laboratory of Advanced Displays and System Application, Ministry of Education,
Shanghai 200072, China
{maran,liudeyang}@shu.edu.cn

Abstract. As one of effective prediction structures of multi-view video (MVV), the Joint Multi-view Video Model (JMVM) has introduced much more prediction structures to reduce the inter-view correlations as well as spatio-temporal correlations. Therefore, this makes compressed bit-streams very sensitive to transmission errors and leads to error propagation easily. In order to against the error propagation, JMVM based error concealment (EC) algorithms are necessary. In this paper, a fast efficient B-view based error concealment algorithm for MVV is proposed, which takes full use of the characteristic of the hierarchical B prediction structure and adjusts the searching range of B-view in neighboring views. Experiment shows that the proposed algorithm can effectively reduce the computation complexity with no reducing the video quality at the same time.

Keywords: Error concealment, Multi-view video, B view.

1   1   Introduction

As the main trend of the 3D video, MVV has been widely applied. And many coding schemes about MVV have been put forward. The hierarchical B frame prediction structure [1], which is proposed by HHI (Fraunhofer Heinrich Hertz Institute), has been adopted by the JVT (Joint Video Team) as the reference prediction structure of JMVM due to its high coding efficiency.

Much more prediction structures have been introduced in the JMVM to reduce the inter-view correlations as well as spatio-temporal correlations. However, the prediction structures make compressed bit-streams very sensitive to transmission errors [2]. If an error occurs in a frame, it propagates to adjacent views and subsequence frames, degrading the reconstructed video quality severely, as shown in Fig. 1 [3]. In order to against the disastrous error propagation, JMVM based error concealment (EC) algorithms for MVV are necessary.

The rest of this paper is organized as follows: Section 2 briefly describes the implementation of temporal EC methods and the disadvantages for JMVM. Section 3 presents the proposed JMVM based EC algorithm. Section 4 evaluates its performance and conclusions are given in Section 5.

W. Zhang et al. (Eds.): IFTC 2012, CCIS 331, pp. 278–283, 2012.

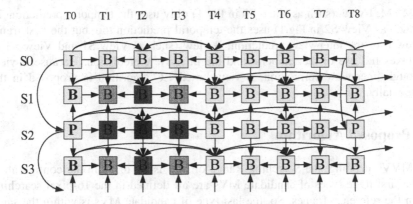

Fig. 1. Error propagation in JMVM

2   Temporal EC Methods and the Characteristic of JMVM

The traditional temporal error concealment (TEC) [4] methods recover the lost blocks of current frame by exploiting the correlations between current frame and the reference frames. The loss of one block means its MV is lost, too. The regain of the lost MV is very important, and then the error block is recovered. The common process is as follows: First, a set of candidate motion vectors (MVs) is formed. The set might include four types of MVs: zero MV, MVs associated with available neighboring macro-blocks (MBs), MVs of the co-located MBs in the reference frames and MVs by a full searching within certain areas in the reference frames. Then, one of matching criterions is adopted (such as Decoder Motion-Vector Estimation Algorithm, DMVE [5]) to find the best MV from the MVs set to replace the missing MV, which minimizes the SAD (Sum of Absolute Difference). Last, the lost MB is recovered by using the corresponding block in the reference frame according to the recovered MV.

In JMVM, there are two kinds of vectors, one is the motion vector and the other is the disparity vector. The way to acquire the two kinds of vectors is the same. So the motion vector and the disparity vector are collectively referred to as vector. In other words, the TEC methods can also be used to recover the disparity vector.

However, due to the difference between the 3D video and the traditional 2D video, two key issues should be considered when using TEC in JMVM. And the two issues are both based on the correction between views. First, MVV exhibits high corrections between views, in addition to the spatio-temporal corrections within each view. So the set of candidate MVs are extended by exploiting these corrections. Second, the motion vector describes the displacement in temporal field, and the disparity vector indicates the displacement of the same object in horizontal or vertical direction in the adjacent view. Because of the difference, the searching range of the motion vector and the disparity vector in the reference frame should be different. So, by adjusting the searching range, we can increase the accuracy of the searching of the best MV and decrease the searching complexity at the same time.

In JMVM, I-view (such as View S0 in Fig.1) only uses the temporal prediction. P-view (such as View S2 in Fig.1) uses the temporal prediction too, but the first frame in P-view uses the inter-view prediction. B-view (such as View S1 and View S3 in Fig.1) takes full use of the temporal and the inter-view prediction. Because B-view has enough inter-view correlation, B-view based EC algorithm is proposed in the paper specially.

3   Proposed Algorithm

In the MVV encoding, the Searching-Range of MV is set to 16 in the configuration file. The first three types of candidate MVs are all defined in the 16-pixel searching range in the reference frames. So, the last type of candidate MVs is within the same searching region in the reference frames. If the lost block is in the I-view or P-view, only the reference frames in the same view are available. If the error block occurs in the B-view, the reference frames from the same view and the neighbor views are all available. The searching range in the I-view or P-view is similar to the one in the traditional 2D video. In this paper, what we should pay more attention is the search area in B-view.

The disparity vector tends to horizontal displacement [6], because the standardized image pairs have little displacement in the vertical direction. Take the first view (I-view), the second view (B-view), and the third view (P-view) in the "exit" sequence for examples. Fig. 2 shows the 146th frames in the three views, in which there are obvious changes in horizontal direction. Every small square indicates one MB, and the unit of one MB is set as 1 in Fig. 2. In Fig. 2 (b), the man's ear is in the left edge position of the picture and the coordinate of the man's ear is (1, 3). In Fig. 2 (a), the man's ear is in the right comparing to (b) and the coordinate is (5, 3). In Fig. 2 (c), the man's ear is shifted left and we cannot see it any more. However, there is little change in the vertical direction. The similar case also exists in other MVV video.

(a) The first view   (b) The second view   (c) The third view

Fig. 2. Comparison of the neighboring views at same time

It can be concluded that in order to conceal the lost MBs in B-view, the search to right is made in the neighboring left view and the search to left is made in the neighboring right view. Therefore, the candidate disparity vector is set to $\{(x, y) \mid x \in [0, 48], y \in [-4, 4]\}$ in the neighboring left view, and $\{(x, y) \mid x \in [-48, 0], y \in [-4, 4]\}$ in the neighboring right view, in which x is the horizontal displacement and y is the vertical displacement.

From Fig.3(b), we know that the searching region of candidate MVs is $\{(x,y)\mid x\in[0,48],y\in[-4,4]\}$. It is about two times larger in the horizontal direction than that in Fig 3(a),   which is $\{(x,y)\mid x\in[-16,16],y\in[-16,16]\}$. Furthermore, it is one fourth of that in Fig 3(a) in the vertical direction. Obviously, the search region of candidate MVs in (b) is smaller than that in (a), which increases the searching speed. In the reference frame of the same view, the motion vector searching times are $(16-(-16)+1)^2=1089$, and $(0-(-48)+1)(4-(-4)+1)=441$ times are needed in a neighboring view. That is to say, searching times in the intre-view approximately decrease by half than that in the intra-view.

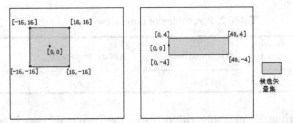

a) searching region [-16,16]×[-16,16]   (b) searching region[0,48]×[-4,4]

Fig. 3. Comparison of the two searching methods

In the searching region, each of the candidate MVs is tested by using matching criterion to find the best candidate MV. Then, the motion compensation is used to find the best replacement for the corrupted block.

4   Experimental Results

4.1   Experimental Conditions

Three test sequences ('Ballroom', 'Exit' and 'Racel') are used to evaluate the performance of the proposed EC algorithm. Each sequence includes 7 views and is encoded by using the hierarchical B prediction structure.

The proposed EC algorithm is simulated on JMVM 6.0. Test condition is shown in Table 1.

Table 1. Test condition

QP(quantization parameter)	Motion estimation resolution	Package model	Coding structure
32	Single-pixel	Scattered type	hierarchical B prediction structure

In order to take full use of the information of the neighboring blocks of the lost block, video stream is generated into packets based on the flexible macroblock order

(FMO) [7]. There are other two assumptions in our experiment: (1) two successive video packets in the same frame cannot be lost at the same time; (2) the error only occurs in B-views.

4.2   Experimental Results

There are two prediction structures in B-view: intra-view prediction structure and the intre-view prediction structure. Table 2 shows the percentage of intre-view prediction in four video sequences. The average proportion is 22%. Therefore, the changes of the searching region in the neighboring views have well effect on the video quality and time-consuming.

Table 2. Percentage of intre-view prediction

Ballroom sequence	Exit sequence	Race1 sequence	average
27%	17%	23%	22%

In our experiment, one algorithm uses the original searching region, i.e. $\{(x, y) \mid x \in [-16,16], y \in [-16,16]\}$. The other algorithm uses the proposed method. The searching region in reference frame in the same view is $\{(x, y) \mid x \in [-16,16], y \in [-16,16]\}$, but $\{(x, y) \mid x \in [0,48], y \in [-4,4]\}$ and $\{(x, y) \mid x \in [-48,0], y \in [-4,4]\}$ are used in the reference frame in the neighboring left and right views respectively.

Table 3 shows the comparison of PSNR of the two algorithms in different packet loss rate. We can see that the proposed method provides a better PSNR performance comparing to the original algorithm. For example, for the "Race1" sequence, the PSNR improves the most with a higher PSNR 0.27 dB. For the "exit" sequence, the PSNR is 0.12 dB higher witch improves the least.

Table 3. Comparison of the PSNR of the two algorithms

sequence	algorithm	Average PSNR(dB) in different loss rate			gain (dB)
		5%	10%	20%	
Ballroom	Original	34.92	33.55	32.26	
	proposed	34.99	33.76	32.59	0.20
	difference	0.07	0.21	0.33	
Race1	Original	32.26	34.55	33.07	
	proposed	32.30	34.88	33.50	0.27
	difference	0.04	0.33	0.43	
Exit	Original	37.26	37.73	36.08	
	proposed	37.30	37.86	36.28	0.12
	difference	0.04	0.13	0.20	

The computation is reduced by about 50%, which has been discussed in Section 3. According to the above PSNR and computational complexity, our proposed algorithm has fast and effective capability to conceal the error in B-view.

5   Conclusion

In the Section 3, we discussed the searching regions in intra-view and the intre-view. Through the mathematical analysis, we concludes that the searching times in the neighboring views is about half of that in the same view. So the proposed algorithm can decrease the complexity effectively. In the Section 4, in the same experimental condition, the proposed algorithm gains a higher PSNR than the traditional method and improves the video quality.

However, the searching region of motion vectors and disparity vectors confine to the limitation of the fixed searching length. The adaptive searching region is more appropriate for the difference contents of the video sequences, which needs further study and improvement.

References

1. Merkle, P., Smolic, A., Muller, K., Wiegand, T.: Efficient Prediction Structures for Multiview Video Coding. IEEE Transactions on Circuits and Systems for Video Technology 17, 1461–1473 (2007)
2. Stockhammer, T., Hannuksela, M.M., Wiegand, T.: H.264/AVC in wireless environments. IEEE Transactions on Circuits and Systems for Video Technology 13, 657–673 (2003)
3. Song, K., Hu, Y., Au, O.C., Li, H.Q., Chen, C.W.: Error concealment of multi-view video sequences using intre-view and intra-view corrections. Journal of Visual Communication and Image Representation 20, 281–292 (2009)
4. Agrafiotis, D., Bull, D.R., Canagarajah, C.N.: Enhanced error concealment with mode selection. IEEE Transactions on Circuits and Systems for Video Technology 16, 960–973 (2006)
5. Zhang, J., Arnold, J.F., Frater, M.R.: A Cell-Loss Concealment Technique for MPEG-2 Coded Video. IEEE Transaction on Circuits and Systems for Video Technology 10, 659–665 (2000)
6. Young, O.P., Chang-Su, K., Sang-Uk, L.: Multi-hypothesis error concealment algorithm for H.26L video. In: 2003 International Conference on Image Processing, South Korea, pp. 14–17 (2003)
7. Lambert, P., De Neve, W., Dhondt, Y., Van de Walle, R.: Flexible macroblock ordering in H.264/AVC. Journal of Visual Communication and Image Representation 17, 358–375 (2006)

Texture and Correlation Based Fast Intra Prediction Algorithm for HEVC

Wenqiang Zhao[1,2], Liquan Shen[1,2], Zhiming Cao[1,2], and Zhaoyang Zhang[1,2]

[1] School of Communication and Information Engineering, Shanghai University,
Shanghai 200072, China
[2] Key Laboratory of Advanced Displays and System Application, Ministry of Education,
Shanghai 200072, China
{zhaowenqiang,shenliquan}@shu.edu.cn

Abstract. As the newest video coding standard, HEVC adopts plenty of state-of-art techniques to improve the coding efficiency. Thus its performance is better than that of all the existing standards. However, these modifications also generate huge computational complexity. To solve this problem, we proposed two fast intra prediction algorithms. By judging the texture complexity of coding unit (CU), a fast CU size decision algorithm can remove some unnecessary CU sizes. Besides, based on the statistic character of intra prediction modes and the correlation of adjacent CUs, a fast intra prediction mode decision algorithm can directly select the optimal intra prediction mode or remove some candidate modes. Compared with the exhaustive intra mode decision method in HEVC, our fast algorithms can effectively save the coding time, while the decrease of coding quality is negligible.

Keywords: HEVC, intra prediction, candidate mode.

1 Introduction

The JCT-VC (Joint Collaborative Team on Video Coding) putted forward the newest video coding standard HEVC (High Efficiency Video Coding) [1] in 2010. Compared with the previous standard H.264, many advanced techniques are introduced into HEVC, such as larger coding blocks, up to 35 intra prediction modes and so on. In addition, HEVC defines three different types of coding blocks: CU (coding unit), PU (prediction unit) and TU (transform unit). In order to get the optimal CU, it needs to recursively exhaust all kinds of CU, PU and TU [2], which produces immense computational burden. Moreover, it would be pretty exaggerated to calculate all of 35 modes during intra mode selection. Therefore, HEVC initially carries out a Hadamard Transform to all available intra prediction modes and calculates the absolute sum of Hadamard Transformed coefficients of residual signal and the mode bits, then selects several modes whose absolute sum are minimum as the candidates. We call this process rough mode decision (RMD) [3]. Even so, the computational complexity is still pretty high. Recently, some fast intra prediction algorithms [4, 5, 6] have been proposed to further reduce the intra coding time. The algorithm in literature [4] reduces the number of candidates obtained by RMD and adds one of optimal modes of neighboring (upper

W. Zhang et al. (Eds.): IFTC 2012, CCIS 331, pp. 284–291, 2012.
© Springer-Verlag Berlin Heidelberg 2012

and left-hand) coded CUs into the candidates to maintain the coding quality. Although the effectiveness is satisfactory, the number of candidates can be further reduced. In [5], instead of Hadamard Transformation based algorithm, a sobel algorithm is adopted to get the candidates. However, due to the inaccuracy of sobel algorithm, the coding quality decreases greatly. Besides, the further splitting of some CU can be terminated in [6] by comparing the optimal mode of previous-depth CU and current CU and the size of CU and TU. This method can ensure a high precision, while its efficiency is very limited.

In our paper, two fast intra prediction algorithms are proposed. The first one is able to skip some CU sizes by judging the texture complexity of CU. The other one firstly calculates the number of neighboring CUs whose optimal modes are next to the candidate mode, then directly select the mode located in the first or second position of candidate array as the optimal mode or except some candidates which have a small probability to be selected as the optimal mode.

The rest of the paper is organized as follows. In section 2, we describe the primary process of intra prediction of HEVC. Then, we present the details of our improved intra mode decision algorithms in section 3. The stimulation results are followed in section 4. Finally, we provide a conclusion of this paper in section 5.

2   Overview of Intra Prediction in HEVC

2.1   Searching for the Optimal CU

In H.264, the coding macro-block for intra prediction has only two types, 16×16 and 4×4 [7], while a quad-tree structure is adopted in HEVC, which is shown in Figure 1.

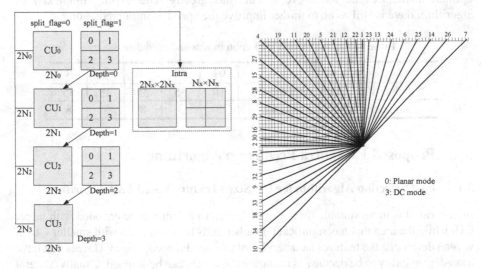

Fig. 1. Quad-tree structure of CU and available PU for intra prediction

Fig. 2. Available intra prediction modes

As shown in Fig. 1, the depth of LCU (largest coding unit) whose size is 64×64 is defined as 0. The depth of four sub-CUs whose size is 32×32 is defined as 1. Recursively, every sub-CU is further split into four small same CUs until the depth is 3. In order to get the optimal CU size (or optimal CU depth), a full searching method is needed to predict the optimal modes of all CUs with different depths. Thus, (1+4+4×4+4×4×4+4×4×4×4)=341 times CU calculation will be required. The calculation burden is so heavy that we must remove some unnecessary CU sizes.

2.2   Searching for the Optimal Intra Prediction Mode

HEVC still utilizes the rate distortion cost (RD cost) as the judgment criteria during the mode selection of intra and inter prediction. However, unlike H.264, there are up to 35 modes for intra prediction of HEVC including 33 directional modes, the DC mode and the Planar mode. These modes are described in Fig. 2.The CUs with different sizes have different numbers of available modes for intra prediction, which is described clearly in table 1.

At the beginning of intra prediction, a rough mode decision (RMD) which has been illustrated in section 1 is adopted to obtain several candidates from all the available modes. The candidates are located in the different positions of a candidate array which is decided by the absolute sum of Hadamard Transformed coefficients of residual signal and the mode bits. That is to say, the less the absolute sum is the more front the location of candidates is. Moreover, the CUs with different sizes have different numbers of candidates, which is also illustrated in Table 1. After getting the candidate modes, all these candidates will be calculated by a rate distortion algorithm. By comparing the RD cost, the candidate with the least RD cost will be selected as the optimal mode. Despite the above scheme has greatly reduced the complexity of algorithm, there is still room to further improve the speed of intra prediction.

Table 1. Number of intra prediction modes and candidate modes

PU size	64	32	16	8	4
Number of available intra modes	19	35	35	35	35
Number of candidate modes	3	3	8	8	8

3   Proposed Fast Intra Prediction Algorithms

3.1   Fast Selection Algorithm for CU Size (Texture Based Fast Algorithm)

In general, it is more suitable for the smooth area of a frame to be encoded with larger CU, while the area that has significant details trends to be encoded with smaller CU. If we can determine the texture characteristic of CU in advanced, some CU sizes that have a small possibility to be decided as the optimal CU size can be skipped. Usually, several classic parameters, such as SSD (Sum of Square Difference) and SAD (Sum of

Absolute Difference), can be used to measure the texture complexity of a CU. In this paper, SSD is chosen as the criterion and defined as:

$$SSD = \frac{1}{N \times N} \sum_{x=0}^{N-1} \sum_{y=0}^{N-1} (p(x,y) - M)^2 \qquad (1)$$

Where N is the size of CU, $p(x,y)$ is the pixel value located in (x,y), M presents the mean of all pixels in this CU. Larger SSD means the texture is complicated, while smaller SSD indicates CU is relatively flat.

If SSD of a CU is less than a specific threshold N_s, it means this CU is smooth enough. Thus, there is no necessary to split current CU into sub-CUs. On the contrary, if SSD of this CU is larger than another specific threshold M_l, we can consider that the texture complexity of this CU is so significant that it is impossible to regard the depth of current CU as the optimal CU depth. Thus, we can skip the coding of CU in current depth and directly encode the sub-CUs within it. And the fast coding process of every sub-CU is similar to that of current CU. However, if the SSD is larger than N_s and smaller than M_l, it means that the CU has no an obvious feature, so we have to encode both CU in current depth and the sub-CUs within it. And this can be illustrated by the following formula,

$$CU \ to \ be \ coded = \begin{cases} current \ CU & , \quad if \ SSD \leq N\_s \\ sub-CUs & , \quad if \ SSD \geq M\_l \\ Both & , \quad else \end{cases} \qquad (2)$$

Because CU in HEVC has five kinds of types, 64×64, 32×32, 16×16, 8×8 and 4×4. Thus, we need to respectively provide four pairs of thresholds for the depths of 0, 1, 2 and 3. Besides, when the QP varies, the judgment based on threshold will not be accurate, so the thresholds should be adaptive with the change of QP.

Fig. 3 illustrates the percentages of 64×64, 32×32, 16×16, 8×8 and 4×4 CU which are chosen as the optimal CUs in different QPs (test sequence is Stockholm-pan, resolution is 1280×720, mode is all-intra). As is revealed in the chart, the percentage of large CU such as 64×64, 32×32, 16×16 increases slowly with the increase of QP, while the percentage of small CU like 4×4 has a rapid decline when the QP decreases.

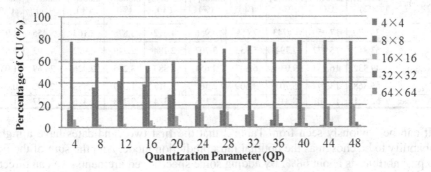

Fig. 3. Percentages of 64×64, 32×32, 16×16, 8×8 and 4×4 CU which are chosen as the optimal CU at different QPs

In our algorithm, the thresholds for QP 24 have been initially selected, then, the thresholds for other QPs are defined as follows:

When $0 \le QP \le 24$,

$$M\_l = \begin{cases} 850 + 4 \times (QP - 24) \,, & \text{if } Depth = 3 \\ 950 + 40 \times (QP - 24), & \text{if } Depth = 2 \\ 1150 + 40 \times (QP - 24), & \text{if } Depth = 1 \\ 1350 + 40 \times (QP - 24), & \text{if } Depth = 0 \end{cases} \quad N\_s = \begin{cases} 120 + 3 \times (QP - 24), & \text{if } Depth = 3 \\ 130 - 3 \times (QP - 24), & \text{if } Depth = 2 \\ 170 - 3 \times (QP - 24), & \text{if } Depth = 1 \\ 0 & \text{if } Depth = 0 \end{cases} \quad (3)$$

When $24 \le QP \le 51$,

$$M\_l = \begin{cases} 850 + 250 \times (QP - 24) \,, & \text{if } Depth = 3 \\ 950 + 250 \times (QP - 24) \,, & \text{if } Depth = 2 \\ 1150 + 250 \times (QP - 24), & \text{if } Depth = 1 \\ 1350 + 250 \times (QP - 24), & \text{if } Depth = 0 \end{cases} \quad N\_s = \begin{cases} 120 + 40 \times (QP - 24), & \text{if } Depth = 3 \\ 130 - 3 \times (QP - 24) \,, & \text{if } Depth = 2 \\ 170 - 3 \times (QP - 24) \,, & \text{if } Depth = 1 \\ 0 & \text{if } Depth = 0 \end{cases} \quad (4)$$

3.2   Fast Selection Algorithm for Intra Prediction Mode (Correlation Based Fast Algorithm)

Through a lot of experiments, we find that most of the candidates determined by the rough mode decision (RMD) are close to each other. If we adopted some classic edge detection methods such as sobel algorithm to reduce the candidates, it would introduce a large coding quality loss. In order to obtain the probability of being chosen as the optimal mode for every candidate, we have encoded four test sequences using exhaustive intra mode decision. For 8×8 CU there are 8 to 10 (two optimal modes of adjacent CUs) candidate modes to be performed with RD cost calculation, and the probability of being chosen as the optimal mode for every candidate mode is illustrated in Table 2. Mode [0] represents the first candidate mode of candidate array, mode [1] represents the second one, and so on.

Table 2. The probability of being chosen as the optimal mode for every candidate modes

Sequence	mode[0] (%)	mode[1] (%)	mode[2] (%)	mode[3] (%)	mode[4] (%)	mode[5] (%)	mode[6] (%)	mode[7] (%)	mode[8] (%)	mode[9] (%)
Bus	38.570	17.959	10.743	7.689	5.956	4.612	3.878	3.163	5.455	1.974
Stefan	53.812	15.777	7.794	5.753	3.707	2.784	2.249	2.022	4.493	1.610
Mobile	49.332	16.733	9.039	6.307	4.654	3.883	3.205	2.926	2.869	1.051
News	66.368	13.797	5.701	3.509	2.462	2.017	1.619	1.553	2.292	0.682
Average	52.021	16.067	8.319	5.815	4.195	3.324	2.738	2.416	3.777	1.329

It can be obviously seen from Table 2 that the first two candidates have a higher probability to be chosen as the optimal intra prediction mode. And the sum of the first two probabilities is about 68%. By adding some specific requirements, we can directly select the first or second candidate mode of candidate array as the optimal mode.

As we known, adjacent CUs within a frame have a strong correlation which can be used to determine the optimal intra prediction type [8]. Besides, the contents of adjacent frames trend to have similarity. Thus, both the corresponding co-located CU in previous frame and the adjacent CUs can be regarded as the reference CUs (RC) to predict the optimal mode. The current CU and RC are shown in Fig. 4. After plenty of observation, we find that the corresponding CU in previous-depth described in Fig. 5 and current CU also have a close correlation. Thus, we can also utilize the corresponding CU in previous-depth to predict the optimal mode of current CU.

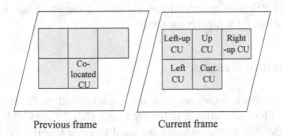

Previous frame   Current frame

Fig. 4. Reference CUs (RC) and current CU

If the optimal modes of most neighboring CUs (including RC illustrated in Fig. 4 and corresponding CU in previous-depth) are the neighboring modes (illustrated in Fig. 5) of a specific candidate mode or just the same as this candidate mode, then this candidate mode would have a high probability to be chosen as the optimal intra prediction mode. However, if the number of such kind of neighboring CUs is very small or just equals zero, we can consider that this candidate mode has a low probability to be chosen as the optimal mode, so we can directly skip the RD cost calculation of this candidate mode.

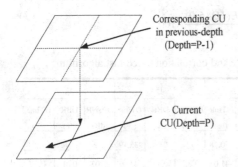

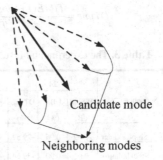

Fig. 5. corresponding CU in previous-depth and current CU (P=1, 2, 3, or 4)

Fig. 6. the neighboring modes of candidate mode

To sum up, the process of fast intra prediction mode decision for a fixed-size CU can be described as follows:

(1) By carrying out RMD to get the candidate array. Mark the first mode of candidate array as mode[0], the second one as mode[1], and so on.

(2) Judge whether the optimal mode of every neighboring CU is the neighboring mode of mode[i] (initially, i=0) or the same as mode[i], mark the number of CUs which

meet this requirement as Z. If Z is less than or equal 1, skip RD cost calculation of mode[i] and go to (4), otherwise, go to (3).

(3) Carry out RD cost calculation of mode[i]. If Z is more than 2 and mode[i] is the first or second mode of candidate array, directly determine mode[i] as the optimal prediction mode and break the whole algorithm. Otherwise, go to (4).

(4) Judge whether mode[i] is the last mode of candidate array. If no, i plus 1 and go to (2). Otherwise, go to (5).

(5) Compare the RD costs of candidates and choose the candidate whose RD cost is the least as the optimal intra prediction mode.

4   Experimental Results

Two fast intra mode decision algorithms are implemented in the reference software HM5.0 of HEVC. The test platform is Intel® Core(TM) 2 Duo CPU-2.53GHz with 2 cores, 1.0 GB RAM. Six test sequences are used to complete the experiment, and 20 frames of every sequence are encoded in all I-frames mode. The quantization parameters are with 24, 28, 32 and 36. The experimental results of proposed algorithm scheme are listed in table 3. Coding efficiency is measured with PSNR and bit rate (BR), while computational complexity is measured with consumed coding time. Positive and negative values represent increments and decrements, respectively. The terms of DPSNR, DBR and DTime are defined as followed:

$$DPSNR = PSNR(Proposed) - PSNR(HM5.0) \tag{5}$$

$$DBR = \frac{BR(Proposed) - BR(HM5.0)}{BR(HM5.0)} \times 100 \tag{6}$$

$$DTime = \frac{TIME(Proposed) - TIME(HM5.0)}{TIME(5.0)} \times 100 \tag{7}$$

Table 3. The experimental results of texture and correlation based fast algorithm

Sequence		24			28			32			36		
		DPSNR	DBR	DTime	DPSNR	DBR	DTime	DPSNR	DBR	DTime	DPSNR	DBR	DTime
		(dB)	(%)	(%)	(dB)	(%)	(%)	(dB)	(%)	(%)	(dB)	(%)	(%)
1280×720	ShipCalender	-0.09	0.96	-29.52	-0.12	0.50	-30.78	-0.11	0.08	-35.19	-0.09	-0.46	-33.04
	Stockholmpan	-0.07	0.90	-39.64	-0.06	0.71	-41.05	-0.05	0.43	-43.06	-0.03	0.01	-42.55
	Jet	-0.04	2.47	-54.61	-0.05	2.00	-55.87	-0.05	1.22	-58.12	-0.03	0.57	-57.45
	Kayak	-0.05	0.40	-29.97	-0.06	0.12	-31.32	-0.05	-0.08	-34.38	-0.03	0.23	-36.42
1920×1080	Mobcal	-0.07	0.60	-33.00	-0.06	0.50	-35.74	-0.06	0.37	-36.74	-0.05	0.14	-39.30
	Tennis	-0.03	1.12	-55.07	-0.03	1.07	-53.93	-0.03	0.80	-54.72	-0.03	0.48	-54.98
	ParkScene	-0.10	0.49	-44.56	-0.12	-0.05	-47.02	-0.11	-0.44	-47.84	-0.07	-0.63	-49.00
	Kayak	-0.04	0.66	-33.07	-0.04	0.33	-33.85	-0.04	0.04	-35.25	-0.03	-0.12	-37.81
	Average	-0.06	0.95	-39.93	-0.07	0.56	-41.20	-0.06	0.30	-43.16	-0.05	0.03	-43.82

Compared with exhaustive mode decision algorithm of HM5.0, the experimental results show that our fast intra prediction algorithm scheme achieves about 40% reduction of encoding time, while the decrease of PSNR and the increase of bite-rate are almost negligible.

5   Conclusion

This paper proposes two fast intra prediction algorithms for HEVC. By calculating the texture complexity of CU, some CU sizes which have a low probability to be determined as the optimal size can be skipped. In addition, by making use of the statistical property of candidates and the correlation between candidate mode and the optimal modes of neighboring CUs, the optimal mode can be directly determined or some candidates can be removed. The simulation results show that the proposed methods can reduce the coding time effectively, while the coding quality loss is negligible. Besides, the proposed two methods can be combined with fast inter prediction algorithm to further improve the coding speed.

Acknowledgment. This paper was supported by Shanghai Science and Technology Development Funds, 11QA1402400 and the National Natural Science Foundation, 661171084.

References

1. JCT-VC, WD4: Working Draft 4 of High-Efficiency Video Coding, JCT-VC Meeting, Torino (2011)
2. JCT-VC, The Reference Software, https://hevc.hhi.fraunhofer.de/svn/svn_HEVCSoftware/tags/HM-5.0
3. Piao, Y., Min, J., Chen, J.: Encoder improvement of unified intra prediction. In: JCTVC-C207, Guangzhou (2010)
4. Zhao, L., Zhang, L.: Fast Mode Decision Algorithm for Intra Prediction in HEVC. In: Visual Communication and Image Processing (VICIP), pp. 1–4 (2011)
5. Jiang, W., Ma, H., Chen, Y.: Gradient Based Fast Mode Decision Algorithm for Intra Prediction in HEVC. In: IEEE International Conference on Consumer Electronics, Communications and Networks (CECNet), pp. 1836–1840 (2012)
6. Kim, J., Yang, J., Lee, H., Jeon, B.: Fast Intra Mode Decision of HEVC based on Hierarchical Structure. In: IEEE International Conference on Information, Communications and Signal Processing (ICICS), pp. 1–4 (2011)
7. Chang, K., Men, A., Zhang, W.: Fast Intra-prediction Mode Decision for H.264/AVC. In: ISECS International Colloquium on Computing, Communication, Control, and Management, pp. 69–73 (2009)
8. Leng, J., Sun, L., Ikenaga, T., Sakaida, S.: Content Based Hierarchical Fast Coding Unit Decision Algorithm For HEVC. In: IEEE International Conference on Multimedia and Signal Processing, pp. 56–59 (2011)

A Fast Intra Prediction Algorithm for HEVC

Yilong Cheng, Guowei Teng, Xuli Shi, and Huosheng Li

School of Communication and Information Engineering,
Shanghai University, Shanghai 200072, China
{chengyilong,tengguowei}@shu.edu.cn

Abstract. A new fast intra-prediction algorithm for HEVC is proposed in this paper. The algorithm makes full use of spatial correlations among video sequences, decides the best size of CU by referring neighboring coded CUs' size and the best prediction mode of PU by referring the up layer PU modes. The experimental results show that the algorithm averagely achieves 45.2% reduction of intra coding time compared to the default encoding scheme in HM2.0 with drops of 0.05dB PSNR and increases of 0.10% bits rate.

Keywords: HEVC, intra prediction, fast algorithm.

1 Introduction

With the fast development of computer technology, videos with high definition are becoming more and more popular which result in an emphasize on developing new video coding techniques better than the current standard of H.264/AVC. In April 2010, a Joint Collaborative Team on Video Coding (JCT-VC)[1] entity was formed to work on the definition of a next video coding standard called High Efficiency Video Coding(HEVC). Test has shown that gains of 30%-40%[2]BD-rate over H.264/AVC can be achieved due to the result of lots of new techniques adopted in the test model, namely HM of HEVC, however the encoding procedure of HEVC is very complex.

Similar to H.264/AVC, HEVC adopts the conventional block-based hybrid video coding framework but with a much more flexible hierarchy of unit representation which includes three block concepts: coding unit (CU), prediction unit (PU) and transform unit (TU). CU is the basic square shaped coding unit, and its size can range from 8x8 to Largest CU (LCU) according to different depth. PU is the elementary unit for prediction and defined after the last level of CU splitting. TU is the unit for transform and quantization, it must be smaller than or equal the CU size but it can be larger than the PU size unlike previous standards.

The intra prediction for HEVC is performed in a recursive manner, as shown in Fig.1. The encoder need to try all the combinations of CU, PU, and TU in the rate distortion optimization (RDO) process to find the best mode with the lowest rate distortion (RD) cost.

W. Zhang et al. (Eds.): IFTC 2012, CCIS 331, pp. 292–298, 2012.
© Springer-Verlag Berlin Heidelberg 2012

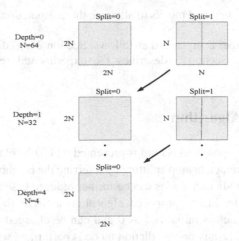

Fig. 1. Quad tree coding structure of HEVC

To reduce the computational complexity of the encoder, a fast intra mode decision algorithm [3] was adopted in HEVC test model HM 2.0: A rough mode decision (RMD) process is first performed to obtain the best candidates. Then, by considering the strong correlation among the neighbors, a most probable mode (MPM) of neighboring blocks is added to the candidate mode set. Only modes in this candidate mode set, $\{Candidate\}$, are needed to perform RD optimization. Though this method can dramatically alleviate the intra prediction complexity, the computational complexity of intra mode decision is still very huge.

$$\{Candidate\} = \{mode_1, mode_2 \ldots \ldots mode_n\} \tag{1}$$

where for CU with size of 4x4, 8x8, 16x16, 32x32, 64x64, the value of n are 8,8,3,3,3.

Many fast intra mode decision algorithm have been proposed for H.264/AVC, the main idea of those algorithm is reducing the prediction modes calculated with RDO and simplifying the RD Cost function. As intra coding block size is highly dependent on the smoothness of the block,intra 4x4 is well suited for a macroblock with the detailed information, while intra 16x16 is well suited for a smooth one,Lin[4] used the ratio of DC to AC to represent the texture complexity of a block and quickly decided the best encoding size of blocks, however, the ratio of DC to AC cannot always correctly represent the texture complexity of blocks, especially for big blocks. F. Pan [5] proposed a fast intra mode decision method based on edge detection. Based on the distribution of the edge direction histogram, only a small part of intra prediction modes are chosen for RDO calculation, but they needed extra pre-processing time to detect edge and analyze edge direction histogram. Therefore, the effects of both fast mode decision algorithms are reduced. The spatial correlation among blocks are also used to reduce the prediction modes.   [6] exploited the inter block correlation in the intra-mode domain to reduce computational complexity. Four modes of neighboring coded blocks are considered as the good candidate intra modes of the current block. If the mode in neighboring blocks is good enough, then it is set to be current block's best prediction mode, else other modes needed to be calculated. The main idea of this paper is also using the correlation of blocks to alleviate the computational complexity of intra prediction.

The rest of this paper is organized as follows: Section 2 introduces the details of the proposed algorithm. Section 3 describes the experimental results and Section 4 concludes this paper.

2   Proposed Algorithm

In this section, the proposed algorithm is presented on CU level and PU level. On CU level, a CU can be skipped or stop splitting by referring the neighboring coded CUs. On PU level, the intra prediction modes can be further reduced based on the up layer PU's best prediction mode. In the proposed algorithm, a SKIP flag is also defined in encoding process which is initialized as 0 and can be changed on CU level. On PU level, If SKIP flag is 1, only one prediction mode is performed with RD Optimization.

2.1   CU Level Algorithm

The CU level fast algorithm relies on the fact that there are strong correlations among current CU and neighboring CU[8], so we can pre-determine the candidate CU depth by referring neighboring CUs' information. Fig. 2 shows the correlations among the referred CUs and current CU. If the above, left-above, left and right-above CUs' best coding size are all 8x8 , then current CU's best coding size is probably 8x8.

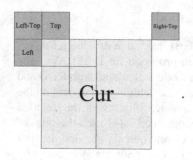

Fig. 2. The relationship among current CU and neighboring CU

Table 1. Correlation among current CU and neighboring CU

Video sequence	Flower Garden720x576	Night 720x576	Spincalendar 1280x720
Rate(%)	42.61	48.84	51.00
Video sequence	Harbour1280 x720	StockholmPan1920x1088	Parkrun1920 x1088
Rate(%)	52.65	46.87	55.92

To demonstrate the assumption above, we test six video sequences with different size. From the test we can see, if current CU's three or more neighboring CU have the same best coding depth, then about 49.65% of current CU's best coding depth is the same as those neighboring CUs'. The correlations among current CU and neighboring CU can be used to early exterminate the split of CU.

The proposed algorithm on CU level is described as follows:

Step1). If all the neighboring CU are available with the same depth-uiDepthx, and current CU's depth is smaller than uiDepthx , then the SKIP flag is set to be 1.

Step2). Else if at least two of the neighboring CUs are available with the same depth uiDepthx, and uiDepthx is larger than current CU's depth plus 1, then set the SKIP flag to be 1.

Step3). Do the intra prediction of current CU.

Step4). If two or more neighboring CUs are available with the same depth,and current CU's RD-Cost is smaller than all of those neighboring CUs' RD-Cost, current CU stop splitting.

Step5). Else do the normal split of current CU.

2.2   PU Level Algorithm

Taking all the directions of each PU size into RDO procedure will cause much computation in the encoder. Therefore, HM2.0 uses a combination of rough mode decision (RMD) and most probable mode(MPM) to boost the encoding speed of intra prediction. In fact, considering the correlation among up layer mode and current mode , intra prediction modes performed with RDO can still be further reduced.

As shown in Fig.3, if the best prediction mode of PU in depth x is 5, then the best mode of PU in depth x+1 is probably 5 or the surrounding modes, for example 4 or 6. To verify this assumption, we test six video sequences with different size for example. As shown in table 2, we define PU whose depth is smaller than current PU but belong to the same CU along with current PU as up layer PU. The test shows that about 70.66% of current PUs' best modes are around the up layer PUs' prediction modes. We can use this property to further reduce the number of prediction modes.

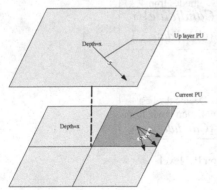

Fig. 3. Correlation between current PU and the up layer PU

Table 2. modes correlation between current PU and   up layer PU

Video sequences	City_1280 x720	Night720 x576	Spincalendar720x576
Rate(%)	68.61	65.40	69.53
Video sequences	Harbour1280x720	StockholmPan1920x1088	City_1280 x720
Rate(%)	70.90	81.95	67.54

The algorithm of this level is as follows: first we obtain a new candidate mode set $\{Candidate_{new}\}$. It's initialized as empty and its elements are derived from $\{Candidate\}$ as depicted in Eq 2. The procedure to obtain $\{Candidate_{new}\}$ is as follows:

$$\{Candidate_{new}\} = \{\text{mode}_{new1}, \text{mode}_{new2} \ldots \text{mode}_{newI}\} \qquad (2)$$

where $\text{mode}_{newI} \in \{Candidate\}$, and I <=n.

Step1). If SKIP flag is 1, then add the first available mode in $\{Candidate\}$ to $\{Candidate_{new}\}$.

Step2). Else if the above layer PU is not available then add the first available mode in $\{Candidate\}$ to $\{Candidate_{new}\}$, and if the first available mode is not DC, add DC mode to $\{Candidate_{new}\}$.

Step3). Else check whether the candidate modes in $\{Candidate\}$ are around the up layer PU's mode. If they are, add the first three of them to $\{Candidate_{new}\}$.

Step4). Check whether the new candidate set $\{Candidate_{new}\}$ is empty. If it is, add all the available modes in $\{Candidate\}$ to $\{Candidate_{new}\}$.

After getting $\{Candidate_{new}\}$, RD Optimization procedure is performed using candidate modes in it and we can then decide mode with the least RD Cost as the best intra prediction mode.

The flow chart of fast algorithm on this level is shown in Fig. 4.

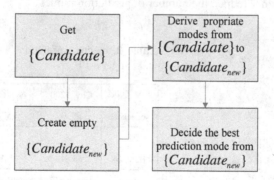

Fig. 4. Fast algorithm on PU level

3   Experimental Results

The proposed algorithm on both CU level and PU level was implemented in HM 2.0. And the results are compared to the original fast mode decision algorithm with different video sequences.

Table 3 shows the experimental results. From the results we can see the proposed algorithm can provide a significant encode time reduction compared to fast mode decision scheme in HM 2.0 with a negligible change of PSNR and bit rate.

Table 3. Experiment Results

Sequence	QP	ΔBits (%)	ΔPSNR (dB)	Δtime reduction (%)	Sequence	QP	ΔBits (%)	ΔPSNR (dB)	Δtime reduction (%)
FlowerGarden_720x576	26	-0.02	-0.08	50.53	City_1280x720	26	+0.12	-0.06	39.49
	32	+0.15	-0.05	51.61		32	+0.15	-0.05	39.72
	38	+0.28	-0.05	52.39		38	+0.02	-0.05	41.97
Spincalendar_720x576	26	-0.17	-0.06	38.04	Parkrun_1920x1088	26	+0.11	-0.05	49.28
	32	-0.07	-0.05	39.75		32	+0.22	-0.05	48.62
	38	+0.04	-0.05	41.59		38	+0.44	-0.05	49.57
BigShips_1280x720	26	-0.02	-0.05	39.43	StockholmPan_1920x1088	26	+0.34	-0.02	45.99
	32	+0.09	-0.04	41.06		32	+0.60	-0.03	47.90
	38	+0.23	-0.04	46.60		38	-0.76	-0.03	49.65

4   Conclusion

In this paper, we propose a fast intra prediction algorithm on CU level and PU level for emerging HEVC. By making use of correlations among CU and PU, we can decide the best CU depth early and further reduce the intra prediction modes. As compared with the previous fast intra mode decision algorithm adopted in HM2.0. Experimental results show that our proposed algorithm can save averagely 45.2% encoding time with negligible coding efficiency loss. Moreover, the proposed algorithm could also be combined with fast inter mode decision to further reduce the encoding time, and it will be our next work.

Acknowledgment. This paper was supported by The Open Subject of Key Laboratory of Advanced Display and System Application (Shanghai University), Ministry of Education, P201104 and Shanghai Science and Technology Development Funds, 11QA1402400 and the National Natural Science Foundation, 661171084.

References

1. JCT-VC.: Architectural Outline of Proposed High Efficiency Video Coding Design Elements. A202, JCT-VC meeting, Dresden, Germany (2010)
2. Han, W., Min, J., et al.: Improved video compression efficiency through flexible unit representation and corresponding extension of coding tools. IEEE Trans. Circus, Syst., Video Technol. 20, 1709–1720 (2010)

3. Marpe, D., Wiegand, T., Sullivan, G.J.: The H.264/MPEG4 advanced video coding standard and its applications. Communications Magazine IEEE 44, 134–143 (2006)
4. Lin, Y., Chang, T.: Fast block type decision algorithm for intra prediction in H.264 FRext. In: IEEE International Conference on Image Processing, vol. 1, pp. 585–588 (2005)
5. Pan, F., Lin, X., et al.: Fast Mode Decision Algorithm for Intraprediction in H.264/AVC Video Coding. IEEE Tran. Circuits syst. Video Technol. 15, 813–822 (2005)
6. Wang, C., Chen, T.-S., Tung, C.: Fast intra-mode decisionin H.264 using inter block correlation. In: IEEE International Conference on Image Processing, vol. 1, pp. 1345–1348 (2006)
7. Teng, S., Hang, H., Cheng, Y.: Fast mode decision algorithm for Residual Quadtree coding in HEVC. In: IEEE Visual Communications and Image Processing (VCIP), vol. 1, pp. 1–4 (2011)
8. Leng, J., Sun, L., et al.: Content Based Hierarchical Fast Coding Unit Decision Algorithm for HEVC. In: IEEE Conference Publication, vol. 1, pp. 56–59 (2011)

A Review of Information Content Metric
for Semantic Similarity[*]

Lingling Meng[1], Junzhong Gu[2], and Zili Zhou[3]

[1] Computer Science and Technology Department,
Department of Educational Information Technology,
East China Normal University, Shanghai, 200062, China
[2] Computer Science and Technology Department,
East China Normal Universtiy, Shanghai, 200062, China
[3] College of Physics and Engineering, Qufu Normal University, Qufu, 273165, China
jzgu@ica.stc.sh.cn, {mengzero,zlzhou999}@163.com

Abstract. All along, Information Content (IC) of concept is a hot topic. It is an important dimension of accessing semantic similarity between two concepts or word senses. Much work has been done. This paper illustrated the use of IC in semantic similarity computing and then focuses on IC metric. It reviews and analyses Corpora-dependent and Corpora-independent IC approach. Hyponym-based, Leaves-based and Relation-based IC Metric is presented respectively. The important related issues are highlighted. Finally further research is outlined for the improvement of IC.

Keywords: Information content, semantic similarity, hyponym-based, leaves-based, relation-based.

1 Introduction

Semantic similarity measure between concepts is a generic issue for many applications of computational linguistics and artificial intelligence, such as information extraction, semantic annotation and question answering. Information Content (IC) of concept provides an estimation of its abstract/specialty. And it is an important dimension in assessing the similarity of two concepts or two words. For a long time, it has been successfully applied in semantic similarity computation [1] [2] [3] [4] [5]. Resnik first proposed an information content-based similarity measure in 1995 [5]. He assumed that similarity between two concepts depended on the extent to which they share information in common. In practice, it is indicated by the specific subsumer in the taxonomy.

$$sim_{Resnik}(c_1,c_2) = -\log p(lso(c_1,c_2)) = IC(lso(c_1,c_2)) \tag{1}$$

---

[*] The work in the paper was supported by Shanghai Scientific Development Foundation (Grant No. 11530700300) and Shandong Excellent Young Scientist Award Fund (Grant No. BS2010DX012).

W. Zhang et al. (Eds.): IFTC 2012, CCIS 331, pp. 299–306, 2012.
© Springer-Verlag Berlin Heidelberg 2012

Where, IC(lso) is the information content value of lso and $lso(c_1,c_2)$ is the most specific common subsumer of c_1 and c_2.

Lin took the self information of the compared concepts into account and proposed another semantic similarity measure [3].

$$sim_{Lin}(c_1,c_2) = \frac{2 * IC(lso(c_1,c_2)))}{IC\ (c_1) + IC\ (c_2)} \tag{2}$$

Jiang proposed a measure from different perspective by calculating semantic distance to obtain semantic similarity [2].

$$dis_{Jiang}(c_1,c_2) = (IC(c_1) + IC(c_2)) - 2IC(lso(c_1,c_2)) \tag{3}$$

We can see that IC plays an important role in semantic similarity measures. How to acquire a proper IC value? Many approaches have been proposed. The main difference is whether to rely on corpora. On the whole, they can be classified in two varieties: corpora-dependent IC model [5] and corpora-independent IC model [6] [7] [8] [9]. Corpora-independent approaches have attracted great concern in the area recently. This paper reviews the different approaches that have been used for IC computing and highlights important related issues. The structure of the paper is as follows. Section 2 gives a general introduction to Corpora-dependent IC metric. Section 3 outlines the different approaches of Corpora-independent for the purpose to compute IC respectively. The further research is described in Section 4 and a summary is given in Section 5.

2   Corpora-Dependent IC Metric

Corpora-dependent IC metric first was proposed by Resnik in 1995 for acquiring semantic similarity between two concepts following information theoretic approach [5]. It obtains IC through statistical analysis of corpora, from where probabilities of concepts occurring are inferred. That is to say, it assumes that, for a concept c in the taxonomy, let p(c) be the probability of encountering and instance of concept c. According to the definition from information theory, the information content of c, that is IC(c), can be quantified as negative the log likelihood, $-\log p(c)$.

$$IC(c) = -\log p(c) \tag{4}$$

Probability of a concept was estimated as follows:

$$p(c) = \frac{freq(c)}{N} \tag{5}$$

Where N is the total number of nouns, and $freq(c)$ is the frequency of instance of concept c occurring in the taxonomy.

When computing $freq(c)$, each noun or any of its taxonomical hyponyms that occurred in the given corpora was included. That is to say, each individual occurrence of any noun in the corpora is recursively counted as an occurrence of each of its taxonomic ancestors.

$$Freq(c) = \sum_{w \in W(c)} count(w) \qquad (6)$$

Where W(c) is the set of words subsumed by concept c.

From formula (4) ~ (6), we can see that,

Firstly, IC is inversely proportional to p(c). When p(c) increases, IC decreases.

Secondly, the more abstract a concept, the lower its information content.

Finally, it relies on corpora analysis, and sparse data problem is inevitable sometimes.

3   Corpora-Independent IC Metric

3.1   Hyponym-Based IC Metric

Hyponym-based IC Metric was proposed by Nuno in 2004. It resumed that in WordNet, IC value of a concept is regarded as the function of the hyponyms it as. A concept with more hyponyms expresses less information than the concepts with less ones. For a concept, the more hyponyms it has, the more abstract it is. Inversely, the less hyponyms it has, the more specified it is .It implies that the leaves nodes have no hyponyms and they are most specified. So the information they convey is maximal However, the root node has the maximal hyponyms and it is the most abstract. Thus it expresses the minimal information [6]. Formally:

$$IC(c) = \frac{\log(\frac{hypo(c)+1}{\max_{wn}})}{\log(\frac{1}{\max_{wn}})} = 1 - \frac{\log(hypo(c)+1)}{\log(\max_{wn})} \qquad (7)$$

Where the function hypo(c) returns the number of hyponyms of a given concept c. And, $\max_{wn}$ is a constant value which is set to the maximum number of concepts that exist in the taxonomy. For example, A is-a relation is shown as Fig.1.

From formula (7) and Fig.1, it is noted that,

Firstly, its main advantage is that IC does not rely on corpora analysis, and avoid the sparse data problem.

Secondly, IC is inversely proportional to the number of hyponyms that a concept has, and range from 0 to1 (IC (root) =0, IC (leaf) =1).

Finally, C_2 and C_6 have the same value 0.699. However, C_6 is deeper than C_2 in the taxonomy tree; and it should convey more information than C_2.

Hence, Zhou considered the depth of each given concept, presented a complement model [7], expressed by:

$$IC(c) = k(1 - \frac{\log(hypo(c)+1)}{\log(node_{max})}) + (1-k)(\frac{\log(deep(c))}{\log(deep_{max})}) \qquad (8)$$

Where $node_{max}$ has the same meaning as max_{wn}. $deep(c)$ returns the depth of concept c in the taxonomy. $deep_{max}$ is the max depth of the taxonomy. k is a changeable factor so as to adjust the weight of the two items. In his experiment, k is 0.5.

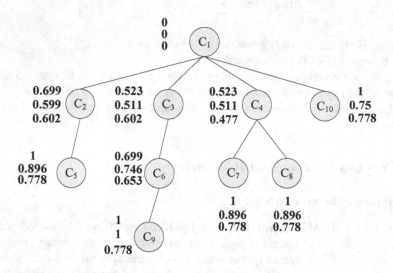

Notes:
Line 1: resulted with Hyponym-based IC Metric(Nuno model)
Line 2: resulted with Hyponym-based IC Metric(zhou model)
Line 3: resulted with Leaves-based IC Metric(David model)

Fig. 1. An example of taxonomy tree

Table 1. IC value of every concept in Fig. 1

concept	$node_{max}$	$deep_{max}$	depth	the number of hypo(c)	$IC(c)_{nunol}$	$IC(c)_{Zhou}$
C_1	10	4	1	9	0	0
C_2	10	4	2	1	0.699	0.599
C_3	10	4	2	2	0.523	0.511
C_4	10	4	2	2	0.523	0.511
C_5	10	4	3	0	1	0.896
C_6	10	4	3	1	0.699	0.746
C_7	10	4	3	0	1	0.896
C_8	10	4	3	0	1	0.896
C_9	10	4	4	0	1	1
C_{10}	10	4	2	0	1	0.75

From formula (8) and Table 1, we find that,

Firstly, the main advantage of Zhou model is that it take depth as considered and tackles the problem that arises in Nuno model. If two concepts have the same number of hyponyms, the deeper one is more concrete and has the higher IC value than the other. Here IC (C_2) =0.599, IC (C_6) =0.746.

Secondly, IC (C_3) = IC (C_4) =0.511. In spite of both C_3 and C_4 have 2 hyponyms, and their depth is equal to 2, the hyponyms of each concept are arranged differently in space structure. Take the factors into considered, such as the depth of every hyponym, it maybe a future research direction.

3.2   Leaves-Based IC Metric

Hypos-based IC Metric was proposed by David in 2011. It's based on the assumption that taxonomical leaves represent the semantic of the most specific concepts of a domain, and they are enough to describe and differentiate the concept from any other one, regardless the amount of inner concepts incorporated in the taxonomy [3]. Leaves-based IC metric argues that the more leaves a concept has the less information it expresses. In other words, a concept with more leaves is more general. Besides this, the depth of concept in taxonomy is considered as Zhou suggested. Here, depth is instead of depth with the number of taxonomical subsumers from a different view [8]. The IC of a concept is defined as:

$$IC(c) = -\log\left(\frac{\frac{|leaves(c)|}{|subsumers(c)|}+1}{max\_leaves+1}\right) \tag{9}$$

Where, let C be the set of concepts of the ontology, for a given concept c,
    leaves(c)={l∈C|l∈hyponyms(c) ∧ l is a leaf}.
    Max_leaves represents the number of leaves corresponding to the root node of the hierarchy. subsumers(c) returns the set of subsumers.
    Subsumers(c)={a∈C | c≤a }∪{c}, c≤a means that c is a hierarchical specialization of a.
    From formula (9) and Fig.1, it is noted that:
    Firstly, Concept's IC is directly proportional to its number of taxonomical subsumers, inversely proportional to the amount of leavers of its hyponym tree.
    Secondly, IC (C_2) =IC (C_3) =0.602. Because of |subsumers(C_2)| = |subsumers(C_3)| = 2, and |leaves(C_2)|=|leaves(C_3)|=1. However, it is noted that hypo(C_2)=1, and hypo(C_3)=2. IC(C_2) and IC(C_3) should convey different information. There is still room for improvement in future research.

3.3   Relation-Based IC Metric

Md. Hanif Seddiqui proposed Relation-based IC Metric in 2010. The approach took concept, properties and their relations of ontology into account. It assumes that every concept is defined with sufficient semantic embedding with the organization, property functions, property restrictions and other logical assertions [9]. Relation-based IC is defined as:

$$IC(c) = \rho \cdot IC_{rel}(c) + (1-\rho) \cdot IC_{nun_o}(c)) \tag{10}$$

$$IC_{rel}(c) = \frac{\log(rel(c)+1)}{\log(total\_rel+1)} \tag{11}$$

$$\rho = \frac{\log(total\_rel+1)}{\log(total\_rel)+\log(total\_concept)} \tag{12}$$

Where rel(c) denotes the number of relations of concept c. And total_rel represents the total number of relations, while total_concept is the maximum of concepts in the ontology. $IC_{nuno}(c)$ is defined with formula (7).

It is obviously that, $IC_{rel}(c)$ is directly proportional to the number of properties it is related to, the more rel(c), the higher $IC_{rel}(c)$. The main advantage of this approach is that it can be applied in not only a simple taxonomy, but also a complex ontology with concept-properties relations.

Different IC models above is defined from different views, Table 2 presents the characteristic respectively.

Table 2. Comparison of different IC models

items	characteristic and the result				
	Corpora dependent IC Metric	Corpora independent IC Metric			
	Resnik model	Nuno model	Zhou model	David model	Md. Hanif model
Depth(c) increase	No	No	Yes IC increase	Yes IC increase	Yes, implicitly IC increase
Hypo(c) increase	No	Yes IC decrease	Yes IC decrease	No	Yes IC decrease
Leaves(c) increase	No	No	No	Yes IC decrease	No
Rel(c) increase	No	No	No	No	Yes $IC_{rel}(c)$ increase
Whether to rely on corpora	Yes	No	No	No	No
Sparse data problem	Yes	No	No	No	No
Improvement suggestions	----	Take every concept's topology into considered, such as, the arrangement of concepts		Take the numbers of hyponyms, depth of leaves into account	Take link type, concept's space structure into considered

4   Discussion and Further Research

IC is crucial in semantic similarity computing. A highly effective IC metric is necessary. There is sparse data problem in Corpora-dependent IC Metric. From the stated above, we can see that Corpora-independent IC Metric still is a hot issue. In Nuno's work, depth is not been taken into considered, and Zhou makes some improvements. However, in Zhou's work when concepts have the same depth and hypo(c), their IC will be equal (eg. IC (C_3) =IC (C_4) in Fig. 1) .There is room for improvement. David argues that leaves are enough to differentiate from other ones, regardless of the inner-detail of the hierarchy. But it is noted that concepts with the same leaves and subsumers will have the same IC value too (eg. IC (C_2) =IC (C_3) in Fig. 1). Yet they have different hyponyms (hypo (C_2) =1, and hypo (C_3) =2). In further work, it would be a good idea to take the topology structure of each concept in considered, such as the depth, the number of hyponyms, the depth of each hyponyms, the arrangements of concepts, etc. Our aim is to highly effective distinguish different concepts and get the most approximate IC value.

5   Summary

This paper reviews various information Content Metric approaches including Corpora-dependent IC model and Corpora-independent IC model. Hyponym-based mode, Leaves-based model and Relation-based IC model are illustrated. The important related issues are highlighted. Finally the area of further research is described.

References

1. Formica, A.: Concept similarity in formal concept analysis: an information content approach. Knowl. -Based Syst. 21(1), 80–87 (2007)
2. Jiang, J.J., Conrath, D.W.: Semantic similarity based on corpus statistics and lexical taxonomy. In: Proceedings of International Conference on Research in Computational Linguistics, Taiwan, pp. 19–33 (1997)
3. Lin, D.: An information-theoretic definition of similarity. In: Proceedings of the 15th International Conference on Machine Learning, Madison, Wisconsin, pp. 296–304 (1998)
4. Pirró, G.: A semantic similarity metric combining features and intrinsic information content. Data Knowl. Eng. 68(11), 1289–1308 (2009)
5. Resnik, P.: Using information content to evaluate semantic similarity in a taxonomy. In: Proceedings of the 14th International Joint Conference on Artificial Intelligence, Montréal, Québec, pp. 448–453 (1995)
6. Seco, N., Veale, T., Hayes, J.: An intrinsic information content metric for semantic similarity in WordNet. In: Proceedings of the 16th European Conference on Artificial Intelligence, Valencia, Spain, pp. 1089–1090 (2004)

7. Zhou, Z., Wang, Y., Gu, J.: A new model of information content for semantic similarity in WordNet. In: Proceedings of Second International Conference on Future Generation Communication and Networking Symposia, China, pp. 85–89 (2008)
8. Sánchez, D., Batet, M., Isern, D.: Ontology-based information content computation. Knowl. -Based Syst. 24, 297–303 (2011)
9. Seddiqui, H., Aono, M.: Metric of intrinsic information content for measuring semantic similarity in an ontology. In: Proceedings of 7th Asia-Pacific Conference on Conceptual Modeling, Australia, pp. 89–96 (2010)

Training Sample Acquisition Strategy Based Digital Pre-distortion

Biao Peng, Lin Gui, and Bo Liu

Department of Electronic Engineering, Shanghai Jiao Tong University, China
{miaozi,guilin,liubo_lb}@sjtu.edu.cn

Abstract. Digital pre-distortion (PD) is a promising technique for power amplifier (PA) linearization and efficiency enhancement. Parameter estimation for both PA and PD models are quite important in all pre-distortion schemes. In this paper we introduce the concept of RCBL (Region Can Be Linearized) and highlight the difference of training sample acquisition strategies (TSAS) for three different pre-distortion schemes. We prove that the improper samples may lead to the inaccuracy of the coefficients, or even an error. Thus we propose to choose the PA modeling and inverse structure as our scheme to do the DPD construction. A 5MHz Wimax signal sampled from a real PA is used to do the loop delay estimation, the PA model identification and the PD construction. Simulation results show that the AM/AM, AM/PM characteristics have been improved much and more than 15 dB of ACPR (Adjacent Channel Power Ratio) has been achieved.

Keywords: Digital Pre-distortion, Power Amplifier, TSAS, RCBL.

1 Introduction

Power amplifiers are very important components of wireless communication systems for both base stations and terminal equipments. Nowadays in order to approach high spectrum efficiency, non-constant envelope modulation technique such as QPSK and high order QAM are widely used, which leads to the problem of high PAPR. Operating PA near its saturation region will generate nonlinear distortion. This can lead to spectrum regrowth which can cause adjacent channel interference and will also bring up in-band distortion which can increase the bit error rate of communication systems. A lot of linearization techniques have been developed to solve this problem [1-5]. Thanks to the cost reduction in digital signal processing (DSP), baseband digital pre-distortion is growing to be a more and more promising scheme. This concept is based on inserting a nonlinear block, the inverse function of the power amplifier, before the power amplifier to compensate its nonlinearity. In order to do digital pre-distortion, a series of issues including loop delay estimation, PA model identification and PD construction must be solved. As the bandwidth goes wider, memory effects should also be taken into consideration.

Volterra series [6] with only odd order kernels is commonly used to model and analyse a PA with memory effect which is actually a nonlinear system with time variance. Because of the inconvenience of too many coefficients in Volterra series, usually only

W. Zhang et al. (Eds.): IFTC 2012, CCIS 331, pp. 307–316, 2012.

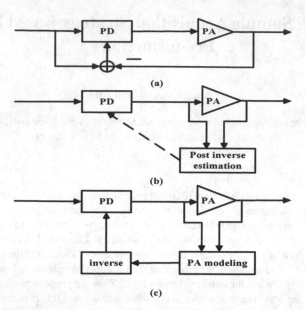

Fig. 1. Three different predistortion schemes(a)the directly learning structure (b)the indirectly learning structure (c)the PA modeling and inverse structure

the coefficient terms along the diagonal are kept. That is known as the memory polynomial model [7][8]. Following analysis of PA and PD model is based on this concept.

This paper is organized as follows, in Section 2 we first introduce the concept of RCBL (Region Can Be Linearized). Based on this concept we highlight the difference of training sample acquisition strategies for three different pre-distortion schemes shown in Fig. 1, the direct learning structure [9], the indirect learning structure [10]and the PA modeling and inverse structure[13]. After comparison and analysis, we propose to choose the third one as our DPD scheme. Section 3 goes on to present our ways to deal with the loop delay estimation, PA model identification and PD construction with data samples from the real PA. Our most work are focused on these three aspects and they are quite important in our pre-distortion scheme. In Section 4 the DPD simulation results are demonstrated. A summary of the work and significant conclusions are given in the final section.

2   Training Sample Acquisition Strategies

2.1   Region Can Be Linearized

Assume the transfer function of a power amplifier is $F(.)$, then the objective is to obtain a pre-distortion function $A(.)$ which when cascaded with the power amplifier can result in a linear transfer function. The system can be constructed as shown in Fig. 1. Assume

x is the original input signal from the baseband transmitter, v is the one after the pre-distorter, y is the output of the PA. The relationship can be given by

$$F(G(x)) = y \qquad (1)$$

The transfer characteristic can be decomposed into an AM/AM component and an AM/PM component. Here we take the first one as an example.

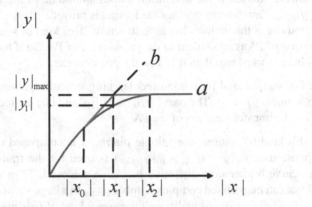

Fig. 2. The AM/AM transfer characteristic

As shown in Fig. 2, the objective of the pre-distorter is to linearize the output of the amplifier up to a certain maximum amplitude of $|y|_{max}$.

$$|y| = \begin{cases} g \cdot |x| & for \quad |x| < |x_1| \\ |y|_{max} & for \quad |x| \geq |x_1| \end{cases} \qquad (2)$$

where g is the open loop gain of the power amplifier.

Definition 1: (Region Can Be Linearized, RCBL): the part of the PA's nonlinear region which can be linearized. Assume a PA has the AM/AM characteristic as shown in Fig. 2. The total nonlinear input amplitude region of the PA is the segment $(|x_0|, |x_2|)$. But not all the nonlinear region of the PA can be linearized, The RCBL is actually the segment $(|x_0|, |x_1|)$, where $|x_1| = |y|_{max}/g$. As for the one $(|x_1|, |x_2|)$, we can do little contribution.

2.2 Training Sample Acquisition Strategies

As shown in Fig. 1, the existed pre-distortion structure or schemes can be classified into three categories. Which are the direct learning structure, the indirect learning structure and the PA modeling and inverse structure. The essence of these schemes is to get the least square solutions for equation $Aw = b$. The difference is that the former two use the samples to directly calculate PD's parameter, however the last one use it to calculate PA's parameter. This kind of difference leads to different training sample acquisition strategies, when we are trying to construct a robust and accurate DPD system.

The first one is the direct learning scheme, which usually uses adaptive algorithms to directly train for the pre-inverse parameters of the amplifier.

Lemma 1: For sample used for the direct learning structure training, we should only choose the segment $(0, |x_1|)$. The part $(|x_1|, |x_2|)$ should be excluded.

Proof: According to Fig. 2, if $x^\dagger$, $|x^\dagger| \in (|x_1|, |x_2|)$ is involved in the training or computation process, it means that there can be a pre-distortion operator G combined with PA's transfer function F mapping the complex number $x^\dagger$ to the complex number $gx^\dagger$. However we know the maximum output amplitude of the PA is $|y|_{max}$, and $g.|x^\dagger| > |y|_{max}$. Thus we can get that the lemma is proved.

The second one is the indirect learning structure. This kind of scheme assumes that the post-inverse of PA is equivalent to the pre-inverse of PA. So if the post-distorter of the PA has been worked out, then it is also the pre-distorter.

Lemma 2: For sample used for the indirect learning structure training, we should only choose the segment $(0, |y_1|)$. The part $(|y_1|, |y_{max}|)$ should be excluded, where $|y_1| = |G(x_1)|$, G is the transfer function of the PA.

Proof: In this kind of scheme, the sample matrix A is composed of y, according to Fig. 2, suppose that $y^\dagger, |y^\dagger| \in (|y_1|, |y|_{max})$ is used for the training process. And the transfer curve b after post-distortion has been achieved. Then we should have a operator G that can map a fixed complex number y_{max} to a large set of complex numbers $\forall x$, $|x| \in (|x_1|, |x_2|)$. Actually we know such kind of G is not existed. Thus the lemma is proved.

The third one is the PA modeling and inverse structure. In this kind of scheme, we do not directly train or calculate the pre-inverse or the post-inverse of PA, instead we use samples to get the positive transfer parameters of PA, then we can use PA's parameter to construct a PD system.

Lemma 3: For sample used for the PA modeling and inverse structure training, we can choose the whole segment $(0, |x_2|)$.

Proof: Due to the existence of the positive transfer curve a, the PA's transfer function G can correctly maps the segment $(0, |x_2|)$ to the segment $(0, |y_{max}|)$. Thus we get the lemma proved.

From above, we can know that compared with the former ones the third one seems to be much more robust and convenient when we do practice construction. That's why we choose the third one as our pre-distortion scheme.

3   PD Algorithm

3.1   Loop Delay Estimation

The loop delay estimation can be divided into two parts, the integer part and the fractional part. In order to do the loop delay estimation simulation, we have gathered 4096 samples from both the input and the output of the power amplifier. The transmitted signal is a Wimax signal with a bandwidth of 5MHz. The DAC's transfer rate is 91MHz, and the ADC's sample rate is 182MHz. The sampled signal is an intermediate frequency signal with a central frequency of 45.5MHz. After the digital down conversion and the low-pass filtering, the input and output data can be used for digital pre-distortion simulations.

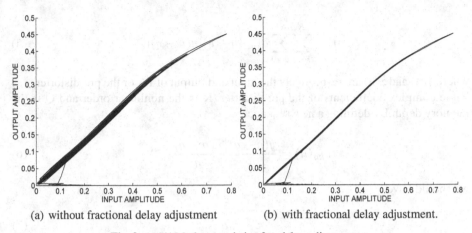

(a) without fractional delay adjustment   (b) with fractional delay adjustment.

Fig. 3. AM/AM characteristic after delay adjustment

We use the input and output sequences to do cross correlation operations to get the integer part of the loop delay. When the two sequences are matched, there will be a peak value.

$$\max\left\{\sum_{n=1}^{N}|x^*(n)y(n-k)|\right\} \tag{3}$$

In order to simplify the computation, we use only the sign bit to do cross correlation operations. The complex multiply operations are instead of bit operations, and this is quite useful when we do implementations. According to the simulation results, using 512 samples of complex data to do the cross correlation operations can effectively do the integer loop delay estimation.

As for the fractional loop delay estimation, there are usually two ways to do the adjustment. One is to do the interpolation, the other is to calculate in the frequency domain. We have done a ten order linear interpolation on the output data.

$$p(x) = f(x_0) + \frac{f(x_1) - f(x_0)}{x_1 - x_0}(x - x_0) \tag{4}$$

As shown in Fig. 3, fractional delay adjustment is really necessary for us to do digital pre-distortion. Without fractional delay adjustment, a certain degree of obvious divergence still existes in the AM/AM characteristic. If we treat this as memory effects, that will certainly weaken the performance of DPD algorithms.

3.2 Memory Polynomial Based PA Identification

For wideband applications, memory effects should be taken into account when we do digital pre-distortions. Memory polynomial [7][8][11] is a common model for both PA modeling and PD construction. The MP model can be described by

$$z(n) = \sum_{k=1}^{K} \sum_{q=0}^{Q} a_{kq} y(n-q)|y(n-q)|^{k-1} \qquad (5)$$

where y(n) and z(n) are respectively the input and output of PA or the pre-distorter, a_{kq} is the complex coefficients of the pre-distorter, K is the nonlinear order and Q is the memory depth.By defining a new sequence

$$u_{kq}(n) = \frac{y(n-q)}{g} | \frac{y(n-q)}{g} |^{k-1} \qquad (6)$$

we should have

$$z = Ua \qquad (7)$$

where $z = [z(0), \cdots, z(N-1)]^T$, $U = [u_{10}, \cdots, u_{K0}, \cdots, u_{1Q}, \cdots, u_{KQ}]$, $u_{kq} = [u_{kq}(0), \cdots u_{kq}(N-1)]^T$ and $a = [a_{10}, \cdots, a_{K0}, \cdots, a_{1Q}, \cdots, a_{KQ}]^T$. The least square solution is

$$\hat{a} = (U^H U)^{-1} U^H z, \qquad (8)$$

where $(.)^H$ denotes the complex conjugate transpose.

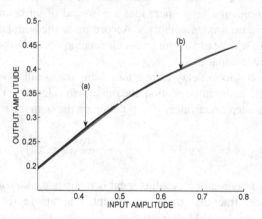

Fig. 4. AM/AM characteristic (a)the real curve (b)the fitting curve

With the input and output data of the PA, we can get the parameter $\hat{a}$ by using adaptive algorithms like LMS,RLS or directly calculation. When $\hat{a}$ is obtained, we have actually built the PA model. The fitting AM/AM and AM/PM curves are shown in Fig. 4 and Fig. 5.

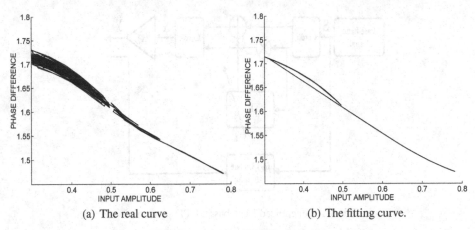

(a) The real curve   (b) The fitting curve.

Fig. 5. The real AM/PM characteristic

3.3 Look Up Table Based Pre-distortion

When the PA model is already obtained, we can use it to do our DPD simulations. A generalized LUT based DPD structure is shown in Fig. 6. With the cordic transform, the input signal is broken into the amplitude and phase components. The amplitude is used as the LUT's index.

$$|\mathrm{x}| = |\mathrm{s}| \cdot I_r(\mathrm{i}, \mathrm{n}) \qquad (9)$$

$$\angle x = \angle s + I_\theta(i, n) \qquad (10)$$

Where $I_r(i, n)$ represents the envelope component of the LUT output with which the incoming data is being multiplied, and $I_\theta(i, n)$ represents the phase component of the LUT output with wich the incoming data is being added. The LUT update algorithm can be described by

$$I_r(i, n + 1) = I_r(i, n) + \lambda_r e_r(n) \qquad (11)$$

$$I_\theta(i, n + 1) = I_\theta(i, n + 1) + \lambda_\theta e_\theta(n) \qquad (12)$$

$$e_r(n) = |s(n)| - |y(n)| \qquad (13)$$

$$e_\theta(n) = \angle s(n) - \angle y(n) \qquad (14)$$

The predistortion LUT will be organized as a set of discrete predistortion coefficients, each spans a certain input amplitude range(referred as a bin). The granularity of each bin limits the amount of adjacent channel reduction that can be achieved. We should do a good compromise between performance and complexity. 256 amplitude bin is enough to obtain a good performance.

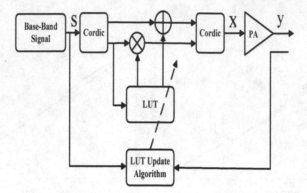

Fig. 6. A generalized LUT based DPD structure

4 Performance Analysis

In this section, we will demonstrate the simulation result of the PA modeling and inverse method. As described above, after doing DDC(digital down conversion), low-pass filtering, loop delay estimation and PA modeling, we can build a digital pre-distortion system. The AM/AM and AM/PM characteristic with and without pre-distortion are shown in Fig. 7 and Fig. 8 respectively.

Power spectral density results are shown in Fig. 9. We can see that more than 15 dB of ACPR (Adjacent Channel Power Ratio) has been achieved by using the PA modeling and inverse method.

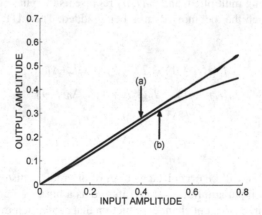

Fig. 7. The AM/AM characteristic(a)with DPD (b)without DPD

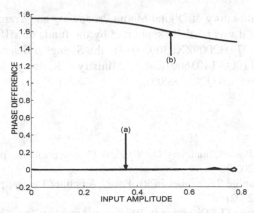

Fig. 8. The AM/PM characteristic(a)with DPD (b)without DPD

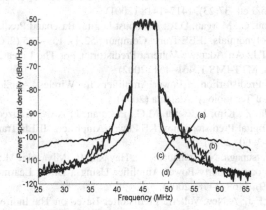

Fig. 9. Power spectral density(a)PA's output without DPD (b)the fitting signal (c)output with DPD (d)the original input signal

5   Conclusion

In this paper, we highlight the difference of training sample acquisition strategies for different pre-distortion schemes. Three different structures are taken into account. We have proved that the improper samples may lead to the inaccuracy of the coefficients for the pre-distorter, or even an error. Based on TSAS, we choose the PA modeling and inverse structure as our PD scheme. Samples from a real PA are used to do the loop delay estimation, PA model identification and PD construction. Simulation results have shown that both the AM-AM, AM/PM characteristic and the power spectrum density have achieved very good performance.

Acknowledgment. This work was supported in part by the Major State Basic Research Development Program of China (973 Program) (No. 2009CB320403), National Natural Science Foundation of China (60902018), the 111 Project (B07022) and the Shanghai Key Laboratory of Digital Media Processing and Transmissions STCSM (12DZ2272600); and it was partially supported by the funds of MIIT of China (Grant No. 2011ZX03001-007-032009ZX03002-014) , the Shanghai Science and technology Development Funds (10QA1403600) and the Ministry of Railways technology research and development programs (J2011X005).

References

1. Cripps, S.C.: RF Power Amplifiers for Wireless Communications, pp. 285–330. Artech House, Norwood (2006)
2. Cripps, S.C.: Advanced Techniques in RF Power Amplifier Design, pp. 153–197. Artech House, Norwood (2002)
3. Vuolevi, J., Rahkonen, T.: Distortion in RF Power Amplifiers, pp. 43–48. Artech House, Norwood (2003)
4. Kim, K.K.: Digital Predistortion of Wideband Signals Based on Power Amplifier Model with Memory. Electron. Lett. 37(23), 1417–1418 (2001)
5. Lei, D., Tong Zhou, G., Morgan, D.R.: A Robust Digital Baseband Predistorter Constructed Using Memory Polynomials. IEEE Trans. Commun. 52(1), 159–165 (2004)
6. Zhu, A., Brazil, T.J.: An Adaptive Volterra Predistorter For The Linearization of RF High Power Amplifiers. MTT-IMS 1, 461–464 (2002)
7. Ding, L.: Digital Predistortion of Power Amplifiers for Wireless Applications, pp. 25–33. Georgia Institute of Technology, Atalanta (2004)
8. Morgan, D.R., Ma, Z., Kim, J., Zierdt, M.G., Pastalan, J.: A Generalized Memory Polynomial Model for Digital Predistortion of RF Power Amplifiers. IEEE Trans. Signal Processing 54(10), 3852–3860 (2006)
9. Horiguchi, K., Matsunaga, N., Yamauchi, K., Hayashi, R., Miyazaki, M.: A Wideband Digital Predistorter For a Doherty Power Amplifier Using a Direct Learning Memory Effect Filter. TMTT 54(9), 3469–3478 (2006)
10. Eun, C., Powers, E.J.: A New Volterra Predistorter Based on The Indirect Learning Architecture. IEEE Trans. Signal Processing 45(1), 223–227 (1997)
11. Raich, R., Qian, H., Zhou, G.T.: Digital Baseband Pre-distortion of Nonlinear Power Amplifier Using Orthogonal Polynomials. In: Proc. IEEE Int. Conf. Acoust, Speech, Signal Processing, pp. 689–692 (2003)
12. Cavers, J.K.: Amplifier Linearization Using a Digital Predistorter With Fast Adaptation And Low Memory Requirements. IEEE Tran. on Vehicular Technology (November 1990)
13. Ma, Y., He, S., Akaiwa, Y., Yamao, Y.: An Open-Loop Digital Predistorter Based on Memory Polynomial Inverses for Linearization of RF Power Amplifier. International Journal of RF and Microwave Computer-Aided Engineering, 589–595 (2011)

Stream Maximization Transmission
for MIMO System
with Limited Feedback Unitary Precoding

Qiu Chen, Chen Peng, and Gui Lin

Department of Electronic Engineering
Shanghai Jiao Tong University, China
{questchen,guilin}@sjtu.edu.cn, cpicey@gmail.com

Abstract. Limited feedback precoding significantly improves multiple-input multiple-output (MIMO) link reliability with a small amount of feedback from the receiver back to the transmitter. One of the key problems linked to LFP is about the selection criteria of the optimal precoder index (PMI) from a codebook. In this paper, we find that the conventional PMI selection criteria under the stream maximization transmission (SMT) will be ineffective when the linear equalizers are employed at the receiver. Inspired by this discovery, a new singular value decomposition (SVD) based criterion activating the PMI selection for the SMT is proposed, which is accessible to both zero-foring (ZF) and minimum mean square error (MMSE) equalizer. Extensive numerical results are provided to substantiate the effectiveness of the proposed criterion.

1   Introduction

Multiple-input multiple-output (MIMO) systems, created by exploiting antenna arrays at the transceiver, offer high capacity and high-quality wireless communication links [1][2]. Primary schemes for exploiting MIMO channels are based on maximizing the capacity by spatial multiplexing [3], or increasing the diversity order by space-time coding [4]. However, the performance of spatial multiplexing is sensitive to the condition of the channel matrix. In order to guard against rank deficiencies in the channel, precoding scheme is proposed to largely improve error rate performance. The core idea of precoding is to use the channel state information at the transmitter side (CSIT) to customize the data stream with a precoding matrix prior to transmission.

In time-division duplex (TDD) systems, it is well known that the CSIT is easily accessible due to the channel reciprocity between the uplink and the downlink transmission. In frequency-division duplex (FDD) system, however, the availability of CSIT requires a feedback operation from the receiver to the transmitter, which introduces huge system overhead and thus is prohibitive in practice. To solve this problem in FDD systems, limited feedback precoding (LFP) schemes [7][8] are proposed. Here, a finite set of precoding matrices, called the codebook, is stored in both the transmitter and the receiver. The merit of LFP is that the

W. Zhang et al. (Eds.): IFTC 2012, CCIS 331, pp. 317–327, 2012.
© Springer-Verlag Berlin Heidelberg 2012

receiver only need to feedback the binary index of the precoding matrix as a function of the current CSI, instead of the full CSI, to the transmitter over a limited feedback channel. As such, the MIMO system promises to benefit from LFP scheme with notably reduced feedback overhead. Some key standards, such as long term evolution advanced (LTE-A), have been introducing LFP in the spatial multiplexing systems [13]. LTE-A established a concept of "layer", which is accordant with that of multiplexed multiple streams. In general precoding schemes, the number of data streams (or layers) is no more than the number of transmit antennas. In order to maximize the capacity of MIMO systems under good channel condition, full spatial multiplexing can be achieved when the number of streams reach up to that of the transmit antenna, referred to the stream maximization transmission (SMT).

The majority works on LFP is the codebook designing and the precoder index selection (PMI). The codebook designing schemes can be divided into unitary codebook and non-unitary codebook according to the power constraints of LFP. If all the matrices of the codebook have orthonormal columns, that is unitary precoding, otherwise that is non-unitary precoding. [12] showed that unitary precoding is more widely used than non-unitary precoding in academics and actual systems, one reason is that it can maintain the load balance of each antenna's power amplifier, the other reason is that it can effectively simplify the calculation of channel quality information (CQI) of the actual communication system such as LTE-A. More crucially, [12] proved that unitary precoding performs as good as non-unitary for small codebooks with MMSE decoder. The PMI criterion is depending on the choice of the system receiver and the performance criterion to be optimized (capacity, average error rate, etc.). ML (Maximum-likelihood) decoder is regarded as the best performance decoder, but its decoding complexity is increasing exponentially with the number of the transmit antennas. Therefore, in practice, linear decoders (including ZF decoder and MMSE decoder) have lower complexity and wider application. [7] proposed four criteria for choosing the optimal matrix from the codebook, three of them optimize the BER (bit error rate) performance: ML-SC for ML decoder, MSV-SC for ZF decoder and MSE-SC for MMSE decoder, the other one optimizes the capacity performance: Capacity-SC, and [11] proposed the precoding criteria for successive interference cancellation (SUC) decoder.

MSV-SC, MSE-SC and Capacity-SC is supposed to be the most widely used PMI criteria in the practical systems when the number of streams is less than the number of transmit antennas. But we discover that in the condition of SMT, these three precoding criteria become ineffectual for limited feedback unitary precoding (LFUP) because the precoding matrix is unitary at this moment. It motives us to propose a new PMI criterion which is a valid alternative in SMT, and we also hope that this new criterion has the common features like upper three criteria - low complexity and practical application.

The rest of paper is organized as follows. In Section 2, the considered system model is presented. Section 3 review the convention precoding criteria and prove that these criteria are inactive in SMT. Section 4 present an in-depth analysis of the precoding criteria for linear decoder in SMT. Simulation results are presented in section 5. Finally, Section 6 concludes the paper.

Notation: $(\cdot)^H$, $(\cdot)^{-1}$, $(\cdot)^+$, $\mathrm{tr}(\cdot)$ and $\det(\cdot)$ denote conjugate transposition, matrix inversion, matrix pseudo-inverse, trace, and determinant, respectively. $\mathbf{I}_M$ is the $M \times M$ identity matrix. $[\cdot]_{nn}$ represents the nth diagonal element. $\{a_{ij}\}_{M \times N}$ is the $M \times N$ matrix with element a_{ij} at entry (i, j). $\| \cdot \|_n$ is the n-dimensional norm, and $\|\mathbf{A}\|_1 = \max_{1 \leq i \leq N} \sum_{j=1}^{N} |a_{ij}|$ is the 1-D norm of matrix $\mathbf{A} = \{a_{ij}\}_{M \times N}$, $\|\mathbf{x}\|_2 = (\sum_{i=1}^{N} |x_i|^2)^{\frac{1}{2}}$ is the 2-D norm of vector $\mathbf{x} = \{x_1, x_2, ..., x_N\}$. $\mathbb{C}^{M \times N}$ represents the set of $M \times N$ in complex field. $\mathcal{CN}(0, \sigma^2)$ represents the complex normal distribution with independent real and imaginary parts distributed according to $\mathcal{N}(0, \sigma^2/2)$. $\mathcal{U}(N, L)$ represents the set of $N \times L$ matrices with orthonormal columns.

2   System Model

First , with the consideration of the single user MIMO (SU-MIMO) systems with N transmit antennas and M receiver antennas, the precoding operating with LFUP can be mathematically described in the sense that

$$\mathbf{x} = \mathbf{Fs}, \tag{1}$$

where $\mathbf{x} \in \mathbb{C}^{N \times 1}$ is the transmitted signal. $\mathbf{F} \in \mathbb{C}^{N \times L}$ is the precoding matrix chosen from the codebook $\mathcal{F} = \{\mathbf{F}_1, \mathbf{F}_2, ..., \mathbf{F}_k\}, k = 2^b$, where k is the precoding matrix index of the codebook, b is the size of the codebook. $\mathbf{s} \in \mathbb{C}^{L \times 1}$ is the data streams vector and the number of the streams L is no greater than the number of transmit antennas ($L \leq N$). For convenience, the data steams $\mathbf{s}$ have uniform power $\mathbb{E}[\mathbf{ss}^H] = \sigma_s^2 \mathbf{I}_L$.

The baseband transmission model for SU-MIMO systems can be always illustrated as

$$\mathbf{y} = \mathbf{Hx} + \mathbf{n} = \mathbf{HFs} + \mathbf{n}, \tag{2}$$

under the condition of ideal synchronous samplings, where $\mathbf{y} \in \mathbb{C}^{M \times 1}$ is the received signal. $\mathbf{H} \in \mathbb{C}^{M \times N}$ is the MIMO channel matrix and we assume that the number of receiver antennas is no less than the number of transmit antennas ($M \geq N$). $\mathbf{H}$ is a Rayleigh fading channel, therefore the entries of $\mathbf{H}$, $h_{ij} \sim \mathcal{CN}(0, 1)$. $\mathbf{n} \in \mathbb{C}^{M \times 1}$ is complex white Gaussian noise with distribution $\mathbf{n} \sim \mathcal{CN}(0, \sigma_n^2 \mathbf{I})$. The input signal-to-noise ratio of this SU-MIMO system is defined as

$$\mathsf{snr} = \frac{\sigma_s^2}{\sigma_n^2}. \tag{3}$$

We assume that each $\mathbf{F} \in \mathcal{F}$ has unit column vectors that are orthogonal, which can be denoted as $\mathbf{F} \in \mathcal{U}(N, L)$ in the setting of LFUP [7]. Further, when the system is operating on SMT mode, i.e. $M = L$, it is clear that $\mathbf{F}$ is actually a unitary matrix with $\mathbf{FF}^H = \mathbf{F}^H \mathbf{F} = \mathbf{I}_N$.

Linear decoder is used for filtering the received signal vector to obtain the decoded data stream vector $\hat{\mathbf{s}}$ as $\hat{\mathbf{s}} = \mathbf{G}\mathbf{y}$. A ZF linear decoder and a MMSE linear decoder can be illustrated as

$$\mathbf{G}_{\text{zf}} = (\mathbf{H}\mathbf{F})^{+}, \tag{4}$$

and

$$\mathbf{G}_{\text{mmse}} = \left(\mathbf{F}^{H}\mathbf{H}^{H}\mathbf{H}\mathbf{F} + \frac{1}{\text{snr}}\mathbf{I}_{N}\right)^{-1}\mathbf{H}^{H}\mathbf{F}^{H}, \tag{5}$$

respectively. Accordingly, the signal to interference plus noise rate (SINR) of the n-th stream can be given by (see [6])

$$\rho_{\text{zf},n}(\mathbf{F}) = \frac{\text{snr}}{[(\mathbf{F}^{H}\mathbf{H}^{H}\mathbf{H}\mathbf{F})^{-1}]_{nn}}, \tag{6}$$

for the ZF decoder and

$$\rho_{\text{mmse},n}(\mathbf{F}) = \frac{\text{snr}}{[(\mathbf{F}^{H}\mathbf{H}^{H}\mathbf{H}\mathbf{F} + \frac{1}{\text{snr}}\mathbf{I}_{N})^{-1}]_{nn}} - 1, \tag{7}$$

for the MMSE decoder. It is clear that the BER performance is totally decide by (6) and (7).

3   Convention Criteria

In [7], three different selection criteria of the optimal precoder from the codebook are proposed, which are presented in Lemma 1-3 detailedly.

Lemma 1. *MSV-SC (Minimum Singular Value Selection Criterion) can optimize the BER performance of the SU-MIMO system with ZF decoder by picking* $\mathbf{F}$ *such that*

$$\mathbf{F} = \arg\max_{\mathbf{F}_i \in \mathcal{F}} \lambda_{\min}\{\mathbf{H}\mathbf{F}_i\}, \tag{8}$$

where $\lambda_{\min}\{\mathbf{H}\mathbf{F}_i\}$ *is the minimum singular value of* $\mathbf{H}\mathbf{F}_i$.

Lemma 2. *MSE-SC (Mean Squared Error Selection Criterion) can optimize the BER performance of the SU-MIMO system with MMSE decoder by picking* $\mathbf{F}$ *such that*

$$\mathbf{F} = \arg\min_{\mathbf{F}_i \in \mathcal{F}} m(\overline{\text{MSE}}(\mathbf{F}_i)), \tag{9}$$

where $m(\cdot)$ *is either* $\text{tr}(\cdot)$ *or* $\det(\cdot)$. $\overline{\text{MSE}}(\mathbf{F}_i)$ *is the mean squared error (MSE) of MMSE of the MMSE decoder which can be shown as*

$$\overline{\text{MSE}}(\mathbf{F}_i) = \sigma_s^2 \left(\mathbf{I}_N + \text{snr}\mathbf{F}_i^{H}\mathbf{H}^{H}\mathbf{H}\mathbf{F}_i\right)^{-1}. \tag{10}$$

Lemma 3. *Capacity-SC (Capacity Selection Criterion) can optimize the capacity performance of the SU-MIMO system by picking* $\mathbf{F}$ *such that*

$$\mathbf{F} = \arg \max_{\mathbf{F}_i \in \mathcal{F}} C(\mathbf{F}_i). \tag{11}$$

where $C(\mathbf{F}_i)$ *denote the capacity of SU-MIMO systems which can be shown as*

$$C(\mathbf{F}_i) = \log_2 \det \left(\mathbf{I}_N + \mathsf{snr} \mathbf{F}_i^H \mathbf{H}^H \mathbf{H} \mathbf{F}_i \right). \tag{12}$$

The effectiveness of aforementioned criteria has been validated in terms of numerical results in [7] when $L < N$. However, we find that all of them are inactive in SMT mode. In the following, these findings will be testified by both theoretical analysis and numerical results.

Theorem 1. *Lemma 1, Lemma 2 and Lemma 3 are ineffective for limited feedback unitary precoding in SMT.*

Proof. In SMT, the precoding matrix herein is unitary. That means for each $\mathbf{F}_i \in \mathcal{F}$,

$$\mathbf{F}_i \mathbf{F}_i^H = \mathbf{F}_i^H \mathbf{F}_i = \mathbf{I}_N. \tag{13}$$

Thus for Lemma 1, SVD of $\mathbf{H}$ and $\mathbf{H} \mathbf{F}_i$ can be expressed as

$$\mathbf{H} = \mathbf{U}^H \mathbf{\Lambda} \mathbf{V}, \tag{14}$$

$$\mathbf{H} \mathbf{F}_i = \mathbf{U}^H \mathbf{\Lambda} \mathbf{V} \mathbf{F}_i, \tag{15}$$

where $\mathbf{U}$, $\mathbf{V}$ and $\mathbf{F}_i$ are all unitary matrices and we can easily observe that $\mathbf{H}$ and $\mathbf{H}\mathbf{F}_i$ have the same singular values. Thus

$$\lambda_{\min} \{\mathbf{H}\mathbf{F}_i\} = \lambda_{\min} \{\mathbf{H}\}. \tag{16}$$

For Lemma 2,

$$\overline{\mathrm{MSE}}(\mathbf{F}_i) = \sigma_s^2 \left(\mathbf{I}_N + \mathsf{snr} \mathbf{F}_i^H \mathbf{H}^H \mathbf{H} \mathbf{F}_i \right)^{-1} = \sigma_s^2 \left(\mathbf{F}_i^H \left(\mathbf{I}_N + \mathsf{snr} \mathbf{H}^H \mathbf{H} \right) \mathbf{F}_i \right)^{-1}$$
$$= \sigma_s^2 \mathbf{F}_i^H \left(\mathbf{I}_N + \mathsf{snr} \mathbf{H}^H \mathbf{H} \right)^{-1} \mathbf{F}_i,$$

and then we can conclude that

$$\mathrm{tr}(\overline{\mathrm{MSE}}(\mathbf{F}_i)) = \mathrm{tr}(\sigma_s^2 \left(\mathbf{I}_N + \mathsf{snr} \mathbf{H}^H \mathbf{H} \right)^{-1}), \tag{17}$$

$$\det(\overline{\mathrm{MSE}}(\mathbf{F}_i)) = \sigma_s^2 \det((\mathbf{I}_N + \mathsf{snr} \mathbf{H}^H \mathbf{H})^{-1}), \tag{18}$$

that means

$$m(\overline{\mathrm{MSE}}(\mathbf{F}_i)) = \sigma_s^2 m((\mathbf{I}_N + \mathsf{snr} \mathbf{H}^H \mathbf{H})^{-1}). \tag{19}$$

For Lemma 3,

$$C(\mathbf{F}_i) = \log_2 \det \left(\mathbf{F}_i^H \left(\mathbf{I}_N + \mathsf{snr} \mathbf{H}^H \mathbf{H} \right) \mathbf{F}_i \right)$$
$$= \log_2 \det \left(\mathbf{I}_N + \mathsf{snr} \mathbf{H}^H \mathbf{H} \right). \tag{20}$$

Clearly, (16), (19) and (20) indicate that the value of $\lambda_{\min}\{\mathbf{H}\mathbf{F}_i\}$, $m(\overline{\mathrm{MSE}}(\mathbf{F}_i))$ and $C(\mathbf{F}_i)$ is unrelated with $\mathbf{F}_i$ if $\mathbf{F}_i$ is unitary matrix. Thus Lemma 1, Lemma 2 and Lemma 3 become ineffective in SMT.

Above observations in the Theorem 1 motive us to design a novel precoding selection criterion for SMT model. Since neither MSV-SC nor MSE-SC optimizes the system BER performance directly, these process provides us additional degree of freedom to design a novel criterion to optimize the BER performance.

4 Novel Precoding Criteria for SMT

In this section, we will propose a new criterion which is effective in SMT for limited feedback unitary precoding. This new criterion is based on MSM-SC introduced as follows.

Lemma 4. *MSM-SC (Minimum SINR Maximization Selection Criterion) can optimize the BER performance of the SU-MIMO system by picking* $\mathbf{F}$ *such that*

$$\mathbf{F} = \arg \max_{\mathbf{F}_i \in \mathcal{F}} \left(\min_{1 \leq n \leq N} \rho_n(\mathbf{F}_i) \right), \qquad (21)$$

where $\rho_n(\mathbf{F}_i)$ *is the SINR of the nth stream whose expression is* $\rho_n(\mathbf{F}_i) = \rho_{zf,n}(\mathbf{F}_i)$ *for ZF decoder and* $\rho_n(\mathbf{F}_i) = \rho_{mmse,n}(\mathbf{F}_i)$ *for MMSE decoder.*

MSM-SC requires the computation and comparison of the SNR of each of the N streams, therefore it is too complex to implement. This motives us to design a low computational complexity sub-optimal criterion which only need one matrix operation for all the streams. Actually, MSV-SC is proposed by simplifying $\rho_{zf,n}(\mathbf{F})$ in (6) and it is the typical example of MSM-SC relaxation for ZF decoder. Our work is proposing another MSM-SC relaxation method which applies to SMT.

Theorem 2. *MN-SC (Minimum 1-D Norm Selection Criterion) can optimize the BER performance of the SU-MIMO system in SMT by picking* $\mathbf{F}$ *such that*

$$\mathbf{F} = \arg \min_{\mathbf{F}_i \in \mathcal{F}} \|\bar{\mathbf{V}}^H \mathbf{F}_i\|_1, \qquad (22)$$

where $\bar{\mathbf{V}} = [\bar{\mathbf{v}}_1, \bar{\mathbf{v}}_2, ..., \bar{\mathbf{v}}_N]$, $\bar{\mathbf{v}}_k \in \mathbb{C}^{N \times 1}$ *is the kth column of* $\bar{\mathbf{V}}$, *and* $\bar{\mathbf{v}}_k = \mathbf{v}_k / \sqrt{\lambda_k}$ *for ZF decoder,* $\bar{\mathbf{v}}_k = \mathbf{v}_k / \sqrt{\lambda_k + 1/snr}$ *for MMSE decoder.*

Proof. Let $\mathbf{F}_i = [\mathbf{f}_1^{(i)}, \mathbf{f}_2^{(i)}, ..., \mathbf{f}_N^{(i)}]$, where $\mathbf{f}_k^{(i)} \in \mathbb{C}^{N \times 1}$ is the kth column of $\mathbf{F}_i$. The singular value decomposition (SVD) of $\mathbf{H}^H \mathbf{H}$ can be expressed as

$$\mathbf{H}^H \mathbf{H} = \mathbf{V} \mathbf{\Sigma} \mathbf{V}^H, \qquad (23)$$

where $\mathbf{V} \in \mathbb{C}^{N \times N}$ is unitary, $\mathbf{V} = [\mathbf{v}_1, \mathbf{v}_2, ..., \mathbf{v}_N]$, $\mathbf{v}_k \in \mathbb{C}^{N \times 1}$ is the kth column of $\mathbf{V}$, and $\mathbf{\Sigma} = diag\{\lambda_1, \lambda_2, ..., \lambda_N\}$, λ_k is the singular value of $\mathbf{H}^H \mathbf{H}$ at entry (k, k).

The SINR of ZF and MMSE decoder - $\rho_{zf,n}(\mathbf{F}_i)$ and $\rho_{mmse,n}(\mathbf{F}_i)$ can be simplified according to (6) and (7) if each $\mathbf{F}_i \in \mathcal{F}$ is unitary:

$$\rho_{zf,n}(\mathbf{F}_i) = \frac{snr}{\left[\left(\mathbf{F}_i^H \mathbf{V} \mathbf{\Sigma} \mathbf{V}^H \mathbf{F}_i \right)^{-1} \right]_{nn}} = \frac{snr}{[\mathbf{F}_i^H \mathbf{V} \mathbf{\Sigma}^{-1} \mathbf{V}^H \mathbf{F}_i]_{nn}} = \frac{snr}{\sum_{k=1}^{N} \frac{|\mathbf{v}_k^H \mathbf{f}_n^{(i)}|^2}{\lambda_k}},$$

$$\rho_{\mathrm{mmse},n}(\mathbf{F}_i) = \frac{\mathrm{snr}}{[\left(\mathbf{F}_i^H \mathbf{V} \mathbf{\Sigma} \mathbf{V}^H \mathbf{F}_i + \frac{1}{\mathrm{snr}}\mathbf{I}_N\right)^{-1}]_{nn}} - 1$$

$$= \frac{\mathrm{snr}}{[\mathbf{F}_i^H \mathbf{V}(\mathbf{\Sigma} + \frac{1}{\mathrm{snr}}\mathbf{I}_N)^{-1}\mathbf{V}^H \mathbf{F}_i]_{nn}} - 1 = \frac{\mathrm{snr}}{\sum\limits_{k=1}^{N} \frac{|\mathbf{v}_k^H \mathbf{f}_n^{(i)}|^2}{\lambda_k + 1/\mathrm{snr}}} - 1.$$

Let $\bar{\mathbf{V}} = [\bar{\mathbf{v}}_1, \bar{\mathbf{v}}_2, ..., \bar{\mathbf{v}}_N]$, $\bar{\mathbf{v}}_k \in \mathbb{C}^{N \times 1}$ is the kth column of $\bar{\mathbf{V}}$, and $\bar{\mathbf{v}}_k = \mathbf{v}_k/\sqrt{\lambda_k}$ for ZF decoder, $\bar{\mathbf{v}}_k = \mathbf{v}_k/\sqrt{\lambda_k + 1/\mathrm{snr}}$ for MMSE decoder, the expression of MSM-SC (21) can be transformed in this form

$$\mathbf{F} = \arg\min_{\mathbf{F}_i \in \mathcal{F}} \left(\max_{1 \leq n \leq N} \sum_{k=1}^{N} |\bar{\mathbf{v}}_k^H \mathbf{f}_n^{(i)}|^2 \right) = \arg\min_{\mathbf{F}_i \in \mathcal{F}} \left(\max_{1 \leq n \leq N} ||\bar{\mathbf{V}}^H \mathbf{f}_n^{(i)}||_2^2 \right). \quad (24)$$

We can easily observe that $\bar{\mathbf{V}}^H \mathbf{f}_n^{(i)}$ is the nth column of matrix $\bar{\mathbf{V}}^H \mathbf{F}_i$. Thus if we let $\bar{\mathbf{V}}^H \mathbf{F}_i = \{f_{ij}\}_{N \times N}$, $\bar{\mathbf{V}}^H \mathbf{f}_n^{(i)}$ can be expressed as $\bar{\mathbf{V}}^H \mathbf{f}_n^{(i)} = \{f_{in}\}_{N \times 1}$, then we can conclude that

$$\max_{1 \leq n \leq N} ||\bar{\mathbf{V}}^H \mathbf{f}_n^{(i)}||_2^2 = \max_{1 \leq n \leq N} \sum_{i=1}^{N} |f_{in}|^2 \leq \max_{1 \leq n \leq N} \left(\sum_{i=1}^{N} |f_{in}| \right)^2$$

$$= \left(\max_{1 \leq n \leq N} \sum_{i=1}^{N} |f_{in}| \right)^2 = ||\bar{\mathbf{V}}^H \mathbf{F}_i||_1^2. \quad (25)$$

With (24) and (25) we get the expression of MN-SC

$$\mathbf{F} = \arg\min_{\mathbf{F}_i \in \mathcal{F}} ||\bar{\mathbf{V}}^H \mathbf{F}_i||_1. \quad (26)$$

Through theorem 2 we propose a consistent criterion suited for both ZF and MMSE decoder. This proposed criterion has lower complexity than MSM-SC, because it's only required one matrix operation for all the streams, and the matrix inverse operation is also canceled. and then we will test whether this criterion is effective in the next section.

5 Simulations

In this section, numerical results are provided to validate the electiveness of the proposed precoding selection criteria. Here, the BER performances of MN-SC, MSM-SC and the original criteria (c.f. Lemma 1-3) are presented. We employ QPSK modulation with Gray mapping. The codebook matrices are chosen in the Grassmann manifold by the codebook design method introduced in [8], and size of the codebook is 6bit.

5.1 Comparisons in Terms of the Same Number of Transmit Antennas

This simulation used two different antenna settings, one is 4×4, the other is 4×6. In these two settings, the MIMO systems have the same power of each stream.

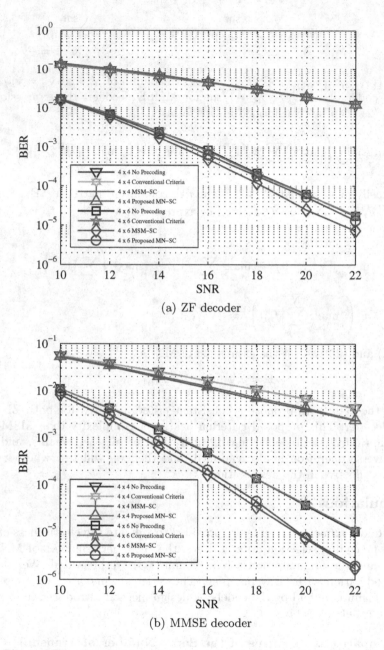

(a) ZF decoder

(b) MMSE decoder

Fig. 1. BER comparison for linear decoder in the same transmit antennas

The results are presented in fig. 1. First, for 4×6 setting we can observe that the conventional criteria is inactive. In the contrast, the proposed criteria have effective precoding gain, which is 0.2dB for ZF decoder and 2.2dB for MMSE decoder. And the performance of MN-SC is closer to MSM-SC for MMSE decoder than that for ZF decoder. Second, for 4×4 setting, although the proposed criteria have precoding gain of 2dB for MMSE decoder, there are no precoding gain for ZF decoder. The reason of this phenomenon is that for ZF decoder, the diversity order is equal to $M - N + 1$ in spatial multiplexing. Therefore in 4×4 setting, the diversity order for ZF decoder is 1. That causes there is no precoding gain for ZF decoder. For MMSE decoder, the diversity order is greater than $M - N + 1$, thus precoding improves the BER performance for MMSE decoder in both 4×4 and 4×6 settings.

This simulation illustrates that in practical, MMSE decoder is more useful than ZF decoder in practical application because MMSE decoder has better BER performance and is adapted for any antenna setting. Actually, most communication systems such as LTE use MMSE decoder or MMSE-SIC decoder in common application.

5.2 Comparisons in Different Number of Transmit Antennas

This simulation used two different antenna settings, one is 4×4, the other is 8×8. MMSE decoder is selected. The results are presented in fig. 2. In these two settings, the power of each stream in 4×4 is higher than that in 8×8, and the diversity order in 4×4 is less than that in 8×8. Thus we can observe that without precoding, the BER performance of 8×8 is 1dB outperform than

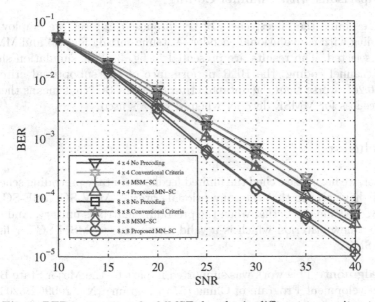

Fig. 2. BER comparison for MMSE decoder in different transmit antennas

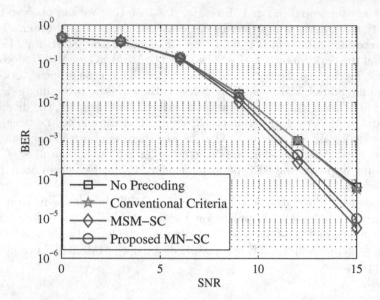

Fig. 3. BER comparison for MMSE decoder with channel coding

4×4. And with precoding, the BER performance of 8×8 is 3dB outperform than 4×4. And fig. 2 also shows that the performance of MN-SC is similar to MSM-SC for MMSE decoder.

5.3   Comparisons with Channel Coding

To further examine the effectiveness of the proposed criteria, we employ the channel coding with convolutional encoder. Antenna setting is 4×4 and MMSE decoder is selected. The results are presented in fig. 3. This simulation shows that with channel coding, the BER performance of the suboptimal criterion MN-SC is 0.2dB worse than the optimal criterion MSM-SC, that means there is performance loss for MMSE decoder when MN-SC is used.

6   Conclusion

In this paper, we have researched the limited feedback unitary precoding schemes in SMT. We have proven that the conventional criteria - MSV-SC, MSE-SC and Capacity-SC become ineffectual when the precoding matrix is unitary. And then we propose a new criterion which is a valid alternative to MSM-SC for linear decoder in SMT.

Acknowledgment. This work was supported in part by the Major State Basic Research Development Program of China (973 Program) (No. 2009CB320403), National Natural Science Foundation of China (60902018), the 111 Project

(B07022) and the Shanghai Key Laboratory of Digital Media Processing and Transmissions; and it was partially supported by the funds of MIIT of China (Grant No. 2011ZX03001-007-032009ZX03002-014) , the Shanghai Science and technology Development Funds (10QA1403600) and the Ministry of Railways technology research and development programs (J2011X005).

References

1. Telatar, I.E.: Capacity of multi-antenna Gaussian channels. Europ. Trans. Telecommun. 10(6), 585–595 (1999)
2. Foschini, G.J., Gans, M.J.: On limits of wireless communications in a fading environment when using multiple antennas. Wireless Personal Commun. 6, 311–335 (1998)
3. Paulraj, A., Kailath, T.: U. S. #5345599: Increasing capacity in wireless broadcast systems using distributed transmission/directional reception (DTDR) (September 1994)
4. Tarokh, V., Seshadri, N., Calderbank, A.R.: Space-time codes for high data rate wireless communication: Performance criterion and code construction. IEEE Trans. Info. Th. 44, 744–765 (1998)
5. Paulraj, A.J., Nabar, R., Gore, D.: Introduction to Space-Time Wireless Communication. Cambridge Univ. Press, U.K. (2003)
6. Heath, R.W., Paulraj, A.: Antenna selection for spatial multiplexing systems based on minimum error rate. In: Proc. IEEE Int. Conf. Communications, Helsinki, Finland, vol. 7, pp. 2276–2280 (June 2001)
7. Love, D.J., Heath, R.W.: Limited feedback unitary precoding for spatial multiplexing systems. IEEE Trans. Inform. Theory 51(8) (August 2005)
8. Love, D.J., Heath, R.W.: Limited feedback unitary precoding for orthogonal space-time block codes. IEEE Trans. Pro. 53(1) (January 2005)
9. Li, P., Paul, D., Narasimhan, R., Cioffi, J.: On the distribution of SINR for the MMSE MIMO receiver and performance analysis. IEEE Trans. Inform. Theory 52, 271–286 (2006)
10. Jiang, Y., Varanasi, M.K., Li, J.: Performance analysis of ZF and MMSE equalizers for MIMO systems: an in-depth study of the high SNR regime. IEEE Trans. Inform. Theory 57(4) (April 2011)
11. Li, Y., Moon, J.: Transmitter precoding with reduced-complexity soft detection for MIMO systems. IEEE Trans. Commun. 6(3) (March 2007)
12. Kapetanovic, D., Rusek, F.: A comparison between unitary and non-unitary precoder design for MIMO channels with MMSE detection and limited feedback. In: IEEE Globecom Conf. (December 2010)
13. 3GPP TS 36.211 V10.4.0 (December 2011)

The Application of Digital Elevation Model in the Coverage Network Planning Software

Ning Ding[*] and Yi-he Dai[**]

Shanghai Oriental Pearl Broadcasting R&D Co., Ltd.
200120 Shanghai, China
{dingn,adai}@opg.cn

Abstract. This paper introduces an analysis method of the digital elevation model map based on the Geotiff format, through the algorithm of data read, coordinate transformation, numerical interpolation of map, convert to the new map format which can be executed efficiently in broadcasting network planning software, to achieve the accurate prediction coverage field strength with radio waves diffractions correction which base on digital elevation model.

Keywords: Geotiff, digital elevation model, format convert.

1   Introduction

With the development of the applications of digital terrestrial television, it need more transmit sites to satisfy the demand of the excellent coverage, so the original single transmit site has transited to transmit network by the technology of single frequency network(SFN). If the configuration of the new additional transmit site, such as transmit power, transmit antenna pattern, site location, is set inappropriately, it will bring unnecessary cost of the network construction, low efficiency of   SFN, and inevitable interference of   the network in the worst case.

Broadcasting Coverage Network Planning Software is a good solution of the network construction. Shanghai Oriental Pearl Broadcasting R&D Co., Ltd had develop a new broadcasting network planning software[1] which support the DTMB(Chinese terrestrial TV standard) and CMMB(Chinese mobile multimedia standard). The software has the function of analysis of field strength, interference and network, and network optimization. The software also integrated the radio waves propagation model correction by drive test data, and network plan criterion correction of receive chips. It is belongs to advanced method of broadcasting network plan by the

---

[*] DING Ning (1986~), male, assistant engineer, graduated from computer science and technology department in Shanghai University in 2009. Bachelor degree, Mayor: data process and software engineering.

[**] Corresponding author. DAI Yihe(1975~) ,senior engineer, graduated from communication engineering department of Shanghai Jiaotong University in 2006, master degree, mayor: radio wave propagation and coverage. mp: 13817682664.

W. Zhang et al. (Eds.): IFTC 2012, CCIS 331, pp. 328–332, 2012.
© Springer-Verlag Berlin Heidelberg 2012

means of Combined with practical experience. In order to gain the high precise of the coverage prediction, it should take the Digital Elevation Model(DEM) which contains area altitude information as calculate factors, usually the DEM become to the obstacle of the widely applications of network planning software attributed to the high price.

This paper analysis the no charge Geotiff format map which is issued by NASA depend on detail information of the new generation global earth observation satellite system TERRA, the map provide the highest resolution of free map in the world now. The related elevation information was been re-sampled, coordination convert and numerical interpolation to achieve format convert and high efficient use in network plan software. It provided convenience of the software widely used.

2   Format Difference

The format difference between Geotiff[2][3] and map of network plan software conclude coordination, reference point, resolution and file configuration structure, more detail can be seen as in tab1

Table 1. The comparison of map format between Geotiff and planning software

	GeoTiff（source file）	Map of plan software（target file）
Coordinate system	Wgs84, Spherical	UTM, orthogonal
Reference point	northwest	southwest
resolution	second	meter
Tile size	1°x 1°	12km*12km
File structure	Private for every file	Public for all
features	Flexible configuration information, low calculate speed	Section block, high speed of loading and calculation

The structure of map data is consisted of three blocks: geographical data, display configure, elevation data. The geographical data describe the parameters of the structure of map layer.

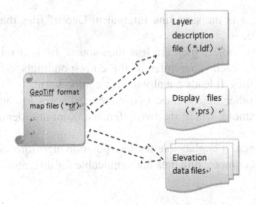

Fig. 1. Structure of source and target files

3   Solutions

3.1   Interpolation Algorithm

For Geotiff files, sampling interval is one second and coordinate system is based on WGS84. According to the radius of earth, 6370km,we can deduce that spherical coordinates is gradient , for the reason that latitude vary from 18° to 53° and sampling interval vary horizontally from 29.4m to 18.6m. However, different completely from Geotiff files, the map files of Planning Software construct geography data, which is sampled metrically at a constant interval, in orthogonal coordinates. As a consequence, it is impossible to obtain exactly the point existing in the map files of Planning Software, corresponding to another point in Geotiff files. To crack this hard nut, we cannot but turn to both the solutions, Projection as well as Interpolation algorithm.

Points:

- The origin of coordinates locates in the lower left corner.
- The origin point is based on UTM.
- Produce each geography point at a constant interval from the origin point, which is constructed in the form of UTM point, but we can convert it to the point in Wgs84 when we use it.
- Search the four specific Point which exist in Geotiff files and keeping the nearest to the target point. All of them are imperative for Interpolation algorithm to compute the height value in the target point.

Two Situation should be under consideration.

For one thing, greater is the sampling interval in Geotiff files than in the map files of Planning Software.

In this situation, object files are more than source files. It may occur that two points Adjacent to each other refer to the same four reference points in Geotiff files. Nonetheless, different positions give rise to different weighting factor, and to different interpolation value. For other object files, two points Adjacent to each other refer to four reference points among which the two reference point are identical and the other are different.

For another, less is the sampling interval in Geotiff files than in the map files of Planning Software.

In this situation, object files are less than source files. It might turn out that two points Adjacent to each other refer to the correspondingly different four reference points in Geotiff files. It leads equally to data compression.

Similarly, for other object files, two points Adjacent to each other refer to four reference points among which the two reference point are identical and the other are different.

As a consequence, it is plausible for Interpolation algorithm accomplish the task of accumulating and compressing data and applicable for different reference files.

3.2   Positioning Algorithm

Deviations occur inevitably when Converting data from spherical coordinates to orthogonal coordinates. The worst thing is that large amounts of data accumulate gradually to such an extent that deviations is increasingly beyond we can bear. There is Positioning Algorithm below, which is able to solve the problem effectively.

Positioning Algorithm follow such a principle that to determine the location of target point and then to go back to the source files, Geotiff files , for computing value. The target points are not based on geography points existing in Geotiff files, and unable to be converted directly into geography points in the object file, the map files of Planning Software. But it is that geography point in the object file, of which the height values is unknown and provided in certain precision on a specific range, that trace to the source files in search of the four specific Point which exist in Geotiff files and keeping the nearest to it, and works out the value of target point.

Positioning Algorithm use the Wgs84 as a bridge connecting different coordinates when tracing to source files. Each unknown target point on the map is required to be converted to an UTM point, then to a wgs84 point. In this way, Positioning Algorithm succeed to capture the four specific Point which exist in Geotiff files and keeping the nearest to it, according to degree, minute, second. By means of Interpolation algorithm, the height value of the target point in object files can be obtained. It ensured the accuracy and eliminate great deviations that results from accumulation.

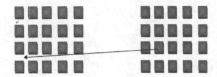

Fig. 2. The schemes of location methods

4   Achievement Apply

Based on the research of above, we develop the map conversion software successfully. The conversion software realized the big map array conversion, data batch import and analysis and merge automatically. Error is small than 1 pix, convert results hand been applied in the Shanxi mobile TV coverage network optimization, and predicted the shadow areas of network successfully.

Fig. 3. Prediction strength coverage map of Shanxi mobile TV

The method of radio wave propagation is under the field strength curves of ITU-R 1546[4], adopt the elevation information, received antenna correction, clearance angle to make the interval of prediction results and the practical test result minimized, finally, it provide the suggestion of additional transmit site configuration.

5   Conclusion

This papers is based on the demand of free use of DEM, discusses the key idea and algorithms of the GeoTiff format convert into planning software format to gain the high efficient application. The study offers a solution for the DEM map conversion, can promote the broadcasting coverage planning and the related work get progress.

References

1. Handbook of Oriental pearl broadcasting network planner, http://rd.opg.cn
2. Adobe Developers Association, TIFF Revision 6 10 (1992),
   http://partners.adobe.com/public/developer/en/tiff/TIFF6.pdf
3. GeoTIFF Format Specification, GeoTIFF Revision 1.0 (2000),
   http://remotesensing.org/geotiff/spec/geotiffhome.html
4. RECOMMENDATION ITU-R P.1546-3 Method for point-to-area predictions for terrestrial services in the frequency range 30 MHz to 3000 MHz (November 2007)

A Novel Dynamic Spectrum Management and Sharing Approach for the Secondary Networks

Haibo Zhou[1], Bo Liu[1], Lin Gui[1], Yongfei Ding[2],
Jianmin Wu[2], and Lifeng Wang[3]

[1] Dept. of Electronic Engineering, Shanghai Jiao Tong University, China
{haibozhou,liubo_lb,guilin}@sjtu.edu.cn
[2] Chinese Aeronautical Radio Electronics Research Institute, China
{dingjia95,jmwuyeah}@gmail.com
[3] China Electronic System Engineering Company, Beijing, China
wlf_box@hotmail.com

Abstract. For the better improvement of spectrum utilization, in this paper, we propose a novel spectrum management and sharing models. For specification, the concept of spectrum database and anxiety level of idle spectrum resource are introduced in dynamic spectrum management model. Accordingly, the QoS requirements are formulated in the spectrum sharing model. In addition, we introduce a multi-hop spectrum relay service scheme that can decrease the spectrum sharing complexity in applications and can be regarded to be more practical and scalable. To improve the spectrum utilization and revenue, the spectrum sharing strategy is combined with the anxiety and matching level of idle spectrum. The simulation results validate that our approach can achieve a high level performance, especially the spectrum sharing revenue.

Keywords: cognitive radio, spectrum management and sharing, multi-hop.

1 Introduction

The fixed spectrum assignment policy for wireless networks is becoming inadequate in addressing the rapidly evolving wireless communication technology [1], due to the growing user demands for wireless bandwidth. For this purpose, how to make flexible dynamic spectrum management (DSM) and sharing strategy have gained growing momentum from both the academia and industry [2][3]. Currently, the significant efforts are beginning to put into many interesting DSM models and spectrum sharing approaches, varied from the centralized or distributed DSM structures to the efficient algorithms for spectrum utilization. Among them, many economic theories and marketing models are used, such as game theory and auction theory, etc.

The share-use model can be categorized as spectrum overlay sharing case and spectrum underlay sharing case [3], some secondary market and spectrum sharing model are proposed [4][5]. In fact, the modeling of DSM and the proposition

W. Zhang et al. (Eds.): IFTC 2012, CCIS 331, pp. 333–340, 2012.
© Springer-Verlag Berlin Heidelberg 2012

of spectrum sharing firstly should combine with different application scenarios, e.g., the TV broadcasting networks, ad-hoc networks and cellular networks etc, because that different scenarios will require distinct models of spectrum management and sharing. In addition, the time-efficiency and some typical QoS metrics should be the basic requirements for the spectrum management and sharing approach. To improve the time-efficiency of the spectrum resource, the strategies with combined considerations for the time-spectrum block are investigated [6][7]. However,the complexity for the proposed strategy is high, and even only focused on some truthfulness problems. Based on the investigated work of [8], the more flexible application scenario should be further considered.

In this paper, we first introduce a novel dynamic spectrum management and sharing model, which consists of the spectrum management network (SMN), the spectrum service relay terminals and common users. In SMN, we denote a spectrum database to establish a centralized spectrum management approach, which can collect all the idle spectrum information and effectively manage them. The spectrum service relay terminals will provide the spectrum application and realtime task transmission for the common users. To better service the common users, the spectrum bid and authorization modeling are based on the spectrum requirements of common users, that is the spectrum leasing rule (SLR). Accordingly, to improve the spectrum utilization and increase the spectrum revenue, we consider the time-efficiency for the idle resource and propose the spectrum management metrics, i. e., the anxiety level and the matching degree for the idle resource. Finally, we formulate the spectrum sharing process. Nevertheless, the paper makes a number of contributions and in particular,

- We propose a factual spectrum management and sharing model, in which the concept of spectrum database and idle anxiety of spectrum resource are introduced. This model is more practical and realizable in the applications.
- We formulate the spectrum sharing problem through the optimization process. Combining with some typical QoS metrics, the optimization results can not only satisfy the requirements of common transmission tasks, but also improve the revenue of spectrum sharing.
- The introduction of multi-hop spectrum relay service can decrease the spectrum sharing complexity in the applications. More importantly, this method can be applied in many kinds of scenarios with strong scalability.

The rest of this paper is organized as follows. The modeling and formulation for dynamic spectrum management and sharing is presented in Section 2. In Section 3, we design the dynamic spectrum sharing scheme. The Section 4 presents the performance analysis and simulation results of the proposed spectrum management and sharing approach. Section 5 concludes this paper.

2   Dynamic Spectrum Management and Sharing Model

2.1   Dynamic Spectrum Management Model

We introduce a general dynamic spectrum management model, which can be applied in the typical communication scenarios, such as the TV broadcasting

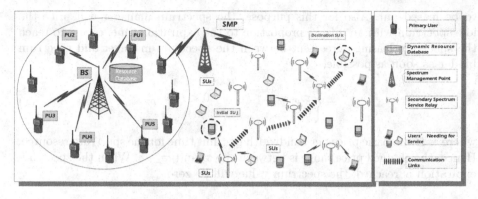

Fig. 1. The dynamic spectrum management and sharing scenario

networks and the cellular networks etc. We regulate that the primary users (PUs) should report the predictable idle spectrum information or confirmed unused spectrum information to the base station (BS). The BS will collect all the realtime idle spectrum and establish a spectrum resource base (SRB). In fact, the realtime unutilized spectrum information for different PUs will have dislike uncertain occurrences, idle durations and spectrum sizes etc. We denote the set of k PUs in the spectrum management model by $\mathbf{P} = \{P_1, P_2, ..., P_k\}$, shown in Fig. 1. According to the fixed spectrum management policy currently, the fixed spectrum resource have been deployed in the k PUs. Any PU who has the idle spectrum resource will have incentive to share or lease the resource for revenue. In the SRB, the definition of available resource record is as follows,

Definition 1: (Available Resource Record, ARR): At time t, the available PU set with idle resource information is denoted as $\mathbf{P}^* = \{\breve{\rho}_1, \breve{\rho}_2, ..., \breve{\rho}_j\}$. The SRB records the ARR of $\breve{\rho}_j$ at time t, including the idle spectrum size k_{ρ_j} and the unoccupied channel time from t to $t + s_{\rho_j}$, $\forall \mathbf{P}^* \subseteq \mathbf{P}$, $\forall t = 1, 2, ..., T$.

For factual applications, the spectrum resource in many types of primary users' networks feature the periodic occupation and variety, even can predict the available resource in advance for a short-term time. We can call this time slot as spectrum reservation time for resource sharing or leasing. Moreover, we regulate that the ARR should include the location information and the interference information of PUs. To void the interference to the other PUs in the communication scenarios, we regulate that the communication link used for spectrum reservation between the SUs and PUs calls a special common narrowband channel (SNC). In addition, the SNC can also be used for the broadcasting and exchanging of other networking information in the unlicensed secondary networks.

As we know that, the time-efficiency is the basic characteristic in the dynamic spectrum database. Hence, for the spectrum manager, the closer approaching expiration time, the largest anxiety that the manager wants to lease the resource out and make revenue. we denote the anxiety level as $I_{\rho_j} = \frac{t}{s_{\rho_j}}$, where I_{ρ_j} is in the range of 0 and 1. The larger I_{ρ_j}, the more anxiety that the spectrum needs to be leased out. Also for this purpose, the spectrum manager will price the idle spectrum with an inverse proportion to the expiration time, trying to reach the spectrum leasing agreement between the spectrum manager and spectrum bidder as soon as possible.

$$\Omega_{\rho_j} = \begin{cases} \varpi_{\rho_j} \cdot e^{(1-\frac{t}{s_{\rho_j}})}, & 0 < t \le s_{\rho_j} \\ 0, & 0 \end{cases} \tag{1}$$

where ϖ is the basic price per bandwidth per unit time for the spectrum resource. Hence, the charged price range is between the ϖ and $\varpi_{\rho_j} \cdot e$. When the spectrum expiration is reached, the spectrum value will be zero.

2.2 The Secondary Spectrum Sharing Model

The secondary spectrum sharing model in the unlicensed networks includes the secondary spectrum service relay terminals, all types of users who need the transmission service and a spectrum management point (SMP). we denote the set of n users by $\mathbf{U} = \{\mu_1, \mu_2, \mu_3, ..., \mu_n\}$. And the set of k spectrum relay nodes by $\mathbf{R} = \{\gamma_1, \gamma_2, \gamma_3, ..., \gamma_k\}$. Different some typical secondary spectrum sharing methods combining with the multi-hop metric and dynamic spectrum leasing approach, we introduce the relay terminal in the model. Because on one hand, the deployment of relay terminals can extend the application range of users, such as the mobile users and static users, and reduce the spectrum accessing requirements for the power and hardware etc. On the other hand, the relay terminals can reduce the complexity of spectrum management for the all types of temporary spectrum leasing applications, due to the uniform services for the relay terminals.

Once one user in the unlicensed secondary networks wants to transmit some data such as multi-media data or pure binary data to one targeted user, which needs the spectrum resource for some time-slots. The initial user only needs to send a spectrum application requirement to the nearby spectrum relay terminal through the SNC. The spectrum relay terminal will find a best routing approach in all the relay terminals to complete the transmission tasks for the initial user. For the factual applications, the users who have some transmission tasks will always propose some requirements for the spectrum leasing services, shown as,

Definition 2:(Spectrum Claim Rule, SCR): Let $\check{r}_{\mu_i}$ be the spectrum requests of SU i, denoted by $\check{r}_{\mu_i} = (\Phi_{\mu_i}, \alpha^{\mu_i}, \triangle^{\mu_i}, \mu_j)$, meaning that the SU μ_i has Φ_{μ_i}-bit burst data to transmit to the SU μ_j, at the service start time α^{μ_i} and with the maximum tolerant service delay time $\triangle^{\mu_i}$.

According to the information about the initial address and destination address, i. e., from the μ_i to the μ_j, the SMP will find a shortest path from the routing source i to destination j. We assume that all the relay terminals have the whole routing information of other relay terminals, and all the relay terminals have got the information that which users are in their communication range. Here, the routing process can be selected according to classical shortest path algorithm, i.

e., the Dijkstra algorithm. The used shortest path algorithm in our paper only considers the distance metric. Based on the *Dijkstra* algorithm, we can quickly and clearly get the hops from the μ_i to the μ_j, denoted as h.

For simplification, and to guarantee the maximum tolerant service delay time, we omit the propagation delay, the queueing delay and some other delays related to the spectrum resource application. We think that the maximum tolerant service delay time $\triangle^{\mu_i}$ is only related to the transmission data-rate of relay terminal, denoted as ν^{μ_i}. We consider that the $h - 1$ selected relay terminals can use the same sizes of spectrum channel ω_{ρ_j} from ρ_j, and assume that the wireless communication parameters in the unlicensed $h - hop$ networks are the same, i.e., the channel gain g_{ρ_j} and the channel noise parameter $(\sigma_{\rho_j})^2$. In fact, the wireless communication parameters can be got from the realtime test. Due to $\triangle^{\mu_i}$, we can get that the minimal data-rate the relay terminal should reach under the fixed wireless communication environments,

$$\triangle^{\mu_i} = \sum_{\lambda=1}^{h} \frac{\Phi_{\mu_i}}{\Theta_{\rho_j}} + o_\lambda \approx \frac{\Phi_{\mu_i} \cdot h}{\Theta_{\rho_j}} + o_\lambda \cdot h \qquad (2)$$

The o_χ is the total estimated delay that can be neglected. Hence, we can easily get the minimal reached data-rate that the applied spectrum can reach, i. e., $\Theta_{\rho_j} = \frac{\Phi_{\mu_i} \cdot h}{\triangle^{\mu_i}}$. According to the Shannon-Hartley theorem and the related wireless communication parameters, if we lease ω_{ρ_j} sizes of spectrum channel from ρ_j, we can get the maximal data-rate as,

$$\Theta_{\rho_j} = \omega_{\rho_j} \cdot \log_2(1 + \frac{\varrho_{\mu_i,\rho_j} \cdot \left|g_{\rho_j}\right|^2}{(\sigma_{\rho_j})^2}), \forall \rho_j \in \mathbf{P}, \mu_i \in \mathbf{U}. \qquad (3)$$

where ϱ_{μ_i,ρ_j} is the allocated power on this channel of ρ_j. To guarantee the minimal reached data-rate i.e., Θ_{ρ_j}, we think the allocated power on this channel of ρ_j can self-adaptive change according to the wireless communication environment. Hence, the needed spectrum sizes applied from the SMP can be calculated as $\omega_{\rho_j} = \Theta_{\rho_j}/\log_2(1 + \frac{\varrho_{\mu_i,\rho_j} \cdot \left|g_{\rho_j}\right|^2}{(\sigma_{\rho_j})^2})$.

According to the SCR, the maximum tolerant service delay time $\triangle^{\mu_i}$ is just the spectrum leasing time in $\mathbf{P}^*$. When the information about the spectrum leasing time and spectrum bandwidth are both obtained, the user who needs the spectrum resource for transmission will send a spectrum requirement information to the local secondary spectrum service relay. Then, the local secondary spectrum service relay will launch a spectrum application to SMP.

3   The Spectrum Management and Sharing Formulation

As the resource manager in the unlicensed networks, for one hand, the SMP will consider the anxiety of unlicensed spectrum resource. i. e., if more than one spectrum resource records can meet the requirements of users, which can be denoted as an available spectrum set $P^\dagger$. The SMP will give the leasing priority to the spectrum resource records with high level anxiety. For the other hand, SMP will choose the fittest spectrum record for this spectrum applicant, considering the benefits of whole spectrum data base, that is, we will choose the best matched one with the minimal gap of $s_{\rho_j} \cdot k_{\rho_j}$ VS. $\omega_{\mu_i} \cdot \Delta^{\mu_i}$. To formulate it, we normalize the gap by dividing the value as $s_{\rho_j} \cdot k_{\rho_j}$. The detailed formulation of secondary spectrum sharing model can be denoted as,

$$\varsigma_{\mu_i}(s_{\rho_j}, k_{\rho_j}) = \arg\max_{\rho_j \in P^\dagger} \quad \alpha \cdot I_{\rho_j} + \beta \cdot \frac{\omega_{\mu_i} \cdot \Delta^{\mu_i}}{s_{\rho_j} \cdot k_{\rho_j}}$$

$$s.t. \quad \begin{array}{ll} (a) \; \alpha + \beta = 1, & 0 \le \alpha \le 1, 0 \le \beta \le 1 \\ (b) \; s_{\rho_j} \ge \omega_{\mu_i}, & \rho_j \in P^\dagger, \; \mu_i \in U \\ (c) \; k_{\rho_j} \ge \Delta^{\mu_i}, & \rho_j \in P^\dagger, \; \mu_i \in U \\ (d) \; \Psi_{\mu_i} \le \Omega_{\rho_j}, & \rho_j \in P^\dagger, \; \mu_i \in U \end{array} \tag{4}$$

where the parameters α and β in the constraint condition (a) are the weighted values to evaluate the spectrum selection priority by the resource manager. If $\alpha > 0.5$, we can get that the spectrum manager will give the priority to the expiring spectrum, once the objective spectrum resource can meet the requirements of users. The constraint condition (b) and (c) are the users' requirements for the spectrum bandwidths and occupation time slots. The constraint condition (d) means that the users and spectrum manager can reach the charging price contract. The detailed spectrum management and sharing algorithm is,

---

Algorithm 1. Algorithm

1: **spectrum application initialization:** For each user i in the unlicensed networks,
   a). Set the spectrum requests of SU i as $\check{r}_{\mu_i}$, denoted by $\check{r}_{\mu_i} = (\Phi_{\mu_i}, \alpha^{\mu_i}, \Delta^{\mu_i}, \mu_j)$.
2: **spectrum bid and authorization:** For μ_i,
   a). SMP will check the spectrum use and lease constraints (b),(c) and (d) in Equation (4) from μ_i.
   b). If $P^\dagger \not\subseteq \emptyset$, SMP will decide the best spectrum resource for μ_i, through the following formulation,
   $$\varsigma_{\mu_i}(s_{\rho_j}, k_{\rho_j}) = \arg\max_{\rho_j \in P^\dagger} \quad \alpha \cdot I_{\rho_j} + \beta \cdot \frac{\omega_{\mu_i} \cdot \Delta^{\mu_i}}{s_{\rho_j} \cdot k_{\rho_j}}$$
   c). Go to the phase of spectrum service relay selection.
   d). Else, ending with the spectrum authorization.
3: **spectrum service relay selection:** For any γ_k in the **R**,
   a). Once got the spectrum lease rule from μ_i, spectrum service relay terminals will decide the best relay routing according to the *Dijkstra* algorithm.
   b). Beginning with a relay transmission task.

---

4 Performance Analysis

In this section, we evaluate the dynamic spectrum management and sharing model with Matlab 2010b. We consider a wireless network with 100m * 100m area, including 15 primary users in the primary user network, 12 spectrum service relay terminals and 80 common users, shown in the Fig. 2.

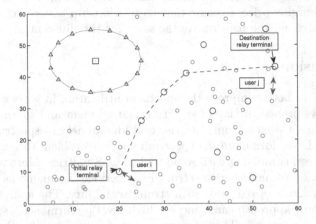

Fig. 2. The factual simulation scenario in for the proposed model

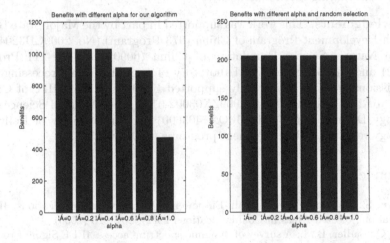

Fig. 3. The benefits comparison between our approach and the randomly resource selection and sharing

We compare the our spectrum management and sharing model with the randomly resource sharing approach, i.e., the spectrum manager does not consider the anxiety level and matching degree of the resource in the spectrum sharing process. Seen from the Fig. 3, firstly, we can get from the figure that in random resource sharing model, the benefits can only reach about 210 price units. However, after the weighted evaluation, the least benefits can also reach about 410 price units. The main reason is that our algorithm can choose the most matched resource and also the spectrum-time block with approaching expiration can be fully utilized. More interesting, From the left figure, we can get that with the increase of the weighted α, more expiration approaching resource can be fully utilized even though the total benefits can be lower, which is related to the time-varied charging price. Because that no relationship between α and random selected resource, all the benefits are the same for the different α.

5   Conclusion

In this paper, to better improve the spectrum utilization in wireless communication area, we propose a factual spectrum management and sharing model, in which the concept of spectrum database and idle anxiety of spectrum resource are introduced. We formulate the spectrum sharing problem through the optimization process, combining with some typical QoS metrics. More importantly, The introduction of multi-hop spectrum relay service in our model can be applied in many kinds of scenarios with strong scalability. The analytical results validate that our approach can achieve a high level performance, especially the spectrum sharing revenue. The different weighted parameters for the anxiety of spectrum resource and the matching degree for the objective resource also affect the spectrum sharing revenue seriously.

Acknowledgments. This work was supported in part by the Major State Basic Research Development Program of China (973 Program) (No. 2009CB320403), National Natural Science Foundation of China (60902018), the 111 Project (B07022) and the Shanghai Key Laboratory of Digital Media Processing and Transmissions; and it was partially supported by the funds of MIIT of China (Grant No. 2011ZX03001-007-032009ZX03002-014) , the Shanghai Science and technology Development Funds (10QA1403600) and the Ministry of Railways technology research and development programs (J2011X005).

References

1. Haykin, S.: Cognitive Radio: Brain-Empowered Wireless Communications. IEEE Journal on Selected Areas in Communications 23(2), 201–220 (2005)
2. Zhao, Q., Sadler, B.M.: A survey of dynamic spectrum access. IEEE Signal Processing Magazine 24(3), 79–89 (2007)
3. Akyildiz, I.F., Lee, W.-Y., Vuran, M.C.: A survey on spectrum management in cognitive radio networks. IEEE Communications Magazine 46(4), 40–48 (2008)
4. Anker, P.: Cognitive Radio, the Market and the Regulator. In: IEEE DySPAN 2010, Delft, Netherlands, pp. 1–6 (2010)
5. Xu, H., Jin, J., Li, B.-C.: A Secondary Market for Spectrum. In: IEEE INFOCOM 2010, Toronto, ON, Canada, pp. 1–6 (2010)
6. Yuan, Y., Bahl, P., Chandra, R., Moscibroda, T.: Allocating dynamic time-spectrum blocks in cognitive radio networks. In: MobiHoc 2007, New York, pp. 130–140 (2007)
7. Sodagari, S., Attar, A., Leung, V.C.M.: Time-Optimized and Truthful Dynamic Spectrum Rental Mechanism. In: IEEE VTC 2010-Fall, PA, USA, pp. 1–5 (2010)
8. Zhou, H., Liu, B., Gui, L., Wang, X., Li, Y.: Fast Spectrum Sharing for Cognitive Radio Networks: A Joint Time-Spectrum Perspective. In: IEEE Globecom 2011, Houston, TX, USA, pp. 1261–1265 (2011)

Wireless Multimedia Communication Requirements for Police and PDT+LTE+3G Solution

Qianjin Tang[1] and Xiaoming Xu[2]

[1] The Third Research Institute of Minitry of Public Security, Engineer, Shanghai, China
tangqj2008@163.com
[2] Wuxi Public Security Bureau, Director, Jiangsu, China
XMXu@sina.com

Abstract. The private wireless multimedia communications (WMC) required by police department is increasing for applications like dispatching, disaster relief, rescue, incident response, traffic management and police's routine patrols. In this paper, we describe the requirements of wireless multimedia communication for public security applications, analyze the difference between the public and private network, and put forward the PDT (Police Digital Trunking) + LTE (Long Term Evolution) + 3G hybrid network solution. This paper only introduces the network frame of solution, the technical details of engineering are out of the scope of the paper.

Keywords: Wireless multimedia communication, Digital trunking, Broadband wireless communication, PDT, LTE.

1 Introduction

In recent years, the tasks of public security departments to preserve public order are increasingly arduous. Natural disasters, accidents are frequent, emergencies are increased sharply, there is also the fight against terrorism, these are highly required for fast reaction and emergency handling ability of the public security departments, and it is very important to establish professional command communication system to transmit voice, data and video information to enable policemen to communicate each other at anywhere and anytime. They need communicate across wide areas, use a massive number of terminals, and coordinate frequently across departments, so a secure, reliable and efficient multimedia communication system is essential for every mission.

Wireless trunking communication system is the uppermost communication means for professional users to command and dispatch, including public security department. But the traditional analog trunking has inherent shortage of low frequency spectrum utilization, small system capacity, single business function, poor secure confidentiality. Digital trunking is an alternative method, such as TETRA system. But the system has limitations including high cost and limited coverage. The status expects a new public security digital trunking standard PDT according to China's actual situation. The narrowband communication still can't meet the police demand

W. Zhang et al. (Eds.): IFTC 2012, CCIS 331, pp. 341–346, 2012.

for video transmission fully. Recent years, the coming generation of wireless communication technology LTE promises a giant leap forward in data rates and has multimedia applications, such mobile telemedicine [1], live TV program, visual talking, et al. We may choose the new technology for public security department as broadband communication system.

2   Requirements of Wireless Multimedia Communication for Police

The requirements include application field and technology specification.

2.1   Application Requirements

There are six typical and basic application requirements as following:

Trunking Talking. System supports voice call between any policeman in stationary or mobile, a diversity of call modes including individual and group calls, inclusive calls.

Real-Time Video Transmission. Stable high-quality images of live video are transmitted to the command center or a mobile command vehicle for helping commanding officers understand the scene immediately.

Query Matching. Policeman can collect information of ID cards, fingerprints, face, match them the background database, and returns the results through the WMC system.

Command and Dispatch Based on Position. With GPS and other positioning means to locate the position of the policeman and vehicles as fast as possible, which helps command center faster command and dispatch in the event of emergencies?

Mobile Police Work. Policemen use the background information system remotely, and the command center officers push multimedia information to the police officers in real time.

Equipment with Zero Manual Configurations. When policemen work together across regions, they need not replace the mobile terminal and reset the parameters of terminal.

2.2   Technology Requirements

To meet the above requirements, the transmission rate, covering range, adaptive mobile ability, roaming switch have special requirements, as follows:

High Data Transmission Rate. The system should have over 10Mbps uplink and downlink data bandwidth.

Wide Coverage Area. Handheld mobile voice transmission distance > 10Km, vehicle platform voice transmission distance > 30Km, the uplink high-speed image transmission distance > 15Km.

Adapt to High Mobility. The system has reliable voice and data communications when the terminal is at speed 200km/h.

Fully Automatic Roaming. The system automatically allows users to roam between multiple base stations and systems without manual intervention.

3 Features of Wireless Multimedia Communication Networks for Police

There may be a doubt. The evolution of public network of the operators is from narrowband to broadband, and multimedia transmission is more and more smooth, why should the police as an industry user need build a private wireless multimedia communication network. In fact, the increasing consumption of mobile video will consume nearly 66% of all mobile data traffic by 2014 [2] , which suggests that public communication bandwidth resources soon will be consumed by public users.

At the same time, the differences between private multimedia communications network for public security and public network as following:

Coverage Parameters Are Different. Private network coverage principle of priority depends on the importance of the region, while public depends on the user number.

Parameter Requirements Are Different. The differences between private network and public network in the system access time, delay time, the system capacity requirements, as shown in Table 1.

Table 1. Parameters difference between private network and public network

Item	Private network	Public network
Access time	<300ms	>1s
System delay time	As short as possible	No strict
System capacity	Performance priority, followed by capacity	Capacity priority, followed by performance

Function Requirements Are Different. Compare with private network, the public network has some special requirements, such as priority level, point-to-point talking mode, higher level requirements, such as dispatch and confidential communications, as shown in Table 2.

Table 2. Function difference between private network and public network

Item	Private network	Public network
Dispatch	Strong	Poor
Priority level	Necessary	No
Confidential communications	Necessary	Poor
Point-to-point talking mode	Yes	No

Reliability Requirements Are Different. Private network must ensure that important users have reliable communications, and the system must be smooth at emergency situations, has ability to withstand natural and man-made damage. Public network provide service as better as possible, but the level of reliability is lower than that of private network for police.

4   Solution of Wireless Multimedia Communication System for Police

4.1   Frame

To achieve the above functionality and performance, the WMC system for police should take into accounts the existing communication facilities and communication technology development status. Figure 1 shows the frame of solution by integrating narrowband and broadband communication systems. The system has two modes of networks: public and private networks. The public network is a 3G mobile network through the VPN transmission channels to meet the data transmission and a small amount of picture or video transmission in the general case. 3G transmission of multimedia is an important tool for police at present, which will later become a supplementary means of the private network after the private broadband network finish. Private network, including 350M analog cluster, PDT, TD-LTE system, which is the coexistence of the narrowband and broadband wireless multimedia transmission system. The PDT is compatible with analog communication system.

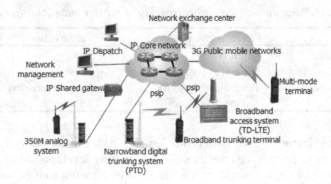

Fig. 1. The framework of the hybrid multimedia communication network solution with narrowband and broadband transmission system

4.2   Key Devices

The key devices of the solution are PDT and LTE multimode terminal, the status is introduced as following:

PDT. From the beginning of 2008, Bureau of Science, Technology and Information under Ministry of Public Security led some capable system providers to begin the discussions on the digital trunking standard PDT. The PDT standards are characterized by powerful function, which is able to achieve a smooth transition from the simulation to the digital, with home-made encryption mechanism, single cell low cost, not only can effectively solve the above problems, but also better protect the investments in existing systems, which satisfy with the actual need of China's vast and complex terrain. After two years of discussion and formulation, the PDT industrial standards have been come out. In addition, the experimental bureaus of multistation system have also put into experiment in some cities [3].

PDT standard technical requirements as follows:

- 12.5 kHz TDMA dual-slot;
- 4 FSK modulation technology, 2.4 kbit/s speech compression rate;
- 9.6 kbit/s transfer rate;
- Support end-to-end voice, data encryption;
- User capacity: 24bit address, supporting 16 million users;
- Data services: short messages, status messages, packet data services;
- Operating modes: direct mode, repeater mode and trunking mode;
- Network model: a large coverage network.

LTE. Compared with some other upgrade options such as HSPA1, HSPA+, and WiMAX2, LTE provides operators with a technically superior and cost effective solution to deliver mobile broadband experience, higher spectral efficiency, lower cost of transmission per megabyte, higher throughput, and lower latency. LTE offers the best potential to address one of the most significant priority of wireless operators, which is, upgrading their capacity constrained networks. Although LTE standards and the ecosystem have not yet evolved fully and upgrade requires significant capital investment, operators can still reap tremendous benefit by formulating the right migration strategy. China has created a larger eco-system for TD-LTE, which has received industry-wide support. Dozens of world leading operators, infrastructure and chipset or terminal vendors, such as Ericsson, Nokia, Motolar, put up demonstrations of their TD-LTE solutions, which reflects their readiness of large-scale deployment. In March 2012, the performance testing of TD-LTE test network in Hangzhou, all tests achieved the desired goal, even more than the current TD-SCDMA network coverage performance. The test network has downlink rate 80Mbit/s and uplink rates up to 10Mbit/s [4].

5   Conclusion

The demand for public security wireless multimedia communications (WMC) is continuously growing. Digital trunking system greatly enhances the emergency communications capability, but there are also inherent weaknesses of narrowband. The integration of narrowband and broadband communication technology is a reality program. Narrowband communication adopts industry communication standard PDT, the broadband adopts LTE standard. At the present stage, 3G network is still used to transmit multimedia for police.

346   Q. Tang and X. Xu

References

1. Lin, C.: An Advance Wireless Multimedia Communication Application: Mobile Telemedicine. Wseas Transactions on Communications 9, 206–215 (2010)
2. Cisco Visual Networking Index, Global Mobile Data Traffic Forecast Update, http://www.sisco.com
3. China Mobile Communication Co., Ltd., http://www.chinamobile.com
4. Hytera Communications Co., Ltd., http://www.hytera.cn/

Modeling and Simulation of Multi-hop Time Synchronization for Underwater Acoustic Networks Based on OPNET

Chuan Sun, Feng Yang, Lianghui Ding, Liang Qian, and Cheng Zhi

Institute of Image Communication and Network Engineering,
Shanghai Jiao Tong University,
No.800 Dongchuan Road, Shanghai, China
{sc0303,yangfeng,lhding,lqian,zhicheng}@sjtu.edu.cn

Abstract. Time synchronization is important for Underwater Acoustic Networks (UANs) to achieve precise scheduling, localization and low energy consumption. Although time synchronization for UANs has been studied for years, corresponding simulation has not been researched in detail. UANs simulation faces some special challenges, such as the accurate channel model and the complex state machine of UANs synchronization algorithm. This paper provides details of the implementation of a multi-hop time synchronization scheme for Underwater Acoustic Networks (MSUAN) based on OPNET. By modifying the pipeline stages of Propdel-Stage, Power-Stage and Bkgnoise-Stage, we make our scheme applicable for underwater channel, and design a project to evaluate synchronization performance of MSUAN.

Keywords: multi-hop, UANs, OPNET, synchronization.

1 Introduction

In the past several years, time synchronization for Underwater Acoustic Networks (UANs) has drawn considerable attention from both academy and industry[1]. Several time synchronization protocols have been developed[2]-[5]. To judge the performance of the proposed time synchronization scheme, a simulation platform is an essential part.

Since channel model and synchronization method for UANs are different from terrestrial environment that, existing wireless channel model and synchronization method cannot be reused, so specific underwater extensions will be needed. The contributions of this paper lie in two aspects: first, we modify the channel property by customizing the 14 stages of OPNET; second, we implement the sophisticated network, node and process model for MSUAN.

The remainder of this paper is organized as follows: we introduce MSUAN in Section 2 and present the network model, node model and process model of MSUAN in Section 3. The performance of MSUAN is evaluated in section 4. Finally, we summarized the paper in section 5.

W. Zhang et al. (Eds.): IFTC 2012, CCIS 331, pp. 347–354, 2012.

2   MSUAN

In this section, we first give the network architecture of MSUAN, then introduce the details of the MSUAN.

2.1   Network Architecture of MSUAN

In this paper, we consider a hierarchical UANs architecture[6], as shown in Fig.1. The network consists of two types of nodes, i.e. Master Node(MN) and Slave Node(SN). MN is a powerful sensor node working as reference clock to SN and all other nodes except MN are SN.

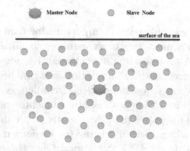

Fig. 1. Underwater Acoustic Network Architecture

2.2   Synchronization Process of MSUAN

We divide MSUAN into two phases: Level Discovery Stage and Synchronization Stage.

Level Discovery Stage. The first stage of the algorithm is to create a hierarchical topology in the network. Every node is assigned a level in this stage.

MN is assigned to level 0 and it initiates this stage by broadcasting a level-discovery packet. After the neighboring Slave Nodes of MN receive the level-discovery packet, Slave Nodes will assign themselves a level one greater than the smallest level they have received. And the source node of the smallest level will be recognized as the node's parent.

Synchronization Stage. After node i assigning its level, a Tri-message synchronization procedure will be carry out between node i and node j. During the Tri-message synchronization procedure, node i may also overhear time-stamps from other nodes. To guarantee the accuracy of the overhearing time-stamps, overhearing time-stamps must be from synchronized nodes which has the smaller or the same level.

We define the unidirectional time-stamps from parent node j or neighboring nodes as one-way time-stamp; we also define time-stamp packets that are sent back and forth between parent node j and node i as two-way time-stamp. As reference[7], in this paper, we also use one-way time-stamps to calculate the skew. After calculating the skew, we use two-way time-stamp to compute the offset.

3 Implementation of MSUAN

In this section, we will give the detail implementation of MSUAN, including the network, node and process model of our simulation.

3.1 Network Model of MSUAN

In this paper, we place sensor nodes randomly in the UANs, MN is set at the center of the topology, and Slave Nodes are randomly placed in the scene as in the Fig.1.

3.2 Node Model of MSUAN

In this paper, we divided MN's node model into 5 components: Master_node_tx0, Master_node_rx0, Master_process, Master_source and Master_sink. Among them, Master_node_tx0 and Master_node_rx0 characterize underwater acoustic channel and the property of transmission and reception; Master_process module decides how to handle the packets from Master_source and Master_node_rx0; Master_source module generates the packets using for time synchronization; Master_sink module destroys the packets which do not belong to MN.

Similarly, we divided SN's node model into 3 components: Slave_node_tx0, Slave_node_rx0 and Slave_process. Slave_node_tx0 and Slave_node_rx0 are used to characterize underwater acoustic channel and the property of transmission and reception; Slave_process module decides how to handle the packets from Slave_node_rx0.

The entire transmitter and receiver modules in this paper are set by the parameters as following table 1:

Table 1. Parameters of Transmitter and Receiver Module

Transmitter Module		Receiver Module	
Parameters	Value	Parameters	Value
Data rate(bps)	1024	Data rate(bps)	1024
Bandwidth(kHz)	3.0	Bandwidth(kHz)	3.0
Modulation	qpsk	Modulation	qpsk
Chanmatch model	Dra_chanmatch	Power model	uwa_power
Propdel model	uwa_propdel	Bkgnoise model	uwa_bkgnoise

OPNET Modeler relies upon 14 computational pipeline stages to evaluate the characteristics of communications. To implement an UANs channel model, we should customize propagation delay stage(stage 5), receiver power stage(stage 7) and background noise stage(stage 8).

Propagation Delay Stage. We designate the acoustic speed as 1500 m/s [8].

Receiver Power Stage. The total absorption coefficient in dB/km is derived in [9, 10]. At frequencies about a few hundreds Hz, the absorption coefficient can be calculated using Thorp's expression as [11]

$$a(f) = 0.11\frac{f^2}{1 + f^2} + 44\frac{f^2}{4100 + f} + 2.75 * 10^{-4} * f^2 + 0.003 \tag{1}$$

In equation (1), f is the signal frequency in kHz.

Background Noise Stage. The overall power spectral density on the ambient noise is given by [12] as follows:

$$NL(I) = NLt(f) + NLs(f) + NLw(f) + NLth(f) \tag{2}$$

In the above equation, NLt(f), NLs(f), NLw(f) and NLth(f) represent the ambient noise caused by turbulence, shipping, waves and thermal noise respectively. They are described by the following equations.

$$\begin{cases} 10logNLt(f) = 17 - 30logf & (3) \\ 10logNLs(f) = 40 + 20(s - 0.5) + 26logf - 60log(f + 0.03) & (4) \\ 10logNLw(f) = 50 + 7.5w^{1/2} + 20logf - 40log(f + 0.4) & (5) \\ 10logNLth(f) = -15 + 20logf & (6) \end{cases}$$

In the above equations, s is the shipping activity factor, the value of which ranges between 0 and 1 for low and high activity, and w is the wind speed in m/s.

3.3   Process Model of MSUAN

In this paper, we use the default packets generate and discard module to generate the initial packets and destroy the useless packets.

We also implement Master_process Model as Fig.2 to decide how to deal with the packets from Master_source and Master_node_rx0.

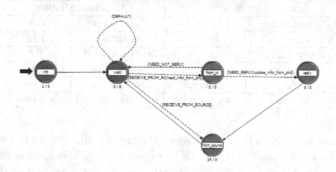

Fig. 2. Process Model of MN's Master_process

Fig.3 depicts the main state machine of our algorithm, which we use the state machine to realize most of the synchronization work.

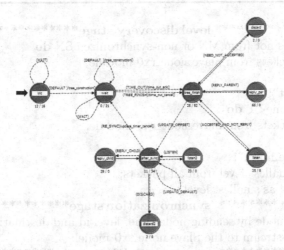

Fig. 3. Process Model of SN's Slave_process

The pseudo code of Master_process and Slave_process model is given as follow:

Pseudo code of MN's Master_process

```
1:  state "wait"
2:  set node id=0, level =0;
3:  while intrpt_type == OPC_INTRPT_STRM do
4:      if packet source == Master_source module then
5:          jump to "from_source" and label the packet with send time;
6:          send packet to the Master_node_tx0 model and jump to "wait";
7:      else if packet source == SN then
8:          jump to "from_rx";
9:          if packets destination == MN then
10:             jump to "reply" and reply the packet by sending out the local time;
11:             send packets to Master_node_tx0 and jump to "from_source";
12:         else
13:             send packets to Master_sink model and jump to "wait";
14:         end if
15:     end if
16: end while
```

Pseudo code of SN's Slave_process

```
1:  state "init"
2:  //***************** level discovery stage*****************//
3:  while packets not from MN or non-synchronized SN do
4:      receive packets from Slave_node_rx0 module;
5:  end while
6:  jump to "wait";
7:  while wait time<T do
8:      receive packets from Slave_node_rx0 module;
9:  end while
10: jump to "tree_finish";
11: search the smallest level from all packets;
12: set node level as smallest level+1;
13: //****************synchronization stage****************//
14: reply parent node by sending node time, level id and destination id;
15: send packets stream to the Slave_node_tx0 model;
16: //****************synchronize with parent****************//
17: while intrpt_type == OPC_INTRPT_STRM do
18:     if packets source== parent && destination ==node itself then
19:         jump to "reply_par" and compute the clock skew and offset;
20:         initial synchronization for higher level SN and jump to "tree_finish";
21:     else if(packet level<=node level&&packet from synchronized node) then
22:         jump to "listen", save packets information and jump to "tree_finish";
23:     else
24:         jump to "discard", destroy the packets and jump to "tree_finish";
25:     end if
26: end while
27: //****************synchronize with child****************//
28: if node has realized synchronization itself then
29:     jump to "after_sync"
30: end if
31: while intrpt_type == OPC_INTRPT_STRM do
32:     if packet level <= node level && packet from synchronized node then
33:         jump to "listen2", save packets information and jump to "after_sync";
34:     else if (parent id ==node id && destination id==node id) then
35:         jump to "reply_child", reply child node by sending node time;
36:         jump to "after_sync";
37:     else then
38:         jump to "discard2", destroy the packets and jump to "after_sync"
39:     end if
40: end while
```

---

4   Simulation Results

In this section, we will evaluate the performance of MSUAN as the number of hops increases. Offset error and skew error are used to evaluate the performance of simulation. We extend Tri-message to multi-hop condition and use it as the reference algorithm. And in our simulation, we set the initial clock skew and offset as 40ppm and 40us respectively.

We vary the number of hops and investigate the influence brought by the varying hops. Fig.4 and Fig.5 show that Tri-message have larger offset and skew errors than MSUAN for every hop. For MSUAN, when the number of hops accumulates up to 8, the average error in offset is maintained at about 70us and the average skew error is below 3.5ppm, while the average offset and skew error for Tri-message is about 82us and 4ppm.

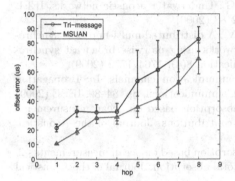   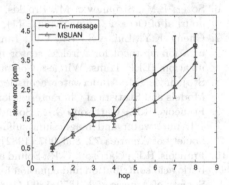

Fig. 4. Offset error on varying hops   **Fig. 5.** Skew error on varying hops

5   Conclusions

In this paper, we proposed a multi-hop time synchronization for UANs (MSUAN). And established a simulation platform by setting up the network model, node model and process model based on OPNET. We also introduce a precise UANs channel model through modifying the pipeline stages of Propdel-Stage, Power-Stage and Bkgnoise-Stage. Finally, we investigate the performance of MSUAN by varying the number of hops. Simulation results show that, when the number of hops accumulates up to 8, for MSUAN, the average error in offset is maintained at about 70s and the average skew error is below 3.5ppm, while the average offset and skew errors for Tri-message are about 82us and 4ppm.

Acknowledgment. This work is supported by National Key Project of China (2010ZX03005-003, 2010ZX03002-007-01), Shanghai Key Laboratory of Digital Media Processing and Transmission(STCSM:12DZ2272600) and National Natural Foundation of China(NO.61102051).

References

1. Akyildiz, I.F., Pompili, D., Melodia, T.: Underwater acoustic sensor networks: research challenges. Ad Hoc Networks Journal, 257–279 (March 2005)
2. Syed, A., Heidemann, J.: Time synchronization for high latency acoustic networks. In: Proceedings of IEEE INFOCOM (2006)
3. Jiang, H., Liu, X., Wang, X., Liu, W., Wang, Y.: Tri-Message, A Lightweight Time Synchronization Protocol for High Latency and Resource-Constrained Networks. In: IEEE International Conference on Communication (2009)
4. Maroti, M., Kusy, B., Simon, G., Ledeczi, A.: The flooding time synchronization protocol. In: Proceedings of the Second International ACM Conference on Embedded Networked Sensor Systems, pp. 39–49. ACM Press, Baltimore (2004)
5. Ganeriwal, S., Kumar, R., Srivastava, M.B.: Timing-sync protocol for sensor networks. In: Proceedings of the First International ACM Conference on Embedded Networked Sensor Systems, pp. 138–149. ACM Press, Los Angeles (2003)
6. Sozer, E.M., Stojanovic, M., Proakis, J.G.: Underwater acoustic networks. IEEE Journal of Oceanic Engineering 25(1), 72–83 (2000)
7. Cheng, K.Y., Lui, K.S., Wu, Y.C., Tam, V.: A distributed multi-hop time synchronization protocol for wireless sensor networks using pairwise broadcast synchronization. IEEE Trans. Wireless Communication 8(4), 1764–1772 (2009)
8. Stojanovic, M.: Underwater acoustic communication channels. In: Propagation Models and Statistical Characterization Communications, pp. 84–89. IEEE (2009)
9. Francois, R.E., Garrison, G.R.: Sound absorption based on ocean measurements - 1. pure water and magnesium sulfate contributions. Journal of the Acoustical Society of America 72, 896–907 (1982)
10. Francois, R.E., Garrison, G.R.: Sound absorption based on ocean measurements - 2. boric acid contribution and equation for total absorption. Journal of the Acoustical Society of America 72, 1879–1890 (1982)
11. Urick, R.J.: Principles of Underwater Sound, 3rd edn. McGraw-Hill, New York (1983)
12. Coates, R.: Noise and reverberation in Underwater Acoustic Systems. John Wiley and Sons, New York (1989)

A Novel Queue Scheduling Scheme for Video Transmission over IEEE 802.11e WLAN

Dong Shao*, Lianghui Ding, Feng Yang, Liang Qian, and Xiangzhong Fang

Institute of Image Communication and Network Engineering,
Shanghai Jiao Tong University,
No.800 Dongchuan Road, Shanghai, China
{shaodong,lhding,yangfeng,lqian,xzfang}@sjtu.edu.cn

Abstract. With the widespread applications of mass media and the rapid development of wireless network, much attention has been paid to wireless video transmission. In this paper, we consider video transmission in IEEE 802.11e WLAN, and propose an adaptive cross-layer scheduling scheme to reduce video distortion. The cross-layer scheduling algorithm propose a scheme, namely, Relative Minimum Distortion Buffer Management (RMDBM). In RMDBM, network loads and service rates are taken into account to realize the cross-layer dynamic queue access. We evaluate the cross-layer scheduling in ns-2 and simulation results demonstrate significant performance gain of the cross-layer scheduling algorithm. In the case of different network loads, our proposed scheduling algorithm achieves lower video distortion than pure 802.11e EDCA, static mapping scheme and conventional adaptive scheme. In the case of non-video influence, the proposed scheduling scheme can effectively reduce the negative impacts on video transmission performance from non-video stream data.

Keywords: WLAN, dynamic queue access, minimum distortion, video transmission, IEEE802.11e.

1 Introduction

With the rapid development of wireless network and widespread application of multimedia, great attention has been devoted to wireless video transmission. It is important to support distortion and delay in widespread broadband access networks, e.g., Wireless Local Area Networks (WLANs). There are mainly two multimedia types. One is non-real-time video streaming, such as medical images, geological mappings and so on. This type of video transmission often pays more attention to video quality rather than delay. The other is real-time video transmission, which is strict in delay like video conference and video calls.

In order to enhance wireless video transmission in WLAN, IEEE puts forward 802.11e standard with Enhanced Distributed Channel Access (EDCA)

* The Project: System and Key Technology of Broadband Wireless Campus Innovation Network(2010ZX03005-003) supported by Shanghai Digital Media Processing and Transmission Key Laboratory(STCSM:12DZ2272600).

W. Zhang et al. (Eds.): IFTC 2012, CCIS 331, pp. 355–362, 2012.
© Springer-Verlag Berlin Heidelberg 2012

mechanism [1], which classifies services into four Access Categories(AC), i.e., AC_VO,AC_VI,AC_BE,AC_BK for voice, video, best effort services and background services respectively. To simplify the notations, we assign AC_VO as AC[3], AC_VI as AC[2], AC_BE as AC[1], and AC_BK as AC[0] in the rest of this paper. Different service priorities access different AC queues according to their categories. Different AC queues can differentiate priorities by MAC protocol parameters including minimum contention window (CWmin), maximum contention window (CWmax) and Arbitration Inter Frame Space (AIFS). The higher the transmission priority, the more the transmission opportunities the service has. EDCA mechanism can treat services differently and is conducive to prior transmission of multimedia.

Although 802.11e EDCA can enhance the video transmission performance to some extent, it is still difficult to guarantee strict delay requirements and deal with unavoidable burst loss. With the fast deployment of hierarchical coding technology, its characteristics should also be taken into consideration to promote the video transmission performance based on EDCA. Two kinds of solutions have been proposed currently. The first is to adjust the parameters of 802.11e MAC, such as Contention Window (CW), Transmission Opportunity (TXOP) to differentiate services [2–5, 8–12]. A slow decrease of CW was proposed to reduce collision and number of retransmitted frames [10]. L.Romdhani and I.Aad introduced a method to modify CW according to different services and priorities [11]. A self-adapting CW scheme based on network conditions is designed to increase the throughput in [2]. In [4], priorities of services are differentiated through changing TXOP. The other kind of solution is cross-layer design. In [6], the characteristics of hierarchical coding in H.264 are taken into account. It shows that Static mapping frame I to AC[2], frame P to AC[1], and frame B to AC[0] can effectively improve the video quality in heavy loads. However, when the network loads are light, static mapping may increase the delay and packet loss due to the overflow of low priority AC queue, and leads to worse performance than EDCA. C.H.Lin and C.H.Ke [7] proposed a cross-layer Dynamic Mapping mechanism which dynamically maps MPEG-4 video stream to appropriate AC queues according to types of video frames and network status. The heavier network loads and lower priority of video packet, the greater opportunity for the packet to be mapped into a lower priority queue. However, they ignored the influence from non-video services. Because the high priority queue, i.e., AC[2] is only accessed by video, the lower priority AC queues will be occupied by non-video streams and lead to overflow of the video stream.

Therefore, in this paper we propose a novel cross-layer scheduling scheme for video transmission in Wireless Local Area Network (WLAN). This scheme propose a algorithm, namely Relative Minimum Distortion Buffer Management (RMDBM). In RMDBM relative distortion about video streams will be estimated and queues are dynamically accessed by the relatively minimum distortion algorithm according to types of services and queue status.We can adequately utilize the queue to enhance the video transmission performance.

The rest of this paper is organized as follows. We first propose our cross-layer scheduling algorithm in Section 2. After that we evaluate the performance of the proposed scheduling algorithm in Section 3 and conclude the whole paper in Section 4.

2 Cross-Layer Scheduling for Video Transmission

2.1 System Framework

The framework of the cross-layer scheduling scheme proposed in this paper is shown in Figure 1. Network loads and service rates are taken into account to realize the cross-layer dynamic queue access for video frames.

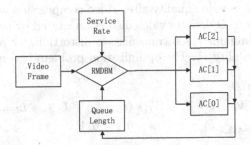

Fig. 1. General System Framework

2.2 Relatively Minimum Distortion Model

As to the wireless video transmission, queue access for both video packets and non-video stream will affect the length of queues and affect video distortion. We use current service rate and queue length to estimate video transmission distortion. Video packets will overflow as the queue length is limited. Let V_i and V denote non-video rate and video rate for AC[i] respectively, W_i denote the output rate of AC[i]. The queue limitation can be written as

$$[V_i + V * P_i - W_i] * (t_i - t_0) + L_i <= L_{limit} \tag{1}$$

Where L_i refers to the current queue length, t_0 refers to the current time, T_i denotes saturate time. When $t_i > T_i$ queue is saturated and video packets will be lost because of overflow which will lead to video distortion. We set L_{limit} as the maximum length of queue.

In the case of multiple queues, different saturate time for different queue lead to different distortion. We assume that queue saturate time is T_i, T_j, T_k for AC[i], AC[j], AC[k]. We set P_i as the probability of video packets to access queue AC[i]. Thus, we can calculate the received video rate U_i at the destination node as

$$U_i = \begin{cases} V * P_i, & t_i <= T_i \\ W_i * \frac{V*P_i}{V*P_i+V_i}, & t_i > T_i \end{cases} \tag{2}$$

Before T_i, video transmission without any overflow. After T_i, video stream and non-video stream share the limited output rate W_i. In the following, we use f_i as the video streams transmitted without lost for AC[i] and write them as

$$f_i = \begin{cases} V * P_i * (T_i - t_0), & T_i <= t_0 \, or \, T_i >= T \\ V * P_i * (T_i - t_0) + W_i * \frac{V*P_i}{V*P_i+V_i}, & t_0 < T_i < T \end{cases} \quad (3)$$

where t_0 refers to the current time, T denotes the total time of video streams. we have the total video distortion in all three access queues can be written as

$$D = D_o - \sum_{i=0,1,2} f_i \quad (4)$$

where D_o is the origin video quality after video compression which is a constant to video transmission, D denotes video distortion caused by packets overflow. In order to realize minimum video transmission distortion, we aim at finding the proper access probability P_i. The optimization problem becomes

$$\begin{cases} min D \\ s.t. [V_i + V * P_i - W_i] * (t_i - t_0) + L_i <= L_{limit} \\ \sum_{i=0,1,2} P_i = 1, P_i >= 0, i = 0, 1, 2 \end{cases} \quad (5)$$

where $i = 0, 1, 2$ denote the queue state for AC[0], AC[1] and AC[2] respectively. L_{limit} is the maximum length of queue and L_i is the current length of AC[i]. As the objective function is nonlinear and difficult to find an analytical solution, we exhaustive search to find the optimal P_i. To find the analytical solution is left as our future work.

3   Simulation Results

3.1   Simulation Setup

In order to evaluate performance of the algorithm proposed in this paper, we adopt a simulation platform based on ns-2 [15] and Evalvid [16]. We compare video transmission performances of 802.11 EDCA, Static Mapping [6], Dynamic Mapping [7] and cross-layer scheduling scheme proposed in this paper. The network topology of the experiment is shown in Figure 2.

The scene size is 500*500m. Wireless nodes A,B,C are connected to AP via IEEE802.11e link. Streams are transmitted from A to C by AP. The routing protocol is AODV. We use Foreman Stream of YUV QCIF(176*144) as the video stream and use MPEG-4 video coding, in which one GOP has nine video frames (I B B P B B P B B).The data rate is 1Mbps. Basic access parameters (CW, TXOP, etc.are set the same as IEEE802.11e EDCA. As for non-video stream, we use CBR and TCP as the background services and map them to AC[1] and AC[0]. We will discuss video transmission performance in two case. In the first case, we discuss the influence of different network loads. In the second case,

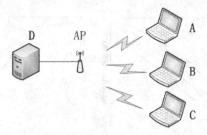

Fig. 2. Network Topology for Simulation

we investigate the influence of non-video streams. We compare the performance of EDCA, Static Mapping, Dynamic Mapping and the cross-layer scheduling scheme proposed in this paper in terms of packet dropping ratio, type of lost frames and PSNR.

Case1: There exist both video streams and non-video streams in the network. The rate of the later one is the half of the former one. We increase their rates with the same ratio to evaluate the impact of network load. Case2: We fix the video stream rate and change non-video stream rates to evaluate their impacts.

3.2   Influence of Network Load

Figure 3 demonstrates packet dropping ratios of four methods with different network loads. When loads are light, because of little collision between queues, the packet dropping ratio of EDCA is lower than that of Static Mapping. When loads are heavy, as a collision between queues is getting heavier, Static Mapping takes advantage of AC[1] and AC[0] and its packet dropping ratio is lower than that of EDCA. Dynamic Mapping further promotes video streams to utilize AC[1] and AC[0] to a certain extent, which makes its packet dropping ratio lower than EDCA and Static Mapping. The packet dropping ratio of RMDBM proposed in this paper is much lower than all EDCA, Static Mapping and Dynamic Mapping. Through Figure 4, we can find that when the network load is heavy, the PSNR of Static Mapping is better than that of other methods because high priority frame I, which can only be accessed to AC[2], is well protected. The RMDBM with the fewest packet dropping ratio obtains better PSNR than Dynamic Mapping. Figure 5 shows a visual comparison of pictures after video streams being decoded in the receiver, displaying advantages of visual effects of the scheme proposed in this paper.

3.3   Influence of Non-video Streams

Non-video data can affect the video transmission performance, especially when they utilize AC[1] and AC[0]. A high non-video stream rate will decrease the queue occupancy of video data, and degrades performance of the video transmission. We choose 0.6Mbps as the constant video rate and 0.1-0.6Mbps as the variable non-video rate and demonstrate PSNRs of four methods in different

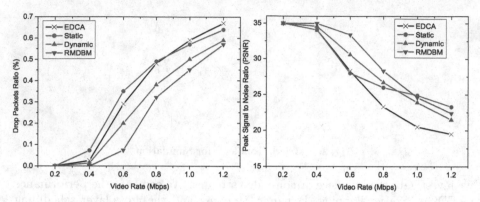

Fig. 3. Packet Dropping Ratio in different loads

Fig. 4. PSNR in Different Loads

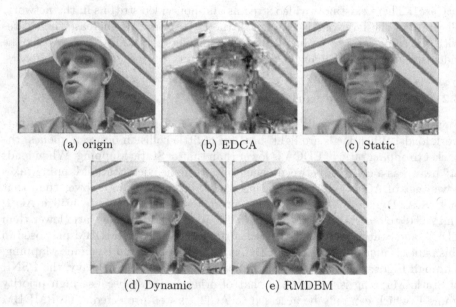

(a) origin   (b) EDCA   (c) Static

(d) Dynamic   (e) RMDBM

Fig. 5. Visual Comparison of Receiving Pictures

non-video stream rates in Figure 6. PSNR of EDCA is stable because video streams can only access to AC[2] and the video rate are constant. Since Static Mapping P frame access to AC[1] and B frame to AC[0], the packet loss of P frame and B frame will rise as the non-video stream rate is increasing, which leads to the lower quality of the video transmission. Dynamic Mapping helps to reduce the influence of non-video stream in heavy loads, while, the performance with light loads are not remarkable. The RMDBM can better control queue access to AC[1] and AC[0]. Therefore, it can reduce the negative effects of the video transmission caused by non-video stream and remains stable.

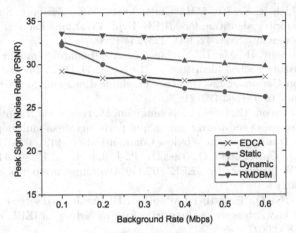

Fig. 6. Influence of the Non-Video Stream Rate

4   Conclusion

Based on the current wireless network standard IEEE802.11e, this paper presents a cross-layer scheduling scheme namely, Relative Minimum Distortion Algorithm. This scheme can access queues dynamically in accordance with the lengths of queues and service rates, improve the utilization of queues and reduce the packet loss. The simulation result show that the scheme proposed in this paper is better than EDCA, Static Mapping and Dynamic Mapping in terms of video transmission performances. In addition, it can effectively control the degradation of video qualities caused by non-video streams.

References

1. IEEE Std 802.11e-2005. In: Wireless LAN medium access control (MAC) and physical layer (PHY) specifications amendment 8:medium access control (MAC) quality of service enhancements (2005)
2. Deng, D.J., Ke, C.H., Chen, H.H., Huang, Y.M.: Contention window optimization for ieee 802.11 DCF access control. IEEE Transactions on Wireless Communications 7(12), 5129–5135 (2008)
3. Kunho, H., Sukyoung, L., Kyungsoo, K., Yoonhyuk, K.: Channel Condition Based Contention Window Adaptation in IEEE 802.11 WLANs. IEEE Transactions on Communications 60(2), 469–478 (2012)
4. Rashwand, S., Misic, J.: IEEE 802.11e EDCA Under Bursty Traffic How Much TXOP Can Improve Performance. IEEE Transactions on Vehicular Technology 60(3), 1099–1115 (2011)
5. Arora, A., Sungguk, Y., Youngjune, C., Bahk, S.: Adaptive TXOP Allocation Based on Channel Conditions and Traffic Requirements in IEEE 802.11e Networks. IEEE Transactions on Vehicular Technology 59(3), 1087–1099 (2010)
6. Ksentini, A., Naimi, M., Gueroui, A.: Toward an improvement of H.264 video transmission over IEEE 802.11e through a cross-layer architecture. IEEE Communications Magazine 44(1), 107–114 (2006)

7. Lin, C.H., Shieh, C.K., Ke, C.H., Chilamkurti, N.K., Zeadally, S.: An adaptive cross-layer mapping algorithm for MPEG-4 video transmission over IEEE 802.11e WLAN. Telecommun. Syst. 42(3-4), 223–234 (2009)
8. Yubin, X., Minghe, H., Ma, L., Yuxiang, Z.: A self-adaptive minimum contention window adjusting backoff algorithm in IEEE 802.11 DCF. In: 2nd International Conference on Consumer Electronics, Communications and Networks (CECNet), vol. 21(23), pp. 1577–1582 (2012)
9. Daewon, J., Jaeseon, H., Hyuk, L., Kyungjoon, P., Hou, J.C.: Adaptive contention control for improving end-to-end throughput performance of multihop wireless networks. IEEE Transactions on Wireless Communications 9(2), 696–705 (2010)
10. Aad, I., Ni, Q., Castelluccia, C., Turletti, T.: Enhancing IEEE802.11 performance with slow CW decrease. In: IEEE 802.11e Working Group Document 802.11-02/674r0 (2002)
11. Romdhani, L., Ni, Q., Turletti, T.: Adaptive EDCF:enhanced service differentiation for IEEE 802.11 wireless ad-hoc networks. In: Proceedings of IEEE WCNC, vol. 2, pp. 1373–1378 (2003)
12. Aad, I., Castelluccia, C.: Differentiation mechanisms for IEEE 802.11. In: Proceedings of IEEE INFOCOM, vol. 1, pp. 209–218 (2001)
13. International Organization for Standardization (1999); Overviewof the MPEG-4 standard
14. Video Group, MPEG-4 video verification model version 18.0 (2001); Coding of moving pictures and associated audio MPEG2001/N3908, ISO/IEC JTC1/SC29/WG11, Pisa, Italy (2001)
15. NS simulator, http://nsnam.isi.edu/nsnam/index.php
16. Evalvid, http://www.tkn.tu-berlin.de/research/evalvid/
17. Zhou, L., Zheng, B., Wei, A., Geller, B., Cui, J.: Joint QoS Control for Video Streaming over Wireless Multihop Networks: A Cross-Layer Approach. International Journal of Electronics and Communications 63(8), 638–647 (2009)

Incentive-Based Bandwidth Auction for Scalable Streaming in Peer-to-Peer Networks

Lin Chen and Junni Zou*

Dept. of Communication Engineering, Shanghai University,
Shanghai 200072, China
chenlin_shu@hotmail.com, zoujn@shu.edu.cn

Abstract. This paper proposes an incentive-based bandwidth allocation for scalable streaming in P2P networks. It is modeled as decentral-
ized dynamic auction games, in which the peers sell and bid the upload
bandwidth for the maximum individual benefit. With the unique characteristic of SVC, the content-aware prioritization of SVC is imposed on the
underlying bandwidth auction in order to avoid bandwidth wastage and
improve the overall video quality at all peers. Also, an incentive mechanism is employed to resolve *free-riding* issue. Finally, the performance
of the proposed scheme is verified by the simulation results.

Keywords: Peer-to-peer, Scalable video coding, Bandwidth auction,
Incentive.

1 Introduction

Peer-to-peer (P2P) media streaming is widely viewed as a promising platform
for delivering high quality media content at the global scale. In such network
settings, peers are expected to operate without control and coordination by a
central agent. In P2P live streaming, peers exchange video chunks they don't
have with neighbor peers. As the number of peers increases, the upload capacity
of the entire system also increases, which may efficiently alleviates the burden
of the media server. However, there are remaining problems in current P2P
networks. For instance, *Free-riding* is a potential problem, where the selfish peer
enjoys the services offered by other peers, but does not make any contribution to
the system. Another problem is how to resolve bandwidth conflicts of different
peers so as to maximize the overall benefits of all peers.

Layered source coding, such as JVT/MPEG scalable video coding (SVC)
[1],[2], provides a convenient way to perform source-based rate adaption to the
changing network conditions. A SVC streaming consists of a base layer which
alone provides an acceptable basic quality, and multiple enhancement layers with
a flexible multi-dimension layer structure to progressively refine the video quality.

* The work was partially supported by Shanghai Young Rising-Star Scientist
Program (11QA1402600), and International Collaboration Program of Shanghai
(11510707000).

W. Zhang et al. (Eds.): IFTC 2012, CCIS 331, pp. 363–371, 2012.
© Springer-Verlag Berlin Heidelberg 2012

Thus, receivers can adapt to their capability by subscribing to certain number of layer streams. Recently, SVC-oriented P2P streaming emerges a promising approach to disseminate scalable video content to a large number of heterogeneous receivers.

The objective of this paper is to design an incentive-based bandwidth auction mechanism to address the following challenges:

1) How to utilize upload capacity efficiently?
2) How to avoid the behavior of free-riding?
3) How to model a bandwidth auction game for scalable streaming?

Many incentive mechanisms in the literature provide various means for discouraging the selfishness. Ma et al. [3] provide service differentiation in a P2P network based on the amount of services each node has provided to the network community. Satsiou et al. [4] introduced a protocol for distributed trust-based policies and regulating the exchange of multiple services. Unlike the works above, Iosifidis et al. [5] design an incentive mechanism by punishing defect behavior and rewarding cooperative behavior. Meanwhile, some solutions have been proposed to address the bandwidth conflict problem. For example, Tareq et al. [6] presented a distributed rate allocation algorithm to achieve optimal layer allocation among peers receiving the same video content. The existing researches on SVC-based P2P streaming mainly consider on one aspect, e.g. optimal bandwidth allocation or efficient incentive mechanism. How to optimize network resource and address *free-riding* issue simultaneously is still an open issue.

The remainder of this paper is organized as follows. An overview of the proposed streaming system is presented in Section 2. In Section 3, we formulate the optimal auction problems for upstream and downstream peers, and discuss the allocation and bidding strategies. Simulation results are shown in Section 4. Finally, Section 5 concludes the paper.

2   SVC Streaming Overlay System

2.1   Network Model and Notations

Suppose that the SVC stream is encoded into a set of M layers at the source node, with layer 1 representing the base layer and $2 \sim M$ representing the progressive enhancement layers. Assume that each video layer m is separately distributed through an overlay m with a maximum transmission rate of R_m. Thus, each peer can access to the particular video layer by joining the corresponding overlay.

The topology of the m-th overlay can be modeled as a directed graph $G_m = (V_m, E_m)$, where V_m is the set of overlay nodes and E_m is the set of weighted links between overlay nodes. Let C_i^u and C_i^d represent the upload and download capacity of peer i, respectively.

Fig. 1 shows a simple P2P network, where six peer $v1$ $v6$ participate in the SVC streaming. Suppose that the video is encode into two layers, with the base layer delivered through overlay 1, and the enhancement layer delivered through overlay 2. It is observed that $v3$ and $v5$ subscribe to the base layer, $v4$ subscribe to the enhancement layer, while $v2$ subscribe to both layers. Also, each peer has different neighbors in each overlay. For example, $v2$ has two neighbors (i.e., $v1$ and $v4$) in overlay 1, and only one neighbor $v1$ in overlay 2.

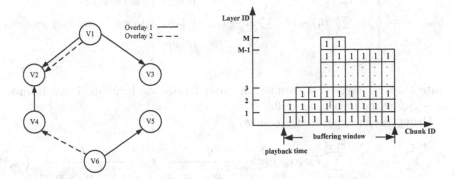

Fig. 1. A P2P topology with two overlays   **Fig. 2.** Buffering window structure

2.2 Buffering Window Structure

Each layer is segmented into chunks. For simplicity, assume the chunks at each layer m are of the same bit rate c_m. Each chunk is identified by a layer ID and a chunk ID. The peer maintains a 2-D buffering window to record what layers and chunks it currently has. As shown in Fig. 2. The buffering window starts at the chunks which are ready to be played, and ends with the maximum chunk it caches. The buffering window moves forward with the playback time of the chunks. The peer categorizes the chunks into informative chunks and non-informative chunks. The former refer to the chunks that it lacks of, the latter are the chunks it has. When a peer newly joins the network, it contacts a centralized directory server for a list of the supplying peers, establishes the neighbor relationship with these supplying peers, and starts requesting the informative chunks from them. Periodically, the peer exchange buffering information with its neighbors to announce the chunk availability.

2.3 Rate-Distortion Model

From the perspective of application-layer QoS, rate-distortion related mode [7] could be picked as the optimized targeted utility for video applications

$$D_e(R_e) = \frac{\theta}{R_e - B_0} + D_0 . \tag{1}$$

where D_e is the distortion of the encoded video sequence, measured by the mean squared error, and R_e is the encoded rate. The variables θ, B_0 and D_0 are the parameters of the R-D model, which can be fitted to empirical data from trial encodings using nonlinear regression techniques.

To characterize the video streaming performance of each layer m, we introduce a utility function $U_m(\cdot)$. It is defined as the absolute value of the distortion decrement when a new layer m is received at arbitrary rate r_m ($0 < r_m \leq R_m$).

$$U_m(r_m) = \begin{cases} D_e(r_m)\,, & \text{if layer } m \text{ is layer 1 ;} \\ D_e(\sum_{l=1}^{m-1} R_l) - D_e(\sum_{l=1}^{m-1} R_l + r_m)\,, & \text{if layer 1 to } m-1 \text{ are fully received ;} \\ 0\,, & \text{otherwise .} \end{cases}$$

$$(2)$$

Note that for layered streaming, in order to decode layer m, layer 1 through $m-1$ must be present as well.

Using Taylor expansion, we have

$$D_e\Big(\sum_{l=1}^{m-1} R_l\Big) - D_e\Big(\sum_{l=1}^{m-1} R_l + r_m\Big) \approx \frac{\theta}{(\sum_{l=1}^{m-1} R_l - B_0)^2} \cdot r_m - \frac{\theta}{(\sum_{l=1}^{m-1} R_l - B_0)^3} \cdot (r_m)^2\,.$$

$$(3)$$

3   Problem Formulation

3.1   Auction Model

The whole bandwidth request and distribution process can be modeled as a series of bandwidth auctions, where each peer i has two roles [8]. As a supplying peer, it organizes an auction i to sell its outgoing bandwidth; As a requesting peer, i.e., a player, it joins the auctions held by the neighbors and bids for bandwidth. Specifically, player j submits a bidding message to peer i in the form of $b_{ij}^m = (p_{ij}^m, r_{ij}^m)$, telling the desired bandwidth r_{ij}^m from peer i for layer m, and the unit price p_{ij}^m it is willing to pay. Upon receiving the message of all the competing players, peer i adopts a particular bandwidth strategy to assign its upload bandwidth resource, and then informs player j of the actual assigned bandwidth x_{ij}^m. To get sufficient bandwidth R_m for layer m, player j is allowed to simultaneously join multiple auctions hosted by different neighbors.

3.2   Credit-Based Incentive Mechanism

To avoid selfish or *free-riding* behavior, we introduce a credit-based incentive mechanism. It is on the common sense of service charges, i.e., the peer uses the bandwidth should be charged and the peer provides the bandwidth should be rewarded. Credit represents a kind of virtual currency that can only be used in P2P networks for payment. If the peer requests a video layer from the neighbor, it has to pay for it in credits. In this way, the peer is motivated to share the bandwidth to earn credits. Assume that when a peer newly joins the network, it is endowed with an initial stock f_i of credits. When player j receives its assignment x_{ij}^m, it pays an amount $p_{ij}^m \cdot x_{ij}^m$ of credits to peer i. Correspondingly, the credits of peer i is increased with equivalent amount.

3.3   Bidding Strategy

Determined by the cumulative decoding nature of the layered streaming, the bandwidth request for video layers should be conducted in sequential order. It implies that the peer is entitled to request a higher layer only if all the lower layers are available. Motivated by this basic idea, we divide the request of upload bandwidth into at most M sequential stages, starting from 1. Each stage is used to fulfill downloading one layer. Further, each stage is partitioned into two sub-stage, with the first one for bidding bandwidth, and the second one for downloading chunks.

When bidding for layer m (i.e., at stage m), the objective of a requesting peer j is to maximize its utility with minimum cost.

$$\textbf{P1:} \quad \max \quad gU_m\left(\sum_{i:(i,j)\in E_m} r_{ij}^m\right) - \sum_{i:(i,j)\in E_m} p_{ij}^m r_{ij}^m$$

s.t.

$$1) \quad r_{ij}^m \le n_{ij}^m \cdot r_m, \forall i:(i,j) \in E_m \ ;$$

$$2) \quad \sum_{i:(i,j)\in E_m} r_{ij}^m \le min(R_m, C_j^d) \ ; \qquad (4)$$

$$3) \quad \sum_{i:(i,j)\in E_m} p_{ij}^m r_{ij}^m \le f_j \ .$$

where g is a constant providing conversion of units, and n_{ij}^m represents the number of layer m's informative chunks peer i can provide for peer j.

The objective function consist of two parts. The first term represents the total quality variation between layers. The second term denotes the payoff for the requested service. Constraint 1) gives the upper bound of the bandwidth requested from peer i. In constraint 2), the total bandwidth requested for layer m is limited by both the maximum layer rate and the available download capacity. Constraint 3) ensures that peer j has enough credits for the requested bandwidth.

3.4   Allocation Strategy

As an supplying peer, it is natural that peer i maximizes its total revenue by selling the upload bandwidth at the highest price. In other words, peer i assigns its upload bandwidth among the players $j, j \in J$ to maximize its revenue. Along with the upload capacity and data rate constraints, the optimal allocation problem for peer i can be formulated as:

P2:

$$\max \quad \sum_{j \in J} p_{ij}^m x_{ij}^m$$

s.t.

$$1) \quad \sum_{j \in J} x_{ij}^m \leq C_i^u \; ;$$

$$2) \quad 0 \leq x_{ij}^m \leq r_{ij}^m \; . \tag{5}$$

The main idea behind this maximization problem is to assign the bandwidth to the player which currently bids the highest price. Thus, peer i picks out the player who declares the highest bidding price, e.g., player j for layer m, and assigns bandwidth quantity $x_{ij}^m = \min(C_i^u, r_{ij}^m)$ to it. And then it switches to the next player with the next highest bid price. This process continues until the upload bandwidth is used up, or the demands of the competing players are fully satisfied.

3.5 Bidding Information Adjustment

In each auction round, peer j takes the following two steps to generate the new bids:

(1) Price update. Peer j adjusts the bidding price based on the relationship between the desired and its upload capacity in the last bidding round. Specifically, if $r_{ij}^m > x_{ij}^m$, it increases the bidding price p_{ij}^m with a small quantity $\varepsilon = \beta \cdot |r_{ij}^m - x_{ij}^m|$, $\beta \in (0,1]$. Or else, decreases p_{ij}^m by ε. If peer j joins overlay m for the first time, it initializes p_{ij}^m to 0 toward all the upstream peers.

(2) Bandwidth request update. After determining the new bidding price, peer j updates the required bandwidth r_{ij}^m from each upstream neighbor by a popular progressive filling algorithm [8]. Actually, the implication of Problem **P2** is to ask for bandwidth from the upstream neighbor which currently has the largest marginal net utility (i.e., the largest $\partial[gU_m(\sum_{i:(i,j)\in E_m} r_{ij}^m) - \sum_{i:(i,j)\in E_m} p_{ij}^m r_{ij}^m]/\partial r_{ij}^m)$.

Peer j first requests bandwidth from the neighbor which currently incursion the largest marginal net utility, e.g., peer i. Since $U_m(r_{ij}^m)$ is continuously differentiable, increasing and strictly concave, $U'_m(r_{ij}^m)$ decrease with the increase of r_{ij}^m. When this marginal net utility is not the largest, peer j choose another neighbor with the present largest marginal utility and request bandwidth from it. This procedure terminates when the desired rate R_m is fulfilled or the credits is used up.

3.6 Game Theoretical Analysis

Theorem 1. The proposed auction model exists a Nash equilibrium.
Proof: Due to space limitation, the proof is omitted in this paper. Interested readers are referred to [9] for the details.

4 Performance Evaluation

This section presents simulation results to evaluate the performance of the proposed bandwidth auction strategies. In our experiments, we randomly select 50

to 300 peers to construct the overlays. To simulate a realistic scenario, we set
the bandwidth capacity as follows: 40% of the peers with 10 Mbps download
capacity and 5 Mbps upload capacity, 60% of the peers with 3 Mbps download
capacity and 1 Mbps upload capacity. $\beta = 0.1$, and the initial credit is randomly
select from 1000 to 1500, $r_1 = 2.56$ Kpbs, $r_2 = 1.28$ Kbps, $r_3 = 1.28$ Kbps, and
n_{ij}^m is randomly select from 10-50. Without a special specification, we choose the
standard test video sequence "Foreman", which is encoded into three layers using
FGS coding, at 256 Kbps on the base layer and 128 Kbps on the enhancement
layers.

Fig. 3 shows that the proposed auction model can achieve Nash equilibrium
in different network sizes and only need less than 25 rounds to achieve Nash
equilibrium. Fig. 4 compares the model($M1$) we proposed with the model ($M2$)
which considers all video layers are of equal importance. Fig. 4 displays in our
model gains higher rates at the base layer, and lower rates in the enhancement
layer. Since with the limited upload bandwidth, $M2$ will receive partial bandwidth at the base layer, which renders a lot of bandwidth reserved for the higher
layers useless.And our bidding strategy considers that the base layer provides
the decisive contribution to video quality, so it guarantees the required bandwidth for the base layer , at the cost of trivial enhancement layer and release
bandwidth for a best video quality.

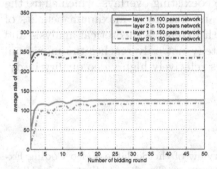

Fig. 3. Average rate for each layer

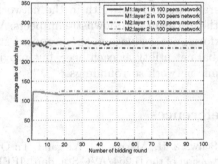

Fig. 4. Average rate for each layer

Fig. 5 shows the convergence speed in different network sizes, where the source
video is encoded into 2 layers and 3 layers, respectively. It is observed that the
convergence speed decreases with the network scales. In Fig. 6 we depict the
evolution of the aggregate utility for a system, which consists of 95% cooperative
peers and 5% selfish peers who don't allocate resource to others, and all 100
peers have the same initial credit. We find that the achieved average rate of
these selfish nodes is lower than that of the cooperative ones. Since they don't
provide resource to others and can't obtain any credit. When the initial credits
are used up, they couldn't receive resource any more.

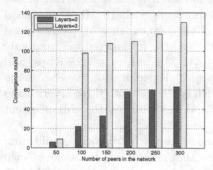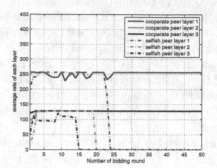

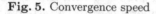

Fig. 5. Convergence speed   **Fig. 6.** Selfish peers vs. cooperative peers

5   Conclusion

In this paper, we propose a game theory strategy which not only optimize the bandwidth allocation of P2P network , but also provide an incentive mechanism which could avoid free-riding. We model the entire distribution network as multiple overlays, with each deliver a video layer. Our optimization scheme aims to resolve bandwidth conflicts among these coexisting overlays, which share the overall upload bandwidth in the network, and guarantee maximum benefits of both upstream and downstream peers. With extensive theoretical analysis and performance evaluation, the proposed strategy not only reaches the maximum global net utility at each peer, but provides relatively high video quality in dynamic network surroundings.

References

1. Schwarz, H., Marpe, D., Wiegand, T.: Overview of the Scalable Video Coding Extension of the H.264/AVC Standard. IEEE Trans. on Circuits and Systems for Video Technology 17(9), 1103–1120 (2007)
2. ISO/IEC.: Scalable Video Coding Shown to be State of the Art. JTC1/SC29/WG11. N9560 (January 2008)
3. Ma, R.T.B., Lee, S.C.M., Lui, J.C.S., Yau, D.K.Y.: Incentive and Service Differentiation in P2P networks: A Game theoretic approach. IEEE/ACM Trans. Networking 14(5), 978–991 (2006)
4. Satsiou, A., Tassiulas, L.: A Trust-Based Exchange Framework for Multiple Services in P2P Systems. In: Proc. 7th IEEE Intern. Conf. on Peerto-Peer Computing (2007)
5. Wang, Y.F., Nakao, A., Ma, J.H.: On the effectiveness of service differentiation based resource-provision incentive mechanisms in dynamic and autonomous P2P networks. Computer Networks 55(17), 3811–3831 (2011)

6. Hossain, T., Cui, Y., Xue, Y.: On the Optimality of Layered Video Streaming Rate in a P2P Mesh Network. In: Proc. of International Conference on Computer Communications and Networks, San Francisco, USA (August 2009)
7. Stuhlmuller, K., Farber, N., Link, M., Griod, B.: Analysis of video transmission over lossy channels. IEEE J. Sel. Areas Commun. 18(6), 1012–1032 (2000)
8. Wu, C., Li, B.C., Li, Z.: Dynamic Bandwidth Auctions in Multi-overlay P2P streaming with Network Coding. IEEE Trans. on Parallel and Distributed Systems 19(6), 806–820 (2008)
9. Mas-Colell, A., Whinston, D.M., Green, R.J.: Microeconomic theory. Oxford University Press (1995)

A Client-Driven Selective Streaming System for Multi-view Video Transmission

Zheng Shi and Junni Zou*

Dept. of Communication Engineering, Shanghai University, Shanghai 200072, China
shizheng136@163.com, zoujn@shu.edu.cn

Abstract. This paper presents a client-driven selective streaming system for multi-view video transmission. For minimizing the total video distortion of all clients, an optimal rate allocation algorithm is proposed in which the views are delivered based on client selections as well as network conditions. In order to achieve a compromise between compression efficiency and view random access, KS-IPP encoding structure is employed where inter-view prediction are only performed for anchor frames. Also, a view and frame streaming priority calculation method is proposed, by which both the frames and views can be dropped according to their streaming priority when the bandwidth is insufficient. Finally, the performance of the proposed scheme is verified by the simulation results.

Keywords: Multi-view video, rate allocation, rate-distortion, streaming priority.

1 Introduction

Three dimensional applications are developing rapidly, multi-view video service draws lots of interests as one of them, which is encoded with different coding methods for different applications [1].

The straightforward encoding method for multi-view video is simulcast encoding, which encodes each view with traditional compression technology independently. Though simulcast encoding provides random access to each view, it contains a large amount of inter-view redundant information. These can be exploited with combined temporal and inter-view prediction, where images are not only predicted from temporally neighboring images but also from corresponding images in adjacent views, referred to as Multi-View Video Coding (MVC), which achieves high compression efficiency. However MVC prediction structure makes the views depend on each others, unnecessary transmission and delay is coursed when the view decoded is far from the reference view, it's difficult for view random access. The MVC with KS-IPP prediction structure achieves a compromise between high compression efficiency and view random access in [2], which only restricts inter-view prediction to anchor frames, the prediction structure is shown in Fig. 1.

* The work was partially supported by Shanghai Young Rising-Star Scientist Program (11QA1402600), and International Collaboration Program of Shanghai (11510707000).

W. Zhang et al. (Eds.): IFTC 2012, CCIS 331, pp. 372–379, 2012.

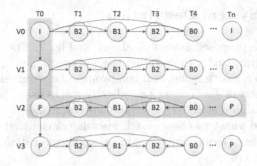

Fig. 1. The prediction structure of KS-IPP coding

Though multi-view video encoding technologies make significant encoding gains, it's impossible to transmit entire multi-view sequences directly when view number is large, since bandwidth requirement is too high for current network. Interactive multi-view video streaming is designed to provide multi-view video service efficiently and flexibly, which can reduce bandwidth requirement by only transmitting the required views.

Interactive multi-view video streaming systems are proposed in [3], [4] and [5]. In [3] multi-view video is encoded with simulcast coding method, each view is encoded and transmitted independently, each client receives as many needed views according to network bandwidth. In [4] MVC and scalable video coding (SVC) are combined to obtain improved compression efficiency and provide selective streaming service, base layer and enhancement layers of two selected views are transmitted. In [5] the system uses successive view motion model, which analyzes the user's motion and then discriminates all frames into potential frames and redundant frames, then frames are encoded and transmitted to client. However, view and frame streaming priority is not considered, it's not clear which views and frames should be dropped when network bandwidth is insufficient, we consider the problem of view and frame streaming priority in this work.

In this paper, we present a client-driven selective streaming system for multi-view video transmission. For minimizing the total video distortion of all clients, an optimal rate allocation algorithm is proposed in which the views are delivered based on client selections as well as network conditions. In order to achieve a compromise between compression efficiency and view random access, KS-IPP encoding structure [2] is employed where inter-view prediction are only performed for anchor frames. Within the context of insufficient system bandwidth, a view and frame streaming priority calculation method is proposed, by which both the frames and views can be dropped according to their streaming priority when the bandwidth is insufficient.

The rest of this paper is organized as follows. After briefly discussing background, the detail of proposed system is described in Section 2. Experimental results are presented in Section 3. We conclude this paper in section 4.

2   Proposed System Description

An overview of the proposed system is shown in Fig. 2. The multi-view video with N views is compressed with encoding method mentioned in [2], the encoding rate of view n is B_n, which achieves a compromise between encoding efficiency and view random access. Each client periodically tracks users' head position and sends request containing selected views and view demands to sever, the server sends the requested views to client. Each view is transmitted over a multicast group formed by clients requesting the same view, client switches view by leaving and joining specific group.

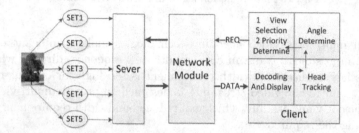

Fig. 2. The overview of the delivery system

We define the content distribution network model as $G = (D, L, C)$, D is the set of nodes, L is the set of directed links between nodes, the capacity of the links can be defined as vector $C = (c_1, c_2, ..., c_n)$. The set D can be further divided into three subsets S, I and R_e, which represent source nodes, interval nodes and receiver nodes respectively. Assuming there are multiple paths $P(r)$ from the source to client r, we use a matrix Z_r to reflect the relationship between its paths j and related links l:

$$Z_{j,l}^r = \begin{cases} 1 \text{ if link } l \text{ is included in path } j, \\ 0 \text{ otherwise.} \end{cases} \tag{1}$$

2.1   View and Frame Streaming Priority

In this section view and frame streaming priority determine method is proposed, it's used to determine which frames should be dropped when bandwidth is insufficient to transmit the whole view or which views should be dropped when bandwidth is even insufficient to transmit all the views.

We use the angles between views and user to calculate view demand for each client, each client selects views by comparing view demand with selection threshold and sends view request to sever, the sever collects requests from all clients and determines view streaming priority, then frame streaming priority is determined according to prediction structure and view streaming priority, the symbols used are defined in Table.1.

Table 1. Important Notations

Symbol	Definition
$F(m)$	The frames of view m in a GOP
E	The number of frames in a GOP of one view
$f(i, m)$	The ith frame of view m
$p_o(m)$	The streaming priority of frame B_2 in view m
$p_v(m)$	The streaming priority of view m
$p_f(i, m)$	The streaming priority of frame i in view m

View streaming priority is determined by requests from all clients. In each client the demand for each view is calculated using the angle between user and view as in [6], the orientation of view m donated as $\mathbf{O_m}$ is given by the normal of its image plane, the user's position is represented by its orientation $\mathbf{O_r}$ referring to the displaying equipment, the angle between user and view θ_m^r is the angle between $\mathbf{O_r}$ and $\mathbf{O_m}$, view demand is defined as $d_v(m, r) = \cos\theta_m^r$. Each client selects views by comparing view demand with selection threshold, view m will be selected when $d_v(m, r)$ is larger than selection threshold $T(T \in [0, 1])$, T is specified by application [6]. The sever collects requests from all clients, view streaming priority is calculated by aggregating all demands for each view:

$$p_v(m) = \sum_{r \in R_e} d_v(m, r). \quad (R_e \text{ is the receiver set}) \tag{2}$$

The multi-view video prediction structure is determined by view streaming priority, view m with the largest $p_v(m)$ is used as v_0 in prediction structure and other views are determined in the same way.

Frame streaming priority is determined by view streaming priority and prediction structure, prediction structure is reflected by frame loss sets coursed by dropping different frame. If an anchor frame is lost, the views depending on it can't be decoded; if a B_0 frame is lost, the frames in the view are useless except the anchor frame; if a B_1 frame is lost, the B_2 frames before and after it are useless; if a B_2 frame is lost, other frames are not affected. The abandon set of frame $f(i, m)$ can be defined as $A(f(i, m))$:

$$A(f(i, m)) = \begin{cases} \{f(g, n) | g = i...E - 1, n = m...N - 1\}, & \text{f(i,m) is I or P frame} \\ \{f(g, m) | g = 1...E - 1\}, & \text{f(i,m) is } B_0 \text{ frame} \\ \{f(g, m) | g = i - 1, i, i + 1\}, & \text{f(i,m) is } B_1 \text{ frame} \\ \{f(i, m)\}. & \text{f(i,m) is } B_2 \text{ frame} \end{cases} \tag{3}$$

The abandon set of frames in view m is donate as $A_I(f(i, m))$ and out of view m is $A_O(f(i, m))$.

The streaming priority of frame $f(i, m)$ considering intra-view prediction structure is the aggregate of streaming priority of frames can't be decoded since the loss of $f(i, m)$, in other words the frames in $A_I(f(i, m))$, which is shown as:

$$p_f(i, m) = \sum_{f(g,m)\in A_I(f(i,m))} p_f(g, m) \quad g \in (0, ...E - 1) \tag{4}$$

For instance, when view streaming priority $p_v(m)$ is obtained, if $f(i, m)$ is a B_2 frame, $p_f(i, m) = p_o(m)$, if $f(i, m)$ is a B_1 frame, $p_f(i, m) = 2 \cdot p_o(m)$ and so on. Here the streaming priority of B_2 frame $p_o(m)$ is used as a basic scalar, since B_2 frame in each view is a hierarchical B frame, it refers to the adjacent frames while encoding and no frame refer to it, so it has the lowest streaming priority, and it's changeable since view streaming priority changes.

The aggregate of streaming priority of all frames in view m equal to view streaming priority $p_v(m)$, which can be shown as:

$$p_v(m) = \sum_{f(g,m)\in F(m)} p_f(g, m) \quad g \in (0, ...E - 1). \tag{5}$$

According to the above two equations, streaming priority of frames in view m considering intra-view prediction structure are obtained.

The calculate of anchor frame streaming priority should consider inter-view prediction structure as well, since only anchor frames are encoded with inter-view prediction structure. The priority of anchor frame $f(0, m)$ is the aggregate of streaming priority of anchor frames can't be decoded since the loss of $f(0, m)$, which are the anchor frames in $A_O(f(0, m))$, it can be expressed as:

$$p_f(0, m) = \sum_{f(0,k)\in A_O(f(0,m))} p_f(0, k) \quad k \in (0, ...N - 1) \tag{6}$$

Views and frames are transmitted according to streaming priority, frames will be dropped according to streaming priority from low to high when network bandwidth is insufficient to transmit the whole view, and views will be dropped in the same way when bandwidth is even insufficient to transmit all the views, the advantage is that some important views and frames are transmitted when bandwidth is insufficient.

2.2   Optimization Problem

In this section we determine the optimal bandwidth allocation and the multicast meshes for multi-view video streaming over network.

Video distortion can be donated by distortion introduced by encoder, the rate-distortion characteristic is donate as $D(R) = D_0 + \frac{\theta}{R-R_0}$, the parameters D_0, θ, R_0 depend on coding scheme and the content of video [7]. We use the scale of streaming priority of one view in the total view streaming priority to determine view importance, the importance of view m in sever side is $w(m) = \frac{p_v(m)}{\sum_{v\in N} p_v(v)}$.

The multi-view video is encoded with KS-IPP structure, view 0 is encoded without referring to any view, the view before is referred while encoding the anchor frame of other views. The average rate difference over simulcast of one view is ΔR_0^{MDE} in [8], the rate difference of view v_n over simulcast can be expressed as:

$$\sigma^n = \begin{cases} 0 & n=0, \\ \Delta R_0^{MDE} & \text{otherwise.} \end{cases} \tag{7}$$

The goal of the optimization problem is to allocate appropriate bandwidth to each client and minimize the total distortion, it can be formulated as:

$$\mathbf{P}\text{:min} \sum_{r \in R_e} \sum_{m \in M(r)} w_r(m) \cdot D(\sigma^m + \sum_{j \in P(r)} x_{m,j}^r)$$

s.t.

1) $\quad \sum_{r \in R_e} \sum_{m \in M} \sum_{j \in P(r)} z_{j,l}^r \cdot x_{m,j}^r \le c_l \quad \forall l \in L;$

2) $\quad 0 \le \sum_{j \in P(r)} x_{m,j}^r \le R_m \quad \forall m \in M(r), \quad r \in R_e;$

3) $\quad x_{m,l}^r \ge 0 \quad \forall m \in M, \quad r \in R_e, \quad l \in L.$

Constraint 1 represents the aggregate flow rate over each link can not exceed link capacity. The receiving rate of each view is constrained no larger than encoding rate by constraint 2.

Since the objective function and constraint set are strictly convex, there exists an unique optimal solution of X, which can be solved with a distributed algorithm using the primal-dual method [9], the stability of the primal-dual algorithm can be proved with the Lyapunov stability theorem.

3 Performance Evaluation

In this section the performance of proposed system is evaluated in a random network as in Fig. 3, there is one source S, five relays and three receivers $(T1...T3)$, the system bandwidth is assumed to be insufficient and link capacity $(Kbps)$ is marked on each link. We compare the proposed system with two reference systems under the same condition, which are: 1) simulcast encoding and streaming the selected views [3] 2) MVC encoding and streaming all views.

Assuming there are three views $(v_0...v_2)$ in multi-view video test sequences "ballroom" with resolution $640 * 480$, which is encoded with KS-IPP structure, the frame rate is $30f/s$ and $QP = 40$, and the length of a GOP is set as 16.

Appropriate bandwidth is allocated to each client with three systems, the average receiving quality of each client is shown in Fig. 4. Since MVC has the highest encoding efficiency and simulcast has the lowest efficiency, the proposed system gets more bandwidth with R-D optimized method and frames with lower streaming priority are dropped when bandwidth is insufficient, so the proposed system gets the highest video quality and simulcast system is the lowest.

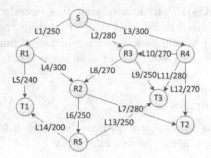

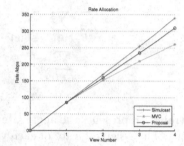

Fig. 3. Topology of the evaluation network

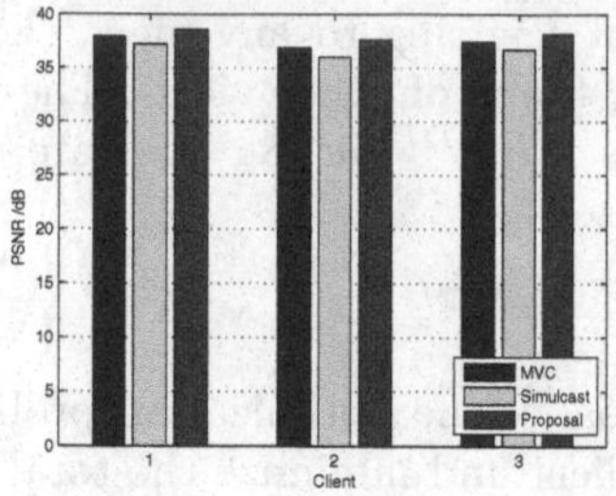

Fig. 4. The average PSNR for three clients in three systems

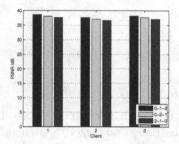

Fig. 5. The average PSNR with different prediction structure

Fig. 6. Rate allocation with the increase of view number

If view demand order is $v_0 - v_1 - v_2$ in each client, so the view prediction structure is $v_0 - v_1 - v_2$ according the proposed method. We compare the average receiving quality when prediction structure is $v_0 - v_1 - v_2$, $v_0 - v_2 - v_1$ and $v_2 - v_1 - v_0$, which is shown in Fig. 5.

View prediction structure $v_0 - v_1 - v_2$ is the same with view streaming priority, frames in view with lower streaming priority will be dropped earlier when bandwidth is insufficient, and frames in other views are not affected, which has the highest video quality. While with $v_0 - v_2 - v_1$ and $v_2 - v_1 - v_0$ structure, frames in view with higher streaming priority are dropped earlier and the decoding of other views are affected, which decreases the receiving video quality. Since $v_2 - v_1 - v_0$ is the reverse of $v_0 - v_1 - v_2$, which has the lowest video quality.

We compare the changes of rate allocation among three systems with the increase of view number, assuming network bandwidth is sufficient and view number changes from 1 to 4, the result is shown in Fig. 6, which indicates the encoding efficiency of three systems. The encoding structure used in the proposed system achieves a balance between compression efficiency and view random access, which only restricts inter-view prediction to anchor frames.

The proposed system is suitable for multi-view video streaming, which realizes a balance between compression efficiency and view random access, video quality is improved with the proposed view and frame streaming priority.

4   Conclusion

In this paper we introduce a rate-distortion optimized interactive multi-view video streaming system. We use a KS-IPP encoding structure, a view and frame priority determine method is proposed to ensure views and frames are transmitted in order. We consider video streaming and network flow control to minimize the total distortion, view streaming priority is considered to determine the optimal paths and rates for each view. Experimental results demonstrate that the proposed system is suitable for multi-view video streaming.

References

1. Gurler, C.G., Gorkemli, B., Saygili, G., Tekalp, A.M.: Flexible Transport of 3-D Video Over Networks. Proceedings of the IEEE 99(4), 694–707 (2011)
2. Joint Video Team of ITU-T VCEG and ISO/IEC MPEG: Comparative Study of MVC Prediction Structures. Doc. JVT-V132-Q (January 2007)
3. Jongryool, K., Kiho, C., Hyunyong, L., Jong, W.K.: Multi-view 3D video transport using application layer multicast with view switching delay constraints. In: 3DTV Conference, pp. 1–4 (2007)
4. Kurutepe, E., Civanlar, M.R., Tekalp, A.M.: Client-driven selective streaming of multiview video for interactive 3DTV. IEEE Trans. on CSVT 17(11), 1558–1565 (2007)
5. Ziyuan, P., Ikuta, Y., Bandai, M., Watanabe, T.: A User Dependent System for Multi-view Video Transmission. In: IEEE International Conference on AINA, pp. 732–739 (2011)
6. Zhenyu, Y., Bin, Y., Klara, N., Ruzena, B.: A Multi-stream Adaptation Framework for Bandwidth Management in 3D Tele-immersion. In: Proceedings of the International Workshop on NOSSDAV (2006)
7. Stuhlmuller, K., Farber, N., Link, M., Girod, B.: Analysis of video transmission over lossy channels. IEEE J. Select. Areas Commun. 18(6), 1012–1032 (2000)
8. Xiaoyu, X., Pang, D., Jie, L.: Rectification-Based View Interpolation and Extrapolation for Multiview Video Coding. IEEE Trans. on CSVT 21(6) (2011)
9. Junni, Z., Hongkai, X., Chenglin, L., Li, S., Zhihai, H., Tsuhan, C.: Prioritized Flow Optimization With Multi-Path and Network Coding Based Routing for Scalable Multirate Multicasting. IEEE Trans. on CSVT 21(3) (2011)

Clear Browser: A Dedicated Embedded Browser for Quality-Affordable Smart TVs

Yuan Liu and Dejian Ye

Multimedia and Networking Laboratory, Software School, Fudan University, China

Abstract. In the recent and following several years, Smart TVs popularly used in most families are likely to be quality-affordable.This kind of Smart TV has the following features: low-performance mainboard, large TV screen, diversified application support and high user-experience demand. As one of the most important fundamentalsoftware, the browser faces great challenges. We designed a dedicated embedded browsernamed Clear Browser and proposed a methodology named SDCBto fit the features of the quality-affordable Smart TV. SDCB is consisted of four steps: tailor the browser's engineers; setup a proxy server for webpages; buildfeedback control module anddiscard secondary information.The experiment results show SDCB can help browserpresent webpages friendly on large screen with limited resources.

Keywords: Quality-affordable, Smart TV, Dedicated embedded browser.

1   Introduction

Smart TV, which is also sometimes referred to as "Connected TV" or "Hybrid TV" is the phrase used to describe the current trend of integration of the internet and Web 2.0 features into modern television sets and set-top boxes, as well as the technological convergence between computers and these television sets/set-top boxes[1]. Through supporting various applications and services, it plays a much more important role in people's normal lifethan the traditional TV set.

There are two main kinds of Smart TVs. One is the high-performance Smart TV with android, for example, Google TV [2]. Another is the quality-affordable Smart TV with Linux, for example, the Hair Integrate-TV. However, there are only several prototype machines of Google TV now and such technique isn't enough mature yet. The majority of market of Smart TV is occupied by the quality-affordable Smart TV. These TVs are sold by millions in the past several years.On the other hand, unlike the smartphones, people are not willing to change this big object in living rooms frequently. Usually,people keep the same TV for 5-10 years.Although the hardware isbecoming cheaper and powerful, high-performance Smart TVs will still occupy a small utilization.Thus, most of the Smart TVs in used are still low-performanceones in the next several years. However, much more applicationswill be pushed to the smart TVs.The contradiction between the low-property mainboard of TVs and the increasing demand of various services became more and more serious. Besides, TV users aren't as

W. Zhang et al. (Eds.): IFTC 2012, CCIS 331, pp. 380–389, 2012.

used to crush and reboot as the smartphone or PC users. So the quality-affordable Smart TV must be robust and stable.

The browser, as one of the most important fundamentalsoftware in quality affordable TV, faces this contradictionextremelysharply.There are two candidate methods to solve this problem for the browser. One way is to use external set-top boxes to improve the processing power of TVs. However, this way needs high cost to buy and install set-top boxes.And users have to use two remote controls to send commands. Furthermore, the signals have to be passed between TV and STB, which may lead slow response. Another way is to solve the problem in software aspect. We may design and implement the browser in the Smart TV's embeddedmainboard.This method could update the quality-affordable Smart TV seamlessly and doesn't need extra cost on hardware.Since the quality-affordable Smart TV has the following features: low-performance mainboard, large screen and high user-experience demand, we need to design a specializedbrowserwhich is able to fitthe features.

The rest of the paper is organized as follows.Section 2 introduces the overall architecture of the Clear Browser. Section 3 presents the methodology ofSDCB (Smart Display of Clear Browser) which is consisted four steps: (1) tailorbrowser's engineers to save resource; (2) set up a proxy server for webpages to fit large TV-screen; (3) build the feedback control module to watch the resource; (4) discard secondary information to shownsmoothly. Section 4 shows some experiment resultsto prove the effectiveness of our method and Section 5 gives a conclusion of this paper.

2   The Architecture of the Clear Browser

In order to fit the features of quality-affordable Smart TV, we need to design a browser which is able to run steady with limited resource and presents contexts properly on large screen. As more services are needed to provide, the browser also needs to support some basic extended functions such as plug-in support, input method, automatic update and so on.

Fig.1 shows the overall architecture of the Clear Browser.

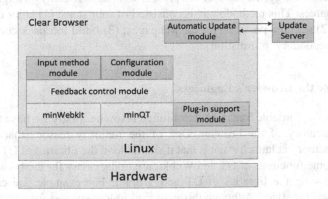

Fig. 1. The architecture of the Clear Browser

The ClearBrowser is consisted of the following modules:

MinWebkit and minQT: The browser use Webkit as the engineer and use QT to implement UI. Qt is a cross platform graphical user interface library that now comes with a user interface design tool that generates C++ code [3]. Webkit is an open-source browser engineer, the corresponding browser including the Gecko (used by Mozilla, Firefox) and Trident (used by IE) [4].Instead of the original QT and Webkit, we use minWebkit and minQTto save resources. This part will be introduced particularly in Section 3.1.

Plugin-in support module: This module implements support for NPAPI (Netscape Plugin Application Programming Interface) plugin-in. With this module, the third party developers can run their plug-ins in our browser conveniently. And they don't need to change their programs to adapt different hardware.

Feedback control module: This module is used to monitor the state of used resource in the mainboard and gives feedback information to the browser. Then the browser will take proper actions to prevent the browser from crushing. This module will be introduced in detail in Section 3.3.

Input method module: This module providessoft keyboard for users. It's implemented based onQTe. With the input method, users can type in Chinese into the browser.

Configuration module: This module is responsible for the configuration of the browser. Users can set the homepage, menu options, languages, max history records and so on.

Automatic Update module: This module support automatic update in two ways: scanning the inserted USB flash disk and contacting with the update server. Smart TVusers can update their browsers easily with this module.

3   The Methodology of SDCB

Based on the design of the browser in Section 2, we proposed a methodology named SDCB to improve the user experiments of quality-affordable Smart TV's browser. With this methodology, the browser can present webpages friendly on large screen with limited resources. This methodology is consisted of four steps: (1) tailor the browser's engineers; (2) set up a proxy server for webpages; (3) build feedback control module; (4) discard secondary information.

3.1   Tailor the Browser's Engineers

As the quality-affordable Smart TV has limited resource, firstly we have to reduce the consumingmemory of the browser. One of the majority reasons that the browser consumes memory at launch stage is that it should load the libraries of QT and Webkit. However, some functions of QT and Webkit are unnecessary for the browser.Thus we consider tailoring the libraries of QT and Webkit. For example, we can tailor the functions used for styles. Although this may lead to less support for complicate styles, but it occupy less memory and the basic necessary functions are remained.

Since version 4.0, QT adopts modularization. It encapsulates the whole libraries into several disparate modules which make it's possible to cut it into a smaller one. We call the minimal collection of QT's libraries that could support our browser as minQT.

The configuration of QT has provided some options to select modules. However, this way can only pick out some general modules; it cannot support more detailed selection. Qt also has a tool named *qconfig* which can let you select the needed components of each module. With these two functions, we can gain a minQT with relatively less libraries. According to our research, a simple application with minQT running on chip Mstar 981 will use over 7MB less than on the original one.

On the other hand, instead of using QT's embedded Webkit, we produce a minWebkit, and then combine the minQT and minWebkit to work together. We generate the minWebkit by compiling the original Webkit with an option "-minimal". According to our research, the size of a single library named "libQtWebKit.so" is smaller 6MB than the original one.

Through the discard of redundant libraries, we save much memory space for the browser.

3.2   Set Up Proxy-Server for Webpages

Since the quality-affordable Smart TV has limited resource and large screen, the common webpages for PC isn't suitable for the Clear Browser. For mobile devices, many web sites provide a mobile version of their pages in order to better fit the content into and better support navigation on the small screen [5]. In general, this kind of Mobile webpages keep the majority context of the original one intended for personal computers while tend to have smaller CSS files and fewer JavaScripts that lead to lighter workload for Style and Scripting [6]. However, few websites have optimized webpages for Smart TV. Thus we need to set up a proxy server to do some transformation of popularwebsites to fit the large TV screen and redirect the browser to the optimized ones.

The proxy server does this transformation for popular websites offline. The server collects the original webpages and then transforms them to fit TVs. The server needs to filter the secondary information, compact the webpages and decreasethe resolution ratiofor the limited resource. Since the common PC webpages have many tabs per line while the change of focus point with remote control is difficult and confused, the optimized webpages also needs to have few tabs per line. And as the TV is far to people, we also need to set bigger font size.

On the other hand, if the requesting website hasn't been optimized for TV screen by the proxy server, we could do some simple change to fit the device. One feasible solution is to override the functions in Class Webpage of QT and set the identification of the browser as "ipad". Then if the visiting website has optimized webpages for ipad, our browser will automatic redirect to the optimized one.

3.3   Build Feedback ControlModule

Although we have done the above improvements, we find that there are still many webpages that may make the browser crushed in limited-resourceSmart TV. According to the research result of [6], over half (56%) of pages visited were not optimized for mobile devices, or non-mobile webpages. And our proxy server can only do transformations for popular websites, there are still a large number of websites aren't optimized for Smart TV. For the TV users, frequently crushes are unbearable. Thus we need a feedback control module which could observe the state of consuming resource and give feedback information.

As the memory is the critical resource, one possible solution is to monitor the memory used and once the available resource is about to be short, the module alarms. However, we find it isn't feasible.

First of all, there is a delay between the point the browser should stop loading and it stops indeed. Many modules of QT are asynchronous. When we find the memory is lack and send signal to make the browser stop loading, the browser doesn't stop immediately. And the painting functions in QT are recursive, it couldn't stop halfway. Thus although the case is detected, the browser's resource runs out. Secondly, the memory of browser will accumulate with time. The resource used may don't release at once. In our experiments, after visiting some pages, no matter whether the actual available memory is enough or not, this method would make the browser couldn't load any webpages. The browser can't judge the point to stop loading exactly. Thirdly, the monitoring of memory isn't accurate. The accuracy is decided by the frequency the monitoring module check the status of memory. However, high accuracy means high frequent check, which would spend lots of resource of Smart TV. It's obviously not suitable.

Another possible solution is to use blacklist. Record the troublesome webpages or URLs in the blacklist and ignore this kind of requests. However, we find it's hard to get the actual URL of current webpage for the functions are asynchronous. The value of URL won't change to the right one until the loading progress has finished 10%-30%. Thus this way also cannot work well.

Since the single memory detection and blacklist detection has lots of shortage, we should find another practical method to monitor the resource. After some experiments, we select some key elements from several candidate targets and find a simple but effective solution. We use the following variables as metrics:

The total request number (TRN): The total number of requests that web page has sent.
The height of web page(HWP): The amount of a web page's vertical pixels.
The progress percentage(PP): The percentage of the loading progress.
The available memory percent(AMP): The percentage of available memory.

The following criteria are used to decide whether it is the point to take action to prevent the resource from lacking.

$TRN>TS_{TRN}/2$ and $HWP>TS_{HWP}$
Or $TRN>TS_{TRN}$
Or $PP>TS_{pp}$ and $AMP<TS_{AMP}$

TS_{TRN} is the largest number of TRN that the browser can accept. TS_{HWP} is a relatively big value of HWP. TS_{pp} means the progress percentage to enable memory checking. TS_{AMP} is the critical available memory percentage that may lead to crush. The value of TS_{TRN}, TS_{HWP} and TS_{pp}, TS_{AMP} can be tested according to your mainboard's processing power and can be set in the configuration file.

As more request connectionsneed more memory used to build connection, download things. Fewer things in the painting buffer means fewer memories used to paint. Thus *TRN* reflect the resource the page has used. So does the height of the webpages.

Furthermore, we can get most of these metrics' values with no delay and judge the condition easily. And *PP*limits the resource occupationof memory checking. Thus this monitoring module wouldn't bring much burden to the memory and CPU.

According to our research, the *TRN* value of web pages like http://tv.babao.comis about 20-30 and the *TRN* value of web pages like http://www.sina.com.cn/ is over 150. A group of empirical value for mainboard such as Mstar 981 is: TS_{pp}=30, M=540*3, AMP =25and TS_{TRN}= 40. You can adjust the critical value to fit the configuration of your mainboard.

3.4   Discard Secondary Information

When the feedback control module detects the resource's incoming lack, a common solution is to simply stop loading the webpage. However, we find it's a bad solution.

If we simply stop loading, few context will be shown on Smart TV. Many elements may be downloaded incompletely and the parse of the webpage would be chaotic. Even the elements being fully downloaded may not be shown.

In order to achieve better user experience, when the feedback control module detects the available resource isn't enough, our browser keep loading the webpage and discard the secondary information through setting this part's URLs as empty. We prefer to treat the resources with more information and smaller size as primary information and think the resources with less information and bigger size as secondary information. For example, we may reserve the texts and drop the pictures, CSS or JS files.

The common syntaxformat of URL is as following [7]:

Protocol://hostname[:port]/path/[;parameters][?query][#fragment]

According to the format, we can judge the type of the request resource by the suffix of path in the URL.

By the way, for some small websites, a server can hold all necessary data. This kind of websites usually adopt relative path to locate the resource. For these websites, the URL using absolute path mostly means secondary information. So we can choose this kind of URL to set empty.

With this method, the browser avoids useless downloading, maintains the main frame of the webpage and presentsinformationas much as possible.

Our methodology won't have much effect on small webpages. For the complicate large webpages, although this way would lose some information of a webpage, it shows the majority of the web page properly and prevents the browser from crush.

4   Experiment Results

We did some experiments to prove the effectiveness of our SDCBmethodology. Here shows some of the experiment results.

4.1   Experiment Set up

We choose a set of webpages, containing some simple pages and the hottest 40 portal websites, as our test webpages set. Then wecarried outfourgroups of comparison experimentswith following settings and record the performance of each:

1)   Visit webpages with the original browser on STB using chip Broadcom.
2)   Visit webpages withthe Clear Browser on Mstar 981;
3)   Visit webpages withthe ClearBrowseron Mstar 988without feedback module;
4)   Visit webpages withthe Clear Browser on Mstar 988;

Table 1 shows the primary hardware configuration of three chips.

Table 1. The hardware configurations of chips

Chip	Mstar 981	Mstar 988	Broadcom
Memory	55356KB	124976KB	105532KB
CPUMip	334.84	447.48	402.43
Processor	Single-core	Single-core	Double-core

Reboot the chip after every test to make sure the experiments have the same initial state.

4.2   Experiment Results and Analysis

We tested every candidate webpages using the four settings in Section 4.1 and recorded the consuming memory and reflection time.

Fig.2.a shows the results of four cases for website "www.sohu.com". Fig.2.b shows the result of four cases for website "www.sina.com".

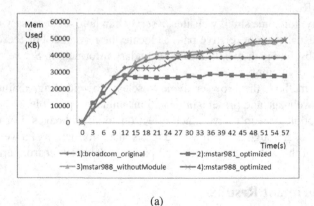

(a)

Fig. 2. Memory used of four experiments for sohu and sina

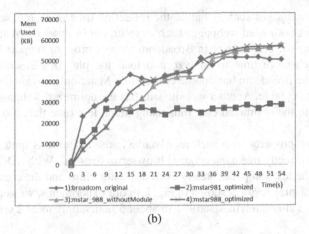

(b)

Fig. 2. *(Continued)*

For complicate webpages such as sohu and sina, the ClearBrowser on Mstar981 uses less than 30M memories.TheClear Browser in Mstar 988 and the original browser on Broadcom consume much more memory than the Clear Browserin mstar981. Because the chip Mstar981 has quite limited resource, it's more sharply affected by SDCBand the used memory is controlled to a low level. The chip Mstar988 has enough resource, thus less restriction is put on it and it can display better. Because our browser supportsplug-in, the used memory of Clear Browser is even a little more than the original onein Broadcom.

For simple webpages such as baidu, since Mstar needs to load lots of its system libs at initial stage and the reflection time is quite short, the Clear Browser in Mstar seems to consume more memory than the orginal one in Broadcom.

We can also find that the memory used by case 3) and case 4) are quite similar.In Mstar988, the browser with feedback module only consumes a little more memory than the one without feedback module. SDCB won't bring much burden to the system.

Fig.3 shows the reflection times that use different chips and browsers to visit different webpages.

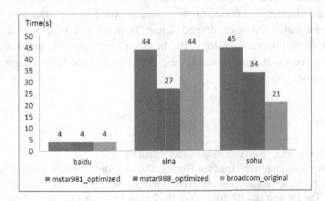

Fig. 3. Webpage reflection times of three cases

For small webpages such as baidu, the reflection time in each case is similar. For complicate not-optimized webpages such as sohu, our browser on Mstar988 will need more time than the original one in Broadcom. As our browser support NPAPI plug-in, we need much more time to analyze and load the plug-in elements. Furthermore, considering the Broadcom has double cores while Mstar only has single core, we think the result is acceptable. Another website sina has the optimized webpages, our browser will redirect to the optimized one, thus using much less time than the original one in Broadcom.

For the low-property chip such as Mstar981, the resource is quite limited. Many websites will directly make the original browser in itrushed. With SDCB, the browser can visit all the test webpages steady even on junior chips and the crush rate decrease greatly. The display result is shown in Fig.4. In our experiments, we kept visit these 40 portal websites alternatelyin Mstar981 in about 5 hours, only meet 2 crushes.

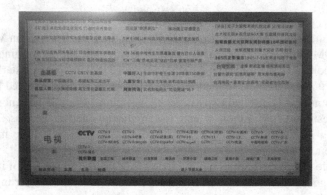

Fig. 4. The display result of Clear-Browser on Mstar 981

5   Conclusion

Since most of the Smart TVs in used in the next several years are quality-affordable Smart TVs, a dedicated embedded browser which could fit their features is needed. We designed a dedicated browser named Clear Browserand proposed a methodology calledSDCB. With this methodology, the browser could provide good user experience on large TV screen with limited resources. We also designed experiments to show the validity of ourmethodology.

References

[1] http://en.wikipedia.org/wiki/Smart_TV
[2] Ferraté, A.: Building Web Apps for Google TV, 1st edn. O'Reilly Media (2011)
[3] Hartness, K.: Graphics and User Interfaces in C++ WITH Qt*. ACM (2005)
[4] Yan, H.: The Design and Realization of the Linux Browser Based on Webkit. IEEE (2009)

[5] Shrestha, S.: Mobile web browsing: usability study. In: Proc. Int. Conf. Mobile Technology, Applications, and Systems and Int. Symp. Computer Human Interaction in Mobile Technology. ACM, Singapore (2007)
[6] Wang, Z.: Why are Web Browsers Slow on Smartphones? In: HotMobile 2011, March 1-2. ACM, Phoenix (2010)
[7] Chen, J.: Optimization Based on DOM Structure Analysis for Mobile Browser (2008)

Model-Based Robust Prediction of Cumulative Participant Curve in Large-Scale Events

Dixin Luo, Rong Xie, Jia Wang, and Wenjun Zhang

Institute of Image Communication, Shanghai Key Lab of Digital Media
Shanghai Jiao Tong University, Shanghai, China
{luodixin,xierong,jiawang,zhangwenjun}@sjtu.edu.cn

Abstract. In this paper, we propose a robust piecewise parametric model for predicting the cumulative number of participants in large-scale events. Based on the analysis of arriving patterns in such events, we establish parametric models for different periods and design an efficient fitting strategy to achieve model parameters from incomplete current data. Moreover, based on historical data, we can train parameters by neural network and get relation prior among parameters and data. With the help of relation prior, we can update the parameters of current data and achieve robust prediction for outlier. Simulation results on the database of Expo 2010 Shanghai show the good performance of our proposed method even in abnormal situations.

Keywords: large-scale event, robust prediction, piecewise parametric model, relation prior.

1 Introduction

In recent years, extensive studies have been devoted to understand human collective behavior in large-scale events [6,7]. The arriving patterns and the cumulative number of participants in the event are the most crucial information for the risk management in large-scale events from the perspective of the organizing committee members. So, to get an accurate and robust prediction of the cumulative curve in large-scale events is a meaningful issue.

The prediction methods can be classified into parametric model based and nonparametric model based methods. The parametric model assumes that there is an explicit relationship existing in data samples, which can be described by an equation with certain parameters. Many approximation algorithms have been proposed, including the Auto-Regressive and Moving Average Model (ARMA) [4] and the Neural Network [2,3]. Nonparametric model estimates the distribution of data instead of estimating the relationship among data, and works well if the relationship among data is not explicit. For example, the nonlocal means in [5] has good performances on image restoration problem. However, both of the two methods above have flaws. Because of the fixed configuration of parameters, parametric model is not robust to outliers. On the other hand, nonparametric

W. Zhang et al. (Eds.): IFTC 2012, CCIS 331, pp. 390–395, 2012.
© Springer-Verlag Berlin Heidelberg 2012

model is robust to outliers to some extent, but the physical meanings of the model is not clear.

The cumulative curve of large scale event has explicit physical explanations, which is suitable to parametric model. However, outliers corresponding to abnormal situations can not be predicted. Nonparametric model based methods can get good regression result, but it is difficult to use in predicting the completed curve from previous data. In this paper, we propose a piecewise parametric model for predicting the number of people in the large-scale event, which is robust to outliers by learning relationships between parameters and data. Figure 1 gives a scheme of the proposed prediction strategy.

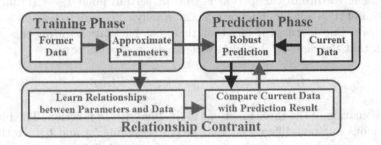

Fig. 1. The scheme of the proposed method

The organization of the rest of the paper is as follows. Section 2 gives the piecewise parametric model. The details about the proposed prediction strategy is presented in section 3. Section 4 describes the experiments we preformed to test our model. Conclusion is in Section 5.

2 Piecewise Parametric Model

Consider a large-scale event E, whose duration time is N days. To the i-th day D_i, $i = 1, 2, ..., N$, the cumulative number of people participating the event can be regarded as a function of time $F_i(t)$.

1) Initial period: Before the beginning of event, it is an universal phenomenon that there are a number of people queuing outside the event sites. Assume the entry speed to be constant to a queue, the initial period of large-scale event, $f_i(t)$ is a linear function.

$$f_i(t) = a_{i1} + b_{i1}t, \quad t_0 \leq t \leq t_{i1}. \tag{1}$$

Here t_0 is the beginning time of event and t_{i1} is the ending time of initial period.

2) Mature period: When people enter the event site with no need to queue or the queue is not continuous, the slope of $f_i(t)$ becomes smaller and converges to 0 with the increase of t. This phenomenon is caused by the spatial and temporal finitude of event. If the number of people increases too fast, the event site will be crowded. The crowdedness of event site naturally suppresses the entry of people. The duration of event is also limited. People will not join in the event if the time left is not enough. According to the feature of mature period, a series of exponential models provide potential fitting functions.

$$f_i(t) = a_{i2} \log(t - b_{i2}) + c_{i2}, \quad t_{i1} < t \leq t_{i2}. \tag{2}$$

t_{i2} is the ending time of the mature period.

3) Secondary mature period: The development of large-scale event is always not stationary because of the change of time and event site itself. For example, the 2010 Shanghai Expo and the Singapore Zoo sell night tickets to tourists. The feature of this period is that at certain point t_{i2}, $f_i'(t)$ increases suddenly and then appears fluctuation, and finally converges to 0 again with the increase of t. Considering the fact that there has fluctuation during this period, we think that the Sigmoidal models will satisfy most situations.

$$f_i(t) = \frac{a_{i3}}{1 + b_{i3} e^{-c_{i3} t}}, \quad t_{i2} < t \leq t_{end}. \tag{3}$$

The combination of the three functions is the final fitting function. The function is continuous but non-differentiable at piecewise points t_{i1} and t_{i2}. To the i-th day, we can get the three fitting functions f_i^n, $n = 1, 2, 3$, and corresponding configurations of parameters, $P_i = \{a_{i1}, ..., c_{i3}\} \in R^8$ based on a small set of data $d = \{d_1, ..., d_k\}$ in D_i, as following algorithm 1 shows. The Feature of the proposed method is that we can get partial model based on incomplete data. Such strong information helps us to achieve robust prediction.

Algorithm 1. 0. $n = 1$.
1. Fit d by f^n and get configuration of parameter p and fitting results $\hat{d}$.
2. Calculate residual $r = \|d - \hat{d}\|_2$.
3. If $r < r_{\max}$, $d = \{d, d_{next}\}$, return step 1; d_{next} is the next data behind d.
4. else the index of d_{next}, m, is a piecewise point, $d = \{d_{m+1}, ..., d_{m+k}\}$, $n = n + 1$.
5. return step 1.

---

3   Robust Prediction Scheme Based on Relation Prior

Given a group of data, we can approximate the configuration of parameter of each sample based on algorithm 1. This group of parameters can be used to train a neural network for approximating the parameters of an unknown variable. According to the parameters getting from samples, we find that although the parameters of outliers are very different from those of normal data, both of them obey similar statistical relationships. Take the data of Shanghai Expo as an example. The relationships among parameters and data can be summarized as follows.

C1) The piecewise points t_{i1}, t_{i2} are significant to describe the development of event. Based on the estimation of parameters, we can get three corresponding curves of different period. According to the regression result, we find that $t_{i1} = b_{i2} + 1.028$, whose deviation is 1.3766%. In other words, the parameter b_{i2} tells us when the initial period finishes.

C2) The number of people in piecewise point t_{i1} can be approximated by parameter c_{i2}. $F_i(t_{i1}) = 1.106c_{i2}$ with deviation 5.0928%.

C3) The value of a_{i3} is also very close to the total number of people attending the event on that day, $F_i(t_{end})$. $a_{i3} = 1.079F_i(t_{end})$ with deviation 0.5031%.

C4) a_{i3} is almost two times of c_{i2}: $a_{i3} = 2.047c_{i2}$ with deviation 0.8943%. Based on the conclusions in **C2)**, **C3)**, we know that $F_i(t_{i1})$ has a close relationship with $F_i(t_{end})$.

The relationships among data and parameters provide us with strong prior knowledge for the prediction of abnormal data. During the capturing of data, we can compare current actual data with the original prediction result gotten by ANN. If prediction result has large errors with actual one, we can consider it as an outlier. Combining algorithm 1 with the relationships mentioned above, we can get new prediction result. This scheme has been illustrated in Figure 1 and a more detailed summary is given as follows.

Algorithm 2. Training Phase: 0. Give former data $\mathbf{D} = \{\mathbf{d}_1, ..., \mathbf{d}_n\} \in R^{k \times n}$.
1. Apply Algorithm 1 to get parameter group $\mathbf{P} = \{\mathbf{p}_1, ..., \mathbf{p}_k\} \in R^{8 \times n}$.
2. Regard $\mathbf{P}$ as training samples and apply ANN to get approximated parameters $\hat{\mathbf{p}}$
Establishing Relationships: 1. Get relationships between the statistics of $\mathbf{D}$ and $\mathbf{P}$.
2. Give constraints $\{\mathbf{C}_1\}$ on the critical parameters.
Prediction Phase: 1. During capturing data, apply Algorithm 1 to get $\hat{\mathbf{p}}_s$.
2. If $\hat{\mathbf{p}}_s$ has large error compared with corresponding elements of $\hat{\mathbf{p}}$,
  regard current data as outlier and predict unknown data again with the help of $\{\mathbf{C}_1\}$.

---

4   Experimental Results

We test the proposed model on the data set of 2010 Shanghai Expo, which is a typical large-scale event. We get the data of the daily number of tourists from May 1 to October 30. The data of each day has 150 samples from 09:05 to 21:00, which form the actual $F_i(t) \in R^{150}$ curve.

Given data samples of 13 consecutive days, we set the former 12-day data as training data and predict data of the 13th day. Using the 12 groups of parameters $\mathbf{P}$, we train GRNN and BP network respectively and apply our method to predict curve of the 13th day. We further compared the results above with the prediction results of neural networks trained by data, and Table 1 gives the mean relative error (MRE) of the four methods on the prediction of a week from Aug.13, 2010 to Aug.19, 2010. Our method can get comparable prediction results compared with traditional methods in normal situations.

Table 1. MRE(%) of prediction methods

Date	Predict by **P**		Predict by data		Date	Predict by **P**		Predict by data	
	GRNN	**BP**	**GRNN**	**BP**		**GRNN**	**BP**	**GRNN**	**BP**
AUG.13	2.102	1.032	1.058	5.474	AUG.17	4.295	4.265	0.902	8.307
AUG.14	1.55	5.175	2.499	1.896	AUG.18	4.121	2.686	0.651	2.899
AUG.15	4.266	2.027	1.259	4.410	AUG.19	3.760	1.549	1.042	1.639
AUG.16	0.830	4.359	1.217	2.897	Average	2.989	3.013	1.233	3.932

Table 2. Comparison on MRE(%) of different prediction methods

Date	GRNN+Relation	BP+Relation	GRNN	BP	Wavelet	AR
May.29	**3.055**	**4.266**	36.913	13.660	57.467	20.084
July.17	**1.814**	**1.926**	16.382	10.378	23.654	12.443
Aug.1	**2.136**	**3.041**	41.132	25.204	49.019	46.240
Aug.31	**3.191**	**2.932**	32.758	11.008	106.320	5.799
Sep.11	**1.855**	**2.143**	43.897	21.992	46.979	23.855
Sep.23	**2.780**	**4.645**	20.111	12.620	26.082	55.649
Oct.16	**4.733**	**2.999**	51.307	26.961	26.046	14.111
Average	**2.795**	**3.136**	34.643	17.403	47.938	25.454

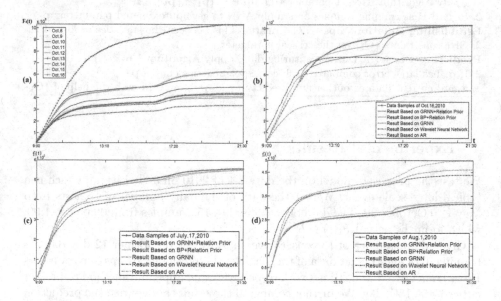

Fig. 2. (a) An outlier and its former normal data. (b-c) The comparison among the prediction result of the proposed method and those of other methods.

The advantage of the proposed method is the robustness to outlier. We detect these abnormal days from Expo data set, including May.29, July.17, Aug.1, Aug.31, Sep.11, Sep.23 and Oct.16. Figure 2(a) gives the participant increase curve of Shanghai Expo in Oct. 16, 2010 and the curves of former days. In such situations, we can update the configuration of parameters with the help of relation priors $\{C_i\}$. When the event experiences the piecewise time point, we can get a prediction to its final situation. If we find the piecewise point t_1 based on current data of $F(t)$ of Expo, we can directly estimate $f(t_{end})$ according to $C4$. Based on the estimated value, we can re-estimate the feasibility of current model and update parameters. Figure 2(b-c) gives some comparison experimental results among our method and other ones, and Table 2 gives numerical results. We can find that our result is much better than those of others in abnormal situations.

5   Conclusion

The proposed method has meaningful applications. Our method gives a robust prediction to abnormal situation, which provides useful information to organizers of large-scale events. The accurate estimation of the total of tourists on that day provides advices on how many ticket-checking channels and security inspectors should be put to work.

Acknowledgments. This work was partially supported by National Basic Research Program of China (2010CB731400 and 2010CB731406) and NSFC project (NO. 60902020).

References

1. Conejo, A.J., Plazas, M.A., Espinola, R., Molina, A.B.: Day-ahead electricity price forecasting using the wavelet transform and ARIMA models. IEEE Transactions on Power Systems 20, 1035–1042 (2005)
2. Specht, D.F.: A General Regression Neural Network. IEEE Trans. on Neural Network 2, 568–576 (1991)
3. Celikoglu, H.B., Cigizoglu, H.K.: Public transportation trip flow modeling with generalized regression neural networks. Advances in Engineering Software 38, 71–79 (2007)
4. Torres, J., Garcia, A., De Blas, M., De Francisco, A.: Forecast of hourly average wind speed with ARMA models in Navarre (Spain). Solar Energy 79, 65–77 (2005)
5. Buades, A., Coll, B., Morel, J.M.: Nonlocal image and movie denoising. International Journal of Computer Vision 76, 123–139 (2008)
6. Eagle, N., Pentland, A.: Reality Mining: Sensing Complex Social System. Personal and Ubiquitous Computing 10, 255–268 (2006)
7. Cristani, M., Murino, V., Vinciarelli, A.: Socially Intelligent Surveillance and Monitoring: Analysing Social Dimensions of Physical Space. In: Proceedings of International Workshop on Society Intelligent Surveillance and Monitoring, San Francisco, USA, pp. 51–58 (2010)

Tourists Flow Prediction
by Clustering-Based GRNN

Yuting Hu, Rong Xie, and Wenjun Zhang

Shanghai Digital Media Processing and Transmission Key Lab.,
Shanghai Jiao Tong University, Shanghai, 200240
{huyuting,xierong,zhangwenjun}@sjtu.edu.cn

Abstract. A new prediction algorithm of tourists flow based on clustering-based generalized regression neural network (GRNN) is proposed in this paper. In order to analyze tourists' behavior, we use the clustering-based GRNN method to estimate the entering rate of each pavilion at Zone D of Shanghai Expo site. The extensive experimental results show that the proposed algorithm exceeds other prediction methods of neural network like back propagation (BP) method on efficiency and correctness.

Keywords: Prediction, Clustering, Generalized Regression Neural Network(GRNN).

1   Introduction

With the wide application of data mining, prediction method, as an important branch of data mining, has become a hot issue today. The prediction methods generally are classified into two categories, the traditional and modern prediction methods, the former including ARMA, ARIMA methods and the latter including neural network, SVM and so on. Neural network is an effective modeling method to deal with non-linear data with the abilities of self-organizing and self-learning. Typical examples of neural network are financial performance prediction, meteorological and network traffic forecasting, learning patterns for anomaly detection and activity prediction [1][2]. However, one main shortcoming for the applications of neural network is the uncertainty of the optimal combination of training parameters [1]. Generalized regression neural network (GRNN), a kind of neural network, which features fast learning and convergence to the optimal regression surface [3], has the advantage of not suffering from the influence of local minima and slow convergence like back propagate (BP) neural network. It also exceeds Radical Basis Function (RBF) neural network on the ability of approximation and learning speed. Moreover, another particularly advantage of GRNN is its better performance with fewer samples because the regression surface can be instantly defined everywhere, even only with just one sample.

Classifying data into different groups arises gradually in many scientific fields such as image segmentation, object recognition, information retrieval and data

W. Zhang et al. (Eds.): IFTC 2012, CCIS 331, pp. 396–402, 2012.

mining. Besides, with the coming of information explosion, models and algorithms for huge volumes of heterogeneous data has become a trend in data clustering [4]. Clustering, as an unsupervised classification method, can divide all patterns into different groups. Generally, there are two kinds of clustering algorithms, hierarchical or partitional clustering. In the hierarchical algorithms, single-link and complete-link are the most widely used methods. As to the partitional algorithm, K-means proposed over 50 years ago is still the simplest and the most popular method because of its easy implementation, simplicity, efficiency, and empirical success. In data mining, K-means clustering is a method of cluster analysis aiming to partition n observations into k clusters in which each observation has the nearest mean. General algorithm for group judgment is realized by calculating the Euclidean distance between the predicted time series and the centroid for each group. The small distance stands for the high similarity. Its corresponding group will be treated as the one which the predicted time series belongs to. Besidesclustering can also be used to detect outlier efficiently [5].

Crowd avoidance is an important part of public safety in theme parks, Expos, traffic surveillance and etc. With the help of sensors for detecting traffic and portable variable message set (PVMS) for issuing warning messages, a queue-end warning system has been proposed based on an artificial neural network (ANN) model to solve the problem of traffic jam [6]. Similarly, we can predict the queuing data by combining clustering and neural networks to analyze tourists' behavior and avoid serious crowd.

In this paper, we propose a new algorithm to predict the entering rate of tourists flow for each pavilion at Zone D Shanghai Expo site by combining clustering and GRNN neural network. We make a comparison of model performance between the proposed clustering-based GRNN prediction and other prediction method, like original GRNN and BP by evaluating the relative prediction errors. The results show that the proposed method performs better. The rest of the paper is organized as follows. Section 2 describes the prediction model. Section 3 shows a typical nonlinear times series, tourists arrival rate of different pavilions in Shanghai Expo 2010, to testify model and make the comparison. Section 4 summaries the paper and discusses issues to be investigated in the future work.

2   Prediction Model

This paper presents a prediction model based on a combination of clustering analysis and GRNN. In order to analyze the tourists flow queuing law and simulate the tourists' behavior, the entering rates of the tourists flow for different pavilions at Shanghai Expo site are predicted based on the clustering-based neural network. The corresponding steps are shown as follows: First, we analyze and preprocess the obtained data to make a preparation for the prediction steps. Secondly, preprocessed samples of different pavilions are divided into different groups by K-means clustering method. Then, each group is used to train GRNN and k different GRNN neural networks are formed. Finally, the predicted time series is classified into a group and input to the neural network with the corresponding time series to gain prediction result.

A. *Data Analysis and Data Preprocessing*

- **Data Analysis.** We have obtained the accurate data of tourists flow for different pavilions in Zone D at Shanghai Expo 2010. In this paper, we choose the data in August for its stability and reliability. Due to the control measures for limiting the tourists flow for some pavilions at Shanghai Expo site, the tourists flow of entering pavilions per hour in one day, which can be treated as a time series, varies from pavilion to pavilion in Zone D. These different time series can be clustered into some groups, each of which stands for a pattern of tourists flow for entering pavilion.

- **Data Preprocessing.** The data preprocessing in the neural network generally ensures all input and output values ranging from zero to one, otherwise the data with different scales will lead to the instability of neural networks [7]. We collect the maximum tourist number of entering each pavilion of zone D every day in August. We sample the data every hour from 10:00 to 22:00 and get 13 sampling points every day. For every sampling point, we divide it by the maximum entering number that day to satisfy the demand of the neutral network.

B. *K-means Clustering among Pavilions*

- **K-means Clustering.** K-means clustering aims at minimizing an object function, the within-cluster sum of squares (WCSS):

$$J = \sum_{j=1}^{k} \sum_{i=1}^{n} \left\| x_i^{(j)} - C_j \right\|^2 \tag{1}$$

where $\left\| x_i^{(j)} - C_j \right\|^2$ represents distance measure between data point $x_i^{(j)}$ and centroid C_j , and n represents n data points. In this paper, we choose the tourists flow of 12 pavilions at Zone D as examples. Referring to clustering results by K-means clustering method and make some adjustment by observing, the 12 pavilions are separated into several groups, in which the sampling data have higher conformity.

C. *Clustering-based Neural Network Prediction*

- **Similarity Calculation for Days of One Pavilion.** In our prediction model, we will firstly calculate the distances between the several sampling points at the beginning of the predicted day and the corresponding portion of other days. Then by making the similarity order, we can decide which group the predicted day belongs to.

- **Clustering-based GRNN prediction.** After preprocessing and classification, we can use the group in which data have high similarity to predict the rest of the sampling points in the predicted day with the method of GRNN.

3   Simulation and Comparison

3.1   K-Means Clustering and Subjective Adjustment

The entering rate for different pavilions of Zone D at Shanghai Expo site can be clustered into three types, that is to say k=3 in k-means clustering, by combining k-means clustering and subjective adjustment. By comparing and synthesizing the clustering results on different days, the final results are shown in Table 1. In Figure 1, we illustrate the three types of the entering rate one day with their representative examples. For the first type, like Coca-Cola pavilion, due to the limitation of tourists' entering, after the sharp rise at the beginning of the day, the flat curve means the entering rate will stay stable. The pavilions of the second type, like China railway pavilion, didn't give any restriction on tourists' entering. Its corresponding curve has more obvious fluctuation than those of pavilions in the first type. Only two pavilions are included in the third type, Republic of Korea business pavilion and people's insurance company of China (PICC) pavilion. In the curve of the entering rate for PICC pavilion, a sharp wave appears during 11:00 to 16:00. By analyzing the curve for Republic of Korea business pavilion, we can find that the great number of tourists who visited the Republic of Korea business pavilion would choose PICC as their next destination considering the neighboring of the two pavilions.

Table 1. Pavilions Classification

Type Number	Pavilion Name & Number
First Type	Japanese Industry Pavilion (#1), Cisco Pavilion (#2), Coca-Cola Pavilion (#6), Oil Pavilion(#7), Space Home Pavilion (#5)
Second Type	Republic of Korea Business Pavilion (#8), People's Insurance Company of China (PICC) Pavilion (#9)
Third Type	China Railway Pavilion (#11), Aurora Pavilion (#12), Shanghai Corporate Joint Pavilion (#10), State Grid Pavilion (#4), City Hall Footprint Pavilion (#3)

3.2   Performance Comparison of Different Prediction Models

Before training the neural network, training samples are selected by making the similarity calculation and choosing the data of five days with the highest similarity. The other following steps are almost the same as the mentioned GRNN prediction. GRNN has a four-layer structure, including input layer, pattern layer, summation layer and output layer. For instance, we select 5 similar sample days with 13 sampling points per day in August to establish GRNN, which means the capacity of the training sample of GRNN is 5. In order to use one third of data in one day to predict data of the whole day, the input layer includes 5 neurons

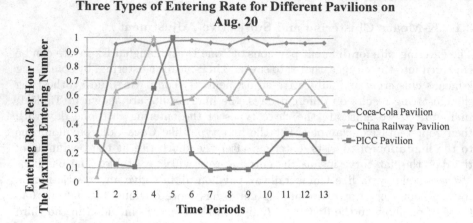

Fig. 1. Three types of entering rate for different pavilions on Aug. 20

representing the entering rate at the initial five sampling points, and the output layer includes 8 neurons standing for the entering rate of the sequential sampling points on the predicted day. A parameter, SPREAD, shows the expansion speed of radial basis function which is sought by optimization method. Moreover, the cross-validation is used in our algorithm to increase the prediction accuracy.

We compare experimental performance of the clustering-based GRNN and other models, and set Coco-cola Pavilion as an example shown in Fig.2 and Table 2. In Fig. 2, the x-axis stands for 13 sampling points in one day and first 5 sampling points are known data on August 16th; the y-axis stands for the actual value and predicted result about entering rate per hour divided by the maximum entering rate. Fig. 2 and Table 2 combined together indicate that in most of the time, the clustering-based neural network performs better than the single neural network and the clustering-based GRNN brings about least prediction errors.

With the table and figure shown above, we can summarize the simulation results as follows:

1. K-means clustering can be used as the reference for classification. The entering rate for different pavilions at Zone D of Shanghai Expo site can be clustered into three types by combining k-means clustering and our subjective adjustment.
2. In contrast with other prediction models, the entering rates predicted by the clustering-based neural network are much closer to the actual values. At most cases, the clustering-based GRNN prediction performs better than the BP prediction with/without clustering with faster speed and higher accuracy.

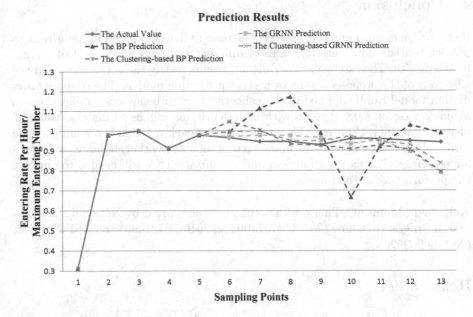

Fig. 2. Compare the different prediction results of Coco-cola Pavilion on Aug. 16

Table 2. Errors of different prediction methods

Date	Method	Relative prediction error
August 11th	GRNN	0.058096
	BP	0.152244
	Clustering-based GRNN	0.035701
	Clustering-based BP	0.043134
August 16th	GRNN	0.045147
	BP	0.124112
	Clustering-based GRNN	0.033968
	Clustering-based BP	0.056512
August 22th	GRNN	0.074652
	BP	0.123005
	Clustering-based GRNN	0.046584
	Clustering-based BP	0.064685
August 28th	GRNN	0.067888
	BP	0.096727
	Clustering-based GRNN	0.035001
	Clustering-based BP	0.083963
Average of Ten Days in August	GRNN	0.072302
	BP	0.144175
	Clustering-based GRNN	0.041610
	Clustering-based BP	0.055952

4   Conclusion

In this paper, we propose a new cluster-based GRNN prediction algorithm to predict tourists flow' entering rates of different pavilions at Zone D of Shanghai Expo site. The extensive experimental results testify the correctness and the efficiency of the proposed model over other prediction models. The proposed prediction model can be applied in the collective human behaviors' applications to avoid congestion risks in zones with high density as well as to increase tourists' visiting efficiency. However, the entering rate of each pavilion is a complex time series which can be affected by many factors such as weather, holiday, and pavilion activities. Therefore, refinement and optimization are still needed to improve the performance of the proposed model.

Acknowledgement. This work was partially supported by National Basic Research Program of China (2010CB731400 and 2010CB731406) and NSFC project (NO. 60902020).

References

1. Lam, M.: Neural network techniques for financial performance prediction: integrating fundamental and technical analysis. Decision Support Systems 37(4), 567–581 (2004)
2. Hu, W., Xie, D., Tan, T., Maybak, S.: Learning Activity Patterns Using Fuzzy Self-Organizing Neural Network. IEEE Transactions on Systems, Man and Cybernetics, Part B: Cybernetics 34(3), 1618–1626 (2004)
3. Specht, D.F.: A general regression neural network. IEEE Transactions on Neural Networks 2(6), 568–576 (1991)
4. Jain, A.K.: Data clustering: 50 years beyond K-means. Pattern Recognition Letters 31(8), 651–666 (2010)
5. Keller, A.: Fuzzy clustering with outliers. In: 19th International Conference of the North American Fuzzy Information Processing Society (NAFIPS), pp. 143–147 (2000)
6. Khan, A.M.: Intelligent infrastructure-based queue-end warning system for avoiding rear impacts. Intelligent Transport Systems 1(2), 138–143 (2007)
7. Yu, L., Wang, S., Lai, K.K.: An integrated data preparation scheme for neural network data analysis. IEEE Transactions on Knowledge and Data Engineering 18(2), 217–230 (2006)

Collision Decoding to Improve the Throughput of OFDM-Based WLAN*

Jingye Cao, Feng Yang, Lianghui Ding, Liang Qian, and Cheng Zhi

Institute of Image Communication and Network Engineering,
Shanghai Jiao Tong University,
No.800 Dongchuan Road, Shanghai, China
{cjy_mii,yangfeng,lhding,lqian,zhicheng}@sjtu.edu.cn

Abstract. When network is congested, packet collisions will happen and lead to severe throughput decrease. In this paper we propose a novel collision decoding method to decode collided packets, and thus increase network throughput. Our method is specifically designed for OFDM-based WLAN network. IFFT/FFT, channel influence and packet collisions effects are formulated as linear processes. Taking into account network features as random-jitter and retransmission, collision can be seen as a group of linear equations and solved. Simulation results show that by adopting collision decoding method, the network throughput can be improved significantly, especially when the network is congested.

Keywords: Collision Decoding, Congestion, Hidden Terminals, OFDM based WLAN, Throughput Improvement.

1 Introduction

Wireless Local Area Network (WLAN) usually applies Carrier Sense Multiple Access and Collision Avoidance (CSMA/CA) to avoid congestion[1]. In CSMA/CA, senders sense the medium at first, then send data when the medium is free or withhold their transmissions when it is occupied. However, collision happens if nodes choose the same transmission time. Without getting feedback from the destination, the collided packets node will retransmit, which may result in repeated collision and network congestion [2–4]. This severely degrades network throughput, especially when the network load is heavy.

Zigzag decoding, proposed by S. Gollakota and D. Katabi in [5], is a promising way to combat collision problem. The basic idea of Zigzag decoding is consecutive interference cancellation utilizing the collision difference of two collided packets. An interference-free chunk of bits in one collision is decoded and cancelled from the other collision, producing another interference-free chunk. Thus, applying an iterative process, interference can all be subtracted and two packets that collide together can be separated and decoded.

* This paper is supported by Research and Development for Commercial LTE-TD Drive Test Equipment Project(2010ZX03002-007-01) and Shanghai Digital Media Processing and Transmission Key Laboratory(STCSM:12DZ2272600).

W. Zhang et al. (Eds.): IFTC 2012, CCIS 331, pp. 403–410, 2012.

However, the consecutive interference cancellation scheme proposed in Zigzag is not suitable for OFDM based systems, which is widely used in 802.11 networks. In OFDM based systems, time domain signals are modulated symbols transformed by IFFT, thus the packets are not chunk-decodable. To decode a packet, the entire interference-free packet must be processed through FFT. That is to say, even if a chunk of bits are interference-free, it still cannot be decoded. When the modulation scheme is OFDM, without FFT transformation, chunks act like noise in time domain and are impossible to decode directly.

In this paper, we propose a novel technique, named as Different Overlap Decoding (DOD), to decode collided packets in OFDM based 802.11 WLAN. We consider the repeated collision of two packets with different time offset, which happens due to the retransmission and random jitter characteristics of WLAN MAC, as shown in Figure 1. In DOD, we formulate IFFT/FFT, channel influence and collision into linear process, thus the received collided packets can be expressed by a group of linear equations. By solving these equations, the collided packets can be decoded successfully. Simulation results show that the proposed method works well in OFDM system, and is robust in multi-path fading channel.

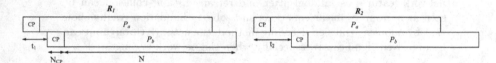

Fig. 1. Packet Collision in WLAN

2   System Model

In this section, we describe the system model used in this paper. For simplicity, we only consider collision of two packets. Extension of our differential overlap decoding algorithm into scenario with more than two collided packets is left as our future work.

2.1   Network Model

We consider the network scenario with an Access Point (AP) and two users, namely, A and B respectively. A and B send data packets to AP with a collision probability of p. When there is no collision, AP can always successfully receive data packets and decode them. When collision happens, collided packets are decoded through the proposed DOD algorithm in this paper.

2.2   Collision Pattern

The collision of two packets is shown in Figure 1. We use R_1, R_2 to denote two received collisions at the AP, respectively, and P_a, P_b to denote the two packets included in collisions, respectively. We assume the lengths of the packets equal to N. Usually, cyclic prefix(CP) is adopted in OFDM system, and the length of CP is denoted as N_{CP}. The time differences of two packets in the two collisions are denoted as t_1 and t_2, respectively. We assume the sample offset is n_1, n_2 and $n_1 \neq n_2$.

In this paper, we assume the channel does not change during transmission and retransmission processes, i.e. P_a and P_b go through the same channel for twice. But note that channels for P_a and P_b are irrelevant.

2.3   Transmitter Model

The transmitter model considered in this paper is ordinary OFDM transmitter which is the cascade of convolutional encoder, bit interleaver, symbol mapper, serial to parallel transformation (S/P), Inverse Fast Fourier Transform (IFFT), and Parallel to Serial transformation (P/S) in sequence. Note that our method can also be implemented in ZP-OFDM with a bit modification [6].

Let $a = [a_0, a_1, \cdots, a_{N-1}]^T, a_M \in \{0,1\}, M = 0 \cdots N - 1$ denote one packet of information bits of node A, where $(\cdot)^T$ denotes matrix transposition. After a being encoded, bit interleaved and symbol mapped, we get

$$X_a = [X_a[0], X_a[1], ..., X_a[N-1]]^T, \quad X_a[K] \in S \tag{1}$$

where $X_a[K]$ represents the symbol at the K_{th} subcarrier in the frequency domain of node A and S denotes the set of symbols. In this paper, we use QPSK symbol mapping method, i.e. $S = \{0.7 \pm 0.7i\}$. Other mapping method can also be applied.

Let F denote an $N \times N$ Inverse Discrete Fourier Transformation Matrix, in which the m_{th} row, n_{th} column entry is

$$F_{mn} = \frac{1}{\sqrt{N}} e^{\frac{2\pi(m-1)(n-1)}{N}i} \tag{2}$$

Let F_{CP} denote an $(N + N_{CP}) \times N$ matrix where the top N_{CP} lines are the bottom N_{CP} lines of F and the other lines are same to F. Thus, the time domain signal will be

$$x_a = F_{CP} X_a \tag{3}$$

Transmitter of Node B works same as that of Node A, and the signal are noted as b, X_b, x_b corresponding to a, X_a, x_a.

2.4   Description of Receiver

Channel behavior can be modeled as a tapped delay line with coefficients $h = [h_0, h_1, ..., h_{L-1}]^T$. Thus, we have the received signal y_n as

$$y_n = \sum_{l=0}^{l=L-1} h_l x_{n-l} + w_n \tag{4}$$

Where y_n, x_n and w_n denotes received signal, transmitted signal and additive Gaussian noise, respectively. We use coefficient sets h_a and h_b to describe the channel for P_a and P_a respectively.

$$h_a = [h_{a,0}, h_{a,1}, ..., h_{a,L_a-1}]^T \tag{5}$$

$$h_b = [h_{b,0}, h_{b,1}, ..., h_{b,L_b-1}]^T \tag{6}$$

The channel behavior can be written in matrix form as follows

$$y = Hx + w \tag{7}$$

where $y = [y_0, y_1, ..., y_{N-1}]^T$, $x = [x_0, x_1, ..., x_{N-1}]^T$
$w = [w_0, w_1, ..., w_{N-1}]^T$, and H is a $(N + N_{CP} + L) \times (N + N_{CP})$ Toeplitz matrix with first column to be a $(N + N_{CP} + L) \times 1$ vector extended from $[h_0, h_1, ..., h_{L-1}]^T$ to $[h_0, h_1, \cdots, h_{L-1}, \underbrace{0, 0, \cdots 0}_{N+N_{CP}}]^T$

$$H = \begin{bmatrix} h_0 & 0 & 0 & \cdots & 0 \\ h_1 & h_0 & 0 & \ddots & 0 \\ \vdots & \ddots & \ddots & \ddots & \vdots \\ h_{L-1} & h_{L-2} & \ddots & \ddots & 0 \\ 0 & h_{L-1} & h_{L-2} & \ddots & 0 \\ \vdots & \ddots & \ddots & \ddots & \vdots \\ 0 & \vdots & \ddots & h_{L-1} & h_{L-2} \\ 0 & \vdots & \ddots & 0 & h_{L-1} \end{bmatrix}_{(N+N_{CP}+L)\times(N+N_{CP})} \tag{8}$$

Combining (3),(7),we get

$$y_a = H_a x_a + w_a = H_a F_{CP} X_a + w_a \tag{9}$$

$$y_b = H_b x_b + w_b = H_b F_{CP} X_b + w_b \tag{10}$$

where H_a and H_b are Toeplitz matrix for channel h_a and h_b.

At the receiver side, in the end, we get two collisions

$$R_1 = y_a + D_{n_1}(y_b) \tag{11}$$

$$R_2 = y_a + D_{n_2}(y_b) \tag{12}$$

where $D_{n_1}(y)$ denotes a function that delays vector y for n_1 samples. The noise terms are omitted for notation simplicity.

We use and $0_{I \times J}$ and E_I to denote $I \times J$ zero matrix and $I \times I$ identity matrix respectively and define

$$D_M \equiv \begin{bmatrix} 0_{M \times (N+N_{CP}+L-M)} & 0_{M \times M} \\ E_{N+N_{CP}+L-M} & 0_{(N+N_{CP}+L-M) \times M} \end{bmatrix}_{(N+N_{CP}+L) \times (N+N_{CP}+L)} \quad (13)$$

With this definition, we can write

$$D_m(y) = D_m y \quad (14)$$

3 Differential Overlap Decoding Algorithm

In order to decode collisions, we separate R_1, R_2 into four parts, i.e., $R_{1,a}$, $R_{1,b}$, $R_{2,a}$, $R_{2,b}$ as shown in Figure 2.

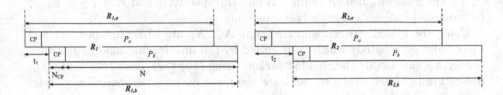

Fig. 2. Packet Separation

According to Figure 2 and (11),(12),(14), we have

$$R_{1,a} = y_a + D_{n_1} y_b = H_a F_{CP} X_a + D_{n_1} H_b F_{CP} X_b + D_{n_1} w_{b,1} + w_{a,1} \quad (15)$$

$$R_{2,a} = y_a + D_{n_2} y_b = H_a F_{CP} X_a + D_{n_2} H_b F_{CP} X_b + D_{n_2} w_{b,2} + w_{a,2} \quad (16)$$

$$R_{1,b} = y_b + F_{n_1} y_a = H_b F_{CP} X_b + D_{n_1}{}^T H_a F_{CP} X_a + D_{n_1}{}^T w_{a,1} + w_{b,1} \quad (17)$$

$$R_{2,b} = y_b + F_{n_2} y_a = H_b F_{CP} X_b + D_{n_2}{}^T H_a F_{CP} X_a + D_{n_1}{}^T w_{a,2} + w_{b,2} \quad (18)$$

Without loss of generality, we suppose $n_1 < n_2$. We combine (15)(18) into one group and (16)(17) into another group.

After some rearrangement and arithmetic calculation, linear equation groups can be solved and the final decoding results are

$$X_{a,1} = F_{CP}{}^H H_a{}^H (E - D_{n_2} D_{n_1}{}^T) G_{a,1} (R_{1,a} - D_{n_1} R_{2,b}) \quad (19)$$

$$X_{b,1} = F_{CP}{}^H H_b{}^H (E - D_{n_1}{}^T D_{n_2}) G_{b,1} (R_{2,b} - D_{n_2}{}^T R_{1,a}) \quad (20)$$

$$X_{a,2} = F_{CP}{}^H H_a{}^H (E - D_{n_1} D_{n_2}{}^T) G_{a,2} (R_{2,a} - D_{n_2} R_{1,b}) \qquad (21)$$

$$X_{b,2} = F_{CP}{}^H H_b{}^H (E - D_{n_2}{}^T D_{n_1}) G_{b,2} (R_{1,b} - D_{n_1}{}^T R_{2,a}) \qquad (22)$$

where

$$G_{a,1} = [(\sigma_a^2 + \sigma_b^2)E + (E - D_{n_1} D_{n_2}{}^T) H_a H_a{}^H (E - D_{n_2} D_{n_1}{}^T)]^{-1}$$

$$G_{b,1} = [(\sigma_a^2 + \sigma_b^2)E + (E - D_{n_2}{}^T D_{n_1}) H_b H_b{}^H (E - D_{n_1}{}^T D_{n_2})]^{-1}$$

$$G_{a,2} = [(\sigma_a^2 + \sigma_b^2)E + (E - D_{n_2} D_{n_1}{}^T) H_a H_a{}^H (E - D_{n_1} D_{n_2}{}^T)]^{-1}$$

$$G_{b,2} = [(\sigma_a^2 + \sigma_b^2)E + (E - D_{n_1}{}^T D_{n_2}) H_b H_b{}^H (E - D_{n_2}{}^T D_{n_1})]^{-1}$$

σ_a^2, σ_b^2 are noise variance for channel A and B respectively and $E \equiv E_{N+L+N_{CP}}$. $(\cdot)^H$ denotes conjugate matrix transposition.

Using the MMSE criteria and assuming X_a, X_b are I.I.D.(Independent and Identically distributed) which is promised by the interleaving module in transmitter, we can decode the collided packets using (19)-(22). Note that some simplification has been made to calculate the noise covariance where we consider the noise covariance to be $(\sigma_a^2 + \sigma_b^2)E$.

When using (19)-(22) to decode collisions, we will get $X_{a,1}, X_{a,2}$ and $X_{b,1}, X_{b,2}$. In order to get the final decoded results a, b, $X_{a,1}, X_{a,2}$ and $X_{b,1}, X_{b,2}$ are transferred into soft values, combined together and passed into channel decoders. The final decoded results are the hard decision of channel decoder outputs.

4   Simulation Results

We evaluate our method in a network with two nodes communicating with AP. Generally speaking, without collision decoding method proposed in this paper, collided packets can hardly be decoded even with the error control code. BER of collision free network represents a lower performance bound of DOD and the difference characterize the ability of DOD to decode collided packets. Thus, the performance of DOD is illustrated by comparing the BER performance of DOD with that of the collision-free case under different Signal to Noise Ratio (Eb/No).

In this paper, we use the 802.11g channel model and assume the channel is invariant in the packet sending period.QPSK modulation is used.We assume n_1 and n_2 are 18 and 50, respectively. We choose N to be 64 according to wifi standard[1]. 1/2 convolution code is used as ECC (Error Control Code), and soft MAP (maximum posterior probability) decoder is applied as channel decoder. The receiver is implemented in MMSE algorithm according to (19)-(22).

The BER performance of DOD under 802.11g channel is shown in Figure 3. In this scenario, the BER performance of DOD is only 5.2db worse than the collision free case when the BER for QPSK is 10^{-5}.

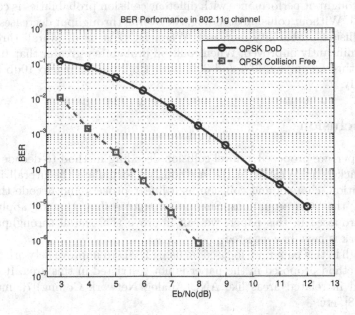

Fig. 3. Comparison of BER performance between DOD and Collision Free case

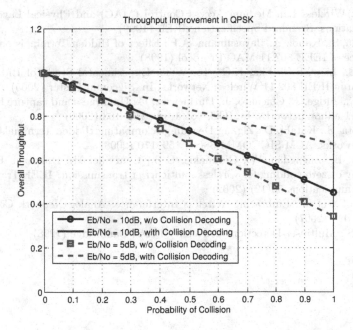

Fig. 4. Throughput Performance Comparison

The throughput performance with different collision probabilities is compared in Figure 4. Without collision decoding, the overall throughput decreases linearly as the collision probability increases. When DOD is used, overall throughput can be significantly improved. When collision probability greater than 0.8, DOD improves throughput by 40% and 30% with Eb/No equaling to 10db and 5db respectively.

5   Conclusion

In this paper, we proposed a novel collision decoding method to decode collided OFDM packets in WLAN. In the method, we formulate the overall influence of modulation, channel and collision as a linear process and decode the signal by solving the linear equations. Simulation results show that by applying the method proposed in this paper, we can improve the overall throughput when the network is heavily congested.

Although in this paper, we focused on using DOD to improve network throughput,the method proposed in the paper is not restricted in this area. It can also be applied in related areas like ANC(Analog Network Coding)[7], multi-user detection[8], etc.

References

1. I. WG.: Wireless Lan Medium Access Control (MAC) and Physical Layer (PHY) Specifications. Standard Specification. IEEE (1999)
2. Khurana, S., Kahol, A., Jayasumana, A.P.: Effect of Hidden Terminals on the Performance of IEEE 802.11 MAC Protocol (1998)
3. Ng, P.C., Liew, S.C., Sha, K.C., To, W.T.: Experimental Study of Hidden node Problem in IEEE 802.11 Wireless Networks. In: Sigcomm Poster (2005)
4. Ware, C., Judge, J., Chicharo, J., Dutkiewicz, E.: Unfairness and capture behaviour in 802.11 adhoc networks. In: ICC, vol. 1, pp. 159–163 (2000)
5. Gollakota, S., Katabi, D.: ZigZag Decoding: Combating Hidden Terminals in Wireless Networks. ACM SIGCOMM 38(4), 159–170 (2008)
6. Muquet, B., Zhengdao, W., Giannakis, G.B., Courville, M., Duhamel, P.: Cyclic Prefixing or zero padding for wireless multicarrier transmission? IEEE Transactions on Communications 50(12) (2002)
7. Kattiet, S., et al.: Embracing Wireless Interference: Analog Network Coding. In: SIGCOMM (2007)
8. Verdu, S.: Multiuser Detection. University Press, Cambridge (1998)

3D Webpage Rendering by Canvas

Shaobo Zhang, Jun Zhou, and Jun Sun

Shanghai Digital Media Processing and Transmission Key Lab
Shanghai 200030, China
{shaobo76,zhoujun,junsun}@sjtu.edu.cn

Abstract. A novel method is proposed to build stereoscopic 3D webpages. This method can bring 3D web experience to 3DTV users with web-based IPTV services. In this method, we use a new HTML5 element, canvas, to accomplish easy downsampling of shapes, images and text. A new JavaScript library is built to accelerate the development process for web designers. A demo webpage with animation is presented to illustrate the capability and potential of this method.

Keywords: 3DTV, IPTV, HTML5, Canvas, Side-by-Side.

1 Introduction

Internet Protocol television(IPTV) provides digital television services over Internet Protocol(IP) for residential and business users at a lower cost. IPTV has two-way interactive communications between operator and users, making it capable of for web applications. Web-based IPTV portal has already been used for easy access and navigation of terminal users. Web-based personalized IPTV services is the upcoming trend of next generation network(NGN)[1]. 3DTV is television that conveys depth perception to the viewer by employing techniques such as stereoscopic display, multi-view display, 2D-plus-depth, or any other form of 3D display. It can be used as the terminal of IPTV systems.

A strong growth in 3DTV and IPTV system has spawned interest in creating 3D webpages viewed on 3DTV, such as 3D video on demand webpages, webpage games, and other 3D web applications. People will enjoy not only 3D movies and TV programs, but also surfing the Internet in 3D and playing 3D games on their 3DTV.

This paper focuses on a new method to create Side-by-Side 3D webpages for entertainment or games on 3DTV. We have built a JavaScript library that works with the new canvas element in HTML5 to help designers creating their own 3D web applications.

The remainder of the paper is structured as follows. Section 2 surveys the recent related work and puts our work in context. Section 3 describes the exact problem and our novel method. Section 4 presents a demo webpage created using our method. Section 5 highlights the main points of the presented work. Section 6 is acknowledgement.

W. Zhang et al. (Eds.): IFTC 2012, CCIS 331, pp. 411–417, 2012.
© Springer-Verlag Berlin Heidelberg 2012

2   Related Work

2.1   Perceived Depth in Stereoscopic Images

Visual fatigue is a common problem when viewing stereoscopic images. Many experiments and researches have been done in order to get a comfortable perceived depth[2][3]. The most commonly used method in industry is to limit the stereoscopic images depth within a certain value related to the size of the screen based on previous subjective experience[4]. In our experiment, we used a 16:9, 42-inch screen with 1920x1080 resolution and set 107 pixels as the maximum disparity between left and right views.

2.2   Stereoscopic 3D on Web

There is a lot of 3D content currently on the web. However, most of it is 2D content generated by 3D models, not stereoscopic 3D.

Since the 1950s, there are sites on Internet using anaglyphic 3D, which achieves the stereoscopic 3D effect by means of encoding each eye's image using filters of different (usually chromatically opposite) colors, typically red and cyan[9][10]. Most of these do not need special web technology and are really curiosities.

On the other hand, the display technology for stereoscopic 3D is available to average consumers today. The urge for stereoscopic 3D content has been growing with this tide of 3D technology. This paper proposes a novice method to achieve stereoscopic 3D effect using HTML5 canvas.

2.3   Webpage on 3DTV

Webpage on 3DTV is pretty much a newly formed field needs fully researching. There is an existing method using CSS to adjust position of elements within a webpage. But it requires an additional downsampling utility in order to get transmitted or displayed. By using our method, one can design a webpage and get the results on any stereo monitor at the same time, thus making it much easier for designer to create their own 3D webpages and games.

2.4   Canvas and HTML5

The canvas element is part of HTML5 and allows for dynamic, scriptable rendering of 2D shapes and bitmap images. It is a low level, procedural model that updates a bitmap and does not have a built-in scene graph[5][6]. Since everything on canvas is bitmapped, downsampling is easily accomplished by built-in functions of canvas. Its integration with JavaScript makes it capable of building graphs, animations, games, and image composition. Nowadays, modern browsers have already achieved most features of canvas. In this paper we present a video on demand 3D webpage with these features.

3   3D Webpage Using Canvas

3.1   Problem Formulation

For notation clarity, we present our method in side-by-side video format. However, our method can be easily extended to top-and-bottom and interlaced video format.

Side-by-Side frame compatible video format is defined in Digital Video Broadcasting(DVB) Frame Compatible Plano-Stereoscopic 3DTV specification. It's an arrangement of the Frame Compatible spatial multiplex such that the horizontally anamorphic left eye picture is placed in a spatial multiplex to occupy the first half of each line, and the right eye picture is placed in the spatial multiplex to occupy the second half of each line, as illustrated in figure 1.

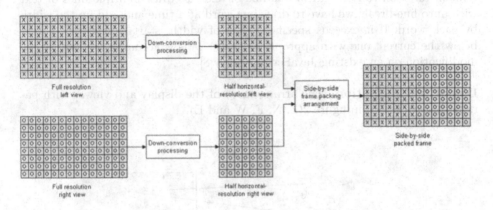

Fig. 1. Side-by-Side video frame composition[7]

To design a webpage viewed on 3DTV using side-by-side video format is to make a webpage with left view on the left half and right view on the right half, both of them down sampled horizontally. Left and right views are slightly different by a horizontal disparity calculated according to the depth of a certain element.

3.2   Our Method

With traditional HTML and CSS, images can be down-sampled by rescaling functions. But it's particularly difficult to get text down-sampled without developing new classes of font with half width of each normal font, which makes it hard to be reused by others. But when it comes to canvas, things become much easier as everything in canvas is bitmapped. One can even retrieve and edit the color of every pixel on canvas. Basic elements supported by canvas include shapes, lines, images and text. Downsampling of these elements can be achieved by different built-in functions.

For rapid development of designers, we have built a JavaScript library named CanvasSBS to provide a layer between web designer and built-in functions of canvas.

Our library defines an additional depth property of canvas elements, with value ranging from -10 to 10. By using our library, web designers only need to specify the value for the depth property of each element and left the work of calculating appropriate disparities to our functions.

Functions in our library calculate appropriate disparity according to the depth value user provided, and then generate left and right views based on the disparity. These two views are then down-sampled horizontally and placed side by side to get the final canvas image.

Text on Canvas. Drawing text on canvas needs a little extra effort since the built-in function can only draw one line of text. To draw multiple lines of text with auto line-break, we have to draw one word at a time and add up the width by each word. If it exceeds specified value of width, start a new line of text below the current one with appropriate space. This is accomplished with some modification on an existing JavaScript library[8].

Disparity Calculation. The arrangement of the display and viewer with parameters are shown in figure 2(Z, N, F, W and E).

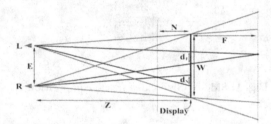

Fig. 2. Notations: Z is the viewing distance. E is eye separation. N and F are the furthest distances each side of the display at which objects should appear to the viewer. W is the width of the display. d_N and d_F are the disparities, on the display, of objects appearing at the limits N and F[2].

Expressions for the screen disparities d_N and d_F are as follows:

$$d_N = \frac{NE}{Z - N} \qquad (1)$$

$$d_F = \frac{FE}{Z + F} \qquad (2)$$

The optimal viewing distance Z is often set as three times the height of the screen. The maximum values of N and F can also be determined according to the height of the screen or through subjective experiments. Once maximum screen disparities d_N and d_F is determined, the maximum value of pixel difference between left and right view is ready for use since pixel density is a constant.

We have defined an additional depth property with value ranging from -10 to 10. Once the depth is specified, a corresponding pixel difference is determined by our function to produce final canvas image.

3.3   Comparison with Traditional Webpages

For a traditional 2D webpage, web designers provide contents and where he wants it to be in order to get a webpage. For our 3D webpage, web designers just need to provide an additional property, depth, to let the browser know where to place elements in 3D. But since the browser only has 2D context, our library will interpret the depth property and get two different views for the browser to render. Different procedures are illustrated in Figure 3.

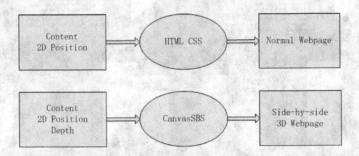

Fig. 3. An illustration of comparison between 2D and 3D webpage designing

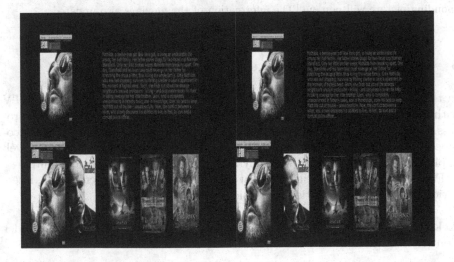

Fig. 4. A demo webpage that users can choose from a list of movies with overview

4   Results

We have made a video on demand webpage using our method shown by Figure 2 and Figure 3. It's tested on a 42-inch 3DTV with a resolution of 1920x1080. Optimal viewing distance is set as three times the height of the screen and maximum pixel difference between left and right views is 107 pixel accordingly.

In the presentation mode of modern browsers, canvas can take full use of the entire screen. The frame of the browser will not been shown on 3DTV. Good animated stereoscopic effect without visual fatigue is achieved in our experiment.

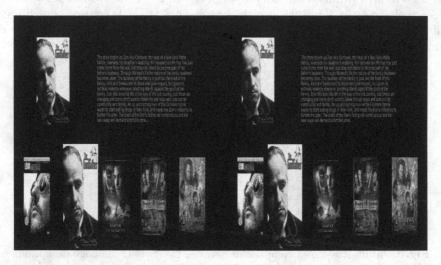

Fig. 5. An illustration of webpage animation. When a movie is selected, the corresponding picture will pop out. The information of the movie is also updated.

5   Conclusions and Future Work

In this paper, we propose a novel 3D webpage development method on 3DTV with a JavaScript library named CanvasSBS to accelerate the development process. By using our method and JavaScript library, web applications with stereoscopic effect can be achieved on 3DTV and IPTV systems. In additional, 3D web applications can be accessed with any 3D monitor connected to a computer.

Future work will include adding features like auto-detecting screen size, interaction by mouse, and solutions to avoid occlusion problems.

Acknowledgement. The work for this paper was supported by MOST under Contact 2011BAH08B01 and 2009AA01A336.

References

1. Choi, J.K., Lee, G.M., Park, H.J.: Web-based Personalized IPTV Services over NGN. In: Proceedings of the 17th International Conference on Computer Communications and Networks 2008 (ICCCN 2008), Virgin Islands (2008)
2. Jones, G., Lee, D., Holliman, N., Ezra, D.: Controlling perceived depth in stereoscopic images. In: Proceedings of SPIE, vol. 4297, pp. 42–53 (2001)
3. Kim, D., Choi, S., Sohn, K.: Depth adjustment for stereoscopic images and subjective preference evaluation. Journal of Electronic Imaging (1017-9909), 033011 (2011)
4. Chen, W., Fournier, J., Barkowsky, M., et al.: New requirements of subjective video quality assessment methodologies for 3DTV. In: Proc. VPQM (2010)
5. Hawkes, R.: Foundation HTML5 Canvas. friendsofED, New York (2011)
6. Fulton, S., Fulton, J.: HTML5 Canvas. O'Reilly, Sebastopol (2011)
7. Digital Video Broadcasting: Frame Compatible Plano-Stereoscopic 3DTV(DVB-3DTV) (2011)
8. CanvasText An easy way to draw styled text into your HTML5 Canvas, http://www.canvastext.com
9. Swell 3D – the anaglyphic 3-D glasses website, http://www.swell3d.com
10. Nokia Maps - 3D WebGL(beta), http://maps.nokia.com/webgl

Context Based Universal Service Recommendation Algorithm

Zhao Zheng-de, Xu Ning, and Zhan Hai-ming

Shanghai University,School of Computer Engineering and Science
zhdzhao@163.com, {295950233,854876775}@qq.com

Abstract. Selecting high quality of service to meet user preferences has become a key issue with the increasing number of services. In this paper, we use the context based universal service recommendation(CBUSR) way to solve the problem of high-quality service. Algorithm proposes a new calculation equation related context factors, such as location and price etc. And this paper also uses the combination of factors to recommend services. Using CBUSR algorithm we can select high quality service that meeting the user preferences. Experiment results gives a strong evidence.

Keywords: Servicing recommendation algorithm, User preferences, Quality of Service.

1 Background

A request can be performed using different services. Facing the increasing number of service, we can't quickly select one service from many services to meet user request. So selecting the optimal services is being studied by scholars[1]. The optimal service selecting theory used to call service recommendation. We studied service recommendation based service discovery in this paper.

Service discovery theory has been studied from two aspects: the semantic information and ontology. Li in [1] proposed an index library-based web service discovery architecture, based the use of semantic mining index database, to search the potential service combinations; Klein in [2] proposed a semantic-based web service discovery technology which using process the process of ontology; Burstein in [3], the technology services function as a process mode defines a process ontology and web services through the index to establish to the ontology(the process ontology). The process of using query language PQL (process query language) to define the query ,so we can use PQL to query the services. Service discovery provides a strong support for the services recommended,

Service recommended theory is more complex because of that not only does service function we concern, but also keep focus on meeting user preferences. TENG Ji in [4] proposed users' personalized service recommendation model that was present state aware, this model can catch the user preferences exactly; DU in [5] used the Bayesian Network and the clustering method to recommend service. Bayesian

W. Zhang et al. (Eds.): IFTC 2012, CCIS 331, pp. 418–424, 2012.

Networks able to handle the uncertainty of user requests' context to match user preferences, and the clustering methods were used to recommended optimization, but it's difficult to guarantee the agents' database real-time updating by using self-learning Agent to track user preferences when the user or service information is increasing fast.

Few years ago, quickly select one service from services is easy. But the situation has greatly changed because of the explosive growth in the number of services, especially similar services increasing. But the problem solved by another way that is recommending some better services instead of selecting a best one to meet user preferences. So the context based pervasive service recommendation is proposed to recommend high quality services to meet user preferences. Here recommended service to meet user preferences is called personalized service recommendation.

2 The Problem Model

With the development of service Universal Computing. On the one hand users require a lot of information services; on the other hand, users are submerged by the huge ocean of services' information. So personalized service is recommended to gradually become a research hotspot[4] when studying the calculation of service Pervasive Computing. How to better meet the user preferences is a crucial key[1].

Assume user request as Req, All services meet Req formed D, which called service area. $Match(Req) = \{Sevice\_D^1, \ldots, Sevice\_D^n\}$ means that Req meet by services that numbers from 1 to n in D. The target is to find the Service = $\{Sevice\_D^k \,|\, Sevice\_D^k \in Match(Req), Sevice\_D^k = BetterMatch(Req)\}$, where BetterMatch is context that needs to define. Context exists in various forms, such as Chen uses the user's context[6]. In this paper, context defined as distance, price and time.

3 Context Based Pervasive Service Recommendation Algorithm

3.1 Service Template and Services Solving Domain

Using the service discovery to collect services' information and using the user-state-aware to analysis the user preferences, after that we should map services' information and user preferences into service template. As following, service template is defined as two parts: main part and personalized part.

Service template=<Main part, Personalized part>

Main part =<ID, <service name, service time, keyword>, < location, frequent periods, prices>

Personalized=< features 1, features 2, ... , features n>

Where: <service name, service time, keyword> is used to find service areas D; < location, frequent periods, prices> is used to calculate services quality in D; personalized supports to recommend service to meet user preferences strongly, then using CSBR algorithm to recommend services.

3.2   The Distance-Related Factor, Price-Related Factor and Time-Related Factor

According to Fig.1, assume that S1,S2 stand for service, Req stands for user request, (x_S1, y_S1),(x_S2, y_S2),(x_Req, y_Req) stand for the coordinates of S1,S2 and Req, the coordinates value are (100,200),(300,100),(100,100). On the map, the points' distance between S1 and Req is $\Delta D(S1, Req) = \sqrt{((100 - 100)^2 + (200 - 100)^2)} = 100$, similarly $\Delta D(S2, Req) = 200 > \Delta D(S1, Req)$, but we can't across the map from S1 to Req, so the real distance between S1 and Req is $\Delta D^{\wedge\prime}(S1, Req) = 100+100+100 = 300 > \Delta D(S2, Req)$, it's clear that S2 is better to satisfied request than S1, but the points' distance between S2 and request is far than S1, so single points' distance can't meet user requests. So using $City_R$, $District_R$ xor $Country_R$, $Road_R$ and (x_R, y_R) express the requestor's location, using $City_S$, $District_S$ xor $Country_S$, $Road_S$ and (x_S, y_S) express the service's location. Distance-related is defined:

$$W\_1 * ((1/1.1)^{\wedge}\Delta D + D\_match) \tag{1}$$

$\Delta D = \log\_x \sqrt{((x\_p - x\_S)^2 + (y\_p - y\_S)^2 + 1)}$, Where x is the scale on the map.

D_match = {0.8,0.3,0.1,0} ,Where   only   if $City_R = City_S$, $District_R = District_S$ xor $County_R = County_S$, $Road_R = Road_S$ then $D_{match} = 0.8$; only if $City_R = City_S$, $District_R = District_S$ or $County_R = County_S$,   then $D_{match} = 0.3$; only if $City_R = City_S$, then $D_{match} = 0.1$; other $D_{match} = 0$.

W_1: distance weighted values, range from 0 to 1

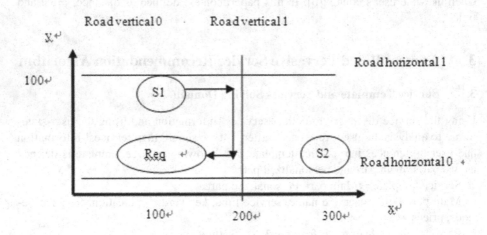

Fig. 1. Distance

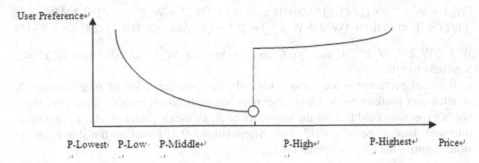

Fig. 2. Price

The price makes the services provided by different businesses with an intuitive comparability. Assume that prices of services is P, the relationship between P and user preferences is "Fig.2". The price is divided into 5 levels: P-Lowest, P-Low, P-Middle, P-High, P-Highest. It's interesting that user do not like P-Lowest or P-Middle, that means too expensive or too cheap things are not likeable. User preferences are inversely proportional to P when P in P-Low, P-Middle, but user preferences and P is unrelated when P in P-High. Price-related is defined:

$$W\_2 * (1/1.1)^\wedge P \tag{2}$$

W_2: price-weighted value ranging from 0 to 1.

We try not to recommend service with lower remaining load capacity in a certain period of time, because it'll give a bad experience. If a service is too busy from morning to night, we try not to recommend it, too. Assume that service frequently used periods as [T_Min, T_Max], user request time as T. Time-related is defined:

$$1/(1 + T\_match) + W\_3 * [(T - (T\_Max - T\_Mix))/24] \tag{3}$$

W_3: time - weighted value of the range of 0 to 1.

T_match = {1,2,3}, [T_Min, T_Max] includes any time in morning, T_match = 1; includes any time in morning and noon, T_match = 2 ; includes any time in morning, noon and night, T_match = 3. For example service frequently using period is [8:00,16:00], Obviously T_match = 2.

3.3   Privilege of the User Preferences

Integration formula(1), (2) and (3) to generate the formula (4).

$$W\_1 * ((1/1.1)^\wedge \Delta D + D\_match) + (W\_2) * (1/1.1)^\wedge P + \{1/(1 + T\_match) + (W\_3) * [(T - (T\_Max - T\_Mix))/24]\} \tag{4}$$

If user preference is distance, price-related or time, the corresponding weight should be increased. This is the privilege of the user preferences is defined:

$$(W\_1 + W\_1^{\wedge\prime}) * ((1/1.1)^{\wedge}\Delta D + D\_match) + (W\_2 + W\_2^{\wedge\prime}) * (1/1.1)^{\wedge}P +$$
$$\{1/(1 + T\_match) + (W\_3 + W\_3^{\wedge\prime}) * [(T - (T\_Max - T\_Mix))/24]\} \qquad (5)$$

$W\_1^{\wedge\prime}, W\_2^{\wedge\prime}, W\_3^{\wedge\prime}$: If user preference is distance, $W\_1^{\wedge\prime}=1$, otherwise $W\_1^{\wedge\prime}=0$; Similarly to others.

But user preferences are variety, not only the distance, price or time. Assume X denotes user preferences in which does not contain distance, price or time. This paper needs experts in field to give the important of X, as user's preferences are reputation, time and price, experts in field gives X(reputation)=0.8. Based on the above discussion, quantify the QoS as formula (6)

$$(W\_1 + W\_1^{\wedge\prime}) * ((1/1.1)^{\wedge}\Delta D + D\_match) + (W\_2 + W\_2^{\wedge\prime}) * (1/1.1)^{\wedge}P +$$
$$\{1/(1 + T\_match) + (W\_3 + W\_3^{\wedge\prime}) * [(T - (T\_Max - T\_Mix))/24]\} + X \qquad (6)$$

4   Logistics Experiment

Established North-East coordinate system on the logistics map Fig.3, "RH" indicate horizontal road, "RV" indicate vertical road, "R + numbers" indicate other types of road. S indicates logistics service, R indicates user request. Labeling rules: S_i for the service delivery area($i \in [1,22]$).Description of service information. The closer the distance from the center of the circle, the more user access in the night, but the more leisure in the morning, such as S4 that is too busy when user access in the night, but S4 is leisure when user access in the morning; service providers: the average user access to the load capacity of 1,000. The area R_i for the service requester is divided into three categories, $R_1 \sim R_6$ in circle, $R_7 \sim R_{11}$ between circle and $R_{12} \sim R_{22}$ outside the circle, $R_i(i \in [1,6])$ is divided into four regions: $R_i^1, R_i^2, R_i^3, R_i^4$.

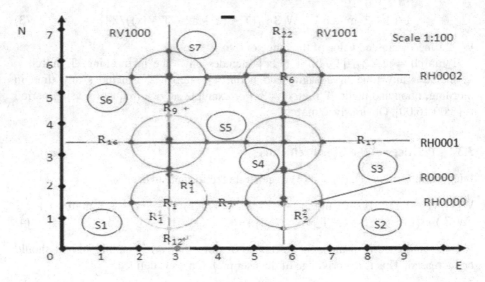

Fig. 3. Road

When the service requester in different regions, the recommended results will be different, due to space reasons, table 1 only displays part of the results, the following table is the same reason. $W_1=W_2=W_3 = 1/3$. Table 1 shows that using the CSBR algorithm to recommend services to meet user preferences at the same time in different locations(P parameter and T parameter are same in (5)).

Table 1. The same request to different locations of service recommended

Area	R_1	R_6	R_7	R_9	R_{16}	R_{17}	R_{22}
Ranking	S1, S7, S2	S7, S4, S6	S2, S1, S4	S7, S5, S6	S5, S4, S6	S4, S5, S3	S4, S7, S5

Table 2 shows that using the CSBR algorithm to recommend services to meet differenct user preferences in same locations at different time.

Table 2. R_2^2 Regional Service Recommendation Form

Requests Numbers	Request time			User preferences		Privilege
-	Morning	Noon	Night	Price($W_2' = 1$)	Time($W_3' = 1$)	Reputation X(Reputation)=1
0-99	S4, S2, S3	S4, S2, S3	S4, S2, S3	S2, S3, S1	S4, S2, S3	S3, S5, S4
100-999	S4, S2, S3	S2, S3,S5	S4, S2, S3	S2, S3, S1	S4, S2, S3	S3, S5, S4
1000-9999	S4, S2, S3	S2, S3,S5	S2, S3,S5	S2, S3, S1	S2, S3, S1	S3, S2, S1
10000-	S2, S3,S1	S2, S3,S1	S2, S3,S1	S2, S3,S1	S2, S3,S1	S3, S2, S1

When request number is high, the result of the request small changes, and better meet the request with the user preferences. Fig.4 shows users' satisfaction with CSBR algorithm (10 is the top).

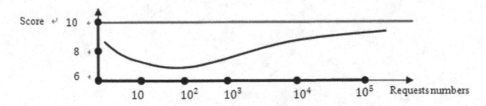

Fig. 4. Users' satisfaction with CSBR algorithm

Using CSBR algorithm to recommend high-quality service can meet most users' preferences strongly.

5 Conclusion

Selecting the high quality of service to meet user preferences has become a key issue with the increasing interests in the servicing of similar functions. In this paper, this paper studies the basic theory of pervasive service recommendation, proposes the context based pervasive service recommendation algorithm to solve the problem of high-quality service selection. Firstly, using user-state-aware to analysis the user preferences, and map user preferences to service template, part of service template is from context, in service template, <service name, service time, keyword> is used to find service set (D) which meets user preference; <location, frequent periods, prices> defined as context, then using context combination to recommend services in D and user preference as a plus.

References

1. Li, C.-B.: Web Service Discovery Recearch Based on Index. Beijing University of Posts and Telecommunications (2011)
2. Klein, M., Bernstein, A.: Searching services on the semantic Web using process ontologies. In: Isabel, C. (ed.) Proc. of the Int'l Semantic Web Working Symp., pp. 159–172. IOS Press, Amsterdam (2001)
3. Burstein, M.H., Hobbs, J.R., Lassila, O., Martin, D., McDermott, D.V., McIlraith, S.A., Narayanan, S., Paolucci, M., Payne, T., Sycara, K.: DAML-S: Web service description for the semantic Web. In: Proc. of the Int'l Semantic Web Conf., pp. 348–363 (2002)
4. Teng, J.: Study of Personalized Recommendation Model Based on the User-State Awareness. Xiangtan University (2009)
5. Du, J., Ye, J., Shi, H.-Z., He, Z., Zhu, Z.-M.: Research on Multi-Agent Service Recommendation Mechanism Based on Bayesian Network. Computer Science 4(37), 208–211 (2010)
6. Chen, A.: Context-awre collaborative filtering system:Predicting the user's preference in the ubiquitous computing environment. In: First International Workshop on Location-and Context-Awareness, pp. 244–253 (2005)

Pointing Hand Distinction by Improved HOG and Wavelet Multi-scale Transform

Yong-Jie Shi[1], Ye-Peng Guan[1,2], and Jin-Hui Du[1]

[1] School of Communication and Information Engineering, Shanghai University
[2] Key Laboratory of Advanced Displays and System Application, Ministry of Education

Abstract. In order to improve the accuracy of distinguish left hands and right ones from a single fixed camera, this paper proposes a new method to deal with it. The method is based on the combination of improved histograms of oriented gradient (HOG) and wavelet multi-scale transform (WMT). By using multi-scale transform to extract the image edge information, the image global edge can be described well. HOG descriptor is improved to simplify the calculating procedure. We use it to extract the detail features of the image edge. Supported vector machine is used to classify left pointing hand, right pointing hand and negative one. Experiment result demonstrates that the proposal increases 23.1% in accuracy rate comparing with the performance of edge orientation histogram. Meanwhile, it is not only less time-consuming than that of HOG, but also has higher performance.

Keywords: Wavelet multi-scale transform, pointing hand distinction.

1   Introduction

Pointing gesture is one of simpler and more effective model for Human Computer Interaction (HCI) among other computer vision gestures [1-4]. It draws much attention from the public. Before recognizing pointing gesture, the first step usually is to judge which person with which hand performs the pointing behavior. When the scene is with multiple persons, the two adjacent with pointing hand, one using left hand, the other using right one. The two hands are close. It is hard to judge which one is the wanted one. Judging which one uses left hand or right hand can mark the two different persons. Therefore, it is a feasible way to judge which person is the wanted one. Discriminating left hands or right hands is a key element to further study the pointing gesture characteristics. There are mainly two kinds of methods to solve this problem. One is based on image sharp of boundary contour. The other is based on image local textural features. The former includes spindle direction descriptor, curvature descriptor, and multiple contours [5]. Snidaro and Foresti [6] proposed fast Euler numbers for shortening the calculating time. Grundmann et al. [7] used shape context algorithm to recognize the spatial and temporal details of human body. Wang et al. [8] took wavelet descriptor to detect edge and it performed well. The latter covered Local Binary Pattern (LBP) descriptor, which was used for texture classification by Guo et al. [9]. Histograms of oriented gradient (HOG) descriptor

W. Zhang et al. (Eds.): IFTC 2012, CCIS 331, pp. 425–431, 2012.

proposed by Dalal and Triggs [10], concerns about the local detail features of an image. It works as making statistics of gradient intensity of image local areas. However, it cannot wholly describe global edge features of an image very well.

To extract image edge information as soon as possible, we propose a method that combines with the image global features and local features. The HOG descriptor is improved to extract image local features and it is less time-consuming than the original one proposed in [10]. Besides, Wavelet Multi-scale Transform (WMT) is used to describe image global edge and edge orientation histogram (EOH) is taken as presentation of global information of an image. The experimental result approves that the proposed algorithm can improve sharply the accuracy rate comparing with that of EOH. Besides, the time-consuming is less than that of HOG algorithm while the performance is higher. The organization of the rest paper is as follows .In the following section, extraction of hand region is discussed. Edge Orientation Histogram with wavelet multi-scale transform and improved HOG are described in section 3 and 4, respectively. Section 5 shows the experimental results and the analysis. Conclusion section is followed.

2   Extraction of Hand Region

The first process of the task about pointing gesture is how to extract hand region [11]. Therefore, it is necessary to extract the whole hand region as soon as possible. The developed approach is based on the skin color segmentation and motion history image detection [12]. Motion information is used to update the motion history image. It can be described as below. Image plane is divided into 360 degree. When the pointing hand rises up, the angle of its motion is limited between angel A_1 and A_2. If the difference of current time label and the older one is larger than threshold M_d, the motion history image will be updated. As pointing gesture happens, pointing arm moves upwards at a certain rate. We can make statistics of numbers of the accumulation motion frames in a video sequence and judge the area of pointing arm. Then, skin color detection [13] is used to extract the hand region from the detected areas. Fig. 1 shows the images of the procedure.

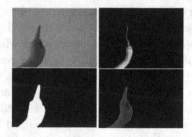

Fig. 1. Extraction of hand region. Original one, motion history image, skin color based binary image of hand, hand region extracted based on skin color and motion history image from left to right and form top to bottom, respectively.

3   Edge Orientation Histogram

Wavelet transform can be used to describe the image edge efficiently [14-15]. The smaller descriptor scale is, the better it can locate the edge. But it is more sensitive to noise. The larger scale descriptor locates the edge worse while it can better suppress noise. The WMT is taken consideration into extracting image edge. In this paper, we use the WMT proposed in [16] to extract the edge gradient information and to make statistics of histograms of edge gradient. The images are performed wavelet decomposition by scale N-1. We can get a C_L as the low-frequency component and D_L^1, D_L^2, D_L^3, each stands for the sub components of high-frequency in vertical direction, horizontal direction and diagonal direction. The 2-D wavelet transformation definition is:

$$W_f(a, b_x, b_y) = \iint f(x, y)\overline{\varphi_{a,b_x,b_y}(x, y)}dxdy \tag{1}$$

$$\overline{\varphi_{a,b_x,b_y}(x, y)} = \frac{1}{|a|}\varphi(\frac{x - b_x}{a}, \frac{y - b_y}{a}) \tag{2}$$

where symbol a stands for scaling factor, reflecting the width of the base function. b_x, b_y mean the shift value of the two dimensions, respectively.

The WMT is used to extract edges in three different directions including horizontal, vertical and diagonal directions. After we get the three different directions edge information, combine them together to get an overfull edge one. The figures are shown in Fig. 2.

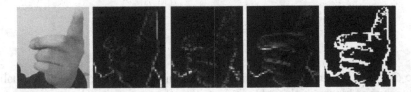

Fig. 2. Extraction of edges based on the WMT. Original image, edge image of vertical components, edge image of horizontal components, edge image of diagonal components, combination of the three components from left to right, respectively.

4   Improved HOG

HOG operator that makes statistics of gradient orientation and magnitude of local areas of an image is a kind of local descriptor which is similar to scale invariant feature transformation (SIFT) [17]. It can present local features of an image very well [18]. However, the calculation procedure is complicated and the running time can hardly satisfy real time demand. To overcome the drawback, it is necessary to simplify the calculation procedure. An improved method is presented that the gradient integral image [19] is used to replace the blocks' further divisions.

Firstly, calculate gradient orientation and magnitude of each pixel in an image. Expressions are as follows.

$$G_x(x, y) = (-1, 0, 1) \otimes I(x, y) \tag{3}$$

$$G_y(x, y) = (-1, 0, 1)^T \otimes I(x, y) \tag{4}$$

$$G(x, y) = \sqrt{G_x(x, y)^2 + G_y(x, y)^2} \tag{5}$$

$$\theta(x, y) = \arctan\left[\frac{G_y(x, y)}{G_x(x, y)}\right] \tag{6}$$

where $G_x(x,y)$, $G_y(x,y)$, $G(x,y)$, $\theta(x,y)$ is horizontal gradient, vertical gradient, total gradient and gradient orientation, respectively, $\otimes$ is convolution operator, T stands for transpose operator.

Secondly, count the histograms of image blocks. An image is divided into several blocks. The range of gradient is set into k bins. We directly accumulate each gradient value with corresponding magnitude value as follows.

$$\psi(x, y) = \begin{cases} G(x, y), & if \quad \theta(x, y) \in bin_k \\ 0, & otherwise \end{cases} \tag{7}$$

$$f(B, k) = \frac{\sum\limits_{(x, y) \in B} \psi_k(x, y)}{\sum\limits_{(x, y) \in I} G(x, y)} \tag{8}$$

where $G(x, y)$ is the gradient with orientation and magnitude, $f(B, k)$ is the normalized HOG feature of block which could eliminate the effects of various lights.

The improved HOG in hand region is shown in Fig. 3.

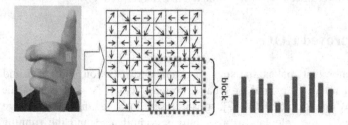

Fig. 3. Improved HOG in hand region. Original image of hand with a sample region in gray, improved HOG in the example region of the hand, the whole example region features of improved HOG from left to right, respectively.

5   Experimental Results and Analysis

The experiments are executed on a PC with 2 GB memory, 2.60 GHz CPU. The code is programmed in C++ with OpenCV under MS VS2010. At the section 4, k is set as 36, B as 16. The block stride is 8. Collect samples of left hands, right hands and negative ones using the single fixed camera off-line. SVM is implemented for training and classification. 1200 images left hands, 1200 right hands, and 1600 no-pointing ones are collected separately. Some examples are given in Fig. 4. They are normalized into size of 48×48 pixels. The proposal algorithm is executed and 1400 features are extracted in each one. We compare the time those kinds of algorithms taken. In Table 1, 1000 features, 900 features, 35-80 features are extracted as EOH, HOG, and SIFT, respectively.

Table 1. Performances of different feature descriptors

Performances	methods			
	EOH[15]	HOG [10]	SIFT[18]	**Proposal**
Left Hands division rate (%)	72.04	98.18	99.32	**98.42**
Right Hands division rate (%)	75.38	98.52	98.89	**99.05**
Time Consuming (ms)	16	17	156	**13**

720 images of each type samples are used for training. We use the left 480 ones for prediction in the test set. Table 1 shows that the performance comparisons of the four methods investigated. One can notice that the developed method outperforms the others by comparisons. The main reason is that it takes both global features and local features into considerations.

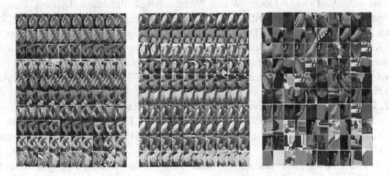

Fig. 4. Some samples collected. Left hand samples, right hand samples and some non-pointing samples from left to right, respectively.

6   Conclusions

A novel method to distinguish pointing left or right hand is proposed. It implements improved HOG and EOH based on the WMT. Motion history image and skin color segmentation are used to extract hand regions at first. Combine the improved HOG descriptor and EOH descriptor to extract the hand image edge information based on the WMT. The experimental results demonstrate that the proposal can effectively and accurately distinguish left hands or right hands. The developed approach can be used in other applications such as pedestrian detection, object distinction, and so on.

Acknowledgements. This work in part is supported by the National Natural Science Foundation of China (Grant No. 11176016, 60872117, 61001162).

References

1. Nickel, K., Stiefelhagen, R.: Visual Recognition of Pointing Gestures for Human-robot Interaction. J. Image Vis. Comput. 25, 1875–1884 (2007)
2. Jaimes, A., Sebe, N.: Multimodal Human–computer Interaction: A Survey. J. Comput. Vis. Image Understand. 108, 116–134 (2007)
3. Sebe, N., Cohen, I., Gevers, T., Huang, T.S.: Emotion Recognition Based on Joint Visual and Audio Cues. In: 18th International Conference on Pattern Recognition, pp. 1136–1139. IEEE Press, New York (2006)
4. Zeng, Z.H., Tu, J.L., Liu, M., Huang, T.S., Pianfetti, B., Roth, D., Levinson, S.: Audio-visual Affect Recognition. IEEE Trans. Multimedia 9, 424–428 (2007)
5. Lankton, S., Tannenbaum, A.: Localizing Region-based Active Contours. IEEE Trans. Image Process. 17, 2029–2039 (2008)
6. Snidaro, L., Foresti, G.L.: Real-time Thresholding with Euler Numbers. J. Pattern Recogn. Lett. 24, 1533–1544 (2003)
7. Grundmann, M., Meier, F., Essa, I.: 3D Shape Context and Distance Transform for Action Recognition. In: 19th International Conference on Pattern Recognition, pp. 1–4. IEEE Press, New York (2008)
8. Wang, K.C.P., Li, Q., Gong, W.G.: Wavelet-based Pavement Distress Image Edge Detection with À Trous Algorithm. Transportation Research Board 2024, 73–81 (2008)
9. Guo, Z.H., Zhang, L., Zhang, D.: A Completed Modeling of Local Binary Pattern Operator for Texture Classification. J. Image Process. 19, 1657–1663 (2010)
10. Dalal, N., Triggs, B.: Histograms of Oriented Gradients for Human Detection. In: IEEE Conf. Comput. Vis. Pattern Recogn., pp. 886–893. IEEE Computer Society, Los Alamitos (2005)
11. Lee, J., Lee, Y.J., Lee, E., Hong, S.H.: Hand Region Extraction and Gesture Recognition from Video Stream with complex Background through Entropy Analysis. In: 26th Annual International Conference of the IEEE EMBS, pp. 1513–1516. IEEE Press, New York (2004)
12. Meng, H.Y., Pears, N., Freeman, M., Bailey, C.: Motion History Histograms for Human Action Recognition. In: Book of Embedded Computer Vision, Part 2, pp. 163–176 (2009)
13. Kakumanu, P., Makrogiannis, S., Bourbakis, N.: A survey of Skin-color Modeling and Detection Methods. J. Pattern Recogn. 40, 1106–1122 (2007)
14. Levi, K., Weiss, Y.: Learning object Detection from A Small Number of Examples: the Importance of Good Features. In: Int. Conf. Comput. Vis. Pattern Recogn., pp. 53–60. IEEE Computer Society, Los Alamitos (2004)
15. Xu, X.W., Ashizawa, K., MacMahon, H., Doi, K.: Analysis of Image Features of Histograms of Edge Gradient for False Positive Reduction in lung Nodule Detection in Chest Radiographs. In: SPIE, pp. 318–326. IEEE Press, New York (1998)

16. Guan, Y.P.: Multi-scale Transform based foreground Segmentation and Shadow Elimination. Open Signal Process. J. 1, 1–6 (2008)
17. Lowe, D.G.: Distinctive image Features from Scale-invariant Keypoints. Int. J. Comput. Vis. 60, 91–110 (2004)
18. Zhang, J.G., Marszalek, M., Lazebnik, S., Schmid, C.: Local Features and Kernels for Classification of Texture and Object Categories: A Comprehensive Study. In: Int. Conf. Comput. Vis. Pattern Recogn., pp. 13–20. IEEE Computer Society, Los Alamito (2006)
19. Baia, J., Liua, X.B., Hua, B.L., Wanga, C.L.: Integration of Sparse Gradient Images for Speeding up Orientation Histogram Extraction. In: Int. Conf. Energy Systems and Electrical Power, pp. 5202–5207. IEEE Press, New York (2011)

Ontology–Based Personalized Service Discovery Algorithm

Zheng-de Zhao, Hai-ming Zhan, and Ning Xu

Computer Engineering and Sciences, Shanghai University, 200072, Shanghai, China
zhanhaiming801@gmail.com

Abstract. To resolve the shortages of current web services discovery algorithm, such as poor matching and difficult to meet personalized needs of users, this paper presents the personalized semantic web service discovery algorithm. Based on the OWL-S semantic web service theory, build personalized domain ontology, and according to its characteristics, to increase semantic factor by gradually, produced three semantic distance calculation methods. Based on this, we designed three personalized semantic web service discovery algorithms, and applied the Online Shopping Mall system. Experimental results show that the algorithm 3 can achieve better service discovery effects.

Keywords: web service discovery, OWL-S, domain ontology, personalized.

1   Background

In recent years, Web services have been becomes a research hot spot in academia and industry, including the important problem of restricting the development of Web service application: how to find the needs of the user accurately and efficiently. The discovery of Semantic Web service is to study how to concept semantic level, parse-and-match user needs and to provide the user the requirement description of Web services. UDDI is one of many developments and solutions that support Web services in one of the most watched. On the UDDI Web service discovery, it is through the UDDI service registrations on keyword that matches the information exactly, mainly on the ID or name of the service, or the service to match the limited values. But as a search engine, people appreciate UDDI Web services registry which brings convenient service, they are often plagued by the low precision for Web services at the same time. The main reason is that WEB service discovery based on keyword matching having the following shortcomings: (1) destination cannot accurately describe the required query; (2) cannot measure coincidence between candidates and query objects; (3) users of personalized information services required cannot be matched.

Efficient and accurate service discovery and meeting the preference of the user has been one focus of our research. Our concepts by building domain ontology, preferences domain ontology, semantic similarity measure method of parameters provided contains personalized semantic search to solve these three problems. It can

W. Zhang et al. (Eds.): IFTC 2012, CCIS 331, pp. 432–439, 2012.

provide a clear object of study for service discovery to describe Web services with Ontology, semantic similarity measure provide interoperability for comparing the candidate services and queries to a degree. The domain name of user preferences can solve users' personalized needs in the service discovery.

2   Related Research

According to which Web services finding and using keywords matching, leading to the problem that service precision recall ratio is not high, the IT industry has quite a few related research: the paper [1] put forward the semantic Web description language DAML describe, using the Prolog language for the reasoning language service discovery system, and the service discovery is based on the predefined service attributes ontology attribute value. Paper [2-5] using the OWL-S defines the semantic web services to create standard vocabulary, and its grammar and semantic are defined by OWL. But this method only pay attention to the service function of the semantic information, do not provide personalized web services discovery, which hard to meet the increasing demand of personalized service.

To sum up, this paper puts forward the individuality of the semantic web service discovery algorithm. On basis of the OWL-S theory of service discovery, it removes the weak impact factor of P (premise condition) in the IOPE framework, establishes the personalized domain ontology, and adds it to the IOPE framework, thereby forming the IOEP framework. And according to the characters of personalized domain ontology, improved traditional semantic similarity method. Based on the above points, it established the personalized semantic web service discovery algorithm.

3   Domain Ontology

According to the different web services description, domain ontology in this paper are divided into four categories, respectively for input domain I, output domain O, the effect domain E, personalized domain P. According to the different conception of each kind of specific fields of application, it can be divided into several domain ontologies. Based on the OWL-S theory, each domain ontology describes the relationship by using tree structure, as shown in Figure 1.

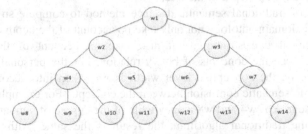

Fig. 1. The structure of domain ontology

Different with other three types of domain ontology, the hierarchy features of personalized domain ontology is not obvious, as the concept of personalized domain mostly parallel concept, shown in figure 2.Represent the different user preference information. The concept on the domain ontology through calculating the semantic distance between the two concepts, and translated into the semantic similarity to quantify the measure of the degree of similarity between the two concepts.

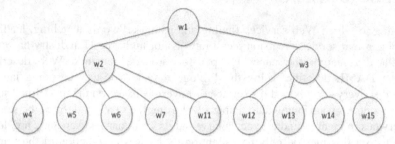

Fig. 2. Personalized domain structure

4   Improved Semantic Similarity Method

Distance in the same ontology refers to the two different concepts exist between the inheritance relationship and binary relationship or the relationship of the shortest length chain of a kind of measure. This method is based on the idea of the concept of distance between semantic with two concepts in the hierarchical distance to quantify the geometric network, giving the corresponding weights to all the items of the tree. The easiest approach is to weight values to the directed edges weight_{edge} to 1.

$$\text{Dis}(w_r, w_s) = \sum_{(w_r, w_s)} \text{weight}_{edge} \tag{1}$$

$$\text{Sim}(w_r, w_s) = \frac{2 * (L - 1) - \text{Dis}(w_r, w_s)}{2 * (L - 1)} \tag{2}$$

$\text{Dis}(w_r, w_s)$ represents the semantic distance. It is equal to the shortest chain path between w_r and w_s. $\text{Sim}(w_r, w_s)$ represents semantic similarity calculated by (1).L represents the maximum depth of the tree.

Application of traditional semantic distance method to compute similarity in the third part of the domain ontology not only take no account of the depth of the concept of the hierarchical tree structure, but also take no account of the inheritance relationship between the concepts of binary relation. For the personalized ontology domain, obviously, the conceptual level width is not taken into account. This will inevitably lead to semantic confusion between the concepts. For example, in Figure 1, the similarity degree of w4 and w8 is inevitable of the degree of similarity of w2 and x4. But with the traditional algorithm, the result is the same. Although meet the principle of quantifiable, but in violation of comprehensiveness and regulatory principles. This article will be based on the domain ontology characteristics to improve the traditional algorithm.

4.1   The Depth Influence of Hierarchical Concept Tree

When two nodes are in the path of the same length, the network structure of the domain ontology level is more close to the top, the semantic distance is more disparity. Otherwise, the closer ontology layer comes to the ontology layer and the description of the more specific, the smaller the semantic distance is and the more similar semantic is. Because in the concept hierarchy tree from the top to bottom, the upper node is relatively lower node sparse and the description of concept is rough. So to define the depth of a concept here in the tree is equal to the concept and the number of edges contained in the roots of the shortest path, namely the level where the concept is in. The concept nodes connected to the side of the weight is calculated as:

$$weight_{edge_i} = \frac{1}{2^{D(w_i)}} \tag{3}$$

The deeper the concept in the level of the domain ontology tree is, the smaller the link to its side of the weight is. It means the similarity of the concept and its upper layer is greater. Formula (3) into equation (1) formed a new semantic distance calculation method. See formula (4):

$$Sim(w_r, w_s) = 1 - \left[\frac{1}{2} * \sum_{(w_r, w_s)} \frac{1}{2^{D(w_i)}}\right]^{\partial} \tag{4}$$

Where ∂ is the semantic similarity adjustment factor, the range is (0, 1).

4.2   The Width Influence of Hierarchical Concept Tree

Based on subjective judgment, the same level concept nodes, the more sibling nodes, and the description of the more specific, the closer the semantic distance is. For example, there are about 380 species of sharks in the world, the same layer of the concept of "Jaws", "whale shark", and "killer whale" should be small in semantic distance. While the essence of certain areas of the concept description is rough, relatively speaking, the semantic distance should be larger. Figure 2, the concept of semantic distance of $w13$ and $w14$ should be greater than the semantic distance of $w8$ and $w9$. So the concept of the classification of the level in detail should also be factors to be considered in the calculation of semantic distance. So, based on the improved of 4.1, we joined the impact of the hierarchical tree width to form a second side of the right formula:

$$weight_{edge_i} = [\frac{1}{2^{D(w_i)}} * \frac{1}{wid(w_i)}]^{\frac{1}{2}} \tag{5}$$

In which, $wid(w_i)$ said the number of the concept w_i brothers concept, namely the width of the conceptual level. Similarly, taking (5) into equation (1), we get the second semantic similarity calculation method:

$$Sim(w_r, w_s) = 1 - \left[\frac{1}{2} * \sum_{(w_r, w_s)} (\frac{1}{2^{D(w_i)}} * \frac{1}{wid(w_i)})^{\frac{1}{2}} \right]^{\partial} \tag{6}$$

4.3   The Edge Type Influence of Hierarchical Concept Tree

Definition 1: 'kind-of' means that the concepts of the relationship between parent and child classes. The parent class contains all the properties and characteristics of sub-class and sub-class has its own special attributes and characteristics. For example, in e-commerce systems, there are "electronic goods", "books", "household appliances" in the category goods, and formed a kind-of relationship with the concept of "commodity".

Definition 2: 'attribute-of' means that a concept is a member of another concept attribute .It is different from the inheritance relationship. The more property is included in the concept or class, such as the concept of 'commodity color', 'red', 'black', 'green', and so on.

We make $type_k$ denotes the kind-of relationship$type_a$, denotes attribute-of relations, under normal circumstances, the degree of similarity of the inheritance relationship between two concepts of the impact of the degree of similarity is greater than the impact of the binary relation of two concepts. Usually take $0 < type_k < type_a < 1$, and $type_k + type_a = 1$. Under the influence of width, we get the third side of the weight of the formula:

$$weight_{edge_i} = [\frac{1}{2^{D(w_i)}} * \frac{1}{wid(w_i)} * type(i)]^{\frac{1}{3}} \tag{7}$$

Where type(i) express edge links two concepts, the value is $type_k$ or $type_a$. Similarly, we get a third semantic similarity calculation method:

$$Sim(w_r, w_s) = 1 - \left[\frac{1}{2} * \sum_{(w_r, w_s)} [\frac{1}{2^{D(w_i)}} * \frac{1}{wid(w_i)} * type(i)]^{\frac{1}{3}} \right]^{\partial} \tag{7}$$

5   Personalized Semantic Web Service Discovery Algorithm

As mentioned above, the web service description contains four types of information: I (input field), O (output field), E (the effect of the domain), P (personalized domain). Each type of information is described by a set of concepts. Each concept is part of domain ontology. By the study of the fourth part, we obtained the third full account of the impact factors of semantic similarity calculation.

Semantic web service discovery algorithms are mainly based on the semantic similarity calculation method. Combined with matrix calculated, it inquires the conditions and the matching of the web services description measure, which according to measure the matching degree that is sorting.

Assume that the concept of user input query:

> Input: A1, A2, A2
> Output: B1, B2
> Effect: C1
> Personalized: D1, D2

Then each service contains its own service description in Registry Center. Assume a service of the service description as follows:

> Input: X1, X2, X3
> Output: Y1, Y2, Y3
> Effect: Z1
> Personalized: P1, P2

First, to calculate the input conditions semantic similarity Sim_I of the concept of A1 to X1, X2, X3 by using semantic similarity algorithm so that the results has been calculated, then do the same operation to A2, A3. We get the input field of the similarity matrix at this time as follows:

$$Sim(A1, X1) \quad Sim(A1, X2) \quad Sim(A1, X3)$$
$$Sim(A2, X1) \quad Sim(A2, X2) \quad Sim(A2, X3)$$
$$Sim(A3, X1) \quad Sim(A3, X2) \quad Sim(A3, X3)$$

The use of matrix screening method for calculating the semantic similarity Sim_I input field, we should take the maximum of the similarity matrix elements each time into the set S, and remove the element where the rows and columns are in ,and do the same operation, until the similarity matrix does not exist, then set the mean of the elements of S . It is the similarity matrix generated in the input field.

Respectively in the same way, we can see Sim_O on the output domain, Sim_E on the effect of domain, and Sim_P on the personalized domain.

Finally, according to the difference in regulating of the semantic web, we get the formula of the personalized semantic web service discovery algorithm:

$$Sim_i = \alpha Sim\_I + \beta Sim\_O + \gamma Sim\_E + \delta Sim\_P \tag{7}$$

Among them, the matching of that query and the i-th candidate services is the real numbers between (0, 1). And that similar metrics in four categories to describe the information on the adjustable weights, usually equal to four parameters, namely web services similar to focus on the same metric in the four categories of description. Calculate and measure all the web services of the candidates, then sort to the similarity measure from the largest to smallest. The top row of web services will be the most one.

6   Experiment

In the web service-based online shopping mall system, we build 12 web services. Each web service description is divided into four categories, respectively are inputs, outputs, effects and personalization. Each category is a concept set, and each concept of in the set is belonging to particular domain ontology, their structures shown in Figure 1 and Figure 2.

The formula (4),(6) and (8) respectively used in the formula (9), formed of Algorithm 1, Algorithm 2 and Algorithm 3.These three algorithms are applied to web services-based Online Shopping Mall system. Set the value of the parameter $\alpha, \beta, \gamma, \delta$ are 0.2, 0.2, 0.2, and 0.4. The algorithms emphasized the great importance on the personalization conditions. Enter the four categories query conditions of "online mall" service. Use these three algorithms to calculate similarity degree of the query conditions and the 12 web services. Calculation results are in the table below.

Table 1. Similarity of the query conditions and services

Service name	Algorithm 1	Algorithm 2	Algorithm 3
S1: online shop	0.923	0.940	0.913
S2: mall shopping	0.930	0.952	0.982
S3: Promotion Services	0.942	0.924	0.859
S4: Ticket Booking	0.828	0.808	0.782
S5: recharge service	0.903	0.832	0.737
S6: Price comparison	0.651	0.672	0.518
S7: Order Search	0.569	0.557	0.499
S8: Help service	0.743	0.647	0.317
S9: Ad service	0.626	0.609	0.349
S10: Account management	0.433	0.419	0.284
S11: Warehouse managemen	0.633	0.608	0.191
S12: entertainment service	0.343	0.308	0.105

From the table1, we can see that all the three algorithms can be calculated the S2 is the best result. But algorithm 1 and algorithm 2 cannot make a clear distinction between the services closer to the best result, such as S1, S3. They also cannot make a greater distinction for not-related services, such as S11, S12, etc. But the algorithm 3 is not present these defects. From Figure 3, we can see more clearly.

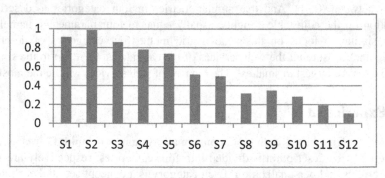

Fig. 3. Similarity calculated by algorithm3

7   Conclusion

Based on OWL-S semantic web services discovery theory, this paper build personalized domain ontology. For the Characteristics of the personalized domain ontology, the authors have made improvements on the traditional semantic distance calculation method. Gradually increase take into account the factors such as depth, width and edge type of ontology tree, design a fully consider semantic similarity calculation method. And based on this method, we proposed the personalized semantic web service discovery algorithm. The advantages are: (1) Service discovery algorithm takes into account the personality factors in making the service discovery algorithm is able to recommend the services closer to the user preferences; (2) Fully consider the influencing factors of semantic, so, the Semantic similarity is very accurate; (3) Service similarity measure is more accurate to distinguish a clear similarity of the different services with the same query.

This study is only a beginning, there are many issues to be studied further. Semantic web service discovery algorithm requires the user to input more information, although the calculated results are better, but the ease of use has to be raised. Next phase we will optimize the use processes of the algorithms to improve the application performance.

References

1. Sivashanmugan, K., Verma, K., Sheth, A.: Discovery of Web Services in a Federated Registy Environment. In: Proceedings of IEEE International Conference on Web Services (ICWS 2004), pp. 270–278. IEEE Computer Society, California (2004)
2. Ankolekar, A., Burstein, M., Hobbs, J.R., Lassila, O., Martin, D., McDermott, D., McIlraith, S.A., Narayanan, S., Paolucci, M., Payne, T.R., Sycara, K.: DAML-S: Web Service Description for the Semantic Web. In: Horrocks, I., Hendler, J. (eds.) ISWC 2002. LNCS, vol. 2342, pp. 348–363. Springer, Heidelberg (2002)
3. W3C.OWL-S: Semantic Markup for Web Services (EB/OL) (November 2004), http://www.w3c.org/submission/owl-s/
4. Peng, H., Chen, L., Chang, L.: Semantic Web Service Matching Based on Dynamic Description Logic. Computer Research and Development 45(12), 2012–2019 (2008)
5. Tao, W., Tao, X., Lv, J.: Rule-based and the similarity of semantic web services matching. Journal of Nanjing University 46(2), 159–167 (2010)
6. Zhang, L., Xia, S., Zhou, Y.: Multi-ontology-based Semantic Web Services Discovery. Computer Engineering and Applications 45(11), 165–167 (2009)

A Circle Detection Method Based on Optimal Parameter Statistics in Embedded Vision

Xiaofeng Lu[1,2], Xiangwei Li[2], Sumin Shen[2], Kang He[2], and Songyu Yu[1]

[1] Shanghai Key Laboratory of Digital Media Processing and Transmissions
Shanghai Jiao Tong University, Shanghai, China
[2] School of Communication and Information Engineering
Shanghai University, Shanghai, China

Abstract. In this paper, we propose a circle detection method based on the optimal parameter statistics (OPSCD). Our method employs fast median filtering based Canny edge detection algorithm (FMFCanny) to obtain edge information. In addition, real-time three points determination circle detection is implemented in FPGA circuit which takes use of the optimal parameters statistics. In this algorithm, the pipeline processing of FIFO and parallelize operation of registers in FPGA detects single circle in videos. Experimental results show that the proposed method is more accurate and robust than the previous algorithm.

Keywords: embedded vision, circle detection, fast median filtering, FPGA.

1 Introduction

Geometry image detection has many applications in embedded vision. The circle detection has been widely used in the areas of product testing, biological information recognition, and integrated circuit boards online quality testing.

As circle detection algorithm inevitably needs to get the edge information, edge detection results play a key role in the follow-up algorithm. Currently, Edge detection algorithm mainly includes the following four categories: (1)classical differential operator, such as Sobel operator and Prewitt operator; (2)optimal operator, such as LOG operator and Canny operator [1]; (3)methods based on local image function; (4)methods based on overall situation. Canny operator is considered as the best edge detection operator as it can obtain single pixel edge. But for the image composed of complex edges, false edges or missing edge information will appear.

Hough transform is a traditional circle detection method introduced by Paul Hough in 1962 [2]. However, it has several shortcomings [3], such as large amount of calculation, high requirement for memory, and quantization interval constraints in parameter space. Since embedded vision system has strict requirement for real-time process, it is difficult to resolve the contradiction between algorithm complexity and detection performance. Additionally, the center of gravity method (CGM) [4] gets a circle's information through calculating mean value of all edge points' coordinates.

W. Zhang et al. (Eds.): IFTC 2012, CCIS 331, pp. 440–447, 2012.

This method will introduce some errors, for the reason that CGM needs to traverse all edge points and some of them may not be on one circle. Chen et al. proposed a fast circle detection method [5], using three non collinear edge points' algebraic relations to determine a circle, on the basis of [6]. However, Chen's approach requires precise coordinates of the three reference points and this condition is hard to be satisfied.

The remainder of this paper is organized as follows. Section 2 introduces the principle of the algorithm and gives a detailed description for their implementation in steps. Experiments are compared in Section 3. Section 4 presents the conclusion.

2   The Proposed Algorithm

2.1   Principle of the Proposed Algorithm

Proposed algorithm consists of two parts in FPGA circuits as shown in Fig.1. The input signal is LVDS serial video signal. First, circle edge image is obtained via FMFCanny module. Then, circle optimal parameters of horizontal coordinate a, vertical coordinate b and circle's radius square r^2 are calculated through OPSCD module based on the input video and circle edge image.

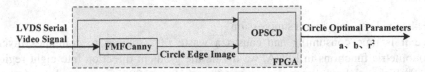

Fig. 1. The algorithm's implementation FPGA architecture

2.2   FMFCanny and Its Implementation in FPGA

Canny edge detection is not good enough especially when the image has complex edges. We improve it in two aspects: (1) Use median filtering instead of Gaussian filtering to suppress grain noise in the image, while edge information is well preserved [7]. In addition, median filtering doesn't need to set a parameter and it is more flexible [8]. (2) In non-maximum suppression, only when the reference point's gradient value is greater than four neighboring points in the gradient direction, it can be viewed as edge point. The algorithm flow chart is shown in Fig.2.

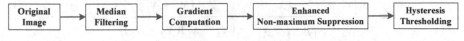

Fig. 2. Flow chart of FMFCanny

1) Fast median filtering
Bubbling method or dichotomy is widely used in sorting elements, while these methods are not conducive to the real-time implementation in FPGA and cannot reflect the parallel processing capabilities of FPGA. Thus, template of 3×3 is used to achieve fast parallel median filtering in this paper. Implementation of median filtering

process in FPGA needs to cache three lines of the image within three FIFOs to get median value of 9 pixels. In order to save resources in FPGA, we use only two FIFOs and one register to get the 3×3 pixel array as Fig.3 shown.

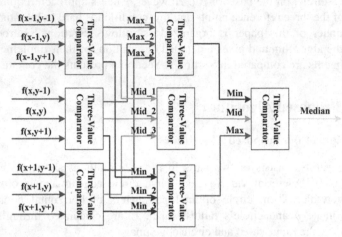

Fig. 3. Schematic diagram of fast median filtering

2) Enhanced non-maximum suppression
Since it is time consuming and causes a waste of resources to computes inverse trigonometric functions in FPGA, we divide the gradient direction into eight regions in 360°. Take gradient direction at 0° to 45° and 180° to 225° for example. In order to suppress the false edge more effectively, the conditions to judge gradient's maximum value need to be enhanced. The pixel will be treated as an edge point, when its $G(x, y)$ is greater than $G(x+1, y-1)$, $G(x, y-1)$, $G(x, y+1)$ and $G(x-1, y+1)$.

2.3   OPSCD and Its Implementation in FPGA

Three points on a circle can determine the circle. Assume that the coordinates of the three points are $(x1, y1)$, $(x2, y2)$ and $(x3, y3)$, the center's horizontal and vertical coordinates of a, b and radius r, can be calculated by formula (1)(2)(3) [5].

$$a = \frac{\begin{vmatrix} x_2^2 + y_2^2 - (x_1^2 + y_1^2) & 2 \times (y_2 - y_1) \\ x_3^2 + y_3^2 - (x_1^2 + y_1^2) & 2 \times (y_3 - y_1) \end{vmatrix}}{4((x_2 - x_1)(y_3 - y_1) - (x_3 - x_1)(y_2 - y_1))} \tag{1}$$

$$b = \frac{\begin{vmatrix} 2 \times (x_2 - x_1) & x_2^2 + y_2^2 - (x_1^2 + y_1^2) \\ 2 \times (x_3 - x_1) & x_3^2 + y_3^2 - (x_1^2 + y_1^2) \end{vmatrix}}{4((x_2 - x_1)(y_3 - y_1) - (x_3 - x_1)(y_2 - y_1))} \tag{2}$$

$$r^2 = (x_i - a)^2 + (y_i - b)^2 \quad i = 1,2,3 \tag{3}$$

Statistical accumulation is presented to choose the largest number of calculated values as the optimal parameters instead of the average value. Fig.4 shows that circle detection algorithm based on optimal parameter statistics consists of three modules.

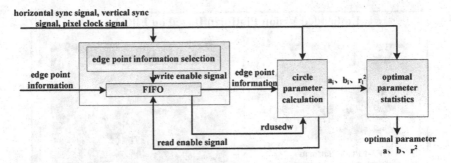

Fig. 4. Circle detection algorithm based on optimal parameter statistics

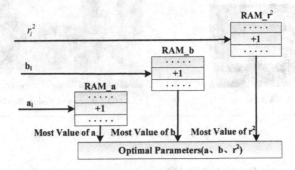

Fig. 5. Key operation of optimal parameter statistics

The optimal parameter statistices is the key module of our method. And we set up 2048 RAMs, whose addresses represent the circle parameters. RAM address is initialized to 0, and accumulate when the same parameter detected. While negative pulse of horizontal sync signal appears, RAMs which have maximum accumulated values will output their addresses as horizontal coordinate a, vertical coordinate b, and radius r as the optimal parameters. The radius can be calculated by square root IP core to parameter r^2.

3   Experimental Results

3.1   FPGA Based Embedded Vision Platform and Its Performance Parameters

This hardware platform is an FPGA based embedded vision system as shown in Fig.6. The camera has resolution of 1300x1024 at 43MHz pixel frequency and captures real-time black and white video. VGA monitor displays in a frame frequency of 60Hz. HD LVDS video signal is captured by Altera DE2 FPGA platfrom through expansion board CLR_HSMC and Camera Link interface protocol. FPGA platform takes advantages of chip internal resources and greatly improves the overall system efficiency. It takes only 0.24 ns to calculate edge information and 17 ms to compute circle optimal parameters, which ensure the real-time processing.

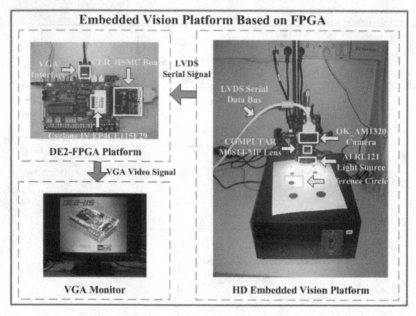

Fig. 6. FPGA based embedded visual platform

3.2   Experimental Results of FMFCanny

In order to have visual comparison between the two edge detection methods, we get simple circle images to do edge detection through method of [1] and proposed FMFCanny respectively, as shown in Fig.7.

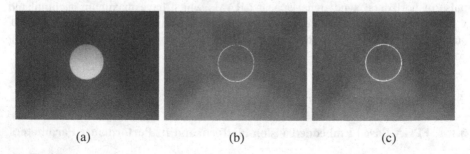

(a)   (b)   (c)

Fig. 7. (a) original image, (b) result of method [1], (c) result of FMFCanny

In Fig.7 (b), there is edge loss in vertical and horizontal directions. In comparison, the edge curve is more continuous and clear without edge loss in Fig.7 (c). According to the results, FMFCanny obtains more continuous and sharp edges, and the false edge is significantly reduced. Experiment results prove the accuracy of our method.

3.3   Experimental Results of OPSCD

Due to optimal parameter statistics, the algorithm gets good results in a simple background, without error caused by circle parameter accumulation and average operations. In order to have visual comparison between CGM [4] and proposed OPSCD, we provide experimental results of black/white circle detection under the white/black background, as shown in Fig.8.

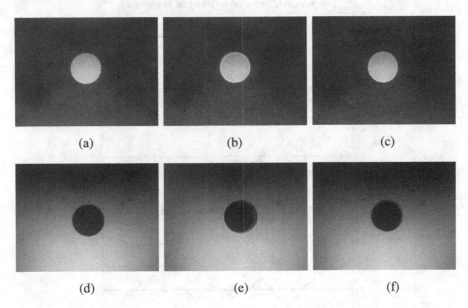

Fig. 8. (a)(d) original images, (b)(e) results of CGM, (c)(f) results of proposed OPSCD

Experimental results shows OPSCD obtains more stable curves and fits the edge of the reference circle compared with CGM. In addition, Signal Tap II is used to record real-time circle parameters and verifies the robustness of the method. There are 20 times computation records as Fig. 9 shown.

According to the analysis of circle parameters, the error ranges of the three circle parameters (a, b, r^2) in CGM are [0 0.59%], [0 0.95%], [0 2.24%], while in our proposed method the corresponding error ranges are [0 0.45%], [0 0.48%], [0 0.96%]. In Fig.9, Experimental results show that, the curves of our method have relative small fluctuation and distributed in the vicinity of the ground truth.

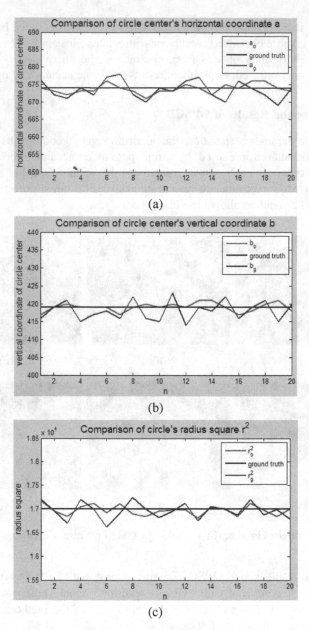

Fig. 9. Comparison between the two circle detection algorithm with actual values in 20 times computation record: (a)circle center's horizontal coordinate, (b)circle center's vertical coordinate, (c)circle's radius square. Where a_g, b_g, r_g^2 represents circle center's horizontal coordinate, vertical coordinate and radius square in CGM, and a_o, b_o, r_o^2 represents circle center's horizontal coordinate, vertical coordinate and radius square in OPSCD.

4   Conclusion

This article puts forward a FPGA based embedded vision platform, and proposes a circle detection algorithm based on optimal parameter statistics. The algorithm takes advantages of pipeline processing and parallel operations in FPGA, and implements real-time single circle detection algorithm. With the module of optimal parameter statistics, it reduces the computational complexity and ensures the accuracy and robustness of the circle detection.

Acknowledgments. This research was supported in part by STCSM (12DZ2272600) and Innovation Foundation of SHU (A10-0107-09-902).

References

1. Canny, J.A.: Computational Approach to Edge Detection. IEEE Trans. on PAMI 8(6), 679–698 (1986)
2. Hough, P.V.C.: Methods and Means for Recognizing Complex Patterns: US, 3069654 (December 18, 1962)
3. Zhang, X., Su, Q.: Fast Algorithm for Circle Detection Using Randomized Hough Transform. Computer Engineering and Applications (22) (2008)
4. Kong, B., Wang, Z., Tan, Y.: Algorithm of Laser Spot Detection Based on Circle Fitting. Infrared and Laser Engineering 3 (2002)
5. Chen, A.-J., Li, J.-Z., Li, D.-D.: Improved Randomized Algorithm for Circle Detection. Opto-Electronic Engineering 12 (2006)
6. Chen, T.C., Chung, K.L.: An Efficient Randomized Algorithm for Detecting Circles. Computer Vision and Image Understanding 83(2), 172–191 (2001)
7. Zeng, J.: An Improved Canny Edge Detector Against Impulsive Noise Based on CIELAB Space. Intelligence Information Processing and Trusted Computing 10 (2010)
8. Peng, F., Lu, X., Lu, H., Shen, S.: An Improved High-speed Canny Edge Detection Algorithm and Its Implementation on FPGA. In: ICMV 2011. Proc. SPIE, vol. 8350, p. 83501 (2011), doi:10.1117/12.920950, (Online Publication Date: January 12, 2012)

Design and Implementation of an Embedded Face Recognition System on DM642

Jianling Hu, Lei Shao, and Honglong Cao

School of Electronic & Information Engineering, Soochow University
215006 Suzhou, P.R. Chian
{jlhu,shaolei,caohonglong}@suda.edu.cn

Abstract. In this paper an embedded system based on TMS320DM642 DSP to implement face recognition in real environment is designed. An AdaBoost based face detection algorithm using Haar features is designed to detect the face. After an active face is detected, cubic interpolation is employed to scale the facial image to the predefined size, and histogram equalization will also be performed to enhance the contrast of the facial image. An embedded hidden Markov model with seven super states and total 36 embedded states is constructed to recognize the detected face. The hardware framework and software design are also illustrated in this paper, and experiments based on simulator and designed hardware platform are performed. The results show that the proposed system can achieve 83% recognition rate under normal lighting condition and meets the requirements of real environment applications.

Keywords: face recognition, EHMM, AdaBoost, DM642.

1   Introduction

Over the last decade, human face recognition has received significant attention because it's useful in varies applications, such as commercial, security and law applications. Notwithstanding the extensive research effort that has gone into computational face recognition algorithms, it still remains a difficult, unresolved problem in general, especially for real environment applications.

Generally, the problem of machine recognition of faces can be formulated as follows: given still or video images of a scene, identify one or more persons in the scene using a stored database of faces [1]. The solution to the problem involves face detection, feature extraction and face recognition. In 2003, a review paper [1] gave a thorough survey of face recognition at that time. Usually there are two kinds of face recognition algorithms. One is appearance-based analysis using eigenface by principal component analysis (PCA) and fisherface by linear discriminant analysis (LDA) [2] or other combinations of features and classifiers. By using those linear analysis methods, the face vectors can be projected to the basis vectors and the dimension of the vector can be reduced greatly. Then the matching score between the test facial image and training images can be achieved by calculation the differences between their projection vectors. The higher the score, more similar these two facial images

W. Zhang et al. (Eds.): IFTC 2012, CCIS 331, pp. 448–458, 2012.

are. The other one is statistical model-based recognition which is aimed at constructing a model of human face that can capture the facial variations. Model-based approaches derive distance and relative position features from the placement of internal facial elements (eyes, nose). One effective model-based approach should be embedded hidden Markov model (EHMM) [3] which extends the hidden Markov model (HMM) to align a 2D image signal with spatial variations. In recent years, face recognition has advanced technically and some new algorithms are published. The representative one is face recognition via sparse representation [4], where a general classification algorithm for image-based face recognition is proposed based on a sparse representation computed by l^1-minimization. Most of the presented algorithms were focused on still face recognition, and usually experiments were performed on some public face databases which consist of fine clipped faces.

This paper pays more attention on video-based face recognition and system integration, where AdaBoost[5] based method is used to detect the face from the acquired video, EHMM based algorithm is used to training the face lib and recognize the detected face, and high performance digital signal processor TMS320DM642 from Texas Instruments Incorporated is selected as implementation platform.

The rest of this paper is organized as follows: In section II, the diagram of the designed face recognition system is presented and the related theories are introduced. Then, Section III illustrates the embedded hardware platform and software design of the system. In section IV we evaluate the proposed system with numerical experiments and the results are also presented. Section V concludes the paper.

2   EHMM Based Face Recognition Algorithm

This paper designed a video-based face recognition system which can be used in real environment, whose diagram is shown in Fig. 1. The input image is acquired from the video scene by a CCD camera or CMOS. Then a face detection algorithm is used to detect whether an active face is existed in the image. After a face is detected, the task of scaling is to transform the detected face to uniform size. And then histogram equalization is performed to adjust the contrast of the facial image. Then the scaled and equalized facial image is input to the model training routine or face recognition routine. For training routine 3 facial images of the same person are needed to train the model. The face recognition routine will give out the identified ID of the input face, and the confidence level of the recognition result will also be shown. Below, each module of the system will be introduced in detail.

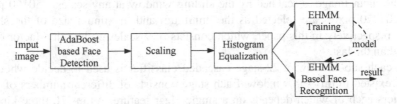

Fig. 1. Diagram of the proposed face recognition system

2.1   Face Detection Module

The first step in any automatic face recognition systems is the detection of faces in images or video clip. Without accurate face location, noticeable degradation in recognition performance is observed. However, face detection is a challenging task because of variability in scale, location, orientation (up-right, rotated), pose (frontal, profile), facial expression, occlusion, and lighting conditions [6]. Though there are many approaches to face detection reported, the AdaBoost based face detection algorithm proposed by Viola [7] is one of the most famous algorithms because of its rapid processing speed and high detection rates, which is adopted by this paper as the face detection algorithm.

The flow chart of face detection module is shown in Fig. 2. For every acquired image, the integral image $ii(x, y)$ for every location (x, y) within the detection region is calculated at first using equ. 1.

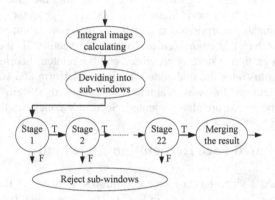

Fig. 2. Flowchart of face detection module

$$ii(x, y) = \sum_{x' < x, y' < y} i(x', y')$$

(1)

Where $i(x, y)$ is the grey level of the pixel (x, y) of the original image [7]. $ii(x, y)$ can be calculated iteratively and is suitable for DSP implementation.

After integral image is calculated, a sliding window across the x and y direction is used to divide the whole image into sub-windows. To be adaptive to different size of face, the input image is scanned by the sliding window at any scales.   50*50 pixels and 120*120 pixels are selected as the minimum and maximum size of the sliding widow respectively in this paper, which consists of 9 scales each with a factor of 1.1 larger than the last.

For each sub-window, a 22-stage cascaded classifier is used to decide whether a face is existed in this sub-window. Each stage consists of different numbers of weak classifiers each of which depends on a single Haar feature. As in [7], three kinds of Haar basis functions with base resolution of 20*20 pixels are used as the features. They are two-rectangle feature, three-rectangle feature and a four-rectangle feature. In each stage, the Haar feature is evaluated according the calculated integral image $ii(x, y)$. Then a weak classifier $h_{j,k}(x, f, \theta)$ consisting of feature f and threshold θ for k^{th} classifier of jth stage is performed.

$$h_{j,k}(x, f, \theta) = \begin{cases} \alpha_0 & if \ f(x) < \theta \\ \alpha_1 & otherwise \end{cases} \tag{2}$$

Here x is a sub-window of the input image. The output of the jth stage O_j is decided by the sum of all results of the K_j classifiers of this stage.

$$S_j = \sum_{k=1}^{K_j} h_{j,k}(x, f, \theta) \tag{3}$$

$$O_j = \begin{cases} F & if \ S_j < T_j \\ T & otherwise \end{cases} \tag{4}$$

Where S_j is the sum of stage j, T_j is the decision threshold for stage j. The output of "F" means the sub-window is a non-face region and will be rejected, and the output of "T" means the sub-window may contain a face and will pass to the next stage. Finally a merging algorithm is used to combine the overlapped sub-windows passed the last stage and output the face location of the input image.

In order to reduce the computation complexity, only 3 and 16 classifiers are introduced in the first and second stage, which rejects the most non-face sub-windows. With the increasing of the stage, more and more classifiers are introduced, and finally a strong classifier is achieved with high detection accuracy. Furthermore, in this paper AdaBoost algorithm [5] is used both to select the features and train the classifiers.

2.2   Scaling and Equalization

The detected face region usually has different size because of the variants of lens, focal length, target distance, and so on. Before input to the EHMM training and recognition module, scaling is performed to transform the detected face to uniform size. Generally, interpolation technique can be used to scale the image by fitting a continuous function to the known samples and evaluating the function at the desired locations. In order to avoid aliasing, an ideal low-pass filter must be used, which is represented as a sinc function with infinite length and isn't realizable in practical application. So this paper selects a cubic low-pass filter [8] as the interpolation filter, whose impulse response hc(x) is shown in Fig. 3 and depicted in equ. 5.

$$h_c(x) = \begin{cases} 1.5|x^3| - 2.5x^2 + 1 & for \ |x| \le 1 \\ -0.5|x^3| + 2.5x^2 - 4|x| + 2 & for \ 1 < |x| \le 2 \\ 0 & for \ |x| > 2 \end{cases} \tag{5}$$

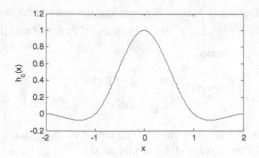

Fig. 3. The cubic interpolation function

Cubic interpolation uses up to four samples of an original signal to calculate the value of an interpolated sample. So it can yield satisfied results while keeping the computing complexity acceptable.

After scaling, histogram equalization (HE) is used to the facial image to improve the quality of low contrast image [9]. The main idea of HE-based methods is to re-assign the intensity values of pixels to make the intensity distribution uniform to utmost extent. In this paper, grey level between 0 and 255 is used to represent the intensity value of pixel. Let $p(x)$ be the density function of intensity distribution of the original image, where x denotes the grey level of the image. So the HE formula is:

$$y = \sum_{i=0}^{x} p(i) * 255 \qquad (6)$$

Where y is the grey level of the output image.

Fig. 4 gives out an example of scaling and HE. Fig. 4(a) is the original image selected from extended Yale face database B [10] and clipped to the size of 120*160 pixels. The detected face has size of 62*77 pixels and is scaled to 88*112 pixels using cubic interpolation as shown in Fig. 4(b). Then HE is performed and the result is shown in Fig. 4(c), whose contrast is enhanced obviously.

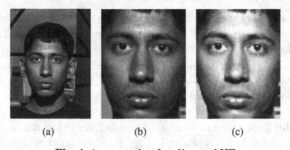

(a)   (b)   (c)

Fig. 4. An example of scaling and HE

2.3   Embedded Hidden Markov Model for Face Recognition

In this paper, Hidden Markov Model (HMM) topology is used to represent the 2D facial image. Different from a fully connected 2D HMM, an embedded HMM

(EHMM) is adopted to reduce the model complexity [3, 11]. An EHMM consists of a set of super states s_n ($n = 1, ..., N_0$, N_0 is the number of super states) along with a set of embedded states $s_{n,i}$ ($i = 1, ..., N_1^n$, N_1^n is the number of embedded states in super state s_n). The super states model the facial image along vertical direction, while the embedded states model the facial image along the horizontal direction. No skipping is allowed between embedded states in different super states. The initial super state probability distribution is defined as $\Pi_0 = \left\{\pi_{s_n}\right\}$, and the state transition matrix between the super states is defined as $A_0 = \left\{a_{s_n s_{n+1}}\right\}$. Each super state s_n is itself a standard HMM defined by the parameter set $\Lambda^n = \left(\Pi_1^n, A_1^n, B^n\right)$, where $\Pi_1^n = \left\{\pi_{s_{n,i}}\right\}$ is the initial state probability distribution of the embedded states, $A_1^n = \left\{a_{s_{n,i} s_{n,i+1}}\right\}$ is the state transition matrix for the embedded states, and $B^n = \left\{b_i^n\left(O_{x,y}\right)\right\}$ is the probability distribution matrix of the observations, which are taken to be finite Gaussian mixtures of the form,

$$b_i^n\left(O_{x,y}\right) = \sum_{m=1}^{M_i^n} w_{i,m}^n N\left(O_{x,y}, \mu_{i,m}^n, \Sigma_{i,m}^n\right) \tag{7}$$

Where $w_{i,m}^n$ is the mixture coefficient for the mth mixture in state i of super state n, and $N\left(O_{x,y}, \mu_{i,m}^n, \Sigma_{i,m}^n\right)$ is a Gaussian density with a mean vector $\mu_{i,m}^n$ and covariance matrix $\Sigma_{i,m}^n$. $O_{x,y}$ is the sequence of observation vectors blocked with spatial indices (x, y).

The structure of the EHMM used for face recognition is illustrated in Fig. 5. From top-to-bottom, there are 7 super states characterizing forehead, eyebrow, eyes, nose, upper lip, mouth and jaw. Unlike in [3] and [11], a super state for eyebrow is introduced for its importance in face recognition [12]. Also a super state for upper lib is introduced to model the mustache's effect. For every super state, there are 3 or 6 embedded states, so total are 36 embedded states considered. And each embedded state has 3 mixtures of Gaussian distributions. The observation sequence is formed from facial image blocks that are extracted by scanning the image from left-to-right and top-to-bottom. The block size is 12*12 pixels and adjacent blocks overlap in the vertical and horizontal direction with 10 pixels. The extracted block is DCT transformed and the DCT coefficients are re-arranged in Zig-Zag form. Then the observation vector is formed using the first 9 re-arranged coefficients.

3   Embedded Face Recognition System

For embedded system, hardware and software usually should be joint-designed to achieve optimum performance while considering the cost at the same time. For the proposed embedded face recognition system, digital signal processor (DSP) is selected as the main processor for its powerful computing capability. The data flow path should be assured by the hardware. And the functionality should be fulfilled by the software in an efficient way.

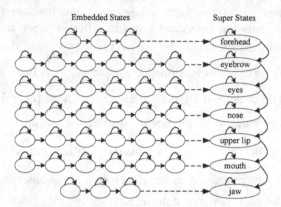

Fig. 5. EHMM representation for facial images

3.1   Hardware Platform Design

Fig. 6 gives out the diagram of the designed hardware platform. The whole platform consists of analog video interface, DSP module, memory module, time-logic control module, communication interface, and power clock module.

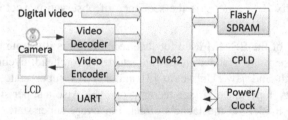

Fig. 6. Diagram of designed hardware system

Analog video interface provides the connection between analog video and digital video through video decoder and video encoder. Two RCA connectors are supplied to input the analog video from a CCD camera and output analog video to a LCD screen. Composite video is selected both for input and output. The video decoder TVP5150AM1 manufactured by TI company converts NTSC, PAL or SECAM video signals into 8-bit YCbCr 4:2:2 component video which input to DSP for further processing. And the video encoder ADV7391 manufactured by Analog Device company receives the 8-bit YCbCr 4:2:2 video from DSP and converts them into composite analog video.

Digital signal processor TMS320DM642 from TI is selected as control and computing core for the system. It connects with TVP5150AM1 and ADV7391 through its VPORT interfaces. The acquired digital video is copied to the memory by DMA and processed by the software.

The platform supports three memory spaces. They are SDRAM space, FLASH space, CPLD and UART space. SDRAM space contains 32M bytes with data bus width of 64 bits which consists of two 4M*32bit SDRAM chip. A 4M*8bit NOR FLASH is used in this platform to store the booting code and application program. The third space is for CPLD registers and UART communication, which is also allocated in the asynchronous memory space of DM642 as FLASH but with different address space.

CPLD is in charge of timing, logic control, data buffering, and so on. Eight control and status registers are implemented in the CPLD to extend the system function. Also the UART communication is under the control of CPLD. A standard DB9 male connector is adopted for UART interface. And the maximum supported baud rate is 115.2k.

The system accepts 5V DC as power supply. And 3 DC-DC voltage regulators are used to generate 3.3V, 1.8V, and 1.4V power sources for different parts.

3.2   Software Design

Structured programming technique is employed in this system. Different functionality is packaged in a module and called by the main routine. A state machine is designed to drive the whole system, which is excited by the event. Four events are employed in the system, including video input, video output, command receiving, and error event. The flags of these events are set by the corresponding interrupt service routines and checked by the main routine. When a flag is set, its processing routine will be called by the main routine and the flag will also be cleared. Fig. 7 gives out the flow chart of the main routine.

After booting from FLASH memory, the main routine initializes the system at first, including hardware initialization and software initialization. The DMA, CACHE, VPORT and other hardware modules will be set to the predefined state during hardware initialization. During software initialization, the lib will be loaded from FLASH memory, the data structures will be initialized, and the state machine will be reset. After initialization, the face detection will be performed on the received video. Then different modules will be called according to the state, which are face recognition module (FACE_REC), face acquisition and face model training (ACQ_TRAIN), and idle operation (IDLE). After that, the command from host through UART will be analyzed and processed. If "Stop" command is received, then the main routine will clear the environment and quit, else it will return to face detection module and execute repetitively.

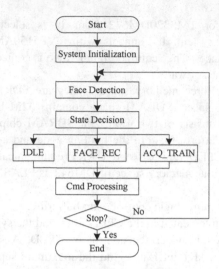

Fig. 7. Flowchart of system software

4   Experiments and Analysis

In this paper, two kinds of experiments are performed to evaluate the system performance. One is based on simulator in CCS, which is an integrated development environment provided by TI,   and the other is based on the designed board.

When in simulator mode, the extended Yale face database B is used to test the recognition performance. Nineteen images of each target in the database are selected, whose light source directions with respect to the camera axis are between -25 to 25 degrees azimuth ($-25 \leq A \leq 25$) and -25 to 25 degrees elevation ($-25 \leq E \leq 25$). Among these 19 images, three images with light source directions of (A=0, E=0), (A= -10, E=0), and (A=10, E=0) are selected to train the EHMM model, and the remained 16 images are used to test the performance. The experiments results show that the recognition rate can be up to 96.6% under such lighting condition. Furthermore, when the light source directions are limited between $-10 \leq A \leq 10$ and $-10 \leq E \leq 10$, the recognition rate can be 100%.

The memory requirements and computing complexity are also evaluated, and the results are shown in Table 1 and Table 2. From Table 1, we can see that total memory requirements are (0x1eafcc+0x8ee8*N) bytes, where N is the number of persons allowed by the system, which is limited by the size of FLASH memory. Table 2 shows that running one time of face detection needs about 30M cycles when the detection region is set to 120*160 pixels. So on the DM642 running in 600MHz clock rate, about 20 frames per second can be performed. The complexity of face recognition is 31.4M cycles, which means for a lib containing 50 persons, only less than 3 seconds are needed to give out the recognition result, which meets the requirement of real environment applications.

The performance of the whole system is also evaluated in the lab. The results show that the average recognition rate can be up to 83% under normal lighting condition.

Table 1. Memory requirements

Content	Memory(Bytes)	Content	Memory(Bytes)
Program	0x16e20	Haar lib	0x440e8
Stack	0x2000	EHMM	0x1b68*N
Heap	0x140400	Face lib	0x7380*N
Table	0x1dc4	i/o buffer	0x4bf00

Table 2. Computing complexity

Module	Cycles
Face detection	29.33M
Face recognition	31.40M

5   Conclusion

In this paper, a DSP based face recognition system is proposed, which consists of video acquisition, video display, face detection, size scaling and histogram equalization, model training, and face recognition. The system accepts NTSC, PAL, SECAM analog video or digital video as input, and recognizes the detected face under the control of the host through UART interface. An EHMM with 7 super states and total 36 embedded states is constructed for face recognition, which can model the human face efficiently. The hardware platform is designed and implemented. Lots of optimizations are performed on software programming and transplanting. Finally variants experiments are carried out to evaluate the performance of the designed system. For extended Yale face database B, 96.6% recognition rate is achieved when the light source direction are limited between ±25 degrees. For real environment, the designed system can achieve up to 83% recognition rate under normal lighting condition, and the recognition time is less than 3 seconds with a lib of 50 persons.

Acknowledgment. This research is partly sponsored by the Applied Fundamental Research Plan of Suzhou, China (SYG201031) and TI's University Program. And the authors would also give thanks to those who provided the public face databases.

References

1. Zhao, W., Chellappa, R., Phillips, P.J., Rosenfeld, A.: Face Recognition: A Literature Survey. ACM Computing Surveys 35(4), 399–458 (2003)
2. Belhumeur, P.N., Hespanha, J.P., Kriegman, D.J.: Eigenfaces vs. Fisherfaces: Recognition Using Class Specific Linear Projection. IEEE Trans. on Pattern Analysis and Machine Intelligence 19(7), 711–720 (1997)
3. Nefian, A., Hayes III, M.H.: Maximum Likelihood Training of the Embedded HMM For Face Detection and Recognition. In: Proc. Int'l Conf. Image Processing (2000)

4. Wright, J., Yang, A.Y., Ganesh, A., Sastry, S.S., Ma, Y.: Robust Face Recognition via Sparse Representation. IEEE Trans. on Pattern Analysis and Machine Intelligence 21(2), 210–227 (2009)
5. Freund, Y., Schapire, R.E.: A Decision-Theoretic Generalization of On-Line Learning and an Application to Boosting. Journal of Computer and System Sciences 55(1), 119–139 (1997)
6. Yang, M., Kriegman, D.J., Ahuja, N.: Detecting Faces in Images: A Survey. IEEE Trans. on Pattern Analysis and Machine Intelligence 24(1), 34–58 (2002)
7. Viola, P., Jones, M.J.: Robust Real-Time Face Detection. International Journal of Computer Vision 57(2), 137–154 (2004)
8. Gallagher, A.C.: Detection of Linear and Cubic Interpolation in JPEG Compressed Images. In: Proceedings of the 2nd Canadian Conference on Computer and Robot Vision, pp. 65–72 (May 2005)
9. Cheng, H.D., Shi, X.J.: A simple and effective histogram equalization approach to image enhancement. Digital Signal Processing 14(2), 158–170 (2004)
10. Georghiades, A., Belhumeur, P., Kriegman, D.: From few to many: Illumination cone models for face recognition under variable lighting and pose. IEEE Trans. on Pattern Analysis and Machine Intelligence 23(6), 643–660 (2001)
11. Chien, J., Liao, C.: Maximum Confidence Hidden Markov Modeling for Face Recognition. IEEE Trans. on Pattern Analysis and Machine Intelligence 30(4), 606–616 (2008)
12. Sinha, P., Balas, B., Ostrovsky, Y., Russell, R.: Face Recognition by Humans: Nineteen Results All Computer Vision Researchers Should Know About. Proc. of the IEEE 94(11), 1948–1962 (2006)

A Local Stereo Matching Algorithm
Based on Region Growing

Pei Wang and Fang Wu*

College of Mechanical and Electronic Engineering
Shanghai Normal University

Abstract. Stereo matching is an important part in stereo vision. For traditional matching algorithm having difficulties to satisfy both accuracy and speed, a novel local stereo matching algorithm is presented in this paper. Firstly, an initial disparity estimation is obtained by using dynamic window of region growing algorithm based on color constraint for matching. On the other side, a simple but efficient way is proposed to further improve matching accuracy without adding additional computational work. Experimental results show that the algorithm we presented can not only get a more accurate disparity map at repetitive areas and depth discontinuities but also meet the need of real-time.

Keywords: color similarity, stereo matching, region connectivity, real-time.

1   Introduction

Stereo matching which gets disparity information from a scene of two images is one of the important problems in stereo vision, it is widely used in many important areas such as robotics, three dimension space object track and model reconstruction [1].

Stereo matching is a major technical method which gets depth information from different view images. Stereo matching algorithm can be categorized into local stereo matching algorithm and global stereo matching algorithm according to different optimal methods. Global matching algorithm including belief propagation, dynamic programming, graph-cut, is too complex to meet the real needs despite of high precision [5].

Local stereo matching algorithm is to find corresponding pixels from two or more images. The size and shape of support window is crucial and difficult to choose since it implies all pixels in a support window are having the similar depth in a scene. The size should be large enough to gain enough intensity variation in order to avoid the image ambiguity. However, it should also be small enough to include only pixels of similar disparities to avoid "foreground-fattening" which is caused at depth discontinuities [6]. In order to assign an appropriate window for each pixel, we hope the support window could include all the pixels that have similar disparities of center pixel and eliminate those pixels of   different disparities. To this end, many methods

---

* Corresponding author.

W. Zhang et al. (Eds.): IFTC 2012, CCIS 331, pp. 459–464, 2012.
© Springer-Verlag Berlin Heidelberg 2012

have been proposed. Kanade and Okutomi [7] proposed an adaptive window method by computing the local variation of intensity and disparity, which is sensitive to initial disparity estimate and computationally expensive. Fusiello [8] designed nine different types of windows for each pixel, and retained the disparity with the smallest matching cost. However, due to its limited windows types, it couldn't represent all the shapes of the windows. YOON [9] proposed an adaptive-weight matching algorithm by assigning different support weights based on color similarity and space distance for each pixel to realize adaptive "segmentation", Though this approach gets a good result, it is time consuming and can't be used in real-time system. Based on what we have talked above, we proposed a novel stereo matching method based on color. Our algorithm can divide into two steps: initial disparity estimate and disparity refinement. Firstly, a dynamic shape and sizes of windows based on region connectivity is presented to improve matching accuracy, Secondly, we proposed a simple but efficient way to improve our algorithm accuracy from initial disparity map based on color information without adding additional computational work.

2   Proposed Algorithm

For traditional matching algorithm having difficulties to meet both accuracy and speed, a region growing algorithm which improved weight factor by using region connectivity and color similarity is presented firstly, then a simple but effective method is proposed for further refinement by using the results of color similarity.

2.1   Region Growing Algorithm

In order to improve the matching accuracy of repetitive area and depth discontinuities, a region growing algorithm is introduced. By using this method we can separate the pixels near to center pixel but not in a region from the center one, and count the number of the pixels which is satisfied to further improve the matching result.

Algorithm [9] thought support weight has close relationship with color similarity and geometric proximity, pixels with similar color and short distance of center pixel would be given high weight. As shown in Fig.1, let's consider weight effect of pixel b and c to pixel a separately. Fig.1(a) is original image. (b) is support-weight map using algorithm [9]. (c) is weight map of ours, w(a,b) is high due to pixel a having similar color and short distance with pixel b. High support weight is also given to pixel c because of similar color and short distance to pixel a. However, pixel c and pixel a are in different depth, in other words, they are not in the same region, according to support weight algorithm [9], they would be given high weight wrongly, see Fig.1(b), support weight of pixel c is bright. If we use region growing method, pixel c couldn't be grown anymore, so we can easily separate pixel c from pixel a by setting color threshold beforehand, see Fig.1(c), support weight of pixel c is dark. Our method focuses on pixels with similar color and proximity but different regions, so it can effectively improve the matching accuracy of repetitive area and some depth discontinues area. To verify the validity of our algorithm, we will give a comparison in experiment section.

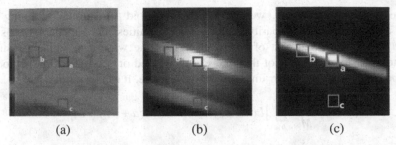

(a)   (b)   (c)

Fig. 1. The support window of Middlebury images. Pixel a is in the center of support window, Fig. 1(a) is original image. Fig. 1 (b) is support-weight map using algorithm [9], Fig. 1 (c) is weight map considering of region connectivity.

Based on the above idea, we propose a stereo matching algorithm of dynamic window based on region growing. We finally get the matching algorithm by using eight neighboring growth which is based on region seed growing method of certain color restraint.

First we construct a support window for every matching pixel which is the center of the window. After region growing, those pixels satisfied are gathered together and grown as a whole, and finally they formed a dynamic window of different sizes and shapes based on color similarity.

The first step of region growing is choosing initial seed, we assume that the pixel which is in the center of the support window is initial seed and compute the distance between the selected seeding pixel and the candidate pixel which is selected on the basis of eight neighborhood connectivity. Here the distance we talked about is calculated in RGB space. The expression is as following:

$$d(p,c) = \sqrt{(r_p - r_c)^2 + (g_p - g_c)^2 + (b_p - b_c)^2} \qquad (1)$$

where p is a candidate point, c is the seed point. r_p g_p b_p is the RGB channel of p.

After comparing the result and given threshold, candidate pixel which is no more than threshold is grown until end.

2.2 Initial Disparity Estimation

After we get the regions which is based on seed growing we talked above, we count the number of pixels in these regions, and mark it as M. We all know the simple way of computing matching cost is AD, which is to calculate the absolute intensity difference of corresponding pixel between the left and right image and choose the disparity value which has the minimum matching cost, it can be expressed as:

$$|L(x,y) - R(x+d,y)| \qquad (2)$$

As the regions we got are irregular in shape, when we calculate the matching cost, we count the number of region pixels, calculate the total intensity difference, and take the average. By doing this way, we can effectively avoid "foreground-fattening" and obtain a more accurate disparity map at discontinuities and repetitive areas. We finally get the matching cost of the pixel(x,y) by the way of dividing the sum of absolute intensity difference of the pixels grown based on seed growing method and corresponding pixel in another image by M for average. It can be written as:

$$C(x,y,d) = \frac{1}{M} \sum_{(a,b) \in r} |L(x+a,y+b) - R(x+a+d,y+b)| \qquad (3)$$

where $a \in [-w/2, w/2]$, $b \in [-h/2, h/2]$. w, h are the width and height of support window, r is the regions of the pixels which is based on seed growing of support window.

2.3   Disparity Adjustment

After initial disparity estimation some mismatches would occur due to outlier. In this section we propose a disparity map adjustment method by assigning suitable disparity value to mismatches using region growing method we have talked above. We finally get disparity value of pixel P by updating the pixel most similar to P in the window W. We use the result of region growing, choosing the one which is in the same region of P as disparity of P.

$$D_p = \min_{q \in W} d(p,q) \qquad (4)$$

where P is the center of window W, $d(p,q)$ is the same distance function like equation (1).

The result shows this method can rebuild the edge and can get more accurate map without adding extra computation cost.

3   Experiment Results and Analysis

In order to verify the validity of our algorithm, we implement by using C language under a 1.83 GHz Intel Core 2 computer running with vista operating system. The tested images and ground truth map are all from Middlebury dataset [10], the size of a support window is 31*31, while in disparity adjustment we take the window size of 15 instead in order to acquire accurate result of discontinuities. We also use command line and parallel processor to improve our operation. It took about 0.87 second for Tsukuba image, so it can meet the need of real-time basically.

Middlebury university provide three parameters to evaluate their results. They represent the percentage of bad pixels of whose absolute disparity error is greater than 1 in different areas. There are: non-occluded(nonocc), the whole(all), depth discontinuities(disc), as shown in table 1, our method is much better than others in these regions, the proposed method have lower rate in both disc and nonocc than any other method. This is coincide with what we have analyzed above, and verify the validity of ours.

We also compare it with algorithm only based on color distance, take Tsukuba image for example, from Fig 3 (a) (b) we can see that because of region growing method, we greatly reduce the mismatches at the top left of the bookshelf(see Fig 3,white areas at the top left), at the same time, the disparity map becomes much sharper at the discontinuities of face and table. It demonstrates that our algorithm can avoid "foreground-fattening" clearly and is much more sharper in repetitive regions and depth discontinues.

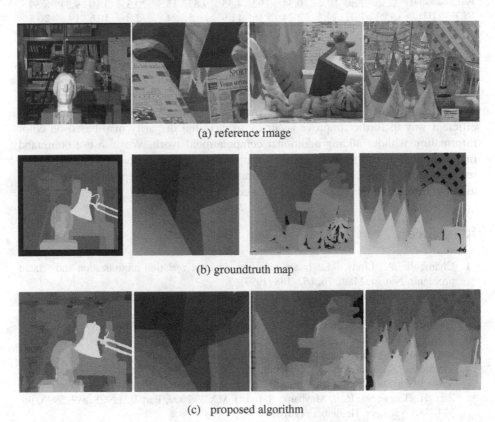

(a) reference image

(b) groundtruth map

(c) proposed algorithm

Fig. 2. The results of standard image Tsukuba, Venus, Teddy, Cones

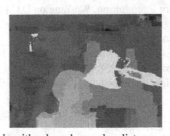
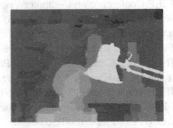

(a) algorithm based on color distance only   (b) our algorithm

Fig. 3. Different methods of Tsukuba image processing

Table 1. Comparison of the proposed algorithm and other algorithms

	Trukuba			Venus			Teddy			Cones		
	nonocc	all	disc	nonocc	all	disc	nonocc	all	disc	nonocc	all	disc
Our algorithm	1.27	1.68	6.84	0.28	0.49	2.67	8.69	14.5	21.9	3.91	9.37	8.76
ReliabilityDP[2]	1.36	3.39	7.25	2.35	3.48	12.2	9.82	16.9	19.5	12.9	19.9	19.7
RealTimeBP[3]	1.49	3.40	7.87	0.77	1.90	9.00	8.72	13.2	17.2	4.61	11.6	12.4
Fast bilateral[4]	2.36	2.80	10.4	0.34	0.92	4.55	9.83	15.3	20.3	3.10	9.31	8.59
SSD+MF[11]	5.23	7.07	24.1	3.74	5.16	11.9	16.5	24.8	32.9	10.6	19.8	26.3

4   Conclusion

In this paper, we propose a novel real-time local stereo matching algorithm. We use region growing method to improve the matching accuracy and propose a simple but efficient way to further improve accuracy from initial disparity map based on color information without adding additional computational work. We also use command line and parallel processor to improve our operation. Experiments show the algorithm we presented can not only get a more accurate disparity map at repetitive areas as well as depth discontinuities but also meet the need of real-time.

References

1. Chambolle, A., Lions, P.L.: Image recovery via total variation minimization and related problems. Numer. Math. 76, 167–188 (1997)
2. Salmen, J., Schlipsing, M., Edelbrunner, J., Hegemann, S., Lüke, S.: Real-Time Stereo Vision: Making More Out of Dynamic Programming. In: Jiang, X., Petkov, N. (eds.) CAIP 2009. LNCS, vol. 5702, pp. 1096–1103. Springer, Heidelberg (2009)
3. Yang, Q., Wang, L., Yang, R., Wang, S., Liao, M., Nister, D.: Real-time global stereo matching using hierarchical belief propagation. In: BMVC (2006)
4. Mattoccia, S., Giardino, S., Gambini, A.: Accurate and Efficient Cost Aggregation Strategy for Stereo Correspondence Based on Approximated Joint Bilateral Filtering. In: Zha, H., Taniguchi, R.-i., Maybank, S. (eds.) ACCV 2009, Part II. LNCS, vol. 5995, pp. 371–380. Springer, Heidelberg (2010)
5. Scharstein, D., Szeliski, R.: A taxonomy and evaluation of dense two-frame stereo correspondence algorithms. Int'l Journal on Computer Vision 47(1/2/3), 7–42 (2002)
6. Felzenszwalb, P.F., Huttenlocher, D.P.: Efficient Belief Propagation for Early Vision. In: IEEE Conference on Computer Vision and Pattern Recognition, Washington D.C (2004)
7. Kanade, T., Okutomi, M.: A stereo matching algorithm with an adaptive window: Theory and experiments. In: IEEE International Conference on Computer Vision (1998)
8. Fusiello, A., Roberto, V., Trucco, E.: Efficient Stereo with Multiple Windowing. In: Proc. IEEE Conf. Computer Vision and Pattern Recognition, pp. 858–863 (1997)
9. Yoon, K.J., Kweon, I.S.: Adaptive support-weight approach for correspondence search. IEEE Trans. PAMI 28(4), 650–656 (2006)
10. Middlebury stereo benchmark dataset,
    http://vision.middlebury.edu/stereo/data
11. Scharstein, D., Szeliski, R.: A taxonomy and evaluation of dense two-frame stereo correspondence algorithms. Int. Jour. Computer Vision (IJCV) 47(1/2/3), 7–42 (2002)

A Key-Frame Selection Method for Semi-automatic 2D-to-3D Conversion

Jiande Sun[1,2,3], Jiangchuan Xie[2], Jing Li[4], and Wei Liu[3]

[1] School of Electronics Engineering and Computer Science,
Peking University, Beijing 100871, China
[2] School of Information Science and Engineering, Shandong University,
Jinan 250100, China
[3] The Hisense State Key Laboratory of Digital-Media Technology, Qingdao 266061, China
[4] Shandong Institute of Trade Unions' Administration Cadres, Jinan 250100, China
jiandesun@hotmail.com, jiejiangchuan@126.com,
lijingjdsun@gmail.com

Abstract. During 2D to 3D conversion, key-frame selection is a very important step as it can directly affect the visual quality of the 3D video. In this paper, a novel key-frame selection method for 2D-to-3D conversion is presented to get fewer errors and much better photorealistic perception. Firstly, the occlusion areas between two consecutive frames are detected and SURF-feature points of the frames are extracted. Secondly, the ratio of feature points to the correspondence is calculated, which is used to select the key-frame candidates. Finally, camera projection matrix in the projective space is computed for every key-frame candidate, and the key-frame candidate that has the least re-projection error is selected as the key-frame. Experimental results show that the propagated depth maps using the proposed method have fewer errors, which is beneficial to generate high quality stereoscopic video.

Keywords: 2D-to-3D Conversion, Key-Frame Selection, Depth Propagation.

1 Introduction

At present, the semi-automatic 2D-to-3D conversion is becoming more and more popular in 3D content production due to its advantage over balancing the tradeoff between manual cost and virtual effect [1-4]. However, there are some challenging issues that determine the quality of the converted 3D video, among which key-frame selection is the most critical one. In the 2D-to-3D conversion of [1] and [5], key-frames are selected at the fixed temporal interval. However, temporal distance is not the only factor, which determines depth propagation error and 3D video quality. There are some other potential factors, such as the occlusion, the location, the total number of key-frames, etc. Nistér selected the key-frames according to the sharpness of frames [6]. The sharpness of a frame, however, is sensitive to its resolution, and the more sharpness is demanded, the more useless frames may be selected. Gibson selected the key-frames taking account of the error that is calculated from the fundamental matrix and the 2D projective transformation matrix [7]. However, it is a

W. Zhang et al. (Eds.): IFTC 2012, CCIS 331, pp. 465–470, 2012.

time consuming work because of the use of iteration. Additionally, the fundamental matrix is very sensitive to noise.

In this paper, a novel key-frames selection method is proposed by using the occlusion area, the correspondence ratio and the re-projection error. At first, the occlusion between two consecutive frames of the input 2D video is detected. The frame with large occlusion can not be selected as key-frame, which can lead the large depth error after propagation. Then, the first frame of the input 2D video is set as the first key-frame, and the correspondence ratio between the first frame and the each of the other frames is calculated. The frames, whose correspondence ratio locates in the specific range, are selected as the key-frame candidates. At last, the re-projection error of each key-frame candidate is calculated and the frame with the least re-projection error will be selected as the key-frame. Fig. 1 shows the key-frames selection algorithm as we proposed.

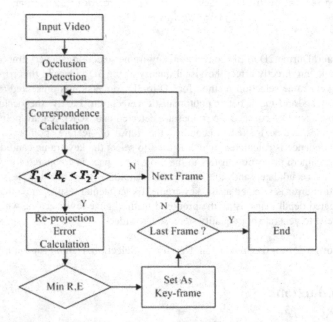

Fig. 1. The framework of the proposed key-frames selection method

2   Key-Frame Selection

2.1   Occlusion Detection

The occlusion between two consecutive frames is an important factor which should be considered first of all. If there is larger occlusion between the key-frame and non-key-frame, the depth of non-key-frames propagated from the key-frames will have larger errors, and the 3D quality will be worse. In the proposed method, the occlusion between two consecutive frames is first detected by applying the stereo correspondence algorithm, and then the accumulative occlusion is calculated as the following [8].

$$O_a(k) = \sum_{i=1}^{k} O_c(i), k = 1,2,3,...,n \tag{1}$$

where $O_c(i)$ is the occlusion area of i th frame, n is the number of frames, which has been done occlusion detection, and $O_a(k)$ is the accumulated occlusion area of the k frames. If the accumulated occlusion area rises steeply, it means that the occlusion area of frames detected is large. In order to avoid large depth propagation error for large occlusion frames, the number of key-frames should be increased.

2.2   Correspondence Calculation

The ratio of feature point to the correspondence is one of the factors for key-frame selection. Let $i_1, i_2, i_3, ..., i_n$ denote the n frames of the input 2D video and i_1 is the first frame which is also taken as the first key-frame. The ratio of feature point to the correspondence of i_1 and i_k is calculated by opensurf algorithm, where i_k belongs to $i_1, i_2, i_3, ..., i_n$. The ratio of correspondence, R_c, can be calculated:

$$R_c = \frac{R_k}{R_1}, k = 2,3,4,...,n. \tag{2}$$

where R_1 and R_k are the total number of feature points of i_1 and i_k respectively. R_c is used to select key-frame candidates. If R_c is too low, the accuracy of camera pose estimation and depth propagation between two frames will decrease so a key-frame candidate should be added. However if too many key-frames are selected, there will be extra labor and time cost. Hence when R_c is between the upper and lower threshold T_1 and T_2, a key-frame candidate should be added. At the same time, when two thresholds are set, accumulative occlusion $O_a(k)$ will also be taken into account to avoid large depth propagation error of non-key-frames.

2.3   Re-projection Error Calculation

After correspondence calculation, the re-projection error of key-frames candidates is calculated to determine the final key-frames. Let $D_i = (X_i, Y_i, Z_i)^T$ denotes the i-th point in 3D space, and $d_i = (x_i, y_i)^T$ is its corresponding pixel in the j-th frame of the 2D video, and the relationship between the two points can be presented as following:

$$x_i = P_j X_i \tag{3}$$

where P_j is a 3×4 camera projection matrix and $P_j = [Rt]$. Here R is a 3×3 matrix, which denotes the rotation matrix and demonstrates the external parameters of camera, while t is the translation matrix and demonstrates the internal parameters of camera. The re-projective error can be calculated as following:

$$R.E = \frac{\sum_i d(P_j X_j^i, x_j^i)^2}{Num} \qquad (4)$$

where *Num* is the number of feature points in the j-th frame. The camera projection matrix is created by the camera calibration algorithm proposed by Tsai in [9] as it has advantages on little iteration parameters, fast calculation and high level accuracy. According to (4), the key-frame candidates with minimum re-projective error are selected as the final key-frames.

3   Experiment Results

In our experiment, in order to verify the feasibility and reliability of the proposed algorithm, the selected key-frames are used in 2D-to-3D conversion. The quality of the generated 3D video can show the performance of the proposed algorithm. During 2D-to-3D conversion, the method in [10] is used for depth assignment, the Shifted bilateral filtering (SBF) algorithm used in [1] and [11] is adopted for depth propagation and the post-processing method for 2D-to-3D conversion in [12] is used here. Mean Square Error (MSE) calculated between the Groudtruth depth and the propagated depth of non-key-frames is used to evaluate the performance of the key-frame selection method. The results on the video of "Beergarden" are shown here. "Beergarden" is a benchmark video in 3D reconstruction with the resolution of 1920*1080. It has 150 frames and each frame has the Groundtruth depth map.

The curve of the accumulative occlusion area of the video "Beergarden" is shown in Fig. 2. It can be seen that the curve is much steeper between the 118th frame and the 140th frame, which means that more key-frames should be selected during the two frames in order to decrease the depth propagation error. The MSE comparison between different methods is shown in Fig. 3 and Table 1. Seven key-frames are selected according to the uniform temporal interval-based method used in [1], and seven key-frames are also selected by the proposed method.

It can be seen from Fig. 3 and Table 1, the MSE of the proposed key-frames selection method is lower than that of SBF. As shown in Fig. 2, the Cumulative occlusion curve is not steep between the 61st and 114th frames, but the MSE shown in Fig. 3 is large. It demonstrates that the distance between two consecutive key-frames is also an important factor. According to this analysis, an extra key-frame is interpolated between the 61st and 114th frames, and lower MSE is obtained as shown in "□" in Fig. 3. In addition, it can be seen clearly from Table 1 that the average MSE decreases significantly.

The experiment results demonstrate that the key-frames selection algorithm is better than temporal interval-based method in term of MSE. Though when one more key-frame is added, the MSE decreased greatly, it will add workload in the depth assignment. So in the practical application, the number of key-frame and MSE should a trade-off.

Table 1. Comparison on average MSE of different key-frame selection methods

Method	Key-frames	Average MSE
SBF	1 25 50 75 100 125 150	31.0583
Proposed Method	1 21 39 61 114 127 142	28.4057
Proposed+Distance	1 21 39 61 87 114 127 142	25.6218

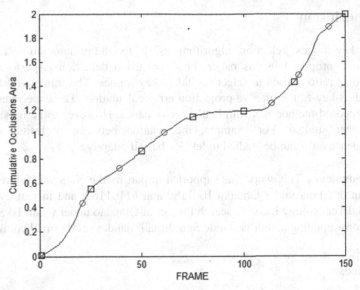

Fig. 2. The Cumulative occlusion curve of input 2D video "Beergarden". The "o" and "□" represent the locations of key-frames selected by proposed method and the fixed temporal interval respectively.

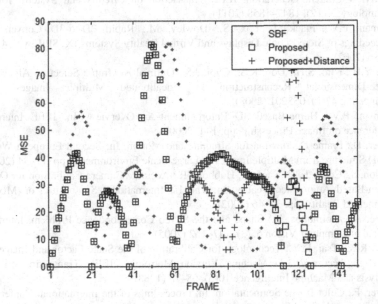

Fig. 3. The MSE comparison between different methods. Here the " · " demonstrates the MSE of SBF, the "+" represents the MSE of proposed method, and the "□" denotes the MSE of proposed method with consideration of distance between every two key-frames.

4   Conclusion

A novel key-frames selection algorithm using for Semi-automatic 2D to 3D conversion is proposed in this paper. First, occlusion detection is performed, and corresponding ratio is used to select candidate key-frames. The frame with least R.E is selected as key-frame after re-projection error calculation. The experiments show that the proposed method has with better performance. However some issues remain to be further studied. For example, the relation between occlusion area and correspondence ratio can be studied to let R_c be self-adaptive.

Acknowledgments. This work was supported in part by the National Nature Science Foundation of China under Grants 61001180 and 61101162, and in part by and the Science and Technology Basic Research Project of Qingdao under Grant 10-3-4-12-1-jch. The corresponding author is Jiande Sun (Email: jiandesun@hotmail.com).

References

1. Cao, X., Li, Z., Dai, Q.: Semi-Automatic 2D-to-3D Conversion Using Disparity Propagation. IEEE Transaction on Broadcasting 57(2), 491–499 (2011)
2. Wang, H., Huang, C., Yang, J.: Block-Based Depth Maps Interpolation for Efficient Multiview Content Generation. IEEE Transaction on Circuits and Systems for Video Technology 21(12), 1847–1858 (2011)
3. Harman, P.V., Flack, J., Fox, S., Dowley, M.: Rapid 2D-to-3D Conversion. In: Proceedings of Stereoscopic Displays and Virtual Reality Systems IX. SPIE, vol. 4669, pp. 78–86 (2002)
4. Seo, Y.H., Kim, S.H., Doo, K.S., Choi, J.S.: Optimal Keyframe Selection Algorithm for Three-Dimensional Reconstruction in Uncalibrated Multiple Images. Optical Engineering 47(5), 053201 (2008)
5. Harman, P.V.: Home-Based 3D Entertainment-An Overview. In: IEEE International Conference on Image Processing, pp. 1–4 (2000)
6. Nistér, D.: Frame Decimation for Structure and Motion. In: Second European Workshop on 3D Structure from Multiple Images of Large-Scale Environments, pp. 17–34 (2000)
7. Gibson, S., Cook, J., Howard, T., Hubbold, R.: Accurate Camera Calibration for Off-Line, Video-Based Augmented Reality. In: The 1st International Symposium on Mixed and Augmented Reality, pp. 37–46 (2002)
8. Ogale, A., Aloimonos, Y.: Shape and the Stereo Correspondence Problem. International Journal of Computer Vision 65(3), 147–162 (2005)
9. Lenz, R.K., Tsai, R.Y.: Technology for Calibration of the Scale Factor and Image Center for High Accuracy 3-D Machine Version Metrology. IEEE Transaction on Pattern Analysis and Machine Intelligence 10(5), 68–75 (1988)
10. Meyer, F.: Color Image Segmentation. In: Proceedings of the International Conference on Image Processing and Its Applications, pp. 303–306 (1992)
11. Ahmad, I., Zheng, W., Luo, J., Lion, M.: A Fast Adaptive Motion Estimation Algorithm. IEEE Transaction on Circuits System for Video Technology 16(3), 420–438 (2006)
12. Fehn, C.: Depth-Image-Based Rendering (DIBR), Compression, and Transmission for a New Approach on 3DTV. In: Proceedings of the SPIE, vol. 5291, pp. 93–104 (2004)

Relationship between Max Stereo Angle and Number of Views in Multi-view Stereo Acquisition/Display System

Hao Cheng, Ping An, and Zhaoyang Zhang

School of Communication and Information Enginerring,
Shanghai University, Shanghai, 200072, China
Chengs99f@163.com

Abstract. This paper establishes the model of multi-view stereo acquisition/display system and proposes the relational model between max stereo angle and number of views. Based on the simulation experiments, the relationship between max stereo angle and number of views can be analyzed qualitatively. Through the results of simulation experiments some characteristics of multi-view acquisition/display system can be found out. They can provide a theoretical basis for building and overall optimizing multi-view acquisition/display system.

Keywords: multi-view acquisition/display system, max stereo angle, number of views.

1   Introduction

The technology of multi-view stereo display is becoming research focus in stereo display technology. Different from traditional 3D viewing, multi-view stereo display can provide stereo image with strong stereo perception and performance without any auxiliary (3D glasses). So, multi-view 3D display has been considered as the future direction of 3D display technology.

Multi-view stereo display technology is not perfect and still in development. At home and abroad, some researchers are partial to expand the stereo angle by increasing views [1]. Some of them are partial to improve the efficiency of multi-view video coding (MVC) by using the correlation between different views[2], and some of them improve the efficiency of stereo perception with horizontal and vertical parallax[3]. All of them rarely consider improving system performance through mathematical modeling [4].

In response to these issues, firstly this paper establishes the model from shooting camera array to multi-view stereo display in Section 2. Then it proposes the relational model between max stereo angle and number of views in Section 3. Section 4 is the simulation experiments and through it the characteristics of relational model can be found out. Section 5 is the conclusion of this paper.

W. Zhang et al. (Eds.): IFTC 2012, CCIS 331, pp. 471–477, 2012.

2   Model of Multi-view Stereo Acquisition/Display System

In order to analyze multi-view stereo acquisition/display system qualitatively, the mathematic model of stereo system should be established. Multi-view stereo acquisition/display is composed of shooting camera array and multi-view stereo display. Shooting camera array can capture the real object from different positions. The stereo images can be synthesized by these images and displayed in multi-view stereoscopic screen.

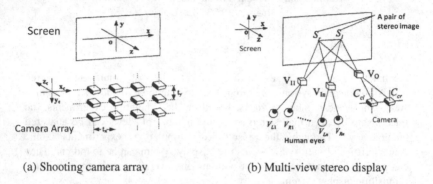

(a) Shooting camera array   (b) Multi-view stereo display

Fig. 1. Model of Multi-view stereo acquisition/display system

Assuming the center of coordinate system is in the center of screen. Screen plane and camera array plane are parallel. Fig.1(a) is the model of shooting camera array. t_x and t_y represent camera spacing in x-axis and y-axis. Fig. 1(b) shows the model of multi-view stereoscopic display. Assume that V_0 is the point of real object. C_{cl} and C_{cr} represent the position of some neighboring cameras in camera array. S_l and S_r represent the pair points in multi-view stereo display screen. If the positions of first viewer's two eyes are at V_{L1} and V_{R1}, he can see the position of virtual objects at V_{I1}. The rest may be deduced by analogy. If the positions of Nth viewer's two eyes are at V_{Ln} and V_{Rn}, he can see the position of virtual objects at V_{In}. So when the viewer stands at the different position to watch multi-view stereo display, he can also see the virtual object in different position.

Assume that one point of real object is $V_0 = (X_0, Y_0, Z_0, 1)$ and the corresponding point in multi-view stereo display screen is $V_I = (X_I, Y_I, Z_I, 1)$. The relationship between V_0 and V_I can be represented by 4×4 homogeneous matrix M:

$$V_I = M \otimes V_O \tag{1}$$

Based on computer vision and binocular parallax theory[5], M includes four transformations. The diagram is in Fig. 2.

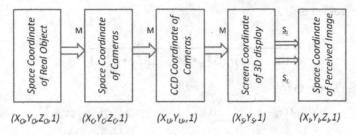

Fig. 2. Diagram of coordinate transformations

In Fig.2, point V_0 $(X_0, Y_0, Z_0, 1)$ in real object can be transformed to the screen point S_{ij} $(X_s, Y_s, 1)$. The relationship between V_0 and S_{ij} can be indicated as:

$$\begin{bmatrix} X_S \\ Y_S \\ 1 \end{bmatrix} = M_{ij} \begin{bmatrix} X_O \\ Y_O \\ Z_O \\ 1 \end{bmatrix} \quad M_{ij} = \begin{bmatrix} pf & 0 & 0 & pf[-x_c-(i-1)t_x] \\ 0 & qf & 0 & qf[-y_c+(i-1)t_y] \\ 0 & 0 & -1 & z_c \end{bmatrix} \tag{2}$$

M_{ij} represents the position of the (i, j)th camera C_{ij} = $(x_{ij}, y_{ij}, z_{ij}, w_{ij})$. f represents the focal length and p (q) represents the zoom factor from CCD sensor to display screen. In general, p and q are equal.

Based on principle of binocular parallax[6], stereo point pair $(X_{sl}, Y_{sl}, 1)$, $(X_{sr}, Y_{sr}, 1)$ can be transformed to one virtual point $V_I = (X_I, Y_I, Z_I, 1)$ in perceived coordinate.

Assume that the positions of left and right eyes are $V_L = (X_L, Y_L, Z_L, W_L)$ and $V_R = (X_R, Y_R, Z_R, W_R)$. In multi-view stereo display screen, left eye can perceive the point $S_l = (X_{sl}, Y_{sl}, 1)$ and right eye can perceive the point $S_r = (X_{sr}, Y_{sr}, 1)$. The relationship between virtual point and stereo point pair can be represented as:

$$V_I = (M_R \bullet S_l - M_L \bullet S_r)/(x_R - x_L) \tag{3}$$

M_R, M_L are decided by two eye positions, which are :

$$M_R = \begin{bmatrix} x_R & 0 & 0 \\ y_R & x_R & 0 \\ z_R & 0 & 0 \\ 1 & 0 & x_R \end{bmatrix} \quad M_L = \begin{bmatrix} x_L & 0 & 0 \\ y_L & x_L & 0 \\ z_L & 0 & 0 \\ 1 & 0 & x_L \end{bmatrix} \tag{4}$$

Based on formula (3) and (4), relationship between real object and virtual object is:

$$\begin{bmatrix} X_I \\ Y_I \\ Z_I \\ 1 \end{bmatrix} = \mathbf{M} \bullet \begin{bmatrix} X_O \\ Y_O \\ Z_O \\ 1 \end{bmatrix} \tag{5}$$

M can be expressed as:

$$M = \frac{1}{(x_R - x_L) \cdot (M_R \cdot M_{cl} - M_L \cdot M_{cr})} \tag{6}$$

Put formula (3), (4) to (6):

$$M = \frac{1}{x_R - x_L} \begin{bmatrix} pf(x_R - x_L) & 0 & 0 & pf(x_L x_{cr} - x_R x_{cl}) \\ pf(y_R - y_L) & qf(x_R - x_L) & 0 & \begin{aligned} pf(y_L x_{cr} - y_R x_{cl}) - \\ qf(x_R y_{cl} - x_L y_{cr}) \end{aligned} \\ pf(z_R - z_L) & 0 & 0 & pf(z_L x_{cr} - z_R x_{cl}) \\ 0 & 0 & x_L - x_R & \begin{aligned} pf(x_{cr} - x_{cl}) + \\ z_c(x_R - x_L) \end{aligned} \end{bmatrix} \tag{7}$$

$C_{cl} = (x_{cl}, y_{cl}, z_{cl}, 1)$ and $C_{cr} = (x_{cr}, y_{cr}, z_{cr}, 1)$ are the position of left and right cameras.

From the above analysis, the relationship between point V_0 $(X_0, Y_0, Z_0, 1)$ in real objects and point V_i in virtual objects can be expressed as:

$$\begin{cases} X_i = \dfrac{pf(x_R - x_L)}{pf(x_{cr} - x_{cl}) + (x_R - x_L)(z_c - Z_0)} X_0 + \dfrac{pf(x_L x_{cr} - x_R x_{cl})}{pf(x_{cr} - x_{cl}) + (x_R - x_L)(z_c - Z_0)} \\ Y_i = \dfrac{pf(y_R - y_L)}{pf(x_{cr} - x_{cl}) + (x_R - x_L)(z_c - Z_0)} X_0 + \dfrac{qf(x_R - x_L)}{pf(x_{cr} - x_{cl}) + (x_R - x_L)(z_c - Z_0)} Y_0 + \dfrac{pf(y_L x_{cr} - y_R x_{cl}) - qf(x_R y_{cl} - x_L y_{cr})}{pf(x_{cr} - x_{cl}) + (x_R - x_L)(z_c - Z_0)} \\ Z_i = \dfrac{pf(z_R - z_L)}{pf(x_{cr} - x_{cl}) + (x_R - x_L)(z_c - Z_0)} X_0 + \dfrac{pf(z_L x_{cr} - z_R x_{cl})}{pf(x_{cr} - x_{cl}) + (x_R - x_L)(z_c - Z_0)} \end{cases} \tag{8}$$

Equation (9) is the model of multi-view stereo acquisition/display system. We can use it to study the system qualitatively.

3   Relationship between Number of Views and Stereo Angle

For multi-view stereo acquisition/display system, people generally consider that the more number of views gets, the better stereo performance is. In order to study this problem, we analyze the relationship between max stereo angle and number of views.

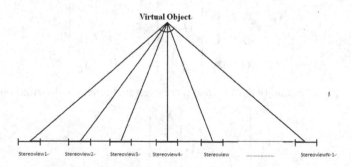

Fig. 3. Stereo angle of multi-view stereo display

Assume that the spacing of human eyes is $e(e = x_R\text{-}x_L)$, spacing of camera array is $a(a = x_{cr}\text{-}x_{cl})$, viewing distance from stereo screen is $z_v(z_L = z_R = z_v)$ and depth of real object is Z_0. So formula (9) can be simplified and depth of virtual object is as follows.

$$Z_I = pfz_v a / (pfa + e(z_c - Z_O))$$ (9)

In ideal case, when parallel camera array are capturing the object, N cameras get N images. N images can transform N-1 stereo image pair. Based on the principle of multi-view stereo display, viewer in different position can see different stereo image pair and stereo image pair can get virtual object in brain. The max stereo angle is the sum of all stereo angles.

$$\text{Angle}_{max} = \sum_{i=1}^{n-1} \text{stereoangle}_i$$ (10)

Now we need to define a parameter---view switching parameter. It is the distance which viewer moves horizontally when viewpoint switches. This parameter is related to the distance between stereo display and viewer. Assume that multi-view stereo display is in ideal case. When viewer moves horizontally at the distance of z_v from the screen, viewpoint switching parameter is a certain value C_{zv}, which depends on the distance between screen and viewer. When viewer who is watching multi-view stereo display stands at the distance of z_v, horizontal moving through the distance of C_{zv} can cause viewpoint switching. In fig.3, when viewer stands at the distance of z_v from the screen, moving from stereo view 1 to stereo view N-1 needs horizontal movement through the distance of $(N\text{-}2) \times C_{zv}$. The max stereo angle is:

$$\text{Angle}_{max} = 2 \cdot \arctan \frac{e + (N - 2) \cdot C_{zv}}{2(z_v - Z_I)}$$ (11)

4   Simulation Experiments and Analyses

To study the relationship between max stereo angle and number of views, we implemented our simulation experiments in MATLAB 7.13. Table 1 is the parameters of shooting and viewing condition, based on formula (12) the relationship between number of views and stereo angle can be expressed.

Table 1. Parameters of shooting and viewing condition (mm)

Num	p	f	z_v	a	Z_O	C_{zv}
1	40	8	800	35	50	32.5
2	40	8	800	35	50	53.3

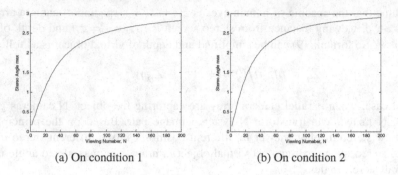

(a) On condition 1   (b) On condition 2

Fig. 4. Relationship between number of views and angle_max

In Fig 4(a) and 4(b), unit of stereo angle is radian. From the figure we can see that with increasing views, max stereo angle is increasing gradually. But growth rate of max stereo is slowing. So when the number of views increases to a certain number, growth of max stereo angle is not obvious. This means that when we use the method what is increasing views to enhance stereo effect, at the beginning it is effective but with increasing views continually, enhancement of stereo effect is not obvious.

5   Conclusion

This paper mainly discuses the rationale model between max stereo angle and number of views. Through simulation experiments, we find out that when views are increasing, max stereo angle becomes larger. But if views increase continually, the growth of max stereo angle is not obvious. That means we do not need to increase number of views blindly for getting more enhanced stereo effect in multi-view stereo acquisition/display system.

Acknowledgment. This work was supported in part by the National Natural Science Foundation of China, under Grants 60832003, 61172096 and 61171084, and the key Project of Shanghai Science and Technology Commission, under Grant 10510500500.

References

1. Zhang, Z., An, P.: 3D Multi-view stereoscopic display and its key technologies. Proc. of Asia Display 1, 460–465 (2007)
2. Yang, Y., Jiang, G., Peng, Z., Yu, M.: User Interaction and Random Accessibility Analysis for Multiview Video System. In: International Conference on Consumer Electronics, ICCE 2008, pp. 1–2. IEEE, Las Vegas (2008)
3. Kang, Y.-S., Lee, C., Ho, Y.-S.: An efficient rectification algorithm for multi-view images in parallel camera array. In: 3DTV Conference: The True Vision - Capture, Transmission and Display of 3D Video 2008, pp. 61–64. IEEE, Istanbul (2008)

4. Bi, J., Zeng, D., Zhang, Z., Dong, Z.: Automultiscopic 3D Displays System Model and Evaluation. In: World Congress on Computer Science and Information Engineering 2009, vol. 6, pp. 514–518. IEEE, Los Angeles (2009)
5. Forsyth, D.A., Ponce, J.: Computer vision, a modern approach, pp. 3–19. Prentice Hall, NJ (2003)
6. Son, J.-Y., Javidi, B., Kwack, K.-D.: Methods for displaying three-dimensional images. Proceedings of IEEE 94, 502–523 (2006)

A New Method of DIBR Based on Background Inpainting

Kui Wang[1,2], Ping An[1,2], Hao Cheng[1,2], Hejian Li[1,2], and Zhaoyang Zhang[1,2]

[1] School of Communication and Information Engineering,
Shanghai University, Shanghai 200072
[2] Key Laboratory of Advanced Displays and System Application,
Ministry of Education, Shanghai 200072

Abstract. Depth image based rendering (DIBR) is key technology in stereo video system to generate virtual view image. Filling holes is a difficult task, especially to no views blending and wide baseline. This paper proposes a new method of DIBR which combines background estimation and image inpainting. Firstly, an effective division rule is presented to distinguish background and foreground in hole-areas, estimated background is used to fill the background holes. At last image inpainting is used to fill the remaining holes. Compared to other methods, our method can use real pixel of the scene to fill the background holes and improve virtual view quality greatly.

Keywords: 3D Video, DIBR, Hole Filling, Background inpainting.

1   Introduction

Depth-Image-Based-Rendering (DIBR) has become a research hotspot because of its advantages of small quantity, adjustable parallax. However, virtual views rendered by DIBR have many holes, which seriously affect virtual views quality.

In order to improve virtual view quality, A series of studies are carried out in recent years. In [1,2], the authors presented methods based on smoothing filter and other improved methods. These methods may bring in serious image geometric distortion, especially to big baseline. [3,4] proposed a series of algorithm based on image inpainting. In these methods, either filling effect is bad, or processing complexity is very high. A method based on background filling was presented in [5], which could fill background holes with real background information. But the method can't distinguish background holes and foreground holes.

In this paper, a new method of DIBR is presented. Firstly we propose a division algorithm to distinguish background holes and foreground holes, and then use background information to fill background holes, and fill remaining small foreground holes by image inpainting algorithm.

2   Proposed Method

Foreground occlusion is major cause of holes, and large parts of holes are in background area. So we can estimate background by inter-frame information, then divide

W. Zhang et al. (Eds.): IFTC 2012, CCIS 331, pp. 478–484, 2012.

background part from hole areas and use background information to fill background holes directly. Image inpainting method is used to fill the remaining holes.

Fig.1 is the block diagram of our method.

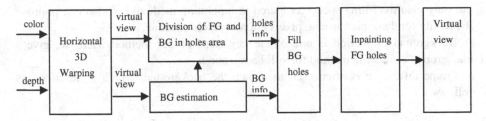

Fig. 1. Block diagram of our method

2.1   Hole Model

The pixels between virtual view and real view have a certain mapping relationship and we can use this relationship to generate virtual view. The mapping relationship between real view and virtual view is defined as below [6]:

$$X_r = X_l + \frac{S_x \times f}{Z} \tag{1}$$

S_x is distance of human eyes, f is camera focus.

The pixels between virtual view and real view are not one-to-one correlation. Holes will be generated in virtual view if there are no correspondence pixels in virtual view for some pixels in real view. There are two types of holes which are background hole and foreground hole. Show as Fig.2. Fig.2 (a) denotes all holes are in background, and Fig.2 (b) is the situation that part holes are in background and the other parts are in foreground.

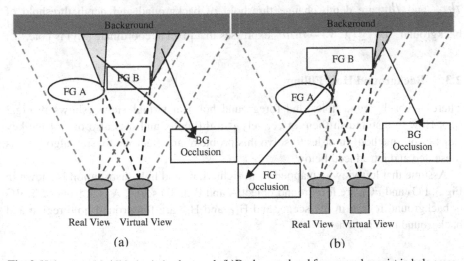

Fig. 2. Hole types:(a) All holes in background; (b)Background and foreground coexist in hole areas

2.2   Background Estimation

Holes are not all in background, but most of holes are in background. So background information can be used to fill holes. Filling holes with background information can not only gain the filling speed compared to inpainting method, but also can improve the reality for these background pixels are real pixels of scene.

Background estimation is one of the key steps of our method. Here we give a background estimation method for still background.

Frame difference is often used to update the background, which is described as follows:

$$D_k(x,y) = \left| depth_{f,c,k}(x,y) - depth_{b,c,(k-1)}(x,y) \right| \tag{2}$$

$D_k(x,y)$ is k-th frame difference image, $depth_{f,c,k}(x,y)$ and $depth_{b,c,(k-1)}(x,y)$ are k-th depth image and (k-1)-th estimated depth image of background.

Below is the background updating method:

$$B_{c,k}(x,y) = \begin{cases} f_{c,k}(x,y); & if\ D_k(x,y) < thr_A\ and\ d_{f,c,k}(x,y) < thr_B \\ f_{c,k}(x,y); & if\ B_{c,k-1}(x,y) = hole\ and\ d_{f,c,k}(x,y) < thr_B \\ B_{c,k-1}(x,y); & if\ D_k(x,y) \geq thr_A \end{cases} \tag{3}$$

$B_{c,k}(x,y)$ and $B_{c,k-1}(x,y)$ are k-th estimated background color image and (k-1)-th estimated background color image, $f_{c,k}(x,y)$ and $d_{f,c,k}(x,y)$ are k-th color image and k-th depth image. $D_k(x,y)$ is frame difference image evaluated by formula (2), thr_A and thr_B are depth change threshold of background and depth threshold of background. $B_{c,k-1}(x,y) = hole$ expresses that pixel at coordinate (x,y) is hole.

2.3   Background Hole Filling

There are background holes and foreground holes in virtual views (shows in Fig.2 (b)), How to distinguish them effectively is a difficulty and it is also one of the key steps of our method. In order to solve this problem, an effective division algorithm is presented and introduced below.

Assume that left view is mapped from right view, and hole distribution is shown in Fig.3. FG_A and FG_B are foreground object A and B in 3D scene, A is at front of B. BG is background region in 3D scene, and H_{FG} and H_{BG} are foreground hole region and background hole region.

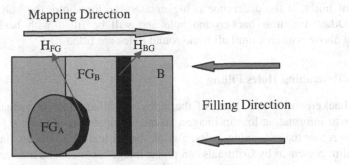

Fig. 3. Distribution of the holes

If mapping direction is from left to right, filling direction is from right to left, and the vice versa (shown in Fig3). Scan by the filling direction until the first hole pixel is met, and calculate the matching degree between current frame and background in right field (red area in Fig.4) of the hole pixel. Sum of absolute difference (SAD) is used to calculate the matching degree shown as below:

$$SAD = \frac{\sum\limits_{\substack{(i,j)\in\Phi \\ F_k(i,j)\notin H \\ B_k(i,j)\notin H}} \left| F_k(i,j) - B_k(i,j) \right|}{n} \tag{4}$$

$F_k(i,j)$ and $B_k(i,j)$ are pixel values of k-th frame and background at the coordinate (i, j), Φ and H are match region and hole regions(shown in Fig.4), n is the number of non-hole pixels.

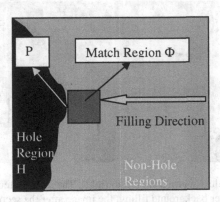

Fig. 4. Schematic diagram of discrimination algorithm

If the SAD of match area is lower than the threshold set by the noise level of camera, we fill the holes with background pixels until the first non-hole pixel in this scan line is met. Otherwise compute the depth difference of non-hole pixels on both sides of holes. If the difference is bigger than the threshold, the hole is foreground hole. Otherwise, it is background hole and will be filled with background pixel. Repeat above scanning until all background holes are filled.

2.4   Remaining Holes Filling

After background filling, most of the holes are filled. Hole in virtual view is very similar to information loss in images, so image inpainting algorithm [7, 8, 9] can be used to repair the remaining holes. Sample-based texture synthesis image inpainting algorithm presented by Criminals can repair image textures, and also can maintain the linear structure of image. This algorithm is simple and developed rapidly in recent years. We use this algorithm[7] to repair the remaining holes.

3   Experimental Results

The proposed method is implemented by C Language, and we use standard ballet sequence and a sequence captured by Kinect to test our algorithm respectively. Fig.5 shows the experimental results of the two scenes. From left to right, the first image of the result is the virtual view generated by 3D warping, in which foreground holes and background holes are all existing. The second image is the estimated background image, the third image is the result after background inpainting, and the last image is the result after foreground inpainting. The experimental results show that our method can distinguish foreground section and background section of the hole areas effectively and fill background section with real pixels of the scene such that the reality of the virtual view is improved.

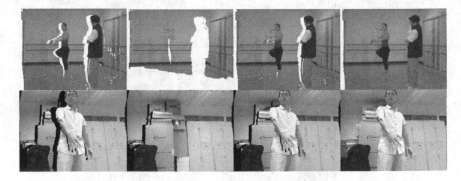

Fig. 5. Experimental Results (in turn from left to right): The image after mapping; the estimated background; the image after background filling; the image after the second inpainting

Fig.6 shows contrast of our method and M. Schmeing's method [5]. Our method can solve the problem of foreground holes effectively.

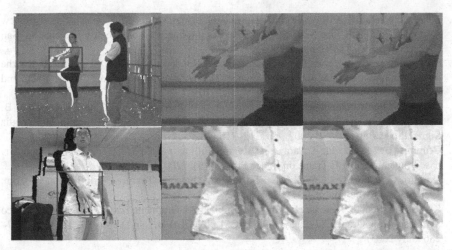

Fig. 6. Contrast results (in turn from left to right): The original virtual view; The M.Schmeing's method; Our method

4   Conclusion

A new method of DIBR combined with background filling and image inpainting is presented in this paper, and the algorithm can improve rendering quality greatly. Background estimation and image inpainting algorithms are used to fill holes in virtual view. On the basis of analyzing the cause of holes, an effective algorithm used to distinguish foreground holes and background holes is presented. Background holes are filled with estimated background information directly, and the remaining holes are inpainted by image inpainting algorithm. Our method can use real pixel of the background to fill the background holes and improve render quality greatly.

Acknowledgments. This work was supported in part by the National Natural Science Foundation of China, under Grants 60832003, 61172096, and the key Project of Science and Technology Commission of Shanghai Municipality, under Grant 10510500500.

References

1. Zhang, L., Tamm, W.J.: Stereoscopic Image Generation Based on Depth Images for 3D TV. IEEE Trans. on Broadcasting 51(2), 191–199 (2005)
2. Lee, P.-J., Effendi: Adaptive Edge-Oriented Depth Image Smoothing Approach for Depth Image Based Rendering. In: Proc. of IEEE Int. Symposium on Broadband Multimedia Systems and Broadcasting, Shanghai, China, pp. 1–5 (March 2010)
3. Daribo, I., Saito, H.: A Novel Inpainting-Based Layered Depth Video for 3DTV. IEEE Transactions on Broadcasting, PP(99) (2011)

4. Fehn, C.: Depth Image Based Rendering (DIBR), Compression and Transmission for a New Approach on 3D-TV. In: SPIE Stereoscopic Displays and Virtual Reality Systems XI, San Jose, USA, pp. 93–104 (January 2004)
5. Schmeing, M., Jiang, X.: Depth Image Based Rendering: A faithful approach for the disocclusion problem. In: 3DTV-Conference: The True Vision – Capture, Transmission and Display of 3D Video (3DTV-CON), pp. 1–4 (2010)
6. Daribo, I.: Ecole Nat. Superieure des Telecommun. Paris Tillier, C.; Pesquet-Popescu, B. Distance Dependent Depth Filtering in 3D Warping for 3DTV. In: IEEE 9th Multimedia Signal Processing (MMSP 2007), pp. 312–315 (2007)
7. Criminisi, A., Perez, P., Toyama, K.: Region Filling and Object Removal by Exemplar-based Inpainting. IEEE Trans. on Image Proc. 13(9), 1200–1212 (2004)
8. Doretto, G., Chiuso, A., Wu, Y.N., Soatto, S.: Dynamic Textures. Int. Journal of Com. Vision, 91–109 (February 2004)
9. Kwatra, V., Schödl, A., Essa, I., Turk, G., Bobick, A.: Graphcut Textures: Image and Video Synthesis using Graph Cuts. In: Proc. of ACM SIGGRAPH, San Diego, CA, USA, pp. 277–286 (July 2003)

Edge-Based Algorithm for Multi-view Depth Map Generation

Yifan Zuo[1], Ping An[1,2], and Zhaoyang Zhang[1,2]

[1] School of Communication and Information Engineering, Shanghai University,
Shanghai, 200072, China
[2] Key Laboratory of Advanced Displays and System Application, Ministry of Education,
Shanghai, 200072, China
kenny0410@sina.com, anping@shu.edu.cn

Abstract. Normalized Cross-Correlation (NCC) is a common matching measure which is insensitive to radiometric differences between stereo images. However, traditional rectangle-based NCC tends to expand the depth discontinuities. An efficient edge-based algorithm with NCC for multi-view depth map generation is proposed in this paper, which preserves depth discontinuity while remaining the advantage of robustness to radiometric differences. In addition, all pixels of initial result are classified into uncover, occlusion, reliable and unreliable by exploiting Left-Right Consistency (LRC) constraint and sequential consistency constraint. Since voting scheme will lead to errors when match windows are lack of reliable information and joint-trilateral filter will blur the depth map if employing fixed window size, especially in depth discontinuities, we combine voting scheme and joint-trilateral filter to get a better result. The experimental results show that our method achieves competitively performance.

Keywords: Depth estimation, edge-preserved, NCC.

1 Introduction

In general, there are two ways to get depth information, one is using depth camera to obtain depth information directly, the other is getting by disparity estimation. Since disparity estimation is widely used to derive depth information in various application fields for its low cost and efficiency, we adopt it in this paper. In stereo matching, common matching costs, which defined based on the brightness constancy assumption, for scene points have similar intensities in different views [1], are Absolute Difference and Squared Difference. Despite using these matching costs, it obtains high accuracy in matching radiometrically similar images for these methods are often quite sensitive to the radiometric differences that violate the brightness constancy prior. Other matching cost functions obtain robustness to radiometric differences by removing or relaxing the brightness constancy assumption, such as Normalized Cross-Correlation (NCC), rank and census transforms, LoG and mean filters. Hirschmuller et al. [5] evaluated many of this kind of functions, in which, NCC has good performance in tolerating common radiometric differences such as bias, gain and vignetting.

W. Zhang et al. (Eds.): IFTC 2012, CCIS 331, pp. 485–491, 2012.

So we choose NCC as the match cost function in this paper. However traditional window-based NCC tends to blur the depth discontinuities because of the pollution introduced by outliers. To obtain depth-discontinuity preserving depth maps, we propose to adapt the shape of the support region to reduce possible outliers. Jiangbo Lu [2] proposed an algorithm based on adaptive window shape aggregating errors using color difference threshold. This method generates adaptive window for each pixel according to the difference in *RGB* color space which is sensitive to the color difference threshold. Based on the fixed threshold, it is hard to find the depth discontinuities accurately. [4] and [7] proposed an effective method based on image segmentation, but image segmentation is time-consuming. In this paper, we propose an algorithm based on edge detection instead of image segmentation to determine the window adaptively, which can be easier and faster than image segmentation and find the depth discontinuities more accurate than [2].

This paper is organized as follows. Section 1 is the introduction. The proposed depth estimation method is detailed in section 2, the experimental results and the corresponding analyses are given in section 3. Finally, section 4 concludes the paper.

2   Proposed Algorithm

To alleviate the adverse impact of occlusion, we use three neighbouring views of images to aggregate errors for the image pairs of center-left and center-right. The proposed algorithm is consists of three steps. All of the images are epipolar rectified. Firstly, Canny operator is used to detect the edges of the center view, which classifies all of the pixels into common pixels and edge pixels. Then determine the certain support region for each pixel. Secondly, the NCC computation procedure is performed and effectively accelerated using an orthogonal integral image technique on the two image pairs independently [9]. The initial result is determined by Winner-Takes-All (WTA). Finally, the two initial depth maps of adjacent views are obtained after the processing above, and are refined by a complex algorithm which combines voting scheme [8] with joint-trilateral filter [6] on reliable estimates. The two adjacent view depth maps are checked by each other iteratively. Figure.1 is the framework of depth estimation of the proposed algorithm. Figure.2 is the framework of the refinement whose two input data is the output of Figure.1.

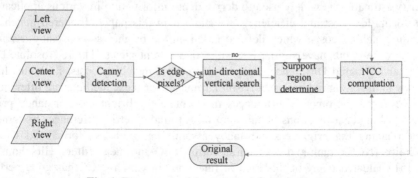

Fig. 1. Framework of the proposed depth estimation

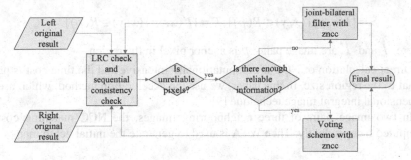

Fig. 2. Framework of the refinement

2.1 Support Region Determine

The one-pixel-wide edge of the center image is obtained by canny operator, which classifies all pixels into common pixels and edge pixels. In the initial window size of 25×25, there are two situations to determine the support regions $R(p)$.

- For each common pixel p, firstly, check the adjacent pixels up and down. Until meet the edge pixel or is out of initial window, stop checking in this direction and let all pixels through checking constitute the vertical range of Support region. Secondly, for each pixel in vertical range, we use the same method to decide the horizontal range. It is obvious that all the pixels in the region are likely to have the similar depth.
- For each edge pixel p, either up or down direction it will be checked to determine the vertical range of support region, since the edge pixel may locate at the depth discontinuity. If the difference in color between the adjacent pixel in previous line and current pixel is smaller than that of next line, we choose up direction and vice versa.

In addition, the support range $R(p)$ is no smaller than 3×3.

2.2 NCC Computing and Initial Result Generation

To measure the correlation between two signals S and T, NCC method is used to compute the following cosine-like correlation coefficient,

$$Cost_{s,t} = \frac{\sum_{i=1}^{N}(s_i - \overline{s})(t_i - \overline{t})}{\sqrt{\sum_{i=1}^{N}(s_i - \overline{s})^2 \sum_{i=1}^{N}(t_i - \overline{t})^2}}, \tag{1}$$

where $\overline{s}$ and $\overline{t}$ are the mean value of the elements from S and T. In our method,

$$S = \{I(x, y) \mid (x, y) \in R(p)\}; T = \{I'(x, y) \mid (x, y) \in R(p)\} \tag{2}$$

where I and I' are image pair, p is anchor pixel in the region.

Direct calculation of NCC is computationally intensive and the time cost is proportional to the region size. In this paper, we use the acceleration method, which use two-dimensional integral image technique [9].

In two image pairs of three neighbouring images, the NCC matching costs are computed independently. Then WTA is used to generate the initial depth map.

2.3   LRC Check and Sequential Consistency Check

The Left-Right Consistency (LRC) check is commonly employed to assess the reliability of disparity estimates. For a point p in the left view, it is checked if the corresponding point $p + d_{left}(p)$ in the right view refers back to the original point p. The potentially remaining distance dis_{L2R} between the back reference and the original point is a measure for the inconsistency and can be calculated as [6]

$$dis_{L2R} = \left| d_{left}(p) + d_{right}(p + d_{left}(p)) \right| \tag{3}$$

The LRC check from right to left is done in the same way. The strength of the LRC check stems from the fact that it combines independent information from the left-to-right and right-to-left estimation process. Here, d_{left} and d_{right} are disparity of point p.

Sequential Consistency check is commonly employed to find occlusion, the detail is shown in Fig. 3.

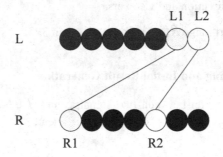

Fig. 3. Sequential Consistency check

In Fig. 3, L and R are corresponding scan lines in the left image and the right image respectively, pixels $L1$, $R1$ and $L2$, $R2$ are reliable corresponding pixels. According to sequential consistency constraint, when the adjacent pixels $L1$ and $L2$ in the left image are reliable points and the disparity of $L1$ is greater than that of

$L2$, the pixels between corresponding pixels $R1$ and $R2$ in the right image are all right occluded pixels. Their disparities are not greater than the disparity of the right pixel $R2$. We have the similar conclusion for detecting left occluded pixels on the base of disparity relationships in the right image.

Based on the constraints above, firstly, we transform initial depth maps of two adjacent views into disparities using camera parameters respectively. Through LRC check, the pixels classified into unreliable, reliable and uncovered which have no corresponding pixels in the other view. Secondly, we employ sequential consistency check to find the occlusion pixels using the reliable pixels detected in LRC check. To combine the results above, three types of pixels need to be refined.

- The pixels can not satisfy the LRC check.
- The pixels satisfy the LRC check, but are considered as occlusion.
- Since there is unavoidable occlusion in two image pair and each virtual image is generated using three neighbouring views, so the uncovered pixels are unchanged by default, except the NCC cost is lower than a threshold. In this paper, we choose 0.65 as the threshold.

2.4 Post Processing

Since voting scheme will lead to errors when match windows are lack of reliable information and joint-trilateral filter will blur the depth map if employing fixed window size, especially in depth discontinuities, we combine them to get a better result. For all pixels which are determined in 2.3, the details of refinement are shown as below.

- If the rate of reliable pixels is larger than 0.6 and the largest value is 20% more than the second largest value in the NCC weighted depth histogram in the support region of current unreliable pixel, it is considered that there is enough information to employ voting scheme. We compute statistical depth of the most pixel in the NCC weighted histogram as correction.
- Otherwise we employ joint trilateral filtering, which is different from [6]. On one hand, the filtering window is the current support region instead of rectangle, on the other hand, W_{NCC} as an additional coefficient weights the reliable pixels to compute the average mean. The weights of unreliable pixels are set to zero.

$$W_{NCC} = \begin{cases} Cost_{s,t}, Cost_{s,t} \geq 0.65 \\ 0, Cost_{s,t} < 0.65 \end{cases} \tag{4}$$

- The results can be used as new image pair to be refined iteratively. In our method, we refine the results three times iteratively.

3 Experimental Results

In this section, we will compare the initial results of our method for the sequences Akko, Lovebird2 and Newspaper with the results of [3] by using a window size of 20×20.

Simultaneously, the refined results of our method will be compared with the results refined by joint-trilateral filter. In Figure.4, the original images are shown in the first column. The corresponding initial depth maps of our method and results of [3] are shown in the second and third column respectively. The refined results of our method and the results of joint-trilateral filter are shown in the fourth and fifth column.

To subjectively evaluate the results, firstly, compare the second with third column, we can notice that the estimated depth maps with our approach seem perceptually more close to the scene. Since lots of edges obtained by canny are not depth discontinuities in Newspaper, it leads the support region being too small. So the result is not as good as the rest sequences. Secondly, compare the fourth with fifth column, we can notice that the results of joint-trilateral filter are fuzzy. Especially at edge position, it is less accurate than our refinement method.

To objectively evaluate the results, in the first place, we render virtual images using the initial depth maps estimated with our method and [3]. In the second place, virtual images using the final depth maps refined by our method and joint-trilateral filter are rendered. Each sequence contains 100 frames in our experiments. We compare the average PSNRs of them. The results are listed in table 1. In the table, each line relates with a sequence, our initial results are in the second column, while results of [3] are in the third column. The fourth column gives the running time of our method for initial depth

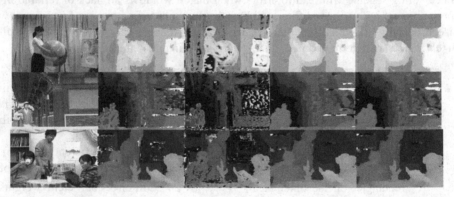

Fig. 4. Comparison of initial and refined depth maps. From the first column to the last column are original images, our initial results, results in [3], our refined results and the results of joint-trilateral filter, respectively.

Table 1. Quantitative evaluation of local stereo matching methods by average PSNR of virtual images and running time cost

SEQUENCES	Our initial results	Paper[3]	Running time of our method	Running time of Paper[3]	Our refined results	Results of joint-trilateral filter
Akko	31.59 dB	31.42 dB	20s	156s	31.87 dB	31.76 dB
Lovebird2	31.18 dB	31.09 dB	25s	167s	31.72 dB	31.66 dB
Newspaper	31.01 dB	30.96 dB	60s	674s	31.30 dB	31.21 dB

estimation while the running time of [3] is given in fifth column. At last, our refined results and results of joint-trilateral filter are list in sixth and seventh column. Generally speaking, our results achieve better performances, not only for the higher average PSNR and subjective quality, but also for the less running time cost.

4 Conclusion

We propose an effective depth map estimation algorithm for multi-view video based on edge detection. Three sequences are used to validate the presented algorithm and the results show that it can not only give accurate depths of the scene but also gain running time.

Acknowledgments. This work was supported in part by the National Natural Science Foundation of China, under Grants 60832003, 61172096, 61171084, and the key Project of Science and Technology Commission of Shanghai Municipality, under Grant 10510500500.

References

[1] Tanimoto, M., Fujii, T., Suzuki, K.: Improvement of Depth Map Estimation and View Synthesis. ISO/IEC JTC1/SC29/WG11, M15090 (January 2008)

[2] Lu, J., Zhang, K., Lafruit, G., Catthoor, F.: Real-time Ste-reo Matching A Cross-Based Local Approach. In: 2009 International Conference on Intelligent Human-Machine Systems and Cybernetics (2009)

[3] Stankiewicz, O.: A soft segmentation matching in Depth Estimation Reference Software (DERS)5.0. ISO/IEC JTC1/SC29/WG11, M17049 (2009)

[4] Liu, Z., Han, Z., Ye, Q., Jiao, J.: A New Segment-Based Algorithm for Stereo Matching. In: International Conference on Mechatronics and Automation, Changchun, China, August 9-12

[5] Hirschmuller, H., Scharstein, D.: Evaluation of cost functions for stereo matching. In: Proc. CVPR, pp. 1–8 (2007)

[6] Jachalsky, J., Schlosser, M., Gandolph, D.: Confidence Evaluation For Robust, Fast-Converging Disparity Map Refinement. In: ICME 2010 (2010)

[7] Tseng, S.-P., Lai, S.-H.: Accurate depth map estimation from video via MRF optimization. In: Visual Communications and Image Processing (VCIP), November 6-9 (2011)

[8] Zhang, K., Lu, J., Lafruit, G., Lauwereins, R., Gool, L.: Accurate and Efficient Stereo Matching with Robust Piecewise Voting. In: ICME 2009 (2009)

[9] Zhang, K., Lu, J., Lafruit, G.: Cross-based local stereo matching using or-thogonal integral images. In: IEEE CSVT 2009 (2009)

Real-Time Rendering Based on GPU
for Binocular Stereo System

Zhuan Zheng[1,2], Ping An[1,2], Bing Zhao[1,2], and Zhaoyang Zhang[1,2]

[1] School of Communication and Information Engineering, Shanghai University,
Shanghai 200072, China
[2] Key Laboratory of Advanced Displays and System Application, Ministry of Education,
Shanghai 200072, China
{zhengzhuan,anping}@shu.edu.cn

Abstract. In binocular real-time stereo system based on depth, how to accurately and quickly fill big holes generated by DIBR is a key problem. This paper presents a real-time rendering algorithm based on GPU. Hole mask image is rendered in order to get the corresponding texture information for big holes at the sending, which can be used to fill the big holes at the receiving. Small holes are filled by linear interpolation algorithm. The experiments show that the proposed method achieves better hole filling effect. In order to meet the real-time requirement, GPU acceleration is applied in this paper. Firstly, per-pixels are projected to 3D space using CUDA, Secondly, these pixels are inversely projected to 2D plane using Open GL. Running on NVIDIA Quadro 600 GPU, with the resolution of 1024×768 and 1920×1080, the proposed method reaches about 45fps and 28fps respectively, meanwhile achieves real-time and better quality.

Keywords: Binocular System, Real-time Rendering, GPU-accelerated, Open GL, CUDA.

1 Introduction

Binocular real-time system based on depth is shown in Fig.1, Depth estimation module generates depth image. Texture image and its corresponding depth image are encoded in encoding module and transmitted through the network to the decoding module. Virtual view image is generated by DIBR (Depth-Image-Based Rendering) [1] in rendering module at the receiving. This system has the advantage of greatly saving transmission bandwidth [2].

3D Image Warping [3] is the key technique in DIBR, but it is too sophisticated and time-consuming and is difficult to be applied to the real-time system. DIBR can theoretically render arbitrary view using a reference color image and its associated depth map which gives the per-pixels depth information [4]. However, DIBR has an inherent problem such as disocclusions. Ismaël [5] proposes an inpainting-based LDV generation method to reduce the amount of residual data to send by retrieving the

W. Zhang et al. (Eds.): IFTC 2012, CCIS 331, pp. 492–499, 2012.

missing pixels from the main layer. Lee [6] preprocesses the depth image by adaptive smoothing filter before warping to reduce the hole occurrence. Inpainting [7] is widely applied in the hole filling, but it is too time-consuming to apply in real-time 3DTV system. Shin [8] uses GPU to accelerate rendering to aim at real-time execution, but it only can handle lower resolution images.

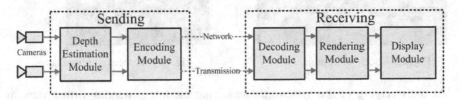

Fig. 1. Binocular real-time stereo system based on depth

This paper presents a real-time rendering algorithm based on GPU applied in binocular real-time stereo system. Hole mask image (HMI) is rendered at the sending of binocular system. Hole filling image (HFI) which can be used to fill the big holes at the receiving of binocular system is generated according to HMI. Small holes are filled by linear interpolation algorithm [9]. In addition, this paper finishes rapidly 3D image warping by combination of CUDA(Compute Unified Device Architecture) technology and Open GL technology based on GPU. The experimental results show that the proposed method greatly improves the rendering speed and achieves better objective and subjective quality. This paper is organized as follows: section 2 presents the problem in binocular real-time system. Section 3 details the proposed algorithm. In section 4 the experimental results are presented. The conclusions are given in section 5.

2   Problem of Binocular Real-Time System

Virtual view generation can be accomplished by warping one color image and its associated depth image in binocular real-time stereo system based on depth. However, the virtual view generated by the DIBR emerges a number of disocclusions, which are shown in Fig.2. Due to the camera shifting horizontally big holes on the right side of Fig.2 lack the necessary texture information, linear interpolation algorithm for filling holes can not achieve better quality, the enlarged section in Fig.3 illustrates the issue.

In order to fill the big holes efficiently in real-time stereo system, the following two points should be considered: Firstly, the sophisticated and time-consuming algorithms should not be acceptable, such as inpainting. Secondly, simple hole filling algorithms can not achieve better effect owing to lack of the necessary texture information. So, HMI, which is used to generate HFI, is rendered at the transmitting of the system. Taking into account the real-time requirement, the CUDA technology and Open GL technology are applied to accelerate rendering HMI.

Fig. 2. Disocclusions problem   **Fig. 3.** Interpolation filling holes

At the receiving of the system, the rendering module generates virtual view by warping one texture image and its corresponding depth image decoded by decoder module. Small holes are filled by linear interpolation algorithm. The decoded HFI is used to fill big holes. Real-time rendering and hole filling are achieved by using the CUDA technology and the Open GL technology.

3   Real-Time Rendering Algorithm Based on GPU

3.1   Project Per-pixels to 3D Space

Depth image uses gray intensity, which ranges from 0 to 255, to present the depth information. So gray-scale depth value should firstly be transformed into the depth of real scene according to the formula (1).

$$Z_c = \frac{1}{\frac{1}{Z_{min}}(\frac{z}{255}) + \frac{1}{Z_{max}}(1 - \frac{z}{255})} \quad z \in [0,...,255] \tag{1}$$

Where Z_c is the depth of real scene, Z_{min} and Z_{max} denote the nearest distance and the furthest distance respectively, z is gray-scale depth value of depth image. Secondly, per pixel is projected to 3D space using formula (2).

$$Z_c \overline{m} = A \cdot \left[R|t \right] \cdot \overline{M} \tag{2}$$

Where Z_c is the depth of real scene, $\overline{m}$ is pixel coordinates in the image coordinate system, $\overline{M}$ is pixel coordinates in the world coordinate system, matrix A and matrix $\left[R|t \right]$ denote 3×3 intrinsic parameters and 3×4 extrinsic parameters respectively.

Fig.4 illustrates that per-pixels are projected to 3D space using CUDA:

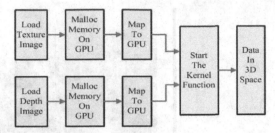

Fig. 4. Per-pixels are projected to 3D space using CUDA

3.2 Inversely Project Per-pixels to 2D Plane

Applying Open GL to transform the three-dimensional coordinates to the screen pixel coordinates, the following steps are necessary:

1) Projection transformation means that the scene in the 3D space is projected onto the screen as the final image. This paper adopts orthographic projection, namely that all objects drawn on the screen are specified according to their relative size and drawn by the same size no matter how far they are.
2) Because the scene is rendered in the rectangular window, objects (pixels) located outside the window will be eliminated, whereby clip operation.
3) The transformed coordinates and the screen pixels must establish the corresponding relation, namely viewport transformation.

Fig.5 illustrates that per-pixels are inversely projected to 2D plane using Open GL:

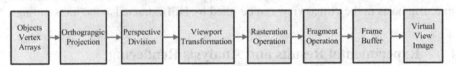

Fig. 5. Per-pixels are inversely projected to 2D plane using Open GL

3.3 Rendering HMI and Generating HFI

To generate HFI, the following steps are necessary:

1) HMI plays a role in recording the hole position, without considering the corresponding color data. Therefore 3D warping can be accomplished only by using the depth image and its corresponding vertex index. The color buffer will be assigned by 0 and 255 respectively, where 0 indicates a hole position and 255 indicates non-hole position. Fig.6 shows HMI.
2) Due to camera shifting horizontally, big holes on the right side of HMI lack the necessary texture information. When the scene suddenly changes, as shown on the right side of Fig.7, a man suddenly appeared in the scene, it is unable to fill holes effectively if not extracting texture information associated big holes. Specific implementation steps are as follows: Firstly, the maximum width of big holes on the right side is computed according to HMI. Secondly, the corresponding HFI is extracted according to the maximum width, as shown in Fig.8.

Fig. 6. HMI   **Fig. 7.** Scene suddenly changes   **Fig. 8.** HFI

3.4   Filling Holes

Holes in virtual view image are divided into two categories: one category is shown on the right side of Fig.6, the rest is considered as small holes. Small holes are filled by linear interpolation algorithm, and the interpolation formula can be written as:

$$P_h = \alpha P_l + (1 - \alpha) P_r \tag{3}$$

Where P_h is the disoccluded pixel, P_l and P_r are the horizontal left and right boundary pixels respectively, α is the weight which is inversely proportional to the distance between P_h and P_l.

The advantage of horizontal interpolation algorithm is high parallelism, so it is easy to achieve by CUDA. Starting a thread for each pixel can greatly reduce the hole filling time. Big holes in the virtual view can be filled by HFI extracted at the transmitting.

4   Experimental Results and Analysis Rendering

The "Book Arrival" test sequence is provided by HHI Academy in German and the "Cafe" test sequence is provided by GIST in Korea. The image resolution is 1024× 768 and 1920 ×1080 respectively. The horizontal distances of the camera array are 6cm and 6.5cm respectively. The focal lengths of the cameras are 140cm and 180cm respectively. The depth estimation reference software DERS5.1 is used to generate depth image, GPU acceleration can be accomplished by using NVIDIA Quadro 600 graphics card. This paper adopts PSNR and SSIM as the objective quality assessment standard.

In order to simulate the binocular real-time system and verify the validity of the proposed algorithm, this paper is based on JM18.0 (H.264/AVC standard reference software) as platform. Table 1 and Table 2 list performance comparison when "Book Arrival" sequence and "Cafe" sequence (QP =22,27,32,37,42,47) apply the proposed algorithm respectively. Bitrate Increase in the table refers to bitrate increase in percentage when transmitting HFI compared to without transmitting HFI. ΔPSNR denotes the difference between PSNR of rendering virtual view when transmitting HFI and PSNR without transmitting HFI. ΔSSIM denotes the difference between SSIM of rendering virtual view when transmitting HFI and SSIM without transmitting HFI. The experimental results show that transmitting HFI improves the rendering quality. The more complex the scene texture is, the better the objective quality of virtual view image is when transmitting HFI. Besides, smaller bitrate increase can be gained with higher image resolutions.

Table 1. Rendered virtual view objective quality comparison of "Book Arrival" sequence

QP	Coding bitrate (unit: kb/s)			Bitrate Increase	ΔPSNR(db)	ΔSSIM
	texture	depth	HFI			
22	4345.82	3049.19	462.79	5.890%	1.159	0.00091
27	1771.26	1478.74	257.51	7.342%	1.111	0.00133
32	946.12	686.58	179.03	9.882%	1.114	0.00107
37	561.00	351.63	129.76	12.448%	1.131	0.00112
42	343.20	200.82	92.47	14.528%	1.218	0.00142
47	220.40	137.76	77.03	17.700%	1.200	0.00112

Table 2. Rendered virtual view objective quality comparison of "Cafe" sequence

QP	Coding bitrate (unit: kb/s)			Bitrate Increase	ΔPSNR(db)	ΔSSIM
	texture	depth	HFI			
22	7021.03	2402.19	112.05	1.175%	0.998	0.00072
27	2779.21	1401.28	72.45	1.704%	0.828	0.00074
32	1516.32	814.81	63.11	2.636%	0.956	0.00076
37	947.41	518.47	57.71	3.788%	0.800	0.00079
42	630.60	346.48	54.28	5.263%	0.741	0.00070
47	459.13	262.87	51.91	6.707%	0.839	0.00074

Fig. 9. "Book Arrival" and "Cafe" original image

Fig. 10. "Book Arrival" and "Cafe" after hole filling

Fig.9 and Fig.10 give the subjective effect comparison. Obviously, virtual view image rendered by proposed method is almost the same as the original image.

Table 3.   Rendering time for the 6~11 frame of "Book Arrival"(unit: ms)

Frame	6	7	8	9	10	11
Sending time	4.974	4.899	4.697	4.616	4.806	4.601
Receiving time	16.961	17.035	16.941	17.174	17.267	17.469
Total time	21.935	21.934	21.638	21.790	22.073	22.070

Table 4. Rendering time for the 14~19 frame of "Cafe" (unit: ms)

Frame	14	15	16	17	18	19
Sending time	8.566	8.549	8.535	8.554	8.725	8.718
Receiving time	26.247	26.078	26.556	26.972	26.350	28.174
Total time	34.813	34.627	35.091	35.526	35.075	36.892

Table 3 and Table 4 list the time consuming for each frame. The proposed method is timed by GPU. Taking into account timing error, this paper accomplishes new viewpoint image rendering for 10 times and computes the average value as the final rendering time. They also show that the speed of rendering "Book Arrival" sequence can reach about 45fps and the speed of rendering "Cafe" sequence can reach about 28fps. So the proposed method can be applied in real-time 3DTV system.

5   Conclusion

This paper presents a real-time rendering algorithm based on GPU to generate virtual view. Firstly, HMI is rendered at the sending of binocular system. Secondly, HFI, which is used to fill the big holes at the receiving of binocular system, is generated according to the maximum width of big holes in the HMI. CUDA and Open GL based on GPU are combined to improve the rendering speed. Firstly, per-pixels are projected to 3D space using CUDA. Secondly, these pixels are inversely projected to 2D plane using Open GL. The experimental results show that the proposed method can not only get high rendering quality, but also satisfy the real-time request of system.

Acknowledgments. This work was supported in part by the National Natural Science Foundation of China, under Grants 60832003, 61172096, and the key Project of Science and Technology Commission of Shanghai Municipality, under Grant 10510500500.

References

1. Shao, F., Jiang, G.Y., Yu, M., Chen, K., Ho, Y.S.: Asymmetric Coding of Multi-View Video Plus Depth Based 3-D Video for View Rendering. IEEE Transactions on Multimedia 14, 157–167 (2012)
2. Xue, J.F., Xi, M., Li, D.X., Zhang, M.: A New Virtual View Rendering Method Based on Depth Image. In: 2010 Asia-Pacific Conference on Wearable Computing Systems, Shenzhen, pp. 147–150 (2010)
3. Feng, Y.M., Li, D.X., Luo, K., Zhang, M.: Asymmetric bidirectional view synthesis for free viewpoint and three-dimensional video. IEEE Transactions on Consumer Electronics 55, 2349–2355 (2009)
4. Wang, Z., Zhou, J.: A novel approach for depth image based rendering, based on non-linear transformation of depth values. In: 2011 International Conference on Image Analysis and Signal Processing (IASP), Shanghai, pp. 138–142 (2011)
5. Ismaël, D., Hideo, S.: A Novel Inpainting-Based Layered Depth Video for 3DTV. IEEE Transactions on Broadcasting 57, 533–541 (2011)
6. Lee, P., Effendi: Nongeometric Distortion Smoothing Approach for Depth Map Preprocessing. IEEE Transactions on Multimedia 13, 246–254 (2011)
7. Jung, C., Jiao, L., Oh, Y., Kim, J.K.: Depth-preserving DIBR based on disparity map over T-DMB. Electronics Letters 46, 628–629 (2010)
8. Shin, H.C., Kim, Y.J., Park, H., Park, J.I.: Fast view synthesis using GPU for 3D display. IEEE Transactions on Consumer Electronics 54, 2068–2076 (2008)
9. Song, G., Xue, J.B., Li, H.: A new double-sided DIBR method for virtual view generation in 3DTV. In: 2011 IEEE 13th International Conference on Communication Technology (ICCT), Jinan, pp. 1099–1102 (2011)

New HVS-Based Stereoscopic Image Watermarking Algorithm for 3D Media

Chunhua Bai, Mei Yu, Gangyi Jiang, Zhongju Peng, and Feng Shao

Faculty of Information Science and Engineering,
Ningbo University, Ningbo, China

Abstract. In this paper, a human visual system (HVS) -based stereoscopic image watermarking algorithm is proposed to protect copyright of three dimensional (3D) media. The proposed algorithm makes use of the features of stereo images. Watermark is embedded in similar areas selected by global disparity. Every bit of watermark is embedded in similar blocks by exploiting relationship embedding. Similar blocks usually have the same change trend when two viewpoints are under the same attack. Experimental results show the effectiveness of the proposed algorithm.

Keywords: three dimensional media, stereoscopic images, stereo image watermark, relationship embedding, global disparity.

1   Introduction

Three dimensional media is becoming the next important developing direction. With 3D multimedia technology develops, there is also a strong necessity for developing robust 3D image watermark techniques, which protect the ownership rights. And effective digital watermark for 3D content protection will play an important role for promoting the 3D entertainment industry [1].

A blind watermarking method is necessary because original stereoscopic images are not available [2] in the consumer side. Blind watermarking for 2D images includes quantization embedding and relationship embedding, etc. Relationship embedding usually changes the coefficients of original images strongly when watermark is different with the relationship defined. Therefore, a blind watermarking algorithm proposed in [3] uses an embedding strategy to adjust the tradeoff between transparency and robustness. The embedding strategy adaptively selects either relationship embedding or quantization embedding. And save the way embedding watermark as a flag matrix. According to the flag matrix, the watermark can be extracted. Human eyes cannot sense any changes below the just noticeable distortion (JND) threshold due to their underlying spatial/temporal sensitivity and masking properties. Several methods for JND have been proposed, some work in image-domain [4], as well as based upon intensive research in subbands, such as discrete cosine transform (DCT) domain[5,6] and wavelet domain [7]. Watson proposed the

W. Zhang et al. (Eds.): IFTC 2012, CCIS 331, pp. 500–507, 2012.

visual pattern based on the Discrete Cosine Transform (DCT) in paper [6]. It is helpful to adjust the tradeoff between transparency and robustness easily. Stereoscopic images studied in this paper are taken by several parallel cameras. So, there exists a disparity called global disparity between adjacent views [8]. Stereoscopic images are similar to 2D images. Moreover stereoscopic images have differences from 2D images, for example, existence at the same time [9], similar content, and so on. Using 2D watermarking method easily can not deal with the content protection problem of stereoscopic images. Taking the similar content of stereoscopic images into consideration, a blind watermarking algorithm is proposed to deal with the content protection problem of stereoscopic images. And the algorithm based on human vision system (HVS) in this paper can adjust the tradeoff between transparency and robustness.

2   Watermarking Algorithm

In this paper, a novel blind watermarking algorithm is proposed, which utilizes theories of global disparity and relationship embedding, is illustrated in Fig.1 (a). According to global disparity of parallel stereoscopic image, choose similar areas of left-view image and right-view image as the watermark embedding area. The extracting algorithm is shown in Fig.1 (b), where the watermark extracted from similar areas of left view image and right-view image by making use of relationship extracting.

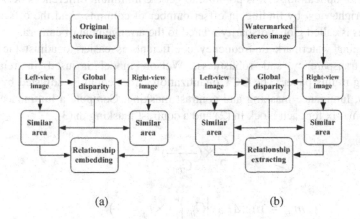

(a)   (b)

Fig. 1. The proposed watermarking algorithm for stereoscopic image. (a) the embedding algorithm and (b) the extracting algorithm.

MAD (Mean Absolute Difference) is employed to calculate the global disparity. Equation (1) shows the equation for global disparity calculation. Fig. 2 shows the global disparity between left-view and right-view. Right-view looks like the shifted version of left-view in the area surrounded by blue pixels.

$$G = \min_{i} \left(\frac{1}{(W-i) \cdot H} \sum_{y=1}^{W-i} \sum_{x=1}^{H} |L(x, y) - R(x, y+i)| \right) \qquad (1)$$

where L and R are left-view and right-view of stereoscopic image. W is the width and H is the height of viewpoint. i is the offset number of columns and i=1,2,...W/2. G is the global disparity by (1).

 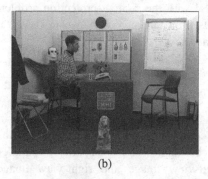

(a)   (b)

Fig. 2. Similar content of stereoscopic image. (a) left-view image and (b) right-view image.

In spite of optical noise, it is possible to get the minimum differences between left-view and right-view by finding an offset number of columns. And the offset number of columns is called global disparity related to the arrangement of camera.

Embedding watermark in frequency coefficients is easier to adjust the tradeoff between transparency and robustness. Watson model is used in relationship embedding in this paper. The DCT quantization errors could be adjusted by contrast sensitivity, luminance masking and contrast masking. Compute a luminance-masked threshold matrix for each block in (2) and a contrast masking in (3).

$$t_{ijk} = \frac{Q}{2} \times \left(\frac{C_{00k}}{C_{00}} \right)^{a_T} \qquad (2)$$

$$m_{ijk} = \max(t_{ijk}, |C_{ijk}|^{w_{ij}} \times t_{ijk}^{1-w_{ij}}) \qquad (3)$$

where Q is quantization matrix of 8×8 block, C_{00k} is the DC coefficient of the DCT for block k, C_{00} is the mean luminance of the whole image. a_T is a suggested value of 0.649. t_{ijk} is the luminance-masked threshold matrix for block k. And in (3), C_{ijk} is the DCT coefficient for block k, w_{ij} is a suggested value of 0.7. m_{ijk} is the masked threshold.

2.1   Embedding Algorithm

Relationship embedding is used in this paper. And balance between robustness and invisibility is achieved by using Watson model. Thus, the embedding algorithm is described as follows.

1)   Compute the global disparity of stereoscopic image and save the global disparity as a key k_1. Similar content of stereoscopic image can be selected by k_1.

2)   The luminance component of similar content is divided into 8×8 non-overlapped blocks. Every block is performed discrete cosine transform (DCT).

3)   Compute DCT quantization errors matrix w_L and w_R of stereoscopic images' luminance component.

4)   Here, according to the size of watermark, the watermark embedded can be divided into three blocks and their block sizes are S_1, S_2, and S_3. The remaining pixels of watermark do not scramble. Arnold scrambling periods of three watermark blocks are k_2, k_3 and k_4, and scrambling order of three blocks are 1, 2 and 3. It is easily to get the scrambled watermark W_1.

5)   Choose the second line and the third coefficient of DCT block as embedded location. The embedded formula is described as follows.

First, $\Delta = L - R$

Then, if $W_1 = 1$ and $\Delta <= 0$

$$\begin{cases} R' = R + a_1 \times \Delta - b_1 \times w_R \\ L' = L - a_2 \times \Delta + b_2 \times w_L \end{cases} \qquad (4)$$

If $W_1 = 0$ and $\Delta > 0$

$$\begin{cases} R' = R + a_3 \times \Delta + b_3 \times w_R \\ L' = L - a_4 \times \Delta - b_4 \times w_L \end{cases} \qquad (5)$$

where L' and R' are DCT coefficients of watermarked stereoscopic images. L and R are DCT coefficients of original stereoscopic images. W_1 is the scrambled watermark. w_L and w_R are DCT quantization errors matrix of two viewpoints. a_1, a_2, a_3, a_4, b_1, b_2, b_3, b_4 are weighted coefficients.

6)   The watermarked coefficients of left-view image and right-view image are performed inverse DCT. The stereoscopic image is the watermarked image.

2.2   Extracting Algorithm

Compute global disparity of watermarked stereoscopic images under attacks and compare global disparity with key k_1. If global disparity of watermarked stereoscopic images is different from k_1, we can draw a conclusion that the stereoscopic image is attacked by serious strikes.

The extracting algorithm of stereoscopic image proceeds as follows.

1)   Compute global disparity and select similar content of stereoscopic image. The luminance component of similar content is divided into 8×8 non-overlapped blocks. Every block of stereoscopic image is performed DCT.

2)   The second line and the third coefficients of two viewpoints' similar content in DCT are chosen as extracted coefficient. The extracted formula is described as follows.

$$\begin{cases} W_1' = 1 & if \ L' > R' \\ W_1' = 0 & else \end{cases} \tag{6}$$

where W_1' is the watermark extracted from stereoscopic image, L' and R' are DCT coefficients of watermarked stereoscopic image.

3)   It is easy to get anti-scrambled watermark W' by three sizes of watermark blocks S_1, S_2, S_3 and arnold scrambling period k_2, k_3, k_4.

3   Experimental Results and Analyses

To demonstrate the effectiveness of the proposed algorithm, simulations are performed. The multi-view video is Book_Arrival [10] obtained from HHI Stereoscopic Dataset. The resolution is 1024×768, camera spacing 65mm.For convenience, the first frames of viewpoint 8 and 9 are taken as an example for stereoscopic image in Fig.2.

According to the similar content of stereoscopic image, a meaningful binary image is chosen as watermark with the size of 125×96. The sizes of three watermark blocks S_1, S_2, S_3 are 64, 88 and 12. Arnold scrambling periods of three watermark blocks k_2, k_3, k_4 are 14,18 and 8.The bit same rate (BSR) of extracting message W_1' from the original watermark W, is denoted as BSR in the rest of this paper. BSR as evaluation parameter is defined as follows. Size of watermark is $M_1 \times N_1$.

$$BSR = \frac{pixels \ number \ of \ (W_1 = W_1')}{M_1 \times N_1} \tag{7}$$

The values of $a_1, a_2, a_3,$ and a_4 range from 0 to 0.5 and the values of $b_1, b_2, b_3,$ and b_4 range from 0 to 1. If the weighted coefficients of Watson model matrix are higher, the robustness is stronger. So, $b_1, b_2, b_3,$ and b_4 are set to 1 in the experiment. Fig.3 shows the watermarks extracted from stereoscopic image under attacks when $a_1, a_2, a_3,$ and a_4 are zero and $b_1, b_2, b_3,$ and b_4 are 1. The ability to resist common signal processing attacks of the proposed algorithm is listed in the figures where data show NC/BSR in the algorithm. And the data show PSNR (dB) of left-view image under attacks / PSNR (dB) of right-view image under attacks. Here the attacks of left-view image and right-view image are the same.

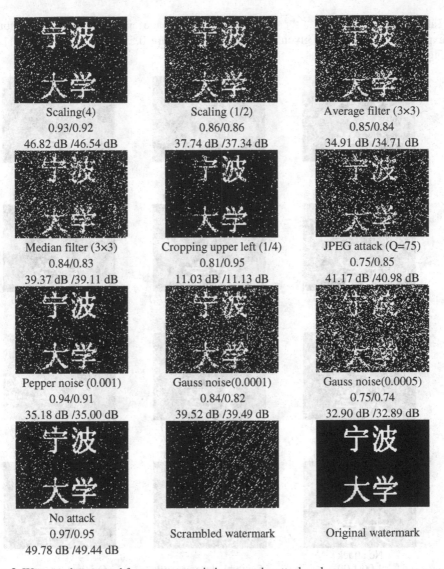

Fig. 3. Watermark extracted from stereoscopic image under attacks when a_1, a_2, a_3, a_4, are zero

From Fig.3, some conclusions are given as

1) The values of NC and BSR are not equal for the same watermark. BSR is not equal to 1 when stereoscopic image under no attack. That is to say, it is not robust enough when a_1, a_2, a_3, a_4, are 0 and b_1, b_2, b_3, b_4 are 1.

2) It is easy to get high transparency by making use of HVS. But Watson model matrix is not enough to resist the difference $\triangle$ in some areas of left-view image and right-view image.

Taking the difference $\triangle$ of stereoscopic image into consideration, some experimental results are given when a_1, a_2, a_3, a_4, are 0.5 and b_1, b_2, b_3, b_4 are 1 in Fig.4.

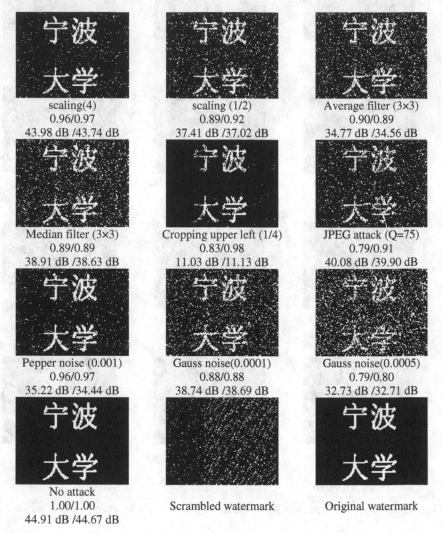

scaling(4)	scaling (1/2)	Average filter (3×3)
0.96/0.97	0.89/0.92	0.90/0.89
43.98 dB /43.74 dB	37.41 dB /37.02 dB	34.77 dB /34.56 dB

Median filter (3×3) 0.89/0.89 38.91 dB /38.63 dB

Cropping upper left (1/4) 0.83/0.98 11.03 dB /11.13 dB

JPEG attack (Q=75) 0.79/0.91 40.08 dB /39.90 dB

Pepper noise (0.001) 0.96/0.97 35.22 dB /34.44 dB

Gauss noise(0.0001) 0.88/0.88 38.74 dB /38.69 dB

Gauss noise(0.0005) 0.79/0.80 32.73 dB /32.71 dB

No attack 1.00/1.00 44.91 dB /44.67 dB

Scrambled watermark

Original watermark

Fig. 4. Watermark extracted from stereoscopic image under attacks when a_1, a_2, a_3, a_4, are 0.5

From Fig.4, some conclusions are given as

1) The robustness is better with the higher values of a_1, a_2, a_3, a_4. But the invisibility is the best when the values of a_1, a_2, a_3, a_4 are zero. The values of a_1, a_2, a_3, a_4 are used to adjust the balance between robustness and invisibility.

2) It is found that if the weighted coefficients of $\triangle$ more than 0.5 in the algorithm, the watermarked stereoscopic images may be detected by subjective observation in edge area.

Divide the similar contents of stereoscopic image's two viewpoints into similar blocks. Similar blocks from left-view image and right-view image usually have the same change trend when the two viewpoints are attacked. It is helpful to enhance the robustness of algorithm. Simulation results show that the algorithm is robust against the attacks such as scaling, filtering, cropping, compression and noise, and it maintains satisfying transparency.

4   Conclusions

A blind watermarking algorithm is proposed to deal with the content protection problem of parallel stereoscopic images in this paper. The proposed scheme exploits the relationship embedding and global disparity existing in parallel views of stereoscopic image. In addition, the scheme is proposed using human vision system. And future work is considered to deal with watermark embedding in edge areas.

Acknowledgments. This work was supported by Natural Science Foundation of China (61171163, 60902096, 61071120), Natural Science Foundation of Zhejiang Province (Y1101240), and Scientific Research Foundation of Graduate School of Ningbo University.

References

1. Zhu, Z., Wang, Y., Jiang, G., Liang, F.: Adaptive digital watermarking algorithm for stereo video. Journal of Image and Graphics 12(1), 68–72 (2007)
2. Lin, Y.-H., Wu, J.-L.: A Digital Blind Watermarking for Depth-Image-Based Rendering 3D Images. IEEE Transactions on Broadcasting 57(2), 602–611 (2011)
3. Ding, Z., Liang, Q.: A blind watermarking algorithm with strong robustness based on relationship and quantization. Journal of Image and Graphics 15(1), 31–36 (2010)
4. Yang, X., Lin, W., Lu, Z., Ong, E., Yao, S.: Motion-compensated residue preprocessing in video coding based on just-noticeable-distortion profile. IEEE Trans. on Circuits and Systems for Video Technology 15(6), 742–752 (2005)
5. Watson, A.B.: DCT quantization matrices visually optimized for individual images. In: Human Vision, Visual Processing, and Digital Display IV, Proc. SPIE, pp. 202–216 (1993)
6. Yang, H., Liang, Y., Liu, L., Ji, S.: HVS-based imperceptibility measure of watermark in watermarked color image. In: International Conference on Software Engineering, Artificial Intelligence, Networking, and Parallel/Distributed Computing, vol. 3, pp. 722–727 (2007)
7. Jin, C., Jin, S.: Image Watermark Algorithm for Copyright Protection Based on Human Visual System. In: International Conference on Information Science and Management Engineering, pp. 64–67 (2010)
8. Oh, K.-J., Ho, Y.-S.: Global Disparity Compensation for Multi-view Video Coding. In: International Workshop on Advanced Image Technology, pp. 18–23 (2007)
9. Bai, C., Yu, M., Wu, A., Luo, T., Jiang, G.: New Relationship-Based Stereo Image Watermarking Algorithm for 3D Media. In: IEEE International Conference on Signal Processing Systems, pp. 339–402 (2011)
10. HHI Book_Arrival sequence, ftp://ftp.hhi.de/HHIMPEG3DV

Model of Relationship among Views Number, Stereo Resolution and Max Stereo Angle for Multi-view Acquisition/Stereo Display System

Hao Cheng, Ping An, and Zhaoyang Zhang

School of Communication and Information Engineering,
Shanghai University, Shanghai, 200072, China
Chengs99f@163.com

Abstract. In the multi-view acquisition/stereo display system, the stereo angle, number of views and stereo image resolution (simply called three points) are very important factors. They can impact the performance of system. This paper introduces stereo angle and explores the model of relationship among number of views, stereo resolution, and max stereo angle. Based on the model, the relationship among this three points is shown. Through the results of simulation experiments, we can get the overall optimizing methods for multi-view acquisition/stereo display system and the model provides a theoretical basis for building and overall optimizing multi-view stereo acquisition/ display system.

Keywords: multi-view acquisition/stereo display system, number of views, stereo resolution, stereo angle.

1 Introduction

Multi-view three-dimensional (3D) display has been considered as future direction of 3D display technology [1], but it is not perfect and still in development. Reference [2] improves the efficiency of stereo sense with horizontal and vertical parallax, reference [3] partially improves the efficiency of multi-view video coding (MVC) with the correlation between different views and reference [4] partially expands the stereo angle by increasing views. All of them rarely consider improving system performance from the overall of FTV.

This paper mainly discusses the relationship among number of views, stereo resolution and stereo angle in multi-view stereo acquisition/display system. Firstly, we introduce the principle of multi-view stereo acquisition/display system and model of relationship between number of views and max stereo angle. Then we analyze synthesis method of stereo image and finds the model of relationship between number of views and stereo resolution. Based on reference [5-6] we propose the model of relationship among number of views, stereo resolution and stereo angle. Finally,

W. Zhang et al. (Eds.): IFTC 2012, CCIS 331, pp. 508–514, 2012.

through the simulation experiments we can   overall optimizing method for multi-view stereo acquisition/ display system.

2   Principle of Multi-view Stereo Acquisition/Display System

Shooting camera array and multi-view stereo display compose multi-view stereo acquisition/display. Shooting camera array can capture the real object from different angle. These images can synthesize stereo image which can be displayed in multi-view stereo screen.

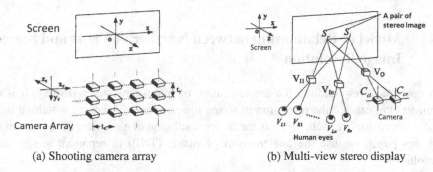

(a) Shooting camera array   (b) Multi-view stereo display

Fig. 1. Model of Multi-view stereo acquisition/display system

Fig.1(a) is the model of shooting camera array and Fig. 1(b) shows the model of multi-view stereo display. t_x and t_y represent camera spacing in x-axis and y-axis. Assume that V_0 is the point of real object. C_{ol} and C_{or} represent the position of some neighboring cameras in camera array. S_l and S_r represent the pair points in multi-view stereo display screen. If the positions of 1th viewer's two eyes are at V_{Ll} and V_{Rl}, he can see the position of virtual objects at V_{l1}. The rest may be deduced by analogy. If the positions of Nth viewer's two eyes are at V_{Ln} and V_{Rn}, he can see the position of virtual objects at V_{ln}. When the viewer stands at different position to see multi-view stereo display, he can see the virtual object at different position.

3   Model of Relationship between Number of Views and Max Stereo Angle

The stereo angle is β which is formed between the two eyes of observer and fixation point of virtual objects. Reference [5] establishes the model of stereo angle.

$$\beta = \arctan \frac{e}{2(z_v - Z_I)} \tag{1}$$

where e is interpupillary distance, z_v is viewing distance and Z_I is the depth of virtual object. Equation (1) calculates every stereo angle for multi-view stereo display and the sum of all stereo angle forms max stereo angle ($\text{Angle}_{\max}$). reference [6] establishes the model which is the relationship between number of views (N) and max stereo angle. It can be expressed as:

$$\text{Angle}_{\max} = 2 \bullet \arctan \frac{e + (N-2) \bullet C_{zv}}{2(z_v - Z_I)} \tag{2}$$

The number of views is N, C_{zv} is viewpoint switching parameter and $\text{Anlge}_{\max}$ is max stereo angle.

4 Model of Relationship between Number of Views and Stereo Image Resolution

Stereo image resolution is not the resolution of multi-view stereo display. It is that human eyes can see the resolution of stereo image when viewers are watching multi-view stereo display. Actually, it is the image resolution of each view each eye can see. In this paper, we use the total number of pixels (TNP) to represent stereo image resolution.

In multi-view stereo display, viewers standing at different position can see different viewpoints because it uses the information of each view to synthesize stereo image. Each view only contributes part of the pixels for synthesizing.

Fig.2 is synthesized diagram of 8-view stereo display. Each view only contributes some pixels. When a viewer stands in front of multi-view stereo display, he can see parts of pixels for some view. With increasing the number of views, the viewer can

	1	2	3	4	5	6	7	8	9	10
	RGB	RGB	RGB	RGB	RGB	RGB	RGB	RGB	RGB	RGB
1	①②③	④⑤⑥	⑦⑧①	②③④	⑤⑥⑦	⑧①②	③④⑤	⑥⑦⑧	①②③	④⑤⑥
2	②③④	⑤⑥⑦	⑧②③	④⑤⑥	⑦⑧②	③④⑤	⑥⑦⑧	②③④	⑤⑥⑦	⑧②③
3	③④⑤	⑥⑦⑧	③④⑤	⑥⑦⑧	③④⑤	⑥⑦⑧	③④⑤	⑥⑦⑧	③④⑤	⑥⑦⑧
4	④⑤⑥	⑦⑧④	⑤⑥⑦	⑧④⑤	⑥⑦⑧	④⑤⑥	⑦⑧④	⑤⑥⑦	⑧④⑤	⑥⑦⑧
5	⑤⑥⑦	⑧⑤⑥	⑦⑧⑤	⑥⑦⑧	⑤⑥⑦	⑧⑤⑥	⑦⑧⑤	⑥⑦⑧	⑤⑥⑦	⑧⑤⑥
6	⑥⑦⑧	⑥⑦⑧	⑥⑦⑧	⑥⑦⑧	⑥⑦⑧	⑥⑦⑧	⑥⑦⑧	⑥⑦⑧	⑥⑦⑧	⑥⑦⑧
7	⑦⑧⑦	⑧⑦⑧	⑦⑧⑦	⑧⑦⑧	⑦⑧⑦	⑧⑦⑧	⑦⑧⑦	⑧⑦⑧	⑦⑧⑦	⑧⑦⑧
8	⑧①②	③④⑤	⑥⑦⑧	①②③	④⑤⑥	⑦⑧①	②③④	⑤⑥⑦	⑧①②	③④⑤

Fig. 2. Synthesized diagram of 8-view stereo display

see more viewpoints. When the resolution of stereo display is a constant, the pixels contributed by each view become less. In order to improve the performance of stereo display, the relationship between number of views and stereo image resolution should be discussed.

In this paper stereo image resolution is represented by total number of image pixels (TNP). TNP means how many pixels each eye of viewer actually sees in multi-view stereo display. Assume that resolution of multi-view stereo display is a constant value. Number of pixels that viewer can see is less than TNP of multi-view stereo display because two eyes only see two views in multi-view stereo display. The relationship between number of views and TNP can be expressed as:

$$TNP_{eachview} = \frac{TNP_{Stereoimage}}{N} \tag{3}$$

$TNP_{eachview}$ is the number of pixels of each view and $TNP_{stereoimage}$ is the number of pixel for synthesized stereo image. For example, 16-view stereo display can support sixteen viewpoints, and each view contributes 1/16 number of pixels. That means the pixels which we can see become less.

5   Simulation Experiments and Analyses

Now we get the relationship model between number of views and stereo image resolution and relationship model between max stereo angle and number of views. To explore their characteristics, we implemented the simulation experiments in MATLAB 7.13 and draw the diagram among max stereo angle, number of views and stereo image resolution. It can be a theoretical foundation for establishing or optimizing multi-view stereo acquisition/ display system.

5.1   Relationship between Number of Views and Total Number of Image Pixel for Each View

Assume that total number of stereo image pixel is a certain value shown as Table 1. Base on table 1 and equation (3) we can get the relationship between number of views and total number of image pixel for each view as Fig.3.

Table 1. Total number of stereo image pixel

	Total Number of Pixels	Resolution
1080P	2073600	1920x1080
720P	921600	1280x720

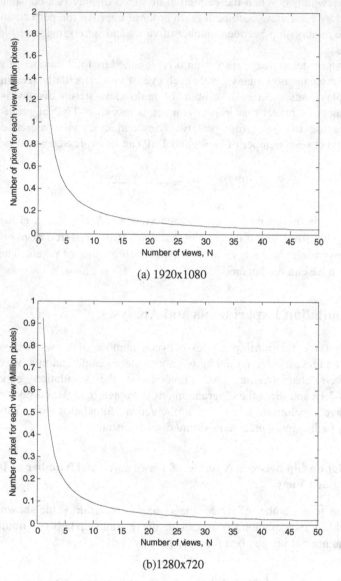

(a) 1920x1080

(b)1280x720

Fig. 3. Relationship between number of views and number of pixels for each view

Fig. 3 show that the number of image pixels for each view declines rapidly with the increase of views. That means the number of pixels which human's eyes can see are reducing. When we watch multi-view stereo display, we feel that the clarity of stereo image declines.

For example, if resolution of multi-view stereo display is 1920x1080, the number of views is 9. According to Equation (3), TNP of each view is 230400. Translating it to resolution is 640x360. In other words, the resolution of image seen by each eye is 640x360. When we see 9-view stereo display with 1920x1080 resolution, each eye actually sees the image whose resolution is 640x360.

5.2   Relationship among Number of Views, Stereo Image Resolution and Max Stereo Angle

Stereo angle, number of views and stereo image resolution are very important three points in multi-view acquisition/stereo display system. They are interrelated and affect the performance of the system.

Based on Equation (1), Equation (2) and the parameters of in Table 2, we draw relationship among stereo image resolution (TNP), number of views and stereo angle as in Fig.4.

Table 2. Parameters of multi-view acquisition/stereo display system (mm)

TNP(million Pixel)	e	C_{ZV}	z_v	Z_I
2.0736	65	106.667	1600	308.966

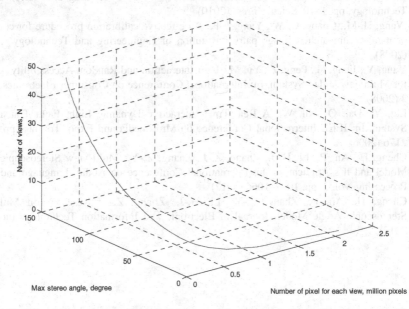

Fig. 4. Relationship among number of views, stereo image resolution and max stereo angle

In Fig.4, x-axis is number of pixels for each view, y-axis is max stereo angle and z-axis is number of views. Stereo angle, number of views and total number of image pixels are associated with each other. When number of views is increasing, max stereo angle is becoming wider. Viewer may feel strong stereo effect in multi-view stereo display. But the clarity of stereo image declines with views increasing. Viewers can clearly feel that image quality deteriorates.

6   Conclusion

This paper mainly discusses the relationship among number of views, stereo angle and stereo image resolution in multi-view acquisition/stereo display system. Firstly, it analyzes the principle of multi-view acquisition/stereo display system and find out the model of relationship between number of views and max stereo angle. Then it gives model of the relationship between number of views and stereo image resolution. Finally, through the simulation experiments, the curve of relationship among the three points is drawn. In designing multi-view stereo acquisition/display system, we should consider the three points comprehensively to improve system quality.

Acknowledgment. This work was supported in part by the National Natural Science Foundation of China, under Grants 60832003, 61172096 and 61171084, and the key Project of Shanghai Science and Technology Commission, under Grant 10510500500.

References

1. Zhang, Z., An, P., Zhang, Z., Shen, L.: 2D/3D Video Processing and Stereo Display Technology, pp. 1–10. Science Press (2010)
2. Wang, H.-M., Chang, C.-W., Yang, J.-F.: An effective calibration procedure for correction of parallax unmatched image pairs. Institution of Engineering and Technology 3, 63–74 (2008)
3. Yang, Y., Jiang, G., Peng, Z., Yu, M.: User Interaction and Random Accessibility Analysis for Multiview Video System. In: International Conference on Consumer Electronics, pp. 1–2 (2008)
4. Liu, Y., Dai, Q., Xu, W.: A Real Time Interactive Dynamic Light Field Transmission System. In: IEEE International Conference on Multimedia and Expo, Toronto, pp. 2173–2176 (2006)
5. Cheng, H., An, P., Li, H.-J., Zhang, Z.-J., Zhang, Z.-Y.: Multi-view Stereoscopic Angle Model and It's Application. In: International Conference on Audio, Language and Image Processing, vol. 2, pp. 1062–1066 (2012)
6. Cheng, H., An, P., Zhang, Z.-Y., Li, H.-J., Zhang, Z.-J.: Research on Multi-view Stereoscopic Angle Model. Journal of Electronic and Information Technology (accepted, 2012)

Author Index